Lecture Notes in Computer Science 3003

Commenced Publication in 1973
Founding and Former Series Editors:
Gerhard Goos, Juris Hartmanis, and Jan van Leeuwen

T0239468

Springer
Berlin
Heidelberg
New York
Hong Kong
London
Milan
Paris
Tokyo

Maarten Keijzer   Una-May O'Reilly
Simon M. Lucas   Ernesto Costa
Terence Soule (Eds.)

Genetic Programming

7th European Conference, EuroGP 2004
Coimbra, Portugal, April 5-7, 2004
Proceedings

Springer

Volume Editors

Maarten Keijzer
KiQ Ltd
De Lairessestraat 150, 1075 HL, Amsterdam, The Netherlands
E-mail: mkeijzer@xs4all.nl

Una-May O'Reilly
Computer Science and Artificial Intelligence Laboratory
Massachusetts Institute of Technology, Cambridge, MA, 02139, USA
E-mail: unamay@ai.mit.edu

Simon M. Lucas
University of Essex, Dept. of Computer Science
Colchester CO4 3SQ,UK
E-mail: sml@essex.ac.uk

Ernesto Costa
University of Coimbra, Department of Computer Science
Polo II - Pinhal Marrocos, 3030-290 Coimbra, Portugal
E-mail: ernesto@dei.uc.pt

Terence Soule
University of Idaho, Department of Computer Science, Moscow, Id 83844-1010, USA
E-mail: tsoule@cs.uidaho.edu

Library of Congress Control Number: 2004102630

Coverillustration: "Embrace" by Anargyros Sarafopoulos

CR Subject Classification (1998): D.1, F.1, F.2, I.5, I.2, J.3

ISSN 0302-9743
ISBN 3-540-21346-5 Springer-Verlag Berlin Heidelberg New York

Springer-Verlag is a part of Springer Science+Business Media

springeronline.com

© Springer-Verlag Berlin Heidelberg 2004
Printed in Germany

Typesetting: Camera-ready by author, data conversion by PTP-Berlin, Protago-TeX-Production GmbH
Printed on acid-free paper   SPIN: 10992999   06/3142   5 4 3 2 1 0

Preface

In this volume we present the accepted contributions for the 7th European Conference on Genetic Programming (EuroGP 2004). The conference took place on 5–7 April 2004 in Portugal at the University of Coimbra, in the Department of Mathematics in Praça Dom Dinis, located on the hill above the old town.

EuroGP is a well-established conference and the sole one exclusively devoted to Genetic Programming. Previous proceedings have all been published by Springer-Verlag in the LNCS series. EuroGP began as an international workshop in Paris, France in 1998 (14–15 April, LNCS 1391). Subsequently the workshop was held in Göteborg, Sweden in 1999 (26–27 May, LNCS 1598) and then EuroGP became an annual conference: in 2000 in Edinburgh, UK (15–16 April, LNCS 1802), in 2001 at Lake Como, Italy (18–19 April, LNCS 2038), in 2002 in Kinsale, Ireland (3–5 April, LNCS 2278), and in 2003 in Colchester, UK (14–16 April, LNCS 2610). From the outset, there have always been specialized workshops, co-located with EuroGP, focusing on applications of evolutionary algorithms (LNCS 1468, 1596, 1803, 2037, 2279, and 2611). This year the EvoCOP workshop on combinatorial optimization transformed itself into a conference in its own right, and the two conferences, together with the EvoWorkshops, EvoBIO, EvoIASP, EvoMUSART, EvoSTOC, EvoHOT, and EvoCOMNET, now form one of the largest events dedicated to Evolutionary Computation in Europe.

Genetic Programming (GP) is evolutionary computation that solves specific complex problems or tasks by evolving and adapting a population of computer programs, using Darwinian evolution and Mendelian genetics as its sources of inspiration. Some of the 38 papers included in these proceedings address foundational and theoretical issues, and there is also a wide variety of papers dealing with different application areas, such as computer science, engineering, language understanding, biology and design, demonstrating that GP is a powerful and practical problem-solving paradigm.

A total of 61 papers were received. A rigorous, double-blind, peer-review selection mechanism was applied to 58 of them. This resulted in 19 plenary talks (31% of those submitted) and 19 research posters. Every paper was reviewed by at least two of the 46 members of the program committee who were carefully selected internationally for their knowledge and competence. As far as possible, papers were matched with the reviewer's particular interests and special expertise. The result of this careful process can be seen here in the high quality of the contributions published within this volume.

Of the 38 accepted papers, 32 have authors who came from European countries (about 85%), confirming the strong European character of the conference. The other 6 came from the USA, Korea, China, New Zealand, and Australia, emphasizing the global nature of our field.

We would like to express our sincere thanks especially to the two internationally renowned speakers who gave keynote talks at the joint conference and workshops plenary sessions: Prof. Stephanie Forrest of the University of New Mexico, and Prof. Zbigniew Michalewicz of the University of North Carolina.

The success of any conference results from the efforts of many people, to whom we would like to express our gratitude. First, we would like to thank the members of the program committee for their attentiveness, perseverance, and willingness to provide high-quality reviews. We would especially like to thank Jennifer Willies who ensured the conference's continued existence and has been greatly influential in sustaining the high quality of the conference organization. Without Jennifer, we would have been lost. Last but not least, we thank the University of Coimbra for hosting the conference.

April 2004   Maarten Keijzer
                                                            Una-May O'Reilly
                                                               Simon Lucas
                                                              Ernesto Costa
                                                              Terence Soule

Organization

EuroGP 2004 was organized by EvoGP, the EvoNet Working Group on Genetic Programming.

Organizing Committee

Conference Co-chairs	Maarten Keijzer (Free University, The Netherland)
	Una-May O'Reilly (MIT, USA)
Publicity Chair	Simon Lucas (University of Essex, UK)
Local Chair	Ernesto Costa (University of Coimbra, Portugal)
Publication Chair	Terence Soule (University of Idaho, USA)

Program Committee

Vladan Babovic, Tectrasys AG
Wolfgang Banzhaf, Memorial University of Newfoundland
Bertrand Braunschweig, Institut Français du Pétrole
Martin C. Martin, MIT
Stefano Cagnoni, University of Parma
Jean-Jacques Chabrier, University of Burgundy
Pierre Colet, Laboratoire d'Informatique du Littoral
Ernesto Costa, University of Coimbra
Marco Dorigo, Université Libre de Bruxelles
Malachy Eaton, University of Limerick
Marc Ebner, Universitaet Wuerzburg
Jeroen Eggermont, Leiden University
Aniko Ekart, Hungarian Academy of Sciences
Daryl Essam, University of New South Wales
Francisco Fernandez de Vega, University of Extremadura
Cyril Fonlupt, Université du Littoral
Alex Freitas, University of Kent
Wolfgang Golubski, University of Siegen
Steven Gustafson, University of Nottingham
Jin-Kao Hao, Université d'Angers
Daniel Howard, QinetiQ
Christian Jacob, University of Calgary
Colin Johnson, University of Kent at Canterbury
Didier Keymeulen, Jet Propulsion Laboratory, CA, USA
Bill Langdon, University College London
Simon Lucas, University of Essex
Evelyne Lutton, INRIA Rocquencourt

Penousal Machado, University of Coimbra
Peter Martin, Naiad Consulting Ltd.
Julian Miller, University of York
Miguel Nicolau, University of Limerick
Michael O'Neill, University of Limerick
Francisco Pereira, Instituto Superior de Engenharia de Coimbra
Riccardo Poli, University of Essex
Conor Ryan, University of Limerick
Bart Rylander, University of Portland
Kazuhiro Saitou, University of Michigan
Marc Schoenauer, INRIA Rocquencourt
Alexei Skourikhine, Los Alamos National Laboratory
Adrian Stoica, Jet Propulsion Laboratory, CA, USA
Matthew Streeter, Carnegie Mellon University
Adrian Thompson, University of Sussex
Marco Tomassini, University of Lausanne
Krister Wolff, Chalmers University of Technology
Edwin de Jong, University of Utrecht

Sponsoring Institutions

Universidade de Coimbra, Portugal
EvoNet: the Network of Excellence in Evolutionary Computation, funded by the
European Commission's IST Programme

Table of Contents

Papers

Posters

Evaluation of Chess Position by Modular Neural Network Generated by Genetic Algorithm

Mathieu Autonès, Ariel Beck, Philippe Camacho, Nicolas Lassabe,
Hervé Luga, and François Scharffe

Institut de Recherche en Informatique de Toulouse, Université Paul Sabatier,
118 route de Narbonne 31062 Toulouse cedex, France

Abstract. In this article we present our chess engine Tempo. One of
the major difficulties for this type of program lies in the function for
evaluating game positions. This function is composed of a large number of
parameters which have to be determined and then adjusted. We propose
an alternative which consists in replacing this function by an artificial
neuron network (ANN). Without topological knowledge of this complex
network, we use the evolutionist methods for its inception, thus enabling
us to obtain, among other things, a modular network. Finally, we present
our results:

- reproduction of the XOR function which validates the method used
- generation of an evaluation function

1 Introduction

The game position evaluation function is a key part in a chess engine. It is composed of a long list of parameters [1], and using a genetic algorithm (GA) [8] to optimise them is relatively efficient, these parameters being obtained from extensive game experience. Another method, which consists of substituting an ANN for this list seems more interesting, because of the generalising capabilities of this model. In practice it is more difficult to implement. Network topology determination is the biggest problem. Evolutionist methods may help us, by evolving a network population which codes this function. We could code the matrix just as it is, in the chromosome [9], connections evolving through successive generations. This coding turns out to be unsatisfactory: the matrix size has to be prefixed and it is hard to predict it a priori. Network encoding then becomes the main problem of our study.

Boers and Kuiper's work [2] allows us, by using L-Systems, to generate modular neural networks whose size is independent of that of the chromosome, and crossover tolerant. We generate a population of L-System construction rules and then mark the resulting networks according to their capabilities to learn game position evaluations from real games. These positions are evaluated more and more deeply in the game tree, along with the increased complexity of the network.

M. Keijzer et al. (Eds.): EuroGP 2004, LNCS 3003, pp. 1–10, 2004.

2   Chess Engine

A chess engine contains three distinct parts: the management of the rules, investigation of the different variant pathways using a search algorithm, and the evaluation function.

2.1   Chess Rules

All chess engines need to know the rules to generate the legal moves or referee a game between two people. All legal moves are pre-calculated in the tables: the engine just needs to confirm that this move is one of them.

2.2   Search Algorithm

The search algorithm explores all the moves from a position and tries to find the best move. In our programme, we use the alphabeta algorithm with various heuristics [10], which are not mentioned here. The values of tree leaves are computed using an evaluation function, which is an ANN in this case.

2.3   Evaluation Function

The evaluation function is very important in all chess engines. It is very complex because it gives the final mark which it uses to select the move to play. The main operation of this function is to count the values of the pieces. After that, it is possible to refine the function, using a series of parameters to define:

- the king's safety
- maintenance of the bishop pair
- domination of the centre
- occupation of the open columns by the rooks.
- ...

We then calculate the sum of all the parameters to obtain the final mark. One of the main limitations of this technique is that we have to define the list of parameters and to set them up correctly, knowing that certain of these values will change during the game and are not self-compensating.

3   Neural Network

3.1   Presentation

Introduction. The human brain is certainly a most amazing organ. It is not a surprise if people try to pierce the secrets of its functioning, to recreate certain of its mechanisms artificially. Neural networks are directly inspired by this vision. The ANN are inspired directly by the structure of the human brain, which is schematically a field of neurons linked together. A Neuron is composed of three parts: dendrites, body and axon. The dendrites get the information (electrical impulses) from the other neurons. The body makes the sum of all this electrical information and if it goes beyond a certain level , the axon is activated, that is to say the neuron sends an electrical impulse to its successors.

The artificial neuron. By starting from these biological considerations, we can find an artificial neural model [12]. The artificial neuron is composed of n inputs which are real numbers and one output (that can be duplicated to power different successor neurons) which is the weighted sum of all the entries. The weights correspond to each one of the connections. It is these weights which will be modified during the learning process.

Learning method: back-propagation. *Principle.* Once a network is created it possesses inputs and outputs. The goal of the learning process is to make sure that, for a given problem, the ANN selects the "correct" outputs as a function of the entries which will be presented. A level is fixed and the learner tries to obtain it.

It is important to note that this learning is supervised. This is like having an expert give a part of some solutions for the entries and the outputs. However, it is impossible to have all the solutions, and one of the properties of the ANN is to generalise. After the learning, it can find the solution for entries which it has never seen (if the structure of the ANN is well adapted). Some other techniques could also be used. Various other learning methods exist. It is also possible to process the learning of a network by a GA. This method could be used once a good topology has beenfound for the network.

Remark. This learning process does not correspond to the humain brain learning process.

3.2   An Example: XOR Function

We have tested a simple example: the learning of XOR function by back-propagation. The particularity of this simple logical function is that it which cannot be learnt by an ANN composed of only one hidden layer.

The logical XOR function is a binary function with two variables:

```
F(0,0) = 0
F(0,1) = 1
F(1,0) = 1
F(1,1) = 0
```

One of the possible topologies for the network is the following matrix (Fig. 1). If we add one connection to it (from 0 to 4), we obtain another topology (Fig. 2) which can resolve the problem.

```
Matrix:        0 1 2 3 4

          0  0 0 1 1 0
          1  0 0 1 1 0
          2  0 0 0 0 1
          3  0 0 0 0 1
          4  0 0 0 0 0
```

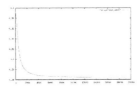

Fig. 1. Topology represented by the matrix

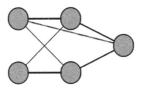

Fig. 2. Topology with one more connection

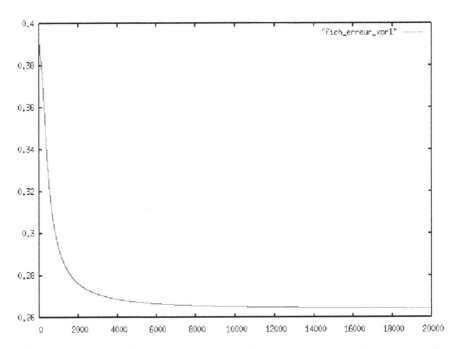

Fig. 3. Learning by the topology of Fig. 1: the graph represents the error on the function for each step of calcul

For the topology of Fig. 1, the error (Fig. 3) does not fall below the local minimum 0.26. In contrast, with the topology of Fig. 2 the learning is better (Fig. 4). This simple example shows how sensitve the learning is to the topology of the neuron.

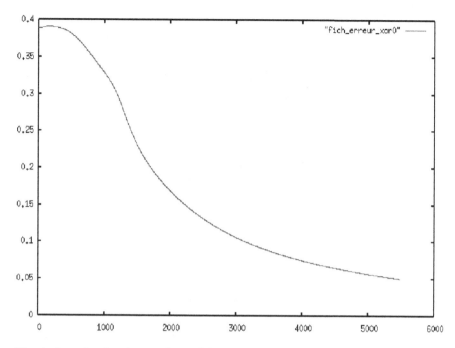

Fig. 4. Learning by the topology of Fig. 2: the graph represents the error on the function for each step of calculation

3.3   Back-Propagation: Limits and Solutions

Problems linked to back-propagation are essentially due to the structure of the network. Regarding this structure, a network will be able to learn, unable to learn, able to learn but need a long time, able to learn but unable to generalise. Another thing is that the net may potentially be able to learn but converges to a local minimum when initial weights are not correctly chosen. It is always the network structure that is responsible for the initial weights sensitivity: some nets are convergent for any set of initial weights, others do not converge every time. We noticed that nets with a modular topology were better for learning. By modularity, we mean the network is made up of many other sub-networks. A connection between two networks is a connection between each output of the first to each input of the second. The next paragraph explains how to create networks with strong modularity.

4   Neural Net Generation with L-Systems

L-Systems [11] are grammar systems generally used for generating artificial plants. They are based on cellular development. We use them to generate modular neural networks. These grammar rules are obtained from a string [4].

Fig. 5. Representation of a green plant by L-System

5   Genetic Algorithms

We originally used this method in order to solve the problem of the network design. How can we find a network topology which can learn the evaluation function? Genetic algorithms [8] provide a solution by exploring the network's possible space.

5.1   Presentation

Coming from Darwinian evolution principles, which maintain that the best individuals, those who adapt, will survive but the others will disappear, GA brings us a new manner of exploring the search space. They consist in manipulating a population of individuals(a byte tab). Each individual can be seen as a gene, carrying a number of L-System rules. Each individual is marked according to how it fits our needs. As in natural selection where better adapted individuals have better chances of surviving and reproducing, individuals we manipulate reproduce proportionally to their fitness. A new generation is created by selecting a number of individuals and recombining them, using some operators. The most commonly used operators are selection, crossover and mutation.

5.2   Implementation

We decided to program our GA library instead of taking an existing one. In this way, we have perfect knowledge of it is functioning and we are more able to set the parameters.

The coding. Respecting the chosen programming language (C++) the program uses three classes:

- class *AlgoG*
- class *Population*
- class *Individual*

An object of the *Population class* represents a population of individuals (or chromosomes) to which selection and crossover operators will be applied. These operators are methods of the class, as well as manipulation functions on the disc. This population is composed of *popSize* individuals including *nbGenes* genes of *genSize* bits. The selection method used is based on the rank.
   rank select algorithm [2]:

1. Selection of two individuals to cross
2. Application of the crossover operator
3. Evaluation of the new individual
4. Repeat points 1,2,3 as long as a percentage of the population has not been cross-referenced

This is done as long as the best individual has not achieved a sufficiently good evaluation, (i.e. as long as the grammatical rules coded in the individual continue to produce a network whose performance is not up to standard). We can follow the evolution of the population by observing the evaluation of individuals as a function of population generation. Parameters allow adjustment of the crossover, inversion and mutation rates. The selection function and percentage of population renewal are set in the same way.

6   Results

We present our results in this section. The computer used was a Pentium III 1.3 GHz.

6.1   XOR Function

First we tested our algorithms to know if they gave good results. We chose to test them on a classic example: the XOR function, which we knew the results of [1]. After one hour, we found two nets similar to those found by Boer and Kuiper.

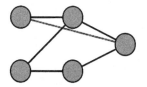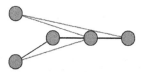

Fig. 6. ANN learning the XOR function perfectly

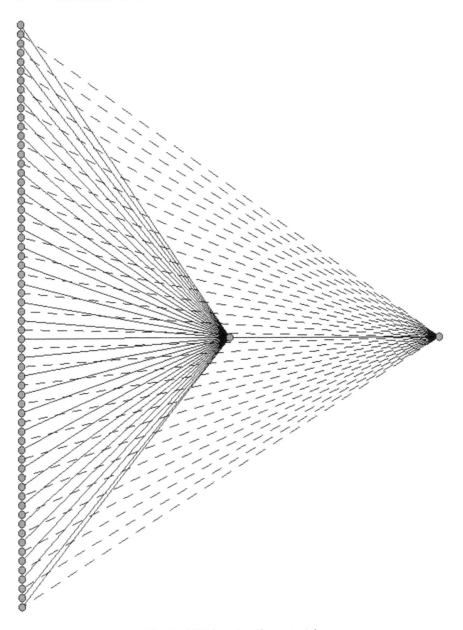

Fig. 7. ANN learning the material

6.2   Chess Evaluation Function

We now have some techniques which allow us to perform the automatic learning of a chess engine evaluation function. As this function is really complex, we decided to proceed by steps. A simple function was learnt at first. The best individuals learnt more and more complex functions.

Material evaluation function. The material plays an important role in the final position mark. A player presenting more material has more chances of winning the game. The learning consists in presenting positions with differences in the materials. It is obviously impossible to present every configuration of a chess position. A hundred positions are necessary in order for our net to generalise. Even if the net seems very simple, it is the most effective one found by GA's. Moreover, it is as fast as an equivalent algorithmic function.

Remark. During the learning process of the XOR function (see Sect. 6.1) most of networks were invalidated because they did not have the right interface. To resolve this problem, we complete the networks which have not the right number of entries to obtain the desired interface. We save time with this solution because almost all networks are used.

Complex evaluation function. Currently we are working on the learning of a more complex evaluation function. The function learned describes the control of the fields by the pieces, the material and some notion of pawn structure. The largest nets found to resolve this probleme have more then two hundred neurons. But solutions of this kind begin to take time to compute so we are working on some optimisation as in Boers and Kuiper's work [5].

7   Conclusion

Although these techniques are costly in terms of computing time, they will become increasingly accessible in the next few years. It seems interesting to continue research on these methods. Optimisation can be performed whatever the problem, which will make the method more efficient It is also possible to combine several topolgy generating techniques depending on how close the solution is. This flexibility seems to indicate that it is easy to generalise these algorithms to many types of problem. The realisation of an evaluation function for a chess program shows the resolving power of these evolutionary thechniques.

References

1. Berliner H.J. Construction of evaluation function for large domains, Artificial Intelligence, vol.14 p.205-220, 1979
2. Boers E.J.W and Kuiper H. Biological metaphors and the design of modular artificial neural networks, Leiden University, 1992

3. Boers E.J.W and Kuiper H. Designing Modular Artificial Neural Networks, Leiden University, 1993
4. Boers E.J.W. Using L-Systems as Graph Grammar: G2L-Systems, Leiden University, 1995
5. Boers E.J.W and Kuiper H. Combined Biological Metaphors, Leiden University, 2001
6. Gruau F. Neural Network Synthesis using Cellular Encoding and the Genetic Algorithm, École Normale Supérieure de Lyon, 1994
7. Happel B.L.M. and Murre J.M.J. The Design and Evolution of Modular Neural Network Architectures, Leiden University, 1994
8. Holland J.H. Adaptation in natural and artificial systems, University of Michigan Press, Ann Harbor, 1975
9. Kitano H. Designing neural networks using genetic algorithms with graph generation system, Complex Systems, vol 4: 461–476, 1990
10. D.E Knuth and R.W. Moore An analysis of alpha-beta pruning Artificial Intelligence, vol.6, nun 4 p.293-326, 1975
11. Lindenmayer A. Mathematical models for celluar interaction and development, parts I and II, Journal of theoritical biology, 18 280–315 1968
12. Mc Culloch W.S. and Pitts W. A logical calculus of the ideas immanent in nervous activity, Bull. Mathem. Biophys, 5, p.115-133. 1943
13. Siddiqi A.A and S.M. Lucas S.M. A comparison of matrix rewriting versus direct encoding for evolving neural networks International Conference on Evolutionary Computation p. 392–397, 1998
14. Yao X. and Liu Y. New Evolutionary System for Evolving Artificial Neural Networks IEEE Transactions on Neural Networks vol: 8 p.694-713, 1997

Coevolution of Algorithms and Deterministic Solution of Equations in Free Groups

Richard F. Booth* and Alexandre V. Borovik**

Department of Mathematics
UMIST
PO Box 88, Manchester M60 1QD
United Kingdom
{richard.booth,borovik}@umist.ac.uk

Abstract. We discuss the use of evolutionary algorithms for solving problems in combinatorial group theory, using a class of equations in free groups as a test bench. We find that, in this context, there seems to be a correlation between successful evolutionary algorithms and the existence of good deterministic algorithms. We also trace the convergence of co-evolution of the population of fitness functions to a deterministic solution.

1 Introduction

Group theory always had a very strong algorithmic component [16] but traditionally ignored the practical complexity of algorithms, and, since many problems in combinatorial group theory are undecidable, was concerned mostly with decidability/undecidability issues. Most known group theoretic algorithms usually have at best exponential complexity by their nature and cannot be executed on modern computers now or in the near future. The same is true for many polynomial algorithms since the power of the polynomial involved is very frequently too big for the computation to be completed in real time.

Applications of genetic/evolutionary algorithms in group theory are relatively new but have already yielded very interesting results [19,20]. This paper discusses the results of an experimental study of the behavior of evolutionary algorithms adapted for solving equations in free groups. The wider aim of the project was an exploration into

- the possible reasons that evolutionary algorithms appear to be so efficient in solving particular classes of group-theoretic problems;
- the limits of their applicability in combinatorial group theory;
- their relation to deterministic algorithms.

More specifically, we attempted to trace how coevolution of an evolutionary algorithm converges to a deterministic algorithm, using equations on free groups with one variable as a test bench.

* Supported by EPSRC grant GR/R29451.
** Partially supported by the same grant.

M. Keijzer et al. (Eds.): EuroGP 2004, LNCS 3003, pp. 11–22, 2004.
© Springer-Verlag Berlin Heidelberg 2004

2 Evolutionary Algorithms for Solving Equations on the Free Group

2.1 Equations on the Free Group

Let F be a free group with free generators $f_1, \ldots, f_k$. Definition and basic properties of free groups could be found in most textbooks on group theory [16]; however, the reader will need only the briefest of descriptions as given in the next few lines. The elements of F are freely reduced words in (non-commutative) letters f_i and f_i^{-1}; "freely reduced" means that the word does not contain occurrences of f_i and f_i^{-1} in adjacent positions. The group operation is concatenation of words followed by the free reduction, that is, cancellation of adjacent occurrences of f_i and f_i^{-1}. The empty word is the identity element 1 of F, while the inversion is given by reversing the word and inverting every letter:

$$(f_{i_1}^{\epsilon_1} \cdots f_{i_k}^{\epsilon_k})^{-1} = f_{i_k}^{-\epsilon_k} \cdots f_{i_1}^{-\epsilon_1}.$$

An *equation* in variables $x_1, x_2, \ldots, x_n$ over F is a formal expression of the form

$$g_1 x_{i_1}^{\epsilon_1} g_2 x_{i_2}^{\epsilon_2} \cdots g_m x_{i_m}^{\epsilon_m} g_{m+1} = 1, \tag{1}$$

where $g_i \in F$, $\epsilon_i = \pm 1$ and $i_j \in \{1, \ldots, n\}$. A *solution* is a substitution $x_i := u_i$ of words $u_i \in F$ for the variables x_i, such that the equation becomes identity in F.

Notice that, by the definition of the free group, the generators $f_1, \ldots, f_k$ do not commute: $f_i f_j \neq f_j f_i$ if $i \neq j$. If we allow commutation $f_i f_j = f_j f_i$ for some (but not all) pairs (f_i, f_j) of generators, we come to the concept of a *partially commutative free group* or *trace group* [8]; this concept is closely related to that of the *trace monoid* [9], which is just the monoid of positive (that is, not involving the inversion of generators) words in (partially commutative) letters $f_1, \ldots, f_k$. The theory of equations on trace monoids and trace groups is of some interest to computer science [9], and the relatively well-developed theory of free groups is an important source of ideas and methods for works on trace groups [8,18].

We briefly outline some known theoretical results about equations on free groups.

Lyndon [15] described all solutions of equations with one variable. Appel [1] simplified Lyndon's description and found upper bounds (unfortunately, at least exponential) on length of minimal solutions. Their results have been improved and clarified by Chiswell and Remeslennikov [5]. Recently Gilman and Myasnikov [10] used context-free languages to give an elementary proof of Appel's results.

Comerford and Edmunds [6] found an algorithm (again, at least exponential) for solving quadratic equations (that is, equations which contain at most two occurrences of each variable x_i) and described all solutions.

In the general case, Makanin [17] showed that solutions of equations over free groups are recursively bounded; this means that there exists a recursive function $f(u)$ such that an arbitrary equation $E = 1$ (over the free group F) has a solution in F if and only if it has a solution of length at most $f(|E|)$, where $|E|$

is the length of equation E. Makanin's method, however, does not provide any practical estimates for f, therefore his algorithm for solving equations amounts to the full search over a set of size beyond any concept of feasibility.

Another theoretical development is the result by Kharlampovich and Myasnikov [12, Theorem 2] who showed that the problem of solving an arbitrary equation over a free group can be reduced to reasonably structured, albeit very big systems of equations, see [12] for the rather technical details. Essentially, their result reduces arbitrary equations to systems of quadratic equations. Again, it does not provide any practical approaches to solving equations.

In this paper, we concentrate on equations with one variable in the free group. This is the case where the "deterministic" theory is already highly non-trivial, while the behaviour of evolutionary algorithms is sufficiently transparent. We look at the coevolution as a bridge between the evolutionary and deterministic algorithms. An alternative and/or complementary approach to semi-deterministic fine-tuning of the evolution by means of *traceback* (some form of an "on the fly" analysis of convergence) is given in [2]. Also, paper [2] discusses some applications of genetic algorithms to solving equations in free semigroups. We note also the work by Craven [7] who applied genetic algorithms to certain classes of equations on trace groups.

2.2 Equations on the Free Group as a Test Bench for the Evolutionary Approach

We refer to [22,24] as general sources for the theory of genetic and evolutionary algorithms.

In most traditional applications of evolutionary algorithms, they are used as optimisation strategies, applied to problems where the concept of an exact solution is not meaningful. (A noticeable exception is constraint satisfaction problems [23,25].)

In the case of equations in groups we aim at finding *exact* solutions of a random problem from a large class of problems. Fortunately, we have a fitness function which provides a mathematically meaningful measure of distance from being a solution.

Our chromosomes are group elements expressed as words in generators; they inevitably reflect the structure of the group. We want to understand what happens in the course of evolution of a population of approximate solutions. Therefore it is natural to pick a group to study in which the mapping from reduced words to the group structure is as transparent as possible. The free group meets this requirement: two reduced words are equal as elements of the group if and only if they are identical as words. In particular, free groups have the advantage that mathematical effects of standard mutation and crossover operators on strings (words) are sufficiently transparent.

In our computational implementation, the chromosomes are made of group elements together with a cache for keeping previously calculated fitness values. The group elements are represented as vectors of integers, n standing for the generator f_n if n is positive, and f_{-n}^{-1}, if n is negative. Members of the initial population are generated as strings of random letters of some fixed length; after free reduction, this gives a moderate variation in the lengths of the initial words.

2.3   Reproduction Operators

Our reproduction operators take two parameters: the existing population of chromosomes, and a number of offspring to produce. They include the following types:

- Mutation: each of these uses a selection function, discussed later, to supply a parent chromosome from the population. This is then passed to the routine producing the new chromosome.
  - Insertion: insert a randomly chosen letter (free generator or inverse) in a randomly chosen position.
  - End insertion: insert a randomly chosen letter at one of the ends of the word.
  - Replacement: replace the letter at a randomly chosen position with a randomly chosen letter.
  - Deletion: remove the letter in a randomly chosen position.
  - Lazy crossover: choose a random position, cut the word in two at that point. Randomly select one part to keep, and discard the other.
- The only recombination operator we have used is one-point crossover; randomly select a real number r between 0 and 1. Cut each of the parent chromosomes into two parts such that the left part is of length approximately r times the length of the original chromosome. Return the chromosome whose left end is the left part of one and right end is the right part of the other.
- Our experience showed that the strict elitist approach to survival is the most suitable for our purposes: to produce n offspring, return the fittest n of the current population unchanged. This is one of the observations which suggest that if the fitness function is chosen in an optimal way, the evolution is guided by the good structure of the search space.

2.4   Selection

Our selection function is a variant of roulette selection. Let the population size be p, the population members be c_i for $1 \leq i \leq p$, and the fitness of a chromosome denoted by $f(c)$. Since we minimise fitness function rather than maximise, with 0 optimally fit, we assign slots on the roulette wheel using the function

$$f'(c) = F - f(c) + s \text{ where } F = \max_i f(c_i)$$

where s is a non-negative integer *smoothing parameter*. To that end, we set the *wheel size* W as

$$W = \sum_1^p f'(c_i).$$

Then an integer j is chosen uniformly at random from the numbers $0, \ldots, W-1$ and the chromosome c_k is selected with k being minimal such that

$$j < \sum_{1}^{k} f'(c_i).$$

2.5   The Population of Fitness Functions

It became clear early on in the project that we need to vary the fitness function and, indeed, treat a collection of suitable functions as a population on its own. Luckily, the nature of the problem allows for a variety of fitness functions. Some terminology will be useful.

For a given problem, a (*loose*) *fitness function* satisfies

$$f(u) \geq 0 \text{ with } f(u) = 0 \text{ if } u \text{ is a solution.}$$

We say that $f(u)$ is a *strict fitness function*, if, in addition,

$$f(u) = 0 \text{ if and only if } u \text{ is a solution.}$$

The sum of any number of fitness functions with positive weights is also a fitness function, and is strict if any of the components is strict. Our fitness functions are normally built from simple components in this way.

We work with a given equation, represented as a word $\mathbf{e}(x)$ in the variable x with solution given by $\mathbf{e}(x) = 1$. Our typical strict component is *length* $f(u) = l(\mathbf{e}(u))$ of the (reduced) word $\mathbf{e}(u)$ obtained by substituting $x := u$.

If we write the equation in the form $L(x) = R(x)$ with the distinguished left side $L(x)$ and right side $R(x)$ (so that $\mathbf{e}(x) = L(x)R^{-1}(x)$), the *cyclic Hamming distance* between $L(u)$ and $R(u)$ is a very useful fitness function.

Here, the *Hamming distance* of two words is the minimal number of differences possible comparing places between the two words with some fixed offset; if differences in length occur, these are thought of as comparisons between letters and the null letter, and are counted as differences between the words. The *cyclic Hamming distance* is the minimal Hamming distance comparing all cyclic shifts of $L(u)$ and $R(u)$. For example, the cyclic Hamming distance of $x_3^{-1}x_1^3x_2x_5$ and $x_5x_2x_1^3x_3^{-1}$ is 2, obtained by aligning $x_3^{-1}x_1x_1x_1x_2x_5$ with $x_2x_1x_1x_1x_3^{-1}x_5$.

We frequently use the following loose fitness functions:

- The total number of letters in the reduced word $\mathbf{e}(u)$ which come from constants (that is, were not part of subwords u resulting from the substitution $x := u$). This is, of course, dependent on the exact sequence of cancellations during the free reduction; we always do them from the leftmost to the rightmost.
- The length of remnants, in the reduced word $\mathbf{e}(u)$, of words u substituted for particular occurrences of x.
- The length of the shortest non-zero remnant of such an occurrence of u.
- Lengths of remnants of particular constants in $\mathbf{e}(u)$.

In addition, given a strict fitness function f', any integer-valued function g, and a positive integer n we can produce a strict fitness function by

$$f(u) = \begin{cases} 0 & \text{whenever } f'(u) = 0 \\ f'(u) + g(u) & \text{when } f'(u), f'(u) + g(u) > 0 \\ n & \text{when } f'(u) > 0, f'(u) + g(u) < 0. \end{cases}$$

One sometimes useful value for $g(u)$ is a multiple of $l(u)$, the length of u.

Clearly, by altering the original, simple, strict fitness functions in these ways, what we are doing is reshaping the geometry of the search space, guiding the search towards and away from particular local minima (some of which are solutions) and even removing non-solution local minima.

2.6   Generation of Problems

Generation of equations is not a trivial problem, taking into account that, for testing our algorithms, we need sufficiently random equations that have solutions.

We say that a word $\mathbf{e} = \mathbf{e}(x)$ in the free generators $f_1, \ldots, f_k$ and the variable x is *solvable* if the equation

$$\mathbf{e}(x) = 1$$

has a solution in the free group F (that is, there is a free group word u which, when substituted for x, reduces the left hand side of the equation to the identity).

Clearly, a random word in the free generators and x is unlikely to be solvable. This can be explicitly proven [21] within the probabilistic framework of [4], and is easy to see in the important special case of *balanced* equations, that is, equations

$$g_1 x^{\epsilon_1} g_2 x^{\epsilon_2} \cdots g_m x^{\epsilon_m} g_{m+1} = 1 \tag{2}$$

with $\epsilon_i = 0$. Indeed, if we consider the natural homomorphism $F \to \mathbb{Z}^k$ from the free group F to the additive group $\mathbb{Z}^k$ freely generated by the *commuting* letters $f_1, \ldots, f_k$, we see that all x^{ϵ_i} cancel out and therefore the necessary condition for solvability of (2) is $g_1 \cdots g_{m+1} = 0$ (in $\mathbb{Z}^k$). Assume that we generate our equations in such a way that the words g_i are random, independent and not freely reduced, and let n be their total length in terms of $f_1, \ldots, f_k$. Then the probability of a random word $g = g_1 \cdots g_{m+1}$ being equal 0 in $\mathbb{Z}^k$ is the classical return probability of a random walk of length n on the k-dimensional lattice $\mathbb{Z}^k$ and is estimated as $(2\pi n)^{-k/2}$ [26, Proposition P9 on p. 75]. Hence, (2) is solvable with probability less than $(2\pi n)^{-k/2}$. This bound, although sufficiently tight for practical purposes, is still very crude and can be improved [21].

One obvious possibility for the mass production is given by (obviously solvable) equations of the form

$$W(x) = W(A), \tag{3}$$

where A is a random word in the free generators, $W(x)$ a random word in constants $B, C, \ldots$ (each of which, in its turn, is a random word in the generators) and x. These always have solution $x = A$, and are very easily solved by using cyclic Hamming distance as the main component of the fitness, and therefore are not very interesting.

We can construct solvable equations from smaller solvable building blocks in several ways:

- Commutator: if one of $\mathbf{a}$ or $\mathbf{b}$ is solvable then their commutator $[\mathbf{a}, \mathbf{b}] = \mathbf{a}^{-1}\mathbf{b}^{-1}\mathbf{ab}$ is solvable.
- Power and conjugation: if $\mathbf{a}$ is solvable then $\mathbf{a}^n$ and $B^{-1}\mathbf{a}B$ are solvable for any word B in $f_1, \ldots, f_k$.
- Inserting a solvable equation at any point or points within a word in $f_1, \ldots, f_k$ that reduces to the identity gives a solvable equation. For example, if $\mathbf{a}$ is solvable and A, B are words in $f_1, \ldots, f_k$ then $A\mathbf{a}BaB^{-1}A^{-1}$ is solvable.

We get more challenging problems by deliberately introducing steep local minima or multiple solutions:

- $[Ax, Bx] = 1$. Multiple solutions $x = A^{-1}, B^{-1}$.
- $(Cx)^{-10}[Ax, B](Cx)^{10} = 1$. Solution $x = A^{-1}$, but a steep local minimum as $x \to C^{-1}$.
- $[Ax, B(Cx)^{10}]$. Solution $x = A^{-1}$, but a steep local minimum as $x \to C^{-1}$.

Using the loose fitness functions discussed earlier, it is easy to "flatten out" these minima and encourage convergence to whichever solution is desired; for example, assigning a very high weight to the size of the remnants of constant A in the equation will solve all of these classes of problems.

2.7   The Primary Evolution

We distinguish between the *primary evolution* aimed at solving equations from a particular class, and the *coevolution* which optimises the primary one. Parameters controlling the primary algorithm are population size p, fitness function f, numbers of offspring to be produced by each type of reproduction operator at each generation (the sum of which must be p), and the maximum number of generations, M. The fitness function is typically represented as a set of weights for various building block functions, as described in the previous subsection.

1. Set $g = 0$. Generate an initial population of random words of size p.
2. Find the fitnesses of the current population. If any are of fitness zero, return g and the solution, the chromosome of fitness zero.
3. Increment g. If $g = M$, terminate, returning failure.
4. Generate a new population by producing the specified number of offspring for each reproduction operator. Loop back to Step 2.

3   Coevolution

3.1   Setup

Optimisation of the primary algorithm by assigning weights to remnants of constants exploits our understanding of the nature and the behaviour of the equation. It turns the primary evolutionary algorithm into little more than a randomised variant on the natural deterministic algorithm (such as "try adding letters to the end of x; replace x with the result whenever $l(xA^{-1}) - l(x)$ improves"). It is natural to suggest that a coevolution of the population of parameters of the primary algorithm might converge to a "good" parameter set.

Our setup for coevolution is very straightforward. We start with a small population of randomly chosen parameter sets of some fixed population size. Fitness is assessed by running the algorithm on each parameter set for up to specified number M of generations; the resulting fitness is given by $M + k - g$, where g is the number of generations taken to solve the problem and k is a non-negative constant; this makes fitter parameter sets more positive. Some small fixed value is assigned as the fitness of parameter sets which do not solve the problem within the time limit.

The next generation is made of the fittest parameter sets from the old population and parameter sets obtained by breeding; we use roulette selection, and the reproduction operator takes mean average of the parameters of the two parents. There are several sensible possibilities for termination criteria. For example, since this is an optimisation algorithm rather than a solution algorithm, we may choose to terminate once the k-th best parameter set reaches some threshold fitness, so that we can compare parameter sets achieving good results.

We have run many small-scale experiments of this type on "difficult" equations discussed in the previous section, and this coevolutionary approach works extremely well. Problems attempted generally converged quickly to the sorts of semi-deterministic solutions expected, and often produced multiple, unexpected ways of expressing much the same approach with different fitness parameters.

3.2   A Brief Case Study

We examine the class of equations given by

$$[(Ax)^2, Bx]Bx = 1 \tag{4}$$

where A and B are random constants, different for each run of the primary evolutionary algorithm. This class of equation is particularly poorly handled by a naive choice of fitness function: its solution is $x = B^{-1}$, while $f(u) = l([(Au)^2, Bu]Bu)$ has a steep local minimum at $u = A^{-1}$. We assigned separate weights to "remnants of A", "remnants of the first appearance of B", "remnants of the last appearance of B", and each of the three appearances of x in the formula written in this manner. We run the primary evolution on equations with coefficients A and B of length 10 in 5 generators. In a first generation of ten randomly chosen parameter sets, typically fewer than half will reach a solution within the allotted 750 generations, but after two or three generations of the coevolution, each generation consisting of eight chosen by crossover, one elitist survivor, and one random parameter set, most parameter sets solve, and only the random parameter set does not solve the equation.

A typical outcome, for the best-performing parameter set in the fifth generation, is the overall reduced length $l([(Au)^2, Bu]Bu)$ being assigned weight 1, weights 4 and 8 assigned to the two occurrences of B, and weight 1 assigned to the second occurrence of x. When this same parameter set is then tested on the same class of equations with words of length 100 and 10 generators, it converges to a solution $x = B^{-1}$ rather quickly – in five consecutive runs, after 351, 354, 419, 444, and 332 generations.

3.3   The Limitations of Our Approach

For an efficient implementation of the coevolution, we need to run it on "short" equations and then apply the optimised parameter sets to "full scale" equations from the same class. Ability to vary the size of an equation (the total length of coefficients) assumes the knowledge of its structure. Our input language includes symbols $[,]$ and ^{n} for commutator $[X, Y] = X^{-1}Y^{-1}XY$ and powers $X^n = X \cdots X$, which allows to reduce the number of coefficients and occurrences of x. In the example above (4), the size of the coevolution problem increases if the equation is rewritten in a equivalent form as

$$x^{-1}Ax^{-1}Ax^{-1}BA^{-1}xA^{-1}xB^{-1}xB^{-1}x = 1.$$

If the coefficients of the equation involve more than two free generators $f_1, \ldots, f_k$ of the ambient free group F_k (which, of course, means that $k > 2$) then we can decrease the size of the equation by specialising it to an equation over a free group $F_l = \langle g_1, \ldots, g_l \rangle$ over a smaller alphabet by killing some of the generators (by mapping $f_i \mapsto 1$) or by identifying some other generators (by mapping $f_i \mapsto g_h$, $f_j \mapsto g_h$). Obviously, the solution of the original equations are mapped to solutions of the specialised one. However, a very small number of generators of the new free group of the specialised equation sometimes slows down the coevolution, since it leads to frequent freak successes of the principal evolution, which does not allow to eliminate efficiently very bad parameter sets.

Equations over a free group with small number of generators are easier for the primary evolution, but harder for the co-evolution since specialisation does not sufficiently reduce the size of the equation.

3.4   Deterministic Solution

The experimental data convincingly demonstrates that the optimal fitness function found by coevolution usually has a relatively large weight for the auxiliary fitness functions measuring the degree of cancellation of the variable x in some "critical" position in the equation. A very recent result, due to Gilman and Myasnikov [10] and Kvaschuk, Myasnikov, Remeslennikov [14] explains why this should be expected.

Theorem 1 ([10,14]). *For any solution x of an equation*

$$A_1 x^{\pm 1} A_2 x^{\pm 1} A_3 x^{\pm 1} \cdots x^{\pm 1} A_n = 1,$$

some occurrence of x is completely cancelled in a subexpression of length at most 4 in terms of A_i and x (such as, say, $A_2 x^{\pm 1} A_3 x^{\pm 1}$ or $x^{\pm 1} A_2 x^{\pm 1} A_3$).

This result already points to a possible deterministic algorithm for solving the equation, and this algorithm is described (and proved to be polynomial) in [14].

We indicate, as a possible direction of further research, that the analysis of the proof in [10] in combination with the probabilistic machinery for languages produce for finite automata as described in [4] might leave to a rigorous proof of the convergence of co-evolution to a deterministic solution.

4   Conclusions

The results of application of evolutionary and genetic algorithms to group theoretic problems, as described in this paper and in [2,7,19,20], lead us to formulate the following heuristic principle:

- The existence of an efficient evolutionary algorithm for solving a class of group-theoretic problems strongly suggests the existence of a good deterministic algorithm for that class.
- Furhtermore, refining the parameters of an evolutionary algorithm, and especially optimising its fitness function, whether manually or by coevolution, can help to discover such an effective algorithm.

We understand that this might seem excessively general. However, one can compare our thesis with the probably better known assertion that the existence of a polynomial algorithm for a reasonable and compact algebraic problem should normally suggest the existence of a good and practically feasible polynomial algorithm. This is how Neal Koblitz put it in [13, p. 37]:

> *The experience has been that if a problem of practical interest is in P, then there is an algorithm for it whose running time is bounded by a small power of the input length.*

We qualify our thesis by emphasising that we are talking about a specific range of problems, and that we impose stringent requirements on the performance of the resulting algorithms.

For us, "efficient" performance of an evolutionary algorithm means that

- the run time of the algorithm (by which we mean, roughly, the product of the number of generations required and the population size in use) depends only moderately, certainly sub-quadratically, on the size of inputs and other complexity-critical parameters such as size of the alphabet (the set of generators of the group).

- The algorithm should work for any input sizes computationally feasible for the underlying algebraic procedures.
- The algorithm is scalable, that is, parameters of an evolutionary algorithm found by running co-evolution of parameter sets on the "small" test problems can be successfully used on large scale problems.

Once we specialise our requirements, it becomes more plausible to suggest that the structure of the search space under the fitness function is the crucial factor in the efficiency of the evolutionary algorithm. Efficient evolutionary algorithms are guided by a "good" structure of the search space, produced by careful adjustment of fitness functions. As we mentioned earlier, his is more likely to be the case when optimal parameters are found by coevolution, with the primary evolution based on strict elitist selection.

It is tempting to suggest further that a good structure, once experimentally discovered, can be described and utilised in a deterministic algorithm. We have to expect, however, that the actual design of a good algorithm might happen to be a much more difficult and time consuming task than a straightforward programming of an evolutionary search. Indeed, in the few cases when the performance of evolutionary algorithms on groups found an explanation in theoretical results, these explanations happen to be non-trivial and very varied by nature.

- In the case of equations on free groups as described in the present paper, the theoretical explanation comes from the theory of context free languages applied to equations in free groups (Gilman and Myasnikov [10]).
- Some of Craven's genetic algorithms for solving simple equations in trace groups (such as the conjugacy equation, $ax = xb$) [7] have very efficient deterministic analogues [27], while for other, more intricate problems, deterministic algorithms have been developed as the result of the analysis of the behaviour of genetic algorithms [3].
- The most intricate example so far is a genetic version of the so-called Whitehead algorithm for free groups (Miasnikov and Myasnikov [20]). Unfortunately, technical details necessary for its discussion are out of scope of the present paper. We notice only that, in the case of the free group with two generators, the underlying structure (the so-called Whitehead graph) has been thoroughly analysed by Khan [11] and shown to have geometric properties so good that they indeed should direct the evolution.

In the light of this experience, coevolution appears to be a useful tool for bridging the gap between the experiment and the theory; in our opinion, this heuristic aspect of coevolution deserves further study. We believe that it might lead to the discovery of new interesting deterministic algorithms.

References

1. Appel, K.: One-variable equations in free groups. Proc. Amer. Math. Soc. **19** (1968) 912–918

2. Booth, R. F., Bormotov, D. Yu., Borovik, A. V.: Genetic algorithms and equations in free groups and semigroups. Contemp. Math. (to appear)
3. Borovik, A. V., Esyp, E. S., Kazatchkov, I. V., Remeslennikov, V. N.: Divisibility theory for free partially commutative groups (preprint)
4. Borovik, A. V., Myasnikov, A. G., Remeslennikov, V. N.: Multiplicative measures on free groups. Int. J. Algebra Comput. (to appear).
5. Chiswell, I. M., Remeslennikov, V. N.: Equations in free groups with one variable: I. J. Group Theory **3** (2000) 445–466
6. Comerford, L. P., Edmunds, C. C.: Quadratic equations over free groups and free products. J. Algebra **68** (1981) 276–297
7. Craven, M.: Genetic algorithms on trace groups (preprint)
8. Diekert, V., Muscholl, A.: Solvability of equations in free partially commutative groups is decidable. Lect. Notes Comp. Sci. **2076** (2001) 543–554
9. Diekert V., Rosenberger, G., eds.: The Book of Traces. World Scientific, Singapore e.a. (1995)
10. Gilman, R., Myasnikov, A.: One variable equations in free groups via context free languages. Contemp. Math. (to appear)
11. Khan, B.: Hyperbolicity of the automorphism graph of the free group of rank two (preprint)
12. Kharlampovich, O., Myasnikov, A. G.: Irreducible affine varieties over a free group. 2: Systems in triangular quasi-quadratic form and description of residually free groups. J. Algebra **200** (1998) 517–570
13. Koblitz, N.: Algebraic Aspects of Cryprography. Springer, Berlin a. o. (1998)
14. Kvaschuk, A., Myasnikov, A. G., Remeslennikov, V. N.: Equations in one variable in free groups (preprint)
15. Lyndon, R. C.: Equations in free groups. Trans. Amer. Math. Soc. **96** (1960) 445–457
16. Lyndon, R. C., Schupp, P. E.: Combinatorial Group Theory. Springer, Berlin a. o. (1977)
17. Makanin, G. S.: Equations in a free group. Izv. Akad. Nauk SSSR Ser. Mat. **46** (1982) 1199–1273 (in Russian; translation: Math. USSR Izv. **21** (1983))
18. Matiyasevich, Yu.: Some decision problems for traces. Lect. Notes Comp. Sci. **1234** (1997) 248–257
19. Miasnikov, A. D.: Genetic algorithms and the Andrews-Curtis conjecture. Internat. J. Algebra Comput. **9** no. 6 (1999) 671–686
20. Miasnikov, A. D., Myasnikov, A. G.: Whitehead method and genetic algorithms. Contemp. Math. (to appear)
21. Myasnikov, A. G., Remeslennikov, V. N.: Random equations in one variable on free groups (in preparation)
22. Michalewicz, Z.: Genetic Algorithms + Data Structure = Evolution Programs (3rd rev. and extended ed.). Springer, Berlin a. o. (1996)
23. Michalewicz, Z., Schoenauer, M.: Evolutionary algorithms for constrained parameter optimization problems. Evolutionary Computation **4** no. 1 (1996) 1–32
24. Mitchell, M.: An Introduction to Genetic Algorithms. The MIT Press, Cambridge, MA (1998)
25. Paredis, J.: Coevolutionary constraint satisfaction. In: Proc. 3rd Ann. Conf. Parallel Problem Solving from Nature. Springer, Berlin a. o. (1994) 46–55
26. Spitzer, F.: Principles of Random Walk. Springer, Berlin a. o. (2001)
27. Wrathall, C.: Free partially commutative groups. In: Combinatorics, Computing and Complexity (Tianjing and Beijing, 1988) Kluwer Acad. Publ., Dordrecht (1989) 195–216

Designing Optimal Combinational Digital Circuits Using a Multiple Logic Unit Processor

Sin Man Cheang[1], Kin Hong Lee[2], and Kwong Sak Leung[2]

[1] Department of Computing
Hong Kong Institute of Vocational Education (Kwai Chung), Hong Kong SAR, China
smcheang@vtc.edu.hk
[2] Department of Computer Science and Engineering
The Chinese University of Hong Kong, Hong Kong SAR, China
{khlee,ksleung}@cse.cuhk.edu.hk

Abstract. Genetic Parallel Programming (GPP) is a novel Genetic Programming paradigm. The GPP Accelerating Phenomenon, i.e. parallel programs are easier to be evolved than sequential programs, opens up a new approach to evolve solution programs in parallel forms. Based on the GPP paradigm, we developed a combinational digital circuit learning system, the GPP+MLP system. An optimal Multiple Logic Unit Processor (MLP) is designed to evaluate genetic parallel programs. To show the effectiveness of the proposed GPP+MLP system, four multi-output Binary arithmetic circuits are used. Experimental results show that both the gate counts and the propagation gate delays of the evolved circuits are less than conventional designs. For example, in a 3-bit multiplier experiment, we obtained a combinational digital circuit with 26 two-input logic gates in 6 gate levels. It utilizes 4 gates less than a conventional design.

1 Introduction

Genetic Programming (GP) [1] has been widely applied to different application areas. There are two main streams in GP, standard GP [2] and Linear structure GP (LGP) [3]. In standard GP, a genetic program is represented in a tree structure. Genetic operators (e.g. crossovers and mutations) manipulate branches and leave nodes of program trees. LGP is based on the principle of register machines. In LGP, a genetic program is represented in a linear list of machine code instructions or high-level language statements. A linear genetic program can run on a targeted machine directly without performing any translation process. Genetic operators manipulate opcodes and operands in a linear genetic program directly.

In recent years, evolvable hardware (EHW) [4] has become an important paradigm for automatic circuit design. EHW uses Evolutionary Algorithms (EA) to evolve hardware architecture extrinsically or intrinsically. Different genetic approaches have been proposed to design combinational digital circuits [5,6,7,8]. They use fixed size two-dimensional phenotypes and fixed length genotypes to represent combinational digital circuits. The drawback of a fixed size genotype is that it prevents introns from building up. Existence of introns in genetic programs in the early and middle stages of

M. Keijzer et al. (Eds.): EuroGP 2004, LNCS 3003, pp. 23–34, 2004.
© Springer-Verlag Berlin Heidelberg 2004

a run can benefit evolution [9]. However, genetic programs bloat continuously in the final stage. Hence, we propose a variable length parallel program structure to represent combinational digital circuits so that introns can be preserved. These parallel programs can run on an optimal Multiple Logic Unit Processor (MLP) (see Fig. 1 below) which is based on the Multi-ALU Processor (MAP) of Genetic Parallel Programming (GPP) [10]. Any combinational digital circuit can be represented by a MLP program (see Program 1 below). Furthermore, the simplicity of the MLP's architecture allows us to place numerous MLPs in a Field Programmable Gate Array (FPGA) to facilitate parallel evaluation of multiple training cases (i.e. rows in a truth table). It will speed up evolution significantly. The details of the MLP's architecture and MLP programs will be discussed in section 2 below.

Besides the MLP, an Evolution Engine (EE) has been developed to manipulate genetic parallel programs and perform genetic operations in the GPP+MLP system. As we have mentioned before, introns cause GP bloat continuously and enlarge solution programs' sizes. We tackle this problem by a two-stage (i.e. design and optimization stages) approach. In the design stage, the GPP+MLP system aims at on finding a 100% functional program (correct program). In this stage, the fitness function only concerns with the functional correctness of genetic parallel programs. All other qualitative indices (i.e. gate count, propagation gate delay and program size) are not considered. After finding the first correct program, the GPP+MLP system proceeds to the optimization stage. In the optimization stage, the GPP+MLP system uses another set of genetic operators together with an optimization-oriented fitness function to optimize correct programs.

The main purpose of this paper is to show the effectiveness of the proposed GPP+MLP system. We have performed experiments on four benchmark Binary arithmetic circuits (i.e. 1-bit full-adder, 2-bit full-adder, 2-bit multiplier and 3-bit multiplier). Experimental results show that the GPP+MLP system can design and optimize multi-output combinational digital circuits automatically. The qualities of evolved combinational digital circuits are better than conventional designs.

The rest of the paper is organized as follows: section 2 contains descriptions of GPP and MLP; section 3 describes details of experiments and experimental settings; section 4 presents results; and finally, section 5 concludes our work.

2   Genetic Parallel Programming

GPP is a LGP paradigm that evolves parallel programs of a MAP. GPP has been used to evolve optimal parallel programs for numeric function regression [10], artificial ant [11] and data classification problems [12]. The GPP Accelerating Phenomenon [13,14] revealed that parallel programs can be evolved with less computational efforts relative to its sequential counterpart. The phenomenon opens up a new two-step approach that: 1) evolves a solution in a highly parallel program format; and 2) serializes the parallel program to a functional equivalent sequential program. Based on the GPP paradigm, we developed a combinational digital circuit learning system, the GPP+MLP system. The core of the GPP+MLP system consists of an Evolution Engine (EE) and a Multiple Logic Unit Processor (MLP). The EE manipulates genetic parallel programs and performs genetic operations. We are going to discuss the MLP in the following sections.

2.1 The Multiple Logic Unit Processor

The MAP used in GPP is a general-purpose, tightly coupled, multi-ALU processor. By eliminating the cross-bar switching network [10] in the MAP, we obtain a MLP shown in Fig. 1 below. In the Figure, Logic Units (LUs) perform logic operations; variable registers store intermediate values and program outputs; and read-only registers store program inputs and logic constants. Each variable register can only be modified by a dedicated LU (e.g. L_0 can write to R_0 only). Read-only registers are preloaded by the EE before execution of a MLP program. In each clock cycle, each LU takes two input values from two registers, then performs a logic operation and finally, writes a single-bit result to its corresponding output register. For the MLP shown in Fig. 1 below, in each clock cycle, at most 16 operations can be performed concurrently and 16 intermediate results can be carried forward to subsequent parallel-instructions through variable registers. In FPGAs, a LU is implemented by a RAM-based look-up table (LUT). The function of a LU can be changed by modifying the RAM contents of the corresponding LUT. With the advances in semiconductor technologies, numerous MLPs can be placed in a high capacity FPGA [15]. Multiple MLPs in a FPGA can be driven by a single MLP program to evaluate multiple training cases concurrently. So, it will reduce fitness evaluation time significantly.

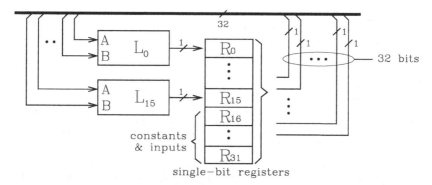

Fig. 1. A MLP is used to perform experiments in this paper. It consists of 16 logic units (L_0-L_{15}), 16 variable registers (R_0-R_{15}), and 16 read-only registers (R_{16}-R_{31})

2.2 The Genotype-Phenotype Mapping

The MLP is a generic evaluator for combinational digital circuit design. Theoretically, any combinational digital circuit can be represented by a MLP program. The MLP is designed to accept any bit pattern (genotype) as a valid program without causing processor fatal errors (e.g. invalid opcodes). The genotype of a genetic parallel program is loaded and executed in the MLP directly without pre-evaluation correction. This closure property is especially important for the GPP+MLP system because of its random nature based on genetic evolutionary techniques. It also saves unnecessary processing time.

	L_0	L_1	...	L_j	...	L_{15}
PI_0	$SI_{0,0}$	$SI_{0,1}$	...	$SI_{0,j}$	...	$SI_{0,15}$
PI_1	$SI_{1,0}$	$SI_{1,1}$	...	$SI_{1,j}$	...	$SI_{1,15}$
				...		
PI_i	$SI_{i,0}$	$SI_{i,1}$	...	$SI_{i,j}$	...	$SI_{i,15}$
				...		
PI_{24}	$SI_{24,0}$	$SI_{24,1}$	...	$SI_{24,j}$	...	$SI_{24,15}$

$SI_{i,j}$	*opcode* (5-bit)	*operandA* (5-bit)	*operandB* (5-bit)

Fig. 2. The genotype of a 25-parallel-instruction (PI_0-PI_{24}), 16-sub-instruction ($SI_{*,0}$-$SI_{*,15}$) MLP program. L_j denotes the j-th LU and $SI_{i,j}$ denotes the sub-instruction for L_j in the i-th parallel-instruction (PI_i)

As shown in Fig. 2 above, the genotype of a MLP program is represented as a sequence of parallel-instructions. Since the MLP shown in Fig. 1 above consists of 16 LUs, each parallel-instruction contains 16 sub-instructions. Each sub-instruction consists of a 5-bit *opcode* (encoding at most 32 functions) and two 5-bit (encoding 32 registers) operands. A total of 240 bits ((5+5+5)×16) are used to encode a parallel-instruction. If we allow at most 25 parallel-instructions in a MLP program, the genotype may contain up to 6,000 (240×25) bits. In all experiments presented in this paper, the function sets of all LUs are identical. The first 16 opcodes (i.e. 00000-01111) encode the 16 two-input logic functions (see Table 1 below) sequentially and the remaining (i.e. 10000-11111) encode *nop* (no operation).

Table 1. All the 16 two-input logic functions. A two-input logic gate can be implemented by a 4-memory-address RAM-based look-up table (LUT) in FPGAs

inputs		16 two-input logic functions															
A	**B**	**b00**	**b01**	**b02**	**b03**	**b04**	**b05**	**b06**	**b07**	**b08**	**b09**	**b10**	**b11**	**b12**	**b13**	**b14**	**b15**
0	0	0	1	0	1	0	1	0	1	0	1	0	1	0	1	0	1
0	1	0	0	1	1	0	0	1	1	0	0	1	1	0	0	1	1
1	0	0	0	0	0	1	1	1	1	0	0	0	0	1	1	1	1
1	1	0	0	0	0	0	0	0	0	1	1	1	1	1	1	1	1
gate symbol		0	A B	A B	A	A B	B	A B	A B	A B	A B	B	A B	A	A B	A B	1

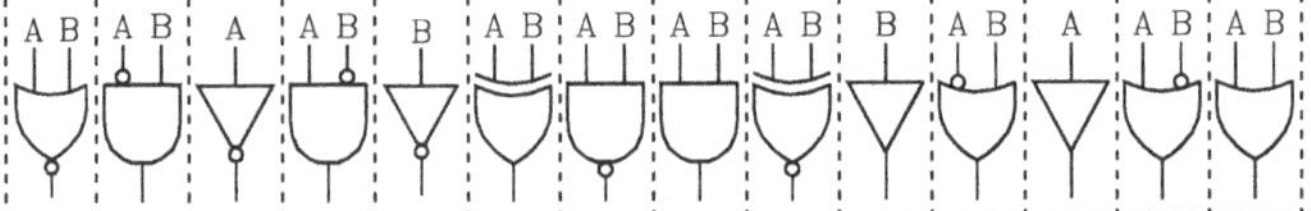

The phenotype of a MLP program can be expressed as a parallel assembly program. Program 1 below shows a MLP program of a 1-bit full-adder.

```
CONSTANTS: (r16-r21)=0, (r22-r28)=1
INPUTS:    (r29,r30,r31)<=(Cin,A,B)
OUTPUTS:   (r00,r01)=>(Cout,S)
[0] b09 r29 r30 r04
[1] b08 r04 r30 r00,b02 r04 r31 r14
[2] b06 r14 r00 r00,b09 r31 r04 r01
```

Program 1. The best 1-bit full-adder. It consists of 5 sub-instructions in 3 parallel-instructions

In Program 1 above, the first three lines instruct the EE to initialize constant, input and output registers. The numbered lines list out three parallel-instructions. A symbolic sub-instruction consists of four parts: 1) a function name (i.e. b00-b15 and nop); 2) a register for input A; 3) a register for input B; and 4) an output register. For example, the **b06 r14 r00 r00** sub-instruction in the last parallel-instruction performs *xor* (b06) on R_{14} and R_0 and then stores the result back to R_0. Before each execution, the EE initializes all variable registers to logic 0. After execution, **Cout** and **S** are stored in R_0 and R_1 respectively. In Fig. 3 below, each gate maps to a sub-instruction in the MLP program shown in Program 1 above.

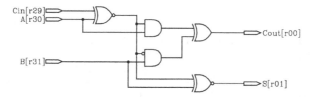

Fig. 3. The 1-bit full-adder (5 gates in 3 levels) shown in Program 1 above

3   Experiments and Settings

In order to investigate the effectiveness of the proposed GPP+MLP system, we have used the system to evolve combinational digital circuits for different benchmark problems. In this section, we shall give a description of the experimental results. Table 2 below lists out four benchmark Binary arithmetic circuits tested in this paper.

Table 2. Four benchmark Binary arithmetic circuits. The N_{input} and N_{output} denote the numbers of inputs and outputs respectively. The N_{row} denotes the number of rows in each truth table. The N_{case} denotes the total number of training cases in each truth table

name	description	N_{input}	N_{output}	$N_{row}(=2^{Ninput})$	$N_{case}(=N_{row} \times N_{output})$
ADD1	1-bit full-adder	3	2	8	16
ADD2	2-bit full-adder	5	3	32	96
MUL2	2-bit multiplier	4	4	16	64
MUL3	3-bit multiplier	6	6	64	384

3.1 The Two-Stage Approach

All combinational digital circuits presented in this paper are evolved by a two-stage (i.e. design and optimization stages) approach. Different sets of genetic operators are used in different stages. In the design stage, the GPP+MLP system aims at finding a 100% functional program (correct program) and the raw fitness is given by

$$f_{ds} = \frac{\text{number of unmatched training cases}}{\text{total number of training cases}} \tag{1}$$

As shown in equation (1) above, a partially correct program has a f_{ds} greater than zero while a correct program has a f_{ds} equal to zero. Having found the first correct program, the evolution proceeds to the optimization stage to optimize the correct program based on optimization-oriented criteria. In the optimization stage, the raw fitness is given by

$$f_{os} = \frac{G}{\text{maxG}} + \frac{D}{\text{maxD}} \cdot \frac{1}{\text{maxG}} + \frac{L}{\text{maxL}} \cdot \frac{1}{\text{maxG}} \cdot \frac{1}{\text{maxD}} \tag{2}$$

In equation (2) above, G, D and L denote the *gate count, propagation gate delay* and *program length* (i.e. the number of parallel-instructions) respectively of a correct program. maxG, maxD and maxL are the maximum allowed values of gate count, propagation gate delay and program length respectively. The f_{os} of a correct program is calculated from G, D and L. For example, in a tournament of two genetic parallel programs, the one with a smaller G will win. If the two genetic parallel programs have same G values, the one with smaller D will win. If the two genetic parallel programs have same G and D values, the one with smaller L will win. In other words, the major objective of the optimization stage is reducing the gate count and then the propagation gate delay. The last term in equation (2) above guides the evolution to shorten the lengths of correct programs.

3.2 Genetic Operators

The GPP+MLP uses the following genetic operations in proper stages:

Crossover: It swaps two segments of parallel-instructions in two MLP programs.
Bit mutation: It mutates bits in the genotype of a MLP program.
Sub-instruction swapping: It swaps two sub-instructions in a MLP program. The purpose is to increase the parallelism of the MLP program.
Dynamic Sample Weighting (DSW) [16,17]: It adjusts the weights of training cases dynamically based on their past fitness evaluation histories. It balances the contributions of training cases to speed up the evolution.
Preselection [18]: A new born child will be discarded if it is functionally equivalent (i.e. matches the same set of training cases) to its parents. The purpose is to increase the diversity of a search.
Gate re-wiring: It intends to eliminate a redundant gate in a correct program by re-wiring an input of a LU to one of its predecessors' inputs (see Fig. 4 below).

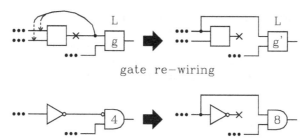

gate re-wiring

Fig. 4. Gate re-wiring. The function of L is mutated from **g** to **g'** and one of its inputs is re-wired to one of its predecessors' inputs

3.3 Experimental Settings

As we mentioned before, a FPGA-assisted MLP can speed up the evolution significantly. However, it does not affect the function of the GPP+MLP system. The main purpose of this paper is to demonstrate that the GPP+MLP system can evolve optimal combinational digital circuits directly from truth tables. Thus, we ran all experiments on a software emulator of the MLP developed in C. Table 3 below shows GP parameters and settings of experiments presented in this paper.

Table 3. GP parameters and settings presented in this paper

	both design and optimization stages	
max. program length (maxL)	25 parallel-instructions	
initialization	bit random, average program length = maxL/2	
selection method	tournament (size=10)	
LU function set	b00, ... , b15, nop	
terminal set	inputs: $R_{32-Ninput}$ ... R_{31}, outputs: R_0 ... $R_{Noutput-1}$	
constants	logic 0, logic 1	
$P_{crossover}$	0.1	
population size	2000	
experiments	50 independent runs	
termination criterion	20,000,000 tournaments	
	design stage	**optimization stage**
$P_{bit\_mutation}$ of each bit	0.002	0.0
$P_{sub-inst. swapping}$ of each program	0.0	0.5
DSW (weights update freq.)	yes (10,000 tournaments)	no
preselection	yes	no
$P_{gate re-wiring}$ of each program	0.0	0.5
fitness	$f = 1.0 + f_{ds}$	$f = f_{os}$
success predicate	$f = 1.0$ (i.e. $f_{ds}=0.0$)	$f \leq 0.0$ (i.e. $f_{os} \leq 0.0$)

Having investigated the difficulties of the four benchmark problems shown in Table 2 above, we set the maximum program length (maxL) to 25 parallel-instructions. This provides enough sub-instructions (for both effective operations and introns) to evolve correct programs. Hence, at most 400 (25×16) operations can be used to build a solution. The constant 1.0 in the fitness row in Table 3 above is used to distinguish the two stages. In the design stage, when *f*=1.0 is achieved, the system proceeds to the optimization stage. Noticeably, in the optimization stage, the success predicate (*f*≤0.0) is unachievable. It forces the system to optimize correct programs as much as possible. Thus, all runs terminate after 20,000,000 tournaments.

4 Results and Evaluations

From the 50 runs of the four individual problems, we obtained many high quality solutions. The best solutions of the four individual problems will be presented and discussed in this section. We have shown the best 1-bit full-adder solution in Program 1 and Fig. 3 in section 2 above. The solution circuit consists of 5 two-input gates in 3 gate levels. The best solution programs of 2-bit full-adder, 2-bit multiplier and 3-bit multiplier are shown in Programs 2 to 4 below respectively. The circuits of the corresponding programs are shown in Figures 5 to 7 below respectively.

```
CONSTANTS:(r16-r21)=0,(r22-r26)=1
INPUTS:  (r27,r28,r29,r30,r31)<=(Cin,A1,A0,B1,B0)
OUTPUTS: (r00,r01,r02)=>(Cout,S1,S0)
[0] b06 r31 r29 r00,b08 r28 r30 r06,b07 r29 r31 r08,
    b09 r28 r30 r11
[1] b08 r00 r27 r01
[2] b06 r08 r01 r03
[3] b06 r03 r11 r01,b06 r00 r27 r02,b01 r03 r11 r14
[4] b14 r14 r06 r00
```

Program 2. The best 2-bit full-adder (10 sub-instructions, 5 parallel-instructions)

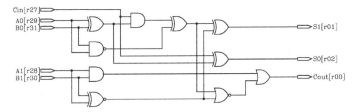

Fig. 5. The 2-bit full-adder (10 gates in 5 levels) shown in Program 2 above

```
CONSTANTS:(r16-r21)=0,(r22-r27)=1
INPUTS:  (r28,r29,r30,r31)<=(A1,A0,B1,B0)
OUTPUTS: (r00,r01,r02,r03)=>(P3,P2,P1,P0)
[0] b08 r29 r30 r00,b07 r28 r31 r02,b08 r31 r29 r03,
    b07 r28 r30 r09
[1] b02 r02 r00 r00,b01 r09 r03 r01,b09 r02 r00 r02
```

Program 3. The best 2-bit multiplier (7 sub-instructions, 2 parallel-instructions)

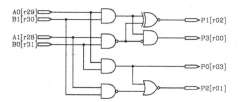

Fig. 6. The 2-bit multiplier (7 gates in 2 levels) shown in Program 3 above

```
CONSTANTS: (r16-r20)=0, (r21-25)=1
INPUTS:  (r26,r27,r28,r29,r30,r31)<=(A2,A1,A0,B2,B1,B0)
OUTPUTS: (r00,r01,r02,r03,r04,r05)=>(P5,P4,P3,P2,P1,P0)
[0] b07 r27 r30 r02,b07 r26 r31 r03,b08 r31 r28 r05,
    b08 r27 r29 r07,b08 r26 r30 r09,b08 r29 r28 r15
[1] b06 r15 r03 r06
[2] b08 r26 r29 r00,b02 r05 r02 r01,b07 r28 r30 r02,
    b09 r06 r02 r03,b01 r09 r07 r07,b07 r31 r27 r08,
    b01 r06 r02 r10,b02 r02 r05 r15
[3] b04 r00 r15 r00,b11 r00 r01 r01,b02 r05 r10 r14
[4] b01 r07 r01 r00,b13 r15 r01 r01,b09 r03 r15 r03,
    b06 r02 r08 r04,b01 r10 r00 r11,b09 r14 r07 r13
[5] b09 r11 r00 r01,b06 r13 r01 r02
```

Program 4. The best 3-bit multiplier (26 sub-instructions, 6 parallel-instructions)

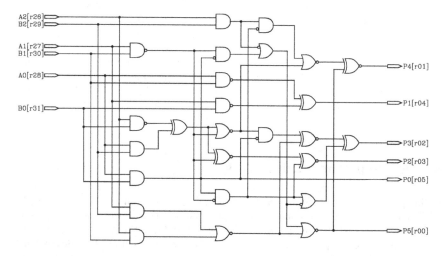

Fig. 7. The 3-bit multiplier (26 gates in 6 levels) shown in Program 4 above

Based on the statistics of the 50 runs, three performance indices: 1) the Koza's minimum computational effort (E) (with z=0.99) [2]; 2) the gate count (G); and 3) the propagation gate delay (D) are calculated and shown in Table 4 below for discussion.

Table 4. Summary of experimental results. The GPP+MLP$_{ds}$ and GPP+MLP$_{os}$ columns list out the results of the design and optimization stages respectively. For comparison, the CGP and CON columns list out the results of Cartesian GP and conventional design reported in [6,19]

problems	GPP+MLP$_{ds}$			GPP+MLP$_{os}$		CGP	CON
	E (×10⁶)	avg G/D	best G/D	avg G/D	best G/D	best G/D	best G/D
ADD1	0.19	161/14	95/9	5/3	<u>5/3</u>	<u>5/3</u>	<u>5/3</u>
ADD2	1.33	203/17	92/10	12/5	<u>10/5</u>	<u>10</u>/6	<u>10</u>/6
MUL2	0.45	193/16	121/9	7/3	<u>7/2</u>	<u>7</u>/3	8/3
MUL3	92.29	179/18	136/16	45/9	26/<u>6</u>	<u>23</u>/8	30/8

In Table 4 above, the E column lists out the minimum numbers of tournaments required to yield correct programs of individual problems (with z=0.99). Obviously, MUL3 is much more difficult than the other three problems. The "avg G/D" values shown under the GPP+MLP$_{ds}$ column present the average qualities of evolved circuits in the design stage. These values are quite large. It implies that the correct programs evolved in the design stage contain many introns. By comparing the "avg G/D" values shown under the GPP+MLP$_{os}$ column, we notice that both G and D decrease significantly after the optimization stage. For example, for the MUL3 problem, the average G decreases from 179 to 45 gates and the average D decreases from 18 to 9 gate levels. It demonstrates the effectiveness of the optimization stage.

In order to compare the qualities of optimal circuits evolved by the GPP+MLP system, we included results of Cartesian GP (CGP) and conventional design (CON) published in [6] and [19]. In Table 4 above, we underlined all minimal values in the last three columns. For ADD1, ADD2 and MUL2, the best circuits evolved by the GPP+MLP system have the minimal gate counts and propagation gate delays. For MUL3, the best circuit evolved by the GPP+MLP system utilizes 3 gates more than CGP but it utilizes 4 gates less than conventional design. Even though the gate count is higher than CGP, the propagation gate delay is the minimum. The underlined values listed in the "best G/D" column under the GPP+MLP$_{os}$ heading show that the GPP+MLP system can design optimal combinational digital circuits for the four problems both in terms of gate count (G) and propagation gate delay (D).

5   Conclusions and Further Work

In this paper, we have presented a Genetic Parallel Programming (GPP) system (the GPP+MLP system) for combinational digital circuit design. It uses a Multiple Logic Unit Processor (MLP) that is based on the Multi-ALU Processor of GPP. The GPP+MLP system applies a two-stage approach to separate the design and optimization processes. In the design stage, the system evolves parallel programs based on a fitness function which aims at evolving a 100% functional program (correct program). When the first correct program is found, the GPP+MLP system proceeds to the optimization stage. In the optimization stage, the GPP+MLP system uses another set of genetic operators to optimize correct programs. Experimental results show that the GPP+MLP system can evolve optimal multi-output combinational digital circuits automatically. The qualities of evolved circuits are better than conventional designs. The advantages of the GPP+MLP system are summarized as follows:

- It uses a generic register machine architecture which can emulate any combination circuits. Moreover, the architecture of MLP is so simple that numerous MLPs can be placed in a FPGA. With this highly parallelized, hardware-assisted fitness evaluation engine, the evolution will be sped up significantly.

- It benefited by the GPP Accelerating Phenomenon. Thus, less computational effort is needed.

- It employs a variable length genotype so that introns can be built up in the early and middle stages of a run to assist evolution.

- A 100% functional program evolved in the design stage can be saved as a seed program for different runs of the optimization stage. For example, different genetic operators and parameters can be used to optimize an identical seed program.

- In the optimization stage, optimization-oriented genetic operators and fitness criteria (e.g. reduce the gate count and the propagation gate delay) is used to guide the optimization. We can also use different fitness functions (e.g. a cost-saving-oriented fitness function) to achieve different optimization objectives.

We are currently evolving combinational digital circuits with four-input and five-input look-up tables (LUTs). These LUTs are commonly used in large scale FPGAs, e.g. Xilin Virtex™ II Platform FPGAs [15]. The preliminary results show that multi-input LUs can evolve circuits more efficient than two-input LUs. Further studies will be conducted to explore the effect of different settings on MLP configurations (e.g. the numbers of registers and inputs of LUs).

Furthermore, we shall develop programs to translate MLP programs into different formats (e.g. gate-level netlists and Hardware Description Language (HDL) statements). With these translators, evolved combinational digital circuits can be ported to other digital circuit design tools.

In the nearly future, we plan to implement a multiple MLPs evaluation engine by using Xilinx FPGAs. We can imagine that the hardware-assisted MLP will speed up the evolution significantly so that more complex combinational digital circuits can be evolved.

Acknowledgements. The work described in this paper was partially supported by a grant from the Research Grants Council of the Hong Kong Special Administrative Region, China (Project No. CUHK4192/03E).

References

1. Banzhaf, W., Koza, J.R., Ryan, C., Spector, L., Jocob, C.: Genetic Programming. IEEE Intelligent Systems Journal, Vol.17, No.3 (2000) 74-84
2. Koza, J.R.: Genetic Programming: On the Programming of Computers by Means of Natural Selection. MIT Press (1992)

3. Banzhaf, W., Nordin, P., Keller, R.E., Francone, F.D.: Generic Programming: An Introduction on the Automatic Evolution of Computer Programs and its Applications. Morgan Kaufmann (1998)
4. Yao, X., Higuchi, T.: Promises and Challenges of Evolvable Hardware. IEEE Transactions on Systems, Man, and Cybernetics – Part C, Vol.29, No.1 (1999) 87-97
5. Kalganova, T.: An Extrinsic Function-Level Evolvable Hardware Approach. Poli R., Banzhaf W., Langdon W.B., Miller J., Nordin P., Fogarty T.C., Eds., Proceedings of the 3rd European Conference on Genetic Programming – EuroGP'2000, LNCS 1802 (2000) 60-75
6. Miller, J.F., Job, D., Vassilev, V.K.: Principles in the Evolutionary Design of Digital Circuits – Part I. Genetic Programming and Evolvable Machines, Vol.1, No.1 (2000) 7-35
7. Coello, C.A., Luna, E.H., Aguirre, A.H.: Use of Particle Swarm Optimization to Design Combinational Logic Circuits. Tyrrell A.M., Haddow P.C., Torresen J., Eds., Proceedings of the 5th International Conference on Evolvable Systems: From Biology to Hardware – ICES'2003, LNCS 2606 (2003) 398-409
8. Torresen J.: Evolving Multiplier Circuits by Training Set and Training Vector Partitioning. Tyrrell A.M., Haddow P.C., Torresen J., Eds., Proceedings of the 5th International Conference on Evolvable Systems: From Biology to Hardware – ICES'2003, LNCS 2606 (2003) 228-237
9. Angeline, P.J.: Two Self-Adaptive Crossover Operators for Genetic Programming. Advanced in Genetic Programming 2. MIT Press (1996) 89-110
10. Leung, K.S., Lee, K.H., Cheang, S.M.: Evolving Parallel Machine Programs for a Multi-ALU Processor. Proceedings of IEEE Congress on Evolutionary Computation – CEC'02 (2002) 1703-1708
11. Leung, K.S., Lee, K.H., Cheang, S.M.: Genetic Parallel Programming – Evolving Linear Machine Codes on a Multiple ALU Processor. Yaacob S., Nagarajan R., Chekima A., Eds., Proceedings of International Conference on Artificial Intelligence in Engineering and Technology – ICAIET'2002 (2002) 207-213
12. Cheang, S.M., Lee, K.H., Leung, K.S.: Evolving Data Classification Programs using Genetic Parallel Programming. Proceedings of IEEE Congress on Evolutionary Computation – CEC'03 (2003) 248-255
13. Leung, K.S., Lee, K.H., Cheang, S.M.: Parallel Programs are More Evolvable than Sequential Programs. Ryan C., Soule T., Keijzer M., Tsang E., Poli R., Costa E., Eds., Proceedings of the 6th European Conference on Genetic Programming – EuroGP'2003, LNCS 2610 (2003) 107-118
14. Cheang, S.M.: An Empirical Study of the GPP Accelerating Phenomenon. Proceedings of the 2nd International Conference on Computational Intelligence, Robotics and Autonomous Systems – CIRAS'03 (2003) PS04-04-03
15. Virtex™ II Platform FPGAs: Introduction and Overview, Xilinx, Inc. (2003)
16. Leung, K.S., Lee, K.H., Cheang, S.M.: Balancing Samples' Contributions on GA Learning. Liu Y., Tanaka K., Iwata M., Higuchi T., Yasunaga M., Eds., Proceedings of the 4th International Conference on Evolvable Systems: From Biology to Hardware – ICES'2001, LNCS 2210 (2001) 256-266
17. Cheang, S.M., Lee, K.H., Leung, K.S.: Applying Sample Weighting Methods to Genetic Parallel Programming. Proceedings of IEEE Congress on Evolutionary Computation – CEC'03 (2003) 928-935
18. Mahfoud, S.W.: Crowding and Preselection Revisited. Parallel Problem Solving from Nature (1992) 27-36
19. Vassilev, V.K., Job, D., Miller, J.F.: Towards the Automatic Design of More Efficient Digital Circuits. Proceedings of NASA/DoD Workshop on Evolvable Hardware (2000) 151-160

A Data Structure for Improved GP Analysis via Efficient Computation and Visualisation of Population Measures

Anikó Ekárt[1] and Steven Gustafson[2]

[1] Computer and Automation Research Institute, Hungarian Academy of Sciences,
1518 Budapest, P.O.B. 63, Hungary
`ekart@sztaki.hu`
[2] School of Computer Science & IT, University of Nottingham,
Jubilee Campus, Wollaton Rd, Nottingham, NG81BB, United Kingdom
`smg@cs.nott.ac.uk`

Abstract. Population measures for genetic programs are defined and analysed in an attempt to better understand the behaviour of genetic programming. Some measures are simple, but do not provide sufficient insight. The more meaningful ones are complex and take extra computation time. Here we present a unified view on the computation of population measures through an information hyper-tree (iTree). The iTree allows for a unified and efficient calculation of population measures via a basic tree traversal.

1 Introduction

"Things should be as simple as possible, but not simpler."
Albert Einstein

A population search method using variable length representation (such as genetic programming) requires expensive measures to collect, mine and visualise dynamics due to the repeated traversal of individuals making up the population. For the researcher, it would be useful to quickly have an overview of population dynamics, which often involves complex computations. However, it is essential to employ measures which are easy to use, intuitive, and efficient to compute in order to reduce the complexity and expense of such analysis. Implementing such measures is usually difficult and time consuming. Instead, the complexity of the analysis, algorithm or problem are typically reduced to allow for detailed analysis.

We introduce an advanced data structure that is efficient to maintain, offers a compact view on a population of tree structured genetic programs and allows for the efficient computation of many population measures. In this way, exploratory analysis beyond simple measures (like fitness, node counts or diversity based on uniqueness) becomes more accessible to the researcher.

Our data structure captures the population information needed to compute several simple and complex measures. The data structure (the information tree, or "iTree") is realised as a "hyper-tree" on the population of trees. The iTree represents the information obtained from a complete traversal of the individuals in the population. The uses of the iTree are two-fold:

M. Keijzer et al. (Eds.): EuroGP 2004, LNCS 3003, pp. 35–46, 2004.
© Springer-Verlag Berlin Heidelberg 2004

- the iTree makes the computation of many useful population measures possible and efficient and
- the iTree can be visualised, offering compact views of the population.

We first introduce the information hyper-tree and demonstrate how it improves the efficiency of several measures. We then discuss several more complex and expensive measures, which become accessible and intuitive with the help of the iTree. We also describe typical situations that call for iTree visualisation.

2   The Information Hyper-tree of a Population

We introduce the information hyper-tree (iTree) for a population as a data structure that collects important details of the individuals making up the population in one easily accessible place. We construct the iTree of a population of genetic programs based on two principles:

1. *The structure of the iTree must be such that it incorporate the structure of any tree in the population.* Therefore, the iTree will have a node at some location if there is at least one member of the population having a node at the same location.
2. *Each node of the iTree should capture the population information related to that particular node position.* In the basic case, this information is the number of trees in the population that have a node at the given location.

In Fig. 1 we show example iTrees for three small populations of genetic trees (for a symbolic regression problem). For simplicity, we only look at binary trees, i.e. problems where all functions accept two arguments. The measures presented in Fig. 1 will be explained later.

The iTree can be constructed for any set of genetic trees, not only for the whole population. For example, the iTree corresponding to the most fit individuals during a run could provide information about the expected structure of the solution to the problem. The iTree corresponding to all individuals visited during a run could provide information about the region of the tree search space covered by the run. The iTree corresponding to the solutions of a number of runs could uncover structural similarities or differences of the found solutions and contribute to the understanding of GP-hardness, for example by complementing Daida et al.'s study [4].

We construct the iTree in a top-down manner, starting from the root. Consequently, the iTree will reflect the top-down structure of the represented trees. This approach is the opposite of Keijzer's bottom-up method [6]. He builds the trees starting from the leaves, and by representing only once the common subtrees that occur in different individuals he can space-efficiently represent a population. In the mean time, the iTree's purpose is to make possible the computation of complex measures for any set of genetic trees. As subtree-based measures are not that straight-forward to compute with the iTree, the two methods could be used in conjunction.

In the subsequent sections we shall describe the computation of population measures based on the iTrees. We shall refer to the iTrees of populations but the measures for iTrees associated to other sets of trees can be computed similarly.

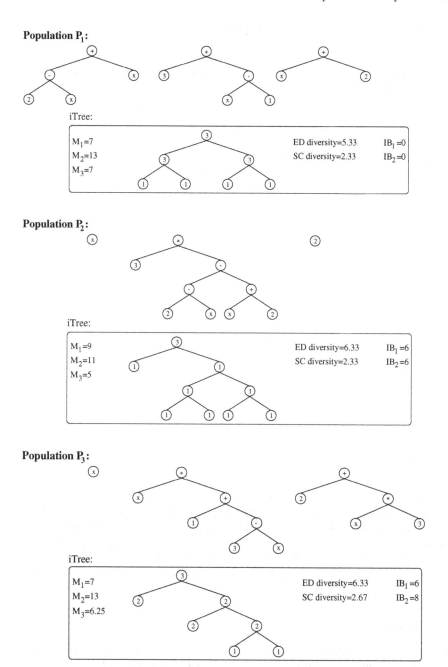

Fig. 1. The iTrees and measures corresponding to three populations of three genetic trees each

3   The Node Coverage of a Population

There are a number of meaningful measures that can be easily computed from the basic information stored in the nodes of the iTree. These measures can be used in analysing how well a population explores the search space of tree structures. We are able to find answers to the following questions related to a population P with corresponding $iTree$:

- How many node positions are being explored in the tree search space? This is the number of node positions in a binary tree that the population samples by at least one member. This measure can be found by simply counting the nodes of the $iTree$,

$$M_1(P) = \sum_{A \in iTree} 1.$$

- How many genetic nodes are there in the population? We only have to sum up the values stored in the nodes of the $iTree$:

$$M_2(P) = \sum_{A \in iTree} n_A.$$

When comparing two populations of trees, we can say which one is larger in terms of node numbers. Note that in order to obtain the total number of nodes in a population without using the iTree, one would have to sum up the sizes of individuals in the population.

- How full is the $iTree$? We can compute the degree of fullness as:

$$M_3(P) = \frac{1}{size(P)} \sum_{A \in iTree} \frac{1}{2^{depth(A)}} n_A.$$

In order to obtain this measure without using the iTree, one would have to do a traversal of all trees in a population. For a full $iTree$, $M_3(P) = depth(iTree)$. For very sparse trees, $M_3(P) \to 1$.

If two populations P_1, P_2 have values $M_1(P_1) < M_1(P_2)$, $M_2(P_1) > M_2(P_2)$ (as in Fig. 1), then the second population explores a larger region of the tree search space, but the first population performs a better exploration through more representatives of the nodes. If $M_1(P_1) = M_1(P_3)$, $M_2(P_1) = M_2(P_3)$ and $M_3(P_1) > M_3(P_3)$ (see Fig. 1) then the first population has more nodes at lower depth, i.e. has more shallower and fuller trees than the second population. Population P_3 may contain deeper and sparser trees than population P_1.

3.1   Entropy

Suppose the iTree also contains information about the distribution of terminal and function values that are covered by each node in the population. We could associate an entropy value to each iTree node that can show how biased the population is toward specific values in the nodes. For a given node A, the distribution of values over the set of functions and terminals $F \cup T$ is given by $D : F \cup T \to \mathbb{N}$, where $D(s)$ is the number of genetic trees in the population containing symbol s in the location corresponding to node A. The entropy of node A is then

$$E(A) = - \sum_{s \in F \cup T} \frac{D(s)}{\sum_{v \in F \cup T} D(v)} log \frac{D(s)}{\sum_{v \in F \cup T} D(v)}$$

where log is the logarithm with the base the total number of functions and terminals $|F \cup T|$. The closer the entropy value is to 1, the more uniform the distribution is and the closer the entropy value is to zero, the more biased the distribution is. The entropy is also a measure of node content diversity: for a given node it has a larger value for a better coverage of the function and terminal sets and a lower value for a worse coverage, respectively.

4 Structural Diversity of a Population

Measuring genotype diversity in tree-based genetic programming can be very time-consuming. Structural diversity is usually measured based on pairwise distances between individuals in a population[1,5,8]. Usually, the average distance of two individuals in a population is employed. Therefore, computing diversity is very expensive: if the population size is N, there are $N \times (N - 1)$ pairs of individuals. For each pair T_1, T_2, the time complexity of obtaining their edit distance is $O(|T_1| \times |T_2|)$. Similarly to Wineberg and Oppacher's results on genetic algorithms [10], we can significantly reduce the computation time of structural diversity when using the iTree.

4.1 Edit Distance

The edit distance of two labeled trees is defined as the cost of shortest sequence of editing operations that transform one tree into the other [7,9]. The editing operations are deleting a node, inserting a node, or changing the label of a node. In the basic case each operation is considered with the same cost. In order to compute the structural diversity of a population, we need to maintain the symbol (terminal and function) distribution in each node of the iTree. Normally, diversity would be calculated as the average edit distance over all pairs of individuals in the population. When comparing two individual trees node by node, three cases can occur:

1. Both trees have the same symbol at the examined position, the node has no contribution to the edit distance;
2. The trees have different symbols at the examined position, so the cost of changing a label is added to the edit distance; or
3. One tree has no node at the given position, so the cost of adding/deleting a node is added to the edit distance.

At the node level in the iTree, each individual is represented by the number of occurrences of the individual's symbol in that position. The same edit distance diversity can be calculated by traversing the iTree and summing up the nodes' contributions. Given the distribution of symbols for a node, obtaining the node's contribution can be formulated as counting the number of pairs of non-identical symbols encountered in that position in the iTree.[1] The number of pairs in a set of N symbols is $N(N-1)/2$. Similarly, the number of pairs in a subset of $D(s)$ identical symbols is $D(s)(D(s)-1)/2$. So, the number of non-identical pairs is

$$N(N-1)/2 - \sum_{s \in F \cup T} D(s)(D(s)-1)/2$$
$$= (1/2)\left(N^2 - N - \sum D(s)^2 + \sum D(s)\right) = (1/2)\left(N \sum D(s) - \sum D(s)^2\right)$$
$$= (1/2)\sum\left(N D(s) - D(s)^2\right) = (1/2)\sum D(s)(N - D(s)).$$

The algorithm for computing diversity as the average edit distance between two individual trees of a population of N trees with corresponding $iTree$ is presented below. We denote by $iNodes$ the number of individuals in the population, which sample the root node of the $iTree$. The time complexity of the algorithm is $O(|F \cup T| \times size(iTree))$.

```
Diversity(iTree, N)
begin
 dist=0;
 if iNodes < N
   dist := dist + iNodes x (N - iNodes);
 for each symbol s encountered in the root of iTree D(s) times
   dist := dist + D(s) x (N - D(s));
 dist := dist / (N x (N - 1));
 if the root has nonempty left child iLeft
   dist := dist + Diversity(iLeft, N);
 if the root has nonempty right child iRight
   dist := dist + Diversity(iRight, N);
 return dist;
end
```

4.2 Distance Based on Structural Comparison

Instead of the edit distance we can use the distance based on structural comparison described in[5]. The distance of two binary trees A and B, with the two subtrees denoted as $.Left$ and $.Right$ is defined as:

$$dist(A, B) = \begin{cases} d(root(A), root(B)) & \text{if both } A \text{ and } B \text{ are leaves} \\ d(root(A), root(B)) + \\ \frac{1}{K} \times (dist(A.Left, B.Left) + dist(A.Right, B.Right)) & \text{otherwise.} \end{cases}$$

In the simple case, when we just count the differences, i.e. $d(x, y) = \delta_{xy}$ (Kronecker delta), if we use the iTree for computing the average distance of two trees in a population, the contribution of a node is the same as in the case of the edit distance. The only difference in the algorithm is that the diversity of subtrees is discounted:

---

[1] For unified treatment, we can assume that each node in the iTree represents $iNodes$ nodes, $N - iNodes$ being the number of "empty" symbols, or number of individuals in the population which have no node at that location.

```
if the root has nonempty left child iLeft
   dist := dist + 1/K x Diversity(iLeft, N);
if the root has nonempty right child iRight
   dist := dist + 1/K x Diversity(iRight, N);
```

In the more general case, computing the contribution of a node becomes more complex, the time needed for this operation becomes $O(|F \cup T|^2)$ and consequently the time complexity of the algorithm becomes $O(|F \cup T|^2 \times size(iTree))$.

5   Distance of Two Populations

As emphasised by Wineberg and Oppacher [10], the distance of two – consecutive – populations can play an important role in understanding the dynamics of evolutionary computation methods. Instead of computing pairwise distances between individuals from the two populations, we can easily obtain the distance of the two populations by traversing their iTrees in parallel.

Normally, the distance between two populations is computed as the average distance between any two individuals from the two populations. Computing the average distance diversity of a population is a special case of computing the distance of two populations, namely, when the two populations are identical and when the distance of an individual to itself is not counted. If we use the iTrees of the two populations, we obtain the following algorithm for computing the edit distance of two populations by generalising the algorithm presented in Section 4.1.[2] The time complexity of the algorithm is $O(|F \cup T| \times (size(iTree1) + size(iTree2)))$.

```
Pop_Dist(iTree1, iTree2, N1, N2)
begin
 dist=0;
 if iNodes1 < N1
   dist := dist + (N1 - iNodes1) x iNodes2
                + iNodes1 x (N2 -iNodes2);
 for each symbol s, D1(s) times in iTree1, D2(s) times in iTree2
   dist := dist + D1(s) x (N2 - D2(s))
                + (N1 -D1(s)) x D2(s);
 dist := dist / (2 x (N1 x N2));
 if at least one root has nonempty left child (iLeft1 or iLeft2)
   dist := dist + Pop_dist(iLeft1, iLeft2, N1, N2);
 if at least one root has nonempty right child (iRight1 or iRight2)
   dist := dist + Pop_dist(iRight1, iRight2, N1, N2);
 return dist;
end
```

In order to obtain the distance based on structural comparison, we only have to modify the recursive calls to include the discounts, similarly to the structural diversity presented in Section 4.2.

6   The Imbalance of a Population

The iTree of a population can provide information about how the population samples different tree structures. A very unbalanced iTree suggests a biased sampling (specific,

---

[2] Whenever one subtree is empty, we make the recursive call for the null subtree representing zero nodes.

mostly sparse tree structures are often present in the population), whereas a balanced iTree suggests uniform sampling of nodes. The imbalance of a population can be seen as an indicator of the structural diversity of the population: (1) A largely unbalanced iTree suggests the presence of many similar trees in a population (low diversity). (2) A balanced iTree corresponds to a population that covers the full tree structure. In an extreme, but very unlikely case this could be the result of the population containing only full trees. Otherwise, the population contains all sorts of structures, which cover together the full tree structure (high diversity).

6.1   Original Imbalance

Colless [2] defines an imbalance measure for a phylogenetic tree as the sum of absolute differences between the sizes of the two subtrees located at each bifurcation in the tree under consideration. We use the same imbalance measure for our data structure and denote it by IB_1. We consider the size of a subtree as the number of nodes contained in it. A fully balanced iTree has the same number of nodes in all subtrees that have the same parent. In the case of binary trees, the only fully balanced tree of some given depth is the complete tree of the same depth. A population of trees corresponding to a fully balanced iTree explores all the possible nodes in the program tree structure to some extent. The more unbalanced an iTree is, the more unexplored regions exist in the "structure space" of program trees. In order to say something about the extent to which the program tree structure is being explored, or more exactly, how uniformly the program tree structure is being explored, we need a more detailed measure of imbalance.

6.2   A More Specific Imbalance

We consider the same imbalance measure for a population's iTree, with the exception that instead of the size of a subtree, we use the total number of genetic tree nodes contained in that subtree (that is, the sum of node numbers for each iTree node). We denote this type of imbalance as IB_2 and show three examples in Fig. 2. The most unbalanced iTree would have all nodes concentrated in one subtree. But if a node of the iTree has any children, it must have two children, both representing the same number of genetic nodes, due to our restriction of binary functions. If we denote by n_i the number of genetic tree

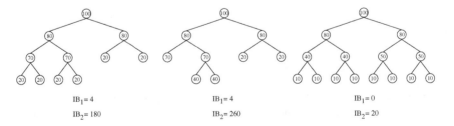

Fig. 2. Examples of different iTrees corresponding to the same total number of nodes

nodes at depth i in an iTree, the largest possible imbalance IB_2 for a tree of depth k is $\sum_{i=2}^{k} (i-1) \times n_i$ (see the example for depth 3 in Fig. 3(a)). [3]

A completely balanced iTree is a full tree with uniformly distributed genetic nodes at each depth, with corresponding $IB_2 = 0$. However, there exist unbalanced iTrees with $IB_2 = 0$, such as the example shown in Fig. 3(b). In such cases, the original imbalance measure $IB_1 > 0$. The two measures are insufficient by themselves, but, taken together, they can show whether a population is exploring all regions of the structure search space (IB_1), and to what extent the actually represented regions are being explored (IB_2). If an iTree has $IB_1 = 0$ and $IB_2 = 0$, the iTree is a full tree of some depth d and all node locations at some depth $i \leq d$ are explored to the same extent in the population. This does not necessarily involve just full trees in the population (see Fig. 1 for example).

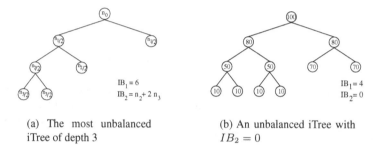

(a) The most unbalanced
iTree of depth 3

(b) An unbalanced iTree with
$IB_2 = 0$

Fig. 3. Examples of unbalanced iTrees

7   Visualisation of the Information Hyper-tree

In order to better analyse and understand the dynamics of genetic programming runs, we could graphically show the iTrees or their parts associated to certain groups of genetic trees. In many cases it is important to see the actual tree structures. For instance, the following questions highlight the need for good, and sometimes complex, visualisation of the population:

1. *What are the most common structures in the best genetic programs that were encountered during a run?* In order to get an answer, we have to first quantify "most common" and "best", such as the nodes that occur in at least 80% of the trees whose fitness is below 0.1 (if we are minimising fitness). Then we construct the iTree corresponding to the genetic trees of desired fitness encountered during the run and visualise the nodes A of the iTree with $\frac{n_A}{n_0} > 0.8$. A small tree would show that the trees are similar only at very low depth, meaning that a diverse set of solutions has been found. A large, perhaps sparse tree would show that genetic programming conducted a local search around one optimum, where the found structure is a good structure. In Fig. 4 we show the most common best tree structure that emerged in a run of a symbolic regression problem. We qualified all trees with fitness below

---

[3] Proof. The difference in node numbers at depth i of a fully unbalanced iTree is $\sum_{j=i+1}^{k} n_j$. We complete the proof by summing up these differences.

0.05 in the best category. Out of the 5100 trees evaluated during the run, 2163 trees were considered best. The large common part suggests a local search around a good structure.

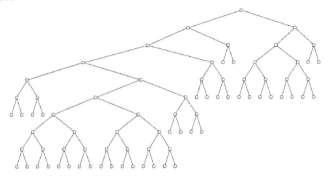

Fig. 4. Example good common structure evolved in a GP run

2. *What makes a good program different from a bad program?* One possibility is to look at the most common part of the iTree corresponding to the best trees and the most common part of the iTree corresponding to the worst trees encountered during the run. One could also do a parallel traversal of the two iTrees and show only the nodes that are common in one group, but not in the other. For the example discussed at (1), 315 trees were very unfit, their most common structure was the full tree of depth 3. The set of unfit trees was quite diverse, so we can only say that the structure shown in Fig. 4 is good, and the structures different from this one might be bad.
3. *How early in the run do the good structures emerge?* Answering this question involves a comparison between the iTree of (1) and the iTrees of populations in subsequent generations.
4. *If there are common structures during the run, do they heavily depend on the initial population?* As in the case of question (2), we first have to look at the iTree of the run (or more exactly its most common parts), and then compare it with the iTrees of populations in subsequent generations. Thus, we could find when these structures first appeared. The earlier these structures emerge, the more likely it is that they depend on the initial population.

8   Case Study

Here we present an analysis based on iTrees for a symbolic regression problem. We use the polynomial $(x + 0.2)^2 (x - 0.5) (x + 0.5) (x - 0.7)$ with $x \in [-1, 1]$. We show the results for 50 independent runs of simple genetic programming. The initialisation method is ramped half and half, populations have size 100, runs are allowed 50 generations. Crossover probability of 90% and mutation probability of 10% are employed. We analyse the iTrees for the runs and the iTrees corresponding to the best and the worst genetic programs encountered during the run, respectively. We classified as best the solution-quality trees (with $fitness \leq 0.03$) and as worst the useless trees (with $fitness > 1$).

Table 1. The measures computed on iTrees of runs, best trees and worst trees encountered during the runs. The average of 50 runs and corresponding confidence interval (with 95% confidence) is presented in each case

	M_1 [$\times 10^2$]	M_2 [$\times 10^3$]	M_3	IB_1 [$\times 10^3$]	IB_2 [$\times 10^4$]
Run	59.7 ± 11.4	389 ± 73.1	4.24 ± 0.26	35.6 ± 6.8	185.6 ± 42.4
Best	31.8 ± 6.5	249.9 ± 53.9	4.93 ± 0.23	23.5 ± 4.7	143.3 ± 33.6
Worst	10.6 ± 2.6	12.8 ± 4.6	3.78 ± 0.22	6.3 ± 1.6	5.1 ± 2.3

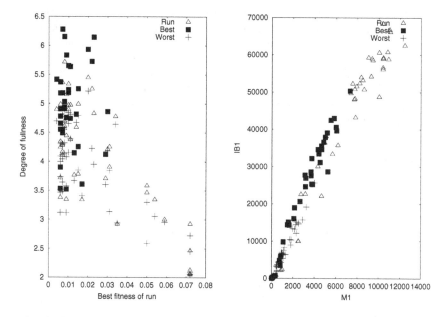

(a) The degree of fullness of the iTrees vs. the quality of solutions

(b) The linear relationship between imbalance and number of nodes

Fig. 5. The resulting iTrees for the runs, best and worst trees. Each triangle represents the iTree of one run, each square the iTree of best trees encountered in one run, and each plus the iTree of worst trees encountered during a run

37 runs were successful, 4 runs had acceptable solution and 9 runs were unsuccessful. In the successful runs, the good trees significantly outnumber the useless trees.

In Table 1 we show the values for five iTree-based measures described in Sections 3 and 6. For all measures, the difference between the value for the best iTree and the worst iTree is significant. The best iTree has more nodes than the worst iTree, the total number of nodes in the best trees is larger than the total number of nodes in the worst trees, meaning that during evolution more time is spent on the good trees than on the bad ones. The best trees are larger and fuller than the worst ones. As shown in Fig. 5(a), the runs producing better solutions evolve a larger range of mostly fuller trees. Also, the best iTrees are fuller than the iTrees of the runs.

An interesting linear relationship emerges between the imbalance (IB_1) and the number of nodes (M_1) in the iTrees for all three cases (Fig. 5(b)). The more nodes are investigated, the more unbalanced the iTree becomes. This is somewhat expected and is in line with the literature on code growth in genetic programming.

9   Conclusions

In this paper, we motivated the need for an intermediate data structure by pointing to the complexity required to conceive and develop population measures and visualisations. In the absence of efficient and intuitive methods, researchers often reduce the complexity of other aspects to make analysis tractable. However, by using the proposed iTree, several population measures become intuitive and more efficient than the traditional traversals of the population. Future genetic programming systems can make use of a standardised data structure, such as the iTree, to allow quicker development and sharing of methods and measures to improve the dissemination of scientific ideas.

References

1. E. Burke, S. Gustafson, G. Kendall, and N. Krasnogor. Advanced population diversity measures in genetic programming. In J. M. Guervós et al., editors, *7th International Conference on Parallel Problem Solving from Nature*, volume 2439 of *LNCS*, pages 341–350, 2002.
2. D. H. Colless. Review of phylogenetics: The theory and practice of phylogenetic systematics. *Syst. Zool.*, 31:100–104, 1982.
3. J. Daida, A. Hilss, D. Ward, and S. Long. Visualizing tree structures in genetic programming. In E. Cantú-Paz et al., editors, *Genetic and Evolutionary Computation – GECCO-2003*, volume 2724 of *LNCS*, pages 1652–1664, 2003.
4. J. Daida, H. Li, R. Tang, and A. Hilss. What makes a problem GP-hard? validating a hypothesis of structural causes. In E. Cantú-Paz et al., editors, *Genetic and Evolutionary Computation – GECCO-2003*, volume 2724 of *LNCS*, pages 1665–1677, 2003.
5. A. Ekárt and S. Németh. Maintaining the diversity of genetic programs. In J. Foster et al., editors, *Proceedings of the 5th European Genetic Programming Conference*, volume 2278 of *LNCS*, pages 162–171, 2002.
6. M. Keijzer. Efficiently representing populations in genetic programming. In P. J. Angeline and K. E. Kinnear, Jr., editors, *Advances in Genetic Programming 2*, chapter 13, pages 259–278. MIT Press, 1996.
7. S.-Y. Lu. The tree-to-tree distance and its application to cluster analysis. *IEEE Transactions on PAMI*, 1(2):219–224, 1979.
8. U.-M. O'Reilly. Using a distance metric on genetic programs to understand genetic operators. In J. R. Koza, editor, *Late Breaking Papers at the 1997 Genetic Programming Conference*, pages 199–206, 1997.
9. S. M. Selkow. The tree-to-tree editing problem. *Information Processing Letters*, 6(6):184–186, 1977.
10. M. Wineberg and F. Oppacher. Distance between populations. In E. Cantú-Paz et al., editors, *GECCO-2003*, volume 2724 of *LNCS*, pages 1481–1492, 2003.

Boosting Technique for Combining Cellular GP Classifiers

Gianluigi Folino, Clara Pizzuti, and Giandomenico Spezzano

ICAR-CNR,
c/o DEIS, Univ. della Calabria
87036 Rende (CS), Italy
{folino,pizzuti,spezzano}@icar.cnr.it

Abstract. An extension of Cellular Genetic Programming for data classification with the boosting technique is presented and a comparison with the bagging-like majority voting approach is performed. The method is able to deal with large data sets that do not fit in main memory since each classifier is trained on a subset of the overall training data. Experiments showed that, by using a sample of reasonable size, the extension with these voting algorithms enhances classification accuracy at a much lower computational cost.

1 Introduction

The explosive growth of information in different domains has spurred the development of data mining techniques [3] for knowledge extraction from massive data sets. The availability of fast, efficient, and accurate data mining algorithms, able to deal with this huge amount of data, too large to fit into the main memory of computers, is becoming a pressing request. To obtain fast methods several parallel data mining algorithms were realized, such as parallel decision trees [18,17], and parallel association rules [20]. On the other hand, to improve the accuracy of any learning algorithm, ensemble techniques, that combine the prediction of multiple classifiers, each trained on a different training set obtained by means of resampling, have been introduced.

Bagging [2] and boosting [8] are well known ensemble techniques that repeatedly run a weak learner on different distributions over the training data. Both methods build *bags* of data of the same size of the original data set by applying random sampling with replacement. Unlike bagging, boosting tries to concentrate on harder examples by adaptively changing the distributions of the training set on the base of the performance of the previous classifiers. It has been shown that bagging and boosting improve the accuracy of decision tree classifiers [2,14,1].

Genetic programming (GP)[10] has showed to be a particularly suitable technique to deal with the task of data classification [7,13,15,11,4] by evolving decision trees. Genetic Programming extended by means of ensemble techniques [9,5] enhances classification accuracy of GP. Genetic programming based classifiers,

M. Keijzer et al. (Eds.): EuroGP 2004, LNCS 3003, pp. 47–56, 2004.

however, involve a lot of computation and their performances may drastically degrade when applied to large problems because of the intensive computation of fitness evaluation of each individual in the population. High performance computing is an essential component for increasing the performances and obtaining large-scale efficient classifiers [19,6]. To this purpose, several approaches have been proposed. The different models used for distributing the computation and to ease parallelize genetic programming, cluster around two main approaches [19]: the well-known *island model* and the *cellular model*. In the island model several isolated subpopulations evolve in parallel, periodically exchanging by migration their best individuals with the neighboring subpopulations. In the cellular model each individual has a spatial location on a low-dimensional grid and the individuals interact locally within a small neighborhood. The model considers the population as a system of active individuals that interact only with their direct neighbors. Different neighborhoods can be defined for the cells and the fitness evaluation is done simultaneously for all the individuals. Selection, reproduction and mating take place locally within the neighborhood. A parallel approach to build predictors speeds up the generation process and, at the same time, allows to deal with large data sets.

Cellular Genetic Programming for data classification ($CGPC$) enhanced with an ensemble bagging-like ($BagCGPC$) technique has been presented in [5] and showed to enhance both the prediction accuracy and the running time of $CGPC$.

In this paper we extend $CGPC$ with a voting classification scheme based on the boosting technique, and present an experimental comparison of $CGPC$ with bagging and boosting voting schemes. The approach can deal with large data sets that do not fit in main memory since each classifier is trained on a subset of the overall training data. Experiments showed that the extension of $CGPC$ with these voting algorithms enhances both accuracy and execution time. In fact, higher accuracy can be obtained by using a sample of reasonable size at a much lower computational cost. The algorithm could also be used to classify distributed data which cannot be merged together. For example, in applications that deal with proprietary, privacy sensitive data, where it is not permitted moving raw data from different sites to a single central location for mining.

The paper is organized as follows. Next section describes Bagging and Boosting algorithms. Section 3 presents the extension of cellular genetic programming with the Boosting technique. In section 4, finally, the results of the method on some standard problems are presented.

2   Ensemble Techniques

Let $S = \{(x_i, y_i) | i = 1, \dots, N\}$ be a training set where x_i, called example, is an attribute vector with m attributes and y_i is the class label associated with x_i. A predictor, given a new example, has the task to predict the class label for it. Ensemble techniques build T predictors, each on a different subset of the training set, then combine them together to classify the test set.

Bagging (bootstrap aggregating) was introduced by Breiman in [2] and it is based on bootstrap samples (replicates) of the same size of the training set S.

Each bootstrap sample is created by uniformly sampling instances from S with replacement, thus some examples may appear more than once while others may not appear in it. T bags $B_1, \ldots, B_T$ are generated and T classifiers $C^1, \ldots, C^T$ are built on each bag B_i. The number T of predictors is an input parameter. A final classifier classifies an example by giving as output the class predicted most often by $C^1, \ldots, C^T$, with ties solved arbitrarily.

Boosting was introduced by Schapire [16] for boosting the performance of any "weak" learning algorithm, i.e. an algorithm that "generates classifiers which need only be a little bit better than random guessing" [8]. The boosting algorithm, called *AdaBoost*, adaptively changes the distribution of the sample depending on how difficult each example is to classify. Given the number T of trials to execute, T weighted training set $S_1, S_2, \ldots, S_T$ are sequentially generated and T classifiers $C^1, \ldots, C^T$ are built to compute a weak hypothesis h_t. Let w_i^t denote the weight of example x_i at trial t. At the beginning $w_i^1 = 1/n$ for each x_i. At each trial $t = 1, \ldots, T$, a weak learner C^t, whose error ϵ^t is bounded to a value strictly less than $1/2$, is built and the weights of the next trial are obtained by multiplying the weight of the correctly classified examples by $\beta^t = \epsilon^t/(1 - \epsilon^t)$ and renormalizing the weights so that $\Sigma_i w_i^{t+1} = 1$. Thus "easy" examples get a lower weight, while "hard" examples, that tend to be misclassified, get higher weights. This induces AdaBoost to focus on examples that are hardest to classify. The boosted classifier gives the class label y that maximizes the sum of the weights of the weak hypotheses predicting that label, where the weight is defined as $ln(1/\beta^t)$. Freund and Schapire [8] showed theoretically that AdaBoost can decrease the error of any weak learning algorithm and introduced two versions of the method. In the next section we present the extension of GP by using AdaBoost.M1.

Regarding the application of ensemble techniques to Genetic Programming, Iba in [9] proposed to extend Genetic Programming to deal with bagging and boosting. A population is divided in a set of subpopulations and each subpopulation is evolved on a training set sampled with replacement from the original data. Best individuals of each subpopulation participate to voting to give a prediction on the testing data. Experiments on some standard problems using ten subpopulations showed the effectiveness of the approach. Another extension of Cellular Genetic Programming for data classification to induce an ensemble of predictors was presented in [5]. Each classifier was trained on a different subset of the overall data, then they were combined to classify new tuples by applying a simple majority voting algorithm, like bagging. Results on a large data set showed that the ensemble of classifiers trained on a sample of the data obtains higher accuracy than a single classifier that uses the entire data set at a much lower computational cost.

3   BoostCGPC

Boost Cellular Genetic Programming Classifier (BoostCGPC), is described in figure 1. Given the training set $S = \{(x_1, y_1), \ldots (x_N, y_N)\}$ and the number P of

Given $S = \{(x_1, y_1), \ldots (x_N, y_N)\}$, $x_i \in X$
with labels $y_i \in Y = \{1, 2, \ldots, k\}$, and a population Q of size q
For j = 1, 2, ..., P (for each processor in parallel)
    Draw a sample S_j with size n for processor j
        Initialize the weights $w_i^1 = \frac{1}{N}$ for $i = 1, \ldots, n$,
        where n is the number of training examples on each processor j.
        Initialize the subpopulation Q_i, for $i = 1, \ldots, P$
        with random individuals
end parallel for
For t = 1,2,3, ..., T
    For j = 1, 2, ..., P (for each processor in parallel)
    Train $CGPC$ on the sample S_j using a weighted
    fitness according to the distribution w^t
    Compute a weak hypothesis $h_{j,t} : X \rightarrow Y$
    Exchange the hypotheses $h_{j,t}$ among the P processors
    let $D_i = 1$ if arg max $h_{j,t}(x_i) \neq y_i$
        0 otherwise
    Compute the error $\epsilon_j^t = \sum_i^n w_i^t D_i$
    if $\epsilon_j^t \geq 1/2$ break loop
    Set $\beta_j^t = \epsilon_j^t/(1 - \epsilon_j^t)$,
    Update the weights $w^t : w_i^{t+1} = 2(1 - \epsilon_j^t) \times w_i^t$ if $h_{j,t}(x_i) = y_i$
        $2\epsilon_j^t \times w_i^t$ otherwise
end parallel for
end for t
output the hypothesis :
    $h_f = arg\ max\ (\sum_j^p \sum_t^T log(\frac{1}{\beta_j^t}) D_j^t)$
    where $D_j^t = 1$ if $h_{j,t}(x_i) = y_i$, 0 otherwise

Fig. 1. The algorithm parallel BoostCGPC

processors to use to run the algorithm, we partition the population in P subpopulations, one for each processor and draw P samples from S of size $n < N$. Each subpopulation is evolved for k generations and trained on its local sample by running $CGPC$. To take advantage of the cellular model of genetic programming, subpopulations are not independently evolved, but they exchange the outmost individuals in an asynchronous way. On each processor at each generation, every tree undergoes one of the genetic operators (reproduction, crossover, mutation) depending on the probability test. If crossover is applied, the mate of the current individual is selected as the neighbor having the best fitness, and the offspring is generated. The current string is then replaced by the best of the two offspring if the fitness of the latter is better than that of the former. After k generations, the individual with the best fitness is selected for participating to vote. In fact the P best individuals of each subpopulation are exchanged among the P subpopulations and constitute the ensemble of predictors that will determine the weights of the examples for the next round.

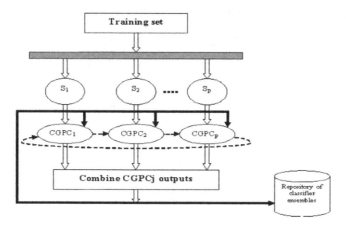

Fig. 2. Implementation of *BoostCGPC* on a distributed memory parallel computer.

Figure 2 illustrates the basic framework for the parallel implementation of the *BoostCGPC* algorithm on a distributed memory parallel computer. We assume that each training sample $S_i, i = 1, \ldots, P$ resides on a different processor within the parallel computer. We use the diffusion model of GP to parallelize in a natural way the implementation of *BoostCGPC*. The size of each subpopulation $Q_i, i = 1, \ldots, P$ present on a node, must be greater than a threshold determined from the granularity supported by the processor. Each processor, using a training sample S_i and a subpopulation Q_i implements a classifier process $CGPC_i$ as a learning algorithm and generates a classifier. For efficiency reasons, the individuals within a subpopulation are combined into a single process that sequentially updates each individual. This reduces the amount of internal communication on each process, increasing the granularity of the application. Communication between processors is local and asynchronous. The configuration of the structure of the processors is based on a ring topology and a classifier process is assigned to each. During the boosting rounds, each classifier process maintains the local vector of the weights that directly reflect the prediction accuracy on that site. At each boosting round the hypotheses generated by each of these classifiers ($CGPC_i$ in Figure 2) are combined to produce the ensemble of predictors. Then, the ensemble is broadcasted at each classifier process to locally recalculate the new vector of the weights and a copy of the ensemble is stored in a repository. After the execution of the fixed number T of boosting rounds, the classifiers stored in the repository are used to evaluate the accuracy of the classification algorithm. Note that, the algorithm can also be used to classify distributed data which cannot be merged together. For example, in applications that deal with proprietary, privacy sensitive data, where it is not permitted moving raw data from different sites to a single central location for mining.

Table 1. Data sets used in the experiments

Dataset	Attr.	Tuples	Classes
Adult	14	48842	2
SatImage	36	6435	6
Segment	20	2310	7
Census	42	299285	2
Covtype	54	581012	7

Table 2. Main parameters used in the experiments

Name	Value
max_depth_for_new_trees	6
max_depth_after_crossover	17
max_mutant_depth	2
grow_method	RAMPED
selection_method	GROW
crossover_func_pt_fraction	0.7
crossover_any_pt_fraction	0.1
fitness_prop_repro_fraction	0.1
parsimony_factor	0

4   Experimental Results

In this section we compare $BagCGPC$, $BoostCGPC$ and classical $CGPC$ using some well known data sets taken from the UCI Machine Learning Repository [12]. The data sets are described in table 1 and present different characteristics in the number and type (continuous and nominal) of attributes, two classes versus multiple classes and number of tuples. In particular, the last two are real large data sets. $Cens$ contains weighted census data extracted from the 1994 and 1995 current population surveys conducted by the U.S. Census Bureau and $CovType$ comprises data representing the prediction of forest cover type from cartographic variables determined from US Forest Service and US Geological Survey. The experiments were performed on a Linux cluster with 16 dual-processor 1,133 Ghz Pentium III nodes having 2 Gbytes of memory connected by Myrinet and running Red Hat v7.2.

The parameters used for the experiments are shown in table 2. All results were obtained by averaging 10-fold cross-validation runs. In order to do a fair comparison among $CGPC$, $BagCGPC$, and $BoostCGPC$ we used 5 processors for all the three algorithms, population size 500 and number of generations 500 for $CGPC$. To obtain the same parameters, $BagCGPC$ was executed 5 times on five processors in parallel, with population size 100 on each processor (for a total size of $100 \times 5{=}500$) and number of generations 100 (for a total number of generations $100 \times 5{=}500$), thus generating 25 classifiers. On the other hand, the number T of rounds of $BoostCGPC$ was 5, again on 5 processors, population size 100 on each processor, number of generations 100 for each round, thus generating the same total population size, number of generations, and number

Table 3. Comparing error, execution time, and size of the best tree for *CGPC* (using the complete data set), *BagCGPC* (20% tuples, 25 classifiers), and *BoostCGPC* (20% tuples, 5 rounds x 5 classifiers)

	Dataset				
CGPC	Adult	Sat	Segment	Census	CovType
Error	17.18	23.02	12.73	5.19	36.27
Time (sec)	4230	1212	1498	32820	66145
Size	233	122	205	389	112
BagCGPC					
Error	17.01	22.33	12.45	5.08	38.03
Time (sec)	528	83	46	3743	11277
Size	6055	3549	2806	14614	1636
BoostCGPC					
Error	16.53	21.22	10.90	8.33	33.65
Time (sec)	796	207	119	4448	16502
Size	4290	2930	755	8328	1467

of classifiers, i.e. 500, 500, and 25, respectively. In table 3 we report the mean error rate over the 10-fold-cross-validations, execution time in seconds, and size of the classifiers. For these experiments *CGPC* used the complete data sets for training, while both *BagCGPC* and *BoostCGPC* employed only the 20% of the overall data sets. Note that in the case of the ensembles, the size is the sum of the 25 classifiers composing the ensemble; thus the average size of a single tree can be obtained dividing this size by 25. From the table we can observe that *BagCGPC* and *BoostCGPC* always obtain better results than *CGPC* in terms of mean error, time and average tree size, the only exception being an error of 8.33 of *BoostCGPC* for the *Cens* data set and an error of 38.03 of *BagCGPC* for the *CovType* data set. Considering that the ensemble methods use only the 20% of the data set, these results are impressive and substantiate the already showed characteristics of this kind of approach in improving accuracy. As regard the comparison between *BagCGPC* and *BoostCGPC*, it is worth to note that *BoostCGPC* obtains always mean error and tree size lower than *BagCGPC*, except for mean error of Census data set. Execution times of *BoostCGPC*, however, are worse than those of *BagCGPC*, though we can observe that while for the smallest data set (Segment, 2310 tuples) the execution time of *BoostCGPC* is 2.5 times more than that of *BagCGPC*, for the biggest data set (CovType, 581012 tuples) the execution time is 1.5 times more than that of *BagCGPC*. Furthermore, in the latter case, *BagCGPC* gives an error of 38.03, while *BoostCGPC* error is 33.65. The running time increase is mainly due to the weight computations and to the necessity of exchanging the hypotheses found after each round.

We wanted also to investigate the influence of the sample sizes on the accuracy of the method. To this end we used the *CovType* data set and run *CGPC* with the overall data set, while *BoostCGPC* was executed with 5%, 10%, and

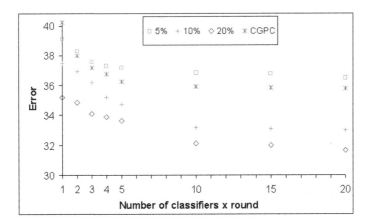

Fig. 3. Mean error for different sample sizes of the training set vs number of classifiers for round. (Covtype dataset)

20% of the tuples for 5 rounds, each round using an increasing number of classifiers. Figure 3 shows the effect of these different sample sizes on accuracy as the number of classifiers generated increases at each round. Parameters are the same of the previous experiments. $CGPC$ used a population size equal to 100 $\times$ *number of classifiers* of the boosting algorithm. From the figure we can note that when $BoostCGPC$ is trained on a sample of size 5% the overall data set, it is not able to outperform $CGPC$ working on the entire data set. But, as the size increases, $BoostCGPC$ is able to obtain an error lower than $CGPC$. An ensemble of two classifiers, 5 round, for a total of 10 classifiers, using the 10% of the data set obtains higher accuracy. Augmenting the sample size and the number of classifiers a further increase can be obtained. Using from 5 to 10 classifier at each round seems to be a good compromise between results obtained and resources employed. In fact figure 3 shows a slow decrease of the mean error after these values.

5   Conclusions

An extension of Cellular Genetic Programming for data classification to induce an ensemble of predictors that uses a voting classification scheme based on boosting technique was presented, and a comparison with bagging like majority voting approach was performed. Experiments showed that the extension of $CGPC$ with these voting algorithm enhances both accuracy and execution time. The approach is able to deal with large data sets that do not fit in main memory since each classifiers is trained on a subset of the overall training data. Experiments on a large real data set showed that, analogously to $BagCGPC$, higher accuracy can be obtained by using a sample of reasonable size at a much lower computational cost, and that sample size influences the achievable accuracy.

References

1. Eric Bauer and Ron Kohavi. An empirical comparison of voting classification algorithms: Bagging, boosting, and variants. *Machine Learning*, (36):105–139, 1999.
2. Leo Breiman. Bagging predictors. *Machine Learning*, 24(2):123–140, 1996.
3. U.M. Fayyad, G. Piatesky-Shapiro, and P. Smith. From data mining to knowledge discovery: an overview. In U.M. Fayyad & al. (Eds), editor, *Advances in Knowledge Discovery and Data Mining*, pages 1–34. AAAI/MIT Press, 1996.
4. G. Folino, C. Pizzuti, and G. Spezzano. A cellular genetic programming approach to classification. In *Proc. Of the Genetic and Evolutionary Computation Conference GECCO99*, pages 1015–1020, Orlando, Florida, July 1999. Morgan Kaufmann.
5. G. Folino, C. Pizzuti, and G. Spezzano. Ensemble techniques for parallel genetic programming based classifiers. In E. Costa C. Ryan, T. Soule, M. Keijzer, E. Tsang, R. Poli, editor, *Proceedings of the Sixth European Conference on Genetic Programming (EuroGP-2003)*, volume 2610 of *LNCS*, pages 59–69, Essex, UK, 2003. Springer Verlag.
6. G. Folino, C. Pizzuti, and G. Spezzano. A scalable cellular implementation of parallel genetic programming. *IEEE Transaction on Evolutionary Computation*, 7(1):37–53, February 2003.
7. A.A. Freitas. A genetic programming framework for two data mining tasks: Classification and generalised rule induction. In *Proceedings of the 2nd Int. Conference on Genetic Programming*, pages 96–101. Stanford University, CA, USA, 1997.
8. Y. Freund and R. Scapire. Experiments with a new boosting algorithm. In *Proceedings of the 13th Int. Conference on Machine Learning*, pages 148–156, 1996.
9. Hitoshi Iba. Bagging, boosting, and bloating in genetic programming. In *Proc. Of the Genetic and Evolutionary Computation Conference GECCO99*, pages 1053–1060, Orlando, Florida, July 1999. Morgan Kaufmann.
10. J. R. Koza. *Genetic Programming: On the Programming of Computers by means of Natural Selection*. MIT Press, Cambridge, MA, 1992.
11. R.E. Marmelstein and G.B. Lamont. Pattern classification using a hybbrid genetic program - decision tree approach. In *Proceedings of the Third Annual Conference on Genetic Programming*, Morgan Kaufmann, 1998.
12. C.J. Merz and P.M. Murphy. In *UCI repository of Machine Learning*, http://www.ics.uci.edu/mlearn/MLRepository.html, 1996.
13. N.I. Nikolaev and V. Slavov. Inductive genetic programming with decision trees. In *Proceedings of the 9th International Conference on Machine Learning*, Prague, Czech Republic, 1997.
14. J. Ross Quinlan. Bagging, boosting, and c4.5. In *Proceedings of the 13th National Conference on Artificial Intelligence AAAI96*, pages 725–730. Mit Press, 1996.
15. M.D. Ryan and V.J. Rayward-Smith. The evolution of decision trees. In *Proceedings of the Third Annual Conference on Genetic Programming*, Morgan Kaufmann, 1998.
16. R. E. Schapire. The strength of weak learnability. *Machine Learning*, 5(2):197–227, 1990.
17. M. Sreenivas, K. AlSabti, and S. Ranka. Parallel out-of-core decision tree classifiers. In H. Kargupta and P. Chan, editors, *in Advances in Distributed Data Mining*, Menlo Park, 1996. AAAI Press.
18. A. Srivastava, E. Han, V. Kumar, and V. Singh. Parallel formulations of decision tree classification algorithms. *Data Mining and Knowledge Discovery*, 3(2):237–261, 1999.

19. M. Tomassini. Parallel and distributed evolutionary algorithms: A review. In P. Neittaanmäki, K. Miettinen, M. Mäkelä and J. Periaux, editors, *Evolutionary Algorithms in Engineering and Computer Science*, J. Wiley and Sons, Chichester, 1999.
20. M. Zaki, S. Parthasarathy, M. Ogihara, and W. Li. Parallel algorithms for discovery of association rules. *Data Mining and Knowledge Discovery, special issue on Scalable High Performance Computing*, 1(4):343–373, 1997.

Co-evolving Faults to Improve the Fault Tolerance of Sorting Networks

Michael L. Harrison and James A. Foster

University of Idaho Computer Science Department
Moscow, ID 83844-1010
{michaelh,foster}@cs.uidaho.edu

Abstract. Fault tolerance is an important objective for circuit design, so it is natural to apply genetic programming techniques that are already being used for circuit design to enhance fault tolerance. We present preliminary evidence that co-evolving faults with circuits enhances the masking of faults in evolved circuits. Our test systems are sorting networks, since these are simple enough to analyze. We show that the overall impact of faults in an evolved sorting network can be reduced proportionally to the strength of co-evolutionary pressure.

1 Introduction

Nature favors robust designs, since fragile designs tend to become extinct. It is logical that evolutionary computing, which takes its inspiration from natural design processes, should also produce robust designs. In designing artificial systems, such as special purpose computing devices, it can be difficult and expensive to design and test complicated fault tolerant systems with traditional techniques. However, naturally inspired design techniques such as genetic programming can be adapted to optimize for design criteria other than correctness, such as fault tolerance.

Several previous studies of fault tolerance in evolved systems have shown that evolutionary design techniques produce fault tolerant designs, often without this particular objective[1,2]. These studies have focused primarily on the inherent fault tolerance due to the evolution process and not on explicit selective pressure. In this paper we show that explicit selective pressure toward fault tolerance in sorting networks increases the fault masking ability of sorting networks. This preliminary evidence demonstrates the possibility of extending the automated design of circuits with evolutionary approaches to produce fault tolerant solutions.

2 Background

FAULT TOLERANCE is the ability of a system to continue normal operation regardless of the presence of faults[3]. The breakdown of a system due to internal failure can be viewed as a chain of events from fault to error to failure. A FAULT

M. Keijzer et al. (Eds.): EuroGP 2004, LNCS 3003, pp. 57–66, 2004.
© Springer-Verlag Berlin Heidelberg 2004

is an internal defect in a software or hardware system, such as a design flaw or a component failure. Incorrect behavior inside a system, caused by a fault, is termed an ERROR. Finally, a FAILURE occurs when a system is unable to perform its specified task or tasks due to errors[4].

A fault will not necessarily cause system failure. If a fault is masked by the system, the system maintains its ability to function despite the presence of a fault. A system with active fault masking has abilities to detect and reconfigure and thereby ignore the effect of the faulty component. A system relying on passive fault masking is characterized by taking no active role in diagnosing or repairing itself, instead relying on internal structure and redundancy to mask faults. This study is concerned with arranging components into passive fault tolerant structures in which the circuit topology provides the tolerance. To explore the evolution of fault tolerant structures we utilize sorting networks as a simple test problem and evolve them using co-evolution.

2.1 Sorting Networks

Sorting networks(SN) have long been of interest to computer scientists. Knuth used nearly 350 pages discussing them in his book *The Art of Computer Programming: Sorting and Searching*[5]. SNs provide a rich search space; even for our small 11 input, 45 gate sorting networks there are $\binom{11}{2}^{45} \approx 2^{260}$ possible networks. Many studies, including the first study using co-evolution by Hillis[6], focus on finding minimally sized sorting networks[7,8,9]. Hillis' work inspired the techniques used in this study, but we emphasize that our goal is to evolve reasonable fault tolerant structures, not minimal sorting networks.

Sorting networks are simple feed forward circuits used to sort values. Figure 1B demonstrates a 5 input, 9 gate sorting network. Values presented to the input lines (horizontal lines) carry the values from left to right. Along the lines the values encounter compare-exchange(CE) gates (vertical lines). CE-gates are simple two input sorting circuits which exchange their input values if they are out of order. The four possible inputs to the simplest of sorting networks (the 2 input, 1 gate network) is displayed in Figure 1A.

(A)   (B)

Fig. 1. (A) A 2x1 (2 inputs with 1 gate) sorting network with all possible inputs and outputs. Values propagate along the horizontal lines until they encounter a gate (vertical line), at that point the gate may switch the values or pass them through. All 1's are sorted to the bottom and all zeros to the top. A valid sorting network will correctly sort all possible inputs. (B) A 5x9 (5 inputs with 9 gates) sorting network demonstrating a larger arrangement of compare exchange gates and inputs.

According to the *0-1 principle* a network topology is valid if it sorts all possible n length bit strings, where n is the number of inputs. Therefore, testing any n input network requires a series of 2^n tests. For our 11 bit networks this means $2^{11} = 2024$ possible test cases[5].

2.2   Co-evolution

A traditional Genetic Algorithm contains a single population with individuals that compete based on some fitness measure. Co-evolution uses multiple populations to aid in the evolution process. There are two main types of co-evolution, competitive and cooperative.

In this study we are concerned with competitive co-evolution[10,6]; pitting two populations against one another, competing for fitness. This is a kind of evolutionary arms-race. One population targets the weaknesses of the other for its own benefit and in this way the fitness measure of each population depends on the other. A major benefit of co-evolution is the ability to evolve without a complete fitness evaluation. During evolution it may only be necessary to use a partial fitness evaluation. Hillis showed that this approach worked well for discovering small sorting networks when compared to full fitness evaluations(too slow) and random test cases[6]. This is particularly useful for sorting networks as there are an exponential number of test cases to be considered. Other studies using competitive co-evolution have demonstrated success as well[11,12,13,14].

3   Methodology

A valid sorting network properly sorts all possible inputs but can be compromised by the presence of faults. A fault is defined as the removal from the network of a CE-gate. If a network depends heavily on a particular CE-gate the faulting of this gate results in many unsorted outputs. It should be noted that we are not concerned with actual electric circuits but with SN at a high level.

To provide selective pressure toward fault tolerance we evolve two populations simultaneously using co-evolution. One population contains sorting networks, the other is a test population containing the input/fault pairs(IFPs). Each IFPs contains two parts; a bit string used as an input to the sorting networks and a fault. The IFPs pressure the sorting networks to evolve correct solutions in the presence of faults. In turn, the sorting networks pressure the IFP population to discover IFPs that cause failures.

Table 1 shows some of the standard parameters for our genetic algorithm. Initially, both populations are generated using random values for CE-gates in the sorting networks, input strings, and faults. Following evaluation, each population is sorted according to fitness. Selection is performed on both populations using a standard 7 member tournament. Tournaments are conducted within the top 30% of each population and continue until the offspring replace the bottom 70%. This preserves the top 30% in each generation.

Table 1. Parameters for algorithm, sorting networks and test string populations.

PARAMETER	VALUE
Elitism(both populations)	top 30%
Selection(both populations)	7 member tournament
Maximum Generations	10,000
Test String Population Size	100
Test String Mutation Probability	0.01
Sorting Network Population Size	15,000
Sorting Network Mutation Probability	0.01
Maximum Gates Allowed	45
Minimum Gates Allowed	9
Parallel Network Stages	9

3.1 Sorting Network Encoding, Crossover, and Mutation

We represent sorting networks as a list of stages, where each stage includes five CE-gates. Each CE-gate is represented by a pair of integers, which indicate the two input lines to that CE-gate. To translate the genotype to its phenotype, a functioning SN, we add CE-gates from left to right in each stage. Each input line is only used once within a stage, so CE-gates that reference previously used lines in the same stage are eliminated from the SN. Our 11 input SNs allow for 9 such stages, resulting in SNs containing between 9 CE-gate (1 in each stage) to 45 CE-gates(5 in each stage). See 2B.

Crossover is standard 2-point crossover with randomly selected crossover points selected along the list of CE-gates. Crossover doesn't split up integers that comprise a CE-gate. Two parent networks produce two child networks. A child may be mutated with some probability (denoted in Table 1) by randomly choosing a CE-gate in the array and randomly modifying one of its input lines.

3.2 Input/Fault Pair(IFP) Encoding, Crossover, and Mutation

A input/fault pair is encoded as a bit string and fault pair as shown in Figure 2A. The binary string on the left is the 11 bit input to the sorting network and the integer on the right is a value from 1 to 45 indicating the index of the CE-gate to be faulted. These refer to CE-gates in the genotype and it is possible for a sorting network to have fewer than 45 CE-gates in the phenotype so these faults may refer to nonexistent CE-gates.

Crossover on input strings is performed using standard 1-point crossover with a random crossover point resulting in 2 children. The faults are then assigned randomly to the two children. After crossover each child may be selected for mutation with the probability noted in Table 1. If selected one of either the fault or the bit string is selected for mutation with even probability. The bit string is mutated by randomly selecting a bit and flipping it. The fault is mutated by randomly assigning its value to another CE gate index.

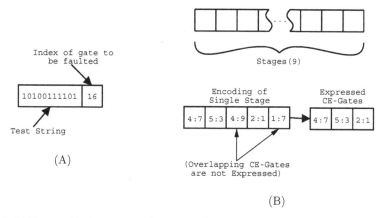

Fig. 2. (A)Integer/fault pair encoding, input string followed by index of gate to fault. (B) Sorting network encoding show 9 stages and demonstration of single stage with some CE-Gates not expressed. Gate [4:9] conflicts with the previous gate [4:7] so it is left unexpressed. Similarly gate [1:7] conflicts with previous gate [2:1] and is left unexpressed.

3.3   Evaluating Sorting Network and Input/Fault Pair Fitness

As described previously, a fault is the removal of a CE-gate from a network. When an IFP is evaluated by a SN the faulty CE-gate associated with that IFP isn't allowed to participate. This missing CE-gate or fault may cause the sorting network to sort its inputs incorrectly which affects the fitness of both the SN(negatively) and the IFP(positively).

The effect of a fault is topology specific, so a input/fault pair may not work well on testing a wide variety of sorting networks. However, we believe the sorting network population will periodically converge on a similar set of solutions which the test strings/faults will exploit.

Sorting networks are evaluated based on their ability to correctly evaluate all the individuals in the IFP population. Every IFP in the test population is applied to every individual in the sorting network population. Given a SN and an IFP we calculate their relative scores in the following manner:

1. Apply the fault from the IFP by removing the CE-gate indicated in the IFP.
2. Sort the input bit string using the sorting network.
3. Determine the bitwise error of the output by calculating the hamming distance between the sorting network's output and the correct output.
4. Add the bitwise error obtained in the previous step to the sorting network's fitness as well as the IFP's fitness.
5. Return the sorting network to pre-fault state by replacing the CE-gate removed in step 1.

Figure 3 shows how a fault is applied to a small example network. The fitness of both populations is calculated simultaneously by applying the above steps to

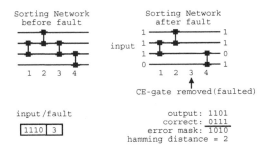

Fig. 3. Evaluation of a sorting network using a input/fault pair. The fault from the IFP is applied to the sorting network and then the input is applied. In this case the number of errors is 2.

Table 2. This table demonstrates the fitness evaluation for a input/fault pair(IFP) population and a sorting network(SN) population. For clarity we use smaller, 4 bit strings. Individual are evaluated by applying each one to all members of the sorting network population and summing the bitwise errors(hamming distance from correct output) in the output. Similarly, sorting networks are evaluated by summing the bitwise errors(hamming distance from correct output) over all test strings in the test string population.

	input	correct	output	score	output	score	output	score	IFP Score
			SN 1		SN 2		SN 3		
IFP1	1010	0011	0011	**0**	0011	**0**	1001	**2**	0+0+2=2
IFP2	0110	0011	0101	**2**	0011	**0**	0101	**2**	2+0+2=4
IFP3	1000	0001	0010	**2**	0001	**0**	0001	**0**	2+0+0=2
SN Scores:			0+2+2=4		0+0+0=0		2+2+0=4		

every possible pairing of IFP and SN. A SN that correctly sorts the entire test string population with no errors would receive a score of 0; the lower the score the better the network. For IFPs the opposite is true; the more errors the better the fitness. Table 2 demonstrates the fitness calculation for 3 test strings and 3 sorting networks using 4 bit inputs, the faults are left out of this example for clarity. From the table we see that SN #2 has the best fitness(lowest value) as it sorts all its inputs correctly(no errors) and thus receives a score of 0. Also, IFP2 is the most fit as it has caused 4 bits to be out of position in the outputs while the other two IFPs have only caused 2.

3.4 Quantifying Fault Tolerance in Sorting Networks

We will introduce a fault tolerance calculation for sorting networks so that we can measure the fault tolerance of a sorting network. This analysis is done after evolution has completed and takes no part in the evolution process. This measurement is used to judge the performance of the evolution process. We define a sorting network fault as the removal of a gate from the network. This is typically referred to as a benign fault because the component simply drops out of the system instead of performing the wrong action or malicious behavior. Benign faults were chosen to simplify the fault analysis and because it is difficult to justify a more complicated fault model for such simple circuits.

When a gate is removed we expect that the network will incorrectly sort some inputs unless the fault is completely masked by the network. Removal of certain CE gates will cause more harm than others. To determine the effect of a fault in the network we simply remove the gate we are interested in and evaluate all possible inputs. Every incorrect bit in output strings is counted and demonstrates the dependence of the network on this particular gate. By evaluating all possible fault(1 fault per gate) and input string(all length 11 bit strings, 2^{11} total strings) combinations and summing the errors we get the total number of possible failures for a network.

4   Results

To demonstrate that co-evolving faults can increase the survivability of a sorting network we performed three separate tests. For the baseline case we evolved sorting networks without using the faults associated with the test string population, no explicit selective pressure toward fault tolerance. Second, we evolved sorting networks and used randomly chosen faults for each evaluation. Third, we co-evolved with the evolved faults associated with the test strings in the IFPs. Each type was run 36 times and each execution produced a correct sorting network(all tests converged on correct solutions). The fault analysis mentioned in Section 3.4 was run on each network which sums the total number of bitwise faults for each gate in the network. The number of failed outputs across all possible inputs and all possible faults is totaled. Figure 4 shows the ranges (one standard deviation) of the total failures for each type. Table 3 shows the same data in tabular form with the addition of the mean, maximum and minimum number of gates per sorting network.

For reference the known minimum size of a 11 input sorting network is 35 gates and 8 parallel stages. Also, one should notice that although there are 45 available gates, they are not all used. We first ran these experiments using parsimony pressure to push down the size of the networks but found that better results were obtained by simply setting a ceiling on the number of gates and parallel stages. All the architectures evolved are constrained to no more that 9 parallel stages. This means that a significant increase in fault tolerance can be obtained in 11 input sorting networks with only 1 additional parallel step. Figure 5 demonstrates one of the evolved sorting network topologies.

5   Conclusion

Figure 4 demonstrates the overall reduction in the number of failures experienced in our evolved sorting networks. Although the *random* and *no fault* experiments overlap, the narrowing of deviations from the mean should indicate an improvement. The deviation of the *random* and *co-evolved* tests are near each other

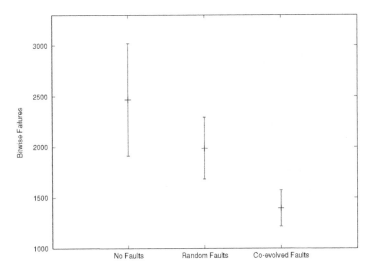

Fig. 4. Average across 36 runs of total bitwise faults for the three types of experiments: no faults, random faults and co-evolved faults. Error bars indicate 1 standard deviation. The number of failures decreases as the selective pressure for fault tolerance is increased.

Table 3. Data collected over 36 runs each based on the fault analysis of the resulting sorting networks. Mean is the average of the total number of failures. Stdev is the standard deviation of these values from the mean. Min and Max are the least and greatest numbers, respectively, of faults observed. Gates category contains the mean number of gates as well as maximum and minimum for each test.

	Failures				Gates		
Fault Pressure	Mean	Stdev	Min	Max	Mean	Max	Min
None	2467	553	1542	4011	40	41	37
Random	1988	304	1418	2292	41	43	39
Co-evolve	1397	178	985	2017	40	43	39

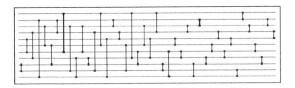

Fig. 5. An example sorting network from the co-evolution runs. This network has 42 gates and total of 1074 total failures over all single point faults. The minimum known 11 input network has 35 gates and 8 stages. This network has 7 more gates but only uses one more stage.

but do not overlap. This demonstrates a statistically significant increase in fault tolerance when using co-evolved faults compared to using random faults and no faults.

One weakness of this approach is the longer run times when introducing faults into the algorithm. The *random* and *co-evolved faults* tests averaged 1.5 times the number of generations as the *no faults* tests. We have not compared the co-evolution approach to using a complete evaluation(fitness based on all inputs and all faults). However, we believe that the complete evaluation approach would be too time consuming given it exponential nature.

5.1   Future Research

Future work includes applying the technique presented here to other systems such as neural networks or circuits with more complicated fault models. Determining if this approach scales to larger problems is also important in determining its usefulness. Another point of interest is the fact that the evolved networks never use all the possible gates they are allowed while there is no parsimony pressure.

Finally, there have been a few theoretical studies on implementing fault tolerant sorting networks with specific techniques that we have yet to compare with[15,16,17]. Although, we are mainly interested in extending this technique to more interesting systems.

References

1. J. Masner, J. Cavalieri, J. Frenzel, and J. A. Foster, "Size verses robustness in evolved sorting networks: Is bigger better?," in *The Second NASA/DoD Workshop on Evolvable Hardware (EH)* (J. Lohn, A. Stoica, and D. Keyeulen, eds.), (Palo Alto, CA, USA), pp. 81–90, IEEE Computer Society, 2000.
2. J. Masner, J. Cavalieri, J. Frenzel, and J. Foster, "Representation and robustness fir evolved sorting networks," in *Proceedings of the 1st NASA/DoD Workshop on Evolvable Hardware* (J. Lohn, A. Stoica, and D. Keyeulen, eds.), (Pasadena, CA, USA), pp. 225–261, 1999.
3. Institute of Electrical and Electronics Engineers, *IEEE Standard Computer Dictionary: A Compilation of IEEE Standard Computer Glossories*, 1990.
4. M. L. Shooman, *Reliability of Computer Systems and Networks: Fault Tolerance, Analysis, and Design.* John Wiley and Sons, Inc., 2002.
5. D. E. Knuth, *The Art of Computer Programming: Sorting and Searching*, vol. 3. Reading, MA, USA: Addison-Wesley, 2 ed., 1975.
6. D. W. Hillis, "Co-evolving parasites improves simulated evolution as an optimization procedure," in *Artificial Life II* (Langton, Taylor, Farmer, and Rasmussen, eds.), vol. 10, pp. 313–324, Addison-Wesley, 1992.
7. K. E. Batcher, "Sorting networks and their applications," in *Conference Proceedings if the 1968 Spring Joint Computer Conference*, vol. 32, (Reston, VA), pp. 307–314, AFIPS Press, May 1968.
8. Gannett, Kothari, and Yen, "On optimal parallelization of sorting networks," *FSTTCS: Foundations of Software Technology and Theoretical Computer Science*, vol. 7, 1987.

9. A. R. Siegel, "Minimum storage sorting networks," *IEEE Transactions on Computers*, vol. C-34, Apr. 1985.
10. M. Mitchell, *An Introduction to Genetic Algorithms*. Complex Adaptive Systems, Cambridge, MA, USA: MIT Press, 1996.
11. F. Seredynski, "Competitive coevolutionary multi-agent systems: The application to mapping and scheduling problems," *Journal of Parallel and Distributed Computing*, vol. 47, pp. 39–57, 25 Nov. 1997.
12. K. O. Stanley and R. Miikkulainen, "Competitive coevolution through evolutionary complexification," Tech. Rep. AI02-298, The University of Texas at Austin, Department of Computer Sciences, Dec. 10 2002. Wed, 10 Sep 103 19:16:38 GMT.
13. C. D. Rosin and R. K. Belew, "New methods for competitive coevolution," Tech. Rep. CS96-491, Cognitive Computer Science Research Group, University of California, San Diego, CA, 1996. to appear in Evolutionary Computation 5:1.
14. J. M. Clavecie, K. De Jong, and A. F. Sheta, "Robust nonlinear control design using competitive coevolution," in *Proc. of the 2000 Congress on Evolutionary Computation*, (Piscataway, NJ), pp. 403–409, IEEE Service Center, 2000.
15. S. Assaf and E. Upfal, "Fault tolerant sorting networks," *SIAM Journal on Discrete Mathematics*, vol. 4, pp. 472–480, Nov. 1991.
16. K. Kantawala and D. L. Tao, "Designing concurrent checking sorting networks," in *Proceedings of the 23rd Annual International Symposium on Fault-Tolerant Computing (FTCS '93)* (J.-C. Laprie, ed.), (Toulouse, France), pp. 250–259, IEEE Computer Society Press, June 1993.
17. T. Leighton and Y. Ma, "Tight bounds on the size of fault-tolerant merging and sorting networks with destructive faults," *SIAM Journal on Computing*, vol. 29, pp. 258–273, Feb. 2000.

Toward an Alternative Comparison between Different Genetic Programming Systems

Nguyen Xuan Hoai, R.I. (Bob) McKay, D. Essam, and H.A. Abbass

School of Information Technology and Electrical Engineering,
Australian Defence Force Academy, University College,
University of New South Wales, ACT 2600, Australia
{x.nguyen,b.mckay,d.essam,h.abbass}@adfa.edu.au

Abstract. In this paper, we use multi-objective techniques to compare different genetic programming systems, permitting our comparison to concentrate on the effect of representation and separate out the effects of different search space sizes and search algorithms. Experimental results are given, comparing the performance and search behavior of Tree Adjoining Grammar Guided Genetic Programming (TAG3P) and Standard Genetic Programming (GP) on some standard problems.

1 Introduction

Since Koza's initial book on genetic programming (GP) [19], a wide range of new systems have been proposed. Typically, when each new system is introduced, it is compared with existing GP systems. The comparisons usually report on the new system's better performance over standard GP when solving particular problems. The reports contain descriptive statistics, such as cumulative frequencies, number of independent runs and the number of individuals that must be processed to yield a success with 99% probability. However, it is generally the case that the new system differs from previous systems over a number of dimensions (search space size, structure and representation, evolutionary operators, feasibility constraints, search algorithm, genotype-to-phenotype map, decoding, evaluation etc). While reporting the above statistics is important, we agree with [7, 8, 15] that it is also necessary to understand the causes of the differences. It is all too easy to assign the improvement from a new system to differences in representation or operators when simple changes in search space size may be more important. In particular, later in the paper we will show how different types of bounds for chromosome complexity in bounded search spaces can be an important contributor to differences between GP systems, potentially masking the effects of the underlying representation changes.

In this paper, we argue that the multi-objective framework can help to solve some of these difficulties. As a test case, we compare a fairly new genetic programming system, Tree Adjoining Grammar Guided Genetic Programming Systems (TAG3P) [12], with standard GP on two standard problems from the literature. The paper proceeds as follows. In Section 2, a brief introduction to TAG3P is given. Section 3 contains our discussion of the use of multi-objective techniques to compare TAG3P and standard GP in search spaces of equivalent size. Our experiments and discussion are presented in Section 4. Finally, Section 5 concludes this paper.

M. Keijzer et al. (Eds.): EuroGP 2004, LNCS 3003, pp. 67–77, 2004.

2   Tree Adjoining Grammar Guided Genetic Programming

In this section, we briefly review tree adjoining grammars and the new GP system, TAG3P (see [11,12] for more details). We also raise concerns about the difficulties of making meaningful comparisons between TAG3P and GP.

2. 1   Tree Adjoining Grammars

Tree Adjoining Grammars (TAGs) are tree-rewriting systems, originally proposed for natural language processing [17]. [18] gives a standard algorithm for converting any Context Free Grammar (CFG) G into a (lexicalised) TAG G_{lex}. Briefly, a TAG system consists of a set of elementary trees $E = I \cup A$ (initial and auxiliary respectively, denoted by α and β). All nodes are labeled grammar symbols, interior labels being restricted to non-terminals. The frontier of an auxiliary tree must contain a 'foot node', with the same label as the root (signified by *). All other non-terminal symbols on the frontier of an elementary tree are available for substitution.

An X-type tree has a root labeled X. TAG systems generate conventional CFG trees (the 'derived' tree) from a derivation tree, encoding the history of substitutions and adjunctions generating the derived tree. Starting from an α tree at the root, each branch records the address for adjunction or substitution, and the elementary tree used

Adjunction takes a tree γ with an interior label A, and an A-type auxiliary tree β, producing a new tree γ' by disconnecting the sub-tree α_1 rooted at A, attaching β to replace it, and finally re-attaching α_1 to the foot node of β.

TAGs have a number of advantages for GP:
– Derivation trees in TAGs are more fine-grained structures than those of CFG.
– They are compact (each elementary node encodes a number of CFG derivations).
– They are closer to a semantic representation [6].
– Derivation and derived trees provide a natural genotype-to-phenotype map.
– In growing a derivation tree f, one can stop anytime and have a valid derived tree.

We call the last property "feasibility". Feasibility helps TAG3P (described in next subsection) control the exact size of its chromosomes, and also to implement a wide range of genetic operators. A number of them are bio-inspired [12].

2.2   Tree Adjoining Grammar Guided Genetic Programming (TAG3P)

To relate TAG3P to previous systems using CFGs [26], we frame the discussion in terms of a CFG G and corresponding LTAG, G_{lex}. TAG3P evolves the derivation trees in G_{lex} (genotype) instead of the derived trees (the derivation trees in G – phenotype), creating a genotype-phenotype map, usually many-to-one. TAG3P may be specified as follows [19]:

Program representation: the derivation trees in LTAG G_{lex}.

Parameters: minimum size of genomes (MIN_SIZE), maximum size of genomes (MAX_SIZE), size of population (POP_SIZE), maximum number of generations (MAX_GEN) and probabilities for genetic operators.

Initialization procedure: Each individual is generated by randomly growing a derivation tree in G_{lex} to a size randomly chosen between MIN_SIZE and MAX_SIZE (unlike most GP systems, which use depth bounds). Because of TAG feasibility, this always generates valid individuals of exact size. An alternative ramped half-and-half initialization generates half of the derivation trees randomly but of full shape.

Fitness Evaluation: an individual derivation is first mapped to the derived CFG tree. The expression defined by the derived tree is semantically evaluated as in grammar guided genetic programming (GGGP) [26].

Main Genetic operators: sub-tree crossover and sub-tree mutation.

In sub-tree crossover, two individuals are selected based on their fitness. Points with the same adjunction label are randomly selected within each tree and the two sub-trees are exchanged. If no such points are found, the two individuals are discarded and the process is repeated until a bound is exceeded.

In sub-tree mutation, a point in the derivation tree is chosen at random and the sub-tree rooted at that point is replaced by a newly generated sub-derivation tree.

2.3   Difficulties in Making Meaningful Comparison between TAG3P and GP

TAG3P differs in many ways from standard GP. It uses grammars (a LTAG and a CFG), can solve typed problem domains; can handle context-sensitive information; has a genotype-to-phenotype map (therefore different search space); has different genetic operators and a different type of bound on chromosomal complexity (length rather than depth). If TAG3P and GP performance differ, it could be a result of any or all of these differences. Consequently, understanding the relationship between TAG3P and GP performance is very challenging.

Firstly, to ensure the grammars give no favorable bias for TAG3P they are chosen as follows. From a description of a GP set of functions and terminals, a context-free grammar, G, is created according to [26] (page 130) thus ensuring G is bias-free and the correspondence, between derivation trees of G and parse trees of GP, is one-to-one. G_{lex} is then derived from G using the algorithm in [18]. Secondly, in order to evaluate fitness of an individual (derivation tree in G_{lex}), it is decoded first into a derivation tree in G, then to the equivalent parse tree in GP. On this final parse tree the evaluation is systematically processed in the same way as in GP. Next, tunable parameters in the two systems are set as uniformly as possible.

However GP systems usually use a bounded search to limit chromosome complexity. In TAG3P, the bound is the maximum number of nodes, whereas in standard GP it is the maximum allowed depth (although some recent GP systems use a maximum number of nodes [20]). It is virtually impossible to adjust these bounds to give the same phenotype space in each, because there is no systematic mapping between nodes in TAG3P – elementary trees – and nodes in GP (see examples in the next section). This problem is not restricted to TAG3P; we believe it applies equally to a range of other GP systems, especially those that use grammars and/or genotype-to-phenotype maps (eg Linear GP [1], GE [24], and GEP [14]). Therefore, while the work in this paper relates only to the problem of making comparison between TAG3P and GP, it has clear implications for other GP systems.

3 The Use of Multi-objective Techniques for Comparisons

To solve the problem of adjusting chromosome complexity bounds, one option might be to remove the bounds. However, unbounded GP systems usually bloat, which is why bounds on the chromosome complexity are usually set. Bloat is a well-documented phenomenon in GP [3, 20, 25]; [20] suggests that code bloat is inevitable for all evolutionary systems that use length-variant chromosomes. But code bloat has serious effects on search performance [3,20,25]; and there is no reason to expect that these effects are invariant between different GP systems. Hence removing bounds simply adds one more confounding variable. Equally, when solving inductive learning problems, one is not indifferent to solution size - short solutions are preferred [23].

One alternative is to use a combined objective. Although there are many ways to combat bloat with single objective selection by integrating chromosome complexity into the fitness function [4, 16, 27], this introduces significant problems for our purpose. When using chromosome complexity as part of a single objective fitness function, some tunable parameters must be defined to determine how much the chromosome complexity of an individual will affect its fitness. It is at least difficult and time-consuming to find an optimal setting for these parameters; it is virtually impossible to find one, which is fair to both systems. Hence we argue that multi-objective selection is more appropriate for this purpose, especially since in [2] it is shown that multi-objective selection can outperform single objective selection in combating bloat. To understand the effect of the difference in search space representation and operators between TAG3P and standard GP, we use an unbounded search space, but apply multi-objective selection, with chromosome complexity as the second objective, to combat bloat. This has two main advantages. Searching with this multi-objective selection pressure can solve the problem of code bloat [2, 5, 9, 10, 21], therefore permit a more meaningful comparison. Moreover, multi-objective selection can unify very different GP-search spaces into a single objective space, providing a common ground for looking into the search performance and behavior of GP systems that use different representations and different genetic operators.

In this paper, we use the strength Pareto evolutionary algorithm (SPEA2) [28, 29], a state-of-the-art evolutionary multi-objective optimization (EMO) algorithm, to implement the comparison between GP and TAG3P. We chose SPEA2 because of its superior performance over other EMO algorithms [28, 29] and its efficiencies in reducing bloat in GP [2]. Moreover, Pareto fitness calculation in SPEA2 uses density estimation techniques, helping to promote diversity in the objective space. In turn, that reduces the common effect whereby the whole population may converge to the individual with minimal chromosome complexity [9]. This was sufficiently effective that in our experiments using SPEA2, we did not observe the effect. It is also possible to use other EMO algorithms, and we intend to investigate alternatives in the future.

4 Experiments

Using the SPEA2 multi-objective selection, we compared TAG3P with standard GP on two standard test problems: the 6-multiplexer, and symbolic regression. In the 6-multiplexer problem [19], a 6-multiplexer uses two address lines to output one of four data lines and the task is to learn this function from its 64 possible fitness cases using function set F={IF, AND, OR, NOT} and terminal set {a0, a1, d0, d1, d2, d3}. In the symbolic regression problem [19], the task is to learn the quadratic function: $X4+X3+X2+X$ from 20 sample points in [-1..1]; the function and terminal set are F={+,-,*,/,sin, cos, exp, rlog} and T={X}. They were chosen as frequently-used GP test-beds, the (shortest) solutions being known. The fitness values of the first are discrete and finite; of the second, continuous and infinite.

4.1 Experimental Design

As in [2], we use weak Pareto non-domination selection. The second objective is the size (in number of nodes) of the parse trees, on which fitness is evaluated. To study the effect of population initialization, for each problem, we ran three systems. The first was TAG3P, the second was GP with the initial population translated from the initial population of TAG3P (GP-I) such that they had the same initial population in the phenotype space, and the third was GP with Ramped-Half-and-Half initialization (GP-RHH). The range of size in the initial population of TAG3P and the maximum depth of the initial population in GP-RHH was calibrated so that on average the size of the final parse trees (phenotype) in the TAG3P initial population was the same as the size of parse trees (genotype) in GP. To investigate the effect of variance in population size, and number of generations, for each problem, we experimented with three settings of population and number of generations. All other parameters (such as genetic operator rates) are the same for all three systems. We can summarize the parameter settings in two categories:

Fixed common settings: Genetic operators – subtree crossover and subtree mutation; crossover rate=0.9; mutation rate=0.1; Calibrated initial size for TAG3P: 10-60 (for 6-multiplexer problem) and 2-60 (for symbolic regression); Calibrated maximal depth for initial population of GP-RHH: 6 (for 6-multiplexer problem – GP-RHH6) and 8 (for symbolic regression – GP-RHH8). In SPEA2 settings, weak dominance was used and the size of the archive was set equal to the size of the main population. No maximal limits were set on the depth or size of any tree. All runs only finished when the maximum number of generations was reached.

Varied common settings: On each problem, three varied settings on population size and number of generations were given to all three systems (TAG3P, GP-I and GP-RHH). The experimented population sizes were 250, 500, and 1000, while the maximum numbers of generations were 101, 51, and 26 respectively.

There were 100 runs allocated for each system for each varied setting, making the total number of runs 1800. The ith run of each setting used the same initial random key as every other ith run. The keys themselves were generated at random. All the runs used the same random generator. The grammars for TAG3P were generated using algorithms in [26] (page 130) and in [18].

The grammars for the 6-multiplexer problem were: G={V={B}, T={a0, a1, d0, d1, d2, d3, d4, and, or, not, if}, P, {B}}, where the rule set P is defined as follows:

B →a0| a1| d0| d1| d2| d3.

B →B and B| B or B | not B | if B B B

G_{lex}={V={B, TL}, T={a0, a1, d0, d1, d2, d3, and, or, not, if}, I, A}, where I ∪ A is depicted in Figure 1. TL is a lexicon that can be substituted by one lexeme in {a0, a1, d0, d1, d2, d3}.

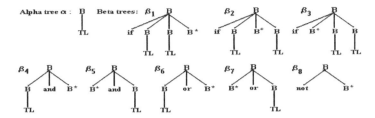

Fig. 1. Elementary trees for G_{lex}

The grammars for the symbolic regression problem were: G = (V={EXP, PRE, OP, VAR,},T= {X, sin, cos, log, ep, +, -, *, /, (,)},P,{EXP}} where ep is the exponential function, and the rule set P is as follows

EXP→EXP OP EXP | PRE (EXP) | VAR

OP→+ | - | * | /

PRE→cos | sin | rlog | ep

VAR→ X

G_{lex} = {V={EXP, PRE, OP,VAR},T={X, sin, cos, log, ep,+, -, *, /, (,)}, I, A) where I∪ A is as in Figure 2.

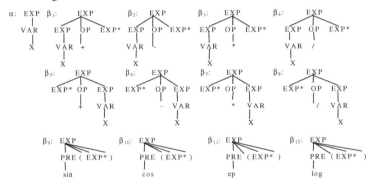

Fig. 2. Elementary trees for G_{lex}.

4.2   Results

For the 6-multiplexer problem, Table 1 summarizes the results of the three systems (TAG3P, GP-I, GP-RHH6) based on 900 runs for three settings. Column 4 contains the percentage of runs that found a solution (i.e first objective value is 0). Column 5 gives the number of runs that found an optimal-size solution. In this problem the optimal size of solutions is 10. An example of such solutions is IF(a0, IF(a1, d3, d2), IF(a1, d1, d0)). Column 6 depicts the average size of solutions, and column 7 is the standard deviation of the data used to calculate column 6.

For the symbolic regression problem, Table 2 summarizes the results of the three systems (TAG3P, GP-I, GP-RHH6) based on 900 runs for three settings. The columns are as above. For this problem, the optimal solution size is 13, (X+X*X)*(X/X+X*X) being an example.

Table 1. 6-Multiplexer Results

GEN	POP	System	Succ	N° perfect	Avg sol. S	Std
101	250	TAG3P	58	35	11.45	2.51
101	250	GP-I	45	35	11.05	3.30
101	250	GP-RHH6	43	15	16.28	9.22
51	500	TAG3P	82	45	11.97	3.27
51	500	GP-I	74	52	11.80	4.05
51	500	GP-RHH6	63	27	18.62	12.62
26	1000	TAG3P	87	59	11.56	4.28
26	1000	GP-I	75	38	13.13	5.85
26	1000	GP-RHH6	62	25	32.37	46.00

Table 2. Symbolic Regression Results

Gen	Pop	Systems	succ	N° perfect	Avg sol.	Std
101	250	TAG3P	46	35	13.85	1.74
101	250	GP-I	34	23	13.74	1.24
101	250	GP-	18	16	13.17	0.50
51	500	TAG3P	57	39	14.37	3.12
51	500	GP-I	39	30	14.00	2.34
51	500	GP-	15	11	13.53	0.96
26	1000	TAG3P	53	23	15.87	4.33
26	1000	GP-I	43	21	15.19	2.71
26	1000	GP-	17	8	17.24	9.40

Figures 3, 4, 5 depict the cumulative frequencies and time series of average fitness of the population in six systems. Due to limited space, only those of the first setting of population and number of generations (population = 250, generations = 101) are given. The corresponding figures for other settings are quite similar.

4.3 Discussion of Results

On the two standard problems, TAG3P was better than GP-I and GP-RHH in finding solutions with (first objective) fitness 0. Moreover, it was also better than the others at finding solutions with optimal size (except one case – table 1, row 4). One reason is TAG3P's faster convergence in the size objective. For GP–I and GP-RHH, the average size also converges to the size of optimal solution in the 6-multiplexer problem but not in the symbolic regression problem. This is explained by the discreteness (only 64 values) of the first objective in the 6-multiplexer problem, so that any large individual has little chance to survive under the multi-objective

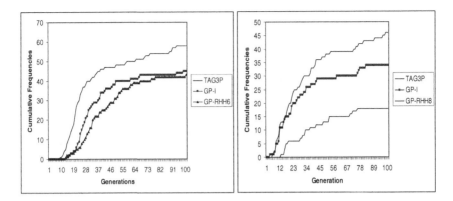

Fig. 3. Cumulative frequencies of success. POP_SIZE=250, MAX_GEN=101. 6-multiplexer results on left, symbolic regression on right.

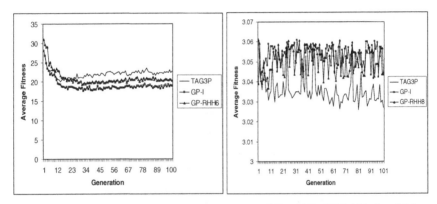

Fig. 4. Time series of average (first) fitness. POP_SIZE=250, MAX_GEN=101; 6-multiplexer results on left, symbolic regression on right.

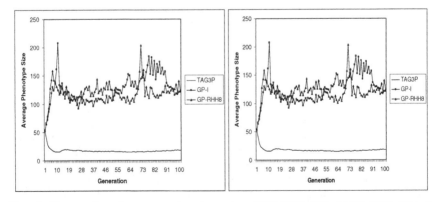

Fig. 5. Time series of average phenotype size. POP_SIZE=250, MAX_GEN=101; 6-multiplexer results on left, symbolic regression on right.

selection pressure. Therefore, the convergence in average size was common for all three systems. On the other hand, the first objective in symbolic regression problems is continuous, so that a large individual has more chance to survive under the multi-objective selection pressure. Since TAG3P converges faster than the others, it finds solutions more frequently in the subspace of smaller trees, whereas GP-I and GP-H search more frequently in the subspace of bigger trees. It can also be seen from the different results of GP-I and GP-RHH, that the method for seeding the initial population is important for the search performance and behavior of GP. This result is contrary to the results found in [22], where the seeding method used to generate the initial population had no significant impact on the search performance and behavior of GP, in a bounded search space and under single objective selection pressure. We see better performance from GP-I than GP-RHH. Since in TAG3P the initial population could be uniformly distributed in size (due to TAG feasibility), the initial population in GP-I (and in TAG3P) was more spread in the objective space than in GP-RHH. The discussions above are also supported by the distribution of tree size over time for all 1800 runs. However, due to limited space, those detailed results are omitted here. In [13], the comparative results on symbolic regression, using single objective and bounded search space, we reported that TAG3P was far better than GP. At that time, we believed that it was because of the new representation and/or operators. The results above show that while those factors did contribute to the better performance of TAG3P, the bound on search spaces in [13] was a greater contributor to TAG3P's better performance compared with GP.

5 Conclusion

In this paper, we have introduced and discussed an alternative type of comparison between different GP systems. In particular, we pointed out that different types of bounds on chromosome complexity, which might derive from different representations, makes it hard to determine the causes of different performance between GP systems. We have argued that the use of multi-objective selection, coupled with an unbounded search space, can help to understand the effects of search space size. Thus, by using an EMO algorithm (SPEA2), we were able to make this alternative type of comparison between our GP system (TAG3P) and standard GP on two standard problems. The results show the differences in search performance and behavior between TAG3P and standard GP. We have also found that setting different types of bounds on search spaces was the prime factor in the better performance of TAG3P compared with GP in [13]. Moreover, the method for seeding the initial population in GP is very important, contrary to previous results.

We now plan to use the same technique to make meaningful comparison between TAG3P and other grammar guided genetic programming systems on typed problems. We also plan to compare other EMO algorithms with SPEA2.

Acknowledgements. The authors would like to express their thanks to Dr. Zitzler for his prompt replies to our questions related to SPEA2.

References

1. Banzhaf W., Nordin P., Keller R.E., and Francone F.D.: *Genetic Programming: An Introduction*. Morgan Kaufmann Pub (1998).
2. Bleuler S., Brack M., Thiele L., and Zitzler E.: Multiobjective Genetic Programming: Reducing Bloat Using SPEA2. *Proc. Congress on Evolutionary Computation* (CEC'2001) (2001) 536-543.
3. Blickle T. and Thiele L.: Genetic Programming and Redundancy. In: *Genetic Algorithms within the Framework of Evolutionary Computation*, Hopf J. (Ed.), (1994) 33-38.
4. Blickle T.: Evolving Compact Solutions in Genetic Programming: A Case Study. In: *PPSN IV*, Voigt H.M., Ebeling W., Rechenberg I,, and Schwefel P. (Eds.), Springer-Verlag (1996) 564-573.
5. Bot M.C.J: Improving Induction of Linear Classification Tree with Genetic Programming. In: *Proc. The Genetic and Evolutionary Computation* (GECCO'2000), Darrell Whitley et al (Eds.). Morgan-Kaufman Publishers (2000) 403-410.
6. Candito M. H. and Kahane S.: Can the TAG Derivation Tree Represent a Semantic Graph? An Answer in the Light of Meaning-Text Theory. In: *Proc. of TAG+4*, Philadelphia, (1999) 25-28.
7. Daida J. M., Ampy D.S., Ratanasavetavadhana M., Li H., and Chaudhri O.A.: Challenges with Verification, Repeatability, and Meaningful Comparison in Genetic Programming: Gibson's Magic. Accessed at http://citeseer.nj.nec.com/257412.html. Date: 11-10-2003.
8. Daida, J.M., Ross S. J., McClain J.J., Ampy D.S., and Holczer M.: Challenges with Verification, Repeatability, and Meaningful Comparison in Genetic Programming. In: *Genetic Programming 97: Proceedings of the Second Annual Conference*, Koza J.R., Deb K., Dorigo M. et al (Eds.), Morgan Kaufman Publishers (1998) 122-127.
9. Dejong E.D. and Pollack J.B.: Multi-Objective Methods for Tree Size Control. *Genetic Programming and Evolvable Machines*, 4 (2003) 211-233.
10. Ekart A. and Nemeth S. Z.: Selection Based on the Pareto Non-domination Criterion for Controlling Code Growth in Genetic Programming *Genetic Programming & Evolvable Machines* 2(1) (2001) 61-73.
11. Nguyen Xuan Hoai and McKay R.I.: A Framework for Tree Adjunct Grammar Guided Genetic Programming. In: *Proceedings of Post Graduate ADFA Conference on Computer Science (PACCS'01)*, H.A. Abbass and M. Barlow (Eds), (2001) 93-99.
12. Nguyen Xuan Hoai, McKay R.I., and Abbass H.A.: Tree Adjoining Grammars, Language Bias, and Genetic Programming. In *Proceedings of EuroGP 2003*, Ryan C. et al (Eds), LNCS 2610, Springer Verlag, (2003) 335-344.
13. Nguyen Xuan Hoai, McKay R.I., Essam, D., and Chau R.: Solving the Symbolic Regression Problem with Tree Adjunct Grammar Guided Genetic Programming: The Comparative Result. In Proceedings of Congress on Evolutionary Computation (CEC'2002), Hawai (2002) 1326-1331.
14. Ferreira C., Gene Expression Programming: A New Adaptive Algorithm for Solving Problems. *Complex Systems*, 13 (2), (2001) 87-129.
15. Haynes, T.: Perturbing the Representation, Decoding, and Evaluation of Chromosomes. In: *Genetic Programming 98: Proceedings of the Third Annual Conference*, Koza J.R et al (Eds.) Morgan Kaufman Publishers (1998) 122-127.
16. Iba H., Garis H., and Sato T.: Genetic Programming Using a Minimum Description Length Principle. In: *Advances in Genetic Programming*, Kinnear Jr K.E. (Ed.), MIT Press (1994), Chapter 12.
17. Joshi A. K., Levy L. S., and Takahashi M.: Tree Adjunct Grammars. *Journal of Computer and System Sciences*, 10 (1), (1975) 136-163.
18. Joshi, A. K. and Schabes, Y.: Tree Adjoining Grammars. In: *Handbook of Formal Languages*, Rozenberg G. and Saloma A. (Eds.) Springer-Verlag, (1997) 69-123.
19. Koza, J. : *Genetic Programming*. The MIT Press (1992).

20. Langdon W.B. and Poli R.: *Foundations of Genetic Programming*. Springer-Verlag (2002).
21. Langdon W.B.: *Genetic Programming + Data Structure =Automatic Programming*. Kluwer Academic (1998).
22. Luke S. and Panait L.: A Survey and Comparison of Tree Generation Algorithms. In: *Proceedings of The Genetic and Evolutionary Computation* (GECCO'2001), Spector L. et al (Eds.), Morgan Kaufman Publishers (2001) 81-88.
23. Michell T.M.: *Machine Learning*. McGraw-Hill (1997).
24. O'Neil M. and Ryan C.: Grammatical Evolution. *IEEE Trans on Evolutionary Computation*, 4 (4), (2000) 349-357.
25. Soule T. and Foster J.: Effects of Code Growth and Parsimony Pressure on Population in Genetic Programming. *Evolutionary Computation*, 6 (4), (1999) 293-309.
26. Whigham P. A.: *Grammatical Bias for Evolutionary Learning*. Ph.D Thesis, University of New South Wales, Australia, (1996).
27. Zhang B.T. and Muhlenbein H.: Balancing Accuracy and Parsimony in Genetic Programming. *Evolutionary Computation*, 3(1), (1995) 17-38.
28. Zitzler E. and Thiele L.: Multi-objective Evolutionary Algorithms: A Comparative Case Study and The Strength Pareto Approach. *IEEE Trans on Evolutionary Computation*, 3 (1), (1999) 257-271.
29. Zitzler E., Laumanns M., and Thiele L.: SPEA2: Improving the Strength Pareto Evolutionary Algorithm. *Technical Report 103*, Computer Engineering and Networks Laboratory (TK), ETH Zurich, Switzerland, 2001.

Lymphoma Cancer Classification
Using Genetic Programming with SNR Features

Jin-Hyuk Hong and Sung-Bae Cho

Dept. of Computer Science, Yonsei University,
134 Shinchon-dong, Sudaemoon-ku, Seoul 120-749, Korea
hjinh@candy.yonsei.ac.kr, sbcho@cs.yonsei.ac.kr

Abstract. Lymphoma cancer classification with DNA microarray data is one of important problems in bioinformatics. Many machine learning techniques have been applied to the problem and produced valuable results. However the medical field requires not only a high-accuracy classifier, but also the in-depth analysis and understanding of classification rules obtained. Since gene expression data have thousands of features, it is nearly impossible to represent and understand their complex relationships directly. In this paper, we adopt the SNR (Signal-to-Noise Ratio) feature selection to reduce the dimensionality of the data, and then use genetic programming to generate cancer classification rules with the features. In the experimental results on Lymphoma cancer dataset, the proposed method yielded 96.6% test accuracy in average, and an excellent arithmetic classification rule set that classifies all the samples correctly is discovered by the proposed method.

1 Introduction

Accurate decision and diagnosis of the cancer are very important in the field of medicine while they are very difficult [1,2]. Exact classification of cancers makes it possible to treat a patient with proper treatments and helpful medicines so as to save the patient's life. Over several centuries, various cancer classification techniques are developed, but most of them are based on the clinical analysis of morphological symptoms for the cancer. With these methods, even a medical expert causes many errors and misunderstandings, because in many cases different cancers show some similar symptoms. In order to overcome these restrictions, classification techniques using human's gene information have been actively investigated, and many good results have been reported recently [1,2,3]

Gene information, usually called gene expression data, is collected by the DNA microarray technique with keen interests. The gene expression data include lots of gene information on living things [2]. Usually, the gene expression data provide useful information for the classification of different kinds of cancers. Since the original format of the data is an array of simple numbers, it is not easy to analyze them directly and to discover useful classification rules of the cancer. Several methods for it have been studied for several years in artificial intelligence [2,3]. Table 1 shows related works on the classification of lymphoma cancer using DNA microarray data.

M. Keijzer et al. (Eds.): EuroGP 2004, LNCS 3003, pp. 78–88, 2004.

Table 1. Related works

Author	Data	Method		Accuracy (%)
		Feature selection	**Classifier**	
Li et al.	Lymphoma	Genetic algorithm	Knn	84.6
Dudoit et al.		The ratio of between-groups to within-groups sum of squares	Nearest neighbor	95.0
			Diagonal linear discriminant analysis	95.0
Nguyen et al.		PCA	Logistic discriminant	98.1
			Boost CART	97.6

It is not easy to obtain a good classification performance with gene expression data, because the data consist of a few samples with a large number of variables. Nevertheless diverse technologies of artificial intelligence have been applied to classify the cancer and shown a superior performance of the classification. However, many conventional approaches such as the neural network and SVMs are not easy to be directly interpreted. In medical area discovered rules should be understandable for people to get a confidence [4]. In this paper, we propose a classification rule generation method which is composed of the SNR feature selection and genetic programming so as to obtain precise and comprehensible classification rules, which also produces an outstanding performance from high dimensional gene expression data by designing the rule with arithmetic operations.

2   Backgrounds

2.1 DNA Microarray

An organism basically has thousands of genes, RNA and protein. Traditional molecular biology has only considered a single gene, so the obtained information is very limited to be applied various problems. DNA microarray has been developed recently, and it successfully deals with the problem. It acquires gene information in terms of microscopic units, and the revelation phase of a total chromosome on a chip is observed by this technique. That is, DNA microarray technique makes it possible to analyze and observe for a complex organism in detail [1,2,3].

DNA microarray fixes cDNA of high density on a solid substrate which is not permeated with a solution, while it attaches thousands of DNA and protein at regular intervals on the solid substrate and combines with the target materials. The phase of the combination can be observed on the chip. Each cell on the array is synthesized with two gene materials collected by different environments and different fluorescent dyes mixed (green-fluorescent dye Cy3 and red-fluorescent dye Cy5 in equal quantities). After the hybridization of these samples with the arrayed DNA probes, the slides are imaged by a scanner that makes the fluorescence measurement for each dye. The overall procedure of DNA microarray technology is as shown in Fig.1 and the log ratio between the two intensities of each dye is used as the gene expression as follows.

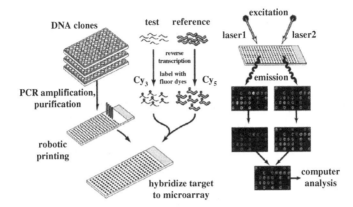

Fig. 1. Overview of DNA microarray technology

$$gene\_expression = \log_2 \frac{\text{Int}(Cy5)}{\text{Int}(Cy3)}$$

where Int(Cy5) and Int(Cy3) are the intensities of red and green colors. Since at least hundreds of genes are put on the DNA microarray, we can investigate the genome-wide information in short time.

2.2 Genetic Programming

Genetic programming is devised to design a program which solves a problem automatically without a user's explicit programming. It regards a program as a structure composed of functions and variables. The program usually has a tree structure to represent the individual's information [13].

Genetic programming is one of evolutionary computation techniques like the genetic algorithm. Basic operations and characteristics are similar to those of the genetic algorithm, but they are different in terms of the representation. The solution space of genetic programming is very wide reaching to problems which can be solved by a program with functions and variables [10,11,14]. There are various functions for genetic programming such as arithmetic operations, logical operations, and user-defined operations. Recently, it has been applied to many problems such as optimization, the evolution of assembly language program, evolvable hardware, the generation of a virtual character's behaviors, etc [13].

3 Classification Rule Discovery

In this paper, we propose a rule discovery method as shown in Fig. 2. First, the SNR feature selection reduces the dimensionality. And then, genetic programming finds out good classification rules with the SNR features.

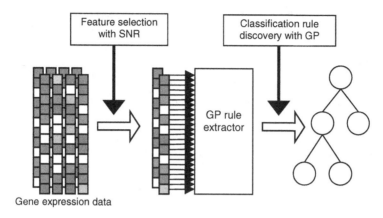

Fig. 2. The proposed method to classify DNA microarray profiles

3.1 Signal-to-Noise Ratio Feature Selection

Since not all the genes are associated with a specific disease, the feature selection often called gene selection is necessary to extract informative genes for the classification of the disease [3,15,16]. Moreover, feature selection accelerates the speed of learning a classifier and removes noises in the data.

There are two major feature selection approaches: filter and wrapper approaches. The former selects informative features (genes) regardless of classifiers. It independently measures the importance of features, and selects some for the classification. On the other hand, the latter selects features together with classifiers. It is simultaneously done by the training of a classifier to produce the optimal combination of features and a classifier. Since the filter approach is simple and fast enough to obtain high performance, we evaluated various filter-based feature selection methods [15]. Finally signal-to-noise ratio ranking method is adopted to select useful features. After measuring the signal to noise ratio of genes, 30 genes are selected based on their ranks.

$$SN(g_i, C) = \frac{\mu_{c1}(g_i) - \mu_{c0}(g_i)}{\sigma_{c1}(g_i) + \sigma_{c0}(g_i)}$$

$\mu_1(g)$: the average of genes in class C

$\mu_2(g)$: the average of genes not in class C

$\sigma_1(g)$: standard deviation of genes in class C

$\sigma_2(g)$: standard deviation of genes not in class C

Signal-to-noise ratio measures how the signal from the defect compares to other background noise. In bioinformatics the signal represents useful information conveyed by genes, and noise to anything else on the genes. Hence a low ratio implies that the gene is not worth for the class C while a high ratio means that the gene is rather related with the class C.

Table 2. Arithmetic operators used in this paper

Arithmetic operator	Function	Description
+	Addition	Positive effect on class 1(Negative effect on class 2)
–	Subtraction	Negative effect on class 1(Positive effect on class 2)
×	Multiplication	Multiplicative correlation
/	Division	Divisive correlation

3.2 Classification Rule Extraction

Conventional rule discovery using genetic programming has usually adopted first-order logic [17] or IF-THEN structure as the rule, while logic operations AND, OR, Not and comparative operations (<, >, =) are frequently used as follows [4,12].

$$Rule1: \text{ IF}((A1 < 0.6) \text{ OR } (A3 > 0.3)) \quad \text{THEN } class1$$
$$Rule2: \text{ IF}((A2 = 0.7) \text{ AND } (A1 > 0.7)) \text{THEN } class2$$

Although these rules are easy to be interpreted, it has a limitation to represent more complex relationships among variables to get a high performance [12]. Mathematical operations have been also tried to construct a rule, but they are difficult in the analysis. Moreover in some applications it is already known that they obtain lower accuracy than arithmetic operations.

In this paper, arithmetic operations are used to construct a more sophisticated rule leading to high accuracy. A rule is designed as a tree with 30 SNR features and basic arithmetic operations (+, -, ×, /). Although numerical value can be also considered as a terminal, it is not used in this experiment. For the easy analysis of rules obtained, the meanings of arithmetic operations for genes are defined in Table 2.

The classification rule is constructed as follows. As shown in Fig. 3, the value of the function eval() represents which class a sample belongs to. Positive value indicates that the sample belongs to class 1, while negative value signifies that the sample is classified into class 2.

$$\text{IF } eval(Individual_i) \geq 0 \text{ THEN } class1 \text{ ELSE } class2$$

We have experimented with three kinds of rule representations. Not all arithmetic operators are used as shown in Table 3, but the 2nd and the 3rd without × and / operators are used to keep the simplicity of the rule. Weights show that which gene is more effective for the classification while the values are from 0 to 1.0. Fig. 4 briefly shows the three rule representations.

Table 3. Rule representations to be tested

No	+	-	×	/	Weighting	Complexity
1	Use	Use	Use	Use	Not-use	High
2	Use	Use	Not-use	Not-use	Use	Middle
3	Use	Use	Not-use	Not-use	Not-use	Low

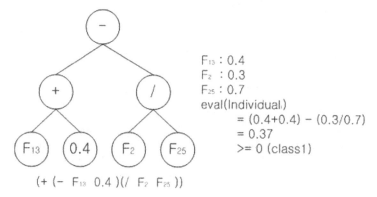

F_{13} : 0.4
F_2 : 0.3
F_{25} : 0.7
eval(Individual.)
$= (0.4+0.4) - (0.3/0.7)$
$= 0.37$
$>= 0$ (class1)

$(+ (- F_{13}\ 0.4\ )(/ \ F_2\ F_{25}\ ))$

Fig. 3. Representation of the proposed method and classification rule

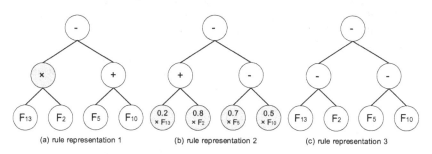

(a) rule representation 1   (b) rule representation 2   (c) rule representation 3

Fig. 4. 3 different rule representations

The performance for the training data is used as the fitness of a rule. The simplicity measure is added on the fitness function to get comprehensible-sized classification rules as follows. It is generally known that a simpler classifier is more general than complicated one with the same accuracy for the training data.

$$fitness\ of\ individual_i = \frac{number\ of\ correct\ samples}{number\ of\ total\ train\ data} \times w_1 + simplicity \times w_2$$

$$where\ \ simplicity = \frac{number\ of\ nodes}{number\ of\ maximum\ nodes},$$

w_1 = weight for training rate, and w_2 = weight for simplicity

Table 4. Experimental environments

Parameter	Value (final)	Parameter	Value (final)
Population size	100	Mutation rate	0.1~0.3 (0.2)
Maximum generation	50,000	Permutation rate	0.1
Selection rate	0.6~0.8 (0.8)	Maximum depth of a tree	3
Crossover rate	0.6~0.8 (0.8)	Elitism	yes

4 Experiments

4.1 Experimental Environment

The proposed method is verified with Lymphoma cancer dataset, which is well known microarray dataset [18]. This dataset (http://llmpp.nih.gov/lymphoma/) is one of popular DNA microarray datasets used in bioinformatics for the benchmark. It consists of 47 samples: 24 samples of GC B-like and 23 samples of activated B-like. Each sample has 4,026 gene expression levels. All features are normalized from 0 to 1.

Since the gene expression data consist of few samples with many features, the proposed method is evaluated by leave-one-out cross-validation. Total 47 experiments are conducted, where each sample is set as the test data and the others are set as the train data. All experiments are repeated 10 times and the average of them is used as the final result.

The parameters for genetic programming are set as shown in Table 4. We use roulette wheel selection with elite preserving strategy, and set the weights w_1 and w_2 of the fitness evaluation function as 0.9 and 0.1, respectively.

4.2 Results Analysis

Fig. 5 shows the accuracy for the test data in terms of the rule representations. We can get 96.6% test accuracy in average with the third rule representation although this is the simplest among the three rule representations.

Fig. 6 shows the classification rules which are the most frequently occurred in the experiments, while they classify all the samples correctly with a few genes. The detailed descriptions of the genes are shown in Table 5~7. The functions of some genes are not known yet, and this gives interest to medical experts to study the functions of those genes. Although the rules are obtained by the cross-validation, we focus on the easy interpretability and the information included in the rules.

The rule shown in Fig. 6(a) is analyzed based on the meaning of the arithmetic operations as described in Table 1. F4 affects a sample to be included into class 2 while negatively into the class 1. F20 and F25 are combined by a multiplicative correlation, so as to push samples to be classified into class1. We can interpret it as follows so to obtain some information from the rule:

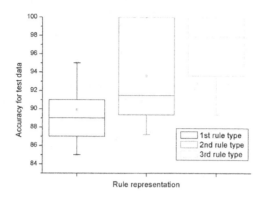

Fig. 5. The accuracy for test data

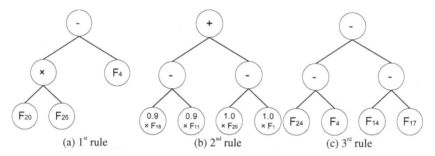

(a) 1ˢᵗ rule   (b) 2ⁿᵈ rule   (c) 3ʳᵈ rule

Fig. 6. The rules for perfect classification with each rule representation

· F4, F20, and F25 are related with lymphoma cancer
· The value of F4 is negatively related with the cancer
· F20 and F25 are positively related with the cancer

We have conducted an additional experiment to compare the proposed method with a neural network, one of promising machine learning techniques. 3-layered multi-layer perceptron is used with 2~10 hidden nodes, 2 output nodes, learning rate of 0.01~0.1 and momentum of 0.7~0.9. The maximum iteration for learning is fixed to 5000. Three features are used as the input of the neural network. The training accuracy is 98%, while the test accuracy is 97.8%. Even with intensive efforts, we could not get 100% accuracy with the neural network. The neural network has been also learned with 30 features, but the result is worse than the first case. It just obtained 95.7% training accuracy and 95.7% test accuracy. This proves that genetic programming also selected useful features among the 30 features. The additional experiment shows the competitive performance of the proposed method in the classification of the dataset.

Fig. 6(b) and Fig. 6(c) are rules for the 2ⁿᵈ and the 3ʳᵈ rule representations. Based on the analysis method, each classification rule includes the following information.

Table 5. The detailed description of genes used in the rule shown in Fig. 6(a)

Feature #	Gene #	Description
F20	75	Unknown UG Hs.169081 ets variant gene 6 (TEL oncogene); Clone=1355435, 14671
F25	2467	*core binding factor alpha1b subunit=CBF alpha1=PEBP2aA1 transcription factor =AML1 Proto-oncogene=translocated in acute myeloid leukemia; Clone=263251, 17823
F4	1277	Unknown UG Hs.136345 ESTs; Clone=746300, 19274

Table 6. The detailed description of the genes used in the rule shown in Fig. 6(b)

Feature #	Gene #	Description
F18	1636	CXCR5=BLR1=B-cell homing chemokine receptor=L1; Clone=31, 4297
F11	1246	*FAK=focal adhesion kinase; Clone=795352, 17333
F29	86	*BCL-2; Clone=342181, 17646
F1	1268	*CD10=CALLA=Neprilysin=enkepalinase; Clone=200814, 15864

Table 7. The detailed description of genes used in the rule shown in Fig. 6(c)

Feature #	Gene #	Description
F24	684	Unknown; Clone=1352715, 14377
F4	1279	*Unknown; Clone=825199, 19288
F14	1914	Lymphotoxin-Beta=Tumor necrosis factor C; Clone=1320296, 13297
F17	680	*Unknown; Clone=1372162, 19541

The classification rule in Fig. 6(b) can be interpreted as follows:
· F18, F11, F29, and F1 are related with the lymphoma cancer
· F18 and F29 affect positively on the GC B-like lymphoma cancer
· F11 and F1 are negatively related with the GC B-like lymphoma cancer
· Each weight signifies the importance on the cancer classification
The classification rule in Fig. 6(c) can be interpreted as follows:
· F24, F4, F14, and F17 are related with the lymphoma cancer
· F24 and F17 affect positively on the GC B-like lymphoma cancer
· F4 and F14 are negatively related with the GC B-like lymphoma cancer

F29 used in the 2nd rule is the *BCL-2 gene, which turned out that it is related with the lymphoma cancer [19]. F14 described in Table 6 is known that it relates with the lymphoma cancer. These imply that the rules discovered by the proposed method are understandable, and there is a possibility that the other features are related with the lymphoma cancer. These rules also need a demonstration by medical experts, but there is a good chance of discovering useful information from them.

5 Concluding Remarks

In this paper, we have proposed an effective rule generation method, which uses genetic programming with SNR features. Since gene expression data have huge-scale feature data with a few samples, it is difficult to generate valuable classification rules from the data directly. The SNR feature selection method used in this paper remarkably reduces the number of features, while genetic programming generates useful rules with those features selected. Moreover we have proposed the analysis method for the arithmetic rule representation. It is very simple but helpful for the interpretation of the rules extracted. The experimental results show that the performance of the proposed method is effective to extract classification rules with 96.6% test accuracy, and also good classification rules have been easily interpreted and provided useful information for the classification.

As the future work, we will verify the obtained results with medical experts and try to combine logical and arithmetic structures in genetic programming for better classification. Each structure has its advantage, and the combination might help to improve the performance and interpretability.

Acknowledgements. This work was supported by Biometrics Engineering Research Center, and a grant of Korea Health 21 R&D project, Ministry of Health & Welfare, Republic of Korea.

References

1. A. Ben-Dor, et al., "Tissue classification with gene expression profiles," *J. of Computational Biology*, vol. 7, pp. 559-584, 2000.
2. A. Brazma and J. Vilo, "Gene expression data analysis," *Federation of European Biochemical Societies Letters*, vol. 480, pp. 17-24, 2000.
3. C. Park and S.-B. Cho, "Genetic search for optimal ensemble of feature-classifier pairs in DNA gene expression profiles," *Int. Joint Conf. on Neural Networks*, pp. 1702-1707, 2003.
4. K. Tan, et al., "Evolutionary computing for knowledge discovery in medical diagnosis," *Artificial Intelligence in Medicine*, vol. 27, no. 2, pp. 129-154, 2003.
5. J. Quinlan, *C4.5: Programs for Machine Learning*, Morgan Kaufmann, 1993.
6. D. Goldberg, *Genetic Algorithms in Search, Optimaization, and Machine Learning*, Addison-Wesley, 1989.
7. K. DeJong, et al., "Using genetic algorithms for concept learning," *Machine Learning*, vol. 13, pp. 161-188, 1993.
8. A. Freitas, "A survey of evolutionary algorithms for data mining and knowledge discovery," *Advances in Evolutionary Computation*, pp. 819-845, 2002.

9. C. Hsu and C. Knoblock, "Discovering robust knowledge from databases that change," *Data Mining and Knowledge Discovery*, vol. 2, no. 1, pp. 69-95, 1998.
10. C. Zhou, et al., "Discovery of classification rules by using gene expression programming," *Proc. of the 2002 Int. Conf. on Artificial Intelligence*, pp. 1355-1361, 2002.
11. C. Bojarczuk, et al., "Discovering comprehensible classification rules using genetic programming: A case study in a medical domain," *Proc. of the Genetic and Evolutionary Computation Conf.*, pp. 953-958, 1999.
12. I. Falco, et al., "Discovering interesting classification rules with genetic programming, " *Applied Soft Computing*, vol. 1, no. 4, pp. 257-269, 2002.
13. J. Koza, "Genetic programming," *Encyclopedia of Computer Science and Technology*, vol. 39, pp. 29-43, 1998.
14. J. Kishore, et al., "Application of genetic programming for multicategory pattern classification," *IEEE Trans. on Evolutionary Computation*, vol. 4, no. 3, pp. 242-258, 2000.
15. H.-H. Won and S.-B. Cho, "Neural network ensemble with negatively correlated features for cancer classification, " *Lecture Notes in Computer Science*, vol. 2714, pp. 1143-1150, 2003.
16. J. Bins and B. Draper, "Feature selection from huge feature sets," *Proc. Int. Conf. Computer Vision 2*, pp. 159-165, 2001.
17. S. Augier, et al., "Learning first order logic rules with a genetic algorithm," *Proc. of the First Int. Conf. on Knowledge Discovery & Data Mining*, pp. 21-26, 1995.
18. A. Alizadeh, et al., "Distinct types of diffuse large B-cell lymphoma identified by gene expression profiling, " *Nature*, vol. 403, pp. 503-511, 2000.
19. O. Monni, et al. "BCL2 overexpression in diffuse large B-cell lymphoma," *Leuk Lymphoma*, vol. 34, no 1-2, pp. 45-52, 1999.

A Practical Approach to Evolving Concurrent Programs

David Jackson

Dept. of Computer Science, University of Liverpool
Liverpool L69 3BX, United Kingdom
d.jackson@csc.liv.ac.uk

Abstract. Although much research has been devoted to devising genetic programming systems that are capable of running the evolutionary process in parallel, thereby improving execution speed, comparatively little effort has been expended on evolving programs which are themselves inherently concurrent. A suggested reason for this is that the vast number of parallel execution paths that are open to exploration during the fitness evaluation of population members renders evolutionary computation prohibitively expensive. We have therefore investigated the potential for minimising this expense by using a far more limited exploration of the execution state space to guide evolution. The approach, involving the definition of sets of schedulings to enable a variety of execution interleavings to be specified, has been applied to the classic 'dining philosophers' problem, and has been found to evolve solutions that are as good as those created by human programmers.

1 Introduction

In his seminal book on the subject, John Koza [1] pointed out the inherently parallel nature of genetic programming. Since that time a number of GP systems have been devised that exploit parallel and distributed hardware to speed up the computationally intensive evolutionary process [2-6].

A related, but entirely distinct, problem is that of evolving programs which are in themselves parallel. Leung et al [7] have described how they evolved parallel programs to run on a Multi-ALU Processor (MAP) machine, and their more recent work [8] suggests that it is actually easier to generate parallel programs for such an architecture than it is to evolve their sequential equivalents. The *Paragen* system of Ryan et al [9,10] does not generate parallel programs *per se*, but it evolves sets of transformations which are capable of converting sequential code to parallel form. Ross [11] describes the evolution of concurrent programs expressed in Milner's CCS formalism. In general, however, comparatively little work has been done on attempting to evolve concurrent programs, particularly those which are restricted to the employment of low-level synchronisation devices such as semaphores, and which may therefore be subject to all the problems of indeterminacy, deadlock and starvation.

A possible reason for this lies in the nature of the fitness evaluation that must be performed. In conventional GP systems for evolving sequential programs, fitness functions tend to take a 'black box' approach. Members of the evolving population are evaluated by executing them over a variety of inputs, and then comparing the

M. Keijzer et al. (Eds.): EuroGP 2004, LNCS 3003, pp. 89–100, 2004.

outputs actually produced with those that were expected. In general, the closer this match, the fitter the candidate. The execution paths a program follows in producing these outputs are irrelevant, and play no part in the fitness decision.

In evolving concurrent programs, however, it is not sufficient to base fitness measures on single executions of population members. Any non-trivial parallel program is non-deterministic; that is, it has many possible parallel paths of execution. An appropriate fitness metric must take these multiple execution interleavings into account, and therein lies the problem. As was made clear in the work by Ross [11], the state space that may arise for even simple programs generated during GP may be huge, making exhaustive evaluation tremendously expensive, perhaps prohibitively so.

The question we wish to investigate in this paper is whether such exhaustive exploration of the state space for concurrent programs is necessary. In other words, can a much more limited exploration be sufficient to guide the evolution of parallel solutions to specific programming problems?

A possible response is that, since a restricted exploration will by definition fail to pursue some parallel execution interleavings, there can be no guarantee that an evolved program is a correct solution. However, in that respect it does not differ from conventional GP, in which exhaustive testing is attainable only for certain small-scale problems. More usually, the evolution process is guided by fitness measures derived from executing candidates over finite, and often small, sets of test data. What purports to be a solution at the end of this process may indeed compute all the correct answers for all the supplied inputs, but that is no guarantee of correctness.

For concurrent programs, then, we propose to take a similarly limited approach to the investigation of the execution state space, in an effort to determine whether this is sufficient to evolve solutions. Despite our acknowledgement that, in general, the approach provides no guarantee of correctness of these programs, we have the additional yardstick of comparing them against human-generated concurrent programs. If the approach can measure up to that standard, then it may be of far more practical use than approaches which attempt exhaustive evaluation.

For the purposes of the study, we will attempt to solve the well-known 'dining philosophers' problem, in a number of variants. In this classic problem, a number of philosophers (usually five) are viewed as being seated around a circular table. The philosophers like to think a lot, but this makes them hungry, so on occasion they also eat. Lying between each pair of philosophers is a single fork, and in the centre of the table is a large bowl of spaghetti. Eating requires the use of two forks, but if a philosopher picks up the forks to both his left and right, then his immediate neighbours are deprived of a fork and cannot eat.

What makes this problem especially suitable as a test-bed is the focus on behaviour (i.e. the state space) rather than inputs and outputs. Moreover, this state space can (depending on the numbers of philosophers and the actions performed) be vast. Interestingly, Godefroid and Khurshid [12] described how they applied genetic algorithms to the task of searching the state space arising from one specific implementation of a dining philosophers program (although they did not attempt to evolve solutions to the problem itself).

2 Experimental Approach

For the experiments which follow, we have developed a GP system that will attempt to evolve solutions to several variants of the dining philosophers problem. For each of those variants, we define a set of actions that the philosophers may perform, e.g.

ACTIONS = {EAT, THINK, GET_LEFT_FORK, ... }

Members of the evolving population encode linear sequences of actions from the above set. Thus, if population member m is of length $mlen$, then:

$m = <a_0, a_1, ..., a_{mlen-1}>$,   where $a_i \in ACTIONS$

For execution purposes, the linear program string is viewed as being the body of an infinite loop:

```
loop
    a0; a1; a2 …
forever
```

In evaluating a program, the fitness function executes the code in pseudo-parallel for a pre-determined number of philosophers (we used five). This pseudo-parallelism is achieved by time-slicing. However, to provide us with the ability to pursue a variety of paths through the parallel execution state space, we also define a set of *schedulings*, which specify the duration of each of a philosopher's actions. These enable us to speed up or slow down a particular philosopher with respect to the others seated around the table, and also to alter the relative speed of a particular activity.

In implementing the scheduling mechanism, we did not want to have to specify the duration of every action for every philosopher, but we desired a system that would be flexible (so that schedulings could be added or altered) and capable of achieving good interleaving coverage. Hence, if *NSCHEDS* is the number of schedulings, and *NPHILS* is the number of philosophers, then the set of schedulings *SCHEDS* is defined as:

$SCHEDS = \{ s_0, s_1, ..., s_{NSCHEDS-1} \}$

For each scheduling $s \in SCHEDS$, $s = < d_0, d_1, ... d_{NPHILS-1} >$, where d_i is a duration associated with philosopher i.

The value of d_i may be positive or negative. If positive, it simply specifies the number of time units taken to execute each action of philosopher i. For example, the scheduling $s = < 1, 20, 20, 20, 20 >$ means that every action performed by philosopher 0 takes just one time unit to complete, while the actions of any other philosopher take 20 time units each.

A negative d_i allows us to slow down a specified action of philosopher i in relation to that philosopher's other actions. To be precise, a value of $-n$ for d_i means that all actions of philosopher i take one time unit to complete, except for action n, which takes a larger, pre-defined time to execute. For example, $s=< -EAT, 1, 2, 3, -THINK>$ means that for philosopher 0, eating takes much longer than any other action, while for philosopher 4, thinking is the slowest activity.

Clearly, there are many other possible ways of defining a scheduling mechanism, but this approach proved simple and powerful enough for our purposes. In evaluating a program, it is executed over all the schedulings specified for that problem. The greater the number of schedulings we specify, the greater the state space coverage we achieve. Each new scheduling we introduce therefore provides increased confidence in the correctness of any purported solution that is evolved. However, adding a new scheduling also greatly increases the computation time, since every population member that is evaluated must be executed with that scheduling.

Since every program is viewed as consisting of an infinite loop, a decision must be made as to when to terminate execution. To this end, execution proceeds until each philosopher has completed a minimum number of cycles of activity (i.e. complete executions of the code string). In general, three cycles was found to be an adequate minimum, bearing in mind that during most evaluations the faster philosophers will execute more than this. Achieving the minimum is of course subject to deadlock avoidance, which may not always be possible.

Another decision that must be made is how to compute fitness scores during evaluation. Given that the main objectives of each philosopher are simply to eat and think, we can define the following rewards for achieving those aims:

RE = reward for eating
RT = reward for thinking

These rewards are doled out once per cycle of a philosopher's execution, and only until the minimum cycle number has been reached. This helps to prevent the evolution of multiple occurrences of eating and thinking within population members. In the case of eating, points are awarded only if the philosopher has possession of both forks when the eat statement is executed.

For each variant of the dining philosophers problem, we also define a number of potential penalties. Common to all of the variants are:

PF = penalty for attempting to drop a fork not currently held
PE = penalty for attempting to eat without holding both forks

Other penalties (for indeterminacy, deadlock, etc.) are described in the next section as each experiment is introduced.

One problem that can arise in concurrent programming scenarios is that of starvation. In general terms this refers to an indefinite exclusion from a shared resource. For our purposes starvation has a more literal meaning, since the shared resources are the forks, and any inability to gain access to them means that one or more philosophers cannot eat. Hence, our approach will be to flag the potential for starvation if there exists a scheduling during which at least one philosopher does not eat in any of its cycles. Note that this is not quite as strong a definition as *indefinite* starvation, but it is a good indicator of a potential problem. It would be possible to define an explicit penalty for starvation, but we avoid this for the simple reason that starvation is self-penalising: an inability to eat means that RE points cannot accrue.

In all the experiments which follow, we have adopted steady-state evolution. Population members are chosen for reproduction, deletion, etc., using tournament selection on a sample size of 5. The population size is 500, and each run comprises 50 generations (generational equivalents). The evolutionary operators are the standard ones of fitness-proportionate reproduction, recombination and mutation, selected probabilistically. For recombination, we use 2-point linear crossover, and 90% of the individuals in the population are generated in this way. Mutation is single-point: that is, only one action in the program code string is affected. Probability of mutation is set at 0.01.

3 The Experiments

3.1 Experiment 1

In this first experiment, no synchronisation primitives are used. The analogy is that of a naïve programmer making a first attempt at the dining philosophers problem, who is unaware of the necessity for such primitives. The action set for this problem is:

ACTIONS={EAT, THINK, GET_LEFT, GET_RIGHT, DROP_LEFT, DROP_RIGHT}

The forks are viewed as unprotected shared variables. Execution of the GET_LEFT or GET_RIGHT statements causes the corresponding fork to be picked up if it is currently on the table; otherwise, nothing happens and the philosopher continues on to the next action.

Since forks are just simple variables, there is no possibility for deadlock. There is, however, ample scope for indeterminacy. This will occur if neighbouring philosophers attempt to access the same fork simultaneously. During fitness evaluation, the execution of a program is monitored to determine whether such access overlaps occur in any of the schedulings. If such a problem is detected, the penalty PI is applied, where

PI = penalty for indeterminacy

If we define 'best program' to mean the shortest-length program of those achieving the highest fitness in a run, then for a low value of PI a typical best program is given in the following (slightly re-formatted) output from our GP system:

Max fitness = 7712, Av fitness = 7474.724000, Best prog = 357
```
repeat
    Think; Think; Think; Think; Think; Think
    Think; Think; Think; Think; Think
    Pick up right fork; Pick up left fork
    Eat
    Drop left fork; Drop right fork
forever
```
Indeterminate; May cause starvation

The first thing to note about this best program is that it is not a particularly good one. It exhibits indeterminacy, and on at least one of the schedulings some of the philosophers went without eating (recall that the execution of an eat statement will not have an effect if both forks are not in possession).

A second thing to note is that the program is quite long, owing mainly to the presence of the repeated think statements. In fact, most of the evolved best programs were of the maximum permitted length. The reason for this is that longer programs probably stand a better chance of avoiding indeterminacy, at least for a time. Forks have to be picked up so that eating can take place and the reward for this received. A small number of fork acquisitions in the midst of a large number of other actions gives a greater chance during parallel execution that a fork acquisition will coincide with an innocuous action rather than another fork acquisition.

The presence of the large number of think actions follows directly on from this. It is not due, as might be thought at first, to evolutionary pressure to achieve high fitness by accumulating lots of RT (reward for thinking) points. As mentioned earlier, the appearance of think statements in population members is promoted by the reward system, but this RT reward is given only once per execution cycle; multiple think occurrences do nothing to gain higher fitness levels. The real reason for the evolution of their repeated appearance is much more mundane: it is simply that they act as a suitable 'filler,' padding out programs to make them longer for the reasons given above. Fork acquisition statements cannot be used for this purpose, as that would increase the probability of indeterminacy arising; eat statements cannot be used, because attempting to eat without both forks is penalised; and fork release statements cannot be used, because attempting to drop a fork not being held is also penalised. Of all the statements in the action set, think is the only one that can be used repeatedly with impunity.

The fact that the best evolved programs lead to the possibility of starvation perhaps requires a little explanation. One of the schedulings is specified as $s = <1,1,1,1,1>$. That is, all actions performed by all philosophers take just a single time unit to execute. This means that the philosophers proceed in lockstep, all performing the first action in parallel, then the second action, and so on. There are no synchronisation primitives to cause any philosopher to fall behind or get ahead of the others. Hence, whenever the left or right fork is picked up, it is picked up by all philosophers simultaneously. The fork on the other side of each philosopher is no longer available, and so nobody gets to eat.

If the penalty for indeterminacy PI is increased beyond a threshold value, the nature of the evolutionary process changes, and a rather different best program tends to emerge:

Max fitness = 4000, Av fitness = 4000.000000, Best prog = 43
```
repeat
    Think
forever
```
No indeterminacy; May cause starvation

This minimal program is produced as the best program on almost all runs. The high PI value has caused the evolutionary process to avoid indeterminacy completely, but at the cost of the philosophers never eating.

In repeated sets of runs, with varying values of fitness parameters, population sizes and generation numbers, it was found that every best program either exhibited indeterminacy or led to starvation. In other words, it was not possible to generate a working solution to the problem as posed. This will be of no surprise to anyone who knows anything about concurrent programming, but it is also encouraging in what it says of the set of schedulings used in fitness evaluation. Had a program evolved which was claimed to be free of indeterminacy and deadlock, it would have cast severe doubt on the adequacy of the scheduling set.

3.2   Experiment 2

Continuing our analogy of a novice programmer working towards a complete solution to the dining philosophers problem, the next step is to equip that programmer with the facility to prevent indeterminacy via the introduction of mutual exclusion. In this experiment, the forks continue to be treated as shared variables, but we now introduce a single binary semaphore for controlling access to those variables. The action set is augmented as follows:

ACTIONS = { EAT, THINK, GET_LEFT, GET_RIGHT, DROP_LEFT, DROP_RIGHT, DOWN_MUTEX, UP_MUTEX }

Picking up and dropping forks work exactly as before. The semaphore operations have their usual semantics, although it should be pointed out that the single semaphore is strictly binary, in the sense that any attempt to raise it above unity will have no effect. Indeterminacy is still a danger; it may arise if the semaphore is improperly used. Use of the semaphore may also cause philosophers to enter a wait state, so we must now include checks in the fitness function for the occurrence of deadlock. Since deadlock is undesirable, we define a penalty:

PD = penalty for deadlock

In practice, the value of PD can be set quite low, since (like starvation) deadlock tends to be self-penalising. If the philosophers are locked in a wait state, they are unable to eat or think, and therefore lose out on the substantial rewards on offer for those activities. During execution, we will record the amount of time that philosophers spend in the wait state. This is expressed as a percentage of the number of execution steps required to run the program in parallel for the minimum number of cycles.

In carrying out the experiment, it was found that a number of runs converged to the minimal repeat-think-forever solution seen in Experiment 1. On other runs, longer programs emerged which still exhibited one or more of the problems of indeterminacy, deadlock or starvation, but which were somewhat fitter than the minimal solution. However, there were some runs which evolved programs that exhibited none of these problems. These working solutions achieved the highest fitness scores of all.

Max fitness = 30400, Av fitness = 28108.914000, Best prog = 37
```
repeat
    Down Mutex
    Pick up right fork; Pick up left fork
    Eat
    Drop left fork; Drop right fork
    Up Mutex
    Think
forever
```
Idle time = 74%; No indeterminacy; Doesn't deadlock; No starvation

In this program, the mutex semaphore has been employed to ensure that only one philosopher at a time can access any of the forks. Despite being a correct solution, however, the high figure for idle time indicates that parallelism is severely restricted, since almost three-quarters of the execution steps were spent by philosophers simply waiting to proceed.

Figure 1 presents the fitness graph for one of the runs leading to a solution. It shows how the maximum fitness and the average fitness of the population as a whole vary as the generation number increases. In this case, a solution was found at generation 38.

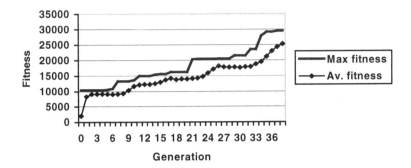

Fig. 1. Fitness graph for Experiment 2

3.3 Experiment 3

Having demonstrated the ability to evolve working solutions to the dining philosophers problem, the next task for our novice programmer is to increase the amount of parallelism (i.e. reduce the amount of idle time) that occurs in the simulations. Clearly, a single semaphore is too blunt an instrument for this. Instead, we introduce a vector of semaphores – one for each of the forks. In this way, the hope is that access to distinct pairs of forks will not cause undue waiting to be enforced. The action set is now:

ACTIONS   =   {EAT,   THINK,   ACQUIRE_LEFT,   ACQUIRE_RIGHT, RELEASE_LEFT, RELEASE_RIGHT }

The global mutex semaphore operations have disappeared, and the terms ACQUIRE and RELEASE are used in preference to GET and DROP to make it clear that these operations are now semaphore-based rather than accesses to simple variables. In programming terms, for philosopher i:

> *acquire left fork* is equivalent to *down(forks[i])*
> *acquire right fork* is equivalent to *down(forks[(i+1) mod NPHILS])*
> ... and similarly for *release*

The absence of shared variables means that indeterminacy is no longer a hazard, but the additional semaphores make deadlock even more of a danger, as was discovered during the GP runs. In fact, in not one of these runs was it possible to evolve a program that was free from both deadlock and starvation. Again, this does not indicate a problem with the approach, but the exact opposite. Experienced parallel programmers will know of the difficulties inherent in situations like these, but novice programmers when faced with this problem will often produce something like the following:

```
repeat
   Think
   Acquire left fork; Acquire right fork
   Eat
   Release left fork; Release right fork
forever
```

At first sight, the code looks promising. The problem is that, if all the philosophers begin more or less in step, they may all acquire the left fork simultaneously, and then be unable to acquire the right fork. With no mechanism for mediation or arbitration, further progress is impossible. The fact that our GP system could not find a way around this situation is again a testament to the adequacy of the scheduling set.

3.4 Experiment 4

In this final experiment, we combine the multiple semaphore approach of Experiment 3 with the global semaphore approach of Experiment 2. The purpose of the global semaphore this time is not to prevent indeterminacy but to avoid deadlock. However, instead of using a binary semaphore we will use a counting semaphore, able to take on any non-negative value. Moreover, we will allow our GP system to evolve the declaration of the semaphore so that it is initialised in the range 1..*NPHILS*. As a further modification, we introduce evolutionary pressure to drive down the idle time of the population, thereby increasing parallelism. To this end we define a new penalty,

PT = penalty based on idle time

On some of the execution runs, the best programs led either to deadlock or starvation. However, other runs generated programs such as the following:

Max fitness = 24086, Av fitness = 22014.632000, Best prog = 268

```
declare sema = 4
repeat
  Think;  Think;  Think;  Think;  Think;  Think;  Think
  Down semaphore
  Acquire right fork; Acquire left fork
  Eat
  Release left fork; Release right fork
  Up semaphore
forever
```

Idle time = 14%; Doesn't deadlock; No starvation

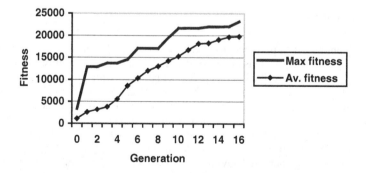

Fig. 2. Fitness graph for Experiment 4

Here, access to the forks is enclosed by operations on the global semaphore which restrict the number of philosophers doing this to at most four. This prevents deadlock occurring, and is in fact a correct solution to the problem (see, for example, Ben-Ari [13]). Note also the extremely low idle time; similar solutions with lower initial values of the global semaphore had longer idle times and were therefore less fit. The fitness graph for one of the successful runs, with a solution obtained at generation 16, is shown in Figure 2.

Some of the best programs that emerged were less easy to understand; for example:

Max fitness = 24013, Av fitness = 22003.594000, Best prog = 157

```
declare sema = 2
repeat
  Think
  Release left fork
  Down semaphore
  Acquire left fork
  Release left fork
  Up semaphore
  Up semaphore
  Acquire right fork
  Acquire left fork
  Eat
  Release right fork
  Up semaphore
  Up semaphore
forever
```

Idle time = 17%; Doesn't deadlock; No starvation

The program begins with a low initial value of the semaphore, but this is compensated for by the multiple 'up' operations in the loop body. As a consequence, the idle time is still very low, and the fitness almost as good as that scored by the solution shown earlier. Although the schedulings that were applied were unable to provoke deadlock or starvation, it is not easy to tell whether this is truly a correct solution to the problem.

4   Conclusions

The dining philosophers problem encapsulates a deceptively simple scenario, in that it requires a good deal of reasoning to develop solutions. The most encouraging outcome of the work described in this paper is that, even with a limited exploration of the parallel execution state space of the form described, it is possible to evolve solutions automatically that are equivalent in standard to those produced by human programmers. In practical terms, this may make it a far more useful approach than those which attempt exhaustive exploration of parallel state spaces. Also interesting is the way in which measures of 'idle time' can be used to guide the GP system towards solutions embodying increased levels of parallelism. This is similar to the way in which parsimony pressure can be used to drive down the size of programs.

Perhaps just as important is the fact that the approach is unable to offer solutions where no solutions are known to exist. In this way, it is able to highlight the inadequacy of certain functions sets for solving the problem; for example, the system was unable to evolve a solution when working with an array of fork semaphores alone, and rightly so. The implication is that the choice of scheduling set, despite its limited size, provides adequate coverage of the state space.

This is not to say that any solution the system evolves is guaranteed to be correct. The limited fitness evaluation we apply is no substitute for, say, rigorous formal analysis and verification of a program. Indeed, it is possible that some of the purported solutions that emerged during our experiments were not solutions at all, but that their failings simply went undetected by the fitness evaluator. The logic of some of these programs is so contorted as to require significant analysis to determine their correctness. However, as we have already tried to make clear, non-exhaustive evaluation is also a feature of GP systems for evolving sequential programs. The key point is that it does not become a less valuable technique on being adopted for parallel code.

Of course, it is always possible to increase confidence in evolved programs by increasing the size of the scheduling set. The penalty for this is an increase in computation time. One possibility would be to apply an additional set of post-processing schedulings to the best program, once it has evolved; a similar method to this was used by Kinnear in evolving sort programs [14]. This and other considerations will play a part in our further research on evolving concurrent programs, in which we hope to consider a much wider range of problems and parallel programming paradigms.

References

1. Koza, J.R.: Genetic Programming: On the Programming of Computers by Means of Natural Selection. MIT Press, Cambridge, MA (1992)
2. Andre, D., Koza, J.R.: Exploiting the Fruits of Parallelism: An Implementation of Parallel Genetic Programming that Achieves Super-Linear Performance. Inform. Sci. J. (1997)
3. Folino, G., Pizzuti, C., Spezzano, G.: CAGE: A Tool for Parallel Genetic Programming Applications. In: Miller, J. et al (eds.): EuroGP 2001, Lecture Notes in Computer Science, vol. 2038. Springer-Verlag, Berlin Heidelberg (2001) 64-73
4. Folino, G., Pizzuti, C., Spezzano, G.: A Scalable Cellular Implementation of Parallel Genetic Programming. IEEE Trans. Evolutionary Computation 7(1) (Feb. 2003) 37-53
5. Fernandez, F., Galeano, G., Gomez, J.A.: Comparing Synchronous and Asynchronous Parallel and Distributed Genetic Programming Models. In: Foster, J.A. et al (eds.): EuroGP 2002, Lecture Notes in Computer Science, vol. 2278. Springer-Verlag, Berlin Heidelberg (2002) 326-335
6. Tomassini, M., Vanneschi, L., Fernandez, F., Galeano, G.: Experimental Investigation of Three Distributed Genetic Programming Models. In: Merelo Guervos, J.J. et al (eds.): PPSN VII, Lecture Notes in Computer Science, vol. 2439. Springer-Verlag, Berlin Heidelberg (2002) 641-650
7. Leung, K.S., Lee, K.H., Cheang, S.M.: Evolving Parallel Machine Programs for a Multi-ALU Processor. Proc. IEEE Congress on Evolutionary Computation (2002) 1703-1708
8. Leung, K.S., Lee, K.H., Cheang, S.M.: Parallel Programs are More Evolvable than Sequential Programs. In: Ryan, C. et al (eds.): EuroGP 2003, Lecture Notes in Computer Science, vol. 2610. Springer-Verlag, Berlin Heidelberg (2003) 107-118

9. Ryan, C., Ivan, L.: Automatic Parallelization of Arbitrary Programs. In: Poli, R. et al (eds.): EuroGP'99, Lecture Notes in Computer Science, vol. 1598. Springer-Verlag, Berlin Heidelberg (1999) 244-254
10. Ryan, C., Ivan, L.: An Automatic Software Re-Engineering Tool Based on Genetic Programming. In: Spector, L. et al (eds.): Advances in Genetic Programming, vol. 3. MIT Press, Cambridge, MA (1999) 15-39
11. Ross, B.J.: The Evolution of Concurrent Programs. Applied Intelligence, vol. 8. Kluwer Academic Publishers, Boston (1998) 21-32
12. Godefroid, P., Khurshid, S.: Exploring Very Large State Spaces Using Genetic Algorithms. In: Katoen, J.-P. and Stevens, P. (eds.): TACAS 2002, Lecture Notes in Computer Science, vol. 2280. Springer-Verlag, Berlin Heidelberg (2002) 266-280
13. Ben-Ari, M.: Principles of Concurrent and Distributed Programming. Prentice-Hall (1990)
14. Kinnear, Jr., K.E.: Generality and Difficulty in Genetic Programming: Evolving a Sort. In: Forrest, S. (ed.): Proc. Fifth International Conf. on Genetic Algorithms. University of Illinois. Morgan Kaufman, San Mateo, CA (1993) 287-294

Evolutionary Induction of Grammar Systems for Multi-agent Cooperation

Clayton M. Johnson and James Farrell

California State University, Hayward
Department of Mathematics and Computer Science
Genetic and Evolutionary Algorithms Research Group
mjohnson@csuhayward.edu, jfarrell@mcs.csuhayward.edu

Abstract. We propose and describe a *minimal cooperative problem* that captures essential features of cooperative behavior and permits detailed study of the mechanisms involved. We characterize this problem as one of language generation by cooperating grammars, and present initial results for language induction by pairs of right-linear grammars using grammatically based genetic programming. Populations of cooperating grammar systems were found to induce grammars for regular languages more rapidly than non-cooperating controls. Cooperation also resulted in greater absolute accuracy in the steady state, even though the control performance exceeded that of prior results for the induction of regular languages by a genetic algorithm.

1 Introduction

Cooperative behavior is a subject of ongoing interest in a diverse spectrum of disciplines, including mathematics, economics, biology, and the social sciences. In computer science it is of fundamental importance to studies of multi-agent systems and distributed artificial intelligence. Researchers have sought to understand how cooperation might have evolved, and attempted to characterize the nature and mechanism of cooperative, coordinated behavior.

Studies pioneered by Axelrod on the Iterated Prisoner's Dilemma [1,2] have led to a good understanding of cooperation in game-theoretic terms, including criteria for the emergence and success of cooperative individuals in a population with fitness-based selection and reproduction, but without recombination. Iterated Prisoner's Dilemma tournaments have provided an overview of different strategies for cooperation, as well as an account of the outcomes of effective cooperative behavior, as exemplified by the simple yet evolutionarily stable "tit-for-tat" strategy.

Various genetic programming investigations of cooperative multi-agent behavior, such as robot navigation tasks and pursuit/capture by groups of "predators", have provided a view of the mechanisms by which cooperative behavior occurs [3,4,5,6]. These studies have emphasized the importance of communication, although the systems are sufficiently complex that the cooperative behavior of the agents sometimes remains difficult to quantify.

M. Keijzer et al. (Eds.): EuroGP 2004, LNCS 3003, pp. 101–112, 2004.

The process of cooperative problem solving has been studied by Wooldridge and Jennings [7], who propose specific criteria for cooperative behavior, outline stages in the cooperative solution of a problem, and present a system of formal logic satisfying their premises. These criteria allow for the possibility that cooperation can fail, and include requirements that agents be autonomous and reactive, cooperate on their own initiative, and act in a mutually supportive manner. They, too, deem communication to be essential, but decline to further characterize it in any way.

We have sought to formulate the simplest multiagent task requiring or rewarding cooperation, which we call a *minimal cooperative problem*. It was straightforward to limit ourselves to two agents, and it seemed, too, that some sort of symbol-based task was most appropriate, which led us to the theory of grammar systems.

2   Grammars and Grammar Systems

2.1   Generative Grammars

A *generative grammar* is a quadruple $G = (V, T, P, S)$, consisting of a non-empty variable alphabet V, a terminal alphabet T, a set of productions P, and a start variable $S \in V$, where $V \cap T = \varnothing$, and we define $\Sigma = V \cup T$, the alphabet containing all symbols in the grammar. Each production $p \in P$ is of the form $a \to b$, where $a \in \Sigma^+$, $b \in \Sigma^*$.

Derivations. Language of a Grammar. A derivation $u \Rightarrow_G \cdots \Rightarrow_G v$ is a sequence of productions applied to transform the sentential form $u \in \Sigma^+$ into $v \in \Sigma^*$. (When unambiguous we may simply write '$\Rightarrow$'.) If $u \Rightarrow v$, then G contains a production $a \to b$, and there are strings $x, y \in \Sigma^*$ for which $u = xay$ and $v = xby$.

For $k \geq 0$, $u \Rightarrow^k v$ indicates derivation in precisely k steps; that is, there is a sequence of strings $u_0, u_1, \ldots, u_k$ such that $u = u_0 \Rightarrow u_1 \Rightarrow \cdots \Rightarrow u_k = v$. Furthermore, $u \Rightarrow^* v$, a derivation in zero or more steps, if $u \Rightarrow^k v$ for some $k \geq 0$.

The language of a grammar is all terminal strings that may be derived from the start symbol:

$$L(G) = \{w \mid w \in T^* \text{ and } S \Rightarrow^* w\} .$$

Right-linearity. *Right-linear* grammars, with which this paper is principally concerned, contain only productions of the forms $v \to wv'$ or $v \to w$, where $v, v' \in V$ and $w \in T^*$. The class of right-linear grammars generates the family of regular languages, computationally equivalent to the class of finite-state automata.

2.2   Cooperating Distributed Grammar Systems

Grammar systems have been developed as formal models of distributed computation and multi-agent cooperation. Our presentation follows the notation of the standard monograph on the subject [8].

A *cooperating distributed (CD) grammar system* Γ is an $(n+2)$-tuple $\Gamma = (T, G_1, \ldots, G_n, S)$, consisting of a terminal alphabet T, a start symbol S, and *components* $G_1, \ldots, G_n$. The components of Γ can be thought of as agents in the system. Each component $G_i = (V_i, T_i, P_i)$ is a grammar, lacking a start symbol, which belongs to the system as a whole. In Section 2.1 above, we required the start symbol to be a variable, $S \in V$. Here, by extension, the start symbol must be a variable in at least one component, $S \in \bigcup_{i=1}^{n} V_i$. A similar expression relates the terminal alphabet of the system to those of its components: $T \subseteq \bigcup_{i=1}^{n} T_i$.

Modes of Derivation. Since CD grammar systems consist of multiple components that can apply productions to a sentential form, several *modes of derivation* are defined. The derivations $u \Rightarrow_{G_i}^{k} v$ and $u \Rightarrow_{G_i}^{*} v$ are as stated previously. In addition, for derivations of at most k steps, $u \Rightarrow_{G_i}^{\leq k} v$ if $u \Rightarrow_{G_i}^{k'} v$ for some $k' \leq k$. Similarly, derivations of at least k steps are denoted $u \Rightarrow_{G_i}^{\geq k} v$. For a derivation that continues as long as a production may be applied, $u \Rightarrow_{G_i}^{t} v$ if $u \Rightarrow_{G_i}^{*} v$ and there is no $v' \neq v$ where $v \Rightarrow_{G_i}^{*} v'$. The *language $L_f(\Gamma)$ of a grammar system* is

$$L_f(\Gamma) = \{w \mid w \in T^* \text{ and } S \Rightarrow_{G_{i_1}}^{f} w_1 \Rightarrow_{G_{i_2}}^{f} \cdots \Rightarrow_{G_{i_r}}^{f} w\} \ ,$$

where $f \in \{*, t, 1, 2, \ldots, \leq 1, \leq 2, \ldots, \geq 1, \geq 2, \ldots\}$. The language consists of all terminal strings reachable from the start symbol by a sequence of components performing derivations in mode f on the sentential form. The different modes of derivation can be thought of as defining the way an agent is expected to work on a partial solution before another agent takes over. We have restricted ourselves to the simplest case, $f = 1$, where each component must apply a single production, after which control passes to another component.

Control Mechanism. To provide a mechanism for passing control between components of the system, we can specify a directed graph U, with vertices consisting of the components of Γ. Control may pass from component G_i to G_j if the edge set $E(U)$ contains the edge (G_i, G_j). The language $L_f^U(\Gamma)$ of Γ controlled by U operating in the f-mode of derivation is then defined as

$$L_f^U(\Gamma) = \{w \mid w \in T^* \text{ and } S \Rightarrow_{G_{i_1}}^{f} w_1 \Rightarrow_{G_{i_2}}^{f} \cdots \Rightarrow_{G_{i_r}}^{f} w$$
$$\text{and } (G_{i_j}, G_{i_{j+1}}) \in E(U), 1 \leq j < r\} \ .$$

Example. Consider a CD grammar system Γ with two components G_0, G_1 that recognizes the language 0^*1^*. The components alternate, each applying a single production to a sentential form, whereby the mode of derivation is $f = 1$ and the control mechanism is the complete digraph $D_2 = (\{G_0, G_1\}, \{(G_0, G_1), (G_1, G_0)\})$. In order that $L_1^{D_2}(\Gamma) = 0^*1^*$, let Γ have:

- $T = \{0, 1\}$, the symbols in the language.
- Start symbol S.
- $G_0 = (V_0, T_0, P_0) = (\{S, A, B, C\}, \{0\}, \{S \to 0A \mid B, C \to B\})$
- $G_1 = (V_1, T_1, P_1) = (\{S, A, B, C\}, \{1\}, \{A \to S, B \to 1C \mid \varepsilon\})$

The string $011 \in L$ can be derived as follows:

$$S \Rightarrow_{G_0} 0A \Rightarrow_{G_1} 0S \Rightarrow_{G_0} 0B \Rightarrow_{G_1} 01C$$
$$\Rightarrow_{G_0} 01B \Rightarrow_{G_1} 011C \Rightarrow_{G_0} 011B \Rightarrow_{G_1} 011$$

Styles of Acceptance. Since the strings in the language of a grammar system consist of terminal symbols $w \in T^*$, the components of Γ must be able, collectively, to produce the entire terminal alphabet. The particular relationship between the terminal alphabet of a CD grammar system and that of its components determines the *style of acceptance* of Γ. A CD grammar system accepts in:

- style(ex) if $T = \bigcup_{i=1}^{n} T_i$, as is the case with the example above.
- style(all) if $T = \bigcap_{i=1}^{n} T_i$
- style(one) if $T = T_i$ for some $1 \leq i \leq n$
- style(arb) if T is an arbitrary subset of $\bigcup_{i=1}^{n} T_i$.

3   Minimal Cooperative Problems

We define a *minimal cooperative problem* (MCP) to be a language $L \subseteq T^*$ with $|T| = 2$, where henceforth $T = \{0, 1\}$. A solution to an MCP is a CD grammar system $\Gamma = (T, G_0, G_1, S)$ such that $L = L_1^{D_2}(\Gamma)$. The grammar system described in the example above is thus a solution to the MCP $L = 0^*1^*$. As with any solution, it consists of a pair of cooperating grammars which alternate productions, beginning from a start variable. In effect, the individual grammars communicate by placing variables in shared partial derivations.

Among the possible classes of solutions to investigate are those with varying styles of acceptance. These correspond to different mechanisms of cooperation and different approaches to distributed, multi-agent problem solving. For example, if $T_0 = T$ and $T_1 \cap T = \varnothing$ (style(one)), then T_0 is the 'master' component, entirely responsible for final production of symbols in a string; for $T \subseteq T_0$ and $T \subseteq T_1$ (style(all)), both components can produce the entire terminal alphabet and cooperation, depending on the problem, may be optional. We chose initially to investigate the case of style(ex), setting $T_0 = \{0\}$ and $T_1 = \{1\}$. This means that a single agent will at best be able to produce only a small subset of a given language. In order to produce any string containing both 0 and 1, the agents *must* cooperate.

Solving a minimal cooperative problem is a grammar induction task. In the context of genetic algorithms, this entails evolving a population of encodings of 2-component CD grammar systems. The fitness of an individual is determined by the accuracy with which it decides strings over T^*. A genetic algorithm has been used to induce regular grammars by searching for the fittest partition of the maximal canonical automaton [9], but this approach cannot obviously be adapted to the case of several grammars cooperatively producing a language.

$$S \rightarrow A1B \mid B1A$$
$$A \rightarrow BB \mid B0B$$
$$B \rightarrow 11B \mid 00 \mid 01$$

(a) An example grammar.

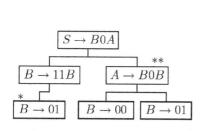

(b) A chromosome of (a).

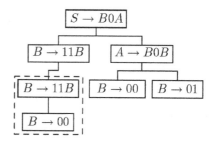

(c) Chromosome of (a) with locus for crossover with (b) indicated by '**'.

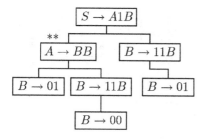

(d) Mutation of (b) at the locus indicated by '*'.

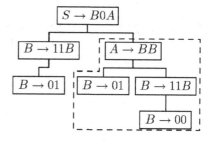

(e) One offspring of crossover between (b) and (c).

Fig. 1. Grammar showing example chromosomes and recombination operations

Others have studied natural language acquisition using a multi-agent evolutionary computation system [10]; this differs from our work in that, among other considerations, parsing is by individual agents.

4 Experimental

Our implementation takes advantage of grammatically-based genetic programming [11,12,13,14]. By using a tree of productions in a context-free grammar (CFG) as our genotype, we were able to encode chromosomes in a manner well suited to evolutionary computation. Grammatically-based genetic programming also introduces a genotype-phenotype distinction. By applying the productions in a chromosome, beginning from the start symbol, the resulting phenotype is a string in the language of the chromosome. As in biology, phenotype, not genotype, determines an individual's fitness.

For a context-free grammar $G = (V, T, P, S)$, we create random individuals by generating a tree headed by a random production $S \rightarrow w \in P$ (see Fig. 1a-b). Then, we recursively create subtrees by choosing, for each variable $v \in V$ in w a random production $v \rightarrow w'$. Mutation (see Fig. 1d) is similar: having randomly selected a locus $v \rightarrow w$, we replace the entire subtree with a randomly generated one headed by a production $v \rightarrow w'$ with the same left-hand variable. We perform crossover between two individuals by swapping randomly choosen subtrees headed by matching productions $v \rightarrow w_1$ and $v \rightarrow w_2$ (see Fig. 1e).

The underlying GA engine of our software is EO (Evolving Objects) [15], a templates-based C++ library, which we used to implement a CFG-based genotype and corresponding crossover and mutation operators. We represent trees as doubly-linked lists, with nodes sequenced according to a pre-order traversal (see Fig. 2). The phenotype is determined by visiting the nodes in the same order, so this process becomes a simple linear traversal of the list. The tree structure is maintained by a pointer from each node to the end of the subtree headed by the node, allowing for efficient splicing of subtrees during crossover and mutation.

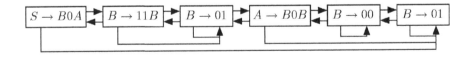

Fig. 2. List representation of the chromosome in Fig. 1b.

NOTE: We are discussing a *grammar system* that we have represented using a context-free *grammar*. In what follows these two terms refer, respectively, to the *phenotype* and the *encoding of the genotype*.

We developed two context-free grammars describing families of grammar systems with one and two regular components, based on the approach described

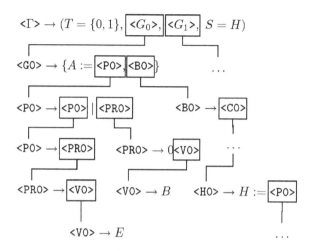

Fig. 3. Example CD grammar system genotype.

in [16]. An example genotype is shown in Fig. 3. Our start variable was fixed for all our experiments, as was the terminal alphabet of the system, $T = \{0, 1\}$. For the one-component control, $T_0 = T$. For two components, $T_0 = \{0\}$, $T_1 = \{1\}$. Productions were of the form $v \to tv' \mid v' \mid \varepsilon$, where $v, v' \in V$, $t \in T$. This subset of the family of right-linear grammars also yields all regular languages. There were eight fixed variables to choose from, of which only the start variable was guaranteed to appear as the left-hand side of a production.

Each grammar system was presented with 200 strings to parse, 1–100 symbols in length. Half were positive examples from the language to be induced, half were negative. Fitness was computed as the number of strings correctly classified plus $1/\text{Prod}(\Gamma)$ where $\text{Prod}(\Gamma)$ is the number of productions in the grammar system, to impose selection pressure for parsimony during evolution.

Existing parallel parsing algorithms [17,18] do not, in general, distribute processing by dividing the grammar into pieces akin to the components of a grammar system. Therefore, to encompass the broadest possible selection of languages and CD grammar systems, we implemented our parsing algorithm as A^* heuristic search. Given a goal string g to be parsed, and an intermediate string $w = w_0 w_1 w_2 \ldots w_{n-1} w_n$, we used the heuristic

$$
h(w) = \begin{cases} 0 & \text{if } w = g \\ 10 & \text{if } |w| - 1 > |g| \\ & \text{or } g \neq w_0 w_1 \ldots w_{n-1} g_n g_{n+1} \ldots \\ & \text{or } w_n \notin V_i \text{ where } G_i \text{ is the next component of } \Gamma \\ \frac{1}{|w|} & \text{otherwise.} \end{cases}
$$

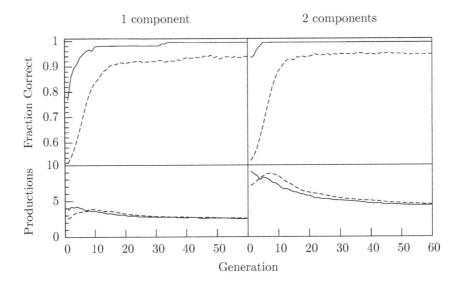

Fig. 4. Induction of $L = \{w \,|\, w \text{ contains at most two 1s}\}$

This heuristic correctly returns a distance estimate of 0 at the goal. If the string w is too long, or does not match the initial characters of the goal (as must be the case for a regular grammar), or if the last character is not a variable in the next component to operate on w, then w is a dead end. Otherwise, the value $h(w) = \frac{1}{|w|} \leq 1$ favors longer strings, in effect performing depth-first search.

For each language, we performed 30 independent runs of 60 generations each, for both a 2-component grammar system and a 1-component control. All reported p-values are the result of one-sample and Welch two-sample t-tests on the best classification rates in the final generation. We used a randomly initialized population of 100 individuals, with 3-tournament selection and no overlap, which appeared to offer the best tradeoff between exploitation and exploration. Our mutation and crossover rates were 0.1 and 0.8, respectively.

5   Results

Representative plots from our language induction experiments are depicted in Fig. 4 and Fig. 5. The solid lines show the fittest individual in the population, the dashed lines the population-wide average; both are averaged over all runs. The upper register shows the fraction of strings correctly classified, while the lower shows the number of productions in the phenotype grammar system. Each figure shows results for a two-component grammar system as well as a single-component control. In both plots, it can be seen that the 2-component system was more rapidly able to induce a grammar for the language. In the case of

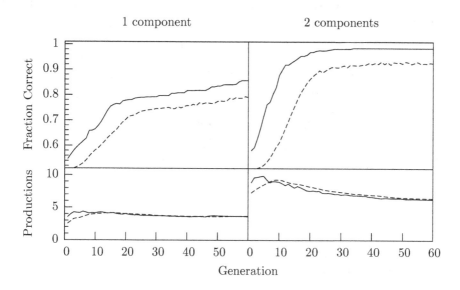

Fig. 5. Induction of $L = \{w \,|\, w$ contains at most two 1s in succession$\}$

Fig. 5, the control never achieved a classification rate comparable to that of the cooperative case ($p < 0.001$).

While a randomly generated genotype for a two-component grammar system will have, on average, twice as many productions as a single-component system, this does not confer any significant initial advantage. Both individuals operate under the same fitness pressure for parsimony, and and the number of productions available at any particular point will be identical on average, since only one component at a time operates on a sentential form. We have confirmed that increasing the average number of productions in the control phenotype does not improve its performance (results not shown).

A summary of the average performance of the fittest individual is shown in Table 1. It can be seen that, regardless of any initial disparity in $\mathrm{Prod}(\Gamma)$, during the course of evolution, this decreases to an average of 64% over the languages examined. In the case of $L = 0^*$, the components were required to cooperate even though one could contribute nothing to the solution. For $L = 0^*1^*0^*$, the apparent failure of cooperation is not statistically significant ($p = 0.065$), and is probably attributable to the limit placed on the total number of variables by the structure of the chromosome. Excluding these languages from consideration, the discrepancy in $\mathrm{Prod}(\Gamma)$ shrinks to 46%. Table 1 also shows that, while the two-component grammar systems out-perform the single-component controls, the success of the control nevertheless matches or exceeds exceeds results obtained by Dupont for the induction of regular grammars using a genetic algorithm [9] ($p < 0.001$).

Table 1. Average performance of fittest individual from the final generation with comparison results (*) from [9].

$L =$	1 Component			2 Components		
	Correct	*	Prod(Γ_1)	Correct	Prod(Γ_2)	$\frac{\text{Prod}(\Gamma_2)}{\text{Prod}(\Gamma_1)}$
0^*	100.0%	100.0%	2.7	100.0%	5.4	1.98
$(01)^*$	100.0	99.7	5.0	100.0	6.3	1.27
0^*1^*	98.9		4.8	99.8	5.6	1.15
$0^*1^*0^*$	98.5		3.4	95.4	6.7	2.00
≤ 2 ones	99.5		2.6	99.5	4.4	1.68
≤ 2 successive 1s	85.7	73.9	3.6	98.5	6.3	1.74
Average						1.64

6   Conclusions

Our results indicate that CD grammar systems can be effectively used to study the evolution and mechanisms of cooperation, and that the relatively simple case of a two-component regular grammar system accepting in style(ex) nevertheless demonstrates cooperative behavior in the context of induction of regular languages using grammatically based genetic programming. The two component grammar system learned several regular languages more rapidly than the single-component, non-cooperative control, and even in the case of $L = 0^*$, where cooperation could confer no advantage, a correct solution was nevertheless found. In addition to acquiring languages faster, the two-component system was also able to learn, with near-perfect accuracy, the most challenging of the languages, for which the single-component control was able to achieve a correct classification rate of only 85%.

It would be straightforward to extend these results by examining the other styles of acceptance and comparing the cooperative behavior of the resulting grammar systems. The initial results we have shown for style(ex) divide the terminal symbols among the components of Γ; in contrast, style(one) and style(all), as described above, assign the complete terminal alphabet to at least one component, and thus might clearly indicate the effectiveness or necessity of cooperation in various situations. We also hope to examine successful individual grammar systems from our experimental populations in more detail. By characterizing the sequence of productions by which they accept or reject strings strings, we hope to better understand the mechanisms of cooperative behavior. While outside the scope of minimal cooperative problems as we have defined them, the functional capabilities of grammar systems with greater than two components is also an area of potential interest. It seems likely, however, that progress in this area would rely on the development of suitable parsing algorithms.

We also plan to investigate induction of grammar systems with regular components to recognize context-free languages [19]. The language $L = \{w \mid w = 0^n 1^n$ for some $n \geq 0\}$, for example, is not in the class of regular languages. Yet $L = L_1^{D_2}(\Gamma)$ for $\Gamma = (\{0,1\}, G_0, G_1, S)$ with $V_0 = \{S, A, B\}$, $T_0 = \{0\}$, $P_0 =$

$\{S \to 0A \mid \varepsilon, B \to \varepsilon\}$, $V_1 = \{A, B, C\}$, $T_1 = \{1, S\}$, $P_1 = \{A \to SB, C \to 1B\}$.
Apart from the attractive emergent properties of such systems, they could offer insight into the challenging task of language acquisition, as an established approach to grammar induction has been to decompose and distribute the problem.

Using the data we have already collected, as well as future experiments, we hope to be able to provide a quantitative, mechanistic analysis of the evolution and execution of cooperative behavior. We have also begun to investigate parallel parsing techniques that appear most analogous to CD grammar systems [20,21], in hopes of expanding and developing the practical uses of this model of multi-agent cooperation.

Acknowledgments. Our implementation of grammar-based genetic programming was developed in collaboration with Marek Nelson. Ward Rodriguez contributed suggestions regarding statistical analysis of our data. This material is based on work for which James Farrell received support from a National Science Foundation Graduate Research Fellowship and an Associated Students of CSU Hayward Research Fellowship.

References

1. Axelrod, R., Hamilton, W.D.: The evolution of cooperation. Science **211** (1981) 1390-1396
2. Axelrod, R., Dion, D.: The further evolution of cooperation. Science **242** (1988) 1385-1390
3. Haynes, T., Sen, S., Schoenefeld, D., Wainwright, R.: Evolving multiagent coordination strategies with genetic programming. Technical Report UTULSA-MCS-95-04, The University of Tulsa (1995)
4. Luke, S., Spector, L.: Evolving teamwork and coordination with genetic programming. In Koza, J.R., Goldberg, D.E., Fogel, D.B., Riolo, R.L., eds.: Genetic Programming 1996: Proceedings of the First Annual Conference, Stanford University, CA, USA, MIT Press (1996) 150-156
5. Iba, H.: Emergent cooperation for multiple agents using genetic programming. In Voigt, H.M., Ebeling, W., Rechenberg, I., Schwefel, H.P., eds.: Parallel Problem Solving from Nature IV, Proceedings of the International Conference on Evolutionary Computation. Volume 1141 of LNCS., Berlin, Germany, Springer Verlag (1996) 32-41
6. Iba, H.: Evolutionary learning of communicating agents. Information Sciences **108** (1998) 181-205
7. Wooldridge, M., Jennings, N.R.: The cooperative problem solving process. Journal of Logic and Computation 9 (1999) 563-592
8. Csuhaj-Varjú, E., Dassow, J., Kelemen, J., Păun, G.: Grammar Systems: A Grammatical Approach to Distribution and Cooperation. Gordon and Breach Science Publishers, London (1994)
9. Dupont, P.: Regular grammatical inference from positive and negative examples by genetic search: the gig method. In: Grammatical Inference and Applications, ICGI'94. Number 862 in Lecture Notes in Artificial Intelligence. Springer-Verlag (1994) 236-245

10. De Pauw, G.: Evolutionary computing as a tool for grammar development. In Cantú-Paz, E., Foster, J.A., Deb, K., Davis, L.D., Roy, R., O'Reilly, U.M., Beyer, H.G., Standish, R., Kendall, G., Wilson, S., Harman, M., Wegener, J., Dasgupta, D., Potter, M.A., Schultz, A.C., Dowsland, K.A., Jonoska, N., Miller, J., eds.: Proceedings of the Genetic and Evolutionary Computation Conference GECCO. Number 2723 in LNCS. Springer Verlag (2003) 549-560

11. Fujiki, C., Dickinson, J.: Using the genetic algorithm to generate lisp source code to solve the prisoner's dilemma. In Grefenstette, J.J., ed.: Genetic Algorithms and their Applications: Proceedings of the second international conference on Genetic Algorithms, MIT, Cambridge, MA, USA, Lawrence Erlbaum Associates (1987) 236-240

12. Johnson, C.M., Feyock, S.: A genetics-based approach to the automated acquisition of expert system rule bases. In: Proceedings of the IEEE/ACM International Conference on Developing and Managing Expert System Programs, IEEE Computer Society Press (1991) 78-82

13. Whigham, P.A.: Grammatically-based genetic programming. In Rosca, J.P., ed.: Proceedings of the Workshop on Genetic Programming: From Theory to Real-World Applications, Tahoe City, California, USA (1995) 33-41

14. O'Neill, M., Ryan, C.: Grammatical Evolution: Evolutionary Automatic Programming in an Arbitrary Language. Kluwer (2003)

15. Keijzer, M., Merelo-Guervós, J.J., Romero, G., Schoenauer, M.: Evolving objects: A general purpose evolutionary computation library. In Collet, P., Fonlupt, C., Hao, J.K., Lutton, E., Schoenauer, M., eds.: Proceedings of the Fifth Conference on Artificial Evolution (EA-2001), Le Creusot, France, Springer-Verlag (2001) 231-244

16. Johnson, C.M.: A Grammar-Based Technique for Genetic Search and Optimization. PhD thesis, College of William and Mary, Virginia (1996)

17. van Lohuizen, M.P.: Survey of parallel context-free parsing techniques. Technical Report IMPACT-NLI-1997-1, Delft University of Technology (1997)

18. Nijholt, A.: Parallel approaches to context-free language parsing. In Adriaens, G., Hahn, U., eds.: Parallel Natural Language Processing. Ablex Publishing Corporation, Norwood, New Jersey (1994) 135-167

19. Kelemen, J., Kelemenová, A.: A grammar-theoretic treatment of multiagent systems. Cybernetics and Systems **23** (1992) 621-633

20. Yonezawa, A., Ohsawa, I.: Object-oriented parallel parsing for context-free grammars. In Adriaens, G., Hahn, U., eds.: Parallel Natural Language Processing. Ablex, Norwood, NJ (1994) 188-210

21. Khanna, S., Ghafoor, A., Goel, A.: A parallel compilation technique based on grammar partitioning. In: Proceedings of the 1990 ACM annual conference on Cooperation, ACM Press (1990) 385-391

Genetic Programming Applied to Mixed Integer Programming

Konstantinos Kostikas and Charalambos Fragakis

Department of Computational Mathematics and Computer Programming
School of Mathematics, Physics and Computational Sciences
Faculty of Technology
Aristotle University of Thessaloniki
54006 Thessaloniki, Greece
{kostikas,fragakis}@gen.auth.gr

Abstract. We present the application of Genetic Programming (GP) in Branch and Bound (B&B) based Mixed Integer Linear Programming (MIP). The hybrid architecture introduced employs GP as a node selection expression generator: a GP run, embedded into the B&B process, exploits the characteristics of the particular MIP problem being solved, evolving a problem-specific node selection method. The evolved method replaces the default one for the rest of the B&B. The hybrid approach outperforms depth-first and breadth-first search, and compares well with the advanced Best Projection method.

1 Introduction

A mixed integer programming (MIP) problem is an optimization problem where some or all of the variables are restricted to take only integer values. General integer and mixed integer programs are NP-hard [1]; even today's state of the art commercial IP solvers have difficulties tackling MIP formulations representing simple engineering or business optimization problems containing more than a few hundred integer variables [2].

The classical and most widely used approach for solving MIP problems is Linear Programming (LP) based Branch and Bound (B&B) which employs LP based relaxations of the MIP problem for exploring the solution space [1]. The implementation of a Branch and Bound algorithm can be viewed as a tree search, where the problem at the root node of the tree is the original MIP; new nodes are formed by branching on an existing node for which the optimal solution of the relaxation is fractional.

In order for Branch and Bound to be successful in solving interesting problems, it needs to 'guide' the search effectively: that is it needs to make correct choices regarding branching (which node to expand next) and node selection (which node to visit next). In this paper we examine the application of Genetic Programming (GP) [3] to node selection.

Several methods for node selection have been proposed since the introduction of B&B for MIP [4]. Most of them offer considerable gains in the execution

M. Keijzer et al. (Eds.): EuroGP 2004, LNCS 3003, pp. 113–124, 2004.

times of the B&B algorithm. However, as Linderoth and Savelsbergh demonstrate in their study of search strategies for MIP [5], no method outperforms all others when a variety of MIP problems is concerned. In particular, Linderoth and Savelsbergh point out that of the 13 different node selection methods, 11 ranked from first to last depending on the particular MIP problem solved.

The above indicate that node selection is a problem domain where (i) no general solutions exist (ii) an approximate solution is acceptable (or is the only result that is ever likely to be obtained) (iii) small improvements in performance are routinely measured and highly prized and (iv) the interrelationships among the relevant variables are poorly understood. According to J. Koza, the founder of Genetic Programming, in his foreword to [6], these are characteristics providing a good indication for applying Genetic Programming to a problem area. More than that, the 'essence' of a node selection method is an expression that can be expressed in Genetic Programming terms.

Consequently, we decided to tackle the problem of node selection in the Branch and Bound method for MIP by applying to it Genetic Programming. Our intention was not to develop node selection methods in a static manner, but to evolve them dynamically in runtime and to apply them during the rest of the B&B search. This study introduces our idea, presents a prototype realization of it and discusses the results obtained.

The rest of the paper proceeds as follows: Section 2 briefly outlines related work. Section 3 is an introduction to the Branch and Bound algorithm for MIP. Section 4 illustrates our modified version of Branch and Bound, and how GP is incorporated in it. Section 5 discusses the experimental parameters of our study, Sect. 6 presents the obtained results, and Sect. 7 summarizes our conclusions.

2 Related Work

The field of metaheuristics for the application to combinatorial optimization problems is a rapidly growing field of research. A recent, general 'overview and conceptual comparison' is [7]. More specifically, metaheuristic algorithms are increasingly being applied to process MIP problems. Most of the time they are used in order to discover 'good' solutions quickly, concluding the search if optimality is not required, or aiding exact approaches, like Branch and Bound, to reach optimality.

Mitchell and Lee [1] cite several references regarding the application of metaheuristics in MIP. Abramson and Randall [8][9] utilize Simulated Annealing, Tabu Search and other metaheuristics for building a 'general purpose combinatorial optimization problem solver'; [9] is also a good reference for related work. A recent example of a Genetic Algorithm based method for finding a first integer solution to MIP problems is contained in [10]. However, to our knowledge, there exists no previous attempt of utilizing metaheuristics or evolutionary computation techniques for evolving node selection methods. We are also not aware of previous uses of Genetic Programming in MIP.

3   Background

3.1   Mixed Integer Programming

A mixed integer program (MIP) is an optimization problem stated mathematically as follows:

$$Maximize \quad z_{MIP} = \sum_{j \in I} c_j x_j + \sum_{j \in C} c_j x_j \tag{1}$$

$$subject\ to \quad \sum_{j \in I} a_{ij} x_j + \sum_{j \in C} a_{ij} x_j \leq b_i \quad i = 1, \ldots m \tag{2}$$

$$l_j \leq x_j \leq u_j \quad j \in N$$
$$x_j \in Z \quad j \in I$$
$$x_j \in R \quad j \in C,$$

where I is the set of integer variables, C is the set of continuous variables, and $N = I \cup C$. The lower and upper bounds l_j and u_j may take on the values of plus or minus infinity. Thus, a MIP is a linear program (LP) plus some integrality restriction on some or all of the variables [5].

3.2   The Branch and Bound Algorithm

The classical approach to solving integer programs is Branch-and-Bound [4]. The B&B method is based on the idea of iteratively partitioning the solution space (branching) to form subproblems of the original (mixed) integer program. The process involves keeping a list of linear programming problems obtained by relaxing some or all of the integer requirements on the variables x_j, $j \in I$.

To precisely define the algorithm, some definitions are needed. We use the term node or subproblem to denote the problem associated with a certain portion of the feasible region of MIP. Define z_L to be a lower bound on the value of z_{MIP}. For a node N^i, let z_U^i be an upper bound on the value that z_{MIP} can have in N^i. The list $\mathcal{L}$ of problems that must still be solved is called the active set. Denote the optimal solution by x^*. The algorithm in Table 1, adopted from [5], is a Linear Programming-based Branch and Bound algorithm for solving MIP.

Branch and Bound is more of a framework, than a specific algorithm: Among other things, every implementation has to provide specific 'rules' regarding how problems are selected for evaluation in step 2 of the algorithm. Although LP based Branch and Bound, being an exact algorithm, is guaranteed to finish whatever choices are made during the run in step 2, 'good' choices are of paramount importance regarding how fast 'acceptable', or even 'optimal' solutions are reached.

Table 1. Linear Programming based Branch and Bound Algorithm

0. **Initialize.** $\mathcal{L}$ = MIP. $z_L = -\infty$. $x^* = \varnothing$.
1. **Terminate?** Is $\mathcal{L} = \varnothing$? If so, the solution x^* is optimal.
2. **Select.** Choose and delete a problem N^i from $\mathcal{L}$.
3. **Evaluate.** Solve the LP relaxation of N^i. If the problem is infeasible, go to step 1, else let z^i_{LP} be its objective function value and x^i be its solution.
4. **Prune.** If $z^i_{LP} \leq z_L$, go to step 1. If x^i is fractional, go to step 5, else let $z_L = z^i_{LP}$, $x^* = x^i$, and delete from $\mathcal{L}$ all problems with $z^j_U \leq z_L$. Go to step 1.
5. **Divide.** Divide the feasible region of N^i into a number of smaller feasible regions N^{i1}, N^{i2}, ..., N^{ik} such that $\cup^k_{j-1} N^{ij} = N^i$. For each $j = 1, 2, \ldots, k$, let $z^{ij}_U = z^i_{LP}$ and add the problem N^{ij} to $\mathcal{L}$. Go to 1.

3.3 Node Selection

The goal of a node selection method is twofold: to find good integer feasible solutions (i), or to prove that no solution better than the current lower bound z_L exists (ii). Integer solutions tend to be found deep into the search tree; as a result, a Depth-First type search (DFS) tends to do well in (i). On the other hand, a Breadth-First type of search (BFS), like best-bound (which chooses the subproblem with the largest value of z^i_U) performs better in (ii) [1].

Estimate-based node selection methods attempt to estimate the value of the best feasible integer solution obtainable from a given node N^i of the B&B tree, and then choose the node with the highest (or lowest in case of minimization) such estimate E_i. There exist many formulae for computing the estimate, and most of them are based around the sum of integer infeasibilities $s^i \equiv \sum_{j \in I} min\left(x^i_j - \lfloor x^i_j \rfloor, 1 - \left(x^i_j - \lfloor x^i_j \rfloor\right)\right)$ of the relaxation solution z^i_U at node N^i of the tree. A popular estimation method, introduced by Mitra [11], is *Best Projection*:

$$E_i = z^i_U + \left(\frac{z_L - z^0_U}{s_0}\right) s^i, \tag{3}$$

where z^i_U is the relaxation solution at node N^i, z_L is the best MIP solution obtained in the search so far, z^0_U is the relaxation solution of the original MIP problem (root node), s_0 is the sum of integer infeasibilities at root node and s^i is the sum of integer infeasibilities at node N^i.

Backtracking methods are based on the idea of combining the advantages of (i) and (ii). They try to go as deep as possible or needed, and then backtrack using for example best bound or best projection as a node selection method. Most commercial MIP solvers utilize such backtracking strategies in their B&B implementation in order to speed up the search [12][13]. Mitchell and Lee [1] and particularly Linderoth and Savelsbergh [5] contain thorough presentations and discussions of node selection methods.

4   Evolving Problem Specific Node Selection Strategies

Node selection methods need to be robust: they need to perform well on a wide variety of MIP problems [5]. If the 'generality' requirement is dropped, maybe much better 'customized' node selection rules could be devised, which would perform optimally for the specific MIP problem at hand. Manually building special purpose selection rules for each data set obviously doesn't make practical and economical sense; however, GP offers the means for doing exactly that: By embedding in the B&B algorithm a Genetic Programming run, customized node selection methods can be evolved, which will consequently replace the initial node selection method. In other words, we are using Genetic Programming for evolving an expression similar to 3 for use in our MIP problem. Our approach consists of three distinct stages:

B&B Stage1 begins with the start of the search and lasts until a criterion is met, i.e. until a specified number of MIP solutions have been found, or until a specified number of nodes has been visited. Stage 1 is ordinary B&B search[1], employing a standard node selection method.

GP Stage is where the GP search takes place: Initially the training set is constructed (Sect. 5.3), and after that the GP run is performed. At the end of the run, the best evolved expression, that is the fittest individual, is selected and replaces the node selection method used in Stage1.

B&B Stage2 resumes the execution of B&B, which was paused in the previous stage, and continues the search by utilizing the GP evolved expression for node selection.

Further GP Stages. In our prototype implementation, only one GP Stage is used during the life-cycle of the B&B search. In other words, the loop starting with B&B Stage1 and finishing with B&B Stage2 is executed once. This needs not be necessarily the case: A design where the node selection method is constantly refined as a result of multiple GP Stages, seems also attractive. More than that, since both B&B and GP are highly parallelisable algorithms, the hybrid architecture is also susceptible to parallelisation.

4.1   GP Building Blocks for Node Selection

The building blocks we used for node selection method construction, that is our terminal set, are listed in Table 2. It contains primitives required for forming node selection expressions. All terminals are readily available from the runtime data structures of the MIP solver we used (GLPK, Sect. 5.1). The terminal set

---

[1] Actually some extra data, required in the GP stage, need to be maintained for each node.

Table 2. GP Terminals for node selection method construction. *Constant Terminals* involve general characteristics of the MIP problem and information regarding the solution of the LP relaxation of the problem. *Dynamic Terminals* concern the specific B&B node being evaluated

Property	Description
	Constant Terminals
intvar_count	Number of integer variables of the problem (including binary variables)
binvar_count	Number of binary variables of the problem
totvar_count	Total number of variables of the problem (integer and continuous)
ii_sumN$_0$	Sum of integer infeasibilities at the root node of the Branch and Bound tree (i.e. of the linear relaxation solution of the MIP problem)
ii_countN$_0$	Count of integer infeasibilities at the root node of the Branch and Bound tree (i.e. of the linear relaxation solution of the MIP problem)
lp_solN$_0$	Value of the solution of the linear programming relaxation of the MIP problem
bonly	TRUE if the problem contains only Binary integer variables, FALSE otherwise
	Dynamic Terminals
ii_sumN$_i$	Sum of integer infeasibilities at the parent problem of node N$_i$
ii_countN$_i$	Count of integer infeasibilities at the parent problem of node N$_i$
lp_solN$_i$	Value of the solution of the linear programming relaxation of the parent problem of node N$_i$
tree_depth_N$_i$	Depth of the tree at node N$_i$

is quite simple, from an LP based B&B perspective; more complicated primitives, i.e. *pseudocosts*, found in methods like *best estimate* [5], would probably enhance the capabilities of GP search. Such primitives were not used however, because they were not readily available in our solver. Besides, at this early point of research, we were primarily interested in testing the soundness of our approach than to fine-tune the performance of our prototype implementation, and employing extravagant terminals would be of no use to the former[2].

5   Experimental Parameters

5.1   Infrastructure

The MIP solver we based our experimentation on is GLPK (Gnu Linear Programming Kit) [14]. GLPK doesn't provide the plethora of options of commercial software like CPLEX [12], but it contains a solid implementation of the simplex method, and, most importantly, comes with full source code. GLPK adopts a backtracking method for node selection: it goes depth first as much as possible,

---

[2] Even expression 3 cannot be formed using the available terminals because z_L is not in the terminal set.

and then backtracks by selecting a node using DFS[3], BFS[4], or Best Projection (see Sect. 3.3). The necessary hooks were placed into GLPK in order to cater for collecting data during B&B Stage1, for performing the GP run, and for replacing the default backtracking method with the one evolved. For Genetic Programming we used strongly typed lilgp[15][16], which was integrated with the GLPK infrastructure.

5.2   GP Run Parameters

The GP parameters we used in our tests are listed in Table 3. GP Stage evolves 1200 individuals for 50 generations. All individuals constituting the first generation are randomly created, and each subsequent generation is formed using individuals resulting from crossover operations, with 80% probability, mutation, with 10% probability, and reproduction with 10% probability. Tournament selection with size seven is used. The maximum depth of each individual is restricted to 10. Finally, the standard arithmetic and boolean logical and comparison primitives listed in Table 3 are used.

Table 3. Control Parameters. Last row contains the termination criteria for B&B Stage1, that is how many B&B nodes need to be visited before GP Stage begins. This mainly affects the construction of the terminal set in the GP Stage, see Sect. 5.3

Objective:	evolve LP based Branch and Bound node selection criterion specialized for MIP problem instance
Function set:	ADD SUB MUL PDIV AND OR NOT IFTRUE IFGTE IFLTE IFEQ
Terminal set:	B&B and LP related runtime data, see Table 2
Fitness cases:	dynamically created based on data obtained in B&B Stage1
Fitness function:	standardized fitness, based on mean error over the fitness cases
Population size:	1200
Initial population:	initialization method: grow, initial depth: 5-7
Crossover probability:	80 percent
Mutation probability:	10 percent
Selection:	tournament, size 7
Termination:	generation 50
Maximum depth of tree:	10
Parameters for B&B Stage1:	MinNodes 100, MaxNodes 1000, MaxMIPsolfound 10, node selection method best bound.

---

[3] DFS selects a node using LIFO: this results in B&B spending most of its time evaluating nodes found to the bottom of the tree; such a strategy is imbalanced.

[4] BFS selects a node using FIFO: This resembles best bound, mentioned in Sect. 3.3.

5.3 Training Sets

Evolving a problem-specific node selection method using Genetic Programming, means that a problem-specific training set is required as well. The training set has to make use of data generated during B&B Stage1, in order to allow GP to evolve a node selection method which will successfully 'guide' the B&B search in Stage2. Since our work is novel, there was little help from MIP bibliography regarding what such a training set could be; consequently we experimented with two different schemes of our own:

The first scheme is based on the observation that B&B with backtracking capabilities (see Sect. 3.3), which is the case in GLPK and most commercial MIP solvers (for example CPLEX [12], FortMP[13]), can be seen as a sequence of 'dives' from some node in the B&B tree to some node further 'down'. Each dive is comprised from one to a maximum of "tree-depth" nodes. By rating the effectiveness of each dive in finding a MIP solution, the dives taking place in B&B Stage1 can be used for the construction of the training set: such a rating R_i for each dive d^i is obtained through (4), corresponding to training set T_1:

$$R_i = \left(\frac{s^i_{start} - s^i_{finish}}{d^i_{finish} - d^i_{start}} \right) V_{bonus} \tag{4}$$

where s^i_{start} is the sum of integer infeasibilities at the node where the dive starts, s^i_{finish} at the node where it ends, d^i_{finish} and d^i_{start} is the depth of the B&B tree at the finishing and starting node respectively, and V_{bonus} is a bonus factor applied if the dive results in a full integer feasible MIP solution. Our rational was that fast reduction of integer infeasibility denotes a promising dive; in addition, dives resulting in full integer feasible solutions deserve to be rewarded with the V_{bonus} factor[5].

We also applied formula 5 for constructing the training set (T_2). T_2 differs from T_1 in that it does not reward dives resulting in full integer feasible MIP solutions.

$$R_i = \frac{s^i_{start} - s^i_{finish}}{d^i_{finish} - d^i_{start}} \tag{5}$$

An effect of utilizing the above scheme for constructing the training set, is that the number of fitness cases is problem dependant.

The second scheme is much simpler: The training set (T_3) is made up of the MIP solutions found in B&B Stage1.

6 Results

For our experimentation we used the problems of the standard MIPLIB3 library [17] listed in Table 4. MIPLIB3 is probably the most widely used IP and MIP

---

[5] For all the experiments we used $V_{bonus} = 3.0$ for integer feasible solutions worst than the lower bound and $V_{bonus} = 5.0$ for solutions better than the lower bound.

Table 4. MIPLIB3 benchmarks used. The set contains MIP and pure 0/1 integer problems

Problem	Rows	Cols	Int vars	0/1 vars	Cont vars	Descriptions
bell3a	123	133	71	39	62	MIP
bell5	91	104	58	30	46	MIP
blend2	274	353	264	231	89	MIP
khb05250	101	1350	24	24	1326	MIP
l152lav	97	1989	1989	1989	0	0/1 IP
lseu	28	89	89	89	0	0/1 IP
misc07	212	260	259	259	1	MIP
mod008	6	319	319	319	0	0/1 IP
qnet1	503	1541	1417	1288	124	MIP
qnet1$_o$	456	1541	1417	1288	124	MIP
rentacar	6803	9557	55	55	9502	MIP
stein45	331	45	45	45	0	0/1 IP

benchmarking suite in the literature [2][5][10]. The criterion for choosing the specific 12 problems, out of the 59 contained in the library, was the capability of 'vanilla' GLPK to find the optimal solution for each problem (and prove its optimality) between the minimum and maximum time limits, which were set to 10 seconds and 20 minutes of cpu time respectively. The rest of the problems were excluded because they were too 'easy', or because they required excessive computational resources. All tests were performed in the same hardware/software system (Pentium 4 at 2.4GHz with 768Mb Ram running Linux 2.4).

Our goal was to compare the performance of 'standard' GLPK with our GP enhanced system. In particular, we wanted to find out if the hybrid system, utilizing each one of T1, T2 and T3 training methods, would be able to compete with GLPK using the simple DFS and BFS node selection methods, or the advanced Best Projection method.

Total execution times are presented in in Table 5; Table 6 shows times for reaching the optimal solution. Time and ranking averages are included in the Tables as well. It can be seen from Tables 5 and 6 that no selection method dominates the others. This is typical for node selection methods and in accordance with [5]. Two winners stand out however, Best Projection and GP1. Best Projection 'solves' on average each problem in 53.10 seconds, being the fastest method, whereas GP1 is the second best with 94.30 seconds. However, as the average ranking of each method demonstrates, GP1 is a more 'solid' performer (average rank 2.81) than Best Projection (3.00).

As far as the time it takes to reach optimality (but not prove it) is concerned, Best Projection is clearly superior to other methods; GP1 comes second. This means however that once optimality is reached, GP1 is, on average, faster to prove that the solution is optimal, than it is Best Projection.

Concerning how the employed training methods perform in respect to the design criteria mentioned in Sect. 5.3, it appears that our rational 'made sense': that is, GP1 takes advantage of the 'bonus factor' applied to the test cases where

Table 5. Execution times in seconds for solving the MIP and IP problems. Bestp, BFS and DFS are standard node selection methods. GP1, GP2 and GP3 are methods dynamically evolved by GP using training methods T1, T2 and T3 accordingly. 'NS' means no optimal solution was found in the available time limit, 'A' means that the solver aborted in B&B Stage1 because no MIP solution, required for building the training set, was found. Results are the average of 5 runs.

Problem	Bestp	BFS	DFS	GP1	GP2	GP3
bell3a	71.69	39.04	21.79	41.79	127.51	23.59
bell5	22.73	577.76	754.81	494.15	512.39	A
blend2	14.94	57.71	NS	26.71	53.99	30.07
khb05250	10.00	13.80	11.94	18.00	16.94	31.17
l152lav	30.04	46.20	33.41	29.81	31.99	84.46
lseu	50.97	29.36	15.60	93.57	93.76	16.89
misc07	82.19	73.88	70.19	69.65	69.68	76.35
mod008	41.34	30.06	87.26	26.21	26.65	26.30
qnet1	72.21	134.00	NS	100.42	245.61	745.85
qnet1$_o$	15.16	71.83	NS	110.28	NS	59.66
rentacar	19.62	246.11	100.05	22.63	23.28	37.85
stein45	206.32	147.62	101.64	98.34	94.06	305.11
Time avg	**53.10**	**122.28**	**399.72**	**94.30**	**207.99**	**219.78**
Ranking avg	**3.00**	**4.27**	**4.27**	**2.82**	**4.00**	**4.45**

Table 6. Times in seconds to obtain the best integer solution for the different node selection methods

Problem	Bestp	BFS	DFS	GP1	GP2	GP3
bell3a	0.02	0.02	0.02	0.02	0.04	0.02
bell5	16.37	564.76	751.50	474.50	486.21	A
blend2	12.79	54.00	924.93	24.50	49.49	27.90
khb05250	0.68	11.77	5.18	16.57	15.94	31.04
l152lav	8.46	41.10	8.46	8.23	9.35	82.32
lseu	0.90	5.47	8.17	50.31	50.54	8.57
misc07	7.05	0.52	3.45	1.99	1.62	3.61
mod008	0.76	8.07	65.78	3.03	3.09	3.04
qnet1	29.85	130.85	600.06	52.19	245.11	743.85
qnet1$_o$	10.81	68.37	16.37	110.27	496.03	50.32
rentacar	18.48	190.58	82.76	22.44	23.09	37.66
stein45	5.89	0.77	12.41	1.26	1.12	1.51
Time avg	**9.34**	**89.69**	**206.59**	**63.77**	**115.13**	**182.49**
Ranking avg	**2.00**	**3.64**	**4.36**	**3.00**	**4.00**	**4.64**

a MIP solution is found, being able to compete head to head with the Best Projection method. GP2, having no such 'boost', performs average. GP3, employing a simplistic design for the training method, portrays mediocre performance.

Finally, it deserves to be mentioned that if the execution times depicted in Tables 5 and 6 were normalized by deducting the runtime overhead introduced by Genetic Programming in cases GP1-GP3[6], the obtained results would be more in favor of the GP-enhanced solver. For the purposes of our study, such normalization was not deemed necessary.

7   Conclusions and Further Research

We used GP as a component in a hybrid MIP Branch and Bound framework, where GP is utilized for generating the node selection method. Although no special GP structures or techniques (i.e. ADFs) were employed, and despite the application of an untested approach for creating problem-specific training sets, GP was able to extract information from the solution space traversed, coming up with effective node selection expressions.

We believe that the experimental results, obtained by our prototype implementation, show that the hybrid B&B-GP architecture we introduce portrays significant potential. Our future research efforts will be directed in two fronts: The first one will be to incorporate multiple GP Stages in our design, as well as to experiment with more elaborate GP structures and techniques. The second one will be to try to increase our understanding of how the training method adopted in the GP Stage affects the search in B&B Stage2, regarding different classes of MIP problems.

Acknowledgments. We would like to thank George Zioutas for the motivating discussions and his aid in MIP bibliography during the early stages of this research. Also, we would like to thank Panagiotis Kanellis and Leonidas Pitsoulis for their suggestions and comments.

References

1. Mitchell, J., Lee, E.K.: Branch-and-bound methods for integer programming. In Floudas, C.A., Pardalos, P.M., eds.: Encyclopedia of Optimization, Kluwer Academic Publishers (2001)
2. Bixby, R., Fenelon, M., Gu, Z., Rothberg, E., Wunderling, R.: MIP: Theory and practice – closing the gap. In: System Modelling and Optimization: Methods, Theory, and Applications. Volume 174 of IFIP INTERNATIONAL FEDERATION FOR INFORMATION PROCESSING. Kluwer Academic Publishers, Boston (2000) 19–49
3. Koza, J.R.: Genetic Programming: On the Programming of Computers by Means of Natural Selection. MIT Press, Cambridge, MA, USA (1992)
4. Land, A.H., Doig, A.G.: An automatic method for solving discrete programming problems. Econometrica **28** (1960) 497–520

---

[6] The runtime overhead introduced is about one second on average for the GP stage, plus minor overheads resulting from data collection operations in B&B Stage1 and the continuous evaluation of the usually complex node selection expression evolved in B&B Stage2.

5. Linderoth, J., Savelsbergh, M.: A computational study of search strategies for mixed integer programming. INFORMS Journal on Computing **11** (1999) 173 – 187

6. Banzhaf, W., Nordin, P., Keller, R.E., Francone, F.D.: Genetic Programming – An Introduction; On the Automatic Evolution of Computer Programs and its Applications. Morgan Kaufmann, dpunkt.verlag (1998)

7. Blum, C., Roli, A.: Metaheuristics in combinatorial optimization: Overview and conceptual comparison. ACM Computing Surveys **35** (2003) 268–308

8. Abramson, D., Randall, M.: A simulated annealing code for general integer linear programs. Annals of Operations Research **86** (1999) 3–24

9. Randall, M., Abramson, D.: A general metaheuristic based solver for combinatorial optimisation problems. Kluwer Journal on Computational Optimization and Applications **20** (2001)

10. Nieminen, K., Ruuth, S.: Genetic algorithm for finding a good first integer solution for milp. Technical report, Department of Computing, Imperial College, London (2003)

11. Mitra, G.: Investigation of some branch and bound strategies for the solution of mixed integer linear programs. Mathematical Programming **4** (1973) 155–173

12. CPLEX: (www.ilog.com/products/cplex)

13. Numerical Algorithms Group Limited and Brunel University: FortMP Manual. 3 edn. (1999)

14. GLPK: (www.gnu.org/software/glpk)

15. Zongker, D., Punch, B.: lilgp 1.01 user's manual. Technical report, Michigan State University, USA (1996)

16. Luke, S.: (Strongly typed lilgp, www.cs.umd.edu/users/seanl/gp/patched-gp/)

17. Bixby, R.E., Ceria, S., McZeal, C.M., Savelsbergh, M.W.P.: An updated mixed integer programming library: MIPLIB 3.0. Optima **58** (1998) 12–15

Efficient Crossover in the GAuGE System

Miguel Nicolau and Conor Ryan

Biocomputing and Developmental Systems Group
Computer Science and Information Systems Department
University of Limerick, Ireland
{Miguel.Nicolau,Conor.Ryan}@ul.ie

Abstract. This paper presents a series of context-preserving crossover operators for the GAuGE system. These operators have been designed to respect the representation of genotype strings in GAuGE, thereby making sensible changes at the genotypic level. Results on a set of problems suggest that some of these operators can improve the maintenance and propagation of building blocks in GAuGE, as well as its scalability, and could be of use to other systems using structural evolving genomes.

1 Introduction

The GAuGE system (Genetic Algorithms using Grammatical Evolution) [12,9] is a recently introduced position-independent genetic algorithm which, through a mapping process, maps a fixed length genotype string onto a fixed-length phenotype string, ensuring no under- or over-specification in the process. By encoding both the position and value of each phenotypic variable on genotype strings, GAuGE has the ability to structure these, to prioritise information, and to group together partial solutions, to minimise the chances of disrupting them.

Until now, a simple genetic algorithm has been used to generate binary strings that, through a mapping process, are interpreted as GAuGE strings, which in turn specify phenotype strings. A side effect of this is the *ripple effect*, by which a change of context for information exchanged between two individuals can lead to severe changes of its interpretation, at the phenotype level.

In this work, a set of crossover operators is presented, which are adapted to the GAuGE representation. These are context-preserving operators; by applying these, the context of information exchanged is the same, and therefore that information will keep its initial meaning. Experiments conducted suggest that, on the problems analysed, some of these operators scale better to problem difficulty, and are better able to discover, maintain and exchange partial solutions. These operators can therefore not only improve the performance of the GAuGE system, but also of other position-independent systems evolving the structure of genomes.

This paper is organised as follows. Section 2 introduces the GAuGE system, and its relation to Grammatical Evolution, and includes a review of previous work and an example of the mapping process employed. Section 3 introduces the newly designed crossover operators. Section 4 describes the experiments conducted and the results obtained, while Section 5 draws conclusions based on those results, and some lines of future research.

M. Keijzer et al. (Eds.): EuroGP 2004, LNCS 3003, pp. 125–137, 2004.

2   GAuGE

The GAuGE system uses many of the biologically inspired features present in Grammatical Evolution (GE) [11], the main ones being a *genotype to phenotype mapping* (GPM), *functional dependency* between genes, and *degenerate code*.

In GE, a GPM process is used to map variable-length binary strings onto syntactically-correct programs, through the use of a grammar. Each binary string is mapped onto an integer string, through a transcription process, and then, through a translation process, those integers are used to choose productions from the grammar, to create a program (phenotype). This process, based on the analogous process in molecular biology, provides a division between the search space (binary strings) and the solution space (evolved programs) [2].

In GAuGE, a similar process is employed. A population of (fixed length) binary strings is created in the genotypic space, and each of these is also transcribed onto an integer string. This integer string is then interpreted as a sequence of (*position, value*) specifications that, through a mapping process, generate a fixed-length phenotype string, which is neither under nor over-specified.

In GE, the function of a gene can affect the function of the genes that follow it. Indeed, the rule from which a gene is used to choose a production depends on the mapping process up to that point; this means that if the functionality of a gene changes, the functionality of subsequent genes is likely to change as well.

This feature, called functional dependency, is present in GAuGE as well. Each position specification across a genotype string is dependent on previous specifications, in order to create a fully specified phenotype string.

Finally, the use of degenerate code plays an important role in GE: by using the *mod* operator to map an integer to a choice of productions from a grammar rule, neutral mutations can take place [7], creating a many-to-one mapping between the search and solution spaces, and introducing variety at the genotypic level.

In GAuGE, this feature is also present, as a direct result of the mapping process employed. It has also been shown that the explicit introduction of degeneracy can reduce structural bias at the genotypic level [9].

2.1   Previous Work

Previous work has used similar techniques as the ones employed in GAuGE. Some of Bagley's [1] simulations used an extended representation to encode both the position and the value of each allele. Some reordering operators were also designed [10], which combine inversion and crossover operators on extended representations. Later on, the so-called messy genetic algorithms [5] applied the principle of separating the *gene* and *locus* specifications with considerable success, and have since been followed by many competent GAs.

The Random Keys Genetic Algorithm [3] introduced a mapping process that ensures an error-free and fully specified sequence of ordinal numbers. More recently, Harik [6] applied the principles of functional dependency in the Linkage Learning Genetic Algorithm, in which the functionality of a gene is dependent on a chosen interpretation point, and the genes between that point and itself.

2.2 GAuGE Mapping

A full description and analysis of the mapping process in GAuGE has already been given elsewhere [9], including the description of a context-sensitive grammar which implements that process [13]. As a simple example, consider the case where one would wish to solve a four-variable problem ($l = 4$). The first step is to create a genotype population G, of N individuals. The length of each individual depends on the chosen values for the variables pfs (position field size) and vfs (value field size). The minimum value for pfs for this problem would be 2 bits, as that is the minimum number of bits required to encode 4 positions, whereas the minimum value for vfs depends on the range of the problem's variables: for a binary problem, 1 bit is sufficient.

Suppose the range of the variables is $0 \ldots 7$, and four bits are used to encode the value specifications ($vfs = 4$) (to introduce degeneracy, as three bits would be sufficient), and two bits are used to encode each position specification ($pfs = 2$). The length of each element G_i of the genotypic space G will then be a binary string of 24 bits ($l * (pfs + vfs)$).

Let us use the following individual as an example for the mapping process:

$$G_i = 011100111000111001100010$$

The mapping process then proceeds in creating a phenotype string P_i. The first mapping step consists in creating an integer string, using the pfs and vfs values:

$$X_i = \left((X_i^j, \tilde{X}_i^j) \right)_{0 \leq j \leq l-1} = \left((1,12), (3,8), (3,9), (2,2) \right)$$

This string is then evaluated as a sequence of four (*position, value*) specification pairs. From this string, a *positions string* R_i and a *values string* $\tilde{R}_i$ can be created, which contain the *real* position and value specifications.

These are created as follows. We start by taking the first position specified, 1, and map it to the number of available positions in the phenotype string (i.e., 4), by using the *mod* operator: $1 \ mod \ 4 = 1$ (i.e. the second position on the phenotype string). We use a similar process to map the value specified, 12, to the *range* specified earlier, giving the *real* value specification $12 \ mod \ 8 = 5$:

$$R_i = (1,?,?,?) \qquad \tilde{R}_i = (5,?,?,?) \qquad P_i = (?,5,?,?)$$

We then take the second pair, $(3,8)$, and perform a similar mapping. As there are now only three positions remaining in the phenotype string, the position field is calculated by $3 \ mod \ 3 = 0$, that is, the first **available** position of that string; the value specification is calculated as before ($8 \ mod \ 8 = 0$), giving:

$$R_i = (1,0,?,?) \qquad \tilde{R}_i = (5,0,?,?) \qquad P_i = (0,5,?,?)$$

The third pair, $(3,9)$, is then processed in the same fashion. Its position specification is calculated by $3 \ mod \ 2 = 1$, that is, the second available position in the phenotype string. Since both positions 0 and 1 have already been taken, the second available position in the phenotype string is now position 3 (that is, the last position of that string). The value is calculated as before:

$$R_i = (1, 0, 3, ?) \qquad \tilde{R}_i = (5, 0, 1, ?) \qquad P_i = (0, 5, ?, 1)$$

Finally, the fourth pair is handled in the same fashion, giving the final *real* specification strings and corresponding phenotype string:

$$R_i = (1, 0, 3, 2) \qquad \tilde{R}_i = (5, 0, 1, 2) \qquad P_i = (0, 5, 2, 1)$$

So the phenotype string, $(0, 5, 2, 1)$, is ready for evaluation. Note the clear functional dependency between the position specifications, and the many-to-one mapping existing *both* in the position specifications and the value specifications.

3 Crossover Operators

Until now, GAuGE has been used as a mapping process, so any search engine can generate the genotypic binary strings. In this work, the advantages of adapting the search operators to the structure of a GAuGE string are explored; to this end, a series of context-preserving crossover operators has been created.

The reason behind the design of these operators is that the functional dependency feature, shown to exist across the position specifications [9], can result in a change of context for certain specified values. This has been shown to be a valid search technique for binary and combinatorial problems [12], but poses certain restrictions for problems where building block maintenance and exchange are critical to finding an optimal solution. By possibly changing the original position associated with a value, interesting sub-solutions found may be lost through the evolutionary search process, and the case may arise where crossover between two individuals, specifying the same value for a given position, may generate two offspring that do not specify the same value for that given position.

The approach taken in this work is to adapt the search algorithm that generates the binary strings to the structure of each individual, by choosing appropriate crossover points between two individuals, or appropriate sections to be swapped. These "context preserving" operators should be able to maintain and exchange partial solutions found during the evolutionary process, thus increasing the parallel exploration and exploitation of those building blocks.

3.1 Standard Crossover

This is the standard crossover operator, used with GAuGE in all experiments up to now. It is a one-point crossover, operating at the genotype level, but with crossover points limited to pair boundaries; that means that there are $l - 1$ possible crossover points between each individual (every $pfs + vfs$ bits).

For example, take the following two individuals, already expressed as a X_i string[1], randomly generated using a problem size of $l = 8$:

X_1=((0,a),(1,b),(3,c),(7,d),(7,e),(0,f),(3,g),(5,h))
X_2=((0,s),(4,t),(1,u),(5,v),(0,w),(2,x),(2,y),(4,z))

---

[1] With values $a \dots h$ for the first individual, and $s \dots z$ for the second individual.

These are the two corresponding *real* specifications strings for these individuals:

R_1=((0,a),(2,b),(5,c),(4,d),(7,e),(1,f),(6,g),(3,h))
R_2=((0,s),(5,t),(2,u),(1,v),(3,w),(7,x),(4,y),(6,z))

A crossover point is then chosen for these two individuals. If the chosen point is after the fourth pair, then the two offspring generated by that operation are:

X_3=((0,a),(1,b),(3,c),(7,d),(0,w),(2,x),(2,y),(4,z))
X_4=((0,s),(4,t),(1,u),(5,v),(7,e),(0,f),(3,g),(5,h))

These generate the following *real* specifications:

R_3=((0,a),(2,b),(5,c),(4,d),(1,w),(7,x),(3,y),(6,z))
R_4=((0,s),(5,t),(2,u),(1,v),(7,e),(3,f),(6,g),(4,h))

As can be seen, each child keeps the information from the first half of one parent, and uses the second half of the other parent to fill in the remaining unspecified positions. This has the side effect that the values specified in the second half of each parent do not necessarily stay in their original positions. In the example, the first parent specified that values (e,f,g,h) should be located at positions (7,0,3,5), respectively, which correspond to the *real* positions R_1=(...,7,1,6,3). However, when those specifications are interpreted within the context of the second child, the *desired* positions (7,0,3,5) are kept, but these now correspond to the *real* positions R_4=(...,7,3,6,4), as the *real* position 1 was already specified in that child's left side, creating a chain of changes.

This change (or adaptation) of the second half specifications to the new context upon which they are now interpreted is known as the *ripple effect* [11]. Although the way those specifications are interpreted can be quite different when in a new context, it is not random; indeed, the ordering relationship between those specifications is kept. In the example provided, this means that since the values (e,f,g,h) appeared in the order (g,h,f,e) in the phenotype string, then this ordering will be kept in the second child's phenotype.

3.2   Homologous Crossover

In the standard crossover, the degree of the ripple effect of changes occurring when a set of specifications is interpreted in a new context depends on how different that new context is. Furthermore, if the new context is equivalent (i.e., the same positions have been specified up to that point), then there is no ripple effect of changes, and all *desired* positions will encode the same *real* positions.

Based on this concept, the *homologous crossover* was designed to restrict the choice of crossover points to those points that share the same context (called *regions of similarity* [13]). For example, taking the previous two example parents, there is a region of similarity after the first pair, as both individuals have encoded the *real* position 0. This means that, if this crossover point were chosen, there would be no change of context for the second halves from the parents, and therefore all position and value associations would be kept.

These two individuals also share a second region of similarity, after their third pair, as both have encoded positions 0, 2 and 5 (although not in the same order). The homologous crossover will then pick one of these two similarity regions at random, and perform its crossover after the selected region. Considering the region up to the third pair were chosen, the resulting offspring would be:

X_3=((0,a),(1,b),(3,c),(5,v),(0,w),(2,x),(2,y),(4,z))
X_4=((0,s),(4,t),(1,u),(7,d),(7,e),(0,f),(3,g),(5,h))

These generate the following *real* specifications:

R_3=((0,a),(2,b),(5,c),(1,v),(3,w),(7,x),(4,y),(6,z))
R_4=((0,s),(5,t),(2,u),(4,d),(7,e),(1,f),(6,g),(3,h))

We can see that no change of context occurred, and therefore the second halves received from each parent keep their original (*position,value*) associations. Should there be no regions of similarity between the two parents, then the standard crossover operator is applied.

3.3 Pascal Crossover

This crossover was designed to deal more effectively with the uneven distribution of regions of similarity between individuals, which occurs due to the mapping process employed in GAuGE. Indeed, the higher the value of l, the more uneven the distribution of those regions, as a region of similarity is simply a combination of position specifications, regardless of their order. Taking $l = 8$, for example, the number of possible different contexts after each pair are:

$pair1 : \binom{8}{1} = 8$ $pair2 : \binom{8}{2} = 28$ $pair3 : \binom{8}{3} = 56$ $pair4 : \binom{8}{4} = 70$
$pair5 : \binom{8}{5} = 56$ $pair6 : \binom{8}{6} = 28$ $pair7 : \binom{8}{7} = 8$

These elements are quite easy to calculate using Pascal's Triangle, hence the name given to this operator. It works as follows: once one or more regions of similarity have been found, each is given a weight, according to their position; regions closer to the center of the genotype strings have a higher weight, as there are more possible different contexts in this area, and therefore fewer regions of similarity. A crossover point is then chosen, through a roulette-wheel choice between the detected regions. Taking the previous example, the first region of similarity will have the weight 8, and the second the weight 56. This means that the first pair has a $8/(8 + 56) = 8/64$ probability of being the chosen crossover point, whereas the third pair has a $56/64$ probability.

The idea behind this weighting is that, by preferring crossover points closer to the center, a more effective search for different structures is performed.

3.4 Structural Crossover

The main theory behind the way individuals are constructed in both GE [11] and GAuGE [13] is that, because of their functional dependency, individuals are firstly defined on their left side, and slowly extend their definition to the whole genome. For that reason, the *structural crossover* was designed to give more importance to the left side of each individual, to the detriment of its right side.

This crossover works as follows: the structure of each parent is kept, that is, each offspring keeps the position specifications of each parent, but after a randomly chosen crossover point, the values specified are replaced by the corresponding values from the other parent. Taking the previous example, if the crossover point is after pair 4, then the generated offspring are as follows:

X_3=((0,a),(1,b),(3,c),(7,d),(7,x),(0,v),(3,z),(5,w))
X_4=((0,s),(4,t),(1,u),(5,v),(0,c),(2,e),(2,d),(4,g))

These generate the following *real* specifications:

R_3=((0,a),(2,b),(5,c),(4,d),(7,x),(1,v),(6,z),(3,w))
R_4=((0,s),(5,t),(2,u),(1,v),(3,c),(7,e),(4,d),(6,g))

As can be seen, the structure of the corresponding parents is kept, and data is taken from the second parent to replace the values associated with the positions specified after the crossover point. For example, the value v, defined in the second parent to be in the *real* position 1, is now defined in the first child's 6th pair, (0,v), as this is the pair that maps to the *real* position 1 in this individual.

It can also be seen that some data occurring in the left side of the parents has been duplicated (the values c, d and v), whereas some of the data from their right side has been dropped (the values f, h and y).

3.5   Pure Crossover

This operator is the equivalent of a simple one-point crossover in a normal GA. It works as follows. The first offspring receives the first half of the first parent (up to a randomly chosen crossover point), and all positions after that point receive the values associated with those same positions from the second parent (as in structural crossover). The second offspring keeps the structure of the second parent, but receives from the first parent the values corresponding to the positions specified in the second half of that parent. Taking the previous example, if the crossover point is after pair 4, then the generated offspring are:

X_3=((0,a),(1,b),(3,c),(7,d),(7,x),(0,v),(3,z),(5,w))
X_4=((0,s),(4,t),(1,u),(5,f),(0,h),(2,e),(2,y),(4,g))

These generate the following *real* specifications:

R_3=((0,a),(2,b),(5,c),(4,d),(7,x),(1,v),(6,z),(3,w))
R_4=((0,s),(5,t),(2,u),(1,f),(3,h),(7,e),(4,y),(6,g))

As can be seen, the *real* positions (1,3,7,6), in the 4th, 5th, 6th and 8th pairs of the second offspring, receive the corresponding values (f,h,e,g) from the first parent, as these are the *real* positions specified in the second half of that parent.

Like structural crossover, in this operator both offspring retain the structure of both parents, but unlike that operator, all information specified is kept, that is, no data is dropped or duplicated.

4   Experiments and Results

In this work, we examined three problems. For each of these, a simple GA was compared to GAuGE, using each of the five crossover operators. The settings across all algorithms were: population size of 800 individuals, 100 generations[2], roulette-wheel selection, steady-state replacement, probability of crossover of .9, and probability of point mutation of .01. No degeneracy was used, so pfs and vfs values were set to the minimum values required by each problem.

4.1   Onemax

This is a standard problem in GA literature. It is defined by the formula:

$$f(x) = \sum_{i=0}^{l-1} x_i \qquad x_i \in \{0, 1\}$$

where l is the phenotype length, and x_i the allele at position i within that string (with positions ranging from 0 to $l-1$). The best individual is a binary string composed of all 1s, and the fitness contribution of each variable is the same.

This is a problem typically used to test the ability of a system to exchange partial solutions, and illustrates the parallel search of building blocks (of size 1) within in each individual (exploration), and their exchange between individuals (exploitation). It was used in this comparison to check if the GAuGE mapping process impairs its performance on problems where the simple GA excels.

Results. This experiment was conducted to test the scalability of the algorithms; to that end, problem lengths of 128, 256 and 512 were chosen. The graph in Fig. 1 shows the results for $l = 256$, and plots the mean best fitness per generation, averaged over 100 random runs, with error bars showing the standard deviation. It shows that both GAuGE systems using the structural and pure crossovers find an optimal solution faster, whereas all the other approaches show a similar behaviour, regardless of their operators. The non-overlapping standard deviation error bars for those two operators with all other systems, from generation 15 all the way to generation 80, show the statistical significance of these results.

The results obtained (not reported) with the other lengths show that, with smaller values of l, all systems have a similar performance, but as the length of strings increases, both the structural and especially the pure crossover seem to scale better to the problem (with length 512, the pure crossover is significantly better than all other systems, including the structural crossover).

---

[2] Except for the n-block problem, where 400 generations were used.

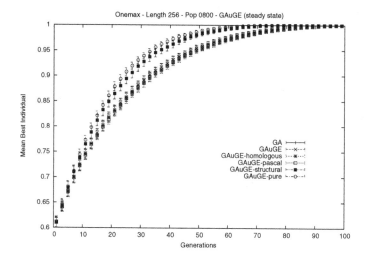

Fig. 1. Results obtained for the Onemax problem. The *x-axis* shows the generation number, and the *y-axis* the mean best individual (from 100 independent runs). The vertical error bars plot the standard deviation for all runs, for each system.

4.2   BinInt

The BinInt problem is an exponentially scaled problem, defined by the formula:

$$f(x) = \sum_{i=0}^{l-1} x_i 2^{l-i-1} \qquad x_i \in \{0,1\}$$

This problem transforms a binary string into its integer equivalent, and uses that value as a fitness reward; the best individual is a string composed of all 1s.

In this problem, the fitness contribution of each allele is higher than the combined fitness of all the following alleles (e.g., $f(0111) = 7$ but $f(1000) = 8$); this means that the salience of each allele decreases from left to right within the phenotype string. It was used in this comparison to test if the structural flexibility of the GAuGE system enhances its performance in this class of problems.

Results. Fig. 2 shows the results for the BinInt problem, using a phenotype length of 64 bits. Error bars for standard deviation could not be plotted, as the *y-axis* is a logarithmic scale; figure analysis however showed that there is no significant difference in the performance of all systems, which is partly due to the high standard deviation in the simple GA results for the 100 runs.

The salience adaptation that occurs as a result of the functional dependency across the position specifications, which has been shown to guide the standard GAuGE approach to finding a suitable representation [8], explains the fact that there is no significant difference in performance between the original GAuGE approach and the GAuGE systems using both the structural and pure crossovers.

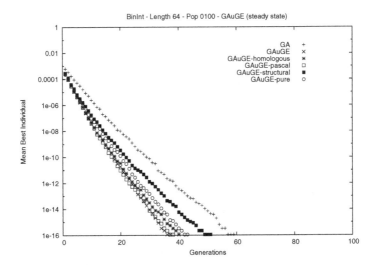

Fig. 2. Results obtained for the BinInt problem. The *x-axis* shows the generation number, and the *y-axis* shows the mean best individual (from 100 independent runs), on a logarithmic scale (lower is better; value plotted is $1 - fitness$).

4.3 n-Block

This is a new problem, designed to test the ability of a system to find, maintain and propagate building blocks. These are deliberately hard to find, making this problem good for testing both the exploration and exploitation of knowledge.

The problem is based on two variables: l, the length of the phenotype strings, and n, the size of each building block, where l is divisible by n. The optimal solution is a string composed of l/n intertwined building blocks, with the first being composed of all 0s, the second of all 1s, the third of all 2s, and so on. The fitness of each building block is $1/(l/n)$ if it is correct, and 0 otherwise.

For example, with $l = 8$ and $n = 2$, the optimal solution is 01230123, whereas with $l = 12$ and $n = 4$, the optimal solution is 012012012012. For this last example, the string 012112012011 would receive a fitness score of $1/(12/4) = 1/3$, has there is only one fully specified building-block (∗1∗∗1∗∗1∗).

Results. For this problem, a block size of $n = 2$ was used, with a phenotype string size of $l = 32$. Fig. 3 shows the results for this experiment; again error bars plot the standard deviation of all results. These show the pure crossover outperforming most other approaches, with a non-overlapping standard deviation compared to all systems except the structural crossover for most generations.

An analysis of the results obtained shows the difficulty of the problem, with most systems showing a large standard deviation across the 100 independent runs. It also shows that the ripple effect of the standard crossover from GAuGE

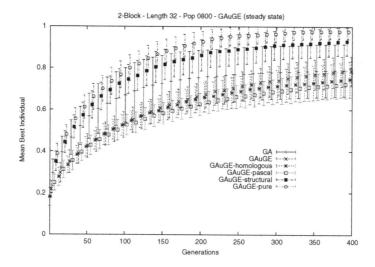

Fig. 3. Results obtained for the n-Block problem, with $n = 2$ and $l = 32$. The x-axis shows the generation number, and the y-axis the mean best individual (from 100 independent runs); error bars plot the standard deviation for each system. The top two plots belong to the systems using the pure and structural crossover, respectively.

impairs its performance in this problem, where it is important to keep previous information, but no saliency exists to guide the structuring of individuals.

Although the pure crossover's error bars are non-overlapping with the simple GA only from generation 220 onward, this is explained by the high variance in the simple GA's results, which shows its dependency in the initial population.

5   Conclusions and Future Work

This paper has introduced a new set of crossover operators, adapted to the way in which GAuGE strings are represented. By keeping the context in which exchanged information is interpreted, some of these operators have been shown to improve the scaling and exchange of partial solutions, in the problems tested. These findings should be useful not only for the further development of the GAuGE system, but for other systems using structure evolving genomes as well.

The homologous and pascal crossovers did not perform better than the standard crossover. An analysis of their behaviour suggests this is due to the exponential number of ways to structure a GAuGE string. On problems with l large, the performance of these crossovers dropped when using smaller populations, as there is less variety in the population. With fewer regions of similarity, the standard crossover is applied quite often, while these operators are applied almost exclusively at the ends of the genotype strings. As the evolutionary process moves on, the standard crossover causes the representations of all genotype strings to converge, leading to the homologous and pascal crossovers being applied on converged sections of these strings, thereby exchanging the same information. The priorities used in the pascal crossover did not seem to improve on this.

The structural and pure crossovers showed a substantial increase in performance on these problems, when compared to the other approaches. The somewhat disappointing performance of the structural crossover can be partially explained by the lack of a context-preserving restructuring operator. This means that prioritising the left side of individuals is of no advantage to the system.

Across all problems, a high standard deviation has been observed for the simple GA, typically double that of the GAuGE systems. This seems to suggest that these are less affected by the random initialisation of the first generation, which in turn suggests more reliability for the GAuGE results.

Future work will see the introduction of context-preserving restructuring operators [4], which should further improve the performance of both the structural and pure crossovers. With these context-preserving operators, the selection pressure can also be lowered, as there is no need to filter the negative results of the ripple effect, so elitist approaches will be considered.

References

1. Bagley, J. D.: The behaviour of adaptive systems which employ genetic and correlation algorithms. Doctoral Dissertation, University of Michigan (1967)
2. Banzhaf, W.: Genotype-Phenotype-Mapping and Neutral Variation - A case study in Genetic Programming. In: Davidor et al., (eds.): Proceedings of the third conference on Parallel Problem Solving from Nature. Lecture Notes in Computer Science, Vol. 866. Springer-Verlag. (1994) 322-332
3. Bean, J.: Genetic Algorithms and Random Keys for Sequencing and Optimization. ORSA Journal on Computing, Vol. 6, No. 2. (1994) 154-160
4. Chen, Y. and Goldberg, D. E.: An Analysis of a Reordering Operator with Tournament Selection on a GA-Hard Problem. In: Cantu-Paz et al., (eds.): Genetic and Evolutionary Computation - GECCO 2003. Springer. (July 2003) 825-836
5. Goldberg, D. E., Korb, B., and Deb, K.: Messy genetic algorithms: Motivation, analysis, and first results. Complex Systems, Vol. 3. (1989) 493-530
6. Harik, G.: Learning Gene Linkage to Efficiently Solve Problems of Bounded Difficulty Using Genetic Algorithms. Doctoral Dissertation, University of Illinois (1997)
7. Kimura, M.: The Neutral Theory of Molecular Evolution. Cambridge University Press. (1983)
8. Nicolau, M., and Ryan, C.: How Functional Dependency Adapts to Salience Hierarchy in the GAuGE System. In: Ryan et al, (eds.): Proceedings of EuroGP-2003. Lecture Notes in Computer Science, Vol. 2610. Springer-Verlag. (2003) 153-163
9. Nicolau, M., Auger, A., and Ryan, C.: Functional Dependency and Degeneracy: Detailed Analysis of the GAuGE System. In: Liardet et al, (eds.): Proceedings of Évolution Artificielle 2003. Lecture Notes in Computer Science (to be published). Springer-Verlag. (2003)
10. Oliver, I. M., Smith, D. J., and Holland, J. R. C.: A Study of Permutation Crossover Operators on the Traveling Salesman Problem. In: Proceedings of the Second International Conference on Genetic Algorithms. (1987) 224-230

11. O'Neill, M. and Ryan, C.: Grammatical Evolution - Evolving programs in an arbitrary language. Kluwer Academic Publishers. (2003)
12. Ryan, C., Nicolau, M., and O'Neill, M.: Genetic Algorithms using Grammatical Evolution. In: Foster et al, (eds.): Proceedings of EuroGP-2002. Lecture Notes in Computer Science, Vol. 2278. Springer-Verlag. (2002) 278-287
13. Ryan, C., and Nicolau, M.: Doing Genetic Algorithms the Genetic Programming Way. In: Riolo, R., and Worzel, B. (eds.): Genetic Programming Theory and Practice. Kluwer Publishers, Boston, MA. (2003)

Grammatical Evolution by Grammatical Evolution: The Evolution of Grammar and Genetic Code

Michael O'Neill and Conor Ryan

Biocomputing and Developmental Systems
Dept. Of Computer Science & Information Systems
University of Limerick, Ireland.
{Michael.ONeill,Conor.Ryan}@ul.ie

Abstract. This study examines the possibility of evolving the grammar that Grammatical Evolution uses to specify the construction of a syntactically correct solution. As the grammar dictates the space of symbols that can be used in a solution, its evolution represents the evolution of the genetic code itself. Results provide evidence to show that the co-evolution of grammar and genetic code with a solution using grammatical evolution is a viable approach.

1 Introduction

This paper details an investigation examining the possibility of evolving the grammar that Grammatical Evolution (GE) [1,2,3,4] uses to specify the construction of a syntactically correct solution. By evolving the grammar that GE uses to specify a solution, one can effectively permit the evolution of the genetic code. The ability to evolve genetic code is important when one has little or no information about the problem being solved, or the environment in which a population exists is dynamic in nature and adaptiveness is essential for survival.

Evolutionary automatic programming methods have, to date, largely focused on problem domains that are static in nature, and while this is perfectly adequate for many, there are a significant number of real world problems that have a dynamic component (e.g. scheduling, robot control, prediction, trading. etc.) and require a more adaptive or open-ended representation that can facilitate progression to different environments.

This paper is concerned with the co-evolution of the *genetic code* along with the very individuals that use the code to guide their mapping. The genetic code typically specifies the symbols that are available for incorporation into a solution and can be used to dynamically incorporate bias towards important symbols at different points in time, and this is the mechanism under investigation in this study. In addition, when the genetic code is represented as a grammar, it can also be used to determine how structures may be legally constructed, and any modification of the code modifies the space in which a particular individual searches. Thus, in theory, co-evolution of the grammar and genetic code could

M. Keijzer et al. (Eds.): EuroGP 2004, LNCS 3003, pp. 138–149, 2004.

be used to dynamically reduce the search space, or even bias individuals towards different regions of the search space.

There have been two previous studies on the evolution of genetic code in the genetic programming literature using the developmental GP representation [6,7]. These studies provide strong evidence demonstrating the effective co-evolution of genetic code and solution. The experiments reported here serve a similar objective, that is, to determine if co-evolution of genetic code (or grammar) and solution is possible using grammatical evolution. The distinguishing feature of this study is that the genetic code is represented by a grammar, and a mechanism to evolve the grammar is presented. Discussions on genetic codes, genetic code evolution and its implications are presented for biology [8,9,10] and for evolutionary computation [11,12].

The remainder of the paper is structured as follows. Section 2 describes the grammatical approach to grammar evolution, section 3 details the experimental approach adopted and results. Section 4 provides some discussion on the results and comparisons to the evolution of genetic code with the developmental GP approach, and finally section 5 details conclusions and examples of future work that is now possible given the success of this study.

2   Grammatical Evolution by Grammatical Evolution

When we have a set of production rules for a non-terminal, such as, for example, `<op>::= + | -`, a codon is used to select the rule to be applied in the development of sentences in the language specified by the grammar. In a similar manner to a biological genetic code, the productions above represent a degenerate genetic code by which a codon is mapped to a symbol in the output language [1].

In biology, a codon (on mRNA), which is comprised of a group of three nucleotides from the set $\{A, U, G, C\}$, is mapped to an amino acid from the set of 20 naturally occurring amino acids. In nature, the code is encoded in transfer RNA (tRNA) molecules, which have a domino like structure, in that one end matches (with a certain affinity dubbed the *wobble hypothesis*) to a codon, while the amino acid corresponding to this codon is bound to the other end of the tRNA molecule [8]. In this sense, the above productions are equivalent to two such tRNA molecules, one matching a set of codons to + while the other matches a different set of codons to −. By modifying the grammar, we are changing the types of tRNA molecules in our system, or to it put another way, we are directly modifying the genetic code by changing the mapping of codon values to different rules (amino acids).

In order to allow evolution of a grammar, grammatical evolution by grammatical evolution $(GE)^2$, we must provide a grammar to specify the form a grammar can take. This is an example of the richness of the expressiveness of grammars that makes the GE approach so powerful. See [13,1] for further examples of what can be achieved with grammars. By allowing an evolutionary algorithm to adapt its representation (in this case through the evolution of the genetic code or grammar) it provides the population with a mechanism to survive in dynamic environments, in particular, and also to automatically incorporate biases into the search process.

In this approach we therefore have two distinct grammars, the *universal grammar* (or grammars' grammar) and the *solution grammar*. The notion of a universal grammar is adopted from linguistics and refers to a universal set of syntactic rules that hold for spoken languages [14]. It has been proposed that during a child's development the universal grammar undergoes modifications through learning that allows the development of communication in their parents native language(s) [15].

In $(GE)^2$, the universal grammar dictates the construction of the solution grammar. Given below are examples of these grammars for solutions that generate expressions, which could be used for symbolic regression type problems.

Universal Grammar (Grammars' Grammar)

```
<g> ::=
      ''<expr> ::= <op> <expr> <expr> | <var>''
      ''<op> ::='' <ops>
      ''<var> ::='' <vars>

<ops> ::= <opt> ''|'' <ops>
      | <opt>

<opt> ::= + | - | * | /

<vars> ::= <vart> ''|'' <vars>
      | <vart>

<vart> ::= m | v | q | a
```

Solution Grammar

```
<expr> ::= <op> <expr> <expr>
      | <var>

<op> ::= ?

<var> ::= ?
```

In the example universal grammar, a grammar, <g>, is specified such that it is possible for the non-terminals <var> and <op> to have one or more rules, with the potential for rule duplication. These are the rules that will be made available to an individual during mapping, and this effectively allows bias for symbols to be subjected to the processes of evolution. The productions <vars> and <ops> in the universal grammar are strictly non-terminals, and do not appear in the solution grammar. Instead they are interim values used when producing the solution grammar for an individual.

The hard-coded aspect of the solution grammar can be seen in the example above with the rules for <op> and <var> as yet unspecified. In this case we have restricted evolution to occur only on the number of productions for <var> and <op>, although it would be possible to evolve the rules for <expr> and even for the entire grammar itself. It is this ability that sets this form of genetic code/grammar evolution apart from previous studies in genetic programming. Notice that each individual has its own solution grammar.

In this study two separate, variable-length, genotypic binary chromosomes were used, the first chromosome to generate the solution grammar from the universal grammar and the second chromosome the solution itself. Crossover operates between homologous chromosomes, that is, the solution grammar chromosome from the first parent recombines with the solution grammar chromosome from the second parent, with the same occurring for the solution chromosomes. In order for evolution to be successful it must co-evolve both the genetic code and the structure of solutions based on the evolved genetic code.

3   Experiments and Results

In this section a number of proof of concept problems are tackled to illustrate the use of grammar and genetic code evolution in $(GE)^2$. For the experiments that follow 100 independent runs are conducted in each case.

The objective of this study is to determine if grammar and code evolution is possible, rather than to test the efficacy of the approach as a method for symbolic regression, so we have not performed comparisons with other approaches. Moreover, the parameters have been chosen to deliberately slow down the evolutionary process to facilitate the observation of the co-evolution of the grammar/code and solution. The evolutionary parameters are as follows: pairwise tournament selection, generational replacement, bit mutation probability 0.01, one-point crossover probability 0.3, codon duplication probability 0.01. Wrapping is turned off, and codon lengths are initialised in the range [1,10], with a codon size of 8-bits. Fitness is minimisation of the sum of errors over the 100 test cases, and a protected division operator is adopted that returns one in the event of a division by zero.

3.1   Quartic Symbolic Regression

An instance of a symbolic regression problem is tackled in order to verify that it is possible for the co-evolution of a genetic code (or grammar) to occur along with a solution. The target function is $f(m, v, q, a) = a + a^2 + a^3 + a^4$ with the three input variables m, v, and q introducing an element of noise. 100 randomly generated input vectors are created for each call to the target function, with values for each of the four input variables drawn from the range [0,1]. Runs are conducted with a population size of 100, for 100 generations. The progress of evolution toward the target solution can be seen in Fig. 1 with ever decreasing error at successive generations.

Fig. 1 shows the increasing frequency of occurrence of the target solution symbols a, + and *. Curiously, after 50 generations the frequency of * is dramatically less than a and +, and even less than /, even though there are double the number of multiplication symbols in the target solution as there are addition operators. It is not until after this point that we begin to see an increase in the frequency of *, which, although it finishes considerably lower than the other two symbols, finishes higher than all others. This could have implications as to how a solution to this problem is constructed, suggesting that firstly terms are added together with the use of multiplication not occurring until much later, perhaps replacing some of the addition operators, or through expansion of terms with the multiplication of a by itself.

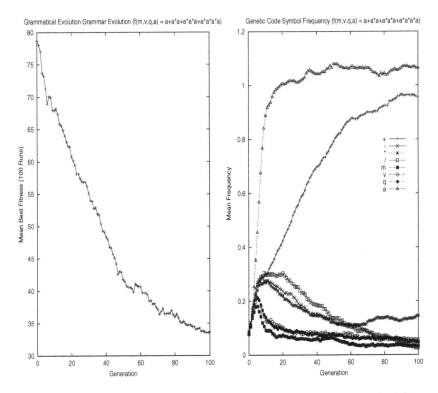

Fig. 1. A plot of the mean best fitness (left) and mean symbol frequency (right) from 100 runs of the quartic symbolic regression problem.

3.2 Dynamic Symbolic Regression I

As indicated in the introduction, dynamic problems are another area in which one could expect to derive some benefit from using evolvable grammars. In this case, one could reasonably expect a system with an evolvable grammar to be able to react more quickly to a change in the environment than a static one could, as a single change in a grammar can reintroduce lost genetic material.

The target functions for the first instance are:

1. $f(m, v, q, a) = a + a^2 + a^3 + a^4$
2. $f(m, v, q, a) = m + m^2 + m^3 + m^4$
3. $f(m, v, q, a) = v + v^2 + v^3 + v^4$
4. $f(m, v, q, a) = q + q^2 + q^3 + q^4$
5. $f(m, v, q, a) = a + a^2 + a^3 + a^4$

The target changes between the functions above every 20 generations. The only difference between each successive function is the variable used. 100 randomly generated input vectors are created for each call to the target function, with values for each of the four input variables drawn from the range [0,1]. The symbols −, and / are not used in any of the target expressions. Runs were conducted with a population size of 500, for 100 generations, with all other parameters as reported earlier. A plot of the average best fitness and average symbol frequencies can be seen in Fig. 2. A sample of evolved grammars from one of the runs is given below, where in each case the grammar selected is the best solution from the generation just prior to a change in target.

Target 1

```
<op>::= +
<var>::= a
<expression>::= + a a
fitness: 34.6511
```

Target 2

```
<op>::= +
<var>::= m
<expression>::= + m m
fitness: 34.2854
```

Target 3

```
<op>::= + | -
<var>::= v
<expression>::= + v v
fitness: 36.6667
```

Target 4

```
<op>::= + | *
<var>::= q
<expression>::= + + q q * * q q * q q
fitness: 22.8506
```

Target 5

```
<op>::= + | *
<var>::= a
<expression>::= + * a + a a * a a
fitness: 7.85477
```

Table 1. Statistics for both the static and evolvable grammars on the first dynamic problem instance. Lower scores indicate better performance.

Fitness Case	mean fixed(dynamic)	median fixed(dynamic)	std. dev fixed(dynamic)	signif.
1	37.33 (40.55)	37.75 (38.22)	7.81 (10.082)	Yes
2	35.48 (36.08)	37.1 (36.57)	6.35 (8.73)	No
3	34.26 (31.53)	36.6 (36.48)	7.54 (10.79)	Yes
4	35.39 (28.74)	37.2 (35.08)	7.96 (12.46)	Yes
5	20.05 (15.1)	22.00 (20.54)	5.99 (10.17)	Yes

The results presented suggest that, when using dynamic grammars, it is possible to successfully preserve and improve solution structure, while still being able to learn appropriate terminal values. This is reflected in the fitness plot where, when the fitness function changes, in most cases there is a decrease in solution fitness for a short period when solutions adjust to the new variable adopted. Later on in the simulations we reach the point where the structure becomes closer to the target and changes in variables alone no longer confer as much damage to fitness, which is again illustrated in the fitness plot (Fig. 2).

A performance comparison of the dynamic and static equivalent of the grammar (given below) for this problem is presented in Fig. 2 and corresponding statistics can be found in Table 1.

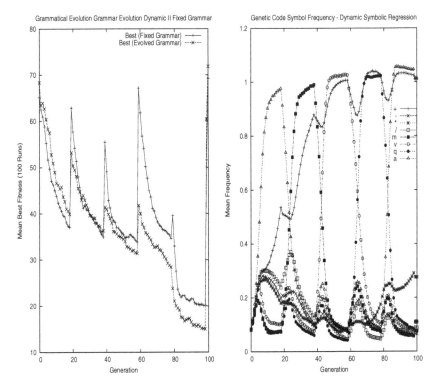

Fig. 2. Plot of the mean best fitness over 100 generations on the first dynamic symbolic regression instance with both static and dynamic grammars (left). Symbol frequency plot (right).

```
<expr> ::= <op> <expr> <expr> | <var>

<op> ::= + | - | * | /

<var> ::= m | v | q | a
```

3.3   Dynamic Symbolic Regression II

The target functions for the second dynamic symbolic regression problem instance are:

1. $f(m, v, q, a) = a + a^2 + a^3 + a^4$
2. $f(m, v, q, a) = m + a^2 + a^3 + a^4$
3. $f(m, v, q, a) = m + m^2 + a^3 + a^4$
4. $f(m, v, q, a) = m + m^2 + m^3 + a^4$
5. $f(m, v, q, a) = m + m^2 + m^3 + m^4$

The target changes between the functions above every 20 generations. The transition used in this problem differs from the previous in that only one term changes each time. However, the change is larger each time (because the power that the new term is raised to increases). 100 randomly generated input vectors are created for each call to the target function, with values for each of the four input variables drawn from the range [0,1]. The symbols q, v, $-$, and $/$ are not used in any of the target expressions. As in the previous dynamic symbolic regression problem instance runs are conducted with a population size of 500, for 100 generations, with all other parameters as per the standard values reported earlier. A plot of the average best fitness and average symbol frequencies can be seen in Fig. 3.

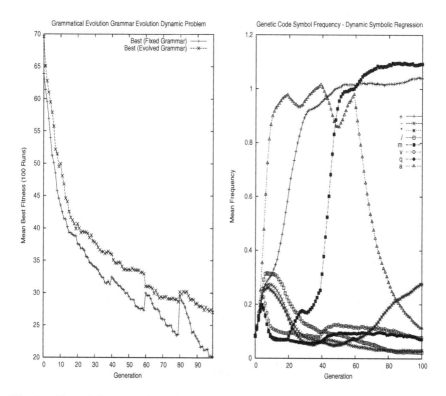

Fig. 3. Plot of the mean best fitness over 100 generations on the second dynamic symbolic regression instance with both dynamic and static grammars (left), and the mean symbol frequency (right).

It is interesting to note that fitness keeps improving over time for the evolvable grammar, with an occasional deterioration corresponding with a change in the fitness function. Notice how the disimprovement is more pronounced later in the runs, particularly for the static grammar, which is due to higher powers being exchanged. These results suggest that the evolvable grammar is more adaptable in scenarios with larger changes facilitating smoother transitions to successive targets. Also evident from Fig. 3 is the manner in which the quantity of a in the population decreases over time while that of m increases. The two plots intersect at around generation 42, shortly after the target has changed to $f(m, v, q, a) = m + m^2 + a^3 + a^4$. However, the plots remain very close until around generation 60, at which time m^3 becomes part of the solution.

A sample of evolved grammars from one of the runs is given below, where the grammars presented represent the best solution at the generation just prior to each fitness change.

Target 1

```
<op>::= + | +
<var>::= a
<expression>::= (+ a a)
fitness: 37.4525
```

Target 2

```
<op>::= +
<var>::= m | a
<expression> = (+ a m)
fitness: 33.8423
```

Target 3

```
<op>::= + | *
<var>::= m | a
<expression> = (+ a (+ m (* a m)))
fitness: 22.9743
```

Target 4

```
<op>::= + | *
<var>::= m
<expression> = (+ m (* (+ (* m m) m ) m) )
fitness: 15.6311
```

Target 5

```
<op>::= + | *
<var>::= m
<expression>::= (+ (* (+ m (* m (+ m (* m m) m) m) ) ) )
fitness: 4.57967e-15
```

Table 2. Statistics for the second dynamic problem instance. Lower numbers indicate a better fitness.

Fitness Case	mean fixed(dynamic)	median fixed(dynamic)	std. dev fixed(dynamic)	signif.
1	39.27 (41.63)	37.98 (38.65)	9.18 (12.59)	No
2	31.55 (36.06)	31.93 (36.60)	6.77 (3.84)	Yes
3	27.62 (33.46)	25.82 (34.52)	6.3 (4.1)	Yes
4	24.05 (29.2)	22.62 (32.17)	5.83 (6.39)	Yes
5	21.34 (27.47)	18.74 (35.2)	11.42 (14.94)	Yes

A performance comparison of the dynamic and static equivalent of the grammar (static grammar as per earlier dynamic problem instance) for this problem is presented in Fig. 3 and corresponding statistics can be found in Table 2. In this case the static grammar outperforms the evolving grammar in terms of best fitness values achieved for all targets but the first. With the evolving grammar there is, as usual, a warm up period where a suitable grammar must be adopted before good solutions can be found. When successive targets are very similar to previous ones this almost negates the potential benefits that a more adaptive representation can bring, as in the case of the evolvable grammars. Clearly, some dynamic problems are more dynamic than others [16], especially in terms of the degree of change. Previous work [17] on genetic algorithms applied to dynamic problems has shown that, when the change is relatively small, a standard GA with high mutation can handle those types of problems. We believe it is likely to be the same for genetic programming.

These results would also lend support to the idea of introducing different operator rates on the grammar chromosome to the solution chromosome, allowing the population to converge towards a similar grammar, facilitating the exploration of solutions based on a similar grammar. If these rates were adaptable, then it may be possible to allow grammars to change more often if the target changes are large, and vice versa.

4   Discussion

In addition to the problems reported in this paper, we tackled two symbolic regression problems taken from the literature on genetic code evolution, where one is a very simple function [6], and the other extremely difficult [7]. For space reasons we have not reported the details of these experiments here, but the results were positive, clearly demonstrating successful grammar/genetic code and solution co-evolution, showing similar trends to those observed for the static quartic symbolic regression instance.

There are a number of differences between this study on genetic code evolution to the Keller & Banzhaf studies [6,7] that are largely representation dependent. These include:

- Variable-length genotypes are adopted with GE as opposed to fixed length in the earlier studies.
- Genetic codes are not seeded at the first generation to be equivalent as was the case for developmental GP; an individuals' binary string is initialised randomly in this case, and thus the genetic code is randomly generated. For developmental GP the code was set such that − was the only symbol represented initially, and thus fitness of an individual was at the lowest possible value.
- The same mutation rate is adopted for the genetic code as for the solutions, whereas independent mutation rates were used in the previous studies. Separate rates of mutation were adopted previously as it was hypothesised that in order for successful evolution to occur changes to the genetic code should occur at a slower rate than a solution, with several different individuals having the same or similar genetic codes at any one point in time. With the current setup of two independent chromosomes it would be possible to implement separate mutation rates for each chromosome, this being an avenue for further investigation.
- Crossover is adopted in this study, which was not present previously.

Despite these differences, the results presented here support the findings of the earlier studies, providing further evidence to support the claim that the co-evolution of genetic code/grammar and solution is possible.

5   Conclusions and Future Work

This study demonstrates the feasibility of the evolution of grammatical evolution's grammar on a number of symbolic regression problem instances. In particular, the results demonstrate the ability of grammatical evolution to learn the importance of the various terminal symbols, and thus the ability to dynamically evolve bias toward individual symbols over the course of a run.

This study opens the door to a number of exciting areas of future investigation using $(GE)^2$, and a sample of possible directions follows.

In this study we have focused on symbolic regression problems, and to test generality beyond symbolic regression it is our intention to extend grammar evolution to other problem domains.

Evolving the genetic code through grammar evolution brings the distinguishing ability to evolve both symbol coding rules (e.g. `<op>` and `<var>` as used in this study) and structural rules (e.g. `<expr>`). In this way it would also be possible to evolve biases towards specific structural configurations of the evolving programs, and also to evolve the complete grammar including the number and type of nonterminals.

The ability to evolve the grammar initially input to grammatical evolution opens up the exploration of a more open-ended form of evolution. For example, it is now possible to dynamically define parameterised functions incorporating their specification into the grammar. A static approach to function definition has been previously tackled [18], however, with the ability to evolve the number of functions along with their respective parameters, outputs and data types, this would represent a powerful extension to grammatical evolution, allowing the dynamic modularisation of code and as a consequence improving its scalability.

In a similar manner to the use of dynamically defined functions using grammar evolution, it would also be possible to extend our earlier investigations on constant generation techniques [19] through the provision of various grammatically based constant generation strategies in the universal grammar. The appropriate strategy could then be incorporated into the grammar and evolved. Investigations are currently underway in each of these directions.

Acknowledgements. The authors would like to thank the various members of the Biocomputing and Developmental Systems Group at the University of Limerick for a number of interesting discussions on this work, and Wolfgang Banzhaf for an insightful discussion on an early draft of this work.

References

1. O'Neill, M., Ryan, C. (2003). *Grammatical Evolution: Evolutionary Automatic Programming in an Arbitrary Language.* Kluwer Academic Publishers.
2. O'Neill, M. (2001). Automatic Programming in an Arbitrary Language: Evolving Programs in Grammatical Evolution. PhD thesis, University of Limerick.
3. O'Neill, M., Ryan, C. (2001). Grammatical Evolution, *IEEE Trans. Evolutionary Computation.* 2001.

4. Ryan, C., Collins, J.J., O'Neill, M. (1998). Grammatical Evolution: Evolving Programs for an Arbitrary Language.*Proc. of the First European Workshop on GP*, 83-95, Springer-Verlag.
5. Koza, J. R. (1992). *Genetic Programming: On the Programming of Computers by Means of Natural Selection.* MIT Press, Cambridge, MA, USA.
6. Keller, R., Banzhaf W. (1999). The Evolution of Genetic Code in Genetic Programming. In *Proc. of GECCO '99*, vol. 2, 1077-1082, Morgan Kaufmann.
7. Keller, R., Banzhaf W. (2001). Evolution of Genetic Code on a Hard Problem. In *Proc. of GECCO 2001*, 50-56, Morgan Kaufmann.
8. Lewin, B. (2000). *Genes VII.* Oxford University Press, 2000.
9. Sella, G., Ardell, D. H. (2001). The Coevolution of Genes and the Genetic Code. *Santa Fe Institute Working Paper* 01-03-015, February 2001.
10. Ardell, D. H.,Sella, G. (2001). On the Evolution of Redundancy in Genetic Codes. *Journal of Molecular Evolution*, 53:269-281.
11. Kargupta, H., Ghosh, S. Toward Machine Learning Through Genetic Code-Like Transformations. *Genetic Programming and Evolvable Machines*, Vol. 3, No. 3., pp.231-258, September 2002.
12. Freeland, S. J. (2002). The Darwinian Genetic Code: An Adaptation for Adapting? *Genetic Programming and Evolvable Machines*, Vol. 3, No. 2., pp.113-128.
13. Ryan, C., O'Neill, M. (2002). How to do anything with Grammars. *Proc. of the Bird of a Feather Workshops, Genetic and Evolutionary Computation Conference 2002*, pp. 116-119.
14. Chomsky, N. (1975). *Reflections on Language.* Pantheon Books. New York.
15. Pinker, S. (1995). *The language instinct: the new science of language and the mind.* Penguin, 1995.
16. Ryan, C., Collins, J.J., Wallin, D. (2003). Non-stationary Function Optimization using Polygenic Inheritance. In Foster et al. (Eds). *GECCO 2003: Proceedings of Genetic and Evolutionary Computation Conference.* Springer-Verlag.
17. K. Ng and K. Wong. (1995). A new diploid scheme and dominance change mechanism for non-stationary function optimisation. In *Proceedings of ICGA-5*, 1995.
18. O'Neill, M., Ryan, C. (2000). Grammar based function definition in Grammatical Evolution. *Proceedings of the Genetic and Evolutionary Computation Conference (GECCO-2000)*, pp. 485-490, Las Vegas, USA. Morgan Kaufmann.
19. O'Neill, M., Dempsey, I., Brabazon, A., Ryan, C. (2003). Analysis of a Digit Concatenation Approach to Constant Generation. In LNCS 2610, *Proceedings of EuroGP 2003, the 6th European Conference on Genetic Programming*, Essex, UK, April 2003. pp. 173-183.

Constrained Molecular Dynamics as a Search and Optimization Tool

Riccardo Poli[1] and Christopher R. Stephens[2]

[1] Department of Computer Science, University of Essex, UK
[2] Instituto de Ciencias Nucleares, UNAM, México

Abstract. In this paper we consider a new class of search and optimization algorithms inspired by molecular dynamics simulations in physics.

1 Introduction

Search and optimization algorithms take inspiration from many different areas of science. For instance, evolutionary algorithms generically take their inspiration from biological systems [1]; simulated annealing from the physics of cooling [2]; Hopfield neural networks from the physics of spin glasses [3,4]; swarm algorithms from social interactions [5,6]. In this paper we consider a class of algorithms that take their inspiration from physics, in the sense that they use of a group of interacting particles to perform the search, and will consider how intuition from there can help in understanding how they work. Systems of this type have been widely studied and simulated in the field of *molecular dynamics.*[1]

Our system is somehow similar to (and partly inspired by) particle swarm optimization (PSO) [5]. Like our system, PSOs use groups of interacting particles. In PSOs such particles *fly over* the fitness landscape, recording the best places seen so far by each particle and by the swarm as a whole. These points are then used to generate pseudo-random forces (produced by springs) which attract the particles towards such points. Although other types of interactions have been recently introduced [9], generally no other information on the fitness landscape is used by PSOs.

Our system differs from a PSO in many ways. Firstly, the motion of our particles is *constrained to be on the fitness landscape*, that is our particles *slide on* the fitness landscape rather than fly over it. Secondly, our simulation is physically realistic, in the sense that a variety of forces may act on our particles such as gravity, friction, centripedal acceleration, in addition to coupling forces such as those generated by springs connecting the particles. As will be shown later some of these forces depend on the topological characteristics of the landscape, such as its gradient and curvatures, in the neighbourhood of each particle. Thirdly, our method does not require the presence of explicit intelligence in the particles,

---

[1] The molecular dynamics method [7], introduced over 40 years ago to study the interactions of hard spheres [8], has since been widely used in physics to understand the behaviour of liquids, proteins, DNA, enzymatic reactions, etc.

M. Keijzer et al. (Eds.): EuroGP 2004, LNCS 3003, pp. 150–161, 2004.

unlike PSOs where this is necessary for observing the motion of the particles and deciding when and how to change the position of the attractors. Fourthly, the method does not rely on the use of pseudo-random forces to perform the search (although these are not excluded).

Given the close relation with molecular dynamics and the constrained nature of the motion of our particles, we have decided to term the class of algorithms considered here *Constrained Molecular Dynamics* (CMD).

The paper is organized as follows. In the next section we describe the basic principles behind CMD. In Section 3 we illustrate the effects of different types of forces on CMD using simple examples. We look at some implementation details in Section 4. In Section 5 we study the behaviour of the algorithm on a small set of benchmark problems. We give our conclusions in Section 6.

2   Constrained Molecular Dynamics

We restrict attention here to continuous search spaces. The search space we denote by $V \subset \mathcal{R}^N$, where $\mathcal{R}^N$ is an N-dimensional Euclidean space and equip it with coordinates $\{x_1, \ldots, x_N\}$. We also consider a fitness function $f : \mathcal{R}^N \to \mathcal{R}^+$. We can now embed V in $\mathcal{R}^{N+1}$, defining the fitness landscape via $y = f(\mathbf{x})$, where y is a height function above V and we use bold face to denote vectors in V. In terms of the embedding coordinates, $\mathbf{r} = \{x_1, \ldots, x_N, x_{N+1}\}$, where $y = x_{N+1}$, the fitness function surface takes the form $g(x_1, \ldots, x_N, x_{N+1}) = y - f(x_1, \ldots, x_N) = 0$. Using a notation that is standard in physics we will denote derivatives of f by $f_{,i_1 \ldots i_m} = \partial^m f / \partial x_{i_1} \ldots \partial x_{i_m}$, e.g. $f_{,i} = \partial f / \partial x_i$, where we use Roman indices for components of vectors associated with V. For indices associated with V we will also use the Einstein summation convention that repeated indices on different objects are considered to be summed over, e.g. $x_i x_i = \sum_i x_i x_i$.

We now consider n particles of mass m^α, $\alpha \in \{1, \ldots, n\}$, where α denotes the particle under consideration[2], moving on the surface $y = f(\mathbf{x})$, with (embedding) coordinates and velocities $\mathbf{x}^\alpha$ and $\mathbf{v}^\alpha$ respectively. In this case the motion of each particle is constrained via an equation $g(\mathbf{x}^\alpha) = 0$. Thus, we have $(N + 1)n$ coordinates and N constraints, which leads to Nn independent degrees of freedom.

The kinetic energy, T^α, of a particle α is

$$T^\alpha = \frac{m^\alpha}{2} |\mathbf{v}^\alpha|^2 = \frac{m^\alpha}{2} \left(\dot{x}_i^\alpha \dot{x}_i^\alpha + \dot{x}_{N+1}^\alpha \dot{x}_{N+1}^\alpha \right) \tag{1}$$

where $\dot{x}_i^\alpha = dx_i^\alpha / dt$ and $\dot{x}_{N+1}^\alpha = f_{,i} \dot{x}_i^\alpha$. (Generally l dots above the symbol will represent l time derivatives.) Then

$$T^\alpha = \frac{m^\alpha}{2} g_{ij}^\alpha \dot{x}_i^\alpha \dot{x}_j^\alpha \tag{2}$$

---

[2] Greek indices will be used to specify the particle of interest.

with $g_{ij}^\alpha = \delta_{ij} + f_{,i}^\alpha f_{,j}^\alpha$ being interpretable as the metric tensor for the space on which the particles are moving. The equations of motion for the particle α are

$$\frac{d}{dt}\left(\frac{\partial T^\alpha}{\partial \dot{x}_i^\alpha}\right) - \frac{\partial T^\alpha}{\partial x_i^\alpha} = \mathbf{F}^\alpha \cdot \frac{\partial \mathbf{r}^\alpha}{\partial x_i^\alpha} \tag{3}$$

where $\mathbf{F}^\alpha$ is the force on the particle. Explicitly

$$\ddot{x}_i^\alpha + \Gamma_{ijk}^\alpha \dot{x}_j^\alpha \dot{x}_k^\alpha = h_{ij}^\alpha \frac{F_k^\alpha}{m^\alpha} r_{k,j}^\alpha \tag{4}$$

where (h_{ij}^α) is the inverse of (g_{ij}^α) and

$$\Gamma_{ijk}^\alpha = \frac{f_{,i}^\alpha f_{,jk}^\alpha}{(1 + f_{,i}^\alpha f_{,i}^\alpha)} \tag{5}$$

The quantity Γ_{ijk}^α is determined solely by geometrical properties of the fitness landscape and gives rise to the "generalized" force that arises due to the constrained motion on the surface. Equation (3) gives a complete description of the dynamics of particle α. The particle trajectories are solutions of (3). The questions now are: can a set of particles like these perform a search, what type of search do these particles carry out and how good are the particles at finding optimal points in the landscape?

3   "Forces for Courses"

If one wishes to use the above physical system for search and optimization it behooves one to think about what would be useful properties to have in order to perform such tasks well. To a large extent this is associated with what type of forces are introduced into the particle dynamics, as well as such obvious characteristics as the number of particles.[3] In the above we have not specified the forces. There are, of course, a huge variety of possibilities. We may fruitfully think of several broad classes however: i) no forces; ii) forces due to particle-particle interactions; iii) forces due to interactions with an external field and iv) friction/viscosity type forces. In the limit when there are no forces then equation (4) becomes

$$\ddot{x}_i^\alpha + \Gamma_{ijk}^\alpha \dot{x}_j^\alpha \dot{x}_k^\alpha = 0 \tag{6}$$

Here the effective generalized force on the particle arises purely due to its constrained motion. This generalized force depends on the geometry of the landscape via Γ_{ijk}^α, which from (5) can be seen to be zero when $f_{,i} = 0$ or $f_{,jk} = 0$. A simple example of this is a particle constrained to move on a half circle (the lower half) of radius R. In V, this is one dimensional motion, hence there is only one degree of freedom. The constraint is $y = -(R^2 - x^2)^{\frac{1}{2}}$. In this case Γ_{ijk}^α only has one component, $\Gamma_{111}^\alpha = x/(R^2 - x^2)$. The equation of motion is

$$\ddot{x} + \left(\frac{x}{R^2 - x^2}\right)\dot{x}^2 = 0 \tag{7}$$

---

[3] In the rest of the paper we will assume $m^\alpha = 1$ for all particles.

This can most easily be solved in a polar coordinate system (r, θ), where we take θ to be the deviation from the direction $-\mathbf{e}_y$ and $\mathbf{e}_y$ is a unit vector in the y direction. In this case (7) becomes

$$\ddot{\theta} = 0 \tag{8}$$

whose solution is $\theta(t) = a + bt$. Thus, in this coordinate system, naturally given the geometry, the particle moves freely as there is no generalized force in the tangential direction. The particle position in terms of the landscape height is $y(t) = -R \cos(a + bt)$. In terms of "optimization", if we are seeking the minimum of the function then obviously if the particle starts with zero velocity we have the trivial situation where the particle does not move. However, moving with angular frequency ω clockwise and starting at $y = 0$ then $y(t) = -R \cos(\pi/2 - \omega t)$. The particle finds the optimum when $\cos(\pi/2 - \omega t) = 1$, i.e. $t = \pi/2\omega$. So in order to find the optimum the particle needs a non-zero initial velocity.

Considering further this simple one-dimensional example we can now introduce the idea of an external force field. A canonical example of that would be gravity, of which the simplest case is that of a constant gravitational field. In the case of particle motion on a surface it is natural to take the gravitational acceleration, g, to be in the y direction. In this case $F_i^\alpha = -g \delta_{i(N+1)}^\alpha$, i.e. the force is "downwards". Once again, taking the case $y = -(R^2 - x^2)^{\frac{1}{2}}$, one finds

$$\ddot{x} + \left(\frac{x}{R^2 - x^2} \right) \dot{x}^2 = \frac{gx}{R}(R^2 - x^2)^{\frac{1}{2}} \tag{9}$$

Passing to a polar coordinate system we have

$$\ddot{\theta} = -g \sin \theta \tag{10}$$

Intuition can be simply gleaned here by considering the case $\theta \ll 1$ so that $\sin \theta \approx \theta$. In this case $\theta(t) = a \cos(g^{1/2}t) + b \sin(g^{1/2}t)$. Starting the particle at $\theta(0) = a$ $(a > 0)$ with inital angular speed zero the particle finds the optimum $\theta = 0$ at $t = \pi/2g^{1/2}$, which is independent of the initial starting point. Thus, adding a constant external force that pulls the particles in the required direction, i.e. to smaller values of the height function, implies that the particle can find the global optimum irrespective of the particle's initial position. Thus, in terms of optimization the advantage of gravity is that it provides a bias for the search to go in the right direction. One might be tempted to think of it as providing a hill climbing type behaviour. This would be wrong however, as (some) *local optima can be avoided*. This can be simply understood in the one-dimensional case by realizing that dropped from a given height with zero velocity the particle will be able to surmount any local maxima that are lower than its starting point as the particle's accumulated kinetic energy is sufficient to take it over the barrier.

In order to consider particle-particle interactions we must go beyond the one particle case, the simplest being that of two particles. An interesting and illustrative example of interparticle interactions would be to connect the particles by attractive spring type forces, where generically the force on particle α would be $\mathbf{F}^\alpha = -\sum_\beta k d_{\alpha\beta}$, where k is a spring constant which in principle could be different for different particles. The sum over β is a sum over those particles β connected to the particle α. This could be all the particles or just nearest neighbors or a random subset, to name but a few. Finally, $d_{\alpha\beta}$ is the "signed" distance between α and β, where $d_{\alpha\beta} = -d_{\beta\alpha}$. This could be the Euclidean distance in the embedding space, the distance in V or the distance as measured by a geodesic curve between the two particles (i.e. the shortest distance on the landscape). In the case of our simple example of a particle constrained to move on a half circle the two equations of motion for the two particles are

$$\ddot{x}^\alpha + \left(\frac{x^\alpha}{R^2 - (x^\alpha)^2} \right) (\dot{x}^\alpha)^2 = -k d_{\alpha\beta} \tag{11}$$

where $\alpha = 1, 2$. In the case where the spring force is associated with the distance between the particles as measured along the curve then passing to polar coordinates (r_1, θ_1) and (r_2, θ_2) and introducing the center of mass and relative coordinates $\Theta = (\theta_1 + \theta_2)/2$ and $\theta_r = (\theta_1 - \theta_2)/2$ one finds

$$\ddot{\Theta} = 0 \qquad\qquad \ddot{\theta}_r = -k\theta_r \tag{12}$$

In this case the center of mass moves with uniform angular speed $\Theta = a + bt$ while the relative angle between the two particles is given by $\theta_r = c\cos(k^{1/2}t) + d\sin(k^{1/2}t)$. A simple example of how such interparticle forces can help in the search process can be to consider the case where both particles start on either side of the optimum at $\theta = 0$, either at rest or with velocities that take them away from the optimum. In this case the attractive force of the spring pulls them in the direction of the optimum. In the explicit example where the particles start with initial positions and velocities $\theta_1 = a$, $\theta_2 = -a$, $\dot{\theta}_1 = \dot{\theta}_2 = 0$ then the particles encounter the optimum at $t = \pi/2k^{1/2}$.

Finally, in discussing the individual forces in the context of simple examples we may consider the case of friction. Taking the particle on the half circle the equation of motion is

$$\ddot{\theta} = -\eta\dot{\theta} \tag{13}$$

which has solution $\theta(t) = (b\eta - a + a\exp(-t))/\eta$, where $\dot{\theta}(0) = -a$ and $\theta(0) = b$, i.e. we start the particle from the right of the optimum and travelling toward it. In the limit of large t the particle will have reached the optimum if $\eta b < a$. Thus, the stronger the friction force the greater the initial velocity in the direction of the optimum must be in order to reach it. It may be though naively then that friction is a bad idea. However, say for example, $b < 0$ then the presence of friction prevents the particle from moving further away from the optimum than it would otherwise do. In this way, in the presence of other forces, friction can have an important role to play in "relaxing" the particle into a good position once an interesting region has been found in the landscape. Increasing the friction then has the character of reducing the explorative component in the search and is somewhat analogous to reducing the temperature in the case of simulated annealing.

Now, in the above we are considering a simple example of a unimodal function in one dimension. We have in mind using the particles for search and optimization on non-trivial multi-dimensional landscapes. So what can we deduce from the above in the more general context? Firstly, consider free particle motion. This is somewhat analogous to random search. There is no "selection" in the sense that there is no systematic tendency to seek fitter (lower) points in the landscape. In this case the particle's trajectory is completely and solely governed by the geometry of the landscape. However, there is a tendency to spend less time in regions of the landscape of high curvature and more time in regions of low curvature. Intuitively this is because the "tighter the bend the quicker the particle has to travel to keep on the track". In this sense the particle motion can be thought of as a potential diagnostic for the size of the basin of attraction of an optimum.

Other type of forces can be included in this framework. For example, particles could be charged as has been proposed for PSOs [9]. In our simulations we have used elasticity (partially unelastic bounces) also to guarantee that the particles would not leave the search area defined by the user.

4   Discretization of the Algorithm

Although Equation (3) gives a complete description of the dynamics of each particle, its explicit solution is generally very hard if not impossible for a generic landscape and a generic set of forces. So, often numerical integration is the only way to determine the trajectory of each particle and, therefore, to run a CMD algorithm. In our implementation we have used the traditional first-order forward difference approximation for derivatives, e.g. we have approximated a continuous velocity $v(t)$ as

$$v(t) = \frac{x(t + \Delta) - x(t)}{\Delta},$$

where Δ is the integration time step.

So, once the initial velocity and position of each particle is given, we update each component of velocity and position of each particle, time step after time step, by using the following recursion:

$$x(t + 1) = x(t) + \Delta \cdot v(t) \qquad (14)$$
$$v(t + 1) = v(t) + \Delta \cdot a(t) \qquad (15)$$

where $a(t)$ is the corresponding component of the acceleration. This is calculated by appropriately adding all the forces (gravity, friction, etc.) acting on the particle. Some such forces depend on the first or second order partial derivatives of the fitness function. These can either be directly computed by differentiation of the fitness functions or be approximated numerically. For simplicity in our experiments we calculated derivatives using central differences. For example, we used the approximation

$$f_{,i} \approx \frac{f(x_1, \ldots, x_i + \Delta, \ldots x_n) - f(x_1, \ldots, x_i - \Delta, \ldots x_n)}{2\Delta}.$$

Naturally, these extra evaluations of the fitness function need to be considered when calculating the computation load of the algorithm.

5   Results

We tested the algorithm on three standard benchmark problems, the De Jong's functions F1 and F2, and the Rastrigin's function, of increasing dimensionality N and with a varying number of masses n. The method we propose is new, and still needs to be understood in depth. So, the purpose of these tests was not to try and beat other well established algorithms, but rather to understand more about what kind of forces are beneficial for what kind of landscapes and why.

The function F1 has the following form:

$$f(\mathbf{x}) = \sum_{i=1}^{N} x_i^2.$$

That is this function represents a symmetric (hyper-)paraboloid, with no local optima and a global optimum in $\mathbf{x} = (0, \dots, 0)$ where $f(\mathbf{x}) = 0$.

The function F2 (also known as Rosenbrook's function) has the following form:[4]

$$f(\mathbf{x}) = \sum_{i=1}^{N-1} ((x_{i+1} - x_i^2)^2 + 0.01(1 - x_i)^2).$$

This function has no local optima and a global optimum in $\mathbf{x} = (1, \dots, 1)$ where $f(\mathbf{x}) = 0$. The function is much harder than F1 since the optimum is effectively at the end of a long, very narrow valley.

Rastrigin's function has the following form:

$$f(\mathbf{x}) = 10N + \sum_{i=1}^{N} (x_i^2 - 10\cos(2\pi x_i))$$

This function has many local optima and one global optimum in $\mathbf{x} = (0, \dots, 0)$ where $f(\mathbf{x}) = 0$.

In the simulations reported here, we initialized all the particles in random positions within the hypercube $[-5.12, +5.12]^N$, all with zero velocities.[5]

For each of the three fitness functions described above we tested a number of different configurations:

- different numbers of particles ($n = 1$, $n = 2$ and $n = 10$),
- different dimensionality of the search space ($N = 1$, $N = 2$ and $N = 3$),
- different configurations for the springs (absence, particles connected so as to form a ring, particles fully connected: s=no, s=ring and s=full, respectively, in Tables 1–3),

---

[4] For simulation convenience we rescaled the original function by dividing it by 100.

[5] Note, however, that providing the particles with non-zero initial velocities can have benefits since it energises the system beyond what's provided by the gravitational and elastic potential energies.

- absence or presence of gravity (g=no and g=yes, respectively, in Table 1–3),
- absence or presence of friction (f=no and f=yes, respectively, in Tables 1–3).

For each setting we performed 30 independent experiments. Each experiment involved the integration of the system of equations in Equation (3) for 5000 time steps with time step $\Delta = 0.01$. Spring stiffness was 0.03, the friction coefficient was 1, gravity acceleration was 0.1, the elasticity coefficient for bounces against the boundaries -5.12 or +5.12 was 0.8. In each run we measured the average and standard deviation of the best fitness value found during the run, as well as the average and standard deviation of the distance between the point where the best value was achieved and the global optimum.

Tables 1–3 report the results of the simulations. Each entry includes four numbers. The first (in italics) represents the average of the best fitness seen in each of the 30 independent runs. The second (in a smaller font and in italics) represent the standard deviation of the best fitness. The third value represents the average distance from the global optimum, while the fourth (in a smaller font) represents the standard deviation for such a distance.

For F1 (see Table 1) we note that, as expected, increasing the number of particles performing the search improves performance. This is true for all our experimental results (i.e. also for Tables 2 and 3). We can also see that, alone, the presence of gravity is sufficient to guarantee near perfect results. This had to be expected since a particle with no initial velocity is bound to pass through the origin in this fitness function. Springs appear not to be too beneficial for the search, particularly in the case of only two particles where the system tends to oscillate in useless directions, unless gravity brings the system (and its oscillations) in the right area. Friction generally helps the search settle in the global optimum.

In Table 2 we report the results obtained with the much harder De Jong's function 2. Generally the comments above apply to this function too, although, due to the long narrow valley leading to the global optimum, the benefits of friction are not as clear in this case. Also, for this function we observe a significant variance in the results for the case $N = 3$. This is due to the fact that, depending on the initial conditions, runs either succeed in finding (and then following until the simulation ends) the bottom of the valley or they oscillate between the "walls" of the valley failing to ever get good fitness values. With enough particles the effect disappears, because there always appear to be some which are well placed to find the valley. For this problem the presence of springs benefits the system when only two particles are present (particularly if gravity is also present). This is because the interaction between the particles help align the trajectories of the particles in the direction of the valley.

The results for the Rastrigin function (Table 3) appear to be the worst of the crop. This is really due to the exceptional multimodality of this function (e.g. for $N = 3$ the function presents around 1000 local optima in the interval of interest). In all cases gravity appears to help bring the system towards the global optimum more than anything else, although the presence of fully connected springs seems to have potential (because the particles can then pull each other out of local

Table 1. Results on De Jong fitness function 1. The cases where no motion could happen are marked as N/A.

Setup	N=1 n=1	N=1 n=2	N=1 n=10	N=2 n=1	N=2 n=2	N=2 n=10	N=3 n=1	N=3 n=2	N=3 n=10
s=no g=yes f=no	*0.0000* *0.0000* 0.0017 0.0012	*0.0000* *0.0000* 0.0010 0.0009	*0.0000* *0.0000* 0.0001 0.0002	*0.0000* *0.0000* 0.0038 0.0029	*0.0000* *0.0000* 0.0023 0.0023	*0.0000* *0.0000* 0.0005 0.0005	*0.0000* *0.0000* 0.0047 0.0032	*0.0000* *0.0000* 0.0031 0.0025	*0.0000* *0.0000* 0.0005 0.0005
s=no g=yes f=yes	*0.0000* *0.0000* 0.0000 0.0000	*0.0000* *0.0000* 0.0000 0.0000	*0.0000* *0.0000* 0.0000 0.0000	*0.0000* *0.0000* 0.0001 0.0002	*0.0000* *0.0000* 0.0000 0.0001	*0.0000* *0.0000* 0.0000 0.0000	*0.0000* *0.0000* 0.0008 0.0014	*0.0000* *0.0000* 0.0002 0.0008	*0.0000* *0.0000* 0.0000 0.0000
s=ring g=no f=no	N/A	*0.6463* *1.5581* 0.3225 0.7364	*0.0000* *0.0000* 0.0001 0.0002	N/A	*0.8151* *3.0105* 0.3449 0.8343	*0.0014* *0.0022* 0.0294 0.0234	N/A	*0.8539* *4.1464* 0.3821 0.8414	*0.0074* *0.0090* 0.0736 0.0441
s=ring g=no f=yes	N/A	*0.8501* *1.8996* 0.2360 0.6492	*0.0000* *0.0000* 0.0001 0.0002	N/A	*1.0403* *3.6969* 0.4165 0.9311	*0.0039* *0.0099* 0.0427 0.0460	N/A	*1.0241* *4.2864* 0.4726 0.8948	*0.0076* *0.0117* 0.0724 0.0485
s=ring g=yes f=no	*0.0000* *0.0000* 0.0018 0.0013	*0.0000* *0.0000* 0.0013 0.0016	*0.0000* *0.0000* 0.0001 0.0002	*0.0000* *0.0000* 0.0038 0.0029	*0.0158* *0.0220* 0.0951 0.0820	*0.0002* *0.0003* 0.0099 0.0080	*0.0000* *0.0000* 0.0047 0.0032	*0.0346* *0.0489* 0.1513 0.1083	*0.0012* *0.0013* 0.0303 0.0172
s=ring g=yes f=yes	*0.0000* *0.0000* 0.0000 0.0000	*0.0000* *0.0000* 0.0000 0.0000	*0.0000* *0.0000* 0.0000 0.0000	*0.0000* *0.0000* 0.0001 0.0002	*0.0010* *0.0045* 0.0120 0.0286	*0.0000* *0.0000* 0.0003 0.0004	*0.0000* *0.0000* 0.0008 0.0014	*0.0028* *0.0067* 0.0309 0.0433	*0.0000* *0.0000* 0.0017 0.0018
s=full g=no f=no	N/A	*0.8058* *1.8267* 0.3661 0.8196	*0.0000* *0.0000* 0.0002 0.0002	N/A	*1.9934* *5.0823* 0.6871 1.2334	*0.0064* *0.0280* 0.0392 0.0698	N/A	*1.2609* *4.5858* 0.5760 0.9639	*0.0073* *0.0132* 0.0687 0.0512
s=full g=no f=yes	N/A	*1.1956* *1.9363* 0.4302 0.6727	*0.0000* *0.0000* 0.0002 0.0002	N/A	*2.8333* *5.6838* 0.8495 1.2733	*0.0505* *0.2465* 0.0876 0.2070	N/A	*1.5146* *4.7949* 0.6795 1.0261	*0.0123* *0.0172* 0.0892 0.0662
s=full g=yes f=no	*0.0000* *0.0000* 0.0018 0.0013	*0.0000* *0.0000* 0.0008 0.0008	*0.0000* *0.0000* 0.0001 0.0002	*0.0000* *0.0000* 0.0038 0.0029	*0.0052* *0.0090* 0.0522 0.0496	*0.0000* *0.0001* 0.0049 0.0039	*0.0000* *0.0000* 0.0047 0.0032	*0.0174* *0.0210* 0.1065 0.0777	*0.0002* *0.0003* 0.0132 0.0078
s=full g=yes f=yes	*0.0000* *0.0000* 0.0000 0.0000	*0.0000* *0.0000* 0.0000 0.0000	*0.0000* *0.0000* 0.0000 0.0000	*0.0000* *0.0000* 0.0001 0.0002	*0.0004* *0.0021* 0.0054 0.0194	*0.0000* *0.0000* 0.0002 0.0002	*0.0000* *0.0000* 0.0008 0.0014	*0.0009* *0.0032* 0.0132 0.0266	*0.0000* *0.0000* 0.0008 0.0005

Table 2. Results on De Jong fitness function 2. This function is not defined for $N = 1$.

Setup	n=1	n=2	n=10	n=1	n=2	n=10	n=1	n=2	n=10
		N=1			N=2			N=3	
s=no g=yes f=no	N/A	N/A	N/A	0.0083	0.0057	0.0008	98.6604	24.5817	0.0540
				0.0063	0.0057	0.0012	168.2136	70.6019	0.1733
				1.5725	1.2344	0.5024	3.2142	2.3850	1.8800
				0.9038	0.8570	0.4947	1.8425	1.1993	0.8406
s=no g=yes f=yes	N/A	N/A	N/A	0.0085	0.0062	0.0011	98.6783	24.5529	0.0281
				0.0063	0.0061	0.0017	168.2172	70.6264	0.0406
				1.8870	1.4017	0.4768	3.2300	2.4520	1.7980
				1.1955	1.0719	0.3980	1.8333	1.1514	0.7935
s=ring g=no f=no	N/A	N/A	N/A	N/A	0.0116	0.0119	N/A	2.0799	0.1160
					0.0101	0.0234		9.4327	0.2155
					1.4533	1.3980		2.0027	1.9016
					0.8073	1.2000		1.0316	0.9785
s=ring g=no f=yes	N/A	N/A	N/A	N/A	0.0093	0.0102	N/A	2.0842	0.0884
					0.0079	0.0186		9.4467	0.1197
					1.4369	1.4064		1.9913	1.9155
					0.8969	1.1284		1.0333	0.9686
s=ring g=yes f=no	N/A	N/A	N/A	0.0083	0.0091	0.0026	98.6604	0.2926	0.0285
				0.0063	0.0091	0.0039	168.2136	0.7559	0.0215
				1.5725	1.3385	0.7636	3.2142	1.8632	1.0944
				0.9038	0.8018	0.6339	1.8425	0.6457	0.5917
s=ring g=yes f=yes	N/A	N/A	N/A	0.0085	0.0096	0.0056	98.6783	0.2768	0.0567
				0.0063	0.0102	0.0140	168.2172	0.7184	0.0711
				1.8870	1.2516	0.7584	3.2300	1.8642	1.7421
				1.1955	0.7705	0.6502	1.8333	0.6534	0.9999
s=full g=no f=no	N/A	N/A	N/A	N/A	1.4072	0.0179	N/A	2.2154	0.1057
					6.6479	0.0279		10.6180	0.3041
					1.5476	1.5874		2.0587	1.5411
					1.0641	1.3333		1.0573	0.6969
s=full g=no f=yes	N/A	N/A	N/A	N/A	1.4429	0.0146	N/A	2.1228	0.1086
					6.7059	0.0233		10.6202	0.2967
					1.5831	1.7296		2.0383	1.5132
					1.0120	1.1779		1.0003	0.7283
s=full g=yes f=no	N/A	N/A	N/A	0.0083	0.0072	0.0020	98.6604	0.2107	0.0345
				0.0063	0.0085	0.0023	168.2136	0.4660	0.0510
				1.5725	1.1053	0.7714	3.2142	1.7438	1.5821
				0.9038	0.6276	0.6215	1.8425	0.7965	0.6131
s=full g=yes f=yes	N/A	N/A	N/A	0.0085	0.0068	0.0016	98.6783	0.2513	0.0346
				0.0063	0.0073	0.0023	168.2172	0.5929	0.0524
				1.8870	1.1092	0.5870	3.2300	1.9117	1.5445
				1.1955	0.6805	0.4682	1.8333	0.8000	0.6408

Table 3. Results on Rastrigin's function.

Setup	N=1			N=2			N=3		
	n=1	n=2	n=10	n=1	n=2	n=10	n=1	n=2	n=10
s=no g=yes f=no	*0.0332*	*0.0266*	*0.0066*	*1.0396*	*0.7361*	*0.3201*	*1.9737*	*1.5414*	*0.8132*
	0.0469	*0.0440*	*0.0248*	*0.5970*	*0.5427*	*0.2693*	*0.9226*	*0.7397*	*0.4943*
	0.3331	0.2669	0.0668	2.8790	2.2777	1.4607	4.0112	3.5864	2.6426
	0.4685	0.4398	0.2481	0.9066	1.0634	0.7793	1.1571	0.9498	0.8851
s=no g=yes f=yes	*0.3980*	*0.2919*	*0.0929*	*1.1536*	*0.7825*	*0.3307*	*2.0360*	*1.5813*	*0.7773*
	0.0000	*0.1518*	*0.1283*	*0.6872*	*0.5866*	*0.2901*	*1.0148*	*0.8024*	*0.4447*
	1.9899	1.5919	0.6633	3.1834	2.4916	1.5797	4.3004	3.7682	2.4908
	0.0000	0.6079	0.6957	1.0348	1.1448	0.7683	1.1970	1.0576	0.8670
s=ring g=no f=no	N/A	*0.3368*	*0.0000*	N/A	*0.9024*	*0.5437*	N/A	*2.1433*	*1.2487*
		0.6520	*0.0000*		*0.6795*	*0.4631*		*0.9289*	*0.5519*
		0.6223	0.0003		2.2698	1.8193		3.5220	3.0507
		1.0560	0.0003		1.1799	0.9733		1.1853	0.9802
s=ring g=no f=yes	N/A	*0.4286*	*0.0000*	N/A	*1.1336*	*0.4475*	N/A	*2.0803*	*1.1415*
		0.6698	*0.0000*		*0.8059*	*0.3490*		*1.0903*	*0.5226*
		0.8941	0.0003		2.5529	1.6278		3.3908	2.9809
		1.1796	0.0004		1.3239	0.7376		1.2126	0.9300
s=ring g=yes f=no	*0.0332*	*0.1029*	*0.0000*	*1.0396*	*1.1870*	*0.3327*	*1.9737*	*1.9231*	*0.8747*
	0.0469	*0.2430*	*0.0000*	*0.5970*	*0.7936*	*0.2492*	*0.9226*	*0.9096*	*0.4806*
	0.3331	0.4322	0.0005	2.8790	2.7213	1.5775	4.0112	3.5778	2.6596
	0.4685	0.9147	0.0006	0.9066	1.2532	0.8007	1.1571	1.2404	0.8376
s=ring g=yes f=yes	*0.3980*	*0.1928*	*0.0000*	*1.1536*	*0.9684*	*0.2835*	*2.0360*	*1.8926*	*0.8497*
	0.0000	*0.3036*	*0.0000*	*0.6872*	*0.6065*	*0.2392*	*1.0148*	*0.8526*	*0.5028*
	1.9899	0.8012	0.0003	3.1834	2.4871	1.4193	4.3004	3.6725	2.6898
	0.0000	1.0773	0.0004	1.0348	1.1120	0.8035	1.1970	1.1526	0.9011
s=full g=no f=no	N/A	*0.3913*	*0.0000*	N/A	*1.1838*	*0.4292*	N/A	*2.1011*	*1.2331*
		0.6669	*0.0000*		*0.9084*	*0.2601*		*1.0658*	*0.5655*
		0.6997	0.0002		2.6754	1.6599		3.7625	2.9868
		1.1208	0.0002		1.3083	0.8089		1.1425	0.9181
s=full g=no f=yes	N/A	*0.4286*	*0.0000*	N/A	*1.1066*	*0.4671*	N/A	*1.8753*	*1.1929*
		0.6698	*0.0000*		*0.8272*	*0.3094*		*1.0624*	*0.5441*
		0.8943	0.0003		2.5687	1.8347		3.6730	2.8970
		1.1796	0.0004		1.3165	0.8264		1.1208	0.8626
s=full g=yes f=no	*0.0332*	*0.0579*	*0.0000*	*1.0396*	*0.8969*	*0.3358*	*1.9737*	*1.5931*	*0.8681*
	0.0469	*0.1306*	*0.0000*	*0.5970*	*0.7295*	*0.2609*	*0.9226*	*0.7710*	*0.4602*
	0.3331	0.3031	0.0005	2.8790	2.3166	1.5941	4.0112	3.5718	2.7054
	0.4685	0.6409	0.0007	0.9066	1.2982	0.7446	1.1571	1.0327	0.8320
s=full g=yes f=yes	*0.3980*	*0.1228*	*0.0166*	*1.1536*	*0.8517*	*0.3373*	*2.0360*	*1.4464*	*0.7913*
	0.0000	*0.1698*	*0.0371*	*0.6872*	*0.7193*	*0.2761*	*1.0148*	*0.7426*	*0.4474*
	1.9899	0.6973	0.1661	3.1834	2.4117	1.6053	4.3004	3.2468	2.5512
	0.0000	0.8572	0.3707	1.0348	1.2834	0.7694	1.1970	1.1666	0.8517

optima, at least in some cases). Judging from the rapid improvements produced by increasing the number of particles from 2 to 10 in all cases, we suspect that further significant improvements could be obtained by using a larger number of particles. Future research will need to clarify this.

6 Conclusions

In this paper we have presented a new search and optimization method inspired by nature: the Constrained Molecular Dynamics method. This method uses the physics of masses and forces to guide the exploration of fitness landscapes. In this paper we have started exploring this idea, using three forces: gravity, interaction via springs, and friction. Gravity provides the ability to seek minima. Springs provide exploration. Friction slows down the search and focuses it.

In the paper we have described experimental results for the De Jong's functions 1 and 2 and for the Rastrigin's function. The results appear to be very encouraging and make us believe that a lot more can come from this method in future research.

Acknowledgements. CRS acknowledges support from DGAPA project ES100201 and Conacyt project 41022-E. RP would like to thank the members of the NEC (Natural and Evolutionary Computation) group for helpful comments and discussion.

References

1. J. Holland. *Adaptation in Natural and Artificial Systems.* University of Michigan Press, Ann Arbor, USA, 1975.
2. S. Kirkpatrick, C. D. Gelatt, and M. P. Vecchi. Optimization by simulated annealing. *Science, Number 4598, 13 May 1983*, 220, 4598:671–680, 1983.
3. J. J. Hopfield. Neural networks and physical systems with emergent collective computational abilities. *Proceedings of the National Academy of Sciences*, 79:2554–2558, 1982.
4. J. J. Hopfield and D. W. Tank. Neural computation of decisions in optimization problems. *Biological Cybernetics*, 52:141–152, 1985.
5. James Kennedy and Russell C. Eberhart. *Swarm Intelligence.* Morgan Kaufmann Publishers, San Francisco, California, 2001.
6. Eric Bonabeau, Marco Dorigo, and Guy Theraulaz. *Swarm intelligence : from natural to artificial systems.* Oxford University Press, New York, 1999.
7. D. C. Rapaport. *The Art of Molecular Dynamics Simulation.* Cambridge University Press, 1997.
8. B. J. Alder and T. E. Wainwright. Phase transition for a hard sphere system. *Journal of Chemical Physics*, 27:1208–1209, 1957.
9. T. M. Blackwell and P. J. Bentley. Dynamic search with charged swarms. In W. B. Langdon *et al.*, editor, *GECCO 2002: Proceedings of the Genetic and Evolutionary Computation Conference*, pages 19–26, New York, 9-13 July 2002. Morgan Kaufmann Publishers.

On the Performance of Genetic Operators and the Random Key Representation

Eoin Ryan, R. Muhammad Atif Azad, and Conor Ryan

Department of Computer Science And Information Systems
University of Limerick
Ireland
{Eoin.Ryan,Atif.Azad,Conor.Ryan}@ul.ie

Abstract. Many evolutionary systems have been developed that solve various specific scheduling problems. In this work, one such permutation based system, which uses a linear GP type Genotype to Phenotype Mapping (GPM), known as the Random Key Genetic Algorithm is investigated. The role standard mutation plays in this representation is analysed formally and is shown to be extremely disruptive. To ensure small fixed sized changes in the phenotype a swap mutation operator is suggested for this representation. An empirical investigation reveals that swap mutation outperforms the standard mutation to solve a hard deceptive problem even without the use of crossover. Swap mutation is also used in conjunction with different crossover operators and significant boost has been observed in the performance especially in the case of headless chicken crossover that produced surprising results.

1   Introduction

Many of the oldest problems historically tackled by the Artificial Intelligence community have been scheduling problems. These problems have been a source of interest both due to their difficulty and the commercial benefits of solving them. This commercial interest has led to the development of many benchmark scheduling problems that focus on various industrial problems [17], as well as many systems developed to solve them.

This paper focuses on solving hard scheduling and permutation problems in a non competent fashion[6]. The Random Key Genetic Algorithm (RKGA)[1] has been chosen as the research focus due to deficiencies observed in the representation and its standard operators. This work attempts to improve the performance of the RKGA and also to understand the dynamics of the system. The aim is to get some clues as to what features a modern, non-competent GA requires in order to solve hard, deceptive scheduling and permutation problems.

The goal of this paper is thus to provide an analysis of the intrinsic behaviour of the RKGA. The unique genotype - phenotype mapping process that exists in this representation has been largely ignored in the literature. We begin our analysis by illustrating the mapping process and then continue, by example, to illustrate the implicit disruptiveness of standard mutation. We follow this with a

M. Keijzer et al. (Eds.): EuroGP 2004, LNCS 3003, pp. 162–173, 2004.

formal analysis of the disruptiveness and show that the bounds of the disruption are maximal. This analysis is then extended to encompass the standard crossover operators and indicates that they too are massively disruptive. With this analysis in mind we develop a new mutation operator that is shown to outperform crossover on a hard deceptive ordering problem from the literature [4].

The remainder of this paper is organised as follows: Section 2 offers a brief background on the most of the historically important evolutionary scheduling systems while Section 3 introduces the representation which will be at the heart of this paper and discusses crossover and mutation operators and their disruptiveness. Section 4 introduces the benchmark problem that is used to test our assertions about the different operators. Finally, Section 5 offers some conclusions and Section 6 presents details of current and future work in this area.

2   Background

Perhaps the most well known scheduling problem is the Travelling Salesman Problem (TSP) [3] which is generally defined as the task of finding the cheapest way of connecting N cities in a closed tour where a cost is associated with each link between the cities. Another class of problems focuses on the scheduling of work in a factory, the most well known being the Job Shop Scheduling Problem (JSSP). In the JSSP we have j jobs and m machines; each job comprises a set of operations each of which must be done on a different machine for a different processing time, in a given job-dependent order. The JSSP is known to be amongst the difficult members of the class of NP-complete problems. Fang [12, 11] offers a thorough and informative discussion of the various forms of Shop Scheduling Problems.

Many historic evolutionary systems employed problem specific representations and great care had to be taken during recombination operations in order to ensure offspring validity. This led to many application and representation specific operators such as the Relative Order Crossover (ROX) [15] and the Edge Assembly Crossover (EAX) [18] in the case of the TSP.

Fang was one of the first to introduce a genotype to phenotype mapping process in the form of a schedule builder. His use of a circular list of uncompleted jobs, akin to the *mod* rule in *Grammatical Evolution* (GE) [2], allowed him to maintain offspring feasibility during crossover operations. In addition the use of the genotype to phenotype mapping process allowed him to incorporate complex dependencies as rules in the schedule builder that eased the burden of the evolutionary process.

Bean [1] was the first to use an encoding scheme that abstracted away from the concept of scheduling and instead treated the problem as a permutation that required solving. He employed the concept that any sequence of numbers can be sorted to provide a valid permutation. He termed this the *Random Key Representation*. This allowed standard search operators to be utilised instead of the problem specific operators as the representation guaranteed offspring validity.

More recently, Hart et. al took a novel approach and used the concept of an *Artificial Immune System* (AIS) [8,7] to evolve *potential antibody libraries*.

The evolved libraries are expressed to form particular antibodies which are then mapped into a schedule using the same process as Fang. An *antigen* describes a set of expected arrival dates for each job in the shop which the antibodies are then matched against. A *match score*, which is equivalent to its fitness, is assigned to the antibody based on how it matches a set of antigens.

Some of the latest research on solving hard permutation problems uses a Competent GA[6], known as the *Ordering Messy Genetic Algorithm* (OMEGA)[4,9,5]. OMEGA uses the robust random key representation in order to guarantee chromosome validity. OMEGA operates by initialising the population with every possible building block up to some maximum size k. Cut and splice operators are then used to recombine pre-existing building blocks to form the global solution. The chromosomes are variable length, hence, the system needs to handle under and over-specification. The former is done by utilising a competitive template which is used to fill in the missing genes. The latter is handled by using a first come first served precedence rule.

3   The Random Key Genetic Algorithm

Bean [1] developed the Random Key GA as a robust method for evolving permutations that guaranteed offspring feasibility after recombination operations. He employed the concept that any sequence of numbers could be sorted to provide a valid permutation. In addition, no matter what recombination or mutation operations are performed on individuals their offsprings are always valid.

His original GA used parametrised uniform crossover instead of traditional one-point or two-point crossover and rather than the traditional gene by gene mutation Bean employed the concept of *immigration*. Immigration is the process of randomly generating new members of the population which he used in order to prevent premature convergence. Immigration will be shown to be of limited value as a search mechanism as the meaning of any particular gene is not easily passed onto offspring via crossover.

Bean's original work focused more on the application of the RKGA to scheduling and resource allocation problems rather than the features of the representation itself and its operators. The goal of our work is to provide an analysis of the intrinsic behaviour of the random key representation and to show how the standard operators interact with it. We investigate both his original immigration operator and the standard point mutation. From there we will develop our own mutation operator which is shown to perform very well on a class of hard deceptive permutation problem.

3.1   The Representation

A Random Key is a real valued number typically in the range $[0, 1]$. In this representation a chromosome is thus a sequence of real valued numbers where each position in the chromosome represents an item in the permutation. A chromosome is transferred into a permutation in two steps. Figure 1 offers a graphical representation of this process.

1	2	3	4	5	6	7	8	
0.66	0.51	0.11	0.98	0.85	0.72	0.22	0.56	Genotype (Unsorted Representation)

0.11	0.22	0.51	0.56	0.66	0.72	0.85	0.98	Genotype (Sorted Representation)

3	7	2	8	1	6	5	4	Phenotype (Permutation)

Fig. 1. The process of mapping an individual from genotype to phenotype. The intermediate (sorted) representation is very important in the mapping process as it provides the order in which genes from the genotype are to be read.

- The chromosome is sorted to provide an intermediate representation termed simply the *sorted representation*. This gives the order in which each gene is to be mapped into a permutation.
- The position of each gene's index in the *unsorted representation* determines where its corresponding item is to be placed.

3.2 Point Mutation

Point, or Key Mutation, operates by randomly selecting a gene along the chromosome, which is then replaced by a randomly generated key. This form of mutation plays a very disruptive role in the evolutionary process due to its unpredictable effects on the phenotype. Let us illustrate by selecting the fourth gene from Fig. 1 for mutation and by randomly generating a new value for this gene (see Fig. 2). Notice that not only does this effect the genotype, but also the intermediate representation.

In order to understand why this is so disruptive, consider the effect this gene has had in the sorted representation and compare this with the sorted representation in Fig. 1. Many of the genes in the sorted representation have been shifted from left to right. Recall that the sorted representation determines the order in which the genes get to code for parts of the permutation, so this seemingly small change has caused a mutation ripple [13] from the mutated point in $[0, 1]$ space to the largest key in $[0, 1]$ space in the chromosome, shifting from left to right, genes in the intermediate representation. This shifting of genes in the intermediate representation causes a knock on effect with how each gene is coded into the phenotype. Thus, even a very small change in the genotype can have a very large effect in the phenotype. This is not always a desirable effect.

Formal Analysis. The previous section exemplifies how disruptive a point mutation event can be. We now present a general case by providing the bounds on the number of genes that a single point mutation can relocate in the ordered representation. We also note that, on average, half the total number of genes are affected by a single point mutation in a randomly generated genotype.

Let $G = g_1, g_2, g_3, \cdots, g_n$ be the *sorted* representation of a genotype containing n genes. Let g_i represent the gene at the ith position in the sorted

1	2	3	4	5	6	7	8	
0.66	0.51	0.11	0.17	0.85	0.72	0.22	0.56	Genotype (Unsorted Representation)

0.11	0.17	0.22	0.51	0.56	0.66	0.72	0.85	Genotype (Sorted Representation)

3	4	7	2	8	1	6	5	Phenotype (Permutation)

Fig. 2. Point Mutation: A gene is selected at random and is replaced by a randomly generated key. This mutation effects the sorted order of the chromosome as well as the final permutation.

representation which may be different from the location it occupies in the unsorted form. Consider a point mutation that changes g_i to g_i'. We assume that $g_i' - g_i$ is effective enough to leave G unsorted. In order to return to a sorted representation G' we have to find k i.e. the number of positions g_i' is shifted left or right. This means that $k + 1$ genes are displaced due to the change $g_i \rightarrow g_i'$. k can be calculated as follows.

$$k = \begin{cases} a = |\{g_j | g_j \in G \wedge g_i' < g_j\}| \text{ if } g_i' < g_i \\ b = |\{g_j | g_j \in G \wedge g_i' > g_j\}| \text{ if } g_i' > g_i \end{cases} \tag{1}$$

Equation 1 shows that if the mutation event decreases the value of g_i to g_i' it is shifted a positions to the left. When $g_i' > g_i$ the modified gene is shifted b positions to the right side. a and b also represent the number of genes displaced in addition to g_i'. The maximum value of k is $n - 1$ when a gene is relocated from one extreme of the sorted genotype to the other and the minimum value is 1 when it is only swapped with one of its immediate neighbours.

In this case, we have assumed that mutation always disrupts the ordered genotype. If we include the possibility that $g_i' - g_i$ is so small that $G' \equiv G$ then $0 \leq k + 1 \leq n$. Thus, for a randomly generated genotype the expected number of relocations is $n/2$.

This analysis gives an indication about the effect of crossover. A crossover event can be viewed as a two step process. In the first step a set of genes moves out of the chromosome leaving behind a number of vacant slots in the genotype. In the second step, the incoming set of genes places itself in the host genotype. The placement of each of the incoming genes can be seen as a mutation event. A single mutation relocates a single gene by moving a block of consecutive genes. Multiple mutation events, on the other hand, can break the blocks themselves. This indicates that crossover can be even more disruptive. However, an analysis that formally quantifies the effects of crossover constitutes a part of the future work.

3.3 Swap Mutation

Swap Mutation operates by randomly selecting two genes along the chromosome which are then swapped. The special characteristic of this form of mutation is that no new genetic material is passed into the chromosome. As a result, the

1	2	3	4	5	6	7	8	
0.66	0.51	0.72	0.98	0.85	0.11	0.22	0.56	Genotype (Unsorted Representation)

0.11	0.22	0.51	0.56	0.66	0.72	0.85	0.98	Genotype (Sorted Representation)

6	7	2	8	1	3	5	4	Phenotype (Permutation)

Fig. 3. Swap Mutation: Two genes are randomly selected in the genotype and are then swapped. This does not affect the intermediate representation but rather has the effect of swapping elements of the permutation.

intermediate representation remains the same. Instead, the effect of this mutation is to reorder the way in which the genes are coded into the phenotype.

To illustrate let us pick the third and the sixth genes in the genotype shown in Fig. 1, swap them and then examine the effects on the phenotype (Fig. 3). Notice that the intermediate representation is identical to that of Fig. 1. The order in which the genes are sorted is not changed. However, as they have swapped places, in effect they have swapped the items they encode for. As a result, items 3 and 6 have exchanged their places in the phenotype in Fig. 3. It should be noted that the rest of the phenotype is the same as in Fig. 1. This is in stark contrast to point mutation which has been shown to affect $k + 1$ positions where $0 \leq k + 1 \leq n$.

4   Problem Definition

In order to understand the performance of the different forms of mutation discussed above as well as the performance of the standard crossover operators, one of the standard benchmark problems from the literature - the Ordering Deceptive Problem [9,5] is used. We have picked the hardest such problem, the Absolute Ordering problem and we use the Loose Coding scheme (see Table 1). The absolute ordering problem tackled is comprised of eight order four deceptive problems concatenated to give a total problem length of 32. In this problem the task is to evolve a permutation such that the first element is one, the second is two, the third is three and so on all the way to 32. We refer the interested reader to the literature for further details on the Ordering Deceptive Problems.

4.1   Performance Results of the Mutation Operators without Crossover

In these experiments we compare the performance of the two forms of mutation discussed above. We make this comparison by examining how different mutation rates affect the evolutionary process without using crossover. The experiments were run using a population size of 600 evolving for 600 generations and all experiments were repeated 50 times. In all cases the evolutionary mechanism used was generational with elitism. An elitism rate of 10% was used and the selection mechanism was roulette wheel. For each mutation type we select an

Table 1. First two columns show the absolute ordering function f_{abs}. These are the fitness scores assigned to each sub-function, depending on their relative ordering. The last two columns show the loose coding scheme used for the problem. The coding scheme determines the placement of each gene, of each sub-problem, in the genotype. The greater the separation, the more difficult it is for the GA to maintain building blocks during recombination.

Absolute Ordering Function		Loose Codings	
f(1 2 3 4) = 4.0	f(2 4 3 1) = 2.0	1	1, 9, 17, 25
f(4 2 3 1) = 1.8	f(3 2 4 1) = 2.0	2	2, 10, 18, 26
f(1 3 2 4) = 1.8	f(1 4 2 3) = 2.0	3	3, 11, 19, 27
f(1 2 4 3) = 1.8	f(4 1 2 3) = 2.6	4	4, 12, 20, 28
f(1 4 3 2) = 1.8	f(3 4 1 2) = 2.6	5	5, 13, 21, 29
f(3 2 1 4) = 1.8	f(2 3 4 1) = 2.6	6	6, 14, 22, 30
f(2 1 3 4) = 1.8	f(2 4 1 3) = 2.6	7	7, 15, 23, 31
f(4 2 1 3) = 2.0	f(2 1 4 3) = 2.6	8	8, 16, 24, 32
f(4 1 3 2) = 2.0	f(4 3 2 1) = 2.6		
f(3 1 2 4) = 2.0	f(4 3 1 2) = 2.6		
f(1 3 4 2) = 2.0	f(3 1 4 2) = 2.6		
f(2 3 1 4) = 2.0	f(3 4 2 1) = 3.3		

individual for mutation with the following probabilities - 10%, 20%, 50% and 80%. The remainder of the time reproduction propagates individuals into the next generation.

As can be seen from Fig. 4 the swap mutation operator clearly outperforms the point mutation operator. In fact on average, swap mutation alone successfully solves the problem in 20 out of the 50 runs in which the experiment was repeated.

4.2   Performance Results of the Mutation Operators with Crossover

In these experiments we compare the performance of the mutation operators by examining how they affect the evolutionary process when using crossover. We compare the standard crossover operators - one point, two point and uniform crossover. In addition, we try headless chicken crossover[10] which operates like one point crossover except the tail of the child chromosome is replaced with randomly generated genes. We experiment with headless chicken crossover in order to compare a truly randomised crossover operator against standard operators which we have already indicated may be extremely disruptive.

The experimental setup was as follows: we evolved a population of 600 individuals to 600 generations and the experiments were repeated 50 times. The evolutionary mechanism used was generational with elitism. An elitism rate of 10% was used and the selection mechanism was roulette wheel. In all cases the probability of a crossover operation was set to 70%, the probability of a mutation was 20% and the probability of reproduction was 10%. In the case of immigration a much higher rate was employed than in Bean's original experiments in order to stimulate more search - an immigration rate of 10% was used.

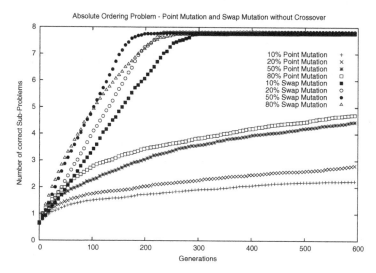

Fig. 4. Plot of the average best fit individual in every generation when using Point and Swap Mutation *without* crossover. We evolve 600 individuals to 600 generations and repeat every experiment 50 times. The superior performance of Swap Mutation can clearly be seen from the graph - on average it solves the problem in 20 out of the 50 runs.

Results from the immigration experiments were as predicted. The extremely poor performance of immigration can clearly be seen from Fig. 5. Uniform crossover is clearly the best solving merely three of the eight subproblems. One and two point crossover are only marginally better than headless-chicken crossover, on average only correctly solving one sub-problem.

The results from the crossover experiments when using point mutation are surprising (see Fig. 6). Referring to Fig. 4 it can be seen that swap mutation alone outperforms the combination of point mutation with crossover. In these experiments uniform crossover is clearly the best - by the end of the evolution it has, on average, correctly solved five of the eight sub-problems. One and two point crossover are identical and on average, only manage to solve four sub-problems and as expected headless chicken crossover is the poorest, on average only managing to correctly solve two of the eight sub-problems.

The results from the crossover experiments when using swap mutation are also extremely interesting (see Fig. 7). The superior performance of *headless-chicken* crossover can clearly be seen; by the end of the evolution it has, on average, correctly solved seven of the eight sub-problems. By comparison there appears to be little difference between uniform crossover, one-point and two-point crossover, on average none of them are able to get to the last sub-problem.

The conclusion that can be drawn from these results is that swap mutation operates in part as an *exploitation* tool. Since swap mutation never actually introduces new genetic material it raises the question as to whether new genetic material is actually required in a permutation based GA. What matters is the

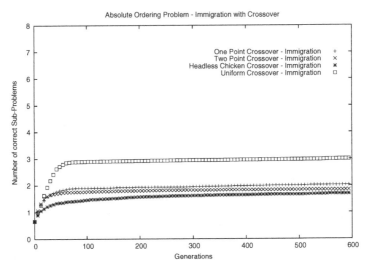

Fig. 5. Plot of the average best fit individual in every generation when using different forms of crossover with immigration. The disappointing performance of this mutation operator can clearly be seen. The best crossover was uniform crossover which only managed to solve three of the eight sub-problems correct.

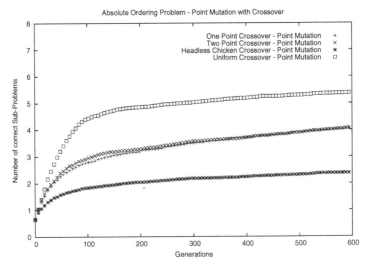

Fig. 6. Plot of the average best fit individual in every generation when using different forms of crossover with point mutation. The disappointing performance of the different crossovers can clearly be seen. The best crossover was uniform crossover which only managed to get five of the eight sub-problems correct.

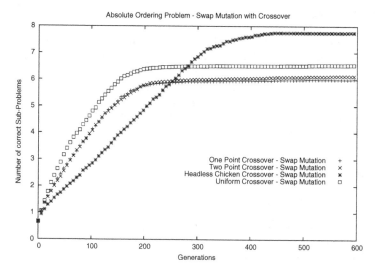

Fig. 7. Plot of the average best fit individual in every generation when using different forms of crossover with swap mutation. The increased performance of the system when using swap mutation can be clearly seen in comparison with 6.

relative ordering of the genes in the chromosome as opposed to the material itself. So, although swap mutation has fixed sized effects and may be limited in its global search abilities, it is systematic enough to beat point mutation.

From these results it is clear that there must exist a synergetic effect between it and the randomised and disruptive headless-chicken crossover. These counter-intuitive results would suggest that headless-chicken crossover is being utilised as an *exploration* operator introducing new combinations of genetic material into the population which swap mutation is then able to exploit.

5   Conclusions

This work examines the intrinsic operation of the RKGA and its representation. The role standard operators play in the evolutionary process is investigated and a formal analysis of the disruptiveness of mutation is presented. Following this analysis a new mutation operator known as swap mutation is suggested that has a controlled effect on the phenotype. Experiments are conducted comparing swap mutation against standard point mutation without using crossover and it is shown that sensible mutation alone is sufficient to solve a hard permutation problem. Furthermore the performance of this new mutation operator is shown in conjunction with various crossover operators and counter-intuitive results are obtained when using headless chicken crossover. These results are interesting for GP Genotype to Phenotype systems such as GE[14] and GADS[16] as they also observe a ripple effect so perhaps a mutation operator similar to swap mutation would be beneficial.

6   Future Work

Current and future work centres around examining different swap mutation rates with different crossovers. A formal analysis of recombination operators in the random key representation is also desirable. Following this it is hoped to develop of a suite of sensible crossovers that aim to propagate the exact meaning of genes from parent to offspring. Once sensible crossovers have been developed it will be interesting to compare the performance of the RKGA to OmeGA. The results of this comparison will guide more future work.

References

1. Bean J. C. Genetic algorithms and random keys for sequencing and optimization. *ORSA Journal on Computing*, 1994.
2. Ryan C., Collins J. J., and O'Neill M. Grammatical evolution: Evolving programs for an arbitrary language. In Wolfgang Banzhaf, Riccardo Poli, Marc Schoenauer, and Terence C. Fogarty, editors, *Proceedings of the First European Workshop on Genetic Programming*, volume 1391, pages 83–95, Paris, 14-15 1998. Springer-Verlag.
3. Johnson D. The travelling salesman problem: A case study in local optimization. In E.H.L. Aarts and J.K. Lenstra, editors, *Local Search in Combinatorial Optimization*, pages 215–310, London, UK, 1997. John Wiley and Sons.
4. Knjazew D. and Goldberg D. E. Large-scale permutation optimization with the ordering messy genetic algorithm. *PPSN 2000*, pages 631–640, 2000.
5. Knjazew D. and Goldberg D. E. Omega - ordering messy ga: Solving permutation problems with the fast messy genetic algorithm and random keys. *ILLiGAL Technical Report No. 2000004*, 2000.
6. Goldberg D. E., Korb B., and K. Deb. Messy genetic algorithms: Motivation, analysis, and first results. *Complex Systems*, pages 493–530, 1989.
7. Hart E. and Ross P. An immune system approach to scheduling in changing environments. In W. Banzhaf et al., editor, *Genetic and Evolutionary Computation Conference - GECCO 1999*, pages 1559–1565, Orlando, Florida, USA, 1999. Morgan Kaufmann.
8. Hart E., Ross P., and Nelson J. Producing robust schedules via an artificial immune system. In *International Conference on Evolutionary Computing, ICEC '98*, pages 464–469, Anchorage, Alaska, USA, 1998. IEEE Press.
9. Kargupta H., Deb K., and Goldberg D. E. Ordering genetic algorithms and deception. In *Parallel Problem Solving from Nature - PPSN II*, pages 47–56, 1992.
10. Angeline P. J. Subtree crossover: Building block engine or macromutation? In J. R. Koza, K. Deb, M. Dorigo, D. B. Fogel, M. Garzon, H. Iba, and R. L. Riolo, editors, *Genetic Programming 1997: Proceedings of the Second Annual Conference*, pages 9–17, San Francisco, CA, 1997. Morgan Kaufmann.
11. Fang H. L. *Genetic Algorithms in Timetabling and Scheduling*. PhD thesis, Department of Artificial Intelligence, University of Edinburgh, 1994.
12. Fang H. L., Ross P., and D. Corne. A promising genetic algorithm approach to job-shop scheduling, rescheduling, and open-shop scheduling problems. In *Proceedings of the Fifth International Conference on Genetic Algorithms*, pages 375–382, 1993.
13. O'Neill M., Ryan C., Keijzer M., and Cattolico M. Crossover in grammatical evolution. *Genetic Programming and Evolvable Machines*, 4, No. 1:67–93, 2003.

14. M. O'Neill and C. Ryan. *Grammatical Evolution - Evolving programs in an arbitrary language.* Kluwer Academic Publishers, 2003.
15. Moscato P. On genetic crossover operators for relative order preservation, 1989.
16. Norman Paterson. *Genetic programming with context-sensitive grammars.* PhD thesis, Saint Andrew's University, September 2002.
17. Ciesielski V. and Scerri P. Real time genetic scheduling of aircraft landing times.
18. J. Watson, C. Ross, V. Eisele, J. Bins, C. Guerra, L. Whitley, and A. Howe. The traveling salesrep problem, edge assembly crossover, and 2-opt, 1998.

Analysis of GP Improvement Techniques over the Real-World Inverse Problem of Ocean Color

Grégory Valigiani, Cyril Fonlupt, and Pierre Collet

LIL,Université du Littoral
BP 719 62228 Calais Cedex, France
{valigian,fonlupt,collet}@lil.univ-littorla.fr

Abstract. This paper is a follow-up of Maarten Keijzer's award-winning EUROGP'03 paper [Kei03], that suggests using *Interval Arithmetic* (IA) and *Linear Scaling* (LS) in Genetic Programming algorithms. The ideas exposed in this paper were so nice that it was decided to experiment with them on a real-world problem on which the LIL research team had some experience and results with: the Ocean Color Inverse Problem.

After extensive testing of IA, LS as well as a progressive learning method using thresholds (T), results seem to show that functions evolved with GP algorithms that do not implement IA may output erroneous values outside the learning set, while LS and T methods produce solutions with a greater generalisation error.

A simple and apparently harmless improvement over standard GP is also proposed, that consists in weighting operands of + and − operators.

1 Introduction

Concentration of phytoplankton over the ocean is a parameter of utmost importance for scientists in order to better understand sea biology and what is called "primary production." Primary production is supposed to play a key role in the evaluation of the global carbon cycle and is thus of great scientific concern, especially to better apprehend the so-called greenhouse effect.

One way to estimate phytoplankton concentration is to measure the energy level reflected by the ocean with a satellite spectrometer. This difficult problem has already been extensively addressed by the LIL team using Genetic Programming[FR00,RF01,Fon01], as it can be seen as a regression problem.

Then, two interesting generic suggestions for improvement in Genetic Programming were brought up by Maarten Keijzer in a recent publication[Kei03] (namely *Interval Arithmetic* and *Linear Scaling*), that received the best paper award at the last EURO-GP conference. It was decided to experiment with them because they were well described, seemed very sound and made a lot of sense.

The primary aim of this work is therefore to assess and analyse those techniques on a tough, real-world problem (the above mentioned ocean color inverse problem), and determine whether they could bring significant improvements over the well polished GP algorithm that had been successfully evolved a couple of

M. Keijzer et al. (Eds.): EuroGP 2004, LNCS 3003, pp. 174–186, 2004.

years ago. Then, during the implementation, the idea of weighting operands of simple operators emerged, and led to positive results.

This paper therefore starts with a short description of the ocean color problem in section 2 and presents the results of Fonlupt *et al.* [RF01]. Section 3 deals with the implementation of the new GP algorithm. Section 4 describes the weighted operands improvement that appeared during this implementation and section 5 presents results obtained with Keijer's suggestions (IA and LS). Section 6 discusses the different techniques, and the paper finishes with a conclusion containing do's and don't's that stemmed from the previous analysis.

2   The Photosynthesis Available Radiation Problem

2.1   PAR Evaluation

The *Photosynthesis Available Radiation* (aka PAR) is the number of photons available for photosynthesis in the visible wavelength range (400 – 700 nm). As explained in the previous section, understanding primary production might help to better evaluate the greenhouse effect and computing the PAR is a step towards the evaluation of the primary production.

It is possible to measure the PAR directly in the middle of the ocean, but this method is impractical, expensive, and only gives local information.

Another idea is to deduce the PAR from an analysis of the light reflected by the ocean. Such analysis could be done on satellite images, therefore removing the constraint of having a boat in the middle of the Pacific Ocean measuring the amount of light coming from the sun. This problem is however quite difficult:

- The light coming from the sun and going down to the ocean is modified by the atmosphere: solar radiance is scattered and absorbed by air molecules and pollution particles in suspension.
- Then, a part of the light is absorbed by water molecules and dissolved particles within the ocean. Only part of it (water-leaving radiance) is scattered back up through the surface,
- Light needs to go through the atmosphere again to reach the satellite sensors.

Usually, less than 10% of the total light detected by the satellite is water-leaving radiance. The inverse problem is also terribly complex due to the fact that water optical properties as well its biological components are spectrally dependent.

2.2   The Inverse Problem

Solutions have been proposed to solve the direct problem, *i.e.* simulating the amount of radiations received by a satellite spectrometer using models of reflectance derived either from empirical data [Mor88,Mor91], or from radiative transfer code such as the OSOA model [CDS00]. These simulations are quite accurate and can be used as a basis to train on the inverse problem.

As the light available for photosynthesis is spectrally dependent, the available energy for each wavelength is modeled using the following formula:

$$K_d(\lambda) = \frac{1}{z} \log(\frac{E_0(\lambda, z)}{E_0(\lambda, z_{\text{surf}})})$$

where z indicates the depth in the water column, $E_0(\lambda, z_{\text{surf}})$ the available energy at the sea surface at wavelength λ and $E_0(\lambda, z)$ the available energy at wavelength λ at depth z for photosynthesis.

So, the estimation of the energy only necessitates the knowledge of the $K_d(\lambda)$ coefficient. Unfortunately, this is far from trivial as this coefficient not only depends on the wavelength but also on the sea components (phytoplankton, yellow substance and sediments).

Therefore, evaluating the K_d coefficient from the measured reflected energy can be formulated as $K_d(\lambda) = f(L_{410}, L_{443}, L_{490}, L_{510}, L_{560}, L_{665})$, a regression problem where L_w indicates the set of monitored wavelengths of the "SeaWIFS" satellite sensor. The table below shows the best results that have been obtained on this problem by the LIL team [RF01] in terms of RMS (Root Mean Square) error that must be minimised.

These results are regarded as very good by biologists:

Wavelength	412	443	490	510	555	620
RMS ERROR (%)	6.5	5.3	2.4	4.7	2.3	1.5

3 New Genetic Programming Implementation

3.1 Framework and Settings

Unfortunately, the code for the original GP program used for [RF01] had been optimized to such degree that it would have been very impractical to precisely determine the impact of Keijzer's improvements on it. It was therefore decided to rapidly develop again a clean GP algorithm using the EASEA fast specification language, so as to have a sound basis for comparison.

In order to compare results, the number of evaluations was kept identical to the original GP program as well as the following choices of the original program:

- A maximum depth, $\mathcal{D}_{max}$ is set in order to avoid bloat.
- The raw fitness of GP individuals is given by the relative RMS error on the training set:

$$\text{Relative RMS error} = \sqrt{\frac{1}{n} \sum_{i=1}^{n} (\frac{K_{\text{computed}} - K_{\text{expected}}}{K_{\text{expected}}})^2}$$

- The fitness cases are built on a data set of 252 samples, based on the OSOA model and generated with a software based on Chami et al [Cha97,CDS97].

Otherwise, extensive tests led to the optimal settings shown below:

Generations	1000
Population	5000
Fitness cases	252
Functions set	$\{+,-,\times,/,\exp,\ln\}$
Terminal set	Cst, $L_{410}, L_{443}, L_{490}, L_{510}, L_{560}, L_{665}$
Recombination rate	0.85
Mutation rate	$0.5 \to 0.05$

Different sets of functions have been tested, and the best results were obtained with $+, -, \times, /$ exp() and ln() only.

One run takes more than one hour on a 2GHz Pentium with 1GB of RAM. All experiments have been done on an average of 10 runs (around 12 hours per test). For the purpose of this paper, most of the figures deal with the 412 nm wavelength which is known to be the most difficult one to approximate.

3.2   Implementation with EASEA

The EASEAv0.6c [CLSL00,Col04] language (EAsy Specification of Evolutionary Algorithms) has been used as a framework for our GP application.

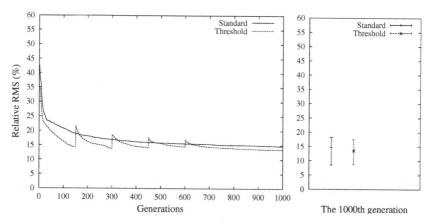

Fig. 1. Comparison between a standard GP and the threshold GP approach for 412 nm. The figure on the right figure shows the best, average and worst of 10 runs.

This language has been designed to make the programming of Evolutionary Algorithms as easy as possible by compiling EA specifications into C++ code using the GALib or EO libraries, or JAVA code using the DREAM library.

It has therefore been possible to quickly write some working code for this application and concentrate on the GP algorithm rather than on the C++ im-plementation of the genetic engine. The implemented algorithm is as simple and straightforward as possible in order to assess Keijzer's suggestions only:

Structure. A common GP tree-structure is used. Each node holds the characteristics of the functions/terminal but also some parameters needed for the GP algorithm, to implement Schwefel's adaptive mutation[Sch95] for instance.

Initialisation. A classical "ramped half-and-half" method is used.

Recombination. The cross-over operator simply exchanges two subtrees of the parents to create the two children. Subtrees are chosen so that the offspring does not have a depth greater than the maximum allowed depth, $\mathcal{D}_{max}$.

Mutation. Mutation of a node is constrained to preserve the arity of the operator in order to keep the tree structure.

Threshold method (T). This method was originally used and described in [RF01] to save on computing time, when only P120s were used. It was decided to keep it, since it is fast, and the best results were obtained with this method. The general principle is based on progressive learning, (a variant of limiting the fitness evaluation to a subpopulation [BNKF99]) or by stopping the evaluation as soon as a threshold of bad individuals has been reached [GR97]. Data is split into n parts corresponding to the number of planned thresholds. New data is given to the algorithm everytime a threshold is reached.

Unfortunately, the good threshold is difficult to find, and varies with the problem to be solved (the wavelength in this case): if it is too high, evolution will have trouble to reach the threshold and go through the different stages. On the contrary, if it is too low, not enough time will be spent on each stage and the progressive method will not achieve its goal.

In the new GP algorithm, it was decided to add data every fixed number of generations (150), which is a parameter that was much easier to find. Results can be seen on fig. 1, which compares the much quicker "threshold" (hereafter called "T") method with standard GP over 10 runs.

4   Weighted Operands

For an efficient evolution, it is known that operators with a great power of variation are needed for the exploration phase while the exploitation phase needs more delicate changes.

In GP however, node mutation usually creates strong alterations in the tree. In order to allow small variations to occur, weighting factors are introduced, that allow to more finely tune operands. $B_1 + B_2$ becomes $\alpha_1 B_1 + \alpha_2 B_2$. α parameters undergo Schwefel's adaptive mutation [Sch95].

Thanks to the weighted + and − operators, evolution seems to have a better dynamics and pass the different stages more easily. Trials with other operators than + and − have not been conclusive.

Since this method always gave slightly better results, (cf. fig. 2) it was kept throughout this paper.

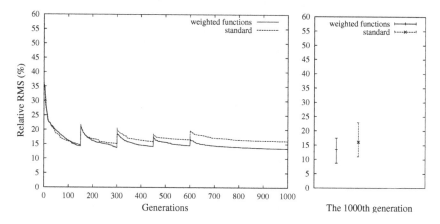

Fig. 2. Influence of the weighted operands on 412 nm for 10 runs.

4.1   Overall Results without Keijzer's Suggestions

Finally, over many runs, the best result was obtained by a great standard run (RMS of 8.5% on the 412 nm wavelength) while the best of all runs with Threshold progressive learning and weighted operands was 8.7%.

These results must be compared with those found by Fonlupt *et al.* in [RF01]: 6.5%, which shows the degree of refinement of the original GP program.

5   Keijzer's Improvements

In his paper [Kei03], Marteen Keijzer proposed two ideas to improve GP symbolic regression: Interval Arithmetic (IA) and Linear Scaling (LS).

5.1   Interval Arithmetic (IA)

M. Keijzer starts with the observation that in symbolic regression problems, used operators should not lead to singular or undefined values. The usual protection for division by zero does not prevent the target value to vary between $+\infty$ or $-\infty$ within a very short range, therefore leading to an approximation that could contain extravagant values within a very narrow interval that could go unnoticed in the sampling of the learning set.

The suggestion is then to avoid using operators on intervals that may contain undefined or singular values, so as to remain into a continuous and derivable domain. This is done by calculating the bounds of a function given the bounds of the operands, while excluding singular values.

New parameters are added: each node n is accompanied with its lower and upper bounds n_l and n_u. With this information, the bounds of the operator are evaluated using basic mathematical knowledge for the different operators:

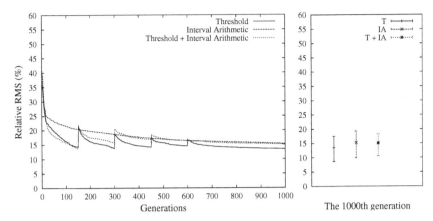

Fig. 3. Results with Interval Arithmetic and Threshold over 10 runs on 412nm.

- If node n represents $a + b$: $n_l = a_l + b_l$ and $n_u = a_u + b_u$.
- If node n represents $a \times b$: $n_l = \min(a_l \times b_l, a_l \times b_u, a_u \times b_l, a_u \times b_u)$ and
  $n_u = \min(a_l \times b_l, u_l \times b_u, a_u \times b_l, a_u \times b_u)$.
- ...

Updating these boundaries from bottom to top allow to exclude singular values from the whole function. With Interval Arithmetic, one can make sure that the second operand of / never contains zero, for instance.

If such a case appears, Keijzer suggests that the individual be either assigned the worst possible fitness value or be deleted. In this implementation, the choice was made to mutate the operator of the offending operand into another one that can accept the operand's interval.

Tests on the Ocean Problem show that IA does not really give better results over threshold GP (cf fig. 3). A probable explanation is that GP evolution using IA is degraded by the additional constraints on singular values exclusion. However, one must keep in mind that the real aim of symbolic regression is not to approximate a function as well as possible on the training set: results on the training set might be slightly worse, but the returned function might present a better behaviour on other values than the training set, which is what GP is all about, after all.

In this respect, scientists should regard GP+IA evolved functions as much safer than GP only evolved functions, since they are sure not to exhibit extravagant results due to an operator returning a near-infinite value on an input that was not part of the training set.

From these results on the training set, implementing IA does not seem a great idea, unless one realises that slightly less good results might be the price to pay for a better-behaved function on the real data.

5.2   Linear Scaling (LS)

The second improvement proposed by Keijzer is Linear Scaling (LS). LS comes from the remark that GP loses time evaluating constants. For instance, GP will easily find x^2 but is not at ease at finding $x^2 + 100$. A lot of time is wasted in determining constant values, although this is an easy problem to solve.

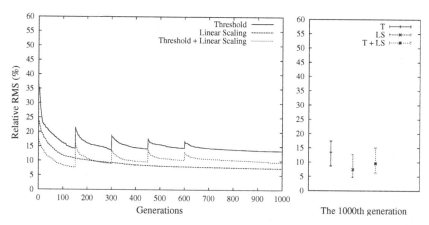

Fig. 4. LS results for the ocean color problem at 412nm

The principle of LS is to let GP find a general form $f(x)$ and then calculate the best $\mathcal{B}$ and $\mathcal{A}$ so that $\mathcal{B} * f(x) + \mathcal{A}$ best fits the data. (Note that the LS idea is close to other research papers like constant fitting [SJK97].)

In [Kei03] the optima $\mathcal{B}$ and $\mathcal{A}$ are defined for MSE error. Since RMS error is used throughout this paper, new optimal values for $\mathcal{B}$ and $\mathcal{A}$ have been computed.

Unlike IA, LS (see fig. 4) greatly improves the performance. On 10 runs, the best average is obtained by LS over T and even T+LS.

Coupling LS with T does not seem to bring any improvement. On the contrary, results are slightly better without T. An interpretation is that LS works too well: $\mathcal{B}$ and $\mathcal{A}$ values quickly adapt, and simplify the task for the GP algorithm that is then able to fit very closely the learning target. As a consequence, whenever new data is added, the structure of the GP-evolved function may need to be changed, which is difficult to do if the population has already converged to solve the previous task that had been simplified by LS.

In other words, LS could be misleading GP for each new data set, with the result that LS works better when the algorithm is provided all the data at once.

This somehow suggests that LS is fitting the learning data very well, but casts doubts on its generalising power, since every time another chunk of data is brought in, results are getting worse rather than improving.

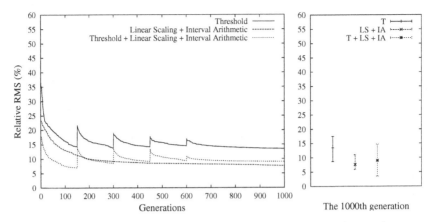

Fig. 5. comparisons of the T, LS+IA, T+LS+IA schemes (412 nm)

5.3   Combining LS and IA

Since T, LS and IA methods are acting on different parts of the GP algorithm, it seems interesting to see how results are affected by combining them. Therefore, T, LS+IA and T+LS+IA methods are compared fig. 5.

Since IA has a tendency to make results worse (cf. section 5.1: IA adds constraints to the GP evolution) the curves are no surprise: *on average*, LS+IA gives worse results than LS alone, and adding the Threshold method to LS+IA is not a good idea, as LS and Threshold are incompatible (cf. section 5.2 above).

5.4   Overall Results on the Training Set for 412 nm

The table below shows all the results for the ocean color inverse problem for the 412 nm wavelength. It is quite obvious that the LS improvement is significant.

Methods	[RF01]	Standard	T	IA	T+IA	LS	T+LS	LS + IA	T+LS+IA
Best run	6.5	8.5	8.7	9.9	10.6	4.8	6.3	5.9	**3.5**
Average	??	14.7	13.5	15.2	15.1	**7.5**	9.5	7.6	9.0

It is worth noting that on the training set, a GP+weighted operands+T+LS+IA method has provided overall best results that are much better than those presented in [RF01] (3.5% rather than 6.5%). Strangely enough (considering that T and LS are incompatible), over all other wavelengths than 410 nm, over 10 runs, the T+LS+IA method has always provided the best result on the training set.

6   Assessment of the Generalisation Capabilities of Functions Obtained through the Different Methods

Up to now, experiments have been made on the training set, meaning that the different GP variants have come up with a solution that matched the training

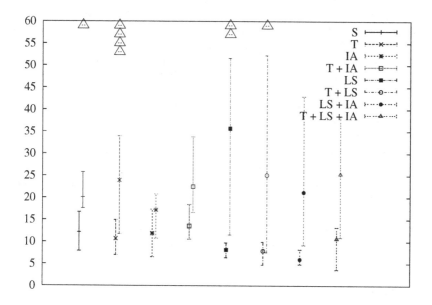

Fig. 6. Each column corresponds to an implemented method. Results over the training set are on the left while results for the validation set are on the right. A little triangle on the upper part of the figure indicates extravagant (more than 60% RMS error) results.

set as closely as possible. However, the aim of this work is to find a function that gives good results on satellite data, and not on the training set only.

Therefore, a final set of experiments has been conducted in order to test the power of generalization of each method, which is what the scientist is really interested in. The result can be seen in fig. 6.

The data file has been randomly split into two subsets. The first set (called the training set) has been used to evolve 10 functions for each method (vertical bars slightly on the left). Then the best evolved functions were tested against the second set, called the validation set (vertical bars slightly on the right).

Results on the training set are of course much better than results on the validation set, but this is no great discovery.

However, it is interesting to note that several functions that performed well on the training set show huge RMS errors on the validation set. For instance, method T alone has come up with a function showing an RMS error of more than 400% ! Those extravagant functions have not been taken into account in the min and max bars, but the information was kept and represented by the small triangles indicating functions with RMS error beyond 60%.

Now, on this validation test, results are quite different than those presented on the training set :

1. Most important result : Although some solutions obtained may be robust in
   the application domain, *all methods that do not include IA (also standard
   GP) have produced functions with triangles (i.e. RMS error beyond 60%).*
   This shows that on 10 runs only, methods (including standard GP) that do
   not include IA have always found functions that work perfectly well on the
   training set but proved absolutely unusable on another data set !
2. Conversely, no functions found by methods that include IA have turned up
   with extravagant error values, meaning that it is very probable that IA is
   doing its job perfectly.
3. Although the IA method alone is one of the worst on the training set, on
   average, it is the best on the validation test.
4. As was sensed in section 5.2, methods using LS do not generalise well, although they certainly give the best results on the training set.
   In fact, LS is the worst method on the validation set although it is one of
   the best on the training set. Worse : all methods using LS (the four on the
   right) are the worst on average on the validation test.
   On this problem, LS presents a strong tendency to overfit the training data.
   It therefore seems that LS cannot rejoin the standard GP toolkit until this
   behaviour is better investigated and understood.
5. The T (progressive learning) method also leads to overfitting. On average,
   T+LS is one of the worst on the validation set.
6. However, it is interesting to see that the best overall value is also obtained
   by T+LS. However, IA is not included, meaning that one does not know if
   this best overall function will not go bezerk on some specific data !
   Maybe T+LS could be used to evolve great functions, only to be verified by
   IA at the end of the evolution. This way of using IA has not been investigated.

7   Conclusion

Although this is not the main subject of the paper, weighting the operands of
the + and − operators is a cheap idea to implement that does not seem to harm
the GP algorithm, at least on the Ocean Color inverse problem.

This said, much more important conclusions can be drawn on Keijzer's suggestions from this test work: although, by essence, the presented results only
apply to the Ocean Color inverse problem, it is very tempting to generalise the
results of section 6 to many problems, where GP is used to find a function that
will be used on real data after it has been evolved on a learning set.

The most important result of this paper is that, on symbolic regression problems, functions obtained with standard GP algorithms may contain narrow infinite branches that may go undetected until the function is used on real data.

Therefore, it is very tempting to conclude that it is a *requirement* for scientists
who want to use GP-evolved functions on real data to implement IA or a similar
technique, even if, on training sets, better results can be obtained without IA.

It seems that any GP algorithm will yield functions that work much better
on real-world data if it implements IA.

Another important remark is that, as on average, IA alone is the best method. This is rather counter-intuitive, as results with IA alone are not good on the training set. Once more, the KISS (Keep It Simple Stupid) principle seems to apply: on the generalisation set, all other clever refinements led to worse results than a simple GP+IA.

Now, conclusions on LS are more problematic to formulate, as it seems terrible to reject a method, on the ground that it works too well on the training set. It seems obvious from the results presented in this paper that LS should not be used without taking some precautions, but what are exactly the precautions that need to be taken ?

A development on this work is certainly needed to explore minutely and methodically the LS improvement and its implications, in order to find if there is a way to use it that does not degrade generalisation. It seems that if a way is found to use the power of LS without losing on generalisation, GP will have found, along with IA, another radical improvement.

Finally, although it leads to much less drastic improvements on the results, the T technique seems to work in the same league as LS. Although techniques seem incompatible in average, the best overall results between LS, LS+IA, T+LS, T+LS+IA have always been obtained with T, meaning that T should certainly be included in the projected work on LS.

The data is available on www-lil.univ-littoral.fr/ valigian/oceancolor for replication, as well as the EASEAv0.6c programs implementing the different methods.

References

[BNKF99] Wolfgang Banzhaf, Peter Nordin, Robert Keller, and Frank Francone. *Genetic Programming An Introduction*. Morgan Kaufmann, 1999.

[CDS97]   Malik Chami, Eric Diligeard, and Richard Santer. A radiative transfer code for the sea-atmosphere system. In *Remote sensing of ocean and sea ice III*, volume 3222, 1997.

[CDS00]   M. Chami, E. Dilligeard, and R. Santer. A radiative transfer model ofr the computation of radiance and polarization in an ocean-atmosphere system. polarization properties of suspended matter for remote sensing purposes. In *submitted to Applied Optics*, 2000.

[CFH+01] Pierre Collet, Cyril Fonlupt, Jin-Kao Hao, Evelyne Lutton, and Marc SChoenauer, editors. *Proceedings of Evolution Artificielle EA'01*, volume 2310 of *LNCS*, Le Creusot, France, oct 2001. Springer.

[Cha97]   Malik Chami. *Développement d'un code de transfert radiatif pour le système océan-atmosphère. Application au détroit du Pas de Calais*. PhD thesis, Université du Littoral - Côte d'Opale, 1997. in French.

[CLSL00] P. Collet, E. Lutton, M. Schoenauer, and J. Louchet. Take it EASEA. In *[SDR+00]*, pages 891–901, 2000.

[Col04]   P. Collet. Easea language, 2004.
          http://www-rocq.inria.fr/EASEA, http://sourceforge.net/projects/easea.

[Fon01]   Cyril Fonlupt. Solving the ocean color problem using a genetic programming approach. *Applied Soft Computing*, 6:1–10, 2001.

[FR00]   Cyril Fonlupt and Denis Robilliard. Genetic programming with dynamic fitness for a remote sensing application. In *[SDR+ 00]*, pages 191–200, 2000.

[GR97]   Chris Gathercole and Peter Ross. Small populations over many generations can beat large populations over few generations in genetic programming. In *[KDD+ 97]*, pages 111–118, 1997.

[KDD+97]   John R. Koza, Kalyanmoy Deb, Marco Dorigo, David B. Fogel, Max Garzon, Hitoshi Iba, and Rick L. Riolo, editors. *Proceedings of the Second Annual Conference on Genetic Programming*, Stanford University, CA, USA, Jul 1997. Morgan Kaufmann.

[Kei03]   Maarten Keijzer. Improving symbolic regression with interval arithmetic and linear scaling. In *[RSK+ 03]*, pages 70–82, 2003.

[Mor88]   A. Morel.   Optical modeling of the upper ocean in relation to its biogenous matter content (case I waters). *Journal of Geophysical Research*, C9(93):10479–10768, 1988.

[Mor91]   A. Morel. Light and marine photosynthesis: a spectral model with geochemical and climatological implications. *Prog. Oceanogr.*, 26:263–306, 1991.

[RF01]   Denis Robilliard and Cyril Fonlupt. Backwarding: An overfitting control for genetic programming. In *[CFH+ 01]*, pages 245–254, 2001.

[RSK+03]   Conor Ryan, Terence Soule, Maarten Keikzer, Edward Tsang, Riccardo Poli, and Enersto Costa, editors. *6th European Conference, EuroGP 2003*, volume 2610 of *LNCS*, Colchester, UK, apr 2003. Springer.

[Sch95]   Hans-Paul Schwefel. *Numerical Optimization of Computer Models*. John Wiley & Sons, 1995. Second Edition.

[SDR+00]   Marc Schoenauer, Kalyanmoy Deb, Günter Rudolph, Xin Yao, Evelyne Lutton, Juan Julian Merelo, and Hans-Paul Schwefel, editors. *Parallel Problem Solving from Nature VI*, volume 1917 of *Lecture Notes in Computer Science*, Paris, France, September 2000. Springer.

[SJK97]   M. Schoenauer, F. Jouve, and L. Kallel. *Evolutionary Computation in Engineering*, chapter Identification of mechanical inclusions, pages 477–494. Springer-Verlag, 1997.

Evolution and Acquisition of Modules in Cartesian Genetic Programming

James Alfred Walker[1] and Julian Francis Miller[2]

[1] School of Computer Science, University of Birmingham,
Edgbaston, Birmingham, UK B15 2TT.
jaw@cs.bham.ac.uk
http://www.cs.bham.ac.uk/~jaw
[2] Department of Electronics, University of York,
Heslington, York, UK, YO10 5DD.
jfm@ohm.york.ac.uk
http://www.elec.york.ac.uk/staff/jfmhome.htm

Abstract. The paper presents for the first time automatic module acquisition and evolution within the graph based Cartesian Genetic Programming method. The method has been tested on a set of even parity problems and compared with Cartesian Genetic Programming without modules. Results are given that show that the new modular method evolves solutions up to 20 times quicker than the original non-modular method and that the speedup is more pronounced on larger problems. Analysis of some of the evolved modules shows that often they are lower order parity functions. Prospects for further improvement of the method are discussed.

1 Introduction

Since the introduction of Genetic Programming (GP) by John Koza [3] researchers have been trying to improve the performance of GP and to develop new techniques for reducing the time taken to find an optimal solution to many different types of evolutionary problems. One such approach, called Evolutionary Module Acquisition is capable of finding and preserving problem specific partial solutions in the genotype of an individual [1]. Since then researchers have been interested in the potential and power that this feature brings to the evolutionary process and have built on this work or taken ideas from it for their own specific situations, to re-use these partial solutions as functions elsewhere in the genotype [2] [7][8][13].

Recently another form of GP called Cartesian Genetic Programming (CGP), has been devised that uses directed graphs to represent programs rather than a tree based representation like that of GP. Even though CGP did not have Automatically Defined Functions (ADFs) it was shown that CGP performed better than GP with ADFs over a series of problems [5][6]. The work reported in this paper implements for the first time in CGP a form of ADFs by automatically acquiring and evolving modules. We call it Embedded CGP (ECGP) as it is a representation that uses CGP to construct modules that can be called by the main CGP code. The number of inputs and outputs to a module are not explicitly defined but result from the application of module encapsulation and evolution.

M. Keijzer et al. (Eds.): EuroGP 2004, LNCS 3003, pp. 187–197, 2004.

The problem of evolving even parity functions using GP with the primitive Boolean operations of AND, OR, NAND, NOR has been shown to be very difficult and has been adopted by the GP research community as good benchmark problems for testing the efficacy of new GP techniques. It also is particularly appropriate for testing module acquisition techniques as even-parity functions are more compactly represented using XOR and EXNOR functions. Also smaller parity functions can help build larger parity functions. Thus parity functions are naturally modular and it is to be expected that they will be evolved more when such modules are provided. It is therefore of great interest to see whether modules that represent such functions are constructed automatically. We show that the new technique evolves solutions to these problems up to 20 times quicker than the original. It also scales much better with problem size. The plan of the paper is as follows. In section 2 we describe CGP. Section 3 is an overview of related work. In section 4 we explain the method of module acquisition and evolution. Our experimental results and comparisons with CGP are presented in section 5. Section 6 gives conclusions and some suggestions for further work.

2 Cartesian Genetic Programming (CGP)

Cartesian Genetic Programming was developed from methods developed for the automatic evolution of digital circuits [5][6]. CGP represents a program as a directed graph (that for feed-forward functions is acyclic). The genotype is a list of integers that encode the connections and functions. It is a fixed length representation in which the number of nodes in the graph is bounded. However it uses a genotype-phenotype mapping that does not require all nodes to be connected to each other. This results in a bounded variable length phenotype. Each of the nodes represents a particular function and the number of inputs and outputs that each node has, is dictated by the arity of function. The nodes take their inputs in a feed forward manner from either the output of a previous node or from one of the initial program inputs (terminals). The initial inputs are numbered from 0 to n-1 where n is the number of initial inputs. The nodes in the genotype are then also numbered sequentially starting from n to m+n-1 where m is the user-determined upper bound in the number of nodes. These numbers are used for referencing the outputs of the nodes and the initial inputs of the program. If the problem requires k outputs then these will be taken from the outputs of the last k nodes in the chain of nodes. In Fig. 1 a genotype is shown and how it is decoded (an even 4-parity circuit). Although each node must have a function and a set of inputs for that function, the output of a node does not have to be used by the inputs of later nodes. This is shown in Fig. 1, where the output of nodes 8, 11 and 13 are not used (shown in grey). This causes areas of the genotype to lie dormant, leading to a neutral effect on genotype fitness (neutrality). When point mutations are carried out on genes representing connections (the mutation is constrained to respect the directed and acyclic nature of the graphs) these dormant genes can be activated or active genes can be made dormant. This unique type of neutrality has been investigated in detail [6][11][14] and found to be extremely beneficial in the evolutionary process for the problems studied.

0 1 0, 1 0 3, 2 3 0, 3 2 3, 2 6 1, 5 4 2, 7 6 2, 7 4 0, 9 10 0, 10 8 2, 10 9 3, 14 12 2

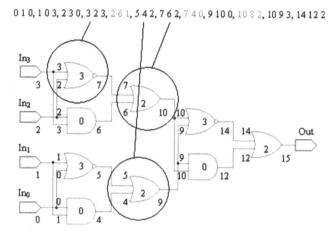

Fig. 1. Cartesian genotype and corresponding phenotype for an even 4-parity program

The evolutionary algorithm used for the experiments is a form of 1+λ evolutionary strategy, where λ=4, i.e. one parent with 4 offspring (population size 5). The algorithm is as follows:

1. Randomly generate an initial population of 5 genotypes and select the fittest;
2. Carry out point-wise mutation on the winning parent to generate 4 offspring;
3. Construct a new generation with the winner and its offspring;
4. Select a winner from the current population using the following rules:
   - If any offspring has a better fitness, the best becomes the winner.
   - Otherwise, an offspring with the same fitness as the best is randomly selected.
   - Otherwise, the parent remains as the winner.
5. Go to step 2 unless the maximum number of generations is reached or a solution is found.

3 Related Work on Module Acquisition

The original idea of Module acquisition [1] was to try and find a way of protecting desirable partial solutions contained in the genotype, in the hope that it might be beneficial in finding a solution. This is because in practice you may find a desirable partial solution in the genotype, but due to the nature of evolution, an operator could modify the partial solution therefore causing the program to take longer to find a solution. Module acquisition does this by introducing another two operators to the evolutionary process, *compress* that selects a section of the genotype to make it immune to manipulation from operators (the module) and *expand* that decompresses a module in the genotype therefore allowing this section of the genotype to be manipulated once more. The fitness of a genotype is unaffected by these operators.

However they affect the possible offspring that might be generated using evolutionary operators. Atomisation [1] not only makes sections of the genotype immune from manipulation by operators but also represents the module as a new component in the genotype therefore allowing the module to be manipulated further by additional compress operators. This allows the possibility of having modules within modules therefore creating a hierarchy organisation of modules. These techniques have been shown to decrease the time taken to find a solution by reducing the amount of manipulations that can take place in the genotype. Rosca's method of Adaptive Representation through Learning (ARL) [7] also extracted program segments that were encapsulated and used to augment the GP function set. The system employed heuristics that tried to measure from population fitness statistics good program code and also methods to detect when search had reached local optima. In the latter case the extracted functions could be modified. More recently Dessi et al [2] showed that *random* selection of program sub-code for re-use is more effective than other heuristics across a range of problems. Also they concluded that, in practice, ARL does not produce highly modular solutions. Once the contents of modules are themselves allowed to evolve (as in this paper) they become a form of automatically defined function (ADF), however in contradistinction to Koza's form of ADFs [4] and Spector's automatically defined macros [8], there is no explicit specification of the number or internal structure of such modules. This freedom also exists in Spector's more recent PushGP [9].

In addition to decreasing computational effort and making more modular code van Belle and Ackley have shown that ADFs can increase the evolvability of populations of programs over time [10]. They investigated the role of ADFs in evolving programs with a time dependent fitness function and found that not only do populations recover more quickly from periodic changes in the fitness function but the recovery rate increases in time as the solutions become more modular.

Woodward [12] showed that the size of a solution is independent of the primitive function set used when modularity is permitted, thus including modules can remove any bias caused by the chosen primitive function set.

4   Algorithm Details and Mutation Operators

The performance of CGP and ECGP were tested on even 4 through to even 8 parity. The output of even parity is one if an even number of inputs are one and zero otherwise. Initially all genotypes are randomly initialized with fifty nodes (150 genes). The fitness is defined as the number of phenotype output bits that differ from the perfect parity function. A perfect solution has score zero. Every generation, any modules in the function list are removed and any modules present in the fittest genotype of the generation are added to the function list. This allows the 1-point mutation operator to randomly choose from any of the modules found in the fittest genotype and the primitive functions to insert into the genotype of the offspring for that generation. The creation of modules allows new functions to be defined from a combination of primitive functions that can then be re-used in other areas of the genotype. For all the experiments, both versions of the program: CGP and ECGP were averaged over fifty independent runs.

4.1 Modules

In this paper we only allowed modules to contain nodes rather than other modules. Also we only allowed the number of nodes in a module to be not greater than a certain user defined value. Modules were required also to have greater than one node for obvious reasons. The modules were required to have a minimum of two inputs and a maximum number of inputs equal to twice the number of nodes contained in the module. This is so that a module has at least the first node, and at most all the nodes, in the module connected to the outputs of earlier nodes or modules or the initial inputs outside the module. It must also have a minimum of one output and a maximum number of outputs equal to the number of nodes contained in the module so that there is at least one output from a node, and at most every output from a node in the module available for connection to the later nodes or modules outside of the module. Modules with no outputs are not allowed, as they would simply contain "junk code" which is not in use and could never be connected, therefore increasing the complexity and size of the genotype. The number of inputs and outputs that a module initially has is determined by the connections between the nodes and modules when a module is created. The nodes within the module whose inputs were connected to the outputs of earlier nodes and modules or the initial inputs when modularisation takes place remain connected to the outputs of the same nodes, modules or initial inputs via the inputs of the module. The later nodes or modules whose inputs were connected to the outputs of the nodes contained in the module before modularisation took place remain connected to the same outputs of the nodes contained within the modules via the module outputs. The module inputs are the initial inputs to the CGP program in the module, therefore they act as pointers to the output of the previous node or module in the genotype which represents their value as an initial input to the CGP program in the module. This means that each module input now has a number and the nodes in the module are now numbered starting from the "number of inputs", as they would be in a CGP program. The outputs of the module are also numbered starting from the "number of inputs + number of nodes" as this allows them to be treated as part of the genotype in the module.

4.2 Operators

ECGP uses four main evolutionary operators: a standard point mutation operator, a compress operator, an expand operator and a module mutation operator.

Mutation. The 1-point mutation operator used for ECGP is the same as the mutation operator used in standard CGP. It selects a node or module from the genotype at random and then chooses randomly one of the inputs or the function of the selected node or module to mutate. If an input of a node or module is chosen for mutation then the new value for the input is chosen at random from the outputs of any of the previous nodes or modules in the genotype so that it preserves the directedness of the graph. If a function of a node is chosen for mutation, then the new value for the function of the node is chosen at random from any of the pre-defined primitive functions or any of the modules contained in the module list. However, if the function of a module is chosen for mutation, there are certain conditions that must be met.

If the function chosen for mutation belongs to a module that was introduced to the genotype by the 1-point mutation operator then the new value for the function of the module is chosen in the same way as the function of a node. This is because these modules are treated just like the primitive functions, they represent a copy of a section of the genotype that has been reused in another area of the genotype. We found that this also helps to stop "bloat", as the total length of the genotype can be made shorter at any point by changing a module to a primitive function. On the other hand, if the function chosen for mutation belongs to a module that was introduced to the genotype by the compress operator (rather than the 1-point mutation operator), the function of the module cannot be changed, as the module is immune from function mutation. This is because it is an original section of the genotype encapsulated in a module, which can only be altered once the module has been decompressed by the expand operator.

Whenever a module in the genotype (with arity m) is mutated to a primitive function (with arity n), the new function uses the first n inputs from the module so that it keeps the number of changes in the genotype to a minimum. The same goes for when a primitive function is mutated to a module, the first "k" inputs of the module use the values of the inputs of the primitive function and the rest of the inputs are randomly generated as required. The new value for either an input or function of a node or module is chosen at random with an equal probability. The 1-point mutation operator has a probability of 0.6 of being used on the fittest parent of the population in each generation and a probability of 0.3 of being used in conjunction with either the compress or expand operator on the fittest parent of the population in each generation. The remaining probability of 0.1 is the chance of a module mutation being used on the fittest parent of the population. This is because every offspring is to be mutated in some way to minimise the chance of two parents in the population having the same genotype.

Compress. The compress operator randomly selects two points in the genotype of the fittest parent, a minimum of two nodes apart and a maximum of the pre-defined maximum module size, and creates a new module containing the nodes between these two selected random points. In the work of this paper it was chosen to disallow modules being called within modules - so the modules can only contain nodes. The module then replaces the sequence of nodes between the two randomly selected points in the genotype but is not added to the module list. The only time modules are added to the module list is in the selection process of the fittest parent of a generation. The compress operator has the effect of making the contents of the module immune from the 1-point mutation operator and also shortening the genotype of the fittest parent but does not affect the fitness of the parent. The compress operator has a probability of 0.1 of being used on the fittest parent in the production of each new member of the population for each generation. This value was chosen because in tests it proved to be optimal when compared with higher and lower values. If the encapsulation process is too frequent too many modules are introduced and they don't have enough time to replicate through the genotype if they are associated with higher fitness. For lower values not enough modules are produced.

Expand. The expand operator randomly selects a module from the genotype of the fittest parent and replaces the module with the nodes contained inside. This operation can only be used on modules that have been made by the compress operator, as the module contents were nodes in the original genotype. We did investigate the possibility of allowing modules created by point mutation to be expanded but found the genotype code grew uncontrollably in length. This operator therefore has a lengthening effect on the genotype. The expand operator has a probability of 0.2 of being applied to the fittest parent of each generation when creating each new member of the population. This value proved to be optimal in tests as it means that modules can only survive if they exist in the genotype more than once. This is because there is a greater chance of a module being destroyed by the expand operator than created by the compress operator, so only the good modules can survive by being replicated (by 1-point mutation) in genotypes with improved fitness.

Module mutation. The module mutation operator consists of five different mutations which all affect the contents or the structure of a module. The operator works by firstly selecting a module at random from the module list and then applying one of the following mutations (at random). Note that the changes only apply to all occurrences of the mutated module in a *single offspring* and not to any occurrences of the module in the whole population.

Add input. The "add input" mutation randomly selects an output of a previous node or module in the genotype and creates a new module input to act as a pointer to the selected node or module output. Once the new input has been created, the operator randomly selects an input of a node contained inside the module and reassigns it to the new module input. An illustration of this process is shown overleaf in Fig. 2.

Remove input. This operator reduces the number of inputs by one each time it is applied but only if there are more than two inputs. This is because the module must have a minimum of two inputs to connect the first node in the module to the previous nodes and modules in the genotype. First the operator randomly selects the module input that it is going to remove. Then it checks through the nodes contained in the module to see if any node inputs are connected to the selected module input. If any inputs are found, they are randomly reassigned to one of the other module inputs or to the output of any previous nodes contained in the module. Once nothing is connected to the module input it is deleted from the module. An example of the remove input operator is the reverse of the example shown above in Fig.2.

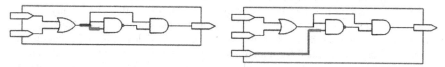

Fig. 2. An illustration of the phenotype of a module before (left) and after (right) the application of the add input operator

Add output. The add output operator increases the number of outputs that a module has by one each time it is applied to a module in the fittest parent, providing that there are fewer outputs than nodes in the module. The add output procedure is started by randomly selecting a node output contained in the module. A module output that points to the chosen node output is then added to the module. The addition of another module output allows later nodes or modules outside the chosen module greater connectivity to the module, but nothing is connected to the modules new output and the fitness of the parent hasn't changed from that of the fittest parent. Therefore the second step of the procedure is to apply the standard mutation operator to the parent, as this will mutate the parent, hence altering its fitness and maybe even creating a connection to the mutated module via its new output.

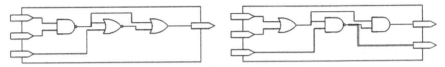

Fig. 3. An illustration of the phenotype of a module before (left) and after (right) the application of the add output operator

Remove output. The remove output operator reduces the number of outputs a module has by one each time it is applied to the fittest parent unless the module only has one output. This is because if the only output of a module were removed it would have no way of allowing latter nodes or modules in the genotype to connect, thus making the module "junk" which can never be used until an add output operator is applied to it. This operator has the effect of limiting the number of connections to nodes contained in the module. The first step of the operator is to randomly select an output of the module that is going to be removed. Before removing the module output however, it is possible that the selected output of the module is in use by later nodes or modules in the genotype. Therefore all the inputs of the nodes or modules that follow the mutated module in the genotype are checked and if an input of a later node or module is using the selected module output, then it is randomly reassigned to one of the other module outputs. The selected module output is deleted once it is no longer in use.

1-point mutation. This mutation operator is essentially the same as the standard mutation operator in CGP but with some limitations. The operator starts by selecting either a node contained in the module or a module output at random. If a node is selected, then it randomly mutates either an input or the function of the node. If an input is selected for mutation then the new value for the input can be any of the module inputs or any output of the previous nodes in the module and is chosen at random. If a function is selected for mutation then the new value can be any of the primitive functions (AND, NAND, OR, NOR) and is chosen at random. No modules from the module list can be used, as this would allow modules inside other modules. If a module output is selected for mutation then its new value can be the output of any of the nodes contained inside the module and is chosen at random. The new value of an output cannot be any of the module inputs as this allows a connection that completely bypasses the contents of the module and is the same as connecting to the output of the node or module previous to the module in the genotype.

5   Results

5.1   What Is the Optimum Maximum Module Size?

We investigated the variation in average evolution time for the even 4 parity problem as a function of maximum module size (varying module size from 3 to 11 primitives). If the maximum module size is too small then it may not be possible to create a good module. If it were possible, it might take a long time to find, as the limited number of nodes would mean exploration would be slow, as there would be very few, if any, unused nodes. If the maximum module size is set too large then the complexity of the modules could be too high. We found a marked improvement in performance for a maximum module size between three and five but performance flattened off for larger modules (with size 8 performing best). This could be due to the fact that one requires a minimum of three primitives to construct either the XOR or EXNOR function.

5.2   Performance Comparison of CGP versus ECGP

The next experiment was a direct comparison between ECGP and CGP to see the differences in speed of solving even-parity functions. The maximum module size was chosen to be five for ECGP. The results are shown in Table 1.

Over all five of the even parity problems tested ECGP varies between 1.25 and 20.27 times faster than standard CGP. Notice that the speedup factor grows with problem size, indicating that ECGP may perform substantially better on even larger problems. It was observed that as the fitness of genotypes improved so the proportion of modules to primitives grew.

Table 1. Average number of generations required to solve even parity problems for CGP and ECGP (to calculate the average number of individuals processed multiply by 4)

	CGP	ECGP	Speedup of ECGP vs. CGP
Even 4-parity	20,432	16,324	1.25
Even 5-parity	73,393	45,480	1.61
Even 6-parity	243,105	71,941	3.38
Even 7-parity	874,883	77,985	11.22
Even 8-parity	2,737,314	135,056	20.27

To give the CGP program a fairer chance against ECGP we looked at how many nodes were contained in the genotype of the final parent when a solution was found. In ECGP the genotype can have grown significantly when all the modules are expanded to nodes. We found that when we ran CGP program using the average number of nodes calculated from ECGP for the corresponding parity problem we found it to be even slower. This suggests strongly that it was not the program size of the phenotypes evolved using ECGP that provided its advantage, but rather, it was the nature of the modules that made the difference. However further investigation is required as it might have been that the mutation rate was too low for the number of nodes so the mutations were being wasted on the junk code in the genotype.

5.3   What Kinds of Modules Evolve?

We examined genotypes that solved the parity problems. In the majority of cases, the genotype consisted mainly of modules and a few primitive functions, which shows that the modules were more desirable in terms of improving fitness. Occasionally we observed modules with few active nodes (sometimes only a single primitive was active).

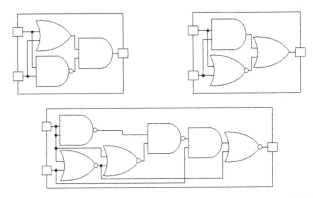

Fig. 4. Evolved modules producing XOR (top left and bottom) and EXNOR.

However, in most cases there were only approximately three to six different modules present, with some modules being used at least ten times in the genotype. The phenotype of modules that were being frequently used almost always constructed the XOR or EXNOR functions. These functions were not always made in the same way, some were made compactly out of three nodes, while others were made in a much more complex way, as shown in Fig. 4.

The average number of modules that were available for re-use per generation was approximately five but this could vary depending on the size of module chosen and length of genotype used, as both of these factors could allow a greater or fewer number of modules to be created respectively.

6   Conclusion

We have presented a form of module acquisition and evolution called ECGP. The new method is able to evolve solutions to even parity problems much quicker than the original non-modular form of CGP. Furthermore the speedup grows with problem difficulty, and we found that ECGP was able to evolve solutions to even 8 parity about 20 times quicker on average. It would be interesting to see if ECGP performs better than CGP and GP on other problems.

Other types of problem that could benefit from this approach are the design of adder and multiplier digital circuits as these are also modular like the even-n-parity problems. Many other problems that are modular could benefit as well. Problems where this approach wouldn't be beneficial are quite simple problems, whether modular or not, as the overhead of having to compress, evolve and expand modules might make this approach slower when compared to a non-modular approach such as CGP.

Currently ECGP does not allow modules within modules. We intend to allow this in future investigations. Our results indicate that success is associated with modules building smaller parity functions, thus we can hope that we might improve performance even further.

References

1.   Angeline, P. J. Pollack, J. (1993) Evolutionary Module Acquisition, Proceedings of the 2nd Annual Conference on Evolutionary Programming, pp. 154-163, MIT Press, Cambridge.
2.   Dessi, A. Giani, A. Starita, A. (1999) An Analysis of Automatic Subroutine Discovery in Genetic Programming, GECCO 1999: Proceedings of the Genetic and Evolutionary Computation Conference, pp. 996-1001, Morgan-Kaufmann, San Francisco.
3.   Koza, J. R. (1993) Genetic Programming: On the Programming of Computers by Means of Natural Selection, MIT Press, London.
4.   Koza, J. R. (1994) Genetic Programming II: Automatic Discovery of Reusable Programs, MIT Press, London.
5.   Miller, J. F. (1999) An Empirical Study of the Efficiency of Learning Boolean Functions using a Cartesian Genetic Programming Approach, GECCO 1999: Proceedings of the Genetic and Evolutionary Computation Conference, Orlando, Florida, pp 1135-1142, Morgan Kaufmann, San Francisco.
6.   Miller, J. F. Thomson, P. (2000) Cartesian Genetic Programming, Proceedings of the 3rd European Conference on Genetic Programming, Edinburgh, Lecture Notes in Computer Science, Vol. 1802, pp 121-132, Springer-Verlag, Berlin.
7.   Rosca, J. P. (1995) Genetic Programming Exploratory Power and the Discovery of Functions, Proceedings of the 4th Annual Conference of Evolutionary Programming, San Diego, pp 719-736, MIT Press, Cambridge.
8.   Spector, L. (1996) Simultaneous evolution of programs and their control structures, Advances in Genetic Programming II, pp. 137-154, MIT Press, Cambridge.
9.   Spector, L. (2001) Autoconstructive Evolution: Push, PushGP, and Pushpop, Proceedings of the Genetic and Evolutionary Computation Conference, GECCO-2001, pp. 137-146. San Francisco, CA: Morgan Kaufmann Publishers
10.   Van Belle, T, and Ackley, D.H. (2001) Code Factoring and the Evolution of Evolvability,. Proceedings of the Genetic and Evolutionary Computation Conference, GECCO-2001, pp. 1383--1390. San Francisco, CA: Morgan Kaufmann Publishers
11.   Vassilev, V. K. and Miller J. F. (2000) The Advantages of Landscape Neutrality in Digital Circuit Evolution, Proceedings of the 3rd International Conference on Evolvable Systems: From Biology to Hardware (ICES2000), Lecture Notes in Computer Science, Vol. 1801, 252-263. Springer, Berlin.
12.   Woodward, J. R. (2003) Modularity in Genetic Programming, Proceedings of the Fifth European Conference on Genetic Programming, Lecture Notes in Computer Science, Vol. 2610, pp. 258--267, Springer-Verlag, Berlin.
13.   Yu, T. Clack, C. (1998) Recursion, Lambda Abstractions and Genetic Programming, Proceedings of the 3rd Annual Conference on Genetic Programming, pp. 422-431, Morgan Kaufmann, San Francisco.
14.   Yu, T. and Miller, J. F. (2001) Neutrality and the evolvability of Boolean function landscape, Proceedings of the 4th European Conference on Genetic Programming, Lecture Notes in Computer Science, Vol. 2038, pp. 204-217, Springer-Verlag, Berlin.

How to Choose Appropriate Function Sets for Gentic Programming

Gang Wang and Terence Soule

University of Idaho, Department of Computer Science, Moscow, ID 83844-1010
tsoule@cs.uidaho.edu
http://www.cs.uidaho.edu/tsoule/index.html

Abstract. The choice of functions in a genetic program can have a significant effect on the GP's performance, but there have been no systematic studies of how to select functions to optimize performance. In this paper, we investigate how to choose appropriate function sets for general genetic programming problems. For each problem multiple functions sets are tested. The results show that functions can be classified into function groups of equivalent functions. The most appropriate function set for a problem is one that is optimally diverse; a set that includes one function from each function group.

1   Introduction

One of the first steps in applying genetic programming (GP) is selecting a function set. Although, the function set appears to have a significant effect upon the performance of the genetic problem, we have not been able to find any studies directly addressing the selection of functions for a particular problem. In his introductory book Koza noted that GP can't solve a problem if the function set is not sufficient to generate a correct solution and that performance will be degraded if too many extraneous functions are included in the function set [4]. Angeline suggests that to devise an optimal function set the programmer must have a reasonable understanding of the problem area to ensure that all necessary operators, variables and range of numerical values are available in the population [1]. This very general advice, plus intuition, are currently the only guidelines a practitioner has to use in choosing a function set for a novel problem.

In this paper we begin to rectify this situation by investigating how to select optimal function sets. Our results demonstrate that functions can be classified into function groups; where a function group is a group that includes one or more functions each of which have the same effect on the GP's performance. The optimal function set appears to consist of exactly one function from each group.

2   Background

In previous work we examined effect of function set selection on the symbolic regression problem, using the sets: F1 $\{+, -, *, \sqrt{||}\}$, F2 $\{+, -*, \sqrt{||} \ /\}$ and F3

M. Keijzer et al. (Eds.): EuroGP 2004, LNCS 3003, pp. 198–207, 2004.

$\{+, -, *, \sqrt{\|}\ /, \text{tangent}\}$[6]. The target function was two full cycles of a sine function, in the range $(-2\pi, 2\pi)$ or $(8\pi, 12\pi)$. The ordering of performance, from best to worst, was F1, F2, F3. F3 is a very interesting case because it can provide a very simple solution to the problem, $sin(x) = tan(x)/\sqrt{(1 + tan^2(x))}$, but the GP performed poorly with this set.

This work demonstrated that, in general, different function sets, even when each set is sufficient to solve the problem, have different effect on GP's performance. However, it didn't determine the best way to chose a function set.

Our preliminary experiments suggested that functions can be divided into function groups in which any function in a group has the same effect on performance and functions from different function groups have different effects on GP's performance. Consider four functions A, B, C and D. If performance is the same for sets {A, B}, {A, C} and {A, B, C}, then functions B and C belong to the same function group. If performance is different for the set {B,D} then functions A and D belong to different groups. Thus, the questions that we are addressing are:

- Do function groups exist?
- How should functions be classified into groups?
- Can the idea of function groups be used to help choose a function set?

Our results show that functions can be divided into groups of equivalent functions, which are useful in choosing GP function sets.

3   The Experiments

Our experiments use three different problems: inter-twined spirals, even-n-parity and symbolic regression. If we can identify rules that are applicable to these problems, the rules are likely apply, for GP, to problems in general. Additionally, these are commonly used problems with standard function sets. The general function set, terminal set and fitness function we used for each of these problems is shown in Table 1.

Table 1. Test problems, functions, terminals and fitness functions.

Problem	Functions	Terminals	Fitness Function
Even-n-Parity	AND,OR XOR,NOT	N inputs	Number of misclassified cases
Inter-twined Spirals	+,-,*,/,sin,cos tan,gtan,iflte	X,Y,random constants (-1,+1)	Number of misclassified points
Symbolic Regression	+,-,*,/,tan, $\sqrt{\|}$	X, random constants (-1,+1)	mean squared error

The even-n-parity problem is the problem of determining whether a sequence of n input bits has an even number of 1's [4,2]. It is a difficult classification problem for GP, especially for increasing n.

The inter-twined spiral problem is a well-known benchmark problem from the field of neural networks. Two inter-twined spirals are used to generate two sets of points, each with 97 members (three complete revolutions at 32 points per revolution, plus endpoints) [5]. The goal is to evolve a computer program that takes as input the x, y coordinates of a point and correctly decides which spiral the current point belongs to.

The division operator used for this problem (see Table 1) is protected; the value ten thousand will be returned if the divisor is less than 0.000001. Iflte is the standard If Less Then Else function. The first two arguments are evaluated and are used to determine whether the value of the third or fourth argument is returned. Gtan() is a sigmoid function for tangent. It is frequently used as a transfer function in artificial intelligence. The formula for gtan() is

$$gtan(x) = \frac{1}{1 + e^{-Ctan(x)}}(a - b) \tag{1}$$

a, b and c are arbitrary constants that define the shape of the function. In general gtan is a version of tan with the undefined points smoothed out by the sigmoid curve.

The goal of the symbolic regression problem is to reconstruct a mathematical function using a set of sample data points. The symbolic regression problem corresponds to many real world problems in which we want to find a function to describe a limited set of actual data and predict future data. Our target function is a sin wave in the range (-2π, 2π). 40 evenly distributed points are used for the training set.

Table 2. GP Parameters

Selection	Tournament, size 3
Population size	800
Initial population	ramped half and half
Crossover	90%, using 9010 rule
Algorithm	Generatonal
Elitism	2
Generations	60
Trials	50
Maximum tree depth	20

The experiments use a generational GP. Table 2 summarizes the GP's parameters. Table 3 summarizes all of the function sets that we tested for this paper. The results obtained with each set are discusses below.

Table 3. Test sets of functions. The number of test sets depends on the number of functions tested.

Set Number	Even-N-Parity	Inter-twinned spirals	Regression
F1	NOT, OR, AND, XOR	+, -, *, /, sin, cos, tan, iflte	+, -, *, $\sqrt{}$, ||
F2	NOT, OR, AND	+, -, *, /, sin, cos, iflte	+, -, *, /, $\sqrt{}$, ||
F3	NOT, OR, XOR	+, -, *, /, sin, tan, iflte	+, -, *, /, $\sqrt{}$, ||, tan
F4	NOT, XOR	+, -, *, /, cos, tan, iflte	Not shown
F5	NOT, AND, XOR	+, -, *, /, tan, iflte	Not shown
F6	NOT, OR	+, -, *, /, sin, cos, iflte, gtan	+, *, $\sqrt{}$, ||, tan
F7	NOT, AND	+, -, *, /,iflte	-, /, $\sqrt{}$, ||
F8		+, -, *, /, sin, cos, tan	-, *, $\sqrt{}$, ||
F9		+, -, *, /	+, *, tan
F10		+, -	
F11		+, *	
F12		+, *, sin, iflte	
F13		-, /, tan, iflte	

4 Results

All of the results described below are for the average of 50 trials. In all cases where the results from two different functions sets are reported as being either the same or different this conclusion is based on a Student's two-tailed, t-test, with a threshold probability of 0.05. E.g. the probability that two results are the same when they are reported as being different (or vice versa) is less than 5%.

4.1 Results for the Even-N-Parity Problem

Set F1, using all of four functions, is the reference set for the even-n-parity problem. Initially we compared it to the sets: F1, F2, F3 and F4 (see Table 3). Figure 1 shows the average fitness of all programs for each of the function sets. (For all of these problems fitness is measured in terms of error, so lower is better.)

Figure 1 shows that F1 and F3 have the best results. F4 and F2 perform significantly worse than F1 and F3. F3 and F1 perform equivalently even though F3 doesn't include AND. There are two possible explanations; AND does not contribute to the solution or AND is equivalent to another function (most likely OR).

From these results we hypothesized that there are three function groups for this problem: {NOT}, {XOR}, and {AND, OR} and that the best performance would result from selecting one function from each group. To test these hypothesizes we ran functions sets F5, F6 and F7. If our hypothesis is correct F5 should have the same performance as F3; F6 and F7 should have the same results as each other but worse than F5 because they don't include XOR. The results (shown in Figure 2) support our hypothesis. F5 has the same performance as F3 and F6 and F7 have the same performance as each other confirming that AND and OR belong to the same function group. If AND and OR were in different groups the results for F3 and F5 and for F6 and F7 would be significantly different.

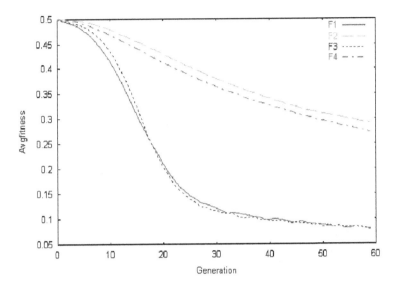

Fig. 1. Average fitness (error) for the Even-N-Parity problem using function sets F1, F2, F3, and F4.

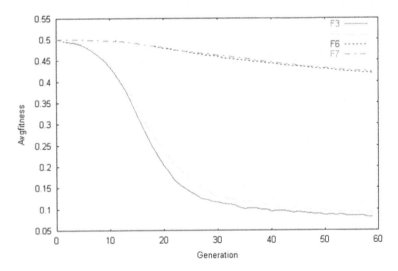

Fig. 2. Average fitness (error) for the Even-N-Parity problem using function sets F3, F5, F6, and F7.

F4 has better result than F6 or F7. So, NOT combines with XOR better than with AND or OR; NOT and XOR interact effectively. This results is significant because it shows that functions from different function groups have different contributions to GP performance.

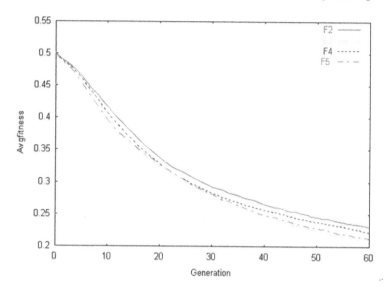

Fig. 3. Average fitness (error) for the inter-twined spirals problem using function sets F2, F3, F4 and F5.

4.2   Results for the Inter-twined Spirals Problem

For the spiral problem, we used three general types of functions: arithmetic (plus, minus, times, divide), trigonometric (sin, cos, tan, gtan) and conditional (iflte). Based on the results with the even-n-parity problem, we hypothesized that there are three or four function groups for this problem, corresponding to the function types, i.e. $\{+, -, *, /\}$, $\{\sin, \cos, \tan, \text{gtan}\}$ and $\{\text{iflte}\}$. Possibly, the first group will separate into two groups: $\{+, -\}$ and $\{*, /\}$.

Out initial test consisted of sets F2, F3, F4, and F5 (see Table 3) to identify whether the trigonometric functions belong to the same group. Figure 3 shows the results of experiments. They support the hypothesis that the trigonometric functions belong to the same group.

Next we tested gtan to determine whether gtan also belongs to the trigonometric group. We compared set F6 to and F1, replacing tan with gtan. The coefficients a, b and c determine the shape of gtan. So, we performed the experiment several times using different values for these coefficients. The results support the conclusion that that gtan() belongs to the trigonometric function group. This is significant because gtan is not a 'pure' trigonometric function and suggests that the function groups are fairly broad.

However, these results didn't provide enough information to support the conclusion that only sin, cos and tan belong to the trigonometric function group, that it is not a subgroup of any other groups, and that iflte belongs to a separate function group. To test these hypotheses, we compared sets F7, F8. and F9. If our hypothesis is correct (i.e. the second group includes only sin, cos, tan and

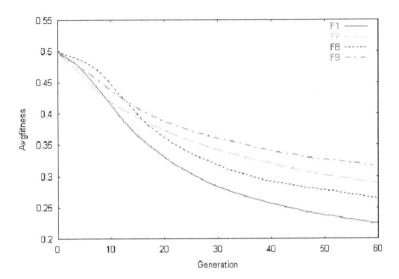

Fig. 4. Average fitness (error) for the inter-twined spirals problem using function sets F1, F7, F8 and F9.

gtan and that iflte belongs to a separate group), then F7, F8 and F9 should have different results. Additionally, these sets should perform worse than F1 because they only include functions from some of the groups. Set F9 should have the poorest performance because it only includes functions from the $\{+,-,*,/\}$ group(s). F7 and F8 should perform differently because F7 include trigonometric functions, but not iflte and F8 includes iflte, but no trigonometric functions. We can not predict in advance which of F7 or F8 will perform better because we do not know the relative value of the trigonometric functions versus iflte. Figure 4 shows the results of this experiment.

The results show in Figure 4 support our grouping hypotheses. F7, F8 and F9 each have significantly different performances, which are significantly worse than F1.

The remaining question is how to divide the four arithmetic functions $\{+, -, *, /\}$. Either they are in the same function group or they form two or more groups. A reasonable alternative hypothesis is that one group includes $\{+, -\}$, the other group includes $\{*, /\}$. We tested sets F9, F10 and F11. If $\{+,-,*,/\}$ can be divided into two groups then F10 should have worse performance than F9 because set F10 does not include a function from the purported $\{*,/\}$ set and F11 should have the same performance as F9. Figure 5 shows the result of this test. The hypothesis that the arithmetic functions form two groups, $\{+,-\}$ and $\{*,/\}$, is clearly supported.

The relationship of the eight functions seems clear. They can be divided into four function groups: Group1 $\{+, -\}$, Group 2 $\{*, /\}$, Group3 $\{sin, cos, tan, gtan()\}$ and Group 4 $\{iflte\}$. There is negligible interaction between functions in

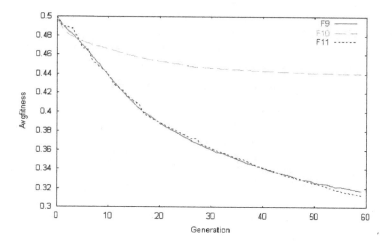

Fig. 5. Average fitness (error) for the inter-twined spirals problem using function sets F9, F10 and F11.

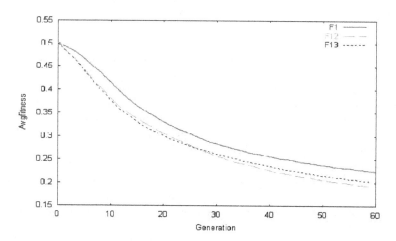

Fig. 6. Average fitness (error) for the inter-twined spirals problem using function sets F1, F12 and F13.

the same function group. There are distinct interactions between functions from different function groups. It appears that the optimal function set includes one function from each group. Thus, two optimal function sets for the inter-twined spirals problem (at least when draw from our eight functions) are F12 {+, *, sin, iflte} and F13 {-, /, tan, iflte}. Figure 6 shows the results for sets F1, F12 and F13.

Based on a Student's t-test sets F12 and F13 do not produce significantly different results, but F1 does perform significantly poorer. Thus, over selection of functions (too many from each function group) can degrade performance.

4.3   Results for the Symbolic Regression Problem

Preliminary results confirmed that a function set include division and tan performed very poorly on the symbolic regression problem (results not shown) even though a perfect solution can be generated using these functions.

From the experience of function classification for the even-n-parity and spirals problems, we hypothesized that the six functions we chose for symbolic regression, $\{+,-,*,/,\tan,\sqrt{||}\}$ can be divided into three groups: $\{+, -\}$, $\{*, /\}$ and $\{\sqrt{||}, \tan\}$. To test the validity of this hypothesis, we tested sets F6, F7, F8 and F9. We avoided combining division and tan because we already know that the combination performs very poorly. If our hypothesis is correct, F6, F7, F8 and F9 should have the same performance because each of them includes at least one function from every function group.

The results (not shown) do not completely support the hypotheses. F6, F8 and F9 have the same performance, supporting the groupings $\{+, -\}$ and $\{\sqrt{||}, \tan\}$. However, F7 performed significantly worse than F8. So, division and times are not in the same function group. In fact, division appears to degrade performance on this problem.

However, the version of protected division used here (which is consistent with our earlier work) returns ten thousand if the absolute value of the divisor is less than 0.000001. A possible disadvantage of this protected function is that it still could create a big output that is far away from sin's domain. So, we reran the previous test using a protected division that returns one. Better methods than protection do exist to handle functions with asymptotes (see for example [3]). However, protection is still a commonly used technique and thus we chose to experiment with it.

F7 with the modified division performs equivalently to F6 and F8 (results not shown). So, the reason for division's poor performance in previous work was the inappropriate protection rule. For this problem / and * are also in the same function group.

5   Conclusions

These results show that for a given problem functions can be separated into function groups. In general, the function set that includes one function from every function group has the best performance; performance may be degraded if too many functions are included from the same group, because the additional functions unnecessarily increase the size of search space. Our results also show that some groups have more important and obvious contribution than others. Thus, in choosing functions it makes sense to consider the more important function groups first. Although we did not observe it in these experiments, it is reasonable to assume that there is also one 'non-functional' functional group that includes all of the functions that do not contribute to a solution.

Our results show that the function grouping for one problem is often the same as for other similar problems that use the same functions. For example, we found that {+, -} belong to the same group for the inter-twined spirals problem and the symbolic regression problem. This rule should be useful for function selection for novel problems that are similar to problems with known function groups.

Based on the results of our experiments, the most appropriate function set for a given problem is a minimal function set: one that selects one and only one function from each function group. This supplies the necessary functions while minimizing the search space. The experiments using function sets F1, F12 and F13 for the inter-twined spirals problem are a clear example of the advantage of minimal function sets. It is worth noting that we used a relatively simple GP for symbolic regression; Keijzer has suggested a significantly more sophisticated and successful approach to symbolic regression problems [3]. An important next step is to determine whether similar results hold for this and other approaches.

References

[1] Angeline, P. J. and Pollack, J. P. "Competitive Environments Evolve Better Solutions for Complex Tasks", In Proceedings of the Fifth International Conference on Genetic Algorithms, Morgan Kaufmann, San Mateo, CA. 264 - 270.1993

[2] Chris Gathercole and Peter Ross, "Tackling the Boolean Even N Parity Problem with Genetic Programming and Limited-Error Fitness", Genetic Programming 1997: Proceedings of the Second Annual Conference, 119–127, San Francisco, CA: Morgan Kaufmann 1997.

[3] Maarten Keijzer, "Improving Symbolic Regression with Interval Arithmetic and Linear Scaling", In Proceedings of the Sixth European Conference on Genetic Programming, Springer, Essex UK., 70-82, 2003.

[4] John R. Koza, Genetic Programming: On the Programming of Computers by Means of Natural Selection,Cambridge, MA: The MIT Press, 1992.

[5] John Koza, "A Genetic Approach to the Truck Backer Upper Problem and the Inter-Twined Spiral Problem", Proceedings of IJCNN International Joint Conference on Neural Networks,310–318, IEEE Press, 1992.

[6] Soule, T. and Heckendorn, R.B., "Function Sets in Genetic Programming," GECCO-2001: Proceedings of the Genetic and Evolutionary Computation Conference, Morgan Kaufmann, 190, 2001.

Improving Grammar-Based Evolutionary Algorithms via Attributed Derivation Trees

Szilvia Zvada[1] and Róbert Ványi[2]

[1] Department of Programming Systems,
Friedrich-Alexander University
Martensstraße 3, D-91058 Erlangen, Germany
szisza@cs.fau.de
[2] Department of Theoretical Computer Science,
Friedrich-Alexander University
Martensstraße 3, D-91058 Erlangen, Germany
vanyi@cs.fau.de

Abstract. Using Genetic Programming difficult optimization problems can be solved, even if the candidate solutions are complex objects. In such cases, it is a costly procedure to correct or replace the invalid individuals that may appear during the evolutionary process. Instead of such post-processing, context-free grammars can be used to describe the syntax of valid solutions, and the algorithm can be modified to work on derivation trees, such that it does not generate invalid individuals. Although tree operators have the advantage of good parameterizability, it is not trivial to construct them correctly and efficiently.

In this paper an already existing method for derivation tree evolution and its extension towards attributed derivation trees are discussed. As the result of this extension the operators are not only faster but they are easy to parameterize, moreover the algorithm is better guided, thus it can converge faster.

1 Introduction

In a usual setup for optimization problems the set of possible solutions S is described by a set of representations R. In general only a part of S, namely S_v, contains the valid solutions. These solutions are produced by evaluating the representations in R_v. In a common EA the operators work on the representations, which implies they may lead out of R_v (as it is outlined in Figure 1). In such cases the validation fails, thus the representation has to be corrected or thrown away. This, usually requires a lot of time. Another option on avoiding invalid individuals can be the restriction of the genetic operators. This, however, may cost the simplicity and randomness of the operators beside the need of a not negligible time. A third possibility is extending the set R_v to be closed under the genetic operators. This approach is followed, for example, by Koza [1], to allow LISP-expressions to be crossed at any point. However, extending R_v to R_v' results in the extension of S_v to S_v' as well, and this is usually not allowed.

M. Keijzer et al. (Eds.): EuroGP 2004, LNCS 3003, pp. 208–219, 2004.

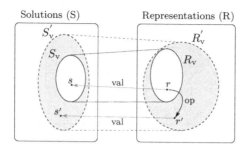

Fig. 1. Common setup for optimization with EA

Our solution used in [2] follows the second approach – the restriction of operators – but keeps simplicity, low costs, and randomness. In order to ensure that during the evolutionary process solely valid individuals, in our case words of a context-free language, are generated the evolutionary operators are not applied directly on the words, but on their derivation trees instead. Thus the operators are simple tree operators where the random tree generator is biased by the underlying context-free grammar. This way every generated derivation tree represents a valid derivation based on the grammar, which implies its frontier is an element of the given language. Furthermore, several attributes are attached to the nodes of the derivation trees, such that the speed and the ability to parameterize the operators will be increased.

We proceed as follows. First, an overview of formal grammars is given. Afterwards, in Section 3 a method for evolving derivation trees is discussed. In Section 4 the derivation trees are extended with attributes and the appropriate genetic operators are outlined. In the last sections the analysis and the experimental results of these operators with respect to their asymptotical costs are detailed and conclusions are drawn.

2   Basics of Formal Grammars

In the followings we briefly summarize the basics of formal grammars and languages. For a detailed description the interested reader might check [3,4], or any basic level textbook.

Context-Free Languages. In this terminology an arbitrary, finite, non-empty set of symbols is considered as an *alphabet*. A finite sequence of symbols from an alphabet Σ is called *string* or *word*. The notation Σ^* stands for the (infinite) set of all strings over Σ, including the *empty string* λ[1], whereas $\Sigma^+ = \Sigma^* \setminus \{\lambda\}$. The subsets of Σ^* are called *languages*. A *context-free language* (*cfl*) denoted by $L(G) \subseteq \Sigma^*$ is generated by a *context-free grammar* G, which means that the elements of $L(G)$ must fulfill the structural requirements described by G.

---

[1] Another usual notation for the empty word is ε.

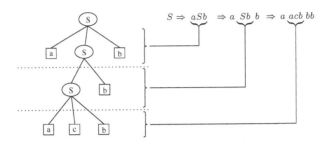

Fig. 2. An example for derivation trees

Context-Free Grammars. Context-free grammars (briefly *cfg*s) are the most widely studied class of *formal grammars* (cf. Chomsky [5]) due to their expressive power and simplicity. A *cfg* is defined as a 4-tuple $G = (N, \Sigma, P, S)$, where N and Σ are finite, non-empty sets of *nonterminal* and *terminal symbols*, respectively. The finite nonempty set $P \subset (N)^+ \times (N \cup \Sigma)^*$ contains the *rewriting rules* in the form of $X \rightarrow \beta$, while $S \in N$ denotes the *start-symbol*. A string w of Σ^* belongs to the language $L(G)$, iff it can be gained by rewriting the start-symbol S according to the rules in P. Thus

$$L(G) = \{w \in \Sigma^* \mid S \Rightarrow^+ w\} \ ,$$

where $\Rightarrow^+$ denotes a *derivation*, that is a finite sequence of rewriting steps.

Derivations and Trees. Formally a *rewriting step* or *immediate derivation* of a string $\gamma = \varphi A \psi$, based on an appropriate rule $A \rightarrow \beta \in P$ is defined as the substitution of A in γ by the right side of the rule, β. It is denoted by $\varphi A \psi \Rightarrow \varphi \beta \psi$. The derivation is then the transitive closure of the immediate derivation relation.

The *derivation trees* (in the sequel *dt*s) are widely-used to represent derivations based on a grammar. As depicted in the Figure 2, the leaves of a *dt* represent terminal symbols of Σ, while the internal nodes of the *dt* stand for nonterminal symbols of N. Having a node in the *dt* that is labeled by X and its children are labeled by $x_1, \ldots, x_n$, respectively, express that at this point of the derivation rule $X \rightarrow x_1 \ldots x_n \in P$ was applied. Consequently, the *frontier* of the *dt*, that is the leaves read in left to right order, gives the derived word.

3   Evolving Derivation Trees

In the real world there are many optimization problems where the solution has to fulfill certain syntactical requirements beside a minimum or maximum criteria. In many cases these requirements can be described by a *cfg*, thus the evolutionary process can be interpreted as a search for a certain element of the generated *cfl*.

In the area of grammatical evolution (GE, [6,7]) bitvector representation and the usual GA bitvector operators are used for evolving elements of a *cfl*. The

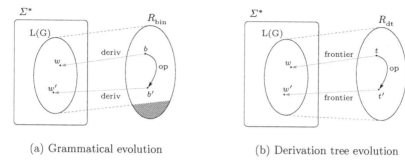

(a) Grammatical evolution (b) Derivation tree evolution

Fig. 3. Methods for evolving elements of a context-free language

outline of this approach is depicted in Figure 3(a). The words of the language are represented by bitvectors, which specify preorder derivations. Some encodings, however, yield an infinite derivation.

In our proposed method outlined in Figure 3(b) derivation trees are evolved, and the candidate solutions, that is the generated words of the context-free language, can be found in the frontiers of these trees.

The individuals of a population are described by derivation trees and special operators that always produce derivation trees are defined over them. This ensures that the search space of the evolutionary algorithm is restricted exactly to the elements of the given *cfl*. Thus an additional syntactical check for "legal solutions" is unnecessary. This also implies that additional costs like those emerged from the derivations in case of bitstrings do not occur at all. Though this method works with large and complex individuals, the costs of the operators may be kept low, and storing more information in the structures may be used to improve the evolutionary process.

Whigham [8] also represents the individuals as derivation trees and applies the operators on them. His limitation is, however, that the operators can not be parameterized, only by global parameters can they be influenced. *Strongly typed genetic programming (STGP)* defined by Montana [9] also uses modified operators, but on parse trees representing expressions. The results are similar, but it is applicable only on a narrower domain.

3.1 Random Tree Generator

Since randomly generated trees are needed both for the initialization and for the evolutionary operators, the *random tree generator* (briefly *rtg*) is a key part of the algorithm. The *rtg* is designed to create a random derivation according to the given *cfg* starting at a certain node of a *dt*. This node is randomly selected by a genetic operator. In general the *rtg* proceeds as follows: it randomly picks up an applicable rewriting rule, that is one with the nonterminal referred by the selected node on the left side, and applies it. The same procedure is performed recursively to each nonterminal symbol on the right side of the rule. The tree

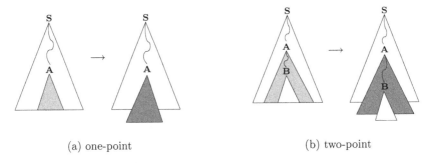

(a) one-point   (b) two-point

Fig. 4. Mutation for derivation trees

generation terminates when every nonterminal symbol has been derived. It is apparent that a *dt* generated this way might be arbitrary large leading to an undesired side-effect of the operator. Therefore, it is preferable to set a limit on the growth of the *dt*s and let the rule selection mechanism of the *rtg* be influenced by this criterion resulting in *dt*s within this limit.

3.2   Mutation

As in the case of regular *genetic programming* [1], mutation replaces a subtree as depicted in Figure 4(a). A two-point mutation can also be defined, it can be seen in Figure 4(b). When two-point mutation is applied, a subtree of the removed tree is inserted back. This operator replaces two syntactically connected, but not necessarily neighboring parts of the word. It is often useful or even necessary, to restrict the size (depth, breadth or both) of the removed and the inserted subtree, such that the mutation remains a local operator.

3.3   Crossover

One-point and two-point crossovers are defined as for GP, but the swapped subtrees must share the same nonterminal symbol in their roots. As with the mutation, the sizes of the involved subtrees may be restricted in the case of a crossover as well.

3.4   Costly Procedures in Derivation Tree Evolution

The first look at these genetic operators might suggest that they have significantly higher costs than those applied on bitvectors due to tree operations, like removing or inserting a subtree. But in general the costs of these operators can easily be kept low by using a pointer-based implementation. So they contribute only a small fraction of the expenses of a genetic operator. The major part is made up by the *random node selection* and the *random tree generation*.

To randomly select an element from a vector is a trivial task, only a random number has to be generated, and the appropriate element can be selected in constant time. A tree can also be transformed into a vector by visiting each node, but the traversal itself requires linear time. Moreover, the random node selection can be constrained by certain subtree properties. This might suggest that to find the candidate nodes the traversal of the whole tree is necessary, thus a significantly better algorithm for the selection cannot be designed. Yet, it is possible, as it will be discussed in the next section.

Another time-consuming operation is the random tree generation. This problem has two sides. On the one hand random tree generation means that complete dts have to be built by deriving words from given nonterminals. On the other hand a derivation has to be done anyway, and the generation of a random subtree in the case of a mutation, for example, means less computational cost than creating a complete dt.

Subtree deletion and insertion are lightweight operators themselves, but when additional information is stored in the nodes, this information must be updated, and thus traversing the whole tree may be necessary. Deeper examination of this case is also subject of the next section.

4   Attributed Derivation Tree Evolution

In the previous section we have described the guidelines of the dt evolution and discussed some of the incurring costs. In the following we show that it is be beneficial if information on the dt or on the context of an arbitrary node (for example its parent node or its subtree) can be accessed in constant time. Namely, it facilitates guided node selection, faster fitness calculation and operators with reduced time-consumption.

4.1   Attributed Derivation Trees

It is clear that such information has to be kept up to date. The only question is how to realize that without additional computational costs.

The answer is quite straightforward: specifying attributes, sort of variables holding the desired information, in the framework of the grammar. Assigning the attributes directly to the symbols of the cfg implies that the attributes will appear in the nodes of the dts as well, since the nodes of a dt represent symbols of the cfg in a context of a rewriting rule. Furthermore, the evaluation rules of the attributes are also defined in the scope of the rewriting rules yielding that the values of the corresponding attributes in a dt may depend solely on attributes in its close context, that is on the attributes of the parent, the children or the neighbors. This extension of the cfgs is based on the *attribute grammars* [3,10].

Nevertheless, these dependencies may still be very complex, so in this paper it is assumed that there is no kind of dependency between neighboring nodes, attributes only in the children may influence attribute values of a node. An often used example for such an attributed derivation tree is when the depth of the subtree rooted at a given node is stored.

The definite advantage of letting the attributes be described by the grammar is that their evaluation can be carried out by the *rtg*. Thus, without any extra computation the genetic operators can get access to information that is stored in the attributes. Note that although the *rtg* ensures that the attribute values of a newly generated sub-derivation tree are correct, attributes depending on changed nodes still have to be updated.

4.2   Random Node Selection

Finding an element in a search tree needs logarithmic time. One can adapt this algorithm for random node selection in *dt*s, such that instead of using a search key, random decisions are made to build a path from the root T down into the tree.

A silly algorithm would choose the target of the next step randomly from the node and its children. Selecting the node itself means the search ends, and the given node is the randomly selected node. When a child is selected, the search is continued in the subtree of the child. The the probability of selecting a child X' of X, that is making a step $X \rightsquigarrow X'$ is

$$P(X \rightsquigarrow X') = \frac{1}{(n+1)} \ ,$$

assumed that node X has n children. This means each subtree has the same probability to be selected, independently from its size. This is obviously not what we want, because to nodes in smaller subtrees proportionally higher probabilities are assigned. However, this outbalanced search can be resolved by giving weights according to the sizes of the subtrees rooted at the nodes. The size of a subtree is defined as usual, it is the number of the nodes in the subtree, which can also be computed recursively. Namely, the size of a subtree is the sum of the sizes of its subtrees plus one, that is

$$S(X) = 1 + \sum_{X' \text{ is a child of } X} S(X')$$

Using this measure, the probability of making a step $X \rightsquigarrow X'$ is

$$P(X \rightsquigarrow X') = \begin{cases} \dfrac{1}{S(X)} & \text{if } X' = X \\ \dfrac{S(X')}{S(X)} & \text{if } X' \text{ is a (direct) child of } X \ . \end{cases}$$

In this way, the probability of selecting a given node X_k from the root T through a path $T = X_0 \rightsquigarrow X_1 \rightsquigarrow X_2 \rightsquigarrow \ldots \rightsquigarrow X_{k-1} \rightsquigarrow X_k \rightsquigarrow X_k$ is the following:

$$P(T \rightsquigarrow^+ X_k) = P(T \rightsquigarrow X_1) \cdot P(X_1 \rightsquigarrow X_2) \cdot \ldots \cdot P(X_{k-1} \rightsquigarrow X_k) \cdot P(X_k \rightsquigarrow X_k)$$
$$= \frac{S(X_1)}{S(T)} \cdot \frac{S(X_2)}{S(X_1)} \cdot \ldots \cdot \frac{S(X_k)}{S(X_{k-1})} \cdot \frac{1}{S(X_k)} = \frac{1}{S(T)} \ .$$

That is each node in the tree has the same probability to be selected. Further-more, the path always descends through the children, thus the maximal length of this path is equal to the depth of the tree, which in turn is logarithmic with respect to the number of nodes. Since the value $S(X)$ depends only on $S(X')$, where X' is a child of X, $S(X)$ can be used as an *attribute*, and as such, it is available for no costs when selecting a node in the attributed dt.

Often, however, not every node is a possible candidate. In case of derivation trees, for example, no mutation or crossover may happen at the leaves. Such restrictions must be taken into consideration during the node selection as well. Therefore, if $C(X)$ denotes the number of the candidate nodes in the subtree rooted in X, and $c(X)$ is 1 when X is a candidate, otherwise 0, then

$$P(X \leadsto X') = \begin{cases} \dfrac{c(X)}{C(X)} & \text{if } X' = X \\ \dfrac{C(X')}{C(X)} & \text{if } X' \text{ is a (direct) child of } X \ . \end{cases}$$

It is easy to see that in this case the probability of a node to be selected is either 0 or $1/C(T)$, that is equally distributed on the set of candidates in the tree. Furthermore $C(X) = c(X) + \sum C(X')$ can be computed as an attribute as well, similarly to $S(X)$.

This concept can also be generalized further, when the condition $c(X)$ is not a binary value, but a non-negative real number indicating that some nodes have higher probabilities to be selected than others. Nevertheless, the computation schema remains the same. As an example, consider a selection criteria, where the depth of a subtree is required to be greater than its breadth. This can be realized by defining $c(X)$ to be 1 whenever $depth > breadth$, otherwise 0. But, it can also be generalized, such that $c(X) = (1 - breadth/depth)$. Thus trees having large depths compared to their breadths will have higher probability to be selected and replaced. Note that this can be achieved without significant additional costs.

As it was seen a logarithmic random node selection can be constructed only by using some additional attributes in the nodes. However, these and the other attributes have to be maintained, first by the random tree generator and then by the operators. This is detailed in the next two sections.

4.3   Random Tree Generation

During the evolutionary process, for the sake of low cost operators, it is assumed that the correct attribute values are present in the nodes. Thus, when a random tree is generated either for initializing the population or for operators like mutation, the *rtg* must initialize the nodes with correct attribute values. This can be done simultaneously to the tree generation, thus without significant additional costs, because the evaluation functions of the attributes are attached to the rules of the *cfg*. Using these functions the attributes are evaluated right after the generation of a subtree. This has another advantage, namely by means of the attributes the random tree generation can be parameterized as well, for example to restrict the size of the created trees.

4.4   Replacing Subtree

By examining the evolutionary operators, one can conclude that besides random node selection and random tree generation, the third base operation is subtree replacement. Mutation replaces a subtree with a randomly generated one, crossover replaces it with a subtree from another tree. Usually subtree replacement is a cheap operation, but when using attributes, the values of these almost always become invalid and they must be updated.

Fortunately attributes depend only on the attributes of the children. Therefore they influence the attributes only of their parents. Thus update can be done by traversing the path from the node back to the root, that is going on the randomly selected path in the reversed direction. Since attributes in a node can be computed in constant time, this yields an algorithm with a logarithmic time-consumption, similarly to random node selection.

5   Usages of Attributes

As it was shown in the previous section, using attributes one can construct a random node selection that needs not linear but only logarithmic time. The tree operators themselves will be slower, however not worse than logarithmic. Thus the accumulated time-consumption of an evolutionary operator that is composed of random node selection and a tree operator, decreases from linear to logarithmic.

When the tree already has a given set of attributes, one can extend this set without increasing the asymptotical time-consumption. These attributes can be then used in many different ways to guide, extend or enhance the evolutionary algorithm. Some possibilities are mentioned in the following.

Parameterized Operators. When several attributes are stored in the nodes, the operators can use these as parameters to change their behavior, for example exchanging subtrees over a given size may be prohibited, or replacing balanced subtrees can be restricted. In these cases the number of the nodes in the subtree and the depth-breadth ratio have to be stored as attributes, respectively.

Fast Frontier Recovery. The frontier of a subtree can be used as an attribute, thus the word represented by the derivation tree can be recovered in constant time, although with an increased memory-consumption.

Faster Fitness Calculation. Sometimes it is possible to calculate a partial fitness value for subtrees. That is certain factors of the fitness function may be precalculated. If these values are stored as attributes, the fitness calculation may be carried out faster, and the recovery of the frontier of the tree might become completely unnecessary.

Protecting Building Blocks. When one can restrict the operators via parameters, it is also possible to restrict or even prohibit the replacement of one or more subtrees. That is certain building blocks that seem to have great contribution on the fitness may be protected, and other subtrees having smaller or no contribution may be promoted for replacement.

6 Results

Our proposed method, which evolves attributed derivation trees, was analyzed theoretically and practically as well.

Analysis of the Operators. In Table 1 the asymptotical costs of the operators with respect to the size of the object used for representation can be seen. As discussed previously, most of the operators for attributed derivation trees have logarithmic costs. Only the random tree generation is worse, but fortunately it is used only for initialization and for generating random subtrees, which are usually much smaller than the individuals themselves.

String representations are usually fast, because their size is relatively small. However, recovering the represented solution does need a linear time with respect to the derivation steps, which is usually asymptotically equal to the size of the solutions. The main difference between strings and trees is that by applying an operator, the string representations completely loose the represented solutions, that is the derived word. Thus using strings a complete derivation is always necessary. In contrast to that trees only loose a small part of the derivation.

Table 1. Asymptotical costs of the operators

	(bit)string			simple derivation tree	attributed derivation tree
	fixed	vector	list		
random individual	constant	constant	linear	linear	linear
random position	constant	constant	linear	linear	*logarithmic*
deletion	constant	linear	constant	constant	logarithmic
insertion	constant	linear	constant	constant	logarithmic
word recovery	linear wrt. steps			linear	*constant*

Experimental Comparisons. In our experiments 12 populations with 1000 trees in each were generated using a fixed tree depth from 5 to 16. The running times needed for 1000 random node selections were averaged over each of these populations. Three node selection operators were examined. The first one is the original version, which inserts the nodes into a vector and selects a node randomly. The second one, the random path, is introduced in Section 4.2 and the last one is the same as the second one, but with the additional costs of updates.

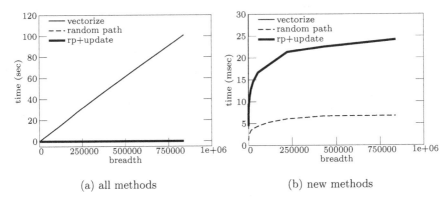

(a) all methods   (b) new methods

Fig. 5. Running times

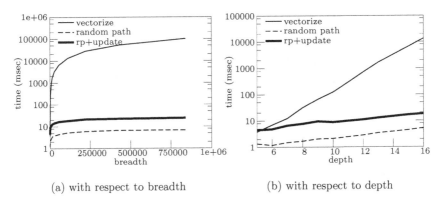

(a) with respect to breadth   (b) with respect to depth

Fig. 6. Logarithmic running times

The running times with respect to the breadth, that is the size of the represented solution can be seen in Figure 5(a) and scaled in Figure 5(b). The running times on a logarithmic scale are plotted against the breadth in Figure 6(a) and against the depth in Figure 6(b). From these figures it is obvious that though our proposed method dramatically reduces the costs for the evolutionary operators in practically useful cases, even if additional parameters are used.

7   Conclusion

In this paper the operators needed for evolving attributed derivation trees were introduced. Using attributes

- the operators can be carried out faster: in logarithmic time instead of linear,
- they can also be parameterized, thus the evolution can be guided, and
- the fitness calculation can be made faster.

One of our future plans is to test these operators on several problems, using various kinds of attributes and compare them with other methods like STGP or GE. Since the attributed derivation trees are already introduced, it would be interesting to use attribute grammars instead of context free grammars. They are more powerful, can describe more complex objects, and the methods, operators introduced in this paper may be applied on them without any significant modifications.

References

1. Koza, J.R.: Genetic Programming: On the Programming of Computers by Means of Natural Selection. MIT Press, Cambridge, Massachusetts (1992)
2. Ványi, R., Zvada, S.: Avoiding syntactically incorrect individuals via parameterized operators applied on derivation trees. In: Proceedings of the 2003 Congress on Evolutionary Computation CEC2003, Canberra, IEEE Press (2003) 2791–2798
3. Moll, R.N., Arbib, M.A., Kfoury, A.J.: An Introduction to Formal Language Theory. Springer Verlag, New York, NY, USA (1988)
4. Hopcroft, J.E., Ullman, J.D.: Introduction to Automata Theory, Language, and Computation. Addison–Wesley, Reading, MA (1979)
5. Chomsky, N.: On certain formal properties of grammars. Information and Control **2** (1959) 137–167
6. Ryan, C., Collins, J., O'Neill, M.: Grammatical evolution: Evolving programs for an arbitrary language. In Bhanzaf, W., et al., eds.: Proceedings of the First European Workshop on Genetic Programming. Volume 1391 of LNCS., Paris, Springer Verlag (1998) 83–95
7. O'Neill, M., Ryan, C.: Grammatical Evolution - Evolving programs in an arbitrary language. Volume 4 of Genetic Programming. Kluwer Academic Publishers (2003)
8. Whigham, P.A.: Grammatically-based genetic programming. In Rosca, J.P., ed.: Proceedings of the Workshop on Genetic Programming: From Theory to Real-World Applications, Tahoe City, California, USA (1995) 33–41
9. Montana, D.J.: Strongly typed genetic programming. Evolutionary Computation **3** (1995) 199–230
10. Alblas, H., Melichar, B., eds.: Proceedings of the International Summer School on Attribute Grammars, Applications and Systems (SAGA'91). Volume 545 of LNCS., Springer Verlag (1991)

Evolved Matrix Operations for Post-processing Protein Secondary Structure Predictions

Varun Aggarwal and Robert M. MacCallum

Stockholm Bioinformatics Center
Stockholm University
106 91 Stockholm
Sweden
{varun,maccallr}@sbc.su.se

Abstract. Predicting the three-dimensional structure of proteins is a hard problem, so many have opted instead to predict the secondary structural state (usually helix, strand or coil) of each amino acid residue. This should be an easier task, but it now seems that a ceiling of around 76% per-residue three-state accuracy has been reached. Further improvements will require the correct processing of so-called "long-range information". We present a novel application of genetic programming to evolve high-level matrix operations to post-process secondary structure prediction probabilities produced by the popular, state-of-the-art neural network-based PSIPRED by David Jones. We show that global and long-range information may be used to increase three-state accuracy by at least 0.26 percentage points – a small but statistically significant difference. This is on top of the 0.14 percentage point increase already made by PSIPRED's built-in filters.

1   Introduction

Proteins are believed to fold to their native states through a process driven by both local sequence preferences and the consequences of long-range interactions which form along the way, for example during β-sheet formation. Currently, secondary structure prediction (SSP) techniques predict, at best, about 76% of residues correctly into one of three states: helix, strand or coil. This quite respectable level of performance can be seen as a reflection of the importance of local sequence information in the formation of structure – the predictors get optimal results when fed information from a sequence window of ± 7 residues only. However it is generally agreed that substantial advances in SSP will require long-range information to be incorporated effectively. In the last few years, a number of efforts have been made in this direction[12, for a review], but it seems difficult to break the 76% ceiling. Very recently however, Meiler and Baker[9] extracted long-range information from predicted three-dimensional structures, and fed this back into their secondary structure predictor. For proteins smaller than 150 residues, they report a substantial improvement in SSP accuracy (around 4-5%), although the computational demands are very high (many hours) for each prediction.

M. Keijzer et al. (Eds.): EuroGP 2004, LNCS 3003, pp. 220–229, 2004.

Here we explore a more modest approach in which we post-process (and hopefully improve) existing secondary structure predictions from the program PSIPRED[4] with the aid of long-range information. While connectionist machine learning techniques, like the neural networks (NNs) used in PSIPRED, have been shown to be the most effective way to map local sequence information into secondary structural state, we propose that a more rule-based approach may be best for the purpose of post-processing. For example, nearly all proteins obey this simple rule: they have either zero or ≥ 2 strands (because unpaired strands cannot exist in isolation). For input data, we may choose between using symbols or continuous variables. We chose the latter, because it is easy to take a $3 \times N$ matrix of helix, strand and coil "probabilities" (for each protein of N residues) directly from PSIPRED. See the left side of Figure 1 for an overview of PSIPRED. Our aim is to produce a set of rules/operations/filters that transform these matrices so that they produce better predictions. Genetic programming[7, for an introduction] (GP) is a convenient tool for this task, since it can produce solutions of varying size and complexity, and we do not have to make many assumptions about the nature of the solution.

Although the idea of evolved matrix operations was introduced to GP some time ago by Montana[10], we have found only one practical application in the literature[6]. Although high-level data manipulation libraries and languages, such as MATLAB, are designed to make life easier for human programmers and scientists, they should also be useful in GP. In this work we claim to be the first to integrate such a data language (namely PDL) seamlessly into GP. We should also point out that another GP system, GPLAB[13], also has the potential to work on matrix data types using MATLAB operators, although as currently provided it handles only scalars.

The following section describes the datasets used to benchmark our post-processors and our novel approach to matrix-manipulating GP. In Section 3 we present some necessary preliminary results concerning discrete filtering of secondary structure predictions. We then investigate the "added value" of long-range information by performing local and global averaging on the inputs for GP runs which evolve matrix transformations. We show that this averaging leads to an improvement in SSP accuracy of around 0.22 percentage points (which is significant when compared to no averaging). The results also suggest an upper limit of about 150 residues to the extent of long-range interactions. Finally, by combining multiple post-processors we can make improvements of at least 0.26 percentage points compared to standard PSIPRED on our datasets.

2 Methods and Data

2.1 Training Data

When benchmarking structure prediction methods it is of critical importance to ensure that the methods have not become good at predicting just one particular group of proteins (unless membership of that group can also be predicted

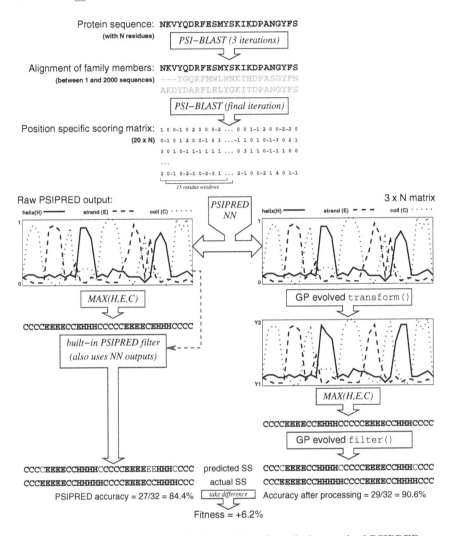

Fig. 1. Fictional example showing the flow of data through the standard PSIPRED approach (left side) and through our evolved matrix `transform()` and symbolic `filter()` functions (right side). *MAX(H,E,C)* represents the simple function which converts a $3 \times N$ matrix of real values for helix, strand and coil into a string of H, E and C characters respectively according to the maximum value for each residue.

confidently). In supervised learning there is the further complication that performance can be overestimated if test-set proteins are related in some way to proteins used for training. We avoid these problems firstly by taking proteins from an ASTRAL[2] subset of protein domain sequences of known structure from SCOP[11] release 1.55. Within this subset, no pair of sequences share more than 10% identical amino acids after being aligned with each other. This is a stringent cutoff which counters the over-representation problem, but we go further and ensure that our training and testing sets do not contain more than 10 members of the same SCOP superfamily (these are believed to have common ancestry). Finally, and most importantly, we ensure that no members of the same SCOP superfamily are present in both training and testing sets. The result is a training set containing 911 domains and a test set with 477 domains. The data is available on request from the authors. Unless otherwise stated, each run uses a unique training set of 500 randomly selected domains (from the original 911 training domains), and performance figures are calculated for the entire test set (for individuals selected on the basis of training performance).

2.2 Baseline PSIPRED Predictions

We used PSIPRED[4] version 2.3 with default parameters to generate our baseline secondary structure predictions. PSIPRED uses PSI-BLAST[1] to find similar sequences in a sequence database (we used the set of non-redundant sequences called "nr", downloaded from the NCBI on 22 July 2002). PSIPRED takes the positional amino acid frequency matrix generated by PSI-BLAST as input, and outputs the prediction in horizontal and vertical format. We need the vertical format file (".ss2" suffix) because it contains the raw NN outputs for each secondary structural state. The vertical format file also contains the "final" three-state prediction which does not correspond exactly to the maximal network output, but is instead the result of applying PSIPRED's filtering rules (discussed in Section 3.1) to the network outputs.

Three-state SSP accuracy is most often reported as the fraction of correctly predicted residues in the entire dataset, and is denoted $Q3$. We use the DSSP program[5] in the same way as Jones[4] to objectively define the "correct" secondary structure from 3D coordinates. The baseline PSIPRED $Q3$ values for the training and test sets used here are 79.89% and 78.69%. It is not surprising that these $Q3$ values are higher than the widely reported 76%, because our training and test sets are likely to include the same or similar proteins that were used to train the PSIPRED NNs. This unavoidable overtraining should not affect our results, because it is consistent across all our data.

2.3 GP Implementation

We have used the open-source PerlGP system[8] in this study. It has a tree representation, is strongly typed, and evolves programs which follow a user-defined grammar. Because the evolved code is evaluated by the Perl interpreter, we can include calls to the powerful Perl Data Language[14] (PDL) with no extra work. The grammar provides production rules for a piece of Perl code containing two subroutine definitions: transform() and filter(). Prior to fitness evaluation, each individual converts its genome to a string of code and evaluates it (with Perl's eval()), thereby redefining these two functions for that individual. During fitness evaluation, these two functions are called (from a non-evolved function) on data for each protein in the training set. The final result is a secondary structure prediction, which is sent to the fitness function. Figure 1 outlines the flow of data and demonstrates how our fitness measure, $\Delta Q3$, is calculated simply as the difference in correctness between our prediction and the original PSIPRED prediction: $\Delta Q3 = Q3_{GP} - Q3_{PSIPRED}$.

PerlGP's default parameters were used throughout (including population size 2000 and tournaments of 50 individuals of which the fittest 20 reproduce), except for crossover and mutation rates, which were set to 1/100 and 1/200 events per node, respectively. In all cases, duplicate runs were performed for fixed times (see Section 3) in parallel on "identical" machines on a Linux cluster. No migration between populations was allowed unless otherwise stated.

2.4   PDL and Evolved Matrix Manipulation

PDL[14] is one of a number of high-level numerical data manipulation languages, of which MATLAB is perhaps the best known. These languages allow effortless use of arithmetic, trigonometric, and other functions on multi-dimensional arrays of data. The arrays are treated just like scalars, in syntactic terms. For example, if x is a $100 \times 100 \times 100$ floating point array, then operations like $y = x + \log(1 + \text{abs}(x)))$ are possible. In this case, operations are performed element-wise and the result is an array with the same dimensions as x. Routines are usually also available for manipulating the matrix dimensions, slicing, rotating, and so on.

For a number of reasons, Perl is highly inefficient at doing calculations on large arrays. This prompted a group of mostly astrophysicists to develop the PDL Perl library so that large arrays could be stored compactly and manipulated easily. The guts of PDL are coded in C (like many Perl modules) and it is very fast.

An outline of the evolved `transform()` function is shown in Figure 2(a). This is where the evolved matrix operations are performed using PDL. The function inputs one or more $3 \times N$ PDL variables, initialises a $3 \times N$ "memory" or register matrix (with the `zeroes` method), makes a copy of the first input, and then manipulates this copy (and the memory array) before returning the result. The inputs are described in more detail in Section 3. The grammar guiding the generation of the PDL manipulating code is explained in Figure 2(b), and a piece of code from a best of run individual is given in Figure 2(c).

The reader should note that the grammar used here does not allow arbitrary matrix arithmetic in the sense that submatrices of different sizes are manipulated (the application does not seem to need this). PerlGP could be used to evolve PDL code for such manipulations however, as long as safeguards were put in place to handle dimension incompatibilities (as in [6]).

3   Results and Discussion

3.1   Symbolic Filters

In the following sections we will be evolving the `transform()` function to manipulate the matrix of NN outputs from PSIPRED, with the aim to produce better

(a)
```
sub transform {

    # get the arguments

    my ($pdl1, $pdl2) = @_;

    # initialise $mem

    my $mem = $pdl1->zeroes;

    # initialise $out

    my $out = $pdl1->copy;

    # modify $out and $mem

    Statement; # expand using

             # grammar  -->

    # then return the result

    return $out;

}
```

(b)
```
Statement ::= Statement ; [newline] Statement
Statement ::= MatrixLHS *= Matrix
Statement ::= slice(MatrixLHS, Column) *= Vector
MatrixLHS ::= $out | $mem
Column    ::= 0 | 1 | 2
Matrix    ::= Matrix * Matrix
Matrix    ::= Matrix * Vector
Matrix    ::= Matrix * Scalar
Matrix    ::= rotate_horiz(Matrix, Scalar)
Matrix    ::= rotate_vert(Matrix, Scalar)
Matrix    ::= $out | $mem | $pdl1 | $pdl2
Vector    ::= slice(Matrix, Column)
Vector    ::= Vector * Vector | Vector * Scalar
Vector    ::= sumover(Matrix) | minimum(Matrix)
Vector    ::= rotate_vert(Vector, Scalar)
Scalar    ::= Scalar * Scalar
Scalar    ::= sum(Vector) | min(Vector)
Scalar    ::= 0 | 1 | 2 | 3 ...
```

(c)
```
$out *= ((($pdl2 + rotate_horiz($pdl2,2) * slice($pdl2, 1)) + ((($pdl2 +
        rotate_horiz($pdl2,2) * slice($pdl2,1)) + pdldiv($mem,$mem)) +
        ($pdl1 * $pdl2))) + (($pdl1 * $pdl2) * $pdl1));
$out -= pow(slice($mem,1),2); # does nothing ($mem still zero)
```

Fig. 2. Generating the PDL `transform()` function. The basic layout of the function is given in (a). The "evolved statements" are generated initially by following production rules from a grammar similar to the one outlined in (b) which is given in Backus-Naur form. The grammar is heavily edited for brevity – for example, all standard arithmetic operations are allowed (not just the element-wise multiplication shown). Note in particular that the `rotate_vert()` function allows access to neighbouring residue information. In (c), an example of evolved contained in `transform()` is given.

predictions. In PSIPRED, the final prediction is not a simple winner-takes-all transformation of the NN outputs, but involves a few hand-coded filters to clean up some of the noise (which would produce infeasible secondary structures). One of these filters involves the NN outputs, while the others are boolean rules to flip the secondary structure (of a lone strand residue surrounded by coil or helix, for example). Unfortunately, it is not possible to re-use PSIPRED's filters in this study (even though the source code is available) because the transformed matrices are not guaranteed to be in the range 0 to 1, and the filter using NN outputs might not function as intended.

Instead we used GP to find a usable set of *symbolic* filters (i.e. discrete state transitions) based on Perl's search-and-replace function (see Fig. 3(b) for an example of the type of filters which could be evolved). We investigated the effect of allowing different numbers of evolved filters. The results are summarised in Figure 3(a). The `filter()` function chosen for use in the rest of this study (and shown in Fig. 3(b)) performs very similarly to PSIPRED's filters ($\Delta Q3 \approx -0.02\%$).

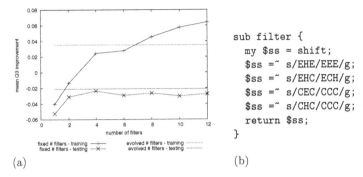

```
sub filter {
    my $ss = shift;
    $ss =~ s/EHE/EEE/g;
    $ss =~ s/EHC/ECH/g;
    $ss =~ s/CEC/CCC/g;
    $ss =~ s/CHC/CCC/g;
    return $ss;
}
```

(a)   (b)

Fig. 3. GP is used to find search-and-replace rules to "clean up" raw PSIPRED output. (a) Mean final fitness values ($\Delta Q3$ after 2h, 15 runs each) for training and test sets are shown for different fixed numbers of filters and for runs where the number of filters was variable/evolved. On the test set, unfiltered PSIPRED output would give $\Delta Q3 = -0.144\%$. Before overtraining becomes a problem, our symbolic filters almost reach $\Delta Q3 = -0.02\%$, which we believe is satisfactory. (b) The evolved filter used in subsequent experiments ($\Delta Q3 \approx -0.02\%$).

3.2   Evolved Transforms and Long-Range Information

Global and local means. In Section 1, the cooperativity of β-sheet formation was discussed, and it was suggested that if the number of predicted strands is very low, then those strands may be incorrectly predicted. In practice though, perhaps the number of residues in predicted strands is more relevant, or maybe the real-valued PSIPRED NN outputs. Our previous unpublished work suggested that the global mean of each PSIPRED NN output was possibly more useful than element-based or residue based information. Back then, our approach was too slow to allow enough data to be gathered to do a proper statistical analysis. Now, with fast, evolved PDL transforms we can perform enough runs to test the null hypothesis that using the mean PSIPRED data makes no difference at all.

But does a global mean make sense from a protein point of view? Natural proteins often contain multiple domains, that is, subunits which can fold independently and may have been swapped around during evolution. β-sheets are rarely shared between domains, and the domains within a protein may have sharply contrasting secondary structural content. Furthermore, very long-range contacts are rare: in our set of training proteins, only 3.2% of intramolecular contacts (including strand-strand pairings) are made between residues more than 300 residues apart. Because it is not always possible to split a sequence correctly into sub-domains prior to SSP, local averaging has also been investigated using various window sizes.

A series of GP runs were performed using the `filter()` function derived in Section 3.1 (and shown in Figure 3(b)), and an evolved `transform()` function taking two inputs, the raw PSIPRED output and a locally or globally averaged version of the same data. The averaging is done separately for helix, strand and

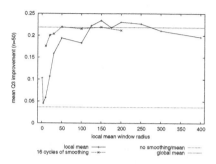

Fig. 4. Locally averaged PSIPRED outputs are given as input for GP evolved `transform()` function. The mean test set fitnesses ($\Delta Q3$) from 50 runs are shown for various windows sizes. Averaging is applied either once, 16 times, or not at all (as a control). The results using a globally meaned input are also given. Local means do not perform significantly better than the global mean at the 5% level (see text), despite the possible peak around window radius 150.

coil in a circular fashion (wrap-around ends). In one set of runs, the second input was identical to the first (no averaging). For each configuration, mean $\Delta Q3$ over 50 runs after 6h was calculated on the test set data using the final best-of-tournament individuals (selected on training fitness).

The somewhat noisy peak in Figure 4 suggests that applying a local mean with radius 150 to the raw PSIPRED outputs could give better results than applying a global mean. We have two estimates of $\Delta Q3$ for each input treatment. They are, with standard deviations, 0.234% (0.0423) and 0.219% (0.0482) for local mean (150 residue window radius) and global mean respectively. A two-sided t-test gives the result $d = 1.724$, from which we conclude that the difference between the two $\Delta Q3$ means is not significant at the 5% level. Iterated local averaging using smaller window radii gives similar results to global averaging (see also Fig. 4). Because our data originates from the mainly domain-based SCOP database, it is possible that more conclusive results could be obtained using datasets containing more multi-domain proteins. Interestingly, the peak at 150 agrees quite well with the mean size of the proteins in our training set (169 residues). With either local or global means, the improvement in $Q3$ after 6h is significantly greater than that obtained using untreated inputs ($d = 17.5$).

Majority post-processors. We performed 50 GP runs for a longer time (24h) using the whole training set (previously this was sampled, see Section 2.1). The inputs were treated with a local mean with window radius 150. Overtraining was judged not to have occurred. The 50 best-of-final-tournament post-processors have a mean $\Delta Q3$ of 0.242% on the test set and 0.264% on training (further details in Table 1). We combine all the post-processors, good and bad, into one using majority voting (at each residue position). The resulting post-processor has a $\Delta Q3$ of 0.30% on test data, and 0.26% on training. From this we conclude that $\Delta Q3$ on a large unseen data set would be approximately 0.26–0.3%.

Put into perspective, however, a 0.3% increase corresponds to just one "improved" residue in every 333 – less than one residue per protein on average! Indeed, there are 122 proteins in our test set which undergo no change in $Q3$ at all. Figure 5 shows a histogram of the non-zero per-protein $\Delta Q3$ values over the

Table 1. Results for the majority post-processor (using 50 individuals trained for 24h)

dataset	individual post-processors			majority post-processor			
	mean $\Delta Q3$	min $\Delta Q3$	max $\Delta Q3$	$\Delta Q3$	ΔQ_{helix}	ΔQ_{strand}	ΔQ_{coil}
training set	0.264	0.203	0.301	0.26	0.22	-1.86	1.31
test set	0.242	0.124	0.299	0.30	0.24	-1.75	1.41

Fig. 5. Histogram of $\Delta Q3$ for 477 test set proteins using a majority predictor which uses 50 individuals evolved for 24h. The bins are the rounded integer values of *per-protein* $\Delta Q3$. The solid bars indicate positive changes, the dashed bars indicate a negative change, and the 122 proteins with zero change in $Q3$ are not shown.

test set. Many larger changes occur in the positive direction, and these are not restricted only to the shorter proteins (for which large changes are more likely). For example, for the SCOP domain d1g73a_ (157 residues) there is a 10.8% rise in $Q3$ (from 67.5% to 78.3%).

Per-state accuracy. If we measure the contribution made by each type of secondary structure to the 0.3% increase in $Q3$ we see (in Table 1) that only the prediction of helix and coil residues are improved, at the expense of strand accuracy (strand residues comprise only 20% of proteins on average). It would clearly be desirable to have a post-processor which made small improvements in all three states. We have performed preliminary experiments with modified fitness functions to encourage this. So far we have evolved a majority post-processor with $\Delta Q3 = 0.24$ ($\Delta Q_{helix} = 0.11$, $\Delta Q_{strand} = 0.11$, $\Delta Q_{coil} = 0.41$). The modified fitness landscapes seem to be harder to search but we anticipate better overall solutions.

4   Final Remarks

We have made a small but statistically significant increase in SSP accuracy, as measured by $Q3$ on our test set, using evolved post-processors for PSIPRED which make use of long-range information (global and local averaging). Indisputable evidence that we have actually improved SSP could only come from extensive blind testing, such as in the EVA continuous evaluation experiment[3]. Because a typical end-user would not appreciate a 0.26% increase in $Q3$, this work should be viewed as the first of a number of steps on the path to better SSP by post-processing. In future work we will provide GP with higher-level matrix manipulation functions, such as window averaging functions (here we applied them offline), or Fourier transforms. We also plan to incorporate other sources of information, including contact map predictions.

References

1. S. F. Altschul, T. L. Madden, A. A. Schaffer, J. H. Zhang, Z. Zhang, W. Miller, and D. J. Lipman. Gapped BLAST and PSI-BLAST: a new generation of protein database search programs. *Nuc. Ac. Res.*, 25:3389–3402, 1997.
2. S. E. Brenner, P. Koehl, and M. Levitt. The ASTRAL compendium for protein structure and sequence analysis. *Nuc. Ac. Res.*, 28(1):254–256, 2000.
3. V. A. Eyrich, M. A. Marti-Renom, D. Przybylski, M. S. Madhusudhan, A. Fiser, F. Pazos, A. Valencia, A. Sali, and B. Rost. EVA: continuous automatic evaluation of protein structure prediction servers. *Bioinformatics*, 17(12):1242–1243, Dec 2001.
4. D. T. Jones. Protein secondary structure prediction based on position- specific scoring matrices. *J. Mol. Biol.*, 292:195–202, 1999.
5. W. Kabsch and C. Sander. Dictionary of protein secondary structure — pattern-recognition of hydrogen-bonded and geometrical features. *Biopolymers*, 22:2577–2637, 1983.
6. M. Keijzer. *Scientific Discovery using Genetic Programming*. PhD thesis, Danish Technical University, Lyngby, Denmark, March 2002.
7. J. R. Koza. *Genetic Programming: On the Programming of Computers by Natural Selection*. MIT press, Cambridge, MA, 1992.
8. R. M. MacCallum. Introducing a Perl Genetic Programming System: and Can Meta-evolution Solve the Bloat Problem? In *Genetic Programming, Proceedings of EuroGP'2003*, volume 2610 of *LNCS*, pages 369–378, 2003.
9. J. Meiler and D. Baker. Coupled prediction of protein secondary and tertiary structure. *Proc. Natl. Acad. Sci. USA*, 100(21):12105–12110, Oct 2003.
10. D. J. Montana. Strongly typed genetic programming. BBN Technical Report #7866, Bolt Beranek and Newman, Inc., 10 Moulton Street, Cambridge, MA 02138, USA, 7 May 1993.
11. A. G. Murzin, S. E. Brenner, T. Hubbard, and C. Chothia. SCOP — a structural classification of proteins database for the investigation of sequences and structures. *J. Mol. Biol.*, 247:536–540, 1995.
12. B. Rost. Review: protein secondary structure prediction continues to rise. *J. Struct. Biol.*, 134(2-3):204–218, 2001.
13. S. Silva. GPLAB - A Genetic Programming Toolbox for MATLAB. http://www.itqb.unl.pt:1111/gplab.
14. C. Soeller, R. Schwebel, T. J. Lukka, T. Jenness, D. Hunt, K. Glazebrook, J. Cerney, and J. Brinchmann. The Perl Data Language. http://pdl.perl.org.

Genetic Programming for Natural Language Parsing*

Lourdes Araujo

Dpto. Sistemas Informáticos y Programación.
Universidad Complutense de Madrid. Spain.
lurdes@sip.ucm.es

Abstract. The aim of this paper is to prove the effectiveness of the genetic programming approach in automatic parsing of sentences of real texts. Classical parsing methods are based on complete search techniques to find the different interpretations of a sentence. However, the size of the search space increases exponentially with the length of the sentence or text to be parsed and the size of the grammar, so that exhaustive search methods can fail to reach a solution in a reasonable time. This paper presents the implementation of a probabilistic bottom-up parser based on genetic programming which works with a population of partial parses, i.e. parses of sentence segments. The quality of the individuals is computed as a measure of its probability, which is obtained from the probability of the grammar rules and lexical tags involved in the parse. In the approach adopted herein, the size of the trees generated is limited by the length of the sentence. In this way, the size of the search space, determined by the size of the sentence to parse, the number of valid lexical tags for each words and specially by the size of the grammar, is also limited.

1 Introduction

The syntactic structure of a sentence represents the way that words in the sentence are related to each other. This structure includes information on how words are grouped, about what words modify other words, etc. The syntactic structure is needed for later processing in very different applications, such as extracting information from documents, translating documents from one language into another, and also to extract the meaning of the sentence. Accordingly, it would be very interesting to be able to perform parsing in an automatic manner.

However, nowadays parsing is still a difficult task which often produces incomplete or ambiguous structures. Because some observations and experiments [1] suggest that human parsing does not perform a complete search, as traditional parsers do, it can be worthwhile to investigate other alternative search methods with heuristic and random components.

The application of Genetic Programming (GP) [2] to this problem is very natural, since GP is an evolution-based search method which processes a population

---

* Supported by projects TIC2003-09481-C04 and 07T/0030/2003.

M. Keijzer et al. (Eds.): EuroGP 2004, LNCS 3003, pp. 230–239, 2004.

of hierarchical structures, or trees, which is the most common and clear representation of a parse. Furthermore, probabilistic grammars provide a way to define a measure of the performance of a parse as a probability. Context Free Grammars (CFG)[1], which represent sentence structure in terms of what components are subparts of other components, are the basis of most syntactic representations of language. The structure of the sentence according to one of these grammars is usually represented as a tree. Probabilistic context free grammars (PCFGs) [3,4,5,6], obtained by supplementing the elements of algebraic grammars with probabilities[2], represent an important part of the statistical methods in computational linguistics. They have allowed important advances in areas such as disambiguation and error correction, being the base for many automatic parsing systems. PCFGs for parsing are automatically extracted from a large corpus [7].

This paper presents the implementation of a probabilistic bottom-up parser based on genetic programming which works with a population of partial parses, i.e. parses of sentence segments. The quality of the individuals is computed as a measure of its probability, which is obtained from the probability of the grammar rules and lexical tags involved in the parse. In the approach adopted herein, the size of the trees generated is limited by the length of the sentence. In this way, the size of the search space, determined by the size of the sentence to parse, the number of valid lexical tags for each words and specially by the size of the grammar, is also limited.

Probabilistic grammar-based genetic programming has been previously proposed [8] to incorporate domain knowledge to the algorithm and also to reduce the bloat phenomenon, resulting from the growth of non-coding branches or introns in the GP individuals. This approach that has been proved effective in other problems is particularly suitable for the parsing problem, in which the domain knowledge is the very grammar of the language. In our case, the initialization step does not represent a problem because the initial population is composed only of trees corresponding to grammar rules of the form *lexical tag → word*, and is limited by the length of the sentence and the lexical tags (noun, verb, etc.) of its words. Furthermore, individuals contains no introns, since only valid parse trees are allowed. The price to pay is the design of more complex genetic operators which only produce valid parses.

Evolutionary Algorithms (EAs) have already been applied to some issues of natural language processing [9], and to parsing in particular. In [10], parse trees are randomly generated and combined. The fitness function is in charge of assigning low probability rates of surviving to those trees which do not match the grammar rules properly. This system has been tested on a set of simple

---

[1] A CFG = (T, N, S, R) is defined by a set of terminals, T, a set of nonterminals, N, an initial symbol $S \in \{N\}$, and a set of rules, $\{N^i \to \eta^j\}$ (η^j is a sequence of terminals and nonterminals).

[2] A PCFG is defined as a CFG along with a set of probabilities on the rules such that

$$\forall i \sum_j P(N^i \to \eta^j) = 1$$

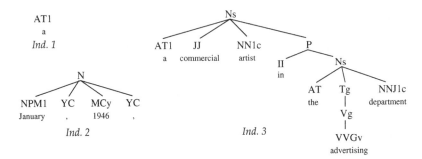

Fig. 1. Examples of individuals for the sentence. The new promotion manager has been employed by the company since January +, 1946 +, as a commercial artist in the advertising department +.

sentences, but the size of the population required to parse real sentences with real grammars, as those extracted from a linguistic corpus, is too large for the system to work properly.

The rest of the paper is organized as follows: Section 2 describes the GP parser, including the main elements of the algorithm. Then Section 3 presents and discusses the experimental setup. The paper ends with some conclusions and perspectives for future work.

2   The Algorithm

Parsing a sentence can be sought as a procedure that searches for different ways of combining grammatical rules to find a combination which could be the structure of the sentence. A bottom-up parser starts with the sequence of lexical classes of the words and its basic operation is to take a sequence of symbols to match it to the right-hand side of the rules. We obtain the grammar from a large collection of hand-processed texts or *corpus* in which grammatical structure has already been marked. Apart from the probabilistic grammar and the genetic parameters, the input data of the algorithm are the sentence to be parsed and the dictionary from which the lexical tags of the words can be obtained along with their frequencies.

Let us now consider each element of the algorithm.

2.1   Chromosome Representation

An important issue in designing a chromosome representation of solutions to a problem is the implementation of constraints on solutions. There are two main techniques to handle this question. One way is to generate potential solutions without considering the constraints, and then to penalize them to reduce their probability of survival. Another way to handle constraints consists in adopting special representations which guarantee the generation of feasible solutions only, and also in defining genetic operators which preserve the feasibility of the solutions. Parsing can be formulated as the search in the set of trees constructed over the grammar alphabet (terminals, P, and nonterminals, N, symbols) of those which satisfies the constraints of the grammar rules. Thus, we can consider any of the two mentioned alternatives to handled this constraint problem.

The first alternative has been adopted in [10]. Though this method works for simple sentences, when we consider real sentences and real grammars extracted from a linguistic corpus, the search space of trees is too large for the GP system to reach a solution in a reasonable amount of time. Accordingly, the algorithm presented herein follows the second alternative.

Individuals in our system are parses of segments of the sentence, that is, they are trees obtained by applying the probabilistic CFG to a sequence of words of the sentence. Each individual is assigned a syntactic category: the left-hand side of the top-level rule of the parse. The probability of this rule is also registered. The first word of the sequence parsed by the tree, the number of words of that sequence and the number of nodes of the tree are also registered. Each tree is composed of a number of subtrees, each of them corresponding to the required syntactic category of the right-hand side of the rule. Figure 1 shows some individuals for the sentence *The new promotion manager has been employed by the company since January +, 1946 +, as a commercial artist in the advertising department +.*, used as a running example, which has been extracted from the Susanne corpus. We can see that there are individuals composed of a single word, such as *1*, while others, such as *3*, are a parse tree obtained by applying different grammar rules. For the former, the category is the chosen lexical category of the word (a word can belong to more than one lexical class); e.g. the category of *1* is *AT1*. For the latter, the category is the left hand-side of the top level rule; e.g. the category of *3* is *Ns*.

Initial Population. The first step to parse a sentence is to find the possible lexical tags of each word. They are obtained, along with their frequencies, from a dictionary. Because parses are built in a bottom-up manner, the initial population is composed of individuals that are leave trees formed only by a lexical category of the word. The system generates a different individual for each lexical category of the word. In order to improve the performance, the initial population also includes individuals obtained by applying a grammar rule provided that all the categories of the right-hand side of the rule are lexical. The individual *2* of Figure 1 is one such example.

2.2   Genetic Operators

Chromosomes in the population of subsequent generations which did not appear in the previous one are created by means of two genetic operators: *crossover* and *cut*. The crossover operator combines a parse with other parses present in the population to satisfy a grammar rule; cut creates a new parse by randomly selecting a subtree from an individual of the population.

At each generation genetic operators produce new individuals which are added to the previous population that in this way is enlarged. The selection

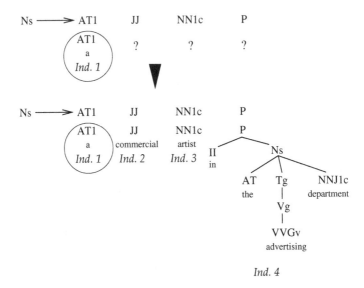

Ind. 4

Fig. 2. Example of application of the crossover operator. Individual 1, whose syntactic category is AT1, is randomly selected for crossover. The rule Ns → AT1 JJ NN1c P is selected among those rules whose right-hand side begins with AT1. Finally, the population is searched for individuals corresponding to the remaining syntactic categories of the rule, provided its sequence of words is appropriate to compose a segment of the sentence.

process is in charge of reducing the population size down to the size specified as an input parameter. Selection is performed with respect to the relative fitness of the individuals, but it also takes into account other factors to ensure the presence in the population of parses containing words that can be needed in later generations. Elitism has also been included to accelerate the convergence of the process. The evolutionary process continues until a maximum number of generations have passed or until the convergence criterion is reached. This criterion requires to have reached a complete parse of the sentence which does not change during a specific number of generations.

Crossover. The crossover operator produces a new individual by combining an individual selected from the population with an arbitrary number of other ones. Notice that the crossover in this case does not necessarily occurs in pairs. The individuals to be crossed are randomly selected. This selection does not consider the fitness of the individuals because some grammar rules may require, to be completed, individuals of some particular syntactic category for which there are no representatives with higher fitness.

Let us assume that the individual *1* of Figure 1 is selected. The syntactic category (label of the root) of this individual is *AT1*. The next step requires selecting among the grammar rules those whose right-hand side begins with this syntactic category, i.e *AT1*. Some examples from the grammar used in this work are (Ns → AT1 JJ NN1c P), (Ns → AT1 JJ NN1n P), (Ns → AT1 JJ Tg NN1c P), etc. Let us assume that we choose the first of these rules. Now, the crossover operator searches in the population for individuals whose syntactic category matches the remaining categories at the right-hand side of the rule, and whose sequence of words is the continuation of the words of the previous individual (Figure 2). In the example, we look for an individual of category *JJ*, another of category *NN1c* and a third one of category *P*. The sequence of words of the individual of category *JJ* must begin with the word *commercial*, the one following the words of individual *1*. Accordingly, the individual *2* of Figure 2 is a possible candidate (likewise, individuals *3* and *4* are also chosen for the crossover). This process produces the individual *3* of Figure 1 whose syntactic category is the left-hand side of the rule (Ns), and which is composed of the subtrees selected in the previous steps. This new individual is added to the population.

With this scheme, the crossover of one individual may produce no descendant at all, or may produce more than one descendant. In this latter case all descendants are added to the population. The process of selection is in charge of reducing the population down to the specified size.

Crossover increases the mean size of the individuals every generation. Though this is advantageous because at the end we are interested in providing as solutions individuals which cover the whole sentence, it may also induce some problems. If the selection process removes small individuals which can only be combined in later generations, the parses of these combinations will never be produced. This situation is prevented by applying some constraints in the selection process, as well as by introducing the *cut* operator.

Cut Operator. This operator produces a new individual out of another one by cutting off a subtree of its parse tree at random. The new individual is added to the population.

The rate of application of the cut operator increases with the length of the individuals. Accordingly, the application of the cut operator depends on two parameters, *per_cut* and *threshold_cut*. *Per_cut* is the percentage of application of cut, while *threshold_cut* is the minimum number of words of the individual required to allow the application of *cut*. It is given as a percentage of the length of the sentence being parsed.

2.3   Fitness: Chromosome Evaluation

Because the system only constructs individuals that are valid parses of the sequence of words considered, we do not need to include in the fitness any measure of feasibility. Thus, the fitness function is basically a measure of the probability of the parse. It is computed as the average probability of the grammar rules used to construct the parse:

$$fitness = \frac{\sum\limits_{\forall s_i \in T} prob(s_i)}{nn(T)}$$

where T is the tree to evaluate, s_i each of its nodes and $nn(T)$ is the number of nodes. For the lexical category, the probability is the relative frequency of the chosen tag.

Selection usually replaces some individuals of the population (preferably those with lower fitness) by others generated by the genetic operators. However, there are two issues that make selection a bit different in our case. First at all, our genetic operators include every new individual in the population, which in this way grows arbitrarily and therefore needs to be reduced to a suitable size. And secondly, if fitness were the only criterion to select the individuals to be eliminated, individuals that are the only ones parsing a particular word of the sentence could disappear, thus making impossible to generate a complete parse of the sentence in later generations. Accordingly, our selection process reduces the size of the population by erasing individuals according to their fitness but always ensuring that each of their words is present in at least another individual.

3   Experimental Results

The GP parser, implemented on a PC in C++ language, has been applied to a set of sentences extracted from the Susanne corpus [11], a database of English sentences manually annotated with syntactic information. The probabilistic grammar for parsing has also been obtained from the Susanne corpus [3]. Each grammar rule is assigned a probability computed as its relative frequency with respect other rules with the same left-hand side [4].

In order to evaluate the quality of the obtained parses, we have used the most common measures for parsing evaluation: recall, precision and accuracy. They are defined assuming a bracket representation of a parse tree. *Precision* is given by the number of brackets in the parse to evaluate which match those in the correct tree; *recall* measures how many of the brackets in the correct tree are in the parse, and *accuracy* is the percentage of brackets from the parse which do not cross over the brackets in the correct parse.

A necessary condition for a parser to produce the correct parse for a sentence is that the required rules are present in the grammar. The Susanne corpus is annotated with very large sets of lexical and syntactic tags, what leads to a lack of statistic for many grammar rules, in such a way that many sentences are parsed with rules which do not appear in any other sentence. Because we are mainly interested in evaluating a parser, this problem can be circumvented by applying the parser to sentences from the training corpus. Thus we have tested the parser on a set of 17 sentences from the training corpus (the average length of the

---

[3] In order to simplify the process, those sentences which make reference to elements outside them (*trace* sentences) have not been used to extract the grammar

[4] If we are considering the rule r of the form $A \rightarrow \cdots$, the probability of r is computed as:

$$P(r) = \frac{\#r}{\sum_{r'=A \rightarrow \cdots} \#r'}$$

where $\#r$ is the number of occurrences of r

Table 1. Results obtained for different sizes of the grammar with a best-first chart parser (BFCP) and with the genetic programming algorithm (GP).

	225 r.		446 r.		795 r.	
	BFCP	GP	BFCP	GP	BFCP	GP
Precision	99.23	100	99.23	99.01	99.23	97.48
Recall	99.23	100	99.23	99.01	99.23	94.86
Accuracy	98.20	100	98.20	99.01	98.20	97.42
Tag. accuracy	100	100	100	100	100	99.61

sentences is 30 words). In order to compare the GP parser with a classic parser, we have implemented a classic *best-first chart parsing* (BFCP) algorithm. It uses a data structure called *chart* to store partial results of matches already done, thus avoiding to try the same matches again and again, and explores the high-probability components first. Table 1 shows the precision, recall, accuracy and tagging [5] results obtained for grammars of different sizes (best results achieved in ten runs). We can observe that the results of the GP parser improve those of a classic chart parser for the first grammar. Though these results get a bit worse when the size of the grammar is enlarged, they can be improved again by modifying the parameters of the GP algorithm (those employed are suitable for the grammar of 225 rules). Anyway, the Susanne corpus produces too large grammars, inappropriate for the GP parser, so we expect to improve the results by using a more appropriate corpus.

The most remarkable point of the obtained results is that GP is able to reach a 100% in all three measures, while the probabilistic chart parsing does not reach this value simply because the correct parse of some sentences is not the most probable one. In this way the heuristic component of the GP algorithm shows its usefulness for parsing.

3.1   Studying the GP Parameters

Some experiments have been carried out in order to determine the most appropriate values for parameters of the GP algorithm. Table 2(a) shows the results obtained for different sizes of the population. A population size of 100 is the minimum required to reach the complete parse of all the sentences in 40 generations. With this number of generations, enlarging the population worsens the results. Table 2(b) shows that results improve with the number of generations for a fixed population size. A number of generations smaller than 30 is insufficient to achieve the complete parse of all sentences with the parameters chosen.

Other parameters which have been investigated are the rates of application of the genetic operators. Table 3(a) shows the results for different rates of the crossover operator and Table 3(b) for different rates of the cut operator. From Table 3(a) we can observe that the results improve with the crossover rate until a certain rate (40%). Enlarging the crossover rate beyond this value slightly

---

[5] Rate of words which have been assigned the correct lexical tag

Table 2. Results obtained for different population sizes with a maximum number of generations of 40 (a) and for different numbers of generations and a population size of 100 individuals (b). Crossover rate is 40%, cut rate %30 and the threshold value to apply cut is |s| / 3, where |s| is the length of the sentence.

Population Size	Precision	Recall	Accuracy
100	100	100	100
150	98.89	98.89	97.42
200	98.89	98.89	97.42

(a)

Generations Number	Precision	Recall	Accuracy
30	98.12	98.12	95.63
35	99.23	99.23	98.20
40	100	100	100
45	100	100	100

(b)

Table 3. Results obtained for different rates of crossover(a) (with a cut rate of %30) and for different rates of the cut operator(b) (with a crossover rate of 40%), a population size of 100 individuals (except the last row, in which it is 120), a maximum number of generations of 40, and a threshold value to apply cut of |s| / 3.

Crossover Rate	Precision	Recall	Accuracy
25	97.14	97.14	94.65
30	97.91	97.91	96.44
40	100	100	100
50(a)	99.23	99.23	98.20
50(b)	100	100	100

(a)

Cut Rate	Precision	Recall	Accuracy
5	97.19	97.19	95.63
10	98.12	98.12	96.44
20	98.12	98.12	96.44
30	100	100	100

(b)

spoils the results, because higher crossover rates require larger populations, as the last row of the table shows. Results also improve with the rate of the cut operator as Table 3(b) shows. Another parameter which has been investigated is the threshold value of the length of the sequence of words parsed by an individual to allow the application of the cut operator to it. The best results are obtained when cut is only applied to individuals which parse a sequence of words longer than a third of the sentence length. Notice that for all the parameters studied, there is at least a value for which precision, recall and accuracy are 100%. This strongly scores for the GP as compared to classical methods.

4   Conclusions

This paper describes a genetic programming scheme for natural language parsing. This parser uses statistical information to select the most appropriate interpretation of an input sentence. This information is given by a probabilistic grammar as well as by the frequencies of the lexical categories corresponding to each word. Because this information is automatically obtained from a linguistic corpus, the parser is language independent.

The described parser has been applied to a number of sentences, some of which present some lexical or grammatical ambiguity which can originate multiple parses. In this situation the GP parser has been able to improve the results of the classical parsers.

The population of the GP parser is composed of partial parses, i.e. parses of sentence segments, which are always valid. In this approach the size of the trees generated is limited by the length of the sentence. In this way, the size of the search space, determined by the size of the sentence to parse, by the number of valid lexical tags for each words and specially by the size of the grammar, is also limited. Because the system is devoted to bottom-up parsing, which builds the parse starting from the words of the sentence, the initial population is composed only of leave trees, corresponding to the assignment of lexical tags to words. In this way, the initialization step does no represent a bottleneck. This incremental approach to build the trees can be applied to other problems in which the size and composition of the programs to be generated by the GP system are limited.

Future experiments are planned to improve the behaviour of the system including the introduction of other genetic operators and the study of other fitness functions, as well as a possible combination of the parsing problem and the tagging problem of assignment of lexical tags to the words of a text.

References

1. Pinker, S.: The Language Instinct. Harper Collins (1994)
2. Koza, J.R.: Genetic Programming: On the Programming of Computers by Means of Natural Selection. MIT Press (1992)
3. Charniak, E.: Statistical Language Learning. MIT press (1993)
4. Brew, C.: Stochastic hpsg. In: Proc. of the 7th Conf. of the European Chapter of the Association for Computational Linguistics, Dublin, Ireland, University College (1995) 83–89
5. Abney, S.: Statistical methods and linguistics. In Klavans, J., Resnik, P., eds.: The Balancing Act. MIT Press (1996)
6. Charniak, E.: Statistical techniques for natural language parsing. AI Magazine **18** (1997) 33–44
7. Charniak, E.: Tree-bank grammars. In: Proc. of the Thirteenth National Conference on Artificial Intelligence. Volume 2., AAAI Press / MIT Press. (1996) 1031–1036
8. Ratle, A., Sebag, M.: Avoiding the bloat with probabilistic grammar-guided genetic programming. In Collet, P., Fonlupt, C., Hao, J.K., Lutton, E., Schoenauer, M., eds.: Artificial Evolution 5th International Conference, Evolution Artificielle, EA 2001. Volume 2310 of LNCS., Creusot, France, Springer Verlag (2001) 255–266
9. Kool, A.: Literature survey (2000)
10. Araujo, L.: A parallel evolutionary algorithm for stochastic natural language parsing. In: Proc. of the Int. Conf. Parallel Problem Solving from Nature (PPSNVII). (2002)
11. Sampson, G.: English for the Computer. Clarendon Press, Oxford (1995)

Comparing Hybrid Systems to Design and Optimize Artificial Neural Networks

P.A. Castillo, M.G. Arenas, J.J. Merelo, G. Romero, F. Rateb, and A. Prieto

Department of Architecture and Computer Technology
University of Granada. Campus de Fuentenueva. E. 18071 Granada (Spain)
pedro@atc.ugr.es

Abstract. In this paper we conduct a comparative study between hybrid methods to optimize multilayer perceptrons: a model that optimizes the architecture and initial weights of multilayer perceptrons; a parallel approach to optimize the architecture and initial weights of multilayer perceptrons; a method that searches for the parameters of the training algorithm, and an approach for cooperative co-evolutionary optimization of multilayer perceptrons.

Obtained results show that a co-evolutionary model obtains similar or better results than specialized approaches, needing much less training epochs and thus using much less simulation time.

1 Introduction

Using artificial neural networks (ANN) requires establishing the structure in layers and connections between them, the parameters (such as initial weights) and a set of learning constants. This is followed by a training method, which is usually an iterative gradient descent algorithm (QuickProp (QP) [7] or RPROP [22]). When using gradient descent methods the convergence tends to be extremely slow, not guaranteed, and depends on the learning constants and other parameters (that must be found heuristically).

Premature convergence and parameter setting problems, have been approached using several optimization procedures, which can be divided into two groups: incremental / decremental [1] or evolutionary algorithms [26]. The main problem with incremental/decremental methods is that they are gradient descent optimization methods, so they suffer the problem that they may reach the local minimum closest to the search space point where the method started.

Evolutionary neural networks are a more efficient way of searching, however, the main problem with these approaches is that they usually concentrate on optimizing only the architecture and the weights, disregarding the learning constants (number of training epochs and learning parameter), in spite of their importance.

On the one hand, a low value of the *training parameter* could make the convergence too slow and the gradient based algorithm could be trapped in a local minimum, whereas a high value could make the training algorithm miss

M. Keijzer et al. (Eds.): EuroGP 2004, LNCS 3003, pp. 240–249, 2004.

the global optimum. Several authors propose values for this constant that makes the algorithm work properly in a wide range of problems [23].

On the other hand, a low *number of training epochs* (number of times the training set is presented to the ANN) could not be sufficient to learn the training data, and conversely a high value could lead to overfitting (the network learns the training patterns, losing generalization ability).

The generalization ability can vary during the training phase, more over, the generalization error could reach an optimum and later it grows [11] as the network is learning certain characteristics not representative of the training set. Overfitting can be avoided by pursuing the generalization error and stopping the training phase when a minimum is reached.

Prechelt [21] uses cross-validation to detect overfitting, obtaining small improvements on the generalization error. In [25,6] a method to calculate the network generalization ability after the training is proposed, using previously not presented data. An advantage of this technique is its speed. Early-stopping can be very effective, nevertheless it is necessary to decide when to stop the training. A way to carry out this technique is by training the network until it overfits and then keep the best set of weights found in the training phase.

An efficient way to solve these problems is using evolutionary algorithms (EA) [26], although in many cases only the network architecture is optimized, to the detriment of the learning constants. Keesing and Stork's experiments [12] show the importance of these parameters, since in an ANN population, training the networks too little or too much implies very slow evolution, whereas an intermediate amount usually is optimal. ANN evolution uses a single population of candidate solutions that encodes all the network parameters.

Several methods [15,18] encode the weights of an individual and learning parameters (having fixed the number of neurons and connectivity). In both cases, the representation has the disadvantage of the lack of precision. The method presented in [14] tries to avoid overfitting coding the number of training times as a bit string in the individual. Another proposal uses simulated annealing for searching for the network learning parameters [2].

These methods focus on the optimization part of the network, since the parameters coded in an individual makes the search space too large. Other authors propose using co-evolution [17], where several populations evolve separately, and obtain the individuals fitness by combining several individuals of the other populations. This kinds of algorithms [10] can solve optimization problems in a more efficient way than classic EAs. In addition, the cooperative model is more adequate when the problem can be decomposed into interrelated subcomponents [19].

Systems proposed by Smalz and Conrad [24] and Moriarty and Miikkulainen [16] carry out the evolution of two populations: a population of nodes, and another of networks. Networks are formed by combining neurons of the first population.

Zhao [27] proposes to decompose a recognition pattern problem in several functions (one per class) and to assign a module (specialized network) to each function. The classifier consists of N specialized networks designed by means of evolution using several EAs. [28] focus on the problem of evaluation of different individual populations, applying a co-evolutionary model to the design of radial basis neural networks.

Garcia-Pedrajas et al. [9] developed SYMBIONT, a model to design sub-networks (modules), that are combined forming complete networks to solve the problem.

These methods focus on the search of the architecture and initial weights of the network, in spite of the importance of the learning constants optimization [12,5].

This paper continues the research on evolutionary optimization of multilayer perceptrons (MLPs) (*G-Prop* method) presented in [3,5], comparing several hybrid systems to optimize MLPs. The G-Prop method leverages the capabilities of two classes of algorithms: the ability of EA to find a solution close to the global optimum, and the ability of the back-propagation algorithm (BP) to tune a solution and reach the nearest local minimum by means of local search from the solution found by the EA.

We propose a co-evolutionary system in which a population of QPs evolve in parallel with a population of MLPs; thus both the network architecture (network structure and weights) and the training parameters (number of training epochs and learning coefficient) are optimized.

The remainder is structured as follows: Section 2 describes the hybrid models proposed in this study. Section 3 describes the experiments, and Section 4 presents the results obtained, followed by a brief conclusion in Section 5.

2   Proposed Hybrid Models

In this work, we are interested in studying four hybrid systems to optimize ANN, that search for the network architecture and the training algorithm parameters, due to the fact that both determine the classification ability and simulation time.

Different models are presented in Figures 1a - 1d, and fully described as follows:

2.1   Sequential Model to Optimize MLPs

In this first model (Figure 1a), an EA evolves a MLP population, searching for the best architecture (structure and network initial weights) for a given problem, trying to optimize the network classification ability.

Usually, an EA needs the individuals to be coded in the chromosomes to be handled by the genetic operators of the EA. Nevertheless, proposed models do not use binary nor another coding; but rather initial network parameters (initial weights and learning rate) are evolved using specific genetic operators (mutation, crossover, addition of neurons to a hidden layer, elimination of neurons of a hidden layer, and training the MLP by means of the application of the QP algorithm).

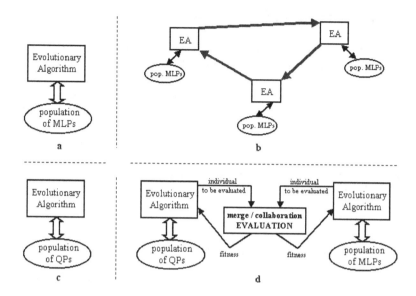

Fig. 1. a) Sequential model to optimize MLPs; an EA evolves a MLP population to search for the architecture and initial weights. b) Parallel EA to optimize MLPs; several processors evolve (in parallel) MLP populations to search for the architecture and initial weights. c) Proposed model to optimize the QP training constants; an EA evolves a QP population to search for the training epoch number and the learning constant. d) Proposed co-evolutive model to optimize MLPs and QPs; two processors evolve (in parallel) a MLP population and another population of QPs, that cooperate to design the MLP and to set the learning parameters.

The fitness calculation takes into account the classification ability and the network size (small networks that generalize well are searched).

Finally, the training algorithm (QP) parameter values along with the EA running parameters (generation number, population size, operator application rates, etc) were set using statistical methods [5].

2.2 Parallel Model to Optimize MLPs

This model (Figure 1b) is based on a parallel system in which the population is distributed between several EAs (run in several processors).

Each EA conforms to the sequential model described in the previous section (see Figure 1a). Several processors work in parallel searching for the solution, sending/receiving population individuals after a certain number of generations following a ring migration scheme (see [4] for details).

2.3 Sequential Model to Optimize QPs

In this case (Figure 1c) we propose to study the evolution of the QP algorithm parameters, trying to minimize the number of training epochs (the fitness calculation time will be smaller, and thus the simulation time too).

Therefore, the EA evolves a population of individuals that encodes the number of training epochs and the learning constant used to apply the QP algorithm.

Each individual-QP can be mutated (increasing or decreasing the number of training epochs and/or the learning constant) and can be crossed with others.

In order to calculate fitness, the model randomly generates several MLPs. Each individual-QP is used to train those MLPs. The fitness value will have as first criteria the average classification ability on those MLPs, and as second criteria the number of training epochs.

2.4 Co-evolutive Model to Optimize MLPs and QPs

We propose a system where two species evolve in a co-operative way (Figure 1d):

- *A population of QPs algorithms evolve to optimize the parameters of the training algorithm.* Each individual encodes, using real number vectors, the QP parameters (number of training epochs and learning constant), and can be mutated (increasing or decreasing some of those parameters) and be crossed with others. This QP, using the specified parameters, is used to train several MLPs: each generation, the EA that evolves the networks will evaluate new MLPs; then, a non evaluated individual-QP is sent to train those MLPs, obtaining the fitness value for those networks and for itself. The fitness function uses as first criteria the average classification ability with those MLPs and as second criteria, the number of training epochs (to minimize simulation time).
- *A population of MLPs evolve to optimize the architecture and initial weights of the network.* The EA optimizes the MLP classification ability and at the time it searches for the network architecture (number of hidden units) and the initial set of weights. This algorithm is identical to the sequential model to optimize MLPs (see subsection 2.1), although to calculate the MLP fitness, a QP (taken from the other population) to train the network is used.

Parallel and co-evolutive models were implemented using the SOAP::Lite module [13] and Perl. SOAP is a standard protocol, proposed by the W3C, that extends the remote call procedures, to allow the remote access to objects. The EAs were implemented using the Algorithm::Evolutionary module , available at http://opeal.sourceforge.net and http://search.cpan.org/author/JMERELO/

Experiments were carried out using up to four processors, whose speeds range between 500 and 800 Mhz, connected using a 10Mbits Ethernet network.

3   Experiments

The tests used to assess the accuracy of a method must be chosen carefully, because some of them (toy problems) are not suitable for certain capacities of the BP algorithm, such as generalization [8].

In these experiments, the **Glass** problem was used (taken from PROBEN1 benchmark proposed by Prechelt [20]). This problem consists of the classification of glass types. The results of a chemical analysis of glass splinters (percent content of 8 different elements) plus the refractive index are used to classify the sample. This dataset was created based on the glass problem dataset from the UCI repository of machine learning databases. The data set contains 214 instances. Each sample has 9 attributes plus the class attribute.

The main data set was divided into three disjoint parts, for training, validating and testing. In order to obtain the fitness of an individual, the MLP is trained with the training set and its fitness is established from the classification error with the validating set. Once the EA is finished (when it reaches the limit of generations), the classification error with the testing set is calculated: this is the result shown.

In order to compare results between models, the sequential EA was executed using a number of generations and with population size so that the number of individuals (MLPs) evaluated in each simulation was equivalent to the number of individuals evaluated in the parallel model.

Thus, whereas the parallel model was run using 1 to 4 populations (EA in a processor) of 100 individuals, and 100 generations, the sequential versions were run using 100 to 400 generations and population size of 100 individuals.

The remaining parameter values (population size, selection rate, operator application rates, number of training epochs, etc) were found by means of statistical methods (see [5] for details).

In the 1st (sequential EA to optimize MLPs) and 3rd (parallel EAs to optimize MLPs) models, 300 training epochs were used and 0,1 as learning constant, whereas in the 2nd (sequential EA to optimize QPs) and 4th (co-evolutionary), these parameters are optimized by the EA.

Average and deviation values shown in tables of results have been obtained after 30 simulations for each case.

4   Obtained Results

Obtained results using the EA for MLP optimization are shown in Table 1. We can see how the classification ability improves and the simulation time grows as the generations number is increased. This model was presented and used in previous papers to solve patern classification problems [3], having obtained better results than other methods.

Obtained results using the parallel model are shown in Table 2. The behavior is similar to the previous model as far as classification ability is concerned, although simulation time does not grow. Figure 2 shows the speedup obtained

Table 1. Results (error %, time and training epochs) obtained using the first model (EA to optimize MLPs).

Generations	Error (%)	Time (min.)	Épochs
100	35 ± 1	**20 ± 2**	300
200	35 ± 1	30 ± 5	300
300	33 ± 2	44 ± 8	300
400	**32** ± 2	70 ± 9	300

Table 2. Results (error %, time and training epochs) obtained using the second model (parallel EA to optimize MLPs), and the speedup for each experiment.

Populations	Error (%)	Time (min.)	Speedup	Épochs
1	35 ± 1	20 ± 2	1	300
2	33 ± 2	**18 ± 1**	1.6	300
3	33 ± 1	20 ± 1	2.2	300
4	**32** ± 1	20 ± 2	3.5	300

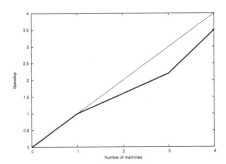

Fig. 2. Speedup obtained using the parallel model.

in these simulations. We can see that classification ability and simulation time can be improved dividing the problem between several processors that work in parallel.

Obtained results using the sequential model for QP optimization are shown in Table 3. The classification ability is worse than in previous cases, because in this one, no architecture or initial weights optimization is carried out (this model focus on the optimization of the training algorithm learning parameters). As we can see, the number of training epochs is reduced and thus the simulation time.

Results obtained using the co-evolutive model can be shown in Table 4. The obtained classification ability is similar to that obtained using other models (MLP optimization is carried out by the EA). At the time, simulation time is lower (as in the sequential EA that optimizes QPs) due to the optimization of the number of training epochs. As can be seen in the last column of the table, better results (errors) are obtained using a learning constant close to 0.03

Table 3. Results (error %, time and training epochs) obtained using the sequential model to optimize QP parameters. It can be seen how the number of training epochs is optimized, in contrast with other models, where this parameter was fixed.

Generations	Error (%)	Time (min.)	Épochs	Learning coefficient
100	39 ± 3	**24 ± 8**	262 ± 13	0.098 ± 0.004
200	38 ± 1	33 ± 6	231 ± 17	0.074 ± 0.006
300	36 ± 3	49 ± 8	194 ± 14	0.040 ± 0.005
400	**35 ± 2**	76 ± 7	**170 ± 19**	0.039 ± 0.006

Table 4. Results (error %, time, training epochs and learning constant) obtained using the co-evolutive model. As can be seen, classification ability is optimized, while obtaining a lower number of training epochs compared to using other models.

Generations	Error (%)	Time (min.)	Épochs	Learning coefficient
100	35 ± 2	**22 ± 5**	175 ± 16	0.094 ± 0.003
200	35 ± 1	31 ± 5	139 ± 19	0.087 ± 0.002
300	33 ± 2	40 ± 4	126 ± 13	0.067 ± 0.003
400	**32 ± 2**	65 ± 6	**114 ± 12**	0.030 ± 0.008

The obtained classification ability using these methods is similar, but for the sequential EA that optimizes QPs, because no network architecture optimization is carried out. On the other hand, simulation time in the co-evolutionary approach is lower due to the fact that optimizing the number of training epochs makes the fitness calculation less expensive on average. It can be seen that the co-evolutionary model obtains MLPs with classification ability similar to others where the main target is the network optimization.

5   Conclusions and Work in Progress

A comparative study between several hybrid models for MLP optimization (architecture, initial weights and learning parameters) has been presented.

We can see the validity of the results obtained with each model:

— The sequential model to optimize the MLP architecture and weights obtains good classification error. Simulation time is slightly higher than in other models since the training parameters are not optimized.
— The parallel version (presented in [4]) obtains similar results to the first model, however, it needs less simulation time.
— The model to optimize the training algorithm parameters improves the simulation time, obtaining worse classification error since it does not optimize the network architecture or weights.
— The co-evolutionary model minimizes the number of training epochs; this makes the MLP training phase faster and the simulation time reduces. At the same time that the QP are optimized, the classification ability improves due to the MLP optimization.

It should be interesting to develop and study the behavior of a distributed co-evolutionary system where a population of QPs and several populations of MLPs evolve in parallel. This way the space search could be explored efficiently due to the advantages of the proposed parallel model. At the same time, the number of training epochs and learning coefficient could be optimized.

We have seen that it is possible to optimize the number of training epochs avoiding network overfitting. At the same time, simulation time was reduced, since the fitness calculation is carried out using less epochs.

Acknowledgements. This work has been supported by project CICYT TIC2003-09481-C04.

The authors are grateful to anonymous referees for their constructive comments and advice about the first revision of our paper.

References

1. E. Alpaydim. GAL: Networks that grow when they learn and shrink when they forget. *International Journal of Pattern Recognition and Artificial Intelligence , 8(1), 391-414*, 1994.
2. P. A. Castillo, J. González, J. J. Merelo, V. Rivas, G. Romero, and A. Prieto. SA-Prop: Optimization of Multilayer Perceptron Parameters using Simulated Annealing. *Lecture Notes in Computer Science, ISBN:3-540-66069-0, Vol. 1606, pp. 661-670, Springer-Verlag*, 1999.
3. P. A. Castillo, J. J. Merelo, V. Rivas, G. Romero, and A. Prieto. G-Prop: Global Optimization of Multilayer Perceptrons using GAs. *Neurocomputing, Vol.35/1-4, pp.149-163*, 2000.
4. P.A. Castillo, M.G. Arenas, J. J. Merelo, V. Rivas, and G. Romero. Optimisation of Multilayer Perceptrons Using a Distributed Evolutionary Algorithm with SOAP. *Lecture Notes in Computer Science, Vol.2439, pp.676-685, Springer-Verlag*, 2002.
5. P.A. Castillo, J.J. Merelo, G. Romero, A. Prieto, and I. Rojas. Statistical Analysis of the Parameters of a Neuro-Genetic Algorithm. *in IEEE Transactions on Neural Networks, vol.13, no.6, pp.1374-1394, ISSN:1045-9227, november*, 2002.
6. D.B. Schwartz; V.K. Samalan; S.A. Solla; J.S. Denker. Exhaustive learning. *Neural Computation 2(3):374-385*, 1990.
7. S. Fahlman. Faster-Learning Variations on Back-Propagation: An Empirical Study. *Proc. of the 1988 Connectionist Models Summer School, Morgan Kaufmann*, 1988.
8. S.E. Fahlman. An empirical study of learning speed in back-propagation networks. Technical report, Carnegie Mellon University, 1988.
9. N. García-Pedrajas, C. Hervás-Martínez, and J. Munoz-Pérez. COVNET: A cooperative coevolutionary model for evolving artificial neural networks. *IEEE Transactions on Neural Networks, vol.14, n.3, pp.575-596*, 2003.
10. P. Husbands. Distributed coevolutionary genetic algorithms for multi-criteria and multi-constraint optimisation. *Evolutionary Computing, Lecture Notes in Computer Science, Vol. 865, pp.150-165, T. Fogarty (Ed.), Springer-Verlag*, 1994.
11. R.D. Reed; R.J. Marks II. *Neural Smithing*. Bradford. The MIT Press, Cambridge, Massachusetts, London, England., 1999.

12. R. Keesing and D. G. Stork. Evolution and Learning in Neural Networks: The number and distribution of learning trials affect the rate of evolution. *Proc. of Neural Information Proc. Sys. NIPS-3 R. P. Lippmann, J. E. Moody and D. S. Touretzky (eds.) pp. 804–810*, 1991.

13. P. Kuchenko. SOAP::Lite. Available from http://www.soaplite.com.

14. H.A. Mayer, R. Schwaiget, and R. Huber. Evolving topologies of artificial neural networks adapted to image processing tasks. *In Proc. of 26th Int. Symp. on Remote Sensing of Environment, pp.71-74, Vancouver, BC, Canada*, 1996.

15. J. J. Merelo, M. Patón, A. Canas, A. Prieto, and F. Morán. Optimization of a competitive learning neural network by genetic algorithms. *Lecture Notes in Computer Science, Vol. 686, pp. 185-192, Springer-Verlag*, 1993.

16. D.E. Moriarty and R. Miikkulainen. Forming neural networks through efficient and adaptive coevolution. *Evolutionary Computation, vol.4, no.5*, 1998.

17. J. Paredis. Coevolutionary computation. *Artificial Life, 2:355-375*, 1995.

18. V. Petridis, S. Kazarlis, A. Papaikonomu, and A. Filelis. A hybrid genetic algorithm for training neural networks. *Artificial Neural Networks, 2, 953-956*, 1992.

19. M.A. Potter and K.A. De Jong. Cooperative coevolution: an architecture for evolving coadapted subcomponents. *Evolutionary Computation, 8(1):1-29*, 2000.

20. L. Prechelt. PROBEN1 — A set of benchmarks and benchmarking rules for neural network training algorithms. Technical Report 21/94, Fakultät für Informatik, Universität Karlsruhe, D-76128 Karlsruhe, Germany, September 1994.

21. L. Prechelt. Automatic early stopping using cross validation: quantifying the criteria. *Neural Networks 11:761-767*, 1998.

22. M. Riedmiller. A direct adaptive method for faster backpropagation learning: The RPROP algorithm. *In IEEE International Conference on Neural Networks (San Francisco), vol. 1, pp.586-591. IEEE, New York*, 1993.

23. D. E. Rumelhart, G. E. Hinton, and R. J. Williams. Learning internal representations by error backpropagation. *In D. E. Rumelhart, J. L. McClelland, and the PDP research group, editors, Parallel distributed processing: explorations in the microstructure of cognition, vol.1, pp.318-362. Cambridge, MA:MIT Press*, 1986.

24. R. Smalz and M. Conrad. Combining evolution with credit apportionment: A new learning algorithm for neural nets. *Neural Networks, vol.7, no.2, pp.341-351*, 1994.

25. E. Levin; N. Tishby; S.A. Solla. A statistical approach to learning and generalization in layered neural networks. *Proc. of the IEEE 78(10):1568-1574*, 1990.

26. X. Yao. Evolving artificial neural networks. *Proceedings of the IEEE, 87(9):1423-1447*, 1999.

27. Q. Zhao. Co-evolutionary learning of neural networks. *Journal of Intelligent and Fuzzy Systems 6, pp.83-90. ISSN 1064-1246*, 1998.

28. Q. F. Zhao, O. Hammami, K. Kuroda, and K. Saito. Cooperative Co-evolutionary Algorithm - How to Evaluate a Module ? *Proc. 1st IEEE Symposium on Combinations of Evolutionary Computation and Neural Networks, pp. 150-157, San Antonio*, 2000.

An Evolutionary Algorithm for the Input-Output Block Assignment Problem

Kit Yan Chan and Terence C. Fogarty

Faculty of Business, Computing and Information Management,
South Bank University, 103 Borough Road,
London, SE1 0AA
{chankf,fogarttc}@sbu.ac.uk

Abstract. In this paper, a procedure for system decompositon is developed for decentralized multivariable systems. Optimal input-output pairing techniques are used to rearrange a large multivariable system into a structure that is closer to the block-diagonal decentralized form. The problem is transformed into a block assignment problem. An evolutionary algorithm is developed to solve this hard IP problem. The result shows that the proposed algorithm is simple to implement and efficient to find the reasonable solution.

1 Introduction

Input-output pairing is an effective and simple pre-design technique in improving inter-channel interactions for multivariable systems. In industrial processes, it is common to apply input-output permutations in order to associate output variables to those most effective control variables [4][15]. The Bristol relative gain array [2] was one of these examples which based on the open-loop dc-gain to determine the best pairing for a closed-loop system. Since then many other interaction measures were proposed to cover wider frequency ranges, such as the relative interaction array [23], the relative dynamic gains [19], the generalized relative dynamic gains [11], dominance measures [4][17] etc.

Various gain array or dominance types interaction measures are frequency dependent. Therefore the measures are dependent on the individual problem and the selected frequency range of interest. The gramians based measures are better alternatives that can be free from the mentioned problems. In [6], the input-state-output interaction measure matrix W is chosen to be

$$W = PQ = \sum_{i,j=1}^{n} P_i Q_j \tag{1}$$

where P, Q are the controllability and observability grammians of a system with the state space realization $S(A, B, C, 0)$, where $A \in R^{n \times n}$, $B \in R^{n \times m}$, $C \in R^{m \times n}$. Here the system is assumed to be proper, and P_i, Q_i satisfying the following Lyapunov functions:

$$AP_i + P_iA + b_ib_i^T = 0; \quad AQ_i + Q_iA + c_ic_i^T = 0 \tag{2}$$

M. Keijzer et al. (Eds.): EuroGP 2004, LNCS 3003, pp. 250–258, 2004.

where b_i and c_i^T are the ith column of the matrix B and C^T respectively. In [21], the interaction matrix is chosen to be:

$$W = \{w_{ij}\}; \tag{3}$$
$$\text{where } w_{ij} = trace(c_j^T c_j P_i)$$

However, gramians based measures only covers impulse type input signals. For other type of control signals, different measures are needed. In this paper, w_{ij} is a measure on the influence of the input-i to the output-j. The matrix W, that contains the information of the controllability and the observability of the system, is used to identify those subsystems which are strongly coupled from those weakly coupled. The objective is to find an optimal input-output permutations so that we can identify the optimal number of strongly bounded sub-systems and to re-group the system matrix into a block decentralized form. If this large system is block diagonal dominant, it can be decomposed into many smaller sub-systems and a simple block diagonal controller can be employed. This decomposed structure is useful in many industrial processes when a true pesudo-decoupled structure are needed. With the newly paired decentralized system matrix, we can use it to design sub-controllers. In the following sections of this paper, it is shown that how the pairing problem can be transformed into a general block assignment problem.

For small multivariable systems, one can often identify the best pairing from various gain arrays by observation. However, for large multivariable systems, it is no longer obvious. Fulkerson et al [10] suggested that this kind of problem could be solved by integer programming because it has far fewer variables than numerous solved problems in the literature. However, experience shows that they are not only hard to compute and verify but also complicated for an engineer without a deep mathematical background. Recent research results showed that evolutionary algorithms were more and more widely used in solving the various of assignment problems [1] [9][13][18][22]. Chu and Beasley [1] indicated that the evolutionary algorithm could be applied successfully to a problem that had traditionally been associated with the operations research. In this paper, an evolutionary algorithm is developed for solving the block assignment problems.

2   Input-Output Block Assignment Problem

If the system consists of a number of strongly bounded subsystems while couplings between these subsystems are weak, such special structural properties can be exploited. If the system is block-diagonal dominant, a large system can be considered as many independent sub-systems. The decentralized controllers yielded from such an approach can be smaller in dimension. In addition, these controllers can be fine tuned independently provided that the dominance condition is maintained. This special properties is important in many process control environments when on-line tuning is essential. Permuting rows/columns of W is equivalent to rearranging output/input variables of the system. This rearrangement problem, consists of permuting and partitioning the W matrix, is an input-output block assignment problem. Let W' be the permuted input-output interaction matrix

$$W' = P^o W P^i, \qquad (4)$$

where P^i and P^o is the column (input) and the row (output) permutation matrices respectively. Both matrices[1] are 2-dimensional binary matrices with a "1" in each column/row. W' can be split into two parts after the partitioning information is given;

$$W' = \bar{W} + V, \qquad (5)$$

where $\bar{W}$ and V are the block-diagonal and the off-block-diagonal part of W' respectively. With this partitions and permutations, the inter-subsystems coupling can be measured by a dominance measure [20]:

$$d = \rho(V\bar{W}^{-1}). \qquad (6)$$

The optimal block assignment problem P_{BA} can now be stated as follows:-

$$P_{BA} : \min_{I^r,\ I^c, N^r, N^c, P^i, P^o} \rho(V\bar{W}^{-1}), \qquad (7)$$

where P^i is the input permutation matrix, P^o is the output permutation matrix, N^r is the number of row partitions, N^c is the number of column partitions, I^r is the position of the row partitions and I^c is the position of column partitions. If the block diagonal matrix is degenerated into a simple diagonal form, the problem is reduced to a general assignment problem, which is much easier to solve.[18][22]. P_{BA} is a hard integer programming problem [10], however, it can be solved by the evolutionary algorithm. In the following section, an evolutionary algorithm is developed for solving this problem.

3   Block Assignment Evolutionary Algorithm

3.1   Chromosome Representation

The first step in designing an evolutionary algorithm for a particular problem is to devise a suitable chromosome representation. In this particular problem, the representation of a chromosome consists of four genes; i.e.:

i. Input permutation gene represents the column permutation of the input-output interaction matrix (P^i).

ii. Output permutation gene represents the row permutation of the input-output interaction matrix (P^o).

iii. Input partition gene represents the number of row partition (N^r) and the position of row partition (I^r).

iv. Output partition gene represents the number of column partition (N^c) and the position of column partition (I^i).

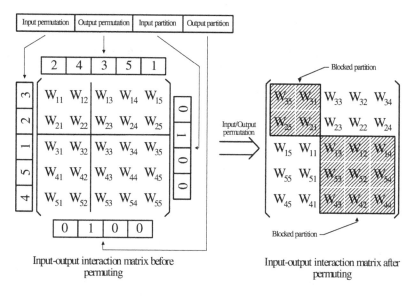

Fig. 1. The chromosome structure of the input/output interaction matrix

Figure 1 shows the chromosome representation for permuting and partition-ing the input-output interaction matrix W.

The length of the chromosome depends on the dimension of the input-output interaction matrix W. For a W matrix with a dimension of $n \times n$, both the input and output partition genes are $n - 1$ bits. They are binary strings in which the value "1" defines a partition at its location. As illustrated in Figure 1, the value "1" is on the second bit of both of the input and output partition genes. Thus the partitions are located between the second and the third row/column of the matrix W. Input and output permutation genes consist of the integer numbers from 1 to n with each number occurring exactly once in the gene. The integer number in the input and output genes define the row and column permutation of the matrix W respectively. As illustrated in Figure 1, the row and column permutation can be represented as $\{1\ 2\ 3\ 4\ 5\} \rightarrow \{2\ 4\ 3\ 5\ 1\}$ and $\{1\ 2\ 3\ 4\ 5\} \rightarrow \{3\ 2\ 1\ 5\ 4\}$ respectively.

3.2   Fitness Function

The fitness function is a measure of goodness of a solution to the cost function. In our algorithm, the fitness of each chromosome is related to the cost function P_{BA} in (6). The dominance measure in (6) involving eigenvalues computation is time-consuming for large matrices. Hence, its associated measure is proposed to

---

[1] Permutation matrix can be represented as a one-to-one map $\pi : I \rightarrow J$, where I and J are set of natural numbers without identical elements [14].

use as the fitness function. The goal of the fitness function can be achieved by satisfing three objectives:

1st objective: Maximize the total sum of the elements inside the block-diagonal matrix $\overline{W}$

$$\max \sum_{i=1}^{n} \sum_{j=1}^{n} \overline{w}_{ij}$$

2nd objective: Minimize the total sum of the elements inside the off-block-diagonal matrix V

$$\min \sum_{i=1}^{n} \sum_{j=1}^{n} v_{ij}$$

3rd objective: Maximize the total number of partitions N^r and N^c.

$$\max \left(N^r + N^c \right)$$

where n is the dimension of the input-output interaction matrix W. To achieve these three objectives, A Parato-based ranking technique [8] is used to evaluate the fitness of the chromosomes.

3.3   Crossover Operation

For the input and output partition genes, one point-crossover operator is applied. However, this operator cannot be applied on the input and output permutation genes, otherwise the matching[2] may not be kept. Thus, for the input and output permutation genes, cycle crossover [16] is applied so as to keep the matching. This operator is very common in the evolutionary algorithm for the matching set problem.

3.4   Mutation Operation

For the input and output partition genes, the bit-by-bit mutation operator for binary string [7] is applied by mutating the gene from "0" to "1" or from "1" to "0". For the input and output permutation genes, the mutation operator can be performed by reordering some region of the gene [12]. For example, consider a gene where two reordering sites position 3 and position 6, are chosen:

$$\{1, 2, 3, 4, 5, 6, 7, 8\}$$

then the newcomer becomes:

$$\{1, 2, 6, 5, 4, 3, 7, 8\}$$

---

[2] The bi-graph $G_n(V, B)$ has a node set V and a branch set B. The index n means there are n pairs of nodes in the bi-graph. A matching of the graph $G_n(V, B)$ is a set of branches such that no two branches of this matching coincide with the same node and each node has a branch connected to it. Therefore a matching is a minimal set of branches to form a cover; some of the nodes will be isolated if any branch of a matching is removed.

3.5 Evolutionary Algorithm for the Block Assignment Problem

In this paper, an evolutionary algorithm for solving the input-output block assignment problem is proposed. We called it as Block Assignment Evolutionary Algorithm (BEA). Assume that we know the input-output interaction matrix W, BEA can find the optimal solution of the input/output block assignment problem as follows:

$$(\overline{W}, V) = \text{BEA}(W)$$

where $\overline{W}$ is the block-diagonal matrix and V is the off-block-diagonal matrix.

The proposed BEA carries out the following five steps.

Algorithm of BEA: Block Assignment Evolutionary Algorithm

Begin

Step 1: Initialization

Generate a population of chromosomes discussed in Section 3.1

Step 2: Evaluation

Evaluate the fitness on each chromosome based on the fitness function discussed in section 3.2.

Step 3: Selection

Give more reproductive chances to the population members with better fitness by performing the roulette wheel selection [12].

Step 4: Reproduction

Reproduction process includes the crossover operations (discussed in Section 3.3) and the mutation operation (discussed in Section 3.4).

Step 5: Termination

Stop if a satisfactory solution is reached, otherwise go to Step 2.

End

4 Examples of Block Assignment Problem for MIMO Systems

Example 1

Let us consider a 5×5 input-output interaction matrix

$$W_1 = \begin{pmatrix} 95 & 2 & 48.5 & 45 & 9 \\ 5 & 93.5 & 4 & 3 & 72 \\ 23 & 6 & 89 & 1.8 & 1.1 \\ 2 & 40 & 9 & 0 & 92 \\ 61 & 6 & 76 & 82 & 4 \end{pmatrix}$$

In the proposed BEA, the crossover rate is set at 0.75 and the mutation rate is set at 0.002. Since the matrix is not too large, the population size is set at 20. By using BEA, the optimal block diagonal matrix $\overline{W}_1$ and the off-block diagonal matrix V_1 are found.

$$\overline{W}_1 = \begin{pmatrix} 92 & 40 & 0 & 0 & 0 \\ 73 & 93.5 & 0 & 0 & 0 \\ 0 & 0 & 95 & 48.5 & 45 \\ 0 & 0 & 23 & 89 & 1.8 \\ 0 & 0 & 61 & 76 & 82 \end{pmatrix}$$

and

$$V_1 = \begin{pmatrix} 0 & 0 & 2 & 9 & 0 \\ 0 & 0 & 5 & 4 & 3 \\ 9 & 2 & 0 & 0 & 0 \\ 1 & 6 & 0 & 0 & 0 \\ 4 & 6 & 0 & 0 & 0 \end{pmatrix}$$

Example 2

Then we consider a a 10×10 input-output interaction matrix.

$$\begin{pmatrix} 1 & 2 & 3 & 1 & 2 & 40 & 2 & 3 & 30 & 40 \\ 2 & 1 & 1 & 2 & 3 & 20 & 2 & 2 & 20 & 3 \\ 1 & 40 & 20 & 3 & 20 & 2 & 2 & 30 & 3 & 1 \\ 20 & 2 & 1 & 30 & 2 & 3 & 20 & 3 & 1 & 1 \\ 1 & 1 & 2 & 1 & 1 & 20 & 3 & 3 & 20 & 20 \\ 30 & 3 & 3 & 40 & 1 & 3 & 20 & 1 & 2 & 2 \\ 3 & 20 & 30 & 1 & 20 & 3 & 1 & 20 & 2 & 1 \\ 1 & 30 & 30 & 3 & 40 & 1 & 2 & 40 & 1 & 1 \\ 40 & 1 & 3 & 40 & 1 & 3 & 30 & 3 & 2 & 1 \\ 1 & 20 & 40 & 1 & 40 & 3 & 1 & 20 & 1 & 3 \end{pmatrix}_{10 \times 10}$$

In this example, the population size of BEA is set at 100. By using BEA, the block diagonal regions which a four-by-four and two three-by-three block diagonal matrices can be found.

$$\begin{pmatrix} \mathbf{20} & \mathbf{20} & \mathbf{30} & \mathbf{20} & 3 & 1 & 2 & 3 & 1 & 1 \\ \mathbf{40} & \mathbf{30} & \mathbf{20} & \mathbf{20} & 2 & 1 & 3 & 1 & 3 & 2 \\ \mathbf{30} & \mathbf{40} & \mathbf{30} & \mathbf{40} & 1 & 1 & 1 & 1 & 3 & 2 \\ \mathbf{20} & \mathbf{20} & \mathbf{40} & \mathbf{40} & 3 & 3 & 2 & 1 & 1 & 1 \\ 1 & 3 & 2 & 1 & \mathbf{20} & \mathbf{20} & \mathbf{20} & 1 & 1 & 3 \\ 2 & 3 & 3 & 2 & \mathbf{40} & \mathbf{40} & \mathbf{30} & 1 & 1 & 2 \\ 1 & 2 & 1 & 3 & \mathbf{20} & \mathbf{30} & \mathbf{20} & 2 & 2 & 2 \\ 3 & 1 & 3 & 1 & 3 & 2 & 2 & \mathbf{30} & \mathbf{40} & \mathbf{20} \\ 1 & 3 & 3 & 1 & 3 & 1 & 2 & \mathbf{40} & \mathbf{40} & \mathbf{30} \\ 2 & 3 & 1 & 2 & 3 & 1 & 1 & \mathbf{20} & \mathbf{30} & \mathbf{20} \end{pmatrix}_{10 \times 10}$$

5   Conclusion

The input-output interaction matrix W has inherited the information of controllability and observability of the system, and it is considered as an inter-channel coupling measure of a multivariable system. Such kind of property is disposed to solve the block assignment problem which is exploited to decompose a large scale system into many weakly coupled subsystems. The row and column permutations on the input-output interaction matrix W are equivalent to rearranging the output and input variables of the multivariable system respectively. Hence the inter-channel coupling of the multivariables in the system could be deduced after permuting the input-output interaction matrix W. Furthermore, a proper partition of W enables to identify the strongly and weakly coupled sub-systems. Thus a large multivariable control system can be decomposed into many weakly coupled sub-systems. In this paper, a NP-hard combinatorial procedure for a large multivariable system is developed. A specified evolutionary algorithm (BEA) is developed for solving this problem. BEA can perform two tasks, i.e., to find the optimal partition and permutation simultaneously. The result shows that BEA is simple to implement and able to find the reasonable solution.

Acknowledgement. Part of the work presented in this paper is taken from the MPhil thesis of the first author [5]. The first author wishes to acknowledge L.F. Yeung, his MPhil supervisor, for many useful discussions and valuable suggestions when he was doing research in City University of Hong Kong. He would also like to thank L.F. Yeung for suggesting him to work on this research topic.

References

1. J.E. Beasley and P.C. Chu, A genetic algorithm for the generalized assignment problem, *Computer Operations Research*, vol. 24, no. 1, pp. 17-23, 1997.
2. E.H. Bristol, On a new measure of interaction for multivariable process control, *IEEE Transactions on Automatic Control*, vol. 11, pp. 133-134, 1966.
3. G.F. Bryant and L.F. Yeung, *Multivariable control system design techniques: dominance and direct methods*, John Wiley and Sons, 1996.
4. G.F. Bryant and L.F. Yeung, Method and concepts of dominance optimization, *IEE Proceedings of Theory and Application*, vol. 130, Pt. D, no. 2, 1983.
5. K.Y. Chan, *New Experimental Design Theoretic Genetic Algorithms for Optimisation Problems and Their Application*, MPhil thesis, City University of Hong Kong, March 2003.
6. A. Conley and M.E. Salgado, Gramian based interaction measure, *Proceeding of the IEEE International Conference of Decision and Control*, vol. 5, pp. 12-15, 2000.
7. L. Davis, *Handbook of genetic algorithm*, New York: Van Nostrand Reinhold, 1991.
8. C.M. Fonseac and P.J. Fleming, Multiobjective optimization and multiple constraint handling with evolutionary algorithms. I. A unified formulation, *IEEE Transactions on Systems, Man and Cybernatics*, Vol. 28, No. 1, pp. 26-37.
9. I.G. French, C.K.S. Ho and C.S. Cox, Genetic algorithms in controller structure selection, *IEE proceeding of Genetic Algorithms in Engineering Systems: Innovations and Applications*, pp. 414-418, 1995.

10. D.R. Fulkerson, L.G. Nemhauser and L.E. Trotter, Two computationally difficult set covering problems that arise in computationally difficult set covering problems that arise in computing the 1-width of incidence matrices of Steiner triple systems, *Mathematical Programming Study 2*, pp. 72-81, 1974.

11. E. Gagnon and A. Desbiens, A. Pomerleau, Selection of pairing and constrained robust decentralized PI controllers, *Proceedings of the American Control Conference*, 1999.

12. E.D. Goldberg, *Genetic algorithms in search, optimization and machine learning*, Addison-Wesley Publishers, 1989.

13. J.N. Amaral and K. Tumer, J. Ghosh, Design genetic algorithm for the state assignment problem, *IEEE Transactions on Systems, Man and Cybernetics*, vol. 254, pp. 687-694, 1995.

14. J.G. Michaels, K.H. Rosen, *Applications of discrete mathematics*, McGraw-Hill International Editions, 1991.

15. N. Munro, Multivariable design using the inverse Nyquist array, *Computer Aided Design*, (4)4, 1972.

16. I.M. Oliver, D.J. Smith and C.R.J. Holland, A study of permutation crossover operators on the traveling salesman problem, *Proceedings of the Second International Conference on Genetic Algorithms*, pp. 224-230, 1987.

17. H.H. Rosenbrock, *State space and multivariable theory*, Nelson, London.

18. J.M. Wilson, A genetic algorithm for the generalized assignment problem, *Journal of the Operational Research Society*, pp. 804-809, 1997.

19. M.F. Witcher and T.J. McAvoy, Interacting control systems: Steady-state dynamic measurement of interaction, *ISA Transactions*, vol. 16, no. 3, pp. 35-41, 1977.

20. L.F. Yeung and G.F. Bryant, New dominance concepts for multivariable control systems design, *International Journal of Control*, vol. 55, no. 4, pp. 969-988, 1992.

21. M. Zhang and L.F. Yeung, Optimization algorithm for input/output structure selection of large multivariable control systems, *IFAC Workshop on Algorithms and Architecture for Real-time Control*, 2000.

22. L. Zhao, Y. Tsujimura and M. Gen, Genetic algorithm for robot selection and work station assignment problem, *Computer Industrial Engineering*, vol. 31, no. 3/4, pp. 599-602, 1996.

23. Z.X. Zhu, Variable pairing selection based on individual and overall interaction measure, *Industrial Engineering in Chemical Research*, vol. 35, pp. 4091-4099, 1996.

Genetic Programming for Subjective Fitness Function Identification

Dan Costelloe and Conor Ryan

Biocomputing and Developmental Systems Group,
Department of Computer Science and Information Systems,
University of Limerick,
Limerick, Ireland
{dan.costelloe,conor.ryan}@ul.ie

Abstract. This work addresses the common problem of modeling fitness functions for Interactive Evolutionary Systems. Such systems are necessarily slow because they need human interaction for the fundamental task of fitness allocation. The research presented here demonstrates that Genetic Programming can be used to learn subjective fitness functions from human subjects, using historical data from an Interactive Evolutionary system for producing pleasing drum patterns. The results indicate that GP is capable of performing symbolic regression even when the number of training cases is substantially less than the number of inputs.

1 Introduction

Interactive Evolutionary Algorithms (IEAs) are given their name because of their need for a user-supplied fitness function. They have found application in design [1], music [2], art [3,4], and even coffee optimisation problems [5], amongst others. All IEAs that rely solely on a user's fitness function suffer from what Biles describes as a "fitness bottleneck" [2]: unlike conventional evolutionary optimisation systems where the fitness function is known and can be automated speedily on a computer, IEAs need to have every solution evaluated by a human, which is a very slow process in comparison.

Attempts to address this issue have been made with varying degrees of success, both Biles [6] and Johanson & Poli [7] used neural networks to try to learn fitness functions in an effort to automate their IEAs for music creation. Other efforts (specific to the musical domain) have included Towsey's [8] identification of musical features that can be objectively defined as a basis for fitness functions for a GA, and later, Truong [9] used a combination of such features and user ratings for his system. A more comprehensive overview of the use of evolutionary techniques for music creation can be found in [10].

This work is a new attempt at the discovery of subjective fitness functions through the use of an IEA for creating pleasing drum rhythms. A fast Genetic Programming system for symbolic regression is run on data collected from several user-runs of the IEA, with results indicating that GP methods may be of considerable merit when it comes to modeling human fitness functions.

M. Keijzer et al. (Eds.): EuroGP 2004, LNCS 3003, pp. 259–268, 2004.

The remainder of this paper is organised as follows; section 2 introduces the IEA, section 3 gives details about the experiments carried out, both on the human evaluators and on their data, section 4 discusses the results obtained and finally, some concluding remarks are made in section 5.

2   Interactive Drumming

In order to investigate whether evolutionary techniques (specifically GP) can be used for learning user-fitness functions, a suitable problem was chosen: the evolution of pleasing drum rhythms. Simple rhythms are relatively easy to represent using a Genetic Algorithm, yet there can also exist a large amount of diversity (and thus quality) in the sounds produced. The Interactive Drumming Evolutionary Algorithm (IDEA) was built for this purpose.

The IDEA breeds a population of simple drum patterns towards fitter states through the use of a human-guided fitness function. An initial population of 12 drum patterns is created and presented to the user, who in turn listens to each pattern and allocates a score, particular to his or her taste. Once all individuals have been rated, the user proceeds to the next generation and repeats the process with an evolved set of patterns. This process continues until the user is satisfied with the quality of the patterns created.

2.1   Representation and Initialisation

The mechanism behind the IDEA is a simple genetic algorithm [11] using fitness proportionate selection, 1-point crossover and bitwise mutation. Each drum pattern is represented as an 80 bit binary string, which is transformed into a sequence of MIDI events [12] that can be sounded using a drum machine or software synthesizer[1]. An example drum pattern created from a bitstring is shown in Figure 1; each of the five 16-bit segments making up an individual are transformed into 16 "ticks" of a drum pattern for a specific instrument. Each set of 16 ticks can be thought of as a bar in musical terms; by default, four bars of each pattern are played back to the user for evaluation.

The initialisation process imposes a certain degree of order on each member of the population. In the initial generation, each pattern has:

  - either ride cymbals or closed hi-hats on every tick or every second tick
  - open hi-hat cymbals only sounding before snare drum sounds
  - all other events randomly created

With most drum patterns across virtually all styles of music, the defining characteristics tend to centre on the placement of the snare, bass drum and (to a lesser extent) open hi-hat sounds, while the closed hi-hat and ride cymbals are usually used to give patterns a continuous feel. The purpose of the initialisation used here is to jump-start the evolutionary process so that all patterns start

---

[1] The synthesizers used here were the deluxe soundbank provided with the Java Runtime Environment, and a Roland TD8 Sound Percussion Module.

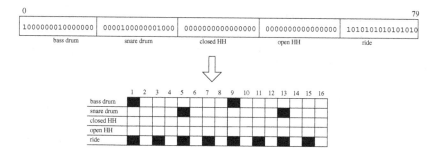

Fig. 1. Individuals are broken into five 16-bit segments and transformed to midi events that can be sounded by the synthesizer. The lower part of the figure shows a "piano-roll" representation of a simple drum pattern. Users of the IDEA have the option to introduce their own changes to evolving patterns through a piano-roll interface.

out with this continuous feel built in. It can also be viewed as a time saving measure; with all events created at random, it can take a significantly larger number of evaluations to get patterns to sound like actual drum beats. With human users acting as fitness functions, "fatigued distraction" becomes an issue, where the users quickly tire and their reactions become increasingly inconsistent in a surprisingly short period of time. This meant that time was very costly and had to be kept to a minimum. After initialisation, however, evolution is free to take patterns in any direction, guided by the user, so if irregular patterns are preferred, they can easily come about.

2.2   Clone Replacement

Early experiments with the IDEA settings indicated that the system was suffering from premature convergence, as the population quickly became saturated with a single pattern, or a set of almost identical patterns. In an effort to deter this from happening, and to give users more freedom to explore the space of possible patterns, the IDEA was extended to incorporate a clone-replacement strategy. After selection, crossover and mutation, each pattern in the population is assigned a checksum value based on the positions and counts of the events it contains. Individuals with identical checksums are then tested for equality and clones removed, for example if a group of n identical individuals is found within the population, $n - 1$ of these are replaced with freshly created patterns (using the initialisation rules) before being presented to the user as part of the next generation.

2.3   Data Collection

As users proceed from one generation to the next, a record of the genetic makeup of each pattern and the score allocated to it is kept in a history file. Later we will see how the history data from users is used as input to a GP system for symbolic regression.

3   Experimental Setup

This section describes how data from user runs of the IDEA was collected from human evaluators and subsequently analysed using GP.

3.1   Obtaining the Data

Unlike many experiments involving evolutionary algorithms where a batch of runs can be set off on a computer and left unsupervised until they are completed with the results neatly tabulated, the experiments carried out here relied on the input of human evaluators. Since no well established dataset for this type of study was publicly available, it was necessary to gather our own dataset for experimental purposes. Nineteen subjects[2] were each given one hour in which to carry out three tasks: complete a questionnaire, perform an "odd-one-out" test and finally, perform the IDEA run. Note that in many studies involving human subjects and computers, typical figures for the number of participants are quite low and it is often acceptable to use four or five subjects for experimental purposes [13].

The questionnaire asked for the following details from the subjects:

- age and gender
- if they would consider their hearing to be normal
- if they are musicians, if so, what level (novice, intermediate, expert)
- level of knowledge of music theory (on a scale of 1–5)
- favourite radio station
- preferred style of music

The purpose of the odd-one-out (or Triangle[3]) test was to establish each subject's ability to tell the difference between similar patterns. For each trial of the test, the subject listened to three drum patterns, two identical and one slightly different and was then asked to choose the odd-one-out. The odd-one-out in each trial of this test differs to the other two by one bit in each 16-bit segment. All subjects were given the same set of patterns for this test, although the location of the odd-one-out was different for each user to prevent subjects from collaborating on the answers. Subjects were given approximately 10 minutes to carry out a maximum of ten trials.

With the remaining time in the session, subjects were then presented with the IDEA and asked to perform one run of as many generations as was comfortably possible. A summary of the data collected from the above experiments is given in Table 1. It is worth noting that working with human subjects almost always means that something unforseen will happen. For example, it was hoped that all subjects would carry out the odd-one-out test, and evaluate fifteen generations

---

[2] All subjects were graduate students from either a Music Technology or Interactive Media course, and paid for their time rather than the quantity and/or quality of data they produced.

[3] Similar to that carried out in [9]

Table 1. Summary of the odd-one-out test results and amount of IDEA history data gathered from 19 subjects.

Subject	Triangle Test #evals, score	IDEA #gens
1	6, 1.0	9
2	7, 0.86	7
3	7, 1.0	11
4	9, 1.0	13
5	10, 0.78	12
6	7, 1.0	13
7	7, 0.71	6
8	7, 0.71	9
9	6, 0.67	12
10	7, 0.71	12
11	8, 0.75	8
12	7, 0.57	12
13	7, 0.57	10
14	7, 0.57	12
15	0, ?	16
16	0, ?	12
17	8, 0.5	16
18	3, 0.67	19
19	6, 0.5	10

worth of drum patterns at the very least, but, unfortunately, two subjects were either unable or unwilling to do the test, and very few managed to get past fifteen generations.

3.2 Analysing the Data

The results from the odd-one-out test were used to split the subjects into four groups as follows:

- Those that performed 6 or more evaluations and acheived a score greater than 0.75 (Group 1)
- Those that performed 6 or more evaluations and scored between 0.55 and 0.75 (Group 2)
- Those whose results from the odd-one-out test were unknown (Group 3)
- Others, who either scored less than 0.55 or performed less than 6 evaluations (Group 4)

The following experiments will only deal with members of groups 1 and 2 as these are the subjects that we feel are most likely to give consistent results. Furthermore, we know the least about groups 3 and 4, making it difficult to draw conslusions about how GP fares ar learning their functions.

Analysis of the history data gathered from each subject focused on the last four generations; of these, three generations were used for training with the final generation used for testing. Tests were performed on both raw and filtered history data.

The raw data was created by taking each boolean value from the 80 bit segment representing a pattern and converting each bit into a numerical value (0.0 or 1.0). For training, 36 cases of 80 variables and 1 target were used. Testing data (the final generation) consisted of 12 cases.

Domain-specific filters were designed and applied to the history files to reduce the number of input variables to 7 using:

- Average distance between closed hi-hat events (x_1).
- Average distance between ride cymbal events (x_2)
- Number of bass drum events (x_3)
- Distance between first and last bass drum events (x_4)
- Number of snare drum events (x_5)
- Distance between first and last snare drum events (x_6)
- Proportion of "correct" open hi-hat events[4] (x_7)

Variables x_1 and x_2 are used to give an indication of the level of continuity within a pattern, while variables x_3 through x_6 focus the bass and snare drum events, which we regard as the defining characteristics of the patterns. The number of such events coupled with the distance between first and last events helps to give an idea of the level of clutter within each pattern. The last variable gives a measure of correctness of the open hi-hat cymbal events; in general these events immediately precede snare drum events across a variety of music styles.

As with the raw data, filtered training data consisted of 36 cases with 12 cases used for testing[5].

Symbolic Regression. The experiments carried out used a fast GP system for symbolic regression that uses interval arithmetic and linear scaling [14]. The system employs a steady state algorithm, tournament selection, subtree crossover and node and branch mutation. Replacement is carried out via an inverse tournament. For each dataset, 30 runs were carried out using varying numbers of generations from 10 to 200. Training performance is calculated using Mean Squared Error:

$$MSE(t, p) = \frac{1}{N} \sum_i^N (t - p)^2 \tag{1}$$

Where t and p are vectors of actual targets and predicted values respectively.

Testing Performance. After each run on the training data, best of run is applied to the testing data. The actual fitness score, t is classified, as either bad $(0 \leq t < 3)$, okay $(3 \leq t < 7)$ or good $(7 \leq t \leq 10)$ as is the predicted score, p.

---

[4] a correct open hi-hat event is judged (by this function) to be one which occurs one tick before a snare drum event, as is commonly found in most drum patterns.

[5] All data files are available at http://bds.ul.ie/danc_egp04/

The performance measure, S, is then calculated as the proportion of successful classifications.

For each data set, two variations of parametric settings were applied. The first used a restricted function set consisting of $\{+, -, *\}$ only, and the second used a larger set of functions, $\{+, -, *, /, x^2, \sqrt{x}, exp(x), ln(x), sin(x), cos(x)\}$. Crossover was applied at a rate 100% and children created always undergo either node or branch mutation.

4 Results

Results from the symbolic regression experiments on the raw data are shown in Tables 2 and 3, while Tables 4 and 5 show the corresponding results from experiments on the filtered data.

Overall, we can see that GP does have the capability to learn the fitness functions, although there is room for improvement in certain cases. Recall that members of group 1 are those that scored highest in the odd-one-out test, and are more likely to be able to distinguish between patterns good, bad and okay. In 3 out of 4 cases, a higher group average is achieved for group 1, indicating a dependency between GP's ability to learn the functions and the subjects' ability to tell patterns apart.

Results from both datasets (raw and filtered) using the larger function set show a slight improvement when using the raw data, indicating that a combination of the summary information provided by the filters and an increased set of functions may hinder fitness function discovery. Furthermore, results for group 1 using the reduced function set show a higher group average using the filtered dataset, which supports this assertion.

5 Conclusions and Future Work

This paper has introduced the use of GP as a new method for discovering subjective fitness functions from an Interactive Evolutionary Algorithm. Results have indicated that GP can be successful at performing this task, although we suspect that the degree of this success depends greatly on the quality and consistency of the data generated by human evaluators.

There are a number of potential future directions for this research, the first of which will involve the derivation of more useful filters from a more focused study of the successful functions produced from the raw history data. Secondly, it is hoped to build a more complex IEA comprising a larger set of instruments (not limited to percussion) that involves on-the-fly learning of fitness functions using GP during the course of the IEA run.

The fact that GP was capable of performing meaningful symbolic regression on real and extremely noisy data is pleasing, if somewhat surprising. Future work will examine other non-linear learning systems, such as a Support Vector Machine [15], to see how it performs on this data.

Table 2. Results from symbolic regression on the raw data with function set $\{+,-,*\}$. Each cell shows the mean testing performance (from 30 runs) achieved on each subject's history file after 10, 20, 50, 100, 150 and 200 generations. High accuracy scores (0.7 or more) are highlighted in bold type.

		Number of Generations						Group Average
		10	20	50	100	150	200	
	1	0.4150	0.4283	0.4033	0.3917	0.3683	0.3683	
	2	**0.8367**	**0.8117**	**0.7567**	**0.7267**	**0.7183**	**0.7117**	
	3	0.2733	0.2633	0.2550	0.2300	0.2033	0.2133	
	4	**0.7233**	0.3217	**0.7233**	**0.7317**	**0.7317**	**0.7333**	0.5519
	5	**0.7250**	0.6967	0.2550	0.2500	0.2400	0.2400	
Group 1	6	**0.8183**	**0.8350**	**0.8817**	**0.8550**	**0.8650**	**0.8667**	
	7	0.3750	0.3883	0.3683	0.3683	**0.7800**	**0.7767**	
	8	0.6583	0.6650	0.6633	0.6817	0.6900	0.6750	
	9	**0.7850**	0.3733	**0.7900**	**0.8000**	0.3883	0.3783	
	10	**0.8417**	**0.8333**	**0.8067**	**0.7783**	**0.7700**	**0.7717**	
	11	**0.9483**	**0.9400**	**0.9417**	**0.9267**	**0.9217**	**0.9283**	0.5635
	12	**0.7050**	0.3117	**0.7133**	**0.7067**	**0.7067**	**0.7033**	
	13	0.1983	0.1767	0.1650	0.1783	0.1767	0.1633	
Group 2	14	0.2400	0.2317	0.1917	0.1633	0.1583	0.1433	

Table 3. Results from symbolic regression on the raw data with function set $\{+,-,*,/,x^2,\sqrt{x},exp(x),ln(x),sin(x),cos(x)\}$. Each cell shows the mean testing performance (from 30 runs) achieved on each subject's history file after 10, 20, 50, 100, 150 and 200 generations. High accuracy scores (0.7 or more) are highlighted in bold type.

		Number of Generations						Group Average
		10	20	50	100	150	200	
	1	0.4383	0.4817	0.4567	0.4183	0.4050	0.4133	
	2	**0.8567**	**0.8417**	**0.7733**	**0.7233**	0.3083	0.3000	
	3	0.2517	0.2233	0.1933	0.1817	0.1683	0.1750	
	4	0.6883	0.6933	**0.7317**	**0.7450**	**0.7583**	**0.7583**	0.5830
	5	**0.7283**	0.6983	0.6667	0.6467	0.6400	0.6300	
Group 1	6	**0.8083**	**0.8383**	**0.8450**	**0.8383**	**0.8367**	**0.8267**	
	7	**0.7717**	**0.8117**	0.4117	0.4050	0.4000	0.0833	
	8	0.1850	0.5950	0.6500	0.6467	0.6483	0.6433	
	9	0.3717	**0.7617**	0.3800	0.3767	**0.7917**	0.3883	
	10	**0.8533**	**0.8083**	0.3350	0.3483	**0.7600**	**0.7583**	
	11	**0.9500**	**0.9483**	**0.9317**	**0.9300**	**0.9217**	**0.9250**	0.5089
	12	**0.7333**	0.3133	0.3200	**0.7033**	0.6933	0.6900	
	13	0.1733	0.1600	0.1617	0.1750	0.1817	0.1683	
Group 2	14	0.2433	0.2217	0.2050	0.1667	0.1583	0.1683	

Table 4. Results from symbolic regression on the filtered data with function set $\{+, -, *\}$. Each cell shows the mean testing performance (from 30 runs) achieved on each subject's history file after 10, 20, 50, 100, 150 and 200 generations. High accuracy scores (0.7 or more) are highlighted in bold type.

		Number of Generations						Group Average
		10	20	50	100	150	200	
	1	0.4633	0.4767	0.4650	0.4500	0.4533	0.4417	
	2	**0.8883**	**0.8933**	**0.8617**	**0.8333**	**0.8083**	**0.7967**	
	3	0.2383	0.2250	0.2217	0.2117	0.2017	0.2133	
	4	**0.7883**	**0.7750**	**0.7783**	**0.7933**	**0.7883**	**0.7867**	0.6153
	5	**0.7500**	**0.7483**	**0.7200**	0.2850	0.6850	0.2700	
Group 1	6	**0.8033**	**0.8417**	**0.8117**	**0.7950**	**0.7917**	**0.7967**	
	7	**0.7817**	0.3650	0.3700	**0.7733**	**0.7683**	**0.7533**	
	8	0.6100	0.5467	0.1283	0.1250	0.1283	0.1317	
	9	0.3650	**0.7667**	0.3383	**0.7200**	**0.7117**	**0.7067**	
	10	0.4667	**0.8600**	**0.8500**	**0.8117**	**0.7817**	**0.7683**	
	11	**0.9383**	**0.9083**	**0.8500**	**0.8650**	**0.8700**	**0.8783**	0.5323
	12	0.6883	0.6750	0.6317	0.6283	0.6150	0.6267	
	13	0.1850	0.1917	0.1950	0.1833	0.1867	0.1933	
Group 2	14	0.2333	0.2600	0.2617	0.2750	0.2867	0.2950	

Table 5. Results from symbolic regression on the filtered data with function set $\{+, -, *, /, x^2, \sqrt{x}, exp(x), ln(x), sin(x), cos(x)\}$. Each cell shows the mean testing performance (from 30 runs) achieved on each subject's history file after 10, 20, 50, 100, 150 and 200 generations. High accuracy scores (0.7 or more) are highlighted in bold type.

		Number of Generations						Group Average
		10	20	50	100	150	200	
	1	0.4633	0.4683	**0.9917**	**0.9900**	**1.0000**	**0.9617**	
	2	**0.8283**	**0.7900**	0.0667	**0.7400**	**0.7150**	0.6983	
	3	0.0433	0.2683	0.0183	0.0250	0.0083	0.0617	
	4	**0.7433**	0.0200	**0.9600**	0.0450	**0.9850**	**0.9717**	0.5598
	5	**0.7417**	**0.7083**	0.2650	0.2500	0.2283	0.2300	
Group 1	6	**0.8000**	**0.7983**	**0.8017**	**0.8117**	**0.8217**	**0.8317**	
	7	0.3217	**0.9783**	**0.9667**	0.0367	**0.9633**	0.0283	
	8	0.6533	0.2050	0.1600	0.1533	0.1633	0.1667	
	9	0.3550	0.3400	0.3250	0.3550	0.3483	0.3433	
	10	**0.8350**	0.4450	0.0300	0.3483	0.3333	0.3050	
	11	**0.9717**	**0.9767**	**0.9783**	**0.9667**	**0.9783**	0.1700	0.4170
	12	0.3283	0.3117	**0.7300**	0.2967	**0.7033**	**0.7017**	
	13	0.2050	0.2300	0.2383	0.2350	0.2383	0.2250	
Group 2	14	0.2300	0.2383	0.2250	0.2300	0.2267	0.2217	

References

1. Peter J. Bentley, editor. *Evolutionary Design by Computers*. Morgan Kaufmann, 1999.
2. J. A. Biles. GenJam: A Genetic Algorithm for Generating Jazz Solos. In *Proceedings of the 1994 International Computer Music Conference*, pages 131–137, ICMA, San Francisco, 1994.
3. K. Sims. Artificial Evolution for Computer Graphics. In *Computer Graphics: Proceedings of SIGGRAPH'91*, volume 25, pages 319–328. ACM Press, 1991.
4. A. E. Eiben, R. Nabuurs, and I. Booij. The Escher Evolver: Evolution to the People. In Peter J. Bentley and David W. Corne, editors, *Creative Evolutionary Systems*, chapter 17, pages 425–439. Morgan Kaufmann, 2002.
5. M. Herdy. Evolutionary Optimization based on Subjective Selection – Evolving Blends of Coffee. In *Proceedings of EUFIT'97*, pages 640–644, 1997.
6. J. A. Biles, P. G. Anderson, and L. W. Loggi. Neural Network Fitness Functions for a Musical IGA. In *Proceedings of the International ICSC Symposium on Intelligent Industrial Automation (IIA '96) and Soft Computing (SOCO '96)*, pages B39–B44, Reading, UK, 1996.
7. B. Johanson and R. Poli. GP-Music: An Interactive Genetic Programming System for Music Generation with Automated Fitness Raters. In *Genetic Programming 1998: Proceedings of the Third Annual Conference*, pages 181–186. Morgan Kaufmann, 1998.
8. M. Towsey, A. Brown, S. Wright, and J. Deiderich. Towards Melodic Extension using Genetic Algorithms. *Educational Technology & Society*, 4(2), 2001.
9. Brian Truong. Trancendence: An Artifical Life Approach to the Synthesis of Music. Master's thesis, School of Cognitive and Computing Sciences, University of Sussex, Brighton, UK, 2002.
10. A. R. Burton and T. Vladimirova. Generation of Musical Sequences with Genetic Techniques. *Computer Music Journal*, 23(4), 1999.
11. David E. Goldberg. *Genetic Algorithms in Search, Optimization and Machine Learning*. Addison-Wesley Publishing Company, Reading, Massachusetts, 1989.
12. MIDI Manufacturers Association (MMA). The complete midi 1.0 detailed specification, v.96.1, 1996.
13. A. von Mayrhauser and A. M. Vans. Program Understanding: Models and Experiments. In Marvin Zelkowitz, editor, *Advances in Computers*, volume 40, pages 1–38. Academic Press, 1995.
14. Maarten Keijzer. Improving Symbolic Regression with Interval Arithmetic and Linear Scaling. In C. Ryan, T. Soule, M. Keijzer, E. Tsang, R. Poli, and E. Costa, editors, *Proceedings of the Sixth European Conference on Genetic Programming (EuroGP-2003)*, volume 2610 of *LNCS*, pages 70–82, Essex, UK, 2003. Springer Verlag.
15. V. Vapnik, S. Golowich, and A. Smola. Support Vector Method for Function Approximation, Regression Estimation and Signal Processing. In *Advances in Neural Information Processing Systems 9*, pages 281–287, Cambridge, MA, 1996.

Saving Effort in Parallel GP by Means of Plagues

F. Fernández and A. Martín

Artificial Evolution Group, Centro Universitario de Mérida,
C/Sta Teresa de Jornet, 38, 0688-Mérida. SPAIN
fcofdez@unex.es, http://gea.unex.es

Abstract. Recently, a new technique that allows Genetic Programming to save computing resources has been proposed. This technique was presented as a new operator acting on the population, and was called plague. By removing some individuals every generation, *plague* aims at compensating for the increase in size of individuals, thus saving computing time when looking for solutions. By means of some test problems, we show that the technique is also useful when employing a parallel version of GP, such as that based on the island model.

1 Introduction

Evolutionary Algorithms (EAs) have been applied to solving optimization problems for several decades. This kind of stochastic techniques are usually employed when the search space features a large size, so that enumerative methods and other classical search techniques are not helpful. Despite their success, researchers know that computational resources required for solving difficult problems, is sometimes prohibitive. This has led to applying efforts to both studying the nature of the algorithms -and the way they work- and also developing new techniques for reducing the computational effort that is required when looking for solutions to problems. If we focus on Genetic Programming (GP), researchers have had to face the problem of bloat. This problem has been deeply studied ([4]), and basically consists of the growing of individuals as generations are computed. The consequence is that computational effort required for evaluating individuals progressively grows as new solutions are generated. Different authors have described and evaluated different reasons that give rise to this effect ([9], [10]). Nevertheless, the problem is not only present in GP, but also in any other EA in which variable size chromosomes are employed.

Researchers have offered during the last few years several proposals aimed at preventing such an inordinate growth ([4]), including the application of multiobjective techniques to GP, in such a way that both size of individuals and fitness are balanced [8]. Nevertheless all of these solutions focus on individuals' size and none of them consider the global problem of population growth as a whole.

During the last year, a new proposal for saving computing resources in GP has been proposed. The idea consist of removing some individuals as generations

M. Keijzer et al. (Eds.): EuroGP 2004, LNCS 3003, pp. 269–278, 2004.

are computed, so that, even in the presence of bloat, computational resources that are required remains constant. This proposal was first presented in [13] and was later described in [2] and [11]. Similar proposals were also described by Monsieurs [15] and Luke [16].

In this paper we try to apply this proposal to a well-known parallel version of Genetic Programming, Parallel GP based on the Island Model. The idea is to test whether it can also save computing effort when using this model. The Island Model -as well as other parallel models- has been proved to be effective for finding better fitness values than the panmictic version of the GP algorithm [12]. The idea now is to maintain the quality of solutions, while at the same time we reduce the required effort for obtaining them.

This paper is structured as follows: section 2 presents the plague operator and also some arguments supporting its usefulness. Section 3 describes some results obtained using plagues and Parallel GP, and section 4, studies how the systematic suppression of individuals from the population affects phenotypic and genotypic diversity. Finally we offer our conclusions in section 5.

2   The Plague Operator

Individuals are usually encoded by means of trees in GP. Although there are other possibilities, Koza's influential work has favoured the use of this structures [7]. Individuals tend to vary in size and complexity when they are generated using genetic operators and variable-size structures -such as trees. There are some reasons that cause large individuals in GP to survive with higher probability than smaller ones [9], [10]. The result is that individuals tend to increase their size as they are evolved, and this is known as the bloat phenomenon. GP is thus affected by the bloat problem.

In previous research, we found that a possibility for fighting bloat at the population level -instead of establishing some kind of control at individual level-was to use *the plague* operator in the population. Plagues work as follows: Some individuals are cyclically removed from the population after a number of generations. Several policies could be employed for selecting individuals to be deleted, although the simplest one chooses bad individuals, according to some criteria, such as their fitness value or size. Our starting point was the panmictic model, and the plague was thus applied to only one population [2].

We are trying now to extend the operator to a parallel version of GP: the island model. We want to know if the operator is also useful when using that model.

The search for solutions by means of Evolutionary Algorithms usually consists of two different operations, exploration and exploitation. While the first one usually requires a large number of individuals -if the search space is not a plateau- the second one can be conveniently performed using a smaller one [17].

The idea behind plagues is to adjust the size of the population as the two steps are performed, so that the process begins with a large number of individuals, and this is progressively reduced by means of the plague. Given that the size of the population is reduced at a linear rate we are also fighting the bloat problem; as said before, this can simply be done by removing a fixed number of individuals from the population each generation, by means of the *plague*.

3   Experimental Results

In the set of experiments that we are presenting, we compute effort as it was first described in [5], as the total number of nodes required for finding a given level of quality in solutions. We compute the effort of computation at a given generation g as the total number of nodes that have been evaluated so far i.e., from generation 1 to generation g. This measure is related to that employed by Poli in [14], although he computed the effort required for obtaining a solution for a problem with a given probability, and the effort was also measured as the total number of nodes computed.

The method described in [5] for measuring results is somehow different because it doesn't take into account probability of success. It just measures the average of the best fitness value obtained in a set of runs, and the effort -number of nodes evaluated- required for obtaining each of the fitness values. This measure possesses several advantages when compared with other commonly used ones [6] and has been recently used by other researchers (see for instance [8]).

The idea is to check whether the plague operator can help to reduce effort when using Parallel GP. In order to do so, we have chosen a couple of representative GP problems: the even parity 5 problem and the ant problem, as described in Koza [7].All the curves presented are the average values obtained over 60 different runs. We use one of the simplest elimination policies: the worst individuals from the fitness point of view are removed at each generation, i.e. we don't take into account the genetic material making up individuals. All of the experiments employ generational GP, tournament selection, 10 individuals per tournament, 1 percent mutation probability, 95 percent crossover probability and elitism.

3.1   Panmictic Model

We present first results that were obtained applying plagues to the Panmictic Model in GP. A more detailed description of results is included in [11].

The Even Parity 5 Problem. Figure 1 (right) was obtained when working with the Even Parity 5 problem. It shows results obtained when comparing a population with 5000 individuals and the same population undergoing plagues: we remove 99 individuals per generation. Standard deviation bars provide statistical significance of these results. We notice that plagues are actually helping to save computational effort when obtaining a given fitness level quality. The same is also true for figure 1(right), which presents results for a population made up of 10000 individuals. Nevertheless, notice that given that all the curves have been computed for the same number of generations in figure 1(right), the final fitness value is slightly worse when using plagues. However, the final value has been

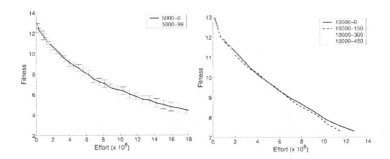

Fig. 1. Even Parity 5 problem. Mean population fitness against computational effort. Black curve: standard GP. Gray and dashed curves: populations undergoing various plagues. The second number in the box is the number of individuals that are suppressed at each generation. Standard deviations are shown as error bars in (a).

obtained using much less effort than the one that has been spent to obtain the same fitness value when population is not affected by plague.

The Ant Problem. Similar experiments have been performed using the ant problem. Figure 2 (left) shows results for the ant problem when using 5000 individuals and several plagues, while Figure 2 (right) shows similar results but now using 10000 individuals. Differences are not so important here, and according to standard deviation measures (not shown in the figure to avoid cluttering it) we cannot state that plague is beneficial, but we can neither say that they are negative events.

The idea under discussion here and results obtained are in agreement with latest research on the size of populations and the way they explore the search space: large population may perform a better exploration phase while small population are best suited for the exploitation step [17]. Depending on the kind of search space, one of the model may be preferred. In the experiments shown above, we have used a large population at the beginning of the search process,

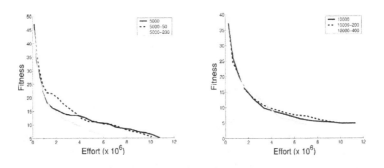

Fig. 2. Left: Ant 5000 individuals. Right: Ant 10000 individuals.

when we try to explore an area of the landscape as large as possible, and we reduce progressively the size of the population, when the exploitation step is performed. Results show that the panmictic model can benefit from the use of plagues.

3.2 The Island Model

We have extended the set of experiments in order to test whether *plagues* are also useful when parallel models are employed. Even when we only check the Island Model, we think that results presented in this section are useful to have an idea about the general behaviour of parallel models under the effect of plagues. Basically the Island Model distributes the population into several island that exchange individuals at specific generations. A more detailed description of this model can be obtained in [12]

All the experiments presented in this section, employ the same parameters described above, and the following ones related to the parallel model: 10 individuals migrating each 10 generations from each population. The individuals selected for migration are the best ones. The individuals that arrive to a population replace the 10 worst ones. Experiments described in the paper employ 2 and 4 populations, although other number and population sizes have been employed obtaining similar results.

Even Parity 5 problem. Figure 3 (left) shows results obtained using 2 populations with 2500 individuals each. We notice that when plague is applied - removing 48 individuals per generation - we obtain better fitness values for similar effort levels. Curves present some small jumps this time, because migration steps helps to improve fitness values at some generations. Similar conclusions can be reached when observing Figure 3 (right): now we employ 4 populations with 1250 individuals each, and two different settings. Removing 24 individuals per generation per population allows us to obtain better fitness values for similar effort levels.

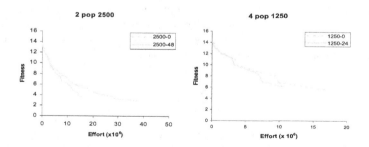

Fig. 3. Evenp 5 problem. Left: 2 populations with 2500 individuals each. Right: 4 populations with 1250 individuals each. Blue dotted line for fixed size populations.

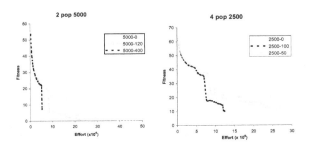

Fig. 4. Ant problem. Left: 2 populations with 5000 individuals each. Right: 4 populations with 2500 individuals each. Blue dotted line for fixed size populations.

The Ant Problem. Similar experiments have been performed using the Island Model for the Ant problem.

Figure 4 (left) presents results obtained when employing 2 populations with 5000 individuals each. We have performed experiments with and without plagues, and again, the best results are obtained with plagues (see 5000-400).

On the other hand, figure 4 (right) shows results obtained using 4 populations with an initial size of 2500 individuals each. The best results are obtained using a plague consisting in removing 100 individual from each population every generation.

4   Diversity Measures

Even when plagues help to save computing time, it is always interesting to study some properties of the evolutionary process that populations undergo when new operators are applied. Researchers are usually interested in monitoring some measures that helps them to know when evolution is progressing or stagnating. For this proposal, several diversity measures have been described and employed.

In this section we try to empirically analyse the evolution of diversity when plagues are employed in Parallel GP, using the Island Model. This kind of experiments will help in the future to even improve the technique presented here.

A rather complete survey of diversity measures in panmictic GP has been presented in [1]. The diversity measures that we use in this paper are based on the concept of *entropy* of a population P, defined as follows:

$$H(P) = \sum_{j=1}^{N} F_j \log(F_j)$$

If we are considering phenotypic entropy, we define F_j as the fraction n_j/N of individuals in P having a certain fitness j, where N is the total number of fitness values in P. If we are considering genotypic entropy, we employ the distance as defined by Ekárt's and Németh's definition [3]. A wider description may also be found in [11]. In the following experiments, the empy tree will be chosen as the origin for measuring purposes.

In previous research, and in agreement with the results of [1], we observed that phenotypic diversity in fixed size populations, after an initial increase, normally tends to decrease with time, while genotypic diversity tends to increase at the beginning of the evolution and to stay constant later in the run. However, as described in [2] and [11], when the population sizes decrease steadily - because of the plague - phenotypic and genotypic population diversities are more correlated, both are decreasing more or less at the same rate when using the panmictic model.

This behaviour indicated that the high genotypic diversity still present at the end of the run in fixed size populations does not help much in finding better solutions. This can be due to bloat and, in general, to the presence of neutral networks of solutions, although the phenomenon should be further investigated. On the other hand, the loss of phenotypic and genotypic diversity for populations undergoing plagues didn't seem to have a negative influence on performance, at least for the problems studied.

4.1   Diversity in Parallel GP Affected by Plagues

This section presents a study of evolution of diversity in Parallel GP when plagues are applied. Figures 5 to 7 shows genotypic and phenotypic entropy obtained for the ant and the evenp problem when plagues have been applied to Parallel GP.

The same trends that were observed with plagues in the panmictic model (see [11]) are found again in the parallel model. Genotypic and phenotypic diversity decrease with time, and this is stressed by the systematic removal of individuals.

In [2] and [11] some proposals to prevent this behaviour were proposed and studied for the panmictic model. Basically, the idea was to carefully select which individuals must be removed for maintaining the diversity as high as possible,

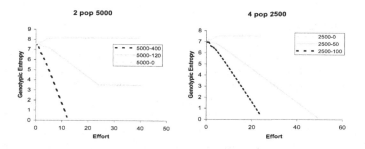

Fig. 5. Left: Evolution of diversity for the ant problem with plagues. 2 population with 5000 individuals each. Right: Evolution of diversity in the ant problem using, 4 population with 2500 individuals each.

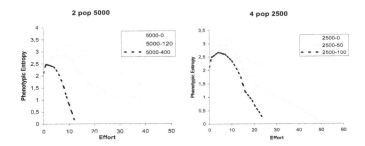

Fig. 6. Left: Evolution of entropy for the ant problem using 4 populations with 2500 individuals. Plagues are applied within each population. Right: Evolution of entropy for the ant problem using 4 populations with 2500 individuals.

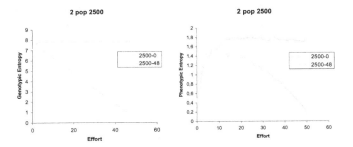

Fig. 7. Evolution of genotypic and phenotypic diversity for the evenp problem using 2 populations with 2500 individuals. Plagues are applied within each population

even when plagues act. In future research we will also try to study and apply several policies to reach a similar goal in Parallel GP, thus allowing to continue improving fitness quality when a low number of individuals are available in the population.

5   Conclusions

In this paper we have applied the concept of *plague* to Parallel GP. *Plagues* act by removing a fixed number of individuals each generation, usually the worst ones. We have experimented on two different problems, and we have found evidence that *plagues*, when applied to Parallel GP, allow to save computing effort. Although removing different number of individuals each generation produce different results, we have seen that the general behaviour is that plagues allows to save computing resources. This technique is only useful if the quality of the solutions found is at least comparable to that of the constant size population GP, which has been the case for the test problems studied here. Results obtained using Parallel GP are completely in agreement with those previously obtained using panmictic GP. We have also found that plagues affect diversity in populations: both genotypic and phenotypic diversity measures decreases as individuals are removed.

We plan to study different elimination techniques for Parallel GP further in the future, in order to avoid diversity to deteriorate.

Acknowledgment. We acknowledge financial support by the Spanish Ministry of Science and Technology (project TRACER) under contract number TIC2002-04498-C05-01.

References

1. Burke, E., Gustafson, S. and Kendall, G. A survey and analysis of diversity measures in genetic programming. In W. B. Langdon et al., editor, *GECCO 2002: Proceedings of the Genetic and Evolutionary Computation Conference*, pages 716–723. Morgan Kaufmann Publishers, San Francisco, CA, 2002.
2. F. Fernandez, M. Tomassini, L. Vanneschi. Saving computational effort in genetic programming by means of plagues. In *Proceeding of the Conference on Evolutionary Computation 2003*, pages 2042–2049. IEEE Press, 2003.
3. Ekárt, A. and Z. Németh, S.. Maintaining the diversity of genetic programs. In J. A. Foster et al., editor, *Genetic Programming, Proceedings of the 5th European Conference, EuroGP 2002*, volume 2278 of *LNCS*, pages 162–171. Springer-Verlag, 2002.
4. Langdon, W. B., Poli, R: Foundations of Genetic Programming. Springer (2001).
5. F. Fernandez, Distributed Genetic Programming Models with Application to Logic Synthesis on FPGAs. PhD thesis, University of Extremadura, 2001.
6. F. Fernandez, G. Galeano, and J. A. Gomez. Comparing synchronous and asynchronous parallel and distributed GP models. In James A. Foster, Evelyne Lutton, Julian Miller, Conor Ryan, and Andrea G. B. Tettamanzi, editors, volume 2278 of LNCS, pages 326–335, Kinsale, Ireland, 3-5 April 2002. Springer-Verlag.
7. Koza, J.R.: Genetic Programming. On the Programming of Computers by Means of Natural Selection, The MIT Press: Cambridge, MA, 1992.
8. de Jong E. D. Multi-Objective Methods for Tree Size Control, Genetic Programming and Evolvable Machines, Vol. 4, pp. 211-233. Kluwer Accademic Press. 2003.
9. Banzhaf, W. Langdon, W. Some considerations on the reason of bloat, in Genetic Programming and Evolvable Machines, Vol 3, N. , Morgan Kaufman (2002) 81-91.
10. Soule, T. Exons and Code Growth in Genetic Programming, in Lecture Notes in Computer Science 2278, Springer-Verlag, 142-151, 2002.
11. F. Fernandez, L. Vanneschi, and M. Tomassini. The effect of plagues in genetic programming:a study of variable-size populations. In M. Keijzer E. Tsang R. Poli E. Costa C. Ryan, T. Soule, editor, *Proceedings of the Sixth European Conference on Genetic Programming (EuroGP-2003)*, volume 2610 of *LNCS*, pages 317–326, Essex, UK, 2003. Springer Verlag.
12. Fernandez, F., Tomassini, M., Vanneschi, L., An Empirical Study of Multipopulation Genetic Programming, in Genetic Programming and Evolvable Machines, vol (4), 2003, pp. 21-51. Kluwer Academic Publishers.
13. Fernandez, F. Estudio de Poblaciones de tamaño variable en Programacion Genetica (Spanish), II Congreso Español sobre Metaheuristicas, Algoritmos Evolutivos y Bioinspirados, Maeb 03, pp.417-423, Gijon, feb. 2003.

14. Poli, R. Some steps towards a form of Parallel Distributed Genetic Programming, In Proceedings of the First On-line Workshop on Soft Computing, 1996.
15. Monsieurs P, Flerackerseddy E, Reducing Populations size while maintaining diversity, LNCS Vol. 2610. Springer.
16. Luke, S, Balan, G. C., Panait, L., Population Implosion in Genetic Programming, Lecture Notes in Computer Science, Vol. 2724, pp. 1729-1739.
17. Fuchs, M. Large populations are not alway the best choice in Genetic Programming, in Proceedings of Genetic and Evolutionary Comptation Conference, Morgan Kaufman (1999), 1033-1038.

Sampling of Unique Structures and Behaviours in Genetic Programming

Steven Gustafson, Edmund K. Burke, and Graham Kendall

School of Computer Science & IT
University of Nottingham, UK
{smg,ekb,gxk}@cs.nott.ac.uk

Abstract. This paper examines the sampling of unique structures and behaviours in genetic programming. A novel description of behaviour is used to better understand the solutions visited during genetic programming search. Results provide new insight about deception that can be used to improve the algorithm and demonstrate the capability of genetic programming to sample different large tree structures during the evolutionary process.

1 Introduction

Genetic programming searches for solutions to a given objective using program-like representations. However, the task of evolving both a solution's structure and content is complex and difficult to understand [1,2,3]. Our previous research has focused on understanding the relationship between diversity and search, particularly on the kind and level of diversity that encourages good performance [4,5]. Recently, we showed how increased diversity negatively and positively effects performance on several problems [6]. A metaphor of hill-climbing search helped explain the results, where deception appeared to be a cause of poor performance. To further understand diversity and search, particularly with respect to deception introduced by the problem and representation, we are interested in the type of structures and behaviours that genetic programming samples during the evolutionary process.

Research into code growth and operator biases can be used to understand the type of structures sampled by genetic programming. Subtree crossover and the representation predispose solutions toward code growth and bloat [7,8,9,10, 11,12,13]. While programs continue to grow, they tend to grow toward deeper and less-bushier structures. Also, the space of tree shapes visited during genetic programming search has been studied [7,11,14,15], showing that there are types of shapes that are more easily sampled than others. If a problem's solution is not within the more easily sampled structures, the problem will be difficult for genetic programming [16].

With respect to the growth of solutions, the subtree crossover operator is shown to be a more "local" operator, where the upper-portion of trees become fixed and variations mainly occur near the leaves [17,18,19,20]. Diversity research

M. Keijzer et al. (Eds.): EuroGP 2004, LNCS 3003, pp. 279–288, 2004.
© Springer-Verlag Berlin Heidelberg 2004

also demonstrates the effects of the convergence of structures [4,5,21]. However, it is also the content of trees (functions and terminals) that provide a solution to a given problem. By using stochastic sampling techniques, the proportion of solutions of increasing size was shown not to increase beyond a certain threshold [14,22]. That is, the space of increasingly larger solutions did not yield a higher proportion of solutions.

As the fitness function is typically a very coarse description of behaviour, it is more difficult to understand the type of solutions sampled by genetic programming. However, comparisons between genetic programming and hill-climbing methods using similar representations and operators can be helpful [22,23,24, 25]. While genetic programming performed better and worse on various problem domains, comparisons emphasised the domains in which more hill-climbing or explorative search is beneficial. These results were particularly useful in explaining the effects of increased genetic diversity [6]. In any case, much of the solutions' *behaviour* remains hidden behind the fitness function value.

To better understand the sampling of structures and behaviours during search, this paper examines the number of unique structures (genotypes without node content) and behaviours (an enriched definition of fitness) sampled. The structure aspect of the following study provides additional views of the search process, while the coarseness of fitness function values is addressed with problem-specific behaviour descriptions that reflect fitness but elucidate the behaviour of the solutions better.

2   Problems and Methods

We use three problem domains that are frequently used to understand genetic programming: The Artificial Ant problem on the Sante Fe Trail, the Even-5-Parity problem and a regression problem using the Binomial-3 function [1]. Each domain causes genetic programming to behave differently and thus experiments spanning all three domains provide a good basis for understanding. The Ant problem attempts to pick up 89 food pellets on a grid with the functions {if-food-ahead, prog2n} and the terminals {left, right, move}. The Parity problem attempts to classify all 2^5 combinations of 5-bit length strings of {1,0} with the functions {and, or, nand} and five boolean terminals. The Binomial-3 regression problem attempts to approximate the function $f(x) = (1+x)^3$ using the terminals x, ephemeral random constants in the range of $[-10, 10]$, and the functions $\{+, -, \times, p/\}$, where division is protected and returns 1.0 if the denominator is extremely small. All problems are minimisation of errors; the number of missed food pellets in the ant problem, the mean squared error in regression of the Binomial-3 function and the number of misclassified bit-strings in the parity problem.

In an evolutionary algorithm, a scalar value is typically used to define a solution's behaviour (although multiobjective methods may use a vector). This value, defined by a fitness function, must be able to distinguish different degrees of solution quality. This coarseness often leads to deception, as in the Artificial

Ant problem [22], or fails to identify solutions that are relatively good in the current population but extremely poor to continue a search with, as in the case of very small solutions in regression problems. Thus, measuring the sampling of behaviours during a run using only the fitness value may not be as informative as one would like, and so we define problem specific definitions of behaviour as follows:

- *Ant:* we label each food item uniquely and create a vector representing the order in which the food is collected,
- *Parity:* a vector of integer values, where the size is the total classified correctly and the contents indicate which of the 2^5 test cases were correctly classified,
- *Regression:* a vector of integer values represents the angles between test points (from the horizontal) taken by a solution.

These definitions capture more information than their typical scalar value fitness would, but are still a reduction of the complete behaviour of a solution. The ant behaviour represents the unique sequence of food collection, where the largest sequence is 89 and the smallest is 0. The parity behaviour describes which specific instances are correctly classified. The definition of behaviour for the regression domain describes the change in angle from the horizontal between each function point in the candidate solution. By casting these angles as integers, when two successive angles in the vector are identical, only the first is kept. Thus, the size of the vector alludes to the complexity of the solution (the number of "bends" in the graph of that function), but not directly to the fitness value as the target function is not considered.

In this paper, the tracking of sampled structures is performed by considering the binary tree structures regardless of tree content. We count the number of unique structures of each size that are sampled during the run of the algorithm. Note that there are many unique tree structures of equal size and depth.

A canonical genetic programming system is run for 51 generations, using a generational algorithm with a population size of 500. Initial tree creation is carried out using ramped half-n-half with tree sizes between depths 2 and 4. Subtree crossover, with internal node selection set at 90% probability and maximum depth of 10, is used for recombination – no mutation or duplication is used. There are 30 random runs collected for each problem domain.

The results for each problem domain are depicted in two graphs showing the average number of unique structures sampled and unique behaviours sampled of a given size. Each line represents the cumulative total of unique structures (or behaviours) in each generation during a run. Each successive ten generations are highlighted with symbols. Thus, the space between two lines represents the number of new unique structures (or behaviours) of a given size that were sampled in a generation. The larger the space, the more effort genetic programming spends on searching unique structures (or behaviours) of that size.

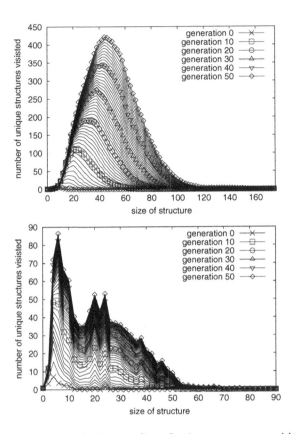

Fig. 1. Ant results, cumulative sampling of unique structures and behaviours.

3   Results

Figure 1 shows the structure and behavioural sampling for the ant problem. There is a distinct trend of the highest number of unique structures sampled toward sizes of 45. The bottom graph in Figure 1 shows the sampled behaviours of each size for the ant problem. Note that the number of unique behaviours sampled of all sizes in each generation is greatly reduced after approximately 10 generations. Also, after two unusual peaks at behaviours of size 20 and 24, the number of unique sampled behaviours greatly decreases for behaviours of large size (which represent more "fit" solutions).

The sampling of structures for the parity problem is shown in the top graph of Figure 2. This problem samples fewer unique structures but at larger sizes. The number of unique behaviours sampled in the parity problem are shown in the bottom graph of Figure 2. A behaviour has a maximum length of 32, which represents all 2^5 correct classifications. However, there are $\binom{32}{k}$ possible unique behaviours for a length of k. For the expected random strategy classification of

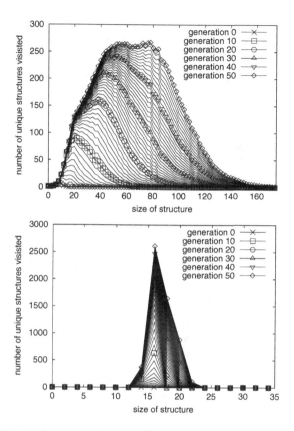

Fig. 2. Parity results, cumulative sampling of unique structures and behaviours.

size 16, nearly 2500 unique behaviours are sampled over the course of a run. Genetic programming spends a large amount of effort searching neutral behaviours equivalent to a random strategy, with slight peaks at fitness 18 and 20. Symmetry in the parity bit-string instances probably rewards the solving of an additional instance with another symmetrical instance also solved correctly, explaining why fitness is concentrated on the random (16) strategy initially, followed by one instance additionally solved (17+1=18) and then another (19+1=20).

The regression problem's sampling of structures is shown in the top graph of Figure 3. A distinct trend is seen toward sampling unique structures of sizes near 40. Fewer unique structures of larger sizes are sampled. The number of unique behaviours sampled in the regression problem, depicted in the bottom graph of Figure 3, shows a strong attraction toward behaviours of size 12. All generations during the run sample unique behaviours of this size. As behaviour does not directly reflect the fitness, these behaviours may or may not have neutral fitness. However, the Binomial-3 fitness function contains 50 equidistant x values that

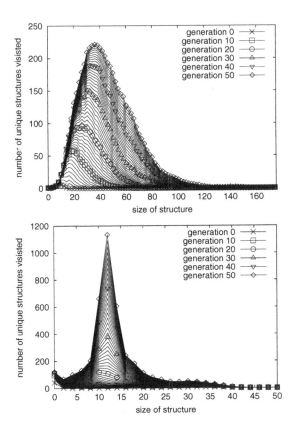

Fig. 3. Regression results, cumulative sampling of unique structures and behaviours.

generate the target y values for testing an individual. The angle gradient between successive y values is nearly always greater than 1. Thus, for our behaviour measure, if a behaviour is to represent the function ideally, it will need close to 50 angle changes between points.

The 95% confidence bars for each of the average distributions from Figures 1 to 3 are shown in Figure 4. From left to right, the ant, parity and regression structures are shown on the top row, and behaviours on the bottom row. The sampling between the 30 runs is fairly uniform with the greatest variations occurring near the peaks in the regression problem.

4   Discussion

How does one search for computer programs, and how do we know if one program is better than the other? The intuitive broad sampling of a complex solution space by a population in genetic programming is one reason why the algorithm may be considered useful. Early work by Cramer [26] and Koza [27] laid the foundations for this procedural representation, where the use of single-value scalars as fitness combined and complex representations were already in use in other evolutionary algorithm domains. While it may have been straightforward to apply these methods to program evolution for genetic programming, the conflicts arising in this representation are well documented [1,2,16,28]. The results presented here, based on the sampling of unique tree structures and unique behaviours, further describe genetic programming's ability to sample a complex solution space.

The behaviour definition used here enriched the description of the sampling of solutions by genetic programming. In the ant problem, the geographic distribution of food pellets on the ant trail may allow for many ant behaviours that are able to collect 20 to 24 pellets, but unable to easily collect more. In this problem, the standard definition of fitness creates deception [22] that has already been shown to negatively impair fitness improvement. However, the more gradual decrease in the ability to sample different behaviours of higher fitness explains why genetic programming often outperforms hill-climbing methods that hill-climb with poor solutions. The peaks of behaviours sampled at size 20 and 24 may represent local optima that trap search. The behaviour distribution for the parity problem is particularly interesting as it shows the ability of genetic programming to sample may different near-random type behaviours. Sampling such high numbers of different behaviours is promising but a likely cause of deception and negative contextual shifts of subtrees, explaining why hill-climbing and elitist strategies are more effective on this problem [23,25].

While the regression problem used a behaviour that did not directly reflect its fitness value, the behaviour did reflect the complexity of solutions. The preference toward sampling behaviours of a small size and complexity could be caused

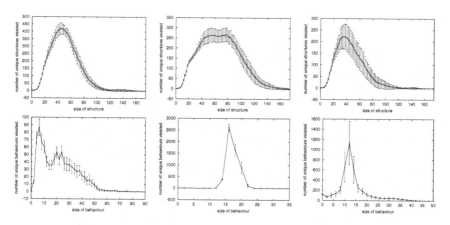

Fig. 4. 95% confidence bars for the average cumulative structure and behaviour sampling distributions. From left to right is the ant, parity and regression problems with structure on top and behaviour below.

by neutrality in the fitness values or the result of a biased structure sampling. In the latter case, the inability to increase structure size is hypothesized to be positively correlated with the inability to increase the complexity of solutions. This hypothesis seems plausible for the regression domain, considering that subtree crossover typically functions near the leaves (terminals).

With respect to the sampling of unique structures of various sizes, all problems showed that while genetic programming is predisposed to code growth (and bloat), unique tree structures of large sizes are sampled less. That is, a fewer number of big tree structures are sampled. The different structures of the same size that are sampled more frequently would appear to be attractive to genetic programming for one reason or another. The depth limit imposed here is one possible cause.

These results also suggest several possibilities to improve performance. The sizes of behaviours that were sampled in high numbers may represent areas of deception in the fitness space. This deception may be reduced by pressuring the search away from areas of neutral fitness. Previous research showing a positive correlation between high fitness-based diversity with good fitness could be the result of avoided deception leading to better fitness. Thus, when a population contains many different but equal in fitness behaviours, we may wish to move the search toward a less deceptive region of the search space. Leading the ant to follow a specific food trail reduced deception and improved fitness [22]. For the regression domain, using a component of complexity in the fitness function may also improve the performance of genetic programming. Similarly, the parity fitness function could be amended to reflect which instances a solution solves correctly to reduce deception. Of course, exploration (global search) and exploitation (local search) ability will be affected when such methods are employed to reduce deception.

5   Conclusions

This paper examined the sampling of unique tree structures and unique behaviours in genetic programming. An enriched definition of behaviour provided more information about solutions than typical fitness functions. As the genetic programming algorithm requires the search of structure and content, it is important to understand issues such as deception and the effort the algorithm spends on searching different types of behaviours and structures. The behaviour sampling results showed sampling trends that help explain previous diversity research and suggests new ways to improve search. The structure sampling results showed that while bloat and code growth occur, fewer different unique structures of these large sizes are sampled. Problems which require specific structures at these large sizes are likely to be more difficult for genetic programming.

Acknowledgments. The authors would like to thank the anonymous reviewers, Natalio Krasnogor and Anikó Ekárt.

References

1. J.M. Daida, R.R. Bertram, S.A. Stanhope, J.C. Khoo, S.A. Chaudhary, O.A. Chaudhri, and J.A. Polito II. What makes a problem GP-hard? analysis of a tunably difficult problem in genetic programming. *Genetic Programming and Evolvable Machines*, 2(2):165–191, June 2001.
2. U.-M. O'Reilly. The impact of external dependency in genetic programming primitives. In *Proceedings of the 1998 IEEE World Congress on Computational Intelligence*, pages 306–311, Anchorage, Alaska, USA, 5-9 May 1998. IEEE Press.
3. J. Hu, K. Seo, S. Li, Z. Fan, R.C. Rosenberg, and E.D. Goodman. Structure fitness sharing (SFS) for evolutionary design by genetic programming. In W.B. Langdon et al., editors, *Proceedings of the Genetic and Evolutionary Computation Conference*, pages 780–787, New York, 9-13 July 2002. Morgan Kaufmann Publishers.
4. E. Burke, S. Gustafson, and G. Kendall. A survey and analysis of diversity measures in genetic programming. In W. B. Langdon et al., editors, *Proceedings of the Genetic and Evolutionary Computation Conference*, pages 716–723, New York, 9-13 July 2002. Morgan Kaufmann Publishers.
5. E. Burke, S. Gustafson, G. Kendall, and N. Krasnogor. Advanced population diversity measures in genetic programming. In J.J. Merelo Guervós et al., editors, *Parallel Problem Solving from Nature*, volume 2439 of *LNCS*, pages 341–350, Granada, Spain, September 2002. Springer.
6. E.K. Burke, S. Gustafson, G. Kendall, and N. Krasnogor. Is increasing diversity in genetic programming beneficial? an analysis of the effects on fitness. In B. McKay et al., editors, *Congress on Evolutionary Computation*, pages 1398–1405, Canberra, Australia, December 2003. IEEE Press.
7. T. Soule and J.A. Foster. Code size and depth flows in genetic programming. In J.R. Koza et al., editors, *Genetic Programming 1997: Proceedings of the Second Annual Conference*, pages 313–320, Stanford University, CA, USA, 13-16 July 1997. Morgan Kaufmann.
8. W.B. Langdon, T. Soule, R. Poli, and J.A. Foster. The evolution of size and shape. In Lee Spector et al., editors, *Advances in Genetic Programming 3*, chapter 8, pages 163–190. MIT Press, Cambridge, MA, USA, June 1999.
9. W.B. Langdon. The evolution of size in variable length representations. In *1998 IEEE International Conference on Evolutionary Computation*, pages 633–638, Anchorage, Alaska, USA, 5-9 May 1998. IEEE Press.
10. W. Banzhaf and W. B. Langdon. Some considerations on the reason for bloat. *Genetic Programming and Evolvable Machines*, 3(1):81–91, March 2002.
11. W.B. Langdon. Quadratic bloat in genetic programming. In D. Whitley et al., editors, *Proceedings of the Genetic and Evolutionary Computation Conference*, pages 451–458, Las Vegas, Nevada, USA, 10-12 July 2000. Morgan Kaufmann.
12. T. Soule and R.B. Heckendorn. An analysis of the causes of code growth in genetic programming. *Genetic Programming and Evolvable Machines*, 3(3):283–309, Sept. 2002.
13. S. Luke. Modification point depth and genome growth in genetic programming. *Evolutionary Computation*, 11(1):67–106, 2003.
14. W.B. Langdon. Scaling of program fitness spaces. *Evolutionary Computation*, 7(4):399–428, 1999.

15. J.M. Daida. Limits to expression in genetic programming: Lattice-aggregate modeling. In D.B. Fogel et al., editors, *Congress on Evolutionary Computation*, pages 273–278, Honolulu, USA, 2002. IEEE Press.

16. J.M. Daida, H. Li, R. Tang, and A.M. Hilss. What makes a problem GP-hard? validating a hypothesis of structural causes. In E. Cantú-Paz et al., editors, *Proceedings of the Genetic and Evolutionary Computation*, volume 2724 of *LNCS*, pages 1665–1677, Chicago, 12-16 July 2003. Springer-Verlag.

17. J. Rosca and D.H. Ballard. Causality in genetic programming. In L. Eshelman, editor, *Genetic Algorithms: Proceedings of the Sixth International Conference (ICGA95)*, pages 256–263, Pittsburgh, PA, USA, 15-19 1995. Morgan Kaufmann.

18. C. Igel and K. Chellapilla. Investigating the influence of depth and degree of genotypic change on fitness in genetic programming. In W. Banzhaf et al., editors, *Proceedings of the Genetic and Evolutionary Computation Conference*, pages 1061–1068, Orlando, Florida, USA, 13-17 July 1999. Morgan Kaufmann.

19. R. Poli and W.B. Langdon. On the search properties of different crossover operators in genetic programming. In J.R. Koza et al., editors, *Proceedings of the Third Annual Genetic Programming Conference*, pages 293–301, Wisconsin, USA, 22-25 July 1998. Morgan Kaufmann.

20. P. D'haeseleer and J. Bluming. Effects of locality in individual and population evolution. In K.E. Kinnear, Jr., editor, *Advances in Genetic Programming*, chapter 8, pages 177–198. MIT Press, 1994.

21. N.F. McPhee and N.J. Hopper. Analysis of genetic diversity through population history. In W. Banzhaf et al., editors, *Proceedings of the Genetic and Evolutionary Computation Conference*, pages 1112–1120, Florida, USA, 1999. Morgan Kaufmann.

22. W.B. Langdon and R. Poli. *Foundations of Genetic Programming*. Springer-Verlag, 2002.

23. U.-M. O'Reilly and F. Oppacher. Program search with a hierarchical variable length representation: Genetic programming, simulated annealing and hill climbing. In Y. Davidor et al., editors, *Parallel Problem Solving from Nature*, number 866 in LNCS, pages 397–406, Jerusalem, 9-14 October 1994. Springer-Verlag.

24. U.-M. O'Reilly and F. Oppacher. A comparative analysis of GP. In P.J. Angeline and K. E. Kinnear, Jr., editors, *Advances in Genetic Programming 2*, chapter 2, pages 23–44. MIT Press, Cambridge, MA, USA, 1996.

25. A. Juels and M. Wattenberg. Stochastic hillclimbing as a baseline method for evaluating genetic algorithms. Technical Report Technical Report CSD-94-834. Computers Science Department, University of California at Berkeley, USA, 1995.

26. N.L. Cramer. A representation for the adaptive generation of simple sequential programs. In J.J. Grefenstette, editor, *Proceedings of an International Conference on Genetic Algorithms and the Applications*, pages 183–187, Carnegie-Mellon University, Pittsburgh, PA, USA, 24-26 July 1985.

27. J.R. Koza. *Genetic Programming: On the Programming of Computers by Means of Natural Selection*. MIT Press, Cambridge, MA, USA, 1992.

28. U.-M. O'Reilly and D.E. Goldberg. How fitness structure affects subsolution acquisition in genetic programming. In J.R. Koza et al., editors, *Proceedings of the Third Annual Genetic Programming Conference*, pages 269–277, Madison, WI, USA, 22-25 July 1998. Morgan Kaufmann.

The Evolution of Concurrent Control Software Using Genetic Programming

John Hart and Martin Shepperd

Bournemouth University
{jhart,mshepper}@bmth.ac.uk

Abstract. Despite considerable progress in GP over the past 10 years, there are many outstanding challenges that need to be addressed before it will be widely deployed for developing useful software. In this paper we suggest a method for the automatic creation of concurrent control software using Linear Genetic Programming (LGP) and a 'divide and conquer' approach. The method involves decomposing the whole problem into a multi-task solution with multiple inputs and multiple outputs – similar to the process used to implement embedded control solutions. We describe the necessary architecture of typical embedded control systems and their relevance to this work, the software evolution scheme used and lastly demonstrate the technique for an embedded software problem, namely a washing machine controller.

1 Introduction

Despite considerable research effort globally towards refining the existing GP techniques, and the development of variants like Grammatical Evolution [8], the ability to create useful, complex and problem-specific programs has remained elusive. Perhaps this is not surprising given that creating computer programs by GP at the individual level, can be seen as a Markov process[1] and, as such, the longer the program is (and so the greater the complexity) then the probability of its discovery will decrease exponentially. The need to search for simpler programs has been identified by other research groups, e.g. Leung *et al.* [7] in their work evolving parallel code.

In this paper we note that the necessary steps required to implement embedded control solutions effectively divide the overall problem into a number of simpler problems. We argue that a similar problem decomposition process can enable EC to automatically generate useful programs for a certain class of problems. This approach is a departure from the original aspirations for GP made by Koza[4] where he suggested that GP can find not only the solution but also

---

[1] A Markov process is a discrete random process whereby the probability of moving onto another state depends solely on the current state of the process and not on any history or other stored information. Thus the choice of the next statement in the construction of a GP tree / string can be viewed as an independent and undirected event. This model has been used to construct analyses of GP operation [6].

M. Keijzer et al. (Eds.): EuroGP 2004, LNCS 3003, pp. 289–298, 2004.

the shape of that solution. Perhaps this is unrealistic for anything beyond trivial problems?

Instead we propose a system that requires the problem shape to be defined in terms of the required program outputs. Thus the target user group for this method of software evolution would include product designers / engineers who wish to add embedded control to their product but who don't have the time, money or interest to write their own software. Instead the contribution made by these users would be the definition of embedded control system inputs and outputs, and the required relationship between these items in operation. Consequently, the primary contribution of this paper is an exploration of the feasibility of a divide and conquer approach to evolving programs for embedded systems and not an exhaustive exploration of different crossover and mutation regimes.

The method described here will only be applicable to a certain class of problems. Suitable targets are defined as non safety-critical, not demanding high precision or guaranteed response timing or reliability. All such targets would still need to be relatively simple, or capable of being decomposed into a solution with such a profile. Hence suitable applications could include fridges, TV remote controls, building environment management systems, dishwashers, etc.

The rest of this paper is organised as follows: Section 2 describes typical characteristics of embedded control systems and how these are relevant; Section 3 outlines the problem decomposition and the EC system used to evolve the solution, Section 4 describes a washing machine controller as an example problem. Section 5 describes the results obtained from tackling this problem, and finally Section 6 draws conclusions from this research, the example problem and ideas for future research.

2 Embedded Control Systems

An embedded control system will typically comprise of dedicated hardware hosting dedicated embedded software or firmware (i.e. between hardware and software). Usually the hardware and software will be optimised or minimised solely to perform the task at hand; there is not usually a requirement for flexibility or expansion. Many embedded applications must guarantee response and execution timing which is possible since the application does not share the hardware and because execution prioritisation is achieved through the use of exception processing i.e. in response to timer or external events. Here, execution will transfer to the code necessary to respond to that event (unless interrupted again by a higher priority event). In effect, structuring the code in this way, segments much of the entire application into a number of execution 'channels' initiated by an event, and linking input to output via the channel code. Since the structure of the problem is inherent within the specification we exploit this outside the search as opposed to allowing the evolutionary search to expend many cycles discovering what is already known.

Another distinct feature of many embedded control applications is the use of multiple inputs and outputs, for example, a robot in a car plant may have inputs for object position, belt speed, object orientation in two dimensions etc., and outputs for tool position in three different planes etc. This is in contrast to PC type applications that might typically only deal with keyboard input and screen output.

Indirectly then, this separation of overall application output into a number of separate outputs, and the demand for temporal as well as structural hierarchies in the code to guarantee response timing, have the effect of decomposing the entire problem into a number of smaller problems, each using a separate channel through execution time and space.

These considerations lead to the approach adopted in this work whereby the overall problem is viewed as a number of smaller code segments each feeding a separate output, such that each isolated code channel is simple enough to evolve automatically using EC techniques.

3   Automatic Software Evolution Method

We obtain a problem decomposition by evolving separate GP code for each channel so that each channel will contribute data for one system output. The channel code is evolved using an isolated population and ultimately the evolved code is intended to be run as a separate concurrent task and synchronised by a multi-tasking OS or implemented on a multi-processor platform.

The goal of this research was to create and evaluate a general purpose software evolution method that could be applied to a range of applications without specific tuning. Consequently relatively little effort has been expended in optimising the performance of the evolutionary method or parameters used, although it turned out that system performance is relatively insensitive to different parameter values within the ranges we studied (see Section 5).

A form of Linear Genetic Programming [1] was chosen because of the relative ease of implementation and inherent problems such as bloat[2] are reduced. Consistent with the desire to build a system with general applicability, the evolutionary language set used was kept simple and general. Effectively, this could be seen as a RISC-type[3] approach, which led to very efficient use of computing

---

[2] Program bloat is mainly a phenomenon manifested in tree-based GP whereby crossover can create trees of excessive size, through the combination of large sub-trees. This will often result in an excessive and possibly inefficient use of computing resources. The bloat, however, can be seen as important in evolutionary terms because the introns (unused code) – that can form the bulk of the bloat – will serve to protect the executed code from mutation. Bloat is often tackled by combining a fitness award for brevity with the existing fitness function.

[3] RISC processors use what is perhaps a counterintuitive approach whereby the machine-level instruction set is limited to simple instructions (Add, OR etc.) and more complex instructions that will perform complex, compound operations are omitted. Generally, this will result in longer machine code programs after compilation because more instructions will be required to accomplish the same task, however, the hardware design of the processor chip becomes simpler. This simplification al-

resources i.e. simple instructions that can be compiled to a single machine code instruction.

As a variant to the standard LGP where execution flow is linear and contiguous, we have implemented a branch instruction to allow the formation of iteration in the evolved code strings if required. The functions available for each language statement are the mathematical operators $(+, -, *, /^4)$ the logical operators (AND, OR, XOR, NOT) and the relational operators $(<, >)$. In addition, a conditional branch instruction is included.

The system can use two data types: continuous and logical. Continuous data type can be positive or negative floating point numbers; the logical data type will only be either '1' or '0'. Here, the same storage class is used for both types and the type to which the stored values are applied is interpreted in context to the instruction at hand. For instance, the logical instructions above will interpret all arguments as unclamped logical values, thus, zero is interpreted as FALSE and everything else as TRUE. These instructions will only produce logical results, storing '0' for FALSE. Similarly, the continuous functions will interpret all arguments as continuous values, and produce continuous results.

The relational operators are a hybrid in that these will treat the arguments as continuous numbers but produce logical results. The conditional branch (IF) statement will interpret the condition as TRUE (take the branch) if the condition evaluates as non-zero. Upon taking the branch, execution will continue at the absolute line number supplied as an argument to this instruction.

By implementing both data types, the system can efficiently cover the input / output requirements of a typical embedded control application. The continuous data types can be used for reading numeric values from various sources e.g. to sample a continuous value such as temperature, position or time. The Boolean type input / output can be used for logic level type sensing e,g, control switches, limit sensors, etc.

The LGP program strings are of variable length (up to a preset maximum) and consist of atomic statements. With the exception of the IF branch instruction, each statement has one or two inputs and an output term. An input source maybe connected to an input terminal, a numbered memory, a constant or a subtotal accumulator. The output term maybe connected to a program output terminal, a numbered memory or to the subtotal accumulator register. The subtotal accumulator was included to facilitate the direct flow and construction of information up through the program i.e. the separate memory registers available are indexed.

Beyond the string length and population size variations, the mechanisms of EC used were basic and were not investigated with a view to optimisation. Evolutionary selection here creates a generational population of constant size. All candidates for the next generation are selected from the current generation by use

---

lows the processor to run faster such that even with a greater number of instructions to process, the overall execution time will usually be reduced.

[4] Note that the divide operator is protected by returning 1 upon attempts to divide by zero.

of a tournament of size two. The developed evolutionary system does, however, allow for the use of different population sizes, and mutation and crossover rates, for each population (task) in case the ability to adjust the evolution process for each output / function became necessary.

To avoid a possibly unhelpful saturation of the population by a single candidate, a maximum fitness 'ceiling' value was employed[5]. This clamp value was used as a candidate's fitness score when the error for the training vector case fell below 0.002. This value was found to be appropriate for the problem at hand by experiment. The tolerance of this value did not seem to be too critical, but the choice for such a value must depend upon both the type of function sought.

One immediate side effect of clamping the maximum fitness score in this way, was to create a 'dead zone'. Within this region, solutions could not be improved upon because the feedback path that leads solutions to improvement through evolution is broken. This potential limit on solution accuracy could be seen as acceptable because of the stated problem class targeted here.

The adopted fitness assessment method used attempts to find useful 'root' solutions that can be improved by evolution. These root solutions will be relatively close to the required solution - but require some refinement. Such solutions can be identified because they produce a minimum, threshold level of fitness in all training vector cases. The size of this threshold will determine how close these candidate solutions will need to be to an ideal solution, in order to be classed as a 'root' solution. This threshold level then, will create a 'capture range' around the ideal solution, within which root solutions can be identified and selected for evolution. This capture range will need to be as large as possible to increase the chances of search success; Simultaneously, the threshold should not be so low (and so the capture range so large) that, for instance, output constants are identified as root solutions.

Crossover action on LGP systems had limited impact. It made little difference (in most cases) in which order unrelated program statements were executed, thus, the action of exchanging the top and bottom halves of two strings, in a converged population contributed little. However, this ordering was certainly more critical in the case of the Output statement. In this case, the sequential execution of the program strings (unless branching occurs) created a situation whereby only the final Output statement executed (and the code that built the data for this) was important. Perhaps not unexpectedly then, the level of crossover used had little impact on the level of success attained. The crossover rate used was 25%.

Subsequent to the initial population, the only way of introducing diversity into the population was through the action of mutation. Mutation becomes especially important then as the population starts to converge – especially if that convergence is upon a sub-optimal solution.

Various methods of mutation were investigated, along with the replacement of the least fit individuals in the population with an equal number of randomly

---

[5] An alternative strategy to obviate population saturation (and loss of diversity) has been suggested by Keijzer [3] Here linear scaling / regression is used to determine the magnitude of the solution first.

created strings. The most effective method used in the experiments was a hybrid approach. The maximum evolutionary time allowed is 20000 generations (interrupted upon success) and this time was divided into four epochs, with the level or type of mutation applied changed according to the current epoch:

- Epoch 0 (the first 40% of evolution time): one single statement is chosen randomly from the string selected for mutation and the entire statement replaced.
- Epoch 1 (40% to 70% of evolutionary time): only one part of the selected statement is altered (either the operation type, the output channel type or one of the two input channels).
- Epoch 2 (70 to 90% of evolution time): only input constants are modified in the chosen statement – if used, the current constant value is retained but adjusted with the addition of a bipolar random number chosen from a Gaussian distribution with a mean of 0, and a standard deviation of 2.
- Epoch 3 (final 10% of evolutionary time): as per epoch 2, but using a standard deviation of 1.

The intention of this approach was to focus down on the solution by using less aggressive mutation over time and concentrating any adaptation only on constants towards the end. Thus, by incrementally adapting the current constant value the solution is slowly improved. A reward for parsimony was not used because program bloat was not a problem.

At just sixteen cases per output, the size of the training set used in the experiments was unusually small for EC. However, because the fitness function adopted required a threshold fitness score in all cases, then the candidate function promoted was most likely to be a useful root function which could map all training cases to some extent. By this process then, a relatively small training set was capable of unambiguously describing the target function (or it's near equivalent) in the example tried.

Table 1 summarises the various parameter values, or ranges of values, that we employed. Relatively little effort was made to optimise them, however, as the next section demonstrates we were able to obtain usable results which did not seem to be particularly sensitive to changes within the ranges we explored.

Table 1. Parameter values for GP search

Parameter	Value
Representation	linear GP
Maximum string length	5-30 words maximum
Population size	200-1000
Initial population	random
Population	steady state
Selection mechanism	tournament
Crossover rate	0.25
Mutation rate	0.4
No. of generations	20000

Table 2. Washing Machine Cycle. N.B. $f(\epsilon_T)$ indicates a function of water temperature error.

	TS0	TS1	TS2	TS3	TS4	TS5	TS6	DrumFull
Heat (cont.)		$f(\epsilon_T)$						
Heat (logic)		X						
Slow		X	X		X	X		
Fast				X			X	
Cold	X			X				X
Hot	X							X
Drain			X			X	X	
Description	Fill	Wash	Drain	Spin	Rinse	Drain	Spin	

4 Washing Machine Controller Problem

This case study followed on from a previous pilot (based on a simple fridge controller) that demonstrated the feasibility of our approach. It targeted a more complex problem with 14 inputs and seven threads plus it introduced temporal sequencing rather than continuous operation.

- **System inputs**
  Timer inputs, TS0 ... TS6 timing sequence inputs, provided by the OS.
  Target temperature the desired wash temperature.
  Water temperature the current water temperature
  Drum Full signals washing drum full of water.
- **System outputs**
  Heat drive for the water heater. This output is to be zero if the current water temperature exceeds the chosen temperature.
  Hot, Cold Boolean signals to open the respective water fill valves.
  Slow, Fast Boolean signals to select drum rotation speed.
  Drain Boolean signal to enable the water drain pump.

Table 2 outlines the required functional relationship between the inputs and outputs for the complete operational cycle of the washing machine. Note that not all time periods (TS0 ... TS6) are necessarily equal in duration.

5 Problem Solution Results

The main problem encountered in the solution of this problem centred on the Heat output because the evolution of the code for this output required that the desired continuous function relating the temperature error and heat drive be found, consequently the results focus upon this aspect of the problem. In addition, the output had to be clamped to zero in the event that the water was too hot or if the current operational time period was not Wash. This overall output required the evolution of a combined continuous and logical function and this proved to be unachievable when tried. The solution adopted was to make the

Table 3. Success rate v. string length in words

Length	5	10	15	20	25	30	Total
Fail	138	138	144	146	143	142	851
Success	12	12	6	4	7	8	49
Total	150	150	150	150	150	150	900

overall Heat output the composite of two evolved tasks: one continuous and one logical. In this way, the fitness landscape of the boolean function did not obscure that for the continuous function. In order to keep the whole system general, we suggest that all continuous outputs functions have an associated logical gating function – whether used or not. This gating would be performed by the OS. For example, the combined Heat function here could be formed using the functions:

```
Heat (continuous) = (Target_temp - Actual_temp) * Span_constant
Heat (logic) = (Target_temp > Actual_temp) & TSO
```

Evolving the washing machine controller problem proved to be relatively straightforward with the evolution of the continuous heat function proving to be the most difficult thread. In order to determine the nature of the relationship between the population size, string length and evolvability, some 900 experiments were performed.

Using longer strings to construct an initial population, one would expect, would generally result in a more diverse population leading to more effective search. However, the results in Table 3 indicate the opposite result. There would seem to be two possible explanations for this unexpected result. First, the evolved program strings were executed sequentially forwards (with the exception that the Branch instruction might cause some instructions to be skipped) and so the contents of the output register would be overwritten by successive output operations. Note that the registersare only sampled at the end of processing. As a consequence, only the code and data directly contributing to the final output operation was relevant, therefore, the overall string length cannot be simply viewed as an indicator of potential. Second, the effect of mutation (and effective search) were diluted in direct proportion to the string length. This is because the probability of selecting the critical instruction for a constructive mutation diminished as the string length increased. These two factors can explain why the counterintuitive observation that string length is negatively proportional to success.

Similarly and, perhaps, even more surprisingly, the experiments also failed to demonstrate any useful *pro rata* advantage in operating with larger population sizes (refer to table 4). Again, the greater diversity afforded by a larger initial population might be expected to increase the probability that a useable root solution will appear in the initial random population. However, it has been shown that, beyond a given threshold, the functional diversity of a random population will tend to a limit irrespective of size [5], but perhaps the dominant factor here is the subsequent loss of diversity.

Table 4. Success rate v. population size

Pop.	200	400	600	800	1000	Total
Fail	172	173	171	167	168	851
Succeed	8	7	9	13	12	49
Total	180	180	180	180	180	900

Due to the fitness assessment measure used the vast majority – or sometimes all – of the candidate solutions in the initial population were scored at zero fitness. As a result, approximately half of the diversity can be lost on selection, and this process will continue with the population starting to converge upon any solution with some fitness.

Unfortunately, premature convergence on any sub-optimal solution in this manner, will effectively block the development of any potentially ideal solution (uncovered by mutation or crossover) unless the fitness of this root solution is sufficiently high. This unexpected indifference to population size (and sometimes other genetic parameters) in some situations, was also noted and investigated by Fuchs [2] in a study where GP and hill climbing (HC) algorithms were compared. Fuchs' conclusion was that this indifference is more an artefact of the particular problem rather than the technique (i.e. another example of the No Free Lunch theorem [9]). Fuchs suggests that in such a situation, the fitness landscape might be flat and (initial) solutions could only be found by 'accident'. In such a situation, a GP search with a population size of one, could be seen as a basic HC search (where the HC can restart at a random point if no progress is made). The conclusion then, is that GP population size can be irrelevant in some situations.

6   Conclusions

In this paper we have identified embedded control programs as a fruitful application domain for GP. We have suggested an approach for using GP to create such programs automatically that differs from other work in that we use the structure inherent in this class of problem to allow a divide and conquer strategy to be effective. The approach has been demonstrated with a relatively complex problem of a washing machine controller involving seven outputs and fourteen inputs. Here the worst thread was soluble about one in every eighteen runs and this took only around half an hour on a three year old PC. The proposed approach proved to be relatively insensitive to variations in the EC parameters used during evolution which we believe to be a positive result for a system aimed at wide application i.e. little or no tuning is required.

There are a number of avenues for future work. Widening the application scope for this system would involve increasing the trustworthiness of such a non-human system. Measures to improve reliability such as schemes whereby an output is the consensus of several (possibly dissimilar) contributors: run time bounds checking of variables (triggering pre-written exception processing within the general OS) and the use of watchdog timers might all be considered. Similarly, automated testing will enhance confidence in this technique. A 'front-end' tool is also needed to capture the problem from the target users so that training and test files may be generated for the EC system. Output could also include parameters values for use during evolution. This could involve graphical, formulaic, algorithmic or truth-table entry of the problem to be tackled.

References

1. Banzhaf, W. Nordin, P. Keller, R. Francone, F. *Genetic Programming: An introduction.* Morgan Kaufmann Publishers Inc. 1998.
2. Fuchs, M. "Large populations are not always the best choice in genetic programming", *GECCO-99. Proceedings of the Genetic and Evolutionary Computation-Conference*, pp1033-8 vol.2, Morgan Kaufmann Publishers, San Francisco, CA, 1999.
3. Keijzer, M. "Improving Symbolic Regression with Interval arithmetic and Linear Scaling", Proc. of EuroGP2003, Springer-Verlag Berlin, 2003.
4. Koza, J. R. *Genetic programming: On the programming of computers by means of natural selection*, Cambridge, MA: MIT Press, 1992.
5. Langdon, W.B. "Convergence of Program Fitness Landscapes", *GECCO-2003. Proceedings of the Genetic and Evolutionary Computation-Conference*, Chicago, 2003.
6. Langdon W.B. Poli R. *Foundations of Genetic Programming*. Springer-Verlag Berlin and Heidelberg, 2002.
7. Leung, K.S., Lee, K.H. Cheang, S.M. "Parallel programs are more evolvable than sequential programs", *Genetic Programming, Proceedings of 6th European Conference.* Springer, Berlin. LNCS 2610, pp107-118, 2003.
8. Ryan, C. Collins, J.J. O'Neill, M. "Grammatical Evolution: evolving programs for an arbitrary language", *Genetic Programming. First European Workshop, EuroGP'98.* Proceedings. Springer-Verlag, Berlin, pp83-96, 1998.
9. Wolpert, D.H. Macready., W.G. "No Free Lunch Theorems for Search", *IEEE Transactions on Evolutionary Computation* 1(1), pp67-82, 1997.

Extending Grammatical Evolution to Evolve Digital Surfaces with Genr8

Martin Hemberg[1] and Una-May O'Reilly[2]

[1] Department of Bioengineering, Bagrit Centre, Imperial College London,
South Kensington Campus, London SW7 2AZ, UK
martin.hemberg@imperial.ac.uk
[2] Computer Science and Artificial Intelligence Lab,
Massachusetts Institute of Technology, Cambridge, MA 02139, USA
unamay@ai.mit.edu

Abstract. Genr8 is a surface design tool for architects. It uses a grammar-based generative growth model that produces surfaces with an organic quality. Grammatical Evolution is used to help the designer search the universe of possible surfaces. We describe how we have extended Grammatical Evolution, in a general manner, in order to handle the grammar used by Genr8.

1 Genr8: The Evolution of Digital Surfaces

We have built a software tool for architects named Genr8. Genr8 'grows' digital surfaces within the modeling environment of the CAD tool Maya. One of Genr8's digital surfaces, is shown on the left of Figure 1. Beside it, is a real (i.e. physical) surface that was evolved first in Genr8 then subsequently fabricated and assembled. A surface in Genr8 starts as an axiomatic closed polygon. It grows generatively via simultaneous, multidimensional rewriting. During growth, a surface's definition is also influenced by the simulated physics of a user defined 'environment' that has attractors, repellors and boundaries as its features. This integration of simulated physics and tropic influences produces surfaces with an organic appearance.

In order to automate the specification, exploration and adaptation of Genr8's digital surfaces, an extended version of Grammatical Evolution (GE) [7] has been developed. The purpose of this contribution is to describe how and why we used and extended GE. We proceed as follows: In Section 2 we explain how Genr8 creates a surface via a generative process. A surface, because of this generative process, is difficult to design by hand and the search space of possible surfaces is vast. In Section 3 we give the reasons why evolutionary computation is ideally suited to address this problem. We also explain why GE, with several extensions, conveniently resolves the issues of representation and mapping we face when using EC. Following, we show some design results and summarize.

M. Keijzer et al. (Eds.): EuroGP 2004, LNCS 3003, pp. 299–308, 2004.
© Springer-Verlag Berlin Heidelberg 2004

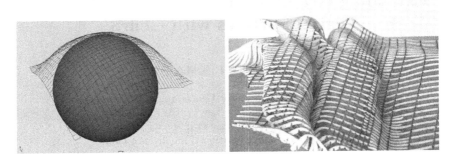

Fig. 1. Left hand side, a Genr8 surface grown in an environment where it has been pulled down by gravity on top of a spherical boundary. Right, a physical model made by Jordi Truco at the Architectural Association in London. The design process started with Genr8 and the evolved digital surface was subsequently exported so that a physical model could be manufactured.

2   Digital Surface Growth

Genr8 simulates organic growth and creates digital surfaces. Its growth process is reactive: it takes place in a simulated physical environment. Surface growth is generated by a HEMLS - a Hemberg Extended Map L-System. A HEMLS is a more complex version of the widely known Lindenmayer System (or L-system) [8]. An L-system is a *grammar*, consisting of a *seed* (or axiom) and a set of *production rules*, plus a *rewrite* process in which productions rules are applied to the seed and its successive states.

An L-system generates strings of symbols and is computer language oriented. It can be transformed into a visual representation by interpreting the seed and rewrite process graphically. The graphical interpretation is based on the metaphor of the seed being drawn in 3D space by a turtle subsequently moving through 3D space according to directions specified by the production rules and (re)drawing lines as it goes along. The turtle's directional movement is based on a set of instructions that are presented in Table 1. An example of a graphical L-system is given in Figure 2. Realistic images of plants, flowers and

Table 1. Turtle commands and their meaning. A parameter δ specifies turn angle

Turtle Command	Meaning
$A_i, B_j, C_k, \dots$	Move forward and draw a line.
+, -	Turn left/right δ.
&, ^	Pitch down/up δ.
/, \	Roll left/right δ.
~	Change direction of the segment.
[,]	Push/pop state on stack.

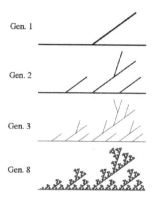

Fig. 2. An example of how a graphical L-system grows from [9]. The top image shows the seed, consisting of three segments. During each growth step, each segment is replaced by the original three segments of the seed. Growth steps 2, 3 and 8 are shown. The rewrite rule is symbolically expressed as F -> F [+ F] F. The F to the left of the arrow is the *predecessor*, i.e., the symbol that will be replaced in the growth step. The sequence to the right is the *successor*; the symbols that will replace the the predecessor. The Fs are segments and the + indicates that the turtle should turn at an angle of $\delta = 36°$ (the numerical value is given as a parameter to the system). The [pushes the current state (ie position) of the turtle on to a stack. When the pop symbol,] is encountered, a state is popped from the stack and the turtle attains that state. This push-pop mechanism enables the branching structure of L-Systems.

trees have been generated as a generated sequence line segments by specially designed L-systems [8].

A Map L-system models 2D cellular structures such as leaves via planar graphs, in contrast to the 3D linear segmented structures of an L-system. All rewrite rules are applied simultaneously to the planar graph (which has an internal representation as a graph) and then any unconnected new edges are either joined or eliminated. An example Map L-system is shown in Figure 3.

Since our goal was creative, responsive surface design, we extended a Map L-system to a HEMLS. The most important feature incorporated into a HEMLS is how the physics of our simulated environment is factored into the rewriting of an edge. The designation of the vertices of the new edge is altered in accordance with how the edge would be pulled by an attractor, pushed by a repellor or deflected by a boundary in the simulated physical environment. With this additional set of environmental factors, the surface growth mimics *tropism*, the response of an organism to external stimuli. Figure 4 shows how a HEMLS surface's growth steps in response to five repellors.

There are additional features in a HEMLS. These include the capacity for the grammar to be context sensitive (e.g. the left hand side of a production rule can express multiple symbols in a specific order), the option of randomly choosing among multiple production rules applying to the same symbol, and rewrite rules that change between time steps.

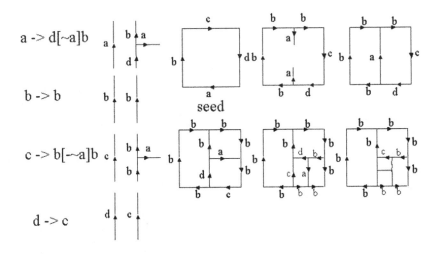

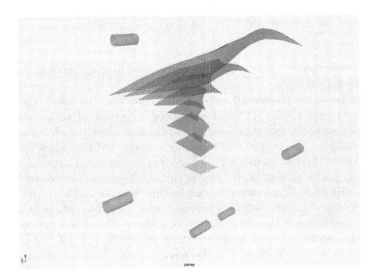

Fig. 3. An example of a Map L-System from [8]. The rewrite rules are shown to the left in symbolic and graphical form. Next, the seed (a square) is shown and the rewrite rules are subsequently applied to it.

Fig. 4. A time series capturing 7 growth steps of a HEMLS surface in an environment with five repellors (here drawn as cylinders). The smallest surface is the axiom. The largest surface is the final growth step.

3 Evolutionary Computation in Genr8

Genr8's means of growing a digital surface implies using any HEMLS within a huge universe. Constructing interesting and useful grammars by hand is a formidable task and is unrealistic to expect of an architect. The EA component of Genr8 serves three purposes related to this need for automation:

- It automatically generates a HEMLS with correct syntax.
- It adaptively explores some of the universe of surfaces following preferred surfaces yet yielding creatively different ones.
- It can be used to explicitize a surface an architect has in mind by allowing its search process to be influenced by the architect.

These reasons are compelling to use EC but they leave open how a HEMLS should be represented within an evolutionary algorithm. Clearly the phenotype, i.e. the outcome, of the EC component is the digital surface. However, should a direct representation of a HEMLS function as the genotype, i.e., the genetic material subject to blind variation, as in [4] and [5]? This is an awkward choice because a HEMLS is a *grammar*. Blind variation on a direct grammar representation would have to be either contrived to adhere to syntax constraints or it would result in offspring genotypes that have to be syntactically repaired or culled afterwards. An alternative is to exploit a powerful approach used in various genetic programming examples such as cellular encoding [1] and embryonic circuit development [6]. In particular, we employ Grammatical Evolution [7] and provide simple effective extensions to it.

3.1 Genr8 Extends Grammatical Evolution

GE provides a means of mapping a fixed length bit string or integer sequence (which is its genotype and thus blindly crossed over or mutated) into a program via the use of a programming language specification given in Backus-Naur Form (BNF). This implies that the genotypic search space is simpler in terms of representation. Also, it implies that GE is a general means of using genetic programming to generate an executable 'program' in an arbitrary language. In our case the 'programming language' is the language that describes any HEMLS. The 'program' is a HEMLS. In Genr8's BNF specification of the HEMLS language we express both syntactic and *semantic* constraints for a HEMLS. These are *implicitly* respected as the BNF is used to derive a HEMLS from the genotype. An example of a syntactic constraint is that a <RewriteRule> must have a <Predecessor>, followed by a arrow towards the right that is followed by a <Successor>. Semantic constraints are more powerful. One example, seen in Figure 5, is a heuristic for symmetry that is expressed in the <Modifier> nonterminal: a turn in one direction along one axis must be subsequently followed by a reciprocal turn on the same axis.

In typical GE systems, the program resulting from mapping the genotype with the BNF is executed and its outputs are compared to desired outputs. In

Genr8 the HEMLS is rewritten via graphical interpretation as a planar graph (in a particular kind of execution) and a set of particular qualities of the resulting digital surface are assessed according to derive a fitness value. Thus, Genr8 has two levels of mappings. Interestingly, each mapping is essentially similar in terms of being generative. A *generative* system has a simple starting point and the procedural means of becoming increasingly complex. The GE mapping from a gentoype to a HEMLS allows a standard genetic algorithm to search in a space of integer strings. This is simpler and more convenient with respect to withstanding the random effects of blind variation than operating directly in the grammar space. The use of GE preserves semantic and syntactic constraints in the more complex representation space of a HEMLS. The HEMLS to surface mapping supports 'growth' and produces a digital representation that is visual.

All Genr8 BNFs have <L-System> as their seed. The <L-system> symbol is rewritten as an <Axiom>, one or more <RewriteRule>'s and, then, some parameters for the turtle. An example HEMLS derived via this BNF is shown in Table 2.

Table 2. An example HEMLS derived from the BNF of Figure 5

Edge0 + Edge1 + Edge2 + Edge3
Edge0 → Edge3 [[+ + Edge0] - - Edge0] Edge1
Edge1 → Edge1
Edge2 → Edge1 [[+ + Edge0] - - Edge0] Edge3
Edge3 → Edge2
Angle 45
Sync
BranchAngle 45

The first line expresses the <Axiom>, i.e., an initial surface of 4 edges each with a different label (e.g. zero through three). The next four lines are the <RewriteRule>s, one for each edge, and the three last rows contain parameters for the turtle. A more detailed description of the derivation and interpretation of the grammar can be found in [2].

The BNFs used in Genr8 use two interpretations of the genome that have not been used in previous implementations of GE. First, if there are many non-terminals in the BNF's production rules, an expanded (or derived) HEMLS is likely to be very large. For instance, in the BNF of Figure 5, six of the nine productions of the non-terminal <Modifier> themselves expand to <Modifier>. Thus, there is a $\frac{2}{3}$ probability of another expansion being required. In Genr8 such very complex rewrite rules in a HEMLS are generally undesirable because they tend to produce less interesting surfaces. The conventional way in GE to prevent this excessive expansion is to restrict the number of times the genome is allowed to wrap around during its decoding. Once the wrapping limit is reached, the individual is assigned the worst fitness fitness possible to make sure that it does not survive the selection process. In Genr8, the problem is addressed differently. A parameter called max_depth limits the maximum depth of the *expanded* syntax tree rather than limiting the mapping of the genotype. When the maximum depth is one short of being reached, only BNF production rules

```
N = { L-System, Axiom, RewriteRule, Predecessor, Successor,
        Modifier, AngleValue, BranchAngleValue }
T = { +, -, &, ^, \, /, ~, [, ], <, >, ->, Edge, Angle, Sync,
        EdgeX, BranchAngle }
S = { <L-System> }
P = {
<L-System> ::= <Axiom> <RewriteRule> { <RewriteRule> } Angle
                AngleValue [ Sync ] BranchAngle
                BranchAngleValue
<Axiom> ::= <Edge> [ ~ ] + <Edge> [ ~ ] + <Edge>
              { [ ~ ] + <Edge> }
<RewriteRule> ::= <Predecessor> -> <Successor>
<Successor> ::= { <Modifier> } <Edge>
<Predecessor> ::= <Edge> { <Edge> } |
                    <Edge> ''<'' <Edge> |
                    <Edge> ''>'' <Edge> |
                    <Edge> ''<'' <Edge> ''>'' <Edge>
<Modifier> ::= { <Edge> } |
                + <Modifier> - |
                - <Modifier> + |
                & <Modifier> ^ |
                ^ <Modifier> & |
                \ <Modifier> / |
                / <Modifier> \ |
                ~ <Modifier> |
                <Edge> ''['' ''['' + <EdgeX> '']'' - <EdgeX>
                '']'' <Edge>
                <Edge> ''['' ''['' + + <EdgeX> '']'' - -
                <EdgeX> '']'' <Edge>
<AngleValue> ::= 30 | 45
<BranchAngleValue> ::= 15 | 30 | 45 | 60 | 75 }
```

Fig. 5. A HEMLS language expressed in Backus Naur Form (BNF). Any derivation of this BNF produces a HEMLS (i.e. a grammar). One derivation is shown in Table 2.

that use terminals are used to rewrite a non-terminal. This scheme still ensures that a HEMLS will not expand indefinitely while it also puts a less abrupt consequence to long expansion.

Second, in a BNF, the symbols {...} and [...] indicate that whatever symbols (terminals or non-terminals) appears between them is to be written zero or more times or one or more times, respectively. For example, in the BNF of Figure 5, <Successor> is rewritten as zero or more <Modifier>'s then an <Edge>.

Because of the importance of genetic inheritance (and the propogation of genetic characteristics) in a GE system, it is important that this optional quantity stay consistent through all decodings of a genotype (i.e., from one generation to the next or within multiple copies of the genotype in the population). The ideal way to achieve this consistency is to use the genotype itself to determine how many times a symbol is written when it is optional. This is accomplished in Genr8 via a simple algorithm that, when a { is encountered, initializes a counter to zero. Next, the following genes on the genome are used, instead of a random number generator, to determine how many times the symbol between the {...} should be written. The algorithm loops and writes the symbol as long as the next gene has a value at least two less than the counter (which itself increments each time through the loop). This leads to a symbol being written again with decreasing probability as it is written more and more, yet there is no fixed upper limit on the quantity. This scheme is deterministic and ensures that the genome will produce the same HEMLS every time it is interpreted.

The <Edge> terminal in a HEMLS BNF is also special in the sense that it requires a label. For convenience a numerical labeling is used in Genr8. Whenever an <Edge> is derived for a HEMLS, the label must be determined. Either an existing label must be used or a new label must be generated. As in the case of optional quantities of symbols, label assignment requires consistency in terms of genotype decoding. The scheme used in Genr8 is similar to the one used for multiple nodes described above. There is a counter that keeps track of the current number of edge labels. The probability of introducing a new edge label decreases with the number of edge labels already existing.

Finally, the BNFs of Genr8 are extended in one way to ensure that branches of a HEMLS will connect. A semantic heuristic enforces the same edge being used in different places in a production rule's successor. For example:

```
<Modifier> ::= <Edge> [ [ + <EdgeX> ] - <EdgeX> ] <Edge>
```

Here, the <EdgeX> terminal is used instead of the <Edge> in order to imply (and enforce) that the edges designated by <EdgeX> need to both have the same label. As the <Modifier> non-terminal is expanded, the first <EdgeX> is assigned a label as described previously. All subsequent <EdgeX> terminals in the production will automatically get the same label as the first one. This informal 'binding' is reminiscent of free variable binding in logic programming.

4   Genr8's Digital and Physical Results

In the case of surface exploration a picture is sometimes worth a thousand words. Genr8 has now been used for two years in a design course within the Emergent Design & Technologies graduate program at the Architectural Association (AA) in London. Figure 7 and 6 is the final example of Genr8 that space permits. Additional images are available on the world wide web at
http://www.ai.mit.edu/projects/emergentDesign/genr8.

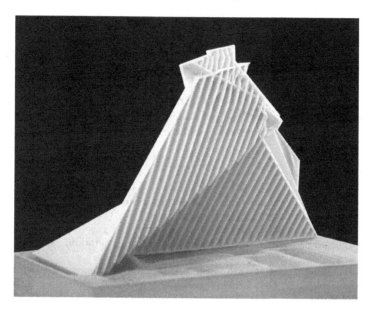

Fig. 6. A physical model, fabricated via CNC milling, based on a Genr8 surface. By Linus Saavedra, AA, London, UK, 2003.

Fig. 7. A rendered image of a design for a pneumatic strawberry/champagne bar. This is Genr8's largest design that has been physically actualized. By Achim Menges, AA, London, UK, 2003.

5   Summary

We have described how evolutionary computation, and in particular, extensions of grammatical evolution, empower a digital surface exploration tool named Genr8. Because of its responsive growth and evolutionary algorithm, Genr8's results are attractive, spontaneous and organic in appearance.

Genr8 also demonstrates how a creative design tool based on evolutionary computation can be effective in three other major respects that are elaborated upon elsewhere (see [2,3]: Genr8's Interrupt, Intervene and Resume (IIR) capability facilitates partner-based design between itself and its human user. Second, the parameterized fitness function allows the user to decide what features of the surface should be selected for. Third, Genr8 is efficiently integrated into a larger design process so that the designer can use its results in subsequent explorations that include, for example, physical model construction.

References

1. Frédéric Gruau. Genetic micro programming of neural networks. In KE Kinnear, editor, *Advances in Genetic Programming*, pages 495–518. MIT Press, Cambridge, MA, 1994.
2. Martin Hemberg. Genr8 - a design tool for surface generation. Master's thesis, Chalmers University of Technology, 2001.
3. Martin Hemberg, Una-May O'Reilly, and Peter Nordin. Genr8 - a design tool for surface generation. In *Late breaking papers, GECCO 2001*, 2001.
4. Gregory S Hornby and Jordan B Pollack. The advantages of generative grammatical encodings for physical design. In *Congress on Evolutionary Computation*, 2001.
5. Gregory S. Hornby and Jordan B. Pollack. Body-brain co-evolution using L-systems as a generative encoding. In *Proceedings of the Genetic and Evolutionary Computation Conference (GECCO-2001)*, pages 868–875, San Francisco, California, USA, 7-11 2001. Morgan Kaufmann.
6. John R. Koza, Forrest H Bennett III, David Andre, and Martin A Keane. Automated design of both the topology and sizing of analog electrical circuits using genetic programming. In John S. Gero and Fay Sudweeks, editors, *Artificial Intelligence in Design '96*, pages 151–170, Dordrecht, 1996. Kluwer Academic.
7. Michael O'Neill and Conor Ryan. *Grammatical Evolution - Evolving programs in an arbitrary language*. Kluwer Academic Publishers, 2003.
8. Przemyslaw Prusinkiewicz and Aristid Lindenmayer. *The algorithmic beauty of plants*. Springer, 1996.
9. David J Wright. Dynamical systems and fractals lecture notes, 1996. http://www.math.okstate.edu/mathdept/dynamics/lecnotes/lecnotes.html.

Evolving Text Classifiers with Genetic Programming

Laurence Hirsch[1], Masoud Saeedi[1], and Robin Hirsch[2]

[1] School of Management, Royal Holloway University of London, Surrey, TW20 OEX, UK
[2] University College London, Gower Street, London, WC1E 6BT, UK

Abstract. We describe a method for using Genetic Programming (GP) to evolve document classifiers. GP's create regular expression type specifications consisting of particular sequences and patterns of N-Grams (character strings) and acquire fitness by producing expressions, which match documents in a particular category but do not match documents in any other category. Libraries of N-Gram patterns have been evolved against sets of pre-categorised training documents and are used to discriminate between new texts. We describe a basic set of functions and terminals and provide results from a categorisation task using the 20 Newsgroup data.

Keywords: Text categorisation, N-Gram, Genetic Programming

1 Introduction

Automatic text categorization is the activity of assigning pre-defined category labels to natural language texts based on information found in a training set of labelled documents. Text categorization can be viewed as a special case of the more general problem of identifying a category in a space of high dimensions so as to define a given set of points in that space. Quite sophisticated geometric systems for categorization have been devised [1]. In recent years it has been recognized as an increasingly important tool for handling the exponential growth in available online texts and we have seen the development of many techniques aimed at the extraction of features from a set of training documents, which may then be used for categorisation purposes.

Classifiers built on the frequency of particular words in a document (sometimes called bag of words) are based on two empirical observations regarding text:

1. the more times a word occurs in a document, the more relevant it is to the topic of the document
2. the more times the word occurs throughout the documents in the collection the more poorly it discriminates between documents.

A well known approach for computing word weights is the inverse document frequency (tf-idf) weighting [2] which assigns the weight to a word in a document in proportion to the number of occurrences of the word in the document and in inverse proportion to the number of documents in the collection for which the word occurs at least once, i.e.

M. Keijzer et al. (Eds.): EuroGP 2004, LNCS 3003, pp. 309–317, 2004.

$$a_{ik} = f_{ik} \log\left(\frac{N}{n_i}\right) \tag{1}$$

where a is the weight of word i in document k, f_{ik} is the frequency of word i in document k, N the number of documents in the collection and n_i equal to the number of documents in which a_i occurs at least once. A standard approach to text categorization makes use of the classical text representation technique [2] that maps a document to a high dimensional feature vector, where each entry of the vector represents the presence or absence of a feature [3]. This approach loses all the word order information only retaining the frequency of the terms in the document. This is usually accompanied by the removal of non-informative words (stop words) and by the replacing of words by their stems, so losing inflection information. Such sparse vectors can then be used in conjunction with many learning algorithms [4].

There are a number of alternative strategies to the reliance on pure word comparison, which can provide additional information for feature extraction. In particular, N-Grams (sequences of N characters) and sequences of contiguous and non-contiguous words (phrases) have also been used for classification [5], [6]. In this paper we describe a method to identify a set of features in the form of N-Gram patterns using Genetic Programming (GP) [7] with fitness based on the tf-idf principle. Although GP has been used in the area of text mining before [8] we are unaware of other implementations that have used GP's to evolve classifiers based on GP created N-Gram patterns. In the next section, we review previous work with N-Grams and with phrases. We then provide information concerning the implementation of our application and the initial results we have obtained on a classification task.

1.1 N-Grams

A character N-Gram is an N-character slice of a longer string so for example the word INFORM can be represented by the 5-grams _INFO, INFOR, NFORM, FORM_ where the underscore represents a blank. If we count N-Grams that are common to two strings, we get a measure of their similarity that is resistant to a wide variety of grammatical and typographical errors. N-Grams have proven a robust alternative to word stemming, having the further advantage of requiring no linguistic preparations [5], [9], [10]. A further useful property of N-Grams is that the lexicon obtained from the analysis of a text in terms of N-Grams of characters cannot grow larger than the size of the alphabet to the power of N. Furthermore, because most of the possible sequences of N characters rarely or never occur in practice for N>2, a table of the N-Grams occurring in a given text tends to be sparse, with the majority of possible N-Grams having a frequency of zero even for very large amounts of texts. Tauritz [11] and later Langdon [12] used this property to build an: adaptive information filtering system based on weighted trigram analysis in which genetic algorithms were used to determine weight vectors. An interesting modification of N-Grams is to generalise N-Grams to substrings which need not be contiguous [13].

1.2 Phrases

The notion of N-Grams of words (i.e. sequences of N words, with N typically equals to 2, 3, 4 or 5) has produced good results both in language identification, speech analysis and in several areas of knowledge extraction from text [14]. Pickens and Croft [6] make the distinction between 'adjacent phrases' where the phrase words must be adjacent and Boolean phrases where the phrase words are present anywhere in the document. They found that adjacent phrases tended to be better than Boolean phrases in terms or retrieval relevance but not in all cases. Restricting a search to adjacent phrases means that some retrieval information is lost.

2 Implementation

Our approach aims to identify sets of both adjacent and non-adjacent sequences of N-Grams found in a text environment that may be useful as classifiers. We use the symbolic capability of GP to combine sequences with functions such as OR, and NAND to provide a set of complex features which may be used as a subtle and sophisticated mechanism for discriminating between documents.

- The basic unit (or phrase unit) we use is an N-Gram (sequence of N characters).
- An N-Gram is said to match a word in a document if it is the same character string as the word or is a substring of the word. We do not include space characters in the N-Grams.
- Sequences of N-Grams can be produced by GP's and evaluate to true or false for a particular document depending on whether a match for the sequence exists in the text of that document.
- Special symbols can be included in the specification produced by the GP's for example a '+' symbol indicates that the two N-Grams which follow must be found in adjacent words in a document i.e. an adjacent phrase in the terminology of Pickens and Croft [6].
- A GP produces N-Gram based schemas which evaluate to true or false (i.e. match or do not match) in any document in the same way as which we can say a particular word occurs or does not occur in a document.
- GP's can also combine schemas using Boolean functions.
- Classifiers must be evolved for each category c of the dataset. Fitness is then accrued for GPs producing Boolean N-Gram schemas which are true for training documents in c but are not true for documents outside c in an tf-idf manner. Thus the documents in the training set represent the fitness cases.

The task involved categorising documents selected from the 20 Newsgroup dataset.

2.1 The 20 Newsgroup Dataset

The 20 Newsgroup corpus collected by Lang [15] contains about 20 000 documents evenly distributed among 20 UseNet discussion groups. This natural language corpus is employed for evaluating text classification techniques [16], [17], [18]. Many of these groups have similar topics (e.g. five groups discuss different issues concerning computers). In addition many of the documents in this corpus are present in more than one group (since people tend to post articles to multiple newsgroups). Therefore, the classification task is typically hard, and suffers from inherent noise, while trying to estimate the relevant probabilities [18].

2.2 Pre-processing

Before the evolution of classifiers a number of pre-processing steps are made.

1. All the text in the document collection is placed in lower case.
2. Numbers are replaced by a special character and non-alphanumeric characters are replaced by a second special character.
3. All the documents in the training data are searched for unique N-Grams which are then stored in sets for size of N=2 to N=max_size. The size of these sets can be reduced by requiring that an N-Gram occur at least σ times (e.g. 2 or more instances of the N-Gram) or that the N-Gram occur in at least σ documents.

Note that the use of N-Grams as features makes word stemming unnecessary and that a stop list is not required because of the natural screening process provided by the fitness test (see below).

2.3 Fitness

GPs are set the task of assembling single letters into N-Gram strings and then forming a Boolean schema of N-Gram patterns. The schema is then evaluated against a set of documents from each category of the training set. An N-Gram matches a word in a document if it is the same as that word or is a substring of that word. Where a schema is simply a sequence of N-Grams it is said to match a document if each element of the schema matches a word in the document and each subsequent element of the schema matches a word further along the document text. The function returns a Boolean value indicating whether the entire sequence has a match in a document. GP's may combine N-Gram sequences with Boolean functions. A library of highly fit Boolean schemas must be evolved for each category of the dataset. For a particular category the GP's are searching for patterns which occur in a number of documents within the category but occur infrequently or not at all in any other document in any other category. A simple fitness measure is summarized by the pseudo code below (where the lower the fitness the better the individual).

```
IF CountOfMatchingDocumentsInTopic=0
  THEN Fitness := High_Value
ELSE Fitness :=
  ((CountOfMatchingDocumentsNotInTopic * penalty)
      + occurrence) / CountOfMatchingDocumentInTopic
```

We generally used a high penalty (e.g. 20) for matching documents not in the topic category and an occurrence around 3 requiring that the N-Gram pattern occur in more than 3 documents to achieve a fitness value below 1. It may also be useful to penalise GP's producing schemas including N-Grams of size 1 as a method of reducing redundant entries in a library.

2.4 GP Types

We use a strongly typed tree based GP system with the following types:

Table 1. GP Types

GP Type	Description
N-Gram	A sequence of one or more characters.
Special Symbol	A symbol used as part of an N-Gram sequence. For example '+' indicates that the following two N-Grams in an N-Gram sequence must be substrings of words which occur together in a document text with no words between them.
N-Gram Sequence	A sequence of one or more N-Grams and special symbols
Boolean	AND, NOT used with N-Gram sequences as arguments

Each GP will output a Boolean N-Gram schema. Any schema output by a GP can be evaluated against a document and the document can be said to match the schema or not match the schema.

2.5 GP Terminals

26 lower case alphabetic characters (a-z).
 # meaning any number.
 ~ meaning any non-alphanumeric character.

2.6 GP Functions

The GP's are provided with a variety of protected string handling functions for combining characters into N-Gram strings, concatenating N-Grams, and adding N-Grams to a sequence of N-Grams. Most combinations of letters above an N-Gram size of 2 are unlikely to occur in any text, for example where N-Gram size =6 only 0.001% of possible N-Grams are found in the 20 Newsgroup data. We therefore guide the GP's through the vast search space of possible N-Gram patterns by the provision of special 'Expand' function. The following function initially forms a new N-Gram by combining two N-Grams (N-Gram1 and N-Gram2). A new N-Gram NewN-Gram is formed by appending N-Gram2 to N-Gram1. If the NewN-Gram is of length l the expand function checks if the NewN-Gram is in the set of N-Grams of size l originally extracted from all the text in the all the training documents used. If it is found in this set NewN-Gram is returned. If not the nearest occurring N-Gram in the set is returned. If the set is empty the original N-Gram N-Gram1 is returned. Note that the 'Expand' function will not return an N-Gram consisting of a sequence of characters which never occurs in the training data. The function is summarised by the following pseudo code

```
SetOfL-Grams = the ordered set of N-Grams of length L
found in documents from the training set
Expand (N-Gram1, N-Gram2)
  NewN-Gram = (concatenate N-Gram1, N-Gram2)
  L = (sizeOf NewN-Gram)

  IF (IsEmpty SetOfL-Grams)
    RETURN N-Gram1
  ELSE IF (IsMember NewN-Gram SetOfL-Grams)
    RETURN NewN-Gram
    ELSE
      RETURN Nearest N-Gram in SetOfL-Grams
```

The size of the N-Gram sets can be reduced by extracting them only from the text of documents belonging to the category for which the library is being evolved. This will greatly reduce the search space of the GP's but some discriminating ability will be lost where a Boolean NOT function is included in the GP function set.

2.7 Measures

We use the following performance measures to test the effectiveness of the evolved classifiers.

$$p = \frac{a}{a+c} \tag{2}$$

$$r = \frac{a}{a+b} \tag{3}$$

where:
- a = the number of documents correctly assigned to the category
- b = the number of documents incorrectly assigned to the category
- c = the number of documents incorrectly rejected from the category
- p = precision
- r = recall

For evaluation we used the F1 performance measure given by

$$F1(p,r) = \frac{2pr}{p+r} \tag{4}$$

Note that then F1 measure gives equal weighting to both precision and recall [19].

2.8 Library Building

When a frequent pattern is found to have a preset minimum fitness (e.g. less than 1) the regular expression is stored in a library. Once a pattern is stored in the library any GP producing such a pattern will accrue a fitness penalty (normally +1). The purpose of this mechanism is to keep the GP population continuously searching for new patterns whilst leaving the GP producing the discovered pattern a good chance of remaining in the population and thus potentially contributing to the evolution of new useful patterns through genetic operators. The graph in Fig. 1. shows a typical pattern of evolution.

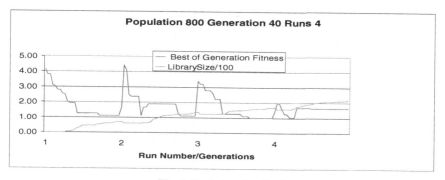

Fig. 1. Evolution of a classifier

Once the GP population has built a library for a particular topic the library can be used for document categorisation purposes. We suggest that a document from the test set which matches patterns stored in the library for a particular category is more likely to be in that category.

3 Experiment

We used a strongly typed, tree based GP system with a population of 800 GP's. The system was run for 4 GP runs of 40 generations for each category. We used 10 categories from the 20 News Group corpus and selected 200 documents per category for training purposes. A library of schemas was evolved for each of the 10 categories with an average size of approximately 300 schemas. Every document from the test set was then assigned to a category based on the number of schemas matching that document from each of the libraries.

Although this is only a subset of the entire corpus (10 out of 20 categories) and cross-method comparison is often problematic [20] the results above would seem to compare favourably with other methods used to categorise this data set [18]. We intend to perform an in-depth comparison with other methods using the complete data set, to identify exactly where the GP system is outperforming other methods and where it may be used to complement other methods of categorization.

Table 2. Results

Category Name	F1	Precision	Recall
Sci.Space	.949	.974	.926
Sci.crypt	.908	.872	.947
Sci.Med	.838	.815	.862
Soc.religion.christian	.841	.860	.823
Alt.atheism	.729	.679	.788
Rec.sport.baseball	.679	.650	.710
Rec.sport.hockey	.751	.787	.719
Rec.motorcyles.	.808	.720	.920
Talk.politics.guns	.816	.890	.754
Talk.politics.mideast	.730	.730	.730

4 Future Work

The regular occurrence of synonyms (different words with the same meaning) and homonyms (words with the same spelling but with distinct meanings) are key problems in the analysis of text data. We are currently trying to assess the usefulness of the Boolean functions OR, AND and NOT to the task of discriminating between texts. We suggest that the OR function may be able to detect synonyms and the AND and NAND functions may be able to detect homonyms by identifying associated words in two N-Gram sequences. We are currently developing the system with the intention of analyzing the use of synonyms and homonyms. We are also investigating the usefulness of new GP functions to insert symbols of the regular expression within the N-Grams, for example a "*" character to mean any sequence of letters. Lastly we are developing a modified fitness test based on the F1 measure.

5 Conclusion

We have produced a system capable of discovering patterns of N-Gram co-occurrence in text and storing specifications for those patterns. We have been able to perform a document categorisation task using these specifications and we believe that there may be many other areas within automatic text analysis where the basic technology described here may be of use.

References

1. Bennet K, Shawe-Taylor J, Wu D.: Enlarging the margins in perceptron decision trees. Machine Learning 41, (2000) pp 295-313
2. Salton, G., and McGill, M.J.: An Introduction to Modern Information Retrieval, McGraw-Hill, (1983)

3. Joachims T.: Text categorization with support vector machines: learning with many relevant features. In Proceedings of the l0th European Conference on Machine Learning (ECML98) , pp 137-142., (1998)

4. Sebastiani F.: Machine learning in automated text categorization, ACM Computing Surveys, 34(1), pp. 1-47, (2002)

5. Cavnar, W., Trenkle, J.: N-Gram-Based Text Categorization In Proceedings of SDAIR-94, 3rd Annual Symposium on Document Analysis and Information Retrieval (1994)

6. Pickens, J., Croft, W.B.: An Exploratory Analysis of Phrases in Text Retrieval, in Proceedings of RIAO 2000 Conference, Paris (2000)

7. Koza, J. R.: Genetic Programming: On the Programming of Computers by Means of Natural Selection. The MIT Press, Cambridge MA, 1992.

8. Bergström, A., JakseticP., Nordin, P.: Enhancing Information Retrieval by Automatic Acquisition of Textual Relations Using Genetic Programming Proceedings of the 2000 International Conference on Intelligent User Interfaces (IUI-00), pp. 29-32, ACM Press, (2000).

9. Damashek, M.: Gauging similarity with n-grams: Language-independent categorization of text, Science, 267 (1995), pp. 843 . 848.

10. Biskri, I., Delisle, S.: Text Classification and Multilinguism: Getting at Words via N-grams of Characters, Proceedings of the 6th World Multiconference on Systemics, Cybernetics and Informatics (SCI-2002), Orlando (Florida, USA), (2002), Volume V, 110-115.

11. Tauritz D.R., Kok J.N., Sprinkhuizen-Kuyper I.G.: Adaptive information filtering using evolutionary computation, Information Sciences, vol.122/2-4, pp.121-140 (2000)

12. Langdon W.B.: Natural Language Text Classification and Filtering with Trigrams and Evolutionary Classifiers, Late Breaking Papers at the 2000 Genetic and Evolutionary (2000) Computation Conference, Las Vegas, Nevada, USA, editor Darrell Whitley, pages 210—217.

13. Lodhi H, Shawe-Taylor J, Cristianini N, Watkins C (2001) Text classification using string kernels. In T. K. Leen, T. G. Dietterich, and V. Tresp, editors, Advances in Neural Information Processing Systems 13, pages 563--569. MIT Press

14. Ahonen-Myka, H.: Finding All Maximal Frequent Sequences in Text. In Proceedings of the 16th International Conference in Machine Learning ICML-99 (1999).

15. Lang, K.: Learning to filter netnews. In Proc. of the 12th Int. Conf. on Machine Learning, pages 331–339, 1995.

16. Schapire, R., and Singer, Y.: BoosTexter: A boosting-based system for text categorization. Machine Learning, 39, (2000)

17. Slonim, N., and Tishby, N.: Agglomerative Information Bottleneck. In Proc. of Neural Information Processing Systems (NIPS-99), pages 617–623, (1999)

18. Slonim, N., and Tishby, N.: The Power of Word Clusters for Text Classification, 23rd European Colloquium on Information Retrieval Research, (2001)

19. Van Rijsbergen C.J.: Information Retrieval, 2nd edition, Department of Computer Science, University of Glasgow (1979)

20. Yang Y, Liu X.: A re-examination of text categorization methods. In Proceedings of the 22nd Annual ACM SIGIR Conference on Research and Development in Information Retrieval, 42-49 (1999)

Automatic Synthesis of Instruction Decode Logic by Genetic Programming

David Jackson

Dept. of Computer Science, University of Liverpool
Liverpool L69 3BX, United Kingdom
d.jackson@csc.liv.ac.uk

Abstract. On many modern computers, the processor control unit is microprogrammed rather than built directly in hardware. One of the tasks of the microcode is to decode machine-level instructions: for each such instruction, it must be ensured that control-flow is directed to the appropriate microprogram for emulating it. We have investigated the use of genetic programming for evolving this instruction decode logic. Success is highly dependent on the number of opcodes in the instruction set and their relationship to the conditional branch and shift instructions offered on the microarchitecture, but experimental results are promising.

1 Introduction

On conventional uniprocessor computers, instruction processing can be viewed as taking place within a fetch-decode-execute cycle that looks something like the following:

```
while TRUE
    issue READ request from address in PC
    PC := PC + 1
    switch (fetched instruction)
        case LOAD:
            issue READ from operand address
            load fetched value into accumulator
        case ADD:
        (etc.)
    end switch
end loop
```

In designing a CPU that may have a couple of hundred opcodes in its instruction set, together with large numbers of complex addressing modes and instruction formats, it is readily appreciated that converting this algorithmic view of the instruction cycle into functioning hardware can be a huge undertaking. It is for this reason that manufacturers often choose to implement the cycle by programming means, rather than building it directly in hardware. The ability to do this requires the introduction of an extra layer of architecture lying just above the hardware level but below the

M. Keijzer et al. (Eds.): EuroGP 2004, LNCS 3003, pp. 318–327, 2004.

assembly-level programmer's view of the machine. This additional layer is known as the microarchitecture, and the low-level code it executes is known as microcode, or firmware. Microarchitecture and microprogramming are topics dealt with in detail in most modern texts on computer organization [1].

For those interested in genetic programming, it is worth pointing out how close GP has approached from both sides of the microarchitectural divide, but never quite entered that twilight world. From below, much research has been done on evolving computer hardware logic, both at the analog and digital levels [2-6]. From above, by far the vast majority of GP problems deal in high-level languages, but some have strayed into the evolution of machine-code programs [7,8]. Others have delved even lower than this; Poli and Langdon [9,10], for example, have suggested the use of what they term 'sub-machine-code programming' to exploit the internal parallelism of a processor. In all of these cases, however, the primary reason for descending to these lower language levels is usually to increase the speed of the evolutionary process, rather than a necessity to obtain solutions which are expressed at those levels.

Creating microcode requires an intimate knowledge of hardware details not normally in view, including the operational characteristics of physical components used to build the processor, the data paths and control signals between those components, and many additional internal registers. Consideration has to be given to the timing properties of components, and to parallelism both within and across microinstructions. An individual microinstruction can be hugely complex, comprising hundreds of bits specifying dozens of operations. Because microcode is highly specific to each processor, few generic tools are available to assist the programmer, and compilation from higher level languages is generally not an option, since the generated code is usually not of sufficient quality. It is imperative that microcode be both correct and efficient, as any deficiencies can have a major impact upon higher machine levels.

It is perhaps not surprising, then, that microcode has received so little attention as a medium for program evolution, and an interesting research question is whether generating microcode in this way is in fact feasible. A partial answer to this is yes. In a set of experiments, the author managed to evolve microprograms capable of emulating a variety of machine code instructions [11]. The microprograms were largely considered in isolation, without regard to the usual context of a fetch-decode-execute cycle.

In this paper, we propose to complete the picture by investigating how GP might be used to evolve the *decode* phase of the instruction processing cycle. In essence, this corresponds to the switch/case statement shown in the algorithm above, but at the level of microcode there is much more involved in ensuring that control flow is directed to the appropriate microprogram for each machine instruction. This is especially true of machines that do not support a jump-table approach, either because such an approach is complicated to implement and perhaps inefficient on the given microarchitecture, or because a suitable table would have to be huge or sparsely populated. For these machines, the decode logic must consist of a sequence of tests and branches to reach the desired destinations. Phrased in those terms, it may be appreciated that the experiments which are described in the subsequent sections of this paper have wider implications for the generation of decision logic in many application areas and at higher programming levels.

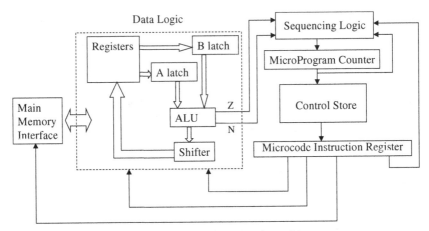

Fig. 1. Overview of the example microarchitecture

2 Example Microarchitecture

The microarchitecture we have used in this paper is based on the one described by Tanenbaum [12]. Although this is a hypothetical machine, it has the virtue of simplicity whilst exhibiting features common to many real microprogrammed processors. A simplified view of this microarchitecture is given in Figure 1.

On each micro-cycle, the next microinstruction is loaded from the control store into the microinstruction register (MIR). The instruction is divided into fields, or microoperations, which control various sub-systems throughout the processor. A complete microinstruction comprises 13 such fields, but only some of these are of relevance to this paper; they are:

A, B: specify inputs to the ALU, usually taken from register bank

ALU: specifies one of four operations to be performed by ALU; these are ADD,AND,COPY, INV, where COPY simply transfers the left ALU input to the output, and INV inverts the bits of the left input

SH: controls the shifter; specifies a shift left (SHL) or right (SHR) by one place

C: optionally specifies a destination register to hold the calculated result

COND, ADDR: optionally specify a jump in the microcode; COND may be JN (jump if negative), JZ (jump if zero), JMP (unconditional jump)

Whereas Tanenbaum used a pseudo-HLL syntax to write microcode, we have chosen to use an assembly-level syntax which more accurately reflects the specific microoperation values, and which is easier to generate via disassembly of evolved microcode sequences. Hence, an example microinstruction is:

A=RA B=SP ADD C=SP JMP LAB1

This instruction selects the RA register and the stack pointer as inputs to the ALU, instructs the ALU to add them, and writes the result back to the stack pointer register. Following this, a jump will be made to address LAB1.

3 Experimental Set-Up

In each of the experiments described in the next section, an initialisation phase creates a population of individuals by randomly selecting both the program length and the operations put together to create microinstructions. There are, however, two important additional aspects to this initialisation stage. Firstly, it is ensured that the address field of each microinstruction refers to a *forward* address. This is to prevent the accidental creation of infinite loops in the code, and is not considered an unnatural restriction, since most decode logic does not require iterative behaviour. Secondly, each population member is 'seeded' with a set of pseudo-instructions representing the microprograms that emulate the opcodes being decoded. These pseudo-instructions are not regarded in the same way as the randomly created microinstructions, in that they are not executable; they are there simply to act as destinations to which control flow can be directed by the evolved decode logic.

In all the experiments which follow, we have adopted steady-state evolution. Population members are chosen for reproduction, deletion, etc., using tournament selection on a sample size of 5. The population size is 2000, and each run comprises 100 generations (generational equivalents). The evolutionary operators are the standard ones of fitness-proportionate reproduction, recombination and mutation, selected probabilistically. Mutation, with a probability of occurrence of 0.01, is single-point: that is, only one field of one microinstruction is affected. For recombination we use 2-point linear crossover. However, because a microinstruction carries out several operations in parallel, and not all of these necessarily contribute positively to an individual's fitness, we introduced a form of crossover that allows segmentation to take place *within* microinstructions rather than merely at instruction boundaries [11]. 90% of the individuals in the population are generated in this way.

Since population members consist of microcode, the fitness function must take the form of a simulator of the microarchitecture. Fitness evaluation of an individual involves executing it multiple times within this simulation environment, and monitoring the state changes that ensue. Because we are interested purely in evolving decode logic, we make the assumption that the fetch phase has already taken place, i.e. an instruction is sitting in the instruction register (IR), ready for decoding. The format of a 16-bit instruction is that the upper 4 bits hold the opcode, and the lower 12-bits contain an operand (which may be an address).

An individual represents a solution to our decode problem if every opcode in the instruction set causes the individual's control flow to land at the corresponding microprogram for that opcode. There must therefore be at least one execution of the individual for each opcode in the set. In early experiments, however, it was discovered that the logic of some individuals could be strongly influenced by the arbitrary value of the *operand* field. To ensure that the correct logic is evolved for the opcode, irrespective of the operand value, it is necessary to test each opcode in conjunction with a variety of operand bit patterns. A 'hit' is tallied only if the correct microprogram (represented as a pseudo-instruction) is reached for each and every operand value. A fitness score can then be based on the number of hits obtained for all opcodes in the instruction set.

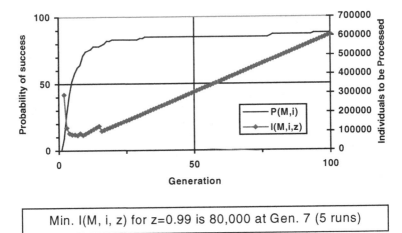

Min. I(M, i, z) for z=0.99 is 80,000 at Gen. 7 (5 runs)

Fig. 2. Performance graph for 3 opcodes {0,7,15}

4   The Experiments

4.1   Three Opcodes

In this first experiment, we test the ability of our GP system to evolve decode logic for just three opcodes. From the 16 possible opcodes that can be represented in the high 4 bits of an instruction, our first set is chosen as {0, 7, 15}. Following Koza [13], the graph presented in Fig. 2 summarises the success rate and the effort needed.

The thin line, plotted against the left axis, indicates the cumulative probability of success (i.e. finding a working solution) P(M,i) for a population size M (=2000) at generation i. The thicker line, plotted against the right axis, indicates the effort required to achieve a solution in terms of the number of individuals processed. This is expressed as I(M, i, z), meaning the number of individuals that are expected to be processed to achieve a solution at generation i with probability z. Conventionally, the value of z is set at 0.99. Below the graph we give the 'minimum computational effort.' For this particular machine instruction, the value is estimated at 80,000 individuals, derived from 5 runs to generation 7.

As the graph suggests, evolving a solution for the opcode set {0, 7, 15} is not that difficult to achieve. Indeed, 88 out of the 100 runs in the experiment produced solutions. A sample solution is:

```
I0: A=IR B=IR ADD JN I2
I1: Microprogram for Opcode 0
I2: A=0 B=IR ADD SHR JN I4
I3: Microprogram for Opcode 7
I4: Microprogram for Opcode F
```

This solution works by firstly adding the instruction register to itself. If the opcode held in the upper four bits is 7 (binary 0111) or 15 (binary 1111), then the result of this addition will be negative, and our code will jump to I2. Otherwise, the opcode

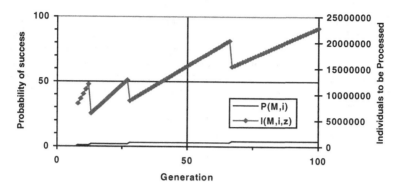

Min. I(M, i, z) for z=0.99 is 6,384,000 at Gen. 13 (228 runs)

Fig. 3. Performance graph for 3 opcodes {1,2,3}

This solution works by firstly adding the instruction register to itself. If the opcode held in the upper four bits is 7 (binary 0111) or 15 (binary 1111), then the result of this addition will be negative, and our code will jump to I2. Otherwise, the opcode must be zero, and the code correctly falls through to the microprogram which handles that opcode. At I2, the instruction register (still holding its original content) is added to zero, and again the result tested for negativity and a branch made if necessary. (The result is also redundantly shifted right, but this has no effect on the negative status flag, which is produced by the ALU *prior* to any shifting).

These initial results are encouraging, but closer scrutiny suggests that the choice of opcodes, although made arbitrarily, may have had an impact on this. The set {0,7,15} contains a zero value, a negative value, and a positive value; this fits in nicely with the conditional branch operations available in the microcode, viz. jump-if-zero and jump-if-negative. The question arises as to what might happen with an opcode set that provides less of a match. We therefore chose to repeat the experiment with the set {1,2,3}, which are all non-zero and non-negative. To make JZ and JN branches usable requires several combinations of shift and test. Fig. 3 shows the resulting graph:

The probability of success curve P(M,i) hardly gets off the ground, and the minimum computational effort is now well over 6 million individuals. In fact, only 4 runs out of 100 managed to evolve solutions which achieved the maximum of 3 hits (i.e. the decode logic always landed at the correct microprogram for each of the 3 opcodes). Of the remaining runs, one scored 2 hits, while the other 95 runs achieved only a single hit. An example solution is the following:

```
I0: A=IR B=IR ADD SHL C=IR
I1: A=IR B=+1 INV SHR JN I5
I2: A=0 B=IR ADD SHL C=IR
I3: A=IR B=+1 INV SHR JN I6
I4: Microprogram for Opcode 3
I5: Microprogram for Opcode 1
I6: Microprogram for Opcode 2
```

In the first microinstruction, the IR is added to itself, shifted left, and then stored back into IR. The GP system has therefore found a way of doing the equivalent of a double left shift in a single instruction. The second microinstruction then inverts the bits of IR (the B=+1 and SHR are just noise here), and jumps on the result. Only if the IR originally contained opcode 1 will the result be negative, and we end up at the correct place at label I5. At I2, the logic effectively performs another (single) left shift of the IR, so that it will now be negative if it originally contained opcode 3, and positive if it held opcode 2. Instruction I3 now repeats the actions of I1, with another inversion and conditional branch to the appropriate destination.

4.2 Six Opcodes

In moving up to six opcodes, we decided to compare the performance of two sets:

Set A = {0,3,6,9,12,15}
Set B = {1,2,3,4,5,6}

Set A contains equally-spaced values drawn from the range of 16 possible opcodes, and contains a mixture of zero, positive and negative values. Set B consists of consecutive non-negative, non-zero values. Fig. 4 shows how the GP system fared for these two sets, in terms of the number of hits achieved over the 100 runs.

The GP system successfully evolved complete solutions for Set A, but only in 2 of the 100 runs. The best that could be managed for Set B was 5 hits out of a maximum of 6. For Set A, a total of 64 runs managed to achieve 4 hits or more, while only 25 runs attained this level for Set B. Hence, it is again clear that the choice of opcodes has a strong influence on the effectiveness of the approach. A solution for Set A is the following:

```
I0:  A=IR B=0 ADD JN I6
I1:  A=IR B=IR ADD SHL C=IR JN I5
I2:  A=IR B=-1 AND JN I4
I3:  Microprogram for Opcode 0
I4:  Microprogram for Opcode 3
I5:  Microprogram for Opcode 6
I6:  A=IR B=IR ADD SHL C=IR JN I8
I7:  Microprogram for Opcode 9
I8:  A=IR B=IR ADD SHR JN I10
I9:  Microprogram for Opcode 12
I10: Microprogram for Opcode 15
```

The first instruction effectively splits the set into two halves, by branching on the sign of the IR. Opcodes {9,12,15} are dealt with from I6 onwards. Meanwhile, I1 represents a neat bit of evolved code: not only does it perform a double left shift as before, but it also manages to test the sign status produced as a result of the *first* of those shifts. This is because the first shift is really an ADD, which, as has already been mentioned, updates the status flags prior to anything done by the shifter itself. Of the three opcodes {0,3,6}, only opcode 6 gives a negative result if shifted left once, and I1 branches appropriately. I2 then examines the sign of the doubly-shifted value of the instruction register (by ANDing with -1), and again branches

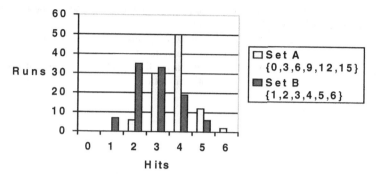

Fig. 4. Hit levels for two 6-opcode sets

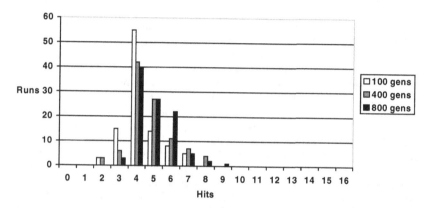

Fig. 5. Hit levels for all 16 opcodes

accordingly. The microcode from I6 onwards operates in a similar way. The triple shift-test-shift action of I1 is repeated at I6, and then a single shift and test is carried out at I8 to complete the decision-making (the SHR in I8 is noise).

4.3 Sixteen Opcodes

The results obtained from the previous experiments gave a good idea of the difficulty that would arise in evolving decode logic for the maximum 16 possible opcodes that can be represented in the 4-bit field of the instruction register. In this experiment, then, we also chose to compare the performance of the GP system over 100 generations with that obtained over 400 and 800 generations. A graph of the number of hits achieved in each case is presented in Fig. 5.

Over 100 generations as used in the earlier experiments, the maximum number of hits that the GP system managed to evolve is 7 out of a possible 16. In other words, the fittest individuals that emerged were capable of directing control flow correctly in all cases for 7 of the opcodes, but not for the others. Only 5 runs managed to achieve these 7 hits. If the number of generations is increased to 400, then 8-hit individuals emerge on 4 of the runs. A further increase to 800 generations leads to the production of a 9-hit program on one of the runs.

For 100 generations, 27 of the runs evolved programs achieving 5 or more hits. For 400 generations, this increased to 49 runs capable of achieving at least 5 hits, while 800 generations gave 57 runs attaining at least 5 hits. Moreover, unlike the 100 and 400-generation cases, none of the 800-generation runs evolved a program that achieved fewer than 3 hits.

5 Conclusions

Writing good quality decode logic at the microcode level is a complex problem even for human programmers, and so the results of the experiments described in this paper should be viewed as encouraging. The fact that the GP system managed to evolve microcode that was capable of dealing with as many as 9 out of 16 opcodes is a significant achievement, and the results appear to suggest that lengthening the evolutionary process by increasing the number of generations has the desired effect of elevating the hit rates. One thing that became clear very early on was that the success rate is greatly influenced by the choice of opcode set, and in particular how well it fits in with the conditions that branch instructions are able to test. Also encouraging was the appearance of microcode that embodies some quite sophisticated programming tricks, which in some cases (such as in the six-opcode example) reached a degree of ingenuity that many human programmers might find difficult to attain.

In performing these experiments, we have adhered to the standard evolutionary operators of fitness-proportionate reproduction, mutation and recombination. It may be the case that the use of alternative operators could improve on the number of hits obtained, and this forms an avenue for possible further investigation. A further observation regarding performance is that, since decode logic contains repeated application of shift-and-test operations, the encapsulation of these operations as single programming entities via the introduction of Automatically Defined Functions (ADFs) [13] could be of benefit.

Also for future work is the way in which some of the techniques described here might be more generally applied or extended. In examining the evolution of decode logic, we have couched the problem as a specific one at a specific programming level. However, as we saw in the Introduction, the instruction decode problem is essentially that of formulating the low-level equivalent of a high-level case statement. The task of generating control flow that always gets to the right destination for any of a set of values is an important problem at any level. Other control flow constructs such as loops and if-statements are also not always easily expressed, especially at low programming levels, and we wish to investigate the problems associated with their evolution.

Finally, one of the things we have glossed over in this paper is the issue of efficiency. Especially at the microarchitectural level it is vital that program code be both correct and efficient. An unnecessary microinstruction in the decode logic can mean an extra clock cycle added to the processing of every machine-code instruction. We therefore intend to look at ways of bringing in measures of execution speed into the fitness function so that efficiency becomes an additional factor driving the evolutionary process.

References

1. Stallings, W.: Computer Organization and Architecture: Designing for Performance. Sixth edn. Prentice Hall (2003)
2. Koza, J.R., Bennett III, F.H., Andre, D., Keane, M.A., Dunlap, F.: Automated Synthesis of Analog Electrical Circuits by Means of Genetic Programming. IEEE Trans. Evol. Comput., vol. 1, no. 2 (July 1997) 109-128
3. Thompson, A., Layzell, P., Zebulum, R.S.: Explorations in Design Space: Unconventional Electronics Design through Artificial Evolution. IEEE Trans. Evol. Comput., vol. 3, no. 3 (Sept. 1999) 167-196
4. Miller, J.F., Job, D., Vassilev, V.K.: Principles in the Evolutionary Design of Digital Circuits – Part I. Genetic Programming and Evolvable Machines, vol. 1. Kluwer, The Netherlands (2000) 7-35
5. Torresen, J.: A Scalable Approach to Evolvable Hardware. Genetic Programming and Evolvable Machines, vol. 3. Kluwer, The Netherlands (2002) 259-282
6. Alpaydin, G., Balkir, S., Dundar, G.: An Evolutionary Approach to Automatic Synthesis of High-Performance Analog Integrated Circuits. IEEE Trans. Evol. Comput. Vol. 7, no. 3 (June 2003) 240-252
7. Nordin, P., Banzhaf, W., Francone, F.D.: Efficient Evolution of Machine Code for CISC Architectures Using Instruction Blocks and Homologous Crossover. In: Spector, L. et al (eds.): Advances in Genetic Programming, vol. 3. MIT Press, Cambridge, MA (1999) 275-299
8. Kühling, F., Wolff, K., Nordin, P.: A Brute-Force Approach to Automatic Induction of Machine Code on CISC Architectures. In: Foster, J.A. et al (eds.): EuroGP 2002, Lecture Notes in Computer Science, vol. 2278. Springer-Verlag, Berlin (2002) 288-297
9. Poli, R., Langdon, W.B.: Sub-machine-code Genetic Programming. In: Spector, L. et al (eds.): Advances in Genetic Programming, vol. 3. MIT Press, Cambridge, MA (1999) 301-323
10. Poli, R.: Sub-machine-code GP: New Results and Extensions. In: Poli, R. et al (eds.): EuroGP'99, Lecture Notes in Computer Science, vol. 1598. Springer-Verlag, Berlin (1999) 65-82
11. Jackson, D.: Evolution of Processor Microcode. In submission.
12. Tanenbaum, A.S.: Structured Computer Organization. Third edn. Prentice Hall (1990)
13. Koza, J.R.: Genetic Programming: On the Programming of Computers by Means of Natural Selection. MIT Press, Cambridge, MA (1992)

Alternatives in Subtree Caching for Genetic Programming

Maarten Keijzer

KiQ Ltd., Amsterdam

Abstract. This work examines a number of subtree caching mechanisms that are capable of adapting during the course of a run while maintaining a fixed size cache of already evaluated subtrees. A cache update and flush mechanism is introduced as well as the benefits of vectorized evaluation over the standard case-by-case evaluation method for interpreted genetic programming systems are discussed. The results show large benefits for the use of even very small subtree caches. One of the approaches studied here can be used as a simple add-on module to an existing genetic programming system, providing an opportunity to improve the runtime efficiency of such a system.

1 Introduction

Implementation issues of genetic programming for imperative languages such as C/C++ have been studied in depth by Keith and Martin [1]. The main focus of the work was on implementing a general genetic programming system, generalized over a large set of possible combinations of functions and terminals. This led to the choice for a prefix jump-table approach as the implementation of choice which combines flexibility and runtime efficiency.

In this work the issue of implementation is revisited for a constrained set of genetic programming problems: those that involve functions without side-effects, evaluated on a fixed set of training data. The prototypical application for this type of genetic programming is symbolic regression. It will be shown that for this domain it is possible to use vectorized evaluation to — for all practical purposes — remove the overhead of a genome interpreter. The additional memory overhead of a system employing vectorized evaluation is a number of arrays the size of the data that needs not exceed the maximal depth of the parse trees.

Because the domain is constrained, it is however possible to extend and outperform this approach. This paper will present a caching approach, where a cache of subtrees and their evaluations is maintained to look up previously evaluated subtrees in order to avoid recalculating commonly occurring subtrees. In contrast with approaches that cache *all* subtrees in a population [2], the current approach will use a cache of a fixed — predetermined — size, which can be set at the beginning of a run. It will be shown that the use of such a cache inside the evaluation routine can greatly speedup a symbolic regression run, even with a limited size of the cache. The results in this paper strongly suggest that

M. Keijzer et al. (Eds.): EuroGP 2004, LNCS 3003, pp. 328–337, 2004.
© Springer-Verlag Berlin Heidelberg 2004

the use of caching together with vectorized evaluation is faster than any system that does not employ caching for this delimited set of problems: in particular it is claimed that this does not in principle exclude genetic programming systems that evolve and execute programs in assembler.

2   Vectorized Evaluation for Symbolic Regression

Symbolic regression is taken to be the search for a symbolic formula that tries to predict some target output t, given a finite set of input vectors $\mathbf{x}$. The size of this dataset is considered to be fixed, and the set of functions applied to the inputs are arithmetic, possibly augmented with other primitive mathematical functions, and possibly conditionals.

The results presented in this paper do not depend on its use in symbolic regression: they apply to any purely functional language that does not have side-effects in the evaluation step, and where there is a notion of independence in the fitness cases: the evaluation of one case does not depend on the evaluation of other cases. Although this limits the applicability of the approach studied here, it is still wide enough to be of practical interest: for instance, regression and classification problems fall into this class.

In most implementations of genetic programming to date, evaluation is done on a case by case basis, where the parse tree is traversed and interpreted for each fitness case separately. The overhead of the genome interpreter is then incurred for each node and each case separately.

Thus, given an individual consisting of M nodes, evaluated over N fitness cases, the number of interpretation steps is $M \times N$. As a fully interpreted genetic programming employs a switch or jump-table to figure out which function to call, the overhead of the switch or lookup and subsequent function call is incurred for each node and each function call. No matter how optimized this step is, it grows with both the size of the population and the number of fitness cases.

When however the loop is reordered such that the the evaluation works on the full *array* of fitness cases for each node, it is possible to reduce the number of interpretation steps to M. With such a *vectorized evaluation* all functions are defined as a simple loop over all fitness cases. By reducing the number of interpretation steps by a factor N, the runtime of a genetic programming system can be massively reduced. In effect, when performing vectorized evaluation, the overhead of the interpreter is *independent* of the number of fitness cases.

This simple trick, where an outer loop over the interpreter is replaced by a (compiled) inner loop over the sub-calculations is known as vectorized evaluation. Interpreted languages such as Matlab and numeric extensions of the languages Python and Perl use vectorized evaluation extensively to reduce the computational impact of the interpreter. Up to date, vectorized evaluation has not been used in genetic programming implementations much, which is surprising given the simplicity and expected gains of this approach. One of the reasons might be that interpreted genetic programming systems are usually set up to be fully general, in that they not only tackle side-effect free programs on a fixed training set, but also dynamic problems with or without side-effects in the training set. For such problems, vectorized evaluation is not or only limitedly applicable.

To give an indication of the impact a non-vectorized genome interpreter has on a system, consider a genetic programming run that evaluates 1000 individuals of average size 200 for 500 generations on a set of 5000 fitness cases. This will mean that the genome interpretation step is invoked a total of 5×10^{10}, or 50 billion times. Even with a heavily optimized genetic programming system such as GPQuick [3], where the overhead of the interpreter reduces to 4 operations (table lookup, pointer dereference, pointer increment and a function call), and furthermore (very optimistically) assuming that each of these four operations take a single clock cycle on a 2 GHz CPU, this leads to a total overhead of 100 seconds per run for the interpreter alone. Contrast this with a vectorized evaluation step that only needs 10 million interpretation steps, and it is clear that with vectorized evaluation the speed of the interpreter itself is much less of an issue. Because the inner loops are all simple loops over arrays of fitness cases, they can run optimally fast on modern day pipelined floating point architectures.

3   Subtree Caching

Due to consistent copying of subtrees by crossover in genetic programming, it is unavoidable that many subtrees will occur multiple times in the population [4]. New individuals created will share many subtrees with their parents, and potentially with many other members of the population. When evaluation is performed in a standard way, these subtrees will be evaluated repeatedly.

It is possible to avoid this continuous re-evaluation of subtrees by storing the entire population in a Directed Acyclic Graph (DAG), and evaluate only those portions of new individuals that are new to the population [2,4]. However, because the size of the population, or more importantly, the number of unique subtrees is a dynamical consequence of the run, the size of the DAG structure and its cached evaluations is dynamic as well. This would not only mean that memory most likely needs to be allocated dynamically (which is another source of overhead), but also that it is hard to limit the number of cached evaluations. Storing all subtrees present in the population can therefore lead to an overflow of the available RAM, and consequently, sub-optimal performance. Furthermore, in symbolic regression type tasks, the number of fitness cases can be very large. Using a subtree caching mechanism such as Handley's [2] is then an all-or-nothing approach.

Here an approach is studied where the maximum size of the subtree cache can be set beforehand; a caching mechanism is introduced that will attempt to exploit such a fixed size cache optimally. Therefore, the following demands are placed on the algorithm.

1. The subtree cache should be of a fixed, user defined size
2. Evaluations are done in a vectorized manner
3. The number of cache hits needs to be maximized
4. Cache lookups should be fast, preferably (amortized) constant time

In this paper descriptions are given of two approaches that will implement these constraints in two different manners. One comes in the form of an add-on module which can conceivably be added to the evaluator of any tree-based genetic programming system. This method uses a postfix traversal of the tree, and keeps the subtree cache local to the module without interfering with the main representation that stores the population. This is a bottom-up approach in the sense that for a subtree to be cached or to remain in the cache, all its children need to be cached as well. The second method follows the DAG approach, where inside the DAG a fixed set of evaluations are cached. The evaluation method is top-down, which enables subtrees to remain in the cache, even when its children are removed from the cache. Both approaches use the same least-recently-used mechanism for updating the cache, the main difference lies in the perceived efficiency of the approaches, the DAG approach expected to be the more efficient, the postfix approach less intrusive.

3.1   Bottom-Up Caching Using a Postfix Representation

For the first version of the caching mechanism, a cache of subtrees will be added to the evaluation function. If a subtree is evaluated, a check will be performed to see if the subtree is present in the cache. If it is, the cached evaluations (an array) will be used instead of re-evaluating the subtree. The implementation makes use of two data-structures: a hash table to store subtrees and cached evaluations, and a linked list to enable a least recently used algorithm for cache additions and removals.

The subtree cache itself is implemented as a DAG stored in a hash table. In the case the subtree is a terminal, it will simply store the identifier and a pointer to the array that contains its values. In the case of an ephemeral random constant it will point simply to the constant value. For functions: an identifier is kept, plus pointers to the children subtrees. Next to the hash table, a linked list is used that stores pointers to the elements in the hash table.

The hash table will thus consist of: (a) the token identifying the function or terminal (or constant), (b) pointers to the arguments (c) a pointer to an array of evaluations, and (d) a pointer to the corresponding element in the list. If we know the locations in the hash table of the children for a certain subtree, a lookup to see if the subtree is contained in the hash table is an O(1) algorithm. Once a hashed subtree is found, its evaluations can be retrieved and the node does not need to be evaluated.

The Update Mechanism. With a caching approach that will maintain a finite cache of evaluations, some mechanism needs to be defined that will select when subtrees should enter the cache, and which subtrees should make place for these. The replacement algorithm chosen here is the fast O(1) least recently used (LRU) mechanism: whenever a subtree needs to enter the cache, the least recently used subtree will be removed. This algorithm can be conveniently implemented using a linked list with pointers to the elements in the cache. Terminals will not enter the LRU mechanism, to make sure that they are never deleted. Although more effective algorithms than the LRU algorithm are known, none of them have constant lookup time. As the mechanism is used inside the evaluator loop, anything above constant time will have a significant impact on the speed of the system.

The cache selection algorithm deserves some more thorough consideration however. If any subtree that is evaluated will enter the cache, many very large subtrees that are not likely to be present multiple times will enter the cache and fill it up to capacity quickly. Although caching large trees can represent large savings, these savings can only be collected when the trees occur frequently. The cache insertion algorithm introduced here will add a subtree to the cache only if all its children are in the cache, and none of these cached children have entered the cache in the current evaluation. In this way, a large tree will only enter the cache when it is encountered many times. Small trees — necessarily occurring more frequently — will enter the cache more rapidly. In this way a balance is struck between the large gains expected of finding a large subtree in the cache and the waste of effort of having only rarely occurring elements in the cache.

For the implementation of this caching mechanism, an individual is traversed in a postfix manner. This enables a stack based implementation. In the description below, a flag is used that signals that an element of the stack is cached. This flag is used for clarity, in an implementation it can easily be replaced by a pointer to the element in the hash table (with zero signalling that it is not cached). Elements on the stack thus contain an array of evaluations, and a pointer to a hash table entry (here represented as a flag).

As an example, consider a postfix representation of a tree:

x y * z + x y * z + *

First the terminals x and y are pushed on the stack and by definition, these are cached, so the flag variable is set to one.

| y | 1 |
| x | 1 |

Then the multiplication operator is processed. Two arguments are popped from the stack, the flags are checked and because both arguments are cached, a check is performed if the subtree y*x is cached as well. As it is not, but both its children are cached, the subtree is added to the cache. Even though after this operation, the subtree is now present in the cache, the flag is set to zero to ensure that any subtrees using this tree will not enter the cache at this time. The stack now contains

| y*x | 0 |

where the symbolic description y*x is used instead of the array of evaluations that is used in the implementation. Subsequently, the terminal z is pushed on the stack

| z | 1 |
| y*x | 0 |

Then the addition operator is processed. It pops the two arguments, and, because the flag is unset for the second argument, it will evaluate the addition,

and pushes the result on the stack. After this operation, the stack will contain
a single uncached element:

| z+y*x | 0 |

Subsequently, the two terminals are pushed on the stack:

y	1
x	1
z+y*x	0

Now the multiplication operator is checked for a second time. As both its
children are cached, and it occurs in the cache itself, its cached evaluations will
be retrieved and the flag will be set. After pushing the variable z on the stack,
the situation is as follows:

z	1
y*x	1
z+y*x	0

The addition operator that follows will be added to the cache, and after
evaluating the root multiplication operator, evaluation is done. This particular
evaluation sequence saved one single evaluation by a lookup. By refraining from
adding all subtrees, the mechanism gradually builds up a cache of subtrees: large
subtrees will be added only when they have occurred many times.

3.2   The LRU-Mechanism

The linked list that stores the cached evaluations is used to implement the LRU
mechanism. Whenever a subtree is found in the cache, the element will be moved
to the top of the list. When a new element is added, the element from the bottom
of the list is taken, and its values are re-used. This new element is again stored
at the top of the list. By using this process, the bottom element of the list is
always the least recently used element. Because the list elements are directly
accessible (as a pointer to it is kept in the hash table of subtrees), and unlinking
and relinking elements from a list can be done in constant time, the overall
complexity of the update mechanism is $O(1)$. As the subtree lookup routine
itself employs a hash table, the overall caching approach described here is $O(1)$
for each cache lookup.

3.3   Top-Down Caching

A second method for caching is to have the population stored as a DAG itself,
such that every distinct subtree occurs only once. Evaluation of an individual in
such a DAG can be done by a standard recursive evaluation function. Because
of the use of vectorized evaluation there is no need to provide an exceptionally
fast genome interpreter. A DAG can be conveniently stored in a hash table for
$O(1)$ access [5]. A similar mechanism as above is employed for caching, albeit it
works in a top-down fashion. When recursively evaluating an individual, first it
is checked if the root node is cached. If it is, the cached evaluations are returned

(while at the same time the position of this root node's cached evaluations in the linked list will become the top of the list). Then a recursive routine is entered where for any node, it is checked if all the children are cached (as a side-effect any of these children that are cached will become the top of the linked list). If all children are cached, the node is evaluated using the cached evaluations of the children, and the evaluations are stored at the top of the linked list. If any of the children are not cached, the routine will enter the recursion. This node will then *not* enter the cache.

The differences between the top-down and bottom-up approach are twofold. Top-down caching is intrusive, in that the elements of the DAG representation need to hold pointers to the linked list. It also presupposes a particular implementation for the population as a DAG. The bottom-up approach only keeps a DAG of the subtrees that are currently cached, and is thus of constant size. The bottom-up approach can conceivably be plugged into the evaluation function oblivious of the actual implementation that is used to store the entire population: be it postfix, prefix or a pointer tree, as long as the representation can be traversed in a postfix manner.

A second difference between the two approaches can be found in the subtrees that can be found inside the cache. In the bottom-up approach, only subtrees whose children are cached can remain cached. Whenever a subtree gets deleted from the cache all the trees that contain it can no longer be accessed and will be flushed. The top-down mechanism works quite different. Whenever a cached subtree is found, it will become the top of the LRU list. However, its subtrees will not be accessed and will therefore remain where they were in the LRU-list. Whenever such a child subtree is removed from the cache, the cached subtree is still accessible, and can be used again. This enables the cache to only contain those subtrees that are (i) large and (ii) occur frequently. In particular, this means that when a subtree only occurs in the context of another subtree, no cache-entry is wasted in storing this subtree, as it will always be the larger tree that will be accessed first. It was expected that this will outperform the bottom-up caching approach. To what extent it does or does not do this is investigated in the experimental section below.

4   Experimental Results

Experiments are performed in order to asses three things: (i) if the caching approach is effective in reducing the number of evaluations, (ii) the impact of the size of the cache on the effectiveness, and (iii) which caching mechanism (top-down or bottom-up) produces best results. To quantify the efficiency of the caching mechanism the ratio of the number of function evaluations performed versus the number of functions that would be needed to evaluated without caching is used. This effectively skips the terminals as in both approaches they will not enter the cache. To perform the experiments, the DAG implementation, including top-down caching, was used as the main representation for the GP runs, while the bottom-up postfix representation was used as an add-on module. The results reported here are thus performed using the same system, which enables a fair comparison. Furthermore, an upper bound on the number of cache hits is calculated by examining the DAG structure and calculating how many new nodes are added to the population after each variation event. This is used to simulate the effort needed for a straightforward DAG implementation where all subtrees are cached at all times and only new subtrees need to be evaluated.

The genetic algorithm that is uses a population of 500 individuals evolving under a regime with 50% crossover and 50% node mutation where selection pressure is implemented using a tournament selection of size three where the worst individual in the tournament is replaced by the offspring of the best two. Note that this setup ensures a fairly diverse run due to the high mutation rate, and caching is thus not expected to be optimally useful.

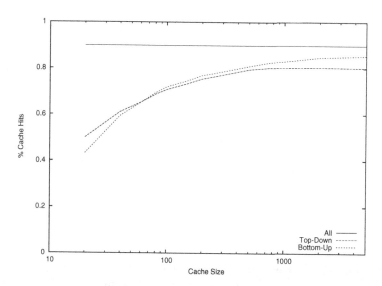

Fig. 1. Caching statistics after 100 generations over 150 runs. Cache sizes ranges from 20 to 5000 subtrees. The average DAG size is 3400 nodes.

Regression of $x^3e^{-x}cos(x)sin(x)(sin^2(x)cos(x) - 1)$. Figure 1 shows the efficiency of the different caching mechanisms for a moderately difficult regression function on a single variable. For small cache sizes the top-down method outperforms the bottom-up method by a significant margin. This indicates the ability of the top-down method to retain large common subtrees in the cache while the bottom-up method flushes them quickly because of space constraints. Already with a cache size of 20 subtrees, the top-down method is capable of saving more than 50% of function evaluations. When the cache size grows, the bottom-up method starts to outperform the top-down method. Because the only difference between the two methods is the treatment of subtrees of cached subtrees, the cause of this must be sought there. In the top-down method, such subtrees are not reinforced and can thus be flushed from the cache, while in the bottom-up method they are reinforced. A frequently occurring subtree with many supertrees in the cache will thus be flushed quickly by the top-down method. Crossover, being frequency driven, samples such a subtree often and will put it in new, uncached, contexts.

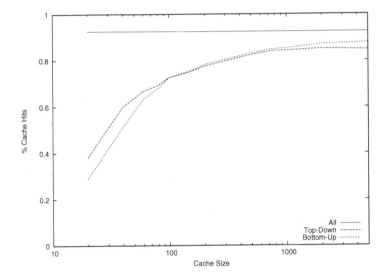

Fig. 2. Caching statistics after 100 generations over 150 runs. The average DAG size is 6500 nodes.

Regression of an 8 variable function. The second test was performed on a 8 variable function that was generated through a hydraulic numerical model for which no closed form solution is known. To give good performance all 8 variables need to be used, which reduces the possibility of extensive subtree sharing. As such, this function is a better representative of regression problems than the single variable function used above. This difference is already reflected in the number of distinct subtrees that are present in the population (6500 versus 3400). The same pattern as above appears: top-down caching is more efficient for small cache sizes while bottom-up caching is the most efficient for large cache sizes. For the smallest cache size tested here, the efficiency of the top-down method was 40%, which signifies already a significant speedup. Also here the benefits of subtree caching are clear.

5 Conclusion

Subtree caching can provide significant benefits, even when memory constraints are present. In this work it was shown that a subtree caching mechanism can provide speedups of up to 50% even when the size of the cache is kept at a very low value of 20 cached subtrees using top-down caching. For moderate values of 500 to 1000 cached subtrees, speedups can rise to levels close to 90%, representing an order of magnitude speedup on vectorized evaluation.

When memory constraints are such that there is space for thousands of cached evaluations, it seems that the caching method proposed by Handley provides the most benefit, however, the inability of this method to control the amount of memory is a clear disadvantage. Also, with large cache sizes, the bottom-up method approaches the efficiency of this optimum within a few percent.

For moderate cache sizes between 100 and 1000 subtrees, the bottom-up caching method seems most efficient. For more heavily memory constrained systems where only a small cache can be used, top-down caching can be preferred. In most practical applications, bottom-up caching is the preferred method: even when the number of fitness cases is in the order of a hundred thousand, it is still feasible to maintain a cache of 500 subtree evaluations on most modern systems. Such a setup would need 50 million floats or doubles, thus 200 or 400 MB of memory for the cache. In such a setting the cache efficiency can easily exceed 70% of the function evaluations, even in diverse populations. Combined with vectorized evaluation, the resulting speed of the system will, although interpreted, approach, if not beat, compiled genetic programming systems.

Bottom-up caching can easily be implemented as an add-on module for any genetic programming representation that can be traversed in a postfix manner. This is an important benefit of the method. Combined with the experimental observation that it approaches the optimal caching efficiency with larger cache sizes makes it the winner in this comparison.

References

1. Keith, M.J., Martin, M.C.: Genetic programming in C++: Implementation issues. In Kinnear, Jr., K.E., ed.: Advances in Genetic Programming. MIT Press (1994) 285–310
2. Handley, S.: On the use of a directed acyclic graph to represent a population of computer programs. In: Proceedings of the 1994 IEEE World Congress on Computational Intelligence, Orlando, Florida, USA, IEEE Press (1994) 154–159
3. Singleton, A.: Genetic programming with C++. BYTE (1994) 171–176
4. Keijzer, M.: Efficiently representing populations in genetic programming. In Angeline, P.J., Kinnear, Jr., K.E., eds.: Advances in Genetic Programming 2. MIT Press, Cambridge, MA, USA (1996) 259–278
5. Tackett, W.A.: Recombination, Selection, and the Genetic Construction of Computer Programs. PhD thesis, University of Southern California, Department of Electrical Engineering Systems, USA (1994)

Structural Risk Minimization on Decision Trees Using an Evolutionary Multiobjective Optimization

DaeEun Kim

Cognitive Robotics
Max Planck Institute for Psychological Research
Munich, 80799, Germany
kim@psy.mpg.de

Abstract. Inducing decision trees is a popular method in machine learning. The information gain computed for each attribute and its threshold helps finding a small number of rules for data classification. However, there has been little research on how many rules are appropriate for a given set of data. In this paper, an evolutionary multi-objective optimization approach with genetic programming will be applied to the data classification problem in order to find the minimum error rate for each size of decision trees. Following structural risk minimization suggested by Vapnik, we can determine a desirable number of rules with the best generalization performance. A hierarchy of decision trees for classification performance can be provided and it is compared with C4.5 application.

1 Introduction

The recognition of patterns and the discovery of decision rules from data examples is one of the challenging problems in machine learning. When data points with numerical attributes are involved, the continuous-valued attributes should be discretized with threshold values. Decision tree induction algorithms such as C4.5 build decision trees by recursively partitioning the input attribute space [14]. Thus, a conjunctive rule is obtained by following the tree traversal from the root node to each leaf node. Each internal node in the decision tree has a splitting criterion or threshold for continuous-valued attributes to partition a part of the input space, and each leaf represents a class depending on the conditions of its parent nodes.

The creation of decision trees often relies on the heuristic information such as information gain measurement. How many nodes are appropriate for classification has been an open question. Mitchell [13] showed the curve of the accuracy rate of decision trees with respect to the number of nodes over the independent test examples. There exists a peak point of the accuracy rate in a certain size of decision trees; larger size of decision trees can increase its classification performance on the training samples but reduces the accuracy over the test samples

M. Keijzer et al. (Eds.): EuroGP 2004, LNCS 3003, pp. 338–348, 2004.
© Springer-Verlag Berlin Heidelberg 2004

which have not been seen before. This problem is related to the overfitting problem to increase the generalization error [1]. Many techniques such as tree growing with stopping criterion, tree pruning or bagging [15,12,14,4] have been studied to reduce the generalization error. However, the methods are dependent upon a heuristic information or measure to estimate the generalization error, and they do not explore every size of trees.

An evolutionary approach to decision trees has been studied to obtain optimal classification performance [9,8,3], since the decision tree is not optimal in structure and performance. Freitas et al. [8] have shown evolutionary multi-objective optimization to obtain both the minimum error rate and minimum size of trees. Their method was based on the information gain measurement; it followed the C4.5 splitting method and selected the attributes with genetic algorithms. They were able to reduce the size of decision trees, but had higher test error rates than C4.5 in some data sets. Recently a genetic programming approach with evolutionary multi-objective optimization (EMO) was applied to decision trees [3,2]. A new representation of decision trees for genetic programming was introduced [2], where the structure of decision trees is similar to linear regression trees [5]. Two objectives, tree size and accuracy rate in data classification, were considered in the method. The method succeeded in reducing both error rates and size of decision trees in some data sets. However, the best structure of decision trees has not been considered in their works.

It has been shown that EMO is very effective for optimization of multi-objectives or constraints in continuous range [17]. Also EMO is a useful tool even when the best performance for each discrete genotype or structure should be determined [11]. There has been no study so far to find what is the best structure of decision trees to have the minimal generalization error, though the EMO approach was used to minimize the training error and the tree size [2,10].

In this paper, the EMO for two objectives, the tree size and the training error, is first used to obtain the Pareto solutions, that is, the minimum training error rate for each size of trees. After the preliminary stage, the structural risk minimization suggested by Vapnik [16] will be applied to find the best structure (tree size) with the minimum generalization error. A special elitism strategy for discrete structures is applied to the EMO. Also an incremental evolution from small to large structures with Pareto ranking is considered, where genetic programming evolves decision trees with variable thresholds and attributes. From the suggested method, we can find the accuracy rate of classification for each size of trees as well as the best structure of decision trees. The result will be compared with the C4.5 method.

2   Method

2.1   Structural Risk Minimization

In structural risk minimization, a hierarchical space of structures is enumerated and then the function to minimize the empirical risk (training error) for each

---

[1] This is also called test error in this paper.

structure space is found. Among a collection of those functions, we can choose the best model function to minimize the generalization error. The number of leaf nodes (rules) in decision trees corresponds to the VC-dimension that Vapnik mentioned in the structural risk minimization [16].

The structure of decision trees can be specified by the number of leaf nodes. Thus, we define a set of pattern classifiers as follows:

$$S_k = \{F(x, \beta) | \beta \in D_k\}$$

where x is a set of input-output vectors, $F(x, \beta)$ is a pattern classifier with parameter vector β, D_k is a set of decision trees with k terminal nodes and S_k is a set of pattern classifiers formed by decision trees with k terminal nodes. Then we have

$$S_1 \subset S_2 \subset \cdots \subset S_n.$$

From the method of structural risk minimization [16], we can easily set the VC dimension into the number of leaf nodes and the VC dimension of each pattern classifier is finite. In this paper, the training error for each set of pattern classifiers, S_k, for $k = 2, ..., n$, is minimized with the EMO method and then the generalization error for each pattern classifier is identified. The best pattern classifier or the best structure of pattern classifiers is the one with the minimum generalization error; 10-fold cross validation will be used to estimate the generalization error.

2.2   Evolutionary Multiobjective Optimization

In the suggested evolutionary approach, a decision tree is encoded in the genotype chromosome; each internal node specifies one attribute for training instances and its threshold. The terminal node defines a class, depending on the conjunctive conditions of its parent nodes through the tree traversal from the root node to the leaf node. Unlike many genetic programming approaches, the current method encodes only a binary tree classification often observed in decision trees (see Fig. 1(d)); the only one function set is a comparison operator for a variable and its threshold, and the terminal set consists of classes determined by decision rules.

The genetic pool in the evolutionary computation handles decision trees as chromosomes. The chromosome size (tree size) is proportional to the number of leaf nodes in a decision tree, that is, the number of rules. Thus, the number of rules will be considered as one objective to be optimized. While an evolutionary algorithm creates a variety of decision trees, each decision tree will be tested on a given set of data for classification. The classification error rate will be the second objective. The continuous-valued attributes require partitioning into a discrete set of intervals. Here the decision tree will have a single threshold for every internal node to partition the continuous-valued attribute into two intervals. Thus, it is assumed that the decision tree is a binary tree.

We are interested in minimizing two objectives, classification error rate and tree size in a single evolutionary run. In the multi-objective optimization, the

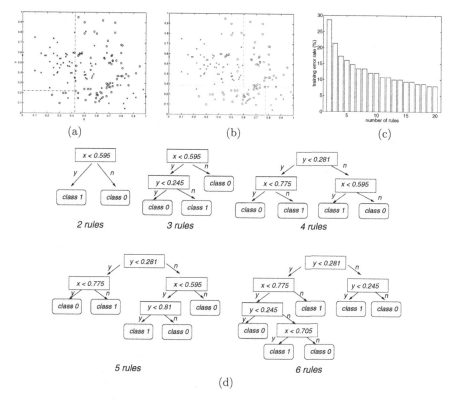

Fig. 1. Artificial data and EMO (a) data set and C4.5 decision boundaries (○ : class 0, × : class 1) (b) 4 rules from EMO (c) an example of EMO result (d) a part of the best chromosomes

rank cannot be linearly ordered. The Pareto scoring in EMO approach has been popular and it is applied to maintain a diverse population over two objectives. A dominance rank is thus defined in the Pareto distribution.

A vector $X = (x_1, x_2, ..., x_m)$ for m objectives is said to *dominate* $Y = (y_1, y_2, ..., y_m)$ (written as $X \prec Y$) if and only if X is partially less than Y, that is,

$$(\forall i \in 1, ..., m, x_i \leq y_i) \land (\exists i \in 1, ..., m, x_i < y_i)$$

A *Pareto optimal set* is said to be the set of vectors that are not dominated by any other vector.

$$\{X = (x_1, ..., x_m) | \neg (\exists Y = (y_1, ..., y_m), Y \prec X)\}$$

To obtain a Pareto optimal set, a dominating rank method [7] is applied to the tournament selection of group size four in this paper. The dominating rank method defines the rank of a given vector in a Pareto distribution as the number of elements dominating the vector. The highest rank is zero, for an element which has no dominator.

A population is initialized with a random size of tree chromosomes. In the experiments, tournament selection of group size four is used for Pareto optimization; a population is subdivided into a set of independent groups and members in each group are randomly chosen among the population. In each group of four members, the two best chromosomes[2] are first selected in a group and then they reproduce with a given mutation rate. A subtree crossover over a copy of two best chromosomes, followed by a mutation operator, will produce two new offspring. These new offspring replace the two worst chromosomes in a group. The crossover operator swaps subtrees of two parent chromosomes where the crossover point can be specified at an arbitrary branch.

The mutation has five different operators. The first operator deletes a subtree and creates a new random subtree. The subtree to be replaced will be randomly chosen in a decision tree. The second operator first picks up a random internal node and then changes the attribute or its threshold. This keeps the parent tree and modifies only one node. The third operator chooses a leaf node and then splits it into two nodes. This will assist incremental evolution by adding one more decision boundary. The fourth operator selects a branch of a subtree and reduces it into a leaf node with random class. It will have the effect of removing redundant subtrees. The fifth operator sets a random attribute in a node and chooses one of the possible candidate thresholds randomly. The candidate thresholds can be obtained at boundary positions[3] by sorting the instances according to the selected variable (the threshold to maximize the information gain is also located at such a boundary position [6]). The last operator has an effect of choosing desirable boundaries based on information gain, but the random selection of the thresholds avoids local optimization only based on information gain. Thus, the last mutation operator[4] accelerates a fast speed of convergence in classification and the other four operators provide a variety of trees in a population. In this paper, crossover rate 0.6 and mutation rate 0.2 were used.

In the initialization of the population or the recombination of trees, we have a limit for the tree size. The minimum size of leaf nodes is 2 and the maximum size of leaf nodes is set to 35; some data set does not need the exploration of as many nodes as 35, because a small number of leaf nodes are sufficient. If the number of leaf nodes in a new tree exceeds the limit, a new random subtree is generated until the limit condition is satisfied. A single run of the EMO method over training examples will lead to the Pareto optimal solutions over classification performance and the number of rules. Each non-dominated solution in a discrete space of tree size represents the minimized error fitness for each number of decision rules. The

---

[2] More than one chromosome may have tie rank scores and in this case chromosomes will be randomly selected among multiple non-dominated individuals.

[3] We first try to find adjacent samples which generates different classification categories and then the middle point of adjacent samples by the selected attribute is taken as a candidate threshold.

[4] There is a possibility of using only information gain splitting, but we use this method instead to allow more diverse trees in structure.

elitism strategy has been significantly effective for EMO methods [17]. In this paper, an elitist pool is maintained, where each member is the best solution for every size of decision trees under progress. For each generation, every member in the elitist pool will be reproduced.

3   Experiments

3.1   Artificial Data

The EMO method was first tested for a set of artificial data with some noise as shown in Fig. 1; we will only show an application of the EMO method to minimize the training error, not generalization error, and the generalization error will be covered in section 3.2. The data set contains 150 samples with two classes. When the C4.5 tree induction program was applied, it generated 3 rules as shown in Fig. 1(a). It produced a 29.3 % training error rate (44 errors). For reference, a neural network (seven nodes in a hidden layer) trained with the back-propagation algorithm achieves a 14.7 % error rate (22 example misclassifications). Evolving decision trees with 1000 generations and a population size 200 by the EMO approach produced a variety of Pareto trees. With only two rules allowed, 43 examples were misclassified (28.7 % error rate) as shown in Fig. 1(c), and it was better than the C4.5 method. Moreover, six rules was sufficient to obtain the same performance as neural networks with seven hidden nodes. As the number of rules increases, decision boundaries are added and the training error performance improves.

In many cases, the best boundaries evolved for a small number of rules also belong to the classification boundaries for a large number of rules; new boundaries can provide better solutions in some cases. A small number of rules are relatively easily evolved since more rules have more parameters to be evolved and it takes longer time. More rules tend to be evolved sequentially from the base of a small number of rules. Thus, incremental evolution from small to large structures of decision trees is operated with the EMO approach.

3.2   Machine Learning Data

For the general case, the suggested evolutionary approach has been tested on several sets of data (*iris, wine, ionosphere, ecoli, pima, wpbc, glass, bupa*) in the UCI repository [1] and the artificial data in Fig. 1. These data sets are mostly for machine learning experiments. Classification error rates are estimated by running the complete 10-fold cross-validation ten times, and for significance statistics, 10 trials are repeated with the EMO approach. For each size of decision trees, 95% confidence intervals of fitness (test error rate) are measured by assuming t-distribution. For each experiment, a population size of 500 with 1000 generations was taken with tournament selection of group size four.

Evolutionary computation was able to attain a hierarchy of structure for classification performance. There exists the best number of rules to show the

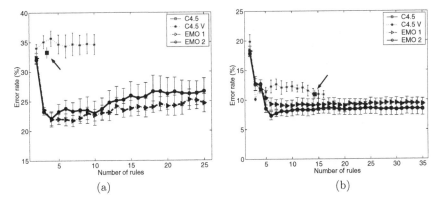

Fig. 2. Examples of EMO result in data classification 1 (arrow: C4.5 with default parameters, *: C4.5 with varying number of nodes, ▷: EMO result with 100 generations, ○: EMO result with 1000 generations) (a) artificial data (b) *ionosphere* data

minimum generalization error as expected from the structural risk minimization. Fig. 2 shows that the artificial data have four decision rules as the best structure of decision trees and that the *ionosphere* data have six rules. If the tree size is larger than the best tree size, then the generalization performance degrades or shows no improvement. More generations tend to show a better curve for the best structure of trees. This test validation process can easily determine a desirable number of rules. The EMO even with 100 generations is better than a C4.5 induction tree in the test error rates for these two sets of data.

In our experiments, the EMO with 100 generations outperforms C4.5 in the test error rate for all the data except *wine* and *glass*. The EMO with 1000 generations improves both the error rate and the number of rules, and it is better than C4.5 in the test error rate for all the data. Table 1 and Fig. 3 show that the EMO is significantly better than C4.5 in error rate with 95 % confidence levels for most of the experimental data. The EMO method with *wine* and artificial data have a little higher number of rules, but it is due to the fact that the EMO finds an integer number of rules in a discrete space. The other data experiments show that the best number of rules in decision trees by the EMO is significantly smaller than the number of rules by C4.5 induction trees.

An interesting result is obtained for the *wpbc* and *pima* data (see Fig. 4). Two sets of data have a bad prediction performance, regardless of the number of rules. The performance of C4.5 is worse than or similar to that of two or three rules evolved. Investing longer training time on *wpbc* and *pima* data does not improve validation performance. It is presumed that more consistent data are required for two sets of data.

In the experiments, the number of rules by C4.5, which is determined by information gain, is mostly larger than that by the suggested approach. It confirms that some rules from C4.5 are redundant and thus C4.5 may suffer from an over-specialization problem. The performance of the suggested method over

Table 1. Data classification errors in C4.5 and the EMO method

data	pattern	attr.	C4.5 error (%)	C4.5 rule	EMO (100 gen.) error (%)	EMO (100 gen.) rule	EMO (1000 gen.) error (%)	EMO (1000 gen.) rule
artificial	150	2	33.3 ± 0.9	3.5 ± 0.3	21.9 ± 1.1	4	22.1 ± 1.2	4
iris	150	4	5.4 ± 0.8	4.8 ± 0.1	3.5 ± 0.7	4	3.3 ± 0.4	4
wine	178	13	6.8 ± 1.0	5.4 ± 0.2	7.1 ± 1.2	8	6.3 ± 1.0	6
ionosphere	351	34	10.9 ± 0.7	14.3 ± 0.3	9.0 ± 0.9	9	7.4 ± 0.7	6
ecoli	336	7	20.0 ± 0.9	24.4 ± 0.7	18.3 ± 1.0	16	17.4 ± 1.2	6
pima	768	8	25.9 ± 1.0	25.4 ± 1.0	25.8 ± 1.0	19	25.2 ± 0.5	3
wpbc	194	32	30.9 ± 2.0	13.1 ± 1.0	24.0 ± 0.6	2	24.2 ± 0.7	2
glass	214	9	32.8 ± 1.6	25.0 ± 0.5	34.2 ± 1.4	27	29.5 ± 1.5	18
bupa	345	6	34.0 ± 2.0	30.4 ± 1.9	33.4 ± 1.1	3	31.9 ± 1.2	3

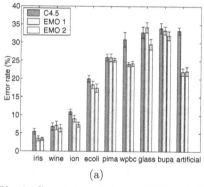
(a)

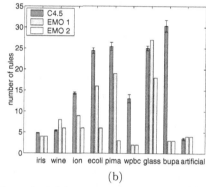
(b)

Fig. 3. Comparison between C4.5 and EMO method (a) error rate in test data with C4.5 and EMO (EMO 1 and EMO 2 represent the EMO running with 100 generations and 1000 generations, respectively) (b) the number of rules with C4.5 and EMO (the number of rules for EMO is determined by selecting the minimum error rate)

decision trees can be influenced by mutation operators. We can add a new mutation operator splitting decision space by information gain in order to see how much it influences the validation performance.

In this paper, we selected the best model for the comparison with C4.5. The comparison can be arguable, because a variety of model complexities for C4.5 are not provided. In fact, C4.5 can also generate varying number of rules by adjusting parameters, for instance, by controlling the parameter of a minimum number of objects in the branches. The performance of C4.5 with varying number of nodes for some data sets is shown in Fig. 2; it is worse than our method in classification performance. With the parameter control, a specific number of decision rules can be missing. Generally it is hard to generate a consecutive number of leaf nodes or a large size of trees with C4.5. It would be a better comparison with the suggested approach if more sophisticated tree induction method with pruning or stopping growing can be tested. As an alternative, other tree induction algorithms that grow trees by one node can be tested and compared with the EMO method. We

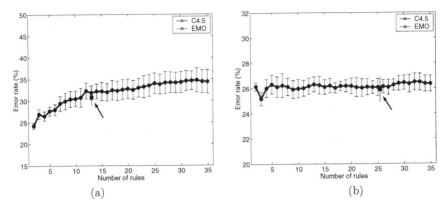

Fig. 4. Examples of EMO result in data classification 2 (arrow: C4.5 with default parameter, ○: EMO result with 1000 generations) (a) *wpbc* data (b) *pima* data

leave the comparison between the suggested approach and other methods in the same model complexities to future work.

The computing time of evolutionary computation requires much more time than C4.5. For example, a single EMO run with a population size of 500 and 100 generations over *pima* data takes about 22 seconds while a single run of C4.5 application takes only 0.1 second (Pentium computer). A single EMO run for *iris, wine, ionosphere, ecoli, wpbc, glass*, and *bupa* took roughly 3 seconds, 6 seconds, 28 seconds, 8 seconds, 12 seconds, 7 seconds, 8 seconds, respectively. Generally the EMO needs much more computing time to find the best performance for every size of trees, but it can improve the classification performance significantly in most of the data sets.

When we wish to have a desirable set of rules over a given set of data, we do not have a prior knowledge about what is the best number of rules to minimize the generalization error. Thus, a two-phase algorithm with the EMO method can be applied to general classification problems. First, we can apply the EMO method to the whole training instances and obtain a set of rules for each size of trees. Then the above method of finding the best structure with 10-fold cross validation can be applied to the training instances. From this information, we can decide the best set of rules among a collection of rule sets for the original data set, which will prevent the overfitting problem.

4   Conclusions

The proposed EMO approach searches for the best accuracy rate of classification for each different size of trees. By structural risk minimization, we can find a desirable number of rules for a given error bound. The performance of the best rule set is better than that of C4.5, although it takes more computing time. In particular, it can reduce the size of trees dramatically. It can also help to evaluate how difficult it is to classify a given set of data examples. Many researchers have used *pima* and *wpbc* in their experiments, but the distribution of error rates over the size of trees implies that these data cannot expect prediction. In addition, we can indirectly determine if a given set of data requires more consistent data or whether it includes many noisy samples.

For future study, the suggested method can be compared with the bagging method [4], which is one of the promising methods to obtain good accuracy rates. The bagging process may also be applied to the rules obtained from the proposed method. The decision tree evolved in this paper has the simple form of a binary tree. The EMO approach can be extended to more complex trees such as trees with multiple thresholds or linear regression trees. The result can also be compared with that obtained from neural networks.

Acknowledgements. The author would like to thank anonymous reviewers for fruitful comments and suggestions. This work is supported by the EU in the project AMOUSE.

References

1. C. Blake, E. Keogh, and C.J. Merz. *UCI* repository of machine learning databases. In *Proceedings of the Fifth International Conference on Machine Learning*, 1998.
2. M.C.J. Bot. Improving induction of linear classification trees with genetic programming. In *Proceedings of the Genetic and Evolutionary Computation Conference (GECCO-2000)*, pages 403–410. Morgan Kaufmann, 2000.
3. M.C.J. Bot and W.B. Langdon. Application of genetic programming to induction of linear classification trees. In *Proceedings of the 3rd European Conference on Genetic Programming*, 2000.
4. L. Breiman. Bagging predictors. *Machine Learning*, 24(2):123–140, 1996.
5. L. Breiman, J. Friedman, R. Olshen, and C. Stone. *Classification and Regression Trees*. Wadsworth International Group., 1984.
6. U.M. Fayyad. *On the induction of decision trees for multiple concept learning*. Ph. D. dissertation, EECS department, University of Michigan, 1991.
7. C. M. Fonseca and P. J. Fleming. Genetic algorithms for multiobjective optimization: Formulation, discussion and generalization. In *Proceedings of the Fifth Int. Conf. on Genetic Algorithms*, pages 416–423. Morgan Kaufmann, 1993.
8. A.A. Freitas G.L. Pappa and C.A.A. Kaestner. Attribute selection with a multiobjective genetic algorithm. In *Proceedings of the 16th Brazilian Symposium on Artificial Intelligence*, pages 280–290. Springer-Verlag, 2002.
9. K.B. Irani and V.A. Khaminsani. Knowledge based automation of semiconductor manufacturing. In *SRC Project Annual Review Report*, The University of Michigan, Ann Arbor, 1991.
10. E.D. De Jong and J.B. Pollack. Multi-objective methods for tree size control. *Genetic Programming and Evolvable Machines*, 4(3):211–233, 2003.
11. D. Kim and J. Hallam. An evolutionary approach to quantify internal states needed for the woods problem. In *From Animals to Animats 7*, pages 312–322. MIT Press, 2002.
12. J. Mingers. An empirical comparison of selection measures for decision-tree induction. *Machine Learning*, 4(2):227–243, 1989.

13. T. M. Mitchell. *Machine Learning*. McGraw Hill, 1997.
14. J.R. Quinlan. Improved use of continuous attributes in *C4.5*. *Journal of Artificial Intelligence Approach*, 4:77–90, 1996.
15. J.R. Quinlan and R. Rivest. Inferring decision trees using the minimum description length principle. *Information and Computation*, 80(3):227–248, 1996.
16. V.N. Vapnik. *The nature of statistical learning theory.* Springer Verlag, 1995.
17. E. Zitzler. *Evolutionary Algorithms for Multiobjective Optimization: Methods and Applications.* Ph. D. dissertation, Swiss Federal Institute of Technology, 1999.

Global Distributed Evolution of L-Systems Fractals

W.B. Langdon

Computer Science, University College, Gower Street, London, WC1E 6BT, UK
http://www.cs.ucl.ac.uk/staff/W.Langdon

Abstract. Internet based parallel genetic programming (GP) creates fractal patterns like Koch's snow flake.
Pfeiffer, http://www.cs.ucl.ac.uk/staff/W.Langdon/pfeiffer.html, by analogy with seed/embryo development, uses Lindenmayer grammars and LOGO style turtle graphics written in Javascript and Perl. 298 novel pictures were produced. Images are placed in animated snow globes (computerised snowstorms) by www web browsers anywhere on the planet. We discuss artificial life (Alife) evolving autonomous agents and virtual creatures in higher dimensions from a free format representation in the context of neutral networks, gene duplication and the evolution of higher order genetic operators.

1 Introduction

For two years we have been running an experiment in distributed evolution in which small local populations within each user's web browser communicate via Javascript with a central server holding a variable sized global population (see Figure 1). Pfeiffer is intended as a prototype to show the feasibility of evolving agents on many small computers running across the Internet under the user's actions as a fitness measure. (A Java based model, albeit without interactive evolution, is sketched in [Chong and Langdon, 1999].) The agents are intended to be attractive and therefore they are animated in a snowstorm. Their form is given by a simple deterministic Lindenmayer grammar, whose initial seed is a Koch fractal snow flake (see Table 1).

The Biomorphs of [Dawkins, 1986] and the work of Karl Sims [Sims, 1994] in evolving virtual creatures are well known. Christian Jacob [Jacob, 2001] used the Mathematica language to evolve many classic Lindenmayer based virtual plants. The Wildwood system [Mock, 1998] allows interactive evolution of static plants, while [Hemberg et al., 2001] uses it for architectural design. More recently [Ortega et al., 2003] has used a linear genetic programming system (grammatical encoding [O'Neill and Ryan, 2001]) to force syntactic correctness of their Lindenmayer grammar. Note these constraints may possibly prevent massive neutral networks from forming in the fitness landscape.

The next two sections describe the GP L-system. Section 4 describes the two month trial. Section 5 describes the results. Section 6 is concerned with implementation problems. (After the trial, some of these were addressed.) The

M. Keijzer et al. (Eds.): EuroGP 2004, LNCS 3003, pp. 349–358, 2004.
© Springer-Verlag Berlin Heidelberg 2004

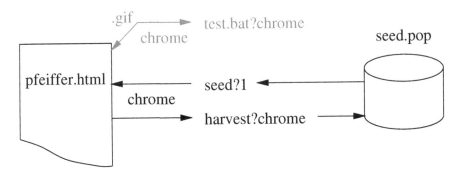

Fig. 1. Overview of Pfeiffer. The user interacts via HTML and Javascript run in their web browser (left hand side). Initial seeds (chromosomes) are either stored locally as a cookie or down loaded via the Internet via cgi program seed running on our web server. Seed returns a randomly chosen member of the global population. Evolution occurs in the user's browser. To visualise modified seeds they are passed to cgi script test.bat which interprets them as Lindenmayer grammars driving turtle graphics. The resulting graphic is convert to a .GIF file and returned to the user's browser for display. Should a user elect to save a seed, it is duplicated, stored on the user's machine as a cookie and added to the global population by cgi program harvest.

penultimate section (7) discusses where evolutionary agents might lead us. We conclude, in Section 8, that worldwide interactive evolution is feasible.

2   How Pfeiffer Works

Pfeiffer (cf. Figure 1) evolves agents and displays them moving in two dimensions across the screen of a www browser. The visual phenotype of each agent is given by a Lindenmayer system grammar. As the agents are moved across the screen they are subject to random encounters and changes which may effect their grammar. Each time the grammar is changed the agent's new shape is drawn on the screen. The user can save pretty shapes and delete ugly ones.

2.1   User Interaction

The primary goal of the user intervention is to use the user to provide selection pressure to drive the evolution of the agents. The user can save an agent by clicking on it. This causes an additional copy of the agent to be stored in the local population, overwriting a deleted agent (if any). Since the local population cannot hold more than 25 agents, if there are no deleted agents, adding an agent means overwriting an existing one. The agent selected by the user is stored in its "cookie" and appended to the global population. (Cookies allow the local population to be stored off line between sessions.) Once in the global population, the agent can be down loaded by other users and so distributed across the world.

These user initiated actions exert selection pressure on the local and global populations.

The user can also use the cursor to "freeze" selected individuals. I.e. prevent them moving for ten seconds. This does not prevent them crossing over. As such it gives the user limited abilities to steer individuals towards each other and so perform mate selection.

While apparently simple, one must bear in mind that all the agents are updated and moved asynchronously. Thus the actual agent's seed can be different (for a short time) from the seed which grew into the fractal (phenotype) displayed on the screen. Time outs are used to make it clearer which user action has been initiated before starting a new one.

2.2   Central Server

The code running on the UCL server splits into two parts. Seed and harvest, which read and write seeds from and to the global population and test.bat.

Javascript has very limited graphics capabilities. It is designed to display predetermined graphics, which it down loads. Pfeiffer needs to be able to display arbitrary Lindenmayer grammars. This cannot be done in Javascript, instead it is done on the server and the results are down loaded. Test.bat interprets each new seed as a Lindenmayer grammar, generating a series of drawing instructions, which are immediately obeyed. The resulting picture is compressed and converted to .GIF format and passed back to the user's browser for display. Because of the data compression, this takes only a few seconds even on low band width connections. The delay appears to be mainly due to network latency, rather than lack of bandwidth.

3   Genetic Programming Configuration

The (up to) 25 individuals in the local population move across the user's web browser display and may run into each other. When this happens and if both individuals are mature (i.e. more than 25 seconds old) crossover occurs and the first parent's seed (chromosome) is replaced by that of its offspring. The new offspring closes up to and remains with the second parent for ten seconds. The 10s delay gives time for the offspring's .GIF to be down loaded from UCL. After 10s the child and parent randomly drift apart.

3.1   Genetic Representation

Each agent seed is a variable length linear text string. The default seed grows into the Koch snow flake (row 6 in Table 1). It is the 56 character string v=60&str=F++F++F & it=2 & sc =5 & rules=('F','F-F++F-F'). So it is no surprise that these characters appear often in both the local and global populations.

Spaces and control codes are removed before each seed is passed across the Internet to be interpreted. The string is split by & characters into parameters. They are are processed left to right. Thus if any parameter is repeated, the second "gene" is "dominant". Note with more flexible genetic operations (only a slight change to our crossover would be needed), this representation would support "gene duplication" and "translocation" [Goldberg, 1989].

Four parameters are recognised. They are v (angle), str (start string of grammar), it (depth of recursive expansion) and sc (side, in units of 0.2 pixels). rules is fixed. Each substring formed by splitting the seed at the & is further split by =. If the first part of the substring exactly matches one of the parameter names then its value is set to the text between the first and second (if any) =. If a parameter is missing, its default is used. The use of the defaults is effectively the same as if the default text where inserted at the start of every seed (albeit protected from genetic operators).

Once parameters have been decoded the Lindenmayer grammar is interpreted. First the start string srt Lindenmayer grammar is expanded it times. At each step every character which matches the left hand symbol of a rule is replaced by the corresponding right hand side. This yields a potentially very long string. To avoid tying up our server with infinite or very long recursions an arbitrary complexity limit of 2000 line segments steps was imposed.

The string is interpreted as a series of "turtle" drawing instructions:

F move forward sc/5 pixels
+ turn clockwise by v degrees,
- turn anti-clockwise by v degrees,

3.2 Example of Interpreting a Grammar

Suppose the initial seed is the 59 characters v=60 & str=F++F++F3t5F+r c sc= 5 & rules = ('F','F-F++F-F'). After removing spaces we are left with 51 characters v=60&str=F++F++F3t5F+rcsc=5&rules=('F','F-F++F-F'). This splits (at &) into two parameters v=60 and str=F++F++F3t5F+rcsc=5. Defaults are given for missing parameter values (it and sc), while rules is fixed. So the grammar is v=60, str=F++F++F3t5F+rcsc, it=2, sc=5 and rules= ('F','F-F++F-F'). Note how the original value of sc had been corrupted but is restored by the default. The start string is expanded twice (it=2) to give the final image.

Iteration	Size	Expansion	Line segments
0	3×3	F++F++F3t5F+rcsc	4
1	6×7	F-F++F-F++F-F++F-F++F-F++F-F++F-F3t5F-F++F-F+r csc	16
2	15×17	F-F++F-F-F-F++F-F++F-F++F-F-F-F++F-F++F-F ++F-F-F-F++F-F++F-F++F-F-F-F++F-F++F-F++F -F-F-F++F-F++F-F++F-F-F-F++F-F3t5F-F++F-F -F-F++F-F++F-F++F-F-F-F++F-F+rcsc	64

3.3 GP Genetic Operations and Other Parameters

Only crossover was active during the two month period. However mutation had been used extensively in the previous two years. Crossover is "homologous" in the sense that the start of the parents' seeds are aligned before two cut points are randomly selected. However to allow seeds to change length, 50% of the time the segment cut from the middle of the second parent is either one character longer or one shorter than the segment in the first parent it replaces. If the second parent is shorter than the second cut point, the inserted fragment must be shorter than the segment it replaces. Leading to a bias towards creating shorter offspring. The first parent is replaced by its offspring.

Wildwood [Mock, 1998] only allows crossover within the L-system production rules and chooses crossover points to ensure [] brackets are matched. Our robust interpreter ensures operation even if crossover violates syntactic rules and allows all the parameters to evolve.

First parent

`v =1-72&strF+'+F+4+F+F&&st F+2& 'c s 5tetulF+ =-F Fe ,- F&F(Fl+&=`

Second parent

`v =1=72&&strF '+F+4+F+F&&st F+2& 'c s 5tetulF+ =-F Fe,,- F&F(Fl++=`

Offspring, replaces first parent

`v =1-72&strF+'+F+4+F+F&&st F+2& 'c s | 5tetulF+ =-F Fe ,- F&F(Fl+&=`

Fig. 2. Example crossover. Length of first parent 67, first cut point at 37, remove 10 characters, insert 11 characters. 68 characters in offspring.

4 How Much Has Pfeiffer Been Used

From December 2001 to November 2003, 43,681 Lindenmayer grammars were evolved by 740 user sessions from 171 different sites. Usage of Pfeiffer has been highly non-uniform. The length of individual sessions is approximately log-normal. However activity also varies in time reflecting the system's development. E.g. usage increased after July 2003 when support for additional browsers (Mozilla, Netscape 6 and Microsoft) was implemented.

In the two months from Wednesday 10 September 2003 to Sunday 9 November, 5,653 Lindenmayer grammars were evolved, interpreted and down loaded by 87 user sessions from 69 different domains. Surprisingly "commercial" sites dominate with only eight obviously academic sites. Usage has been truly international and covers at least 14 countries (be, ca, com edu net org, dk, it, lb, lt, mx, nl, pl, sa, sg, uk, za). The mean number of .GIF down loaded per session was 65. 50% of sessions down loaded 18 or more (corresponding to loading all or nearly all of the initial population from the network). It is disappointing to note that half user sessions last 39 seconds or less. This suggests a serious problem in starting Pfeiffer. Possibly many users are not prepared to wait the 38 seconds on average needed to down load the initial population and start the HTML page.

5   What Has Pfeiffer Learnt

The global population grew roughly linearly during the two month trial. Table 1 tabulates the changes. Of the 43 new seeds, 29 can be attributed to genuine users and 14 to web spiders. 298 totally new phenotypes were evolved by local populations however only one was saved in the global population by a user.

Most users added none or only one seed to the global population but two users added five each. If we group the seeds in the global population by their appearance (phenotype) the new members have been allocated roughly in proportion to the the increase in population (145/102). This suggests no clear user preference. Perhaps this was in part due to poor user interface, leading the Javascript to misinterpret the user's intention.

The asynchronous nature of the update of the agent's phenotype after crossover leads to a lack of direct connection between the user and the system. After the trial the user interface was improved. E.g. various measures such as time outs and visual cues have been implemented to address the problems of the user "clicking but nothing happens" and to overcome the inherent delay in updating an agent's appearance after crossover.

While there were fluctuations in program size, lengths did not change dramatically. This lack of bloat is also consistent with noisy or weak selection.

During the two months, 5653 seeds were interpretted and down loaded. Apart from a few special cases, these contained the same characters as the initial global population, in the same proportions (within 2%). Most (3279 58%) of the .GIF images were copies of the default Koch snow flake. 1531 (27%) images where identical to another image held in the global population. 843 (15%) new images were down loaded. As usual there was a degree of overlaping phenotypes, with these 843 down loads consisting of 298 totally new .GIF files. The usage of these novel shapes was very varied. Two novel .GIF files account for 307 (36%) of down loads but others were evolved just once.

Three .GIF are evolved much more often than their frequency in the initial global population. These are the given in rows 6 (default, Koch, 10×12), 3 (invisible, 49×1) and 4 (10×3) of Table 1. While this may be a response to user preference, another explanation is that crossover is finding many different Lindenmayer grammars with these phenotypes. E.g. by damaging the parameters, so either the defaults are used or v is set to a small value.

14 junk seeds were inserted into the global population by software robots or web spiders. Spider unknown.thorn.net was responsible for inserting rogue characters <PLAINTEXT> into the global population. Similarly % managed to slip in. Note while unwanted, Pfeiffer continues to function satisfactorily despite these.

6   Practicalities

The server software needs greater protection against web spiders and software agents. (This was added after the trial.)

Table 1. Global population at start and end of the two month trial.

Where a grammar does not specify a value, or the value is illegal the default (Koch) is used. There are considerable variations in start symbol **str** but in most cases the specified value is illegal and so replaced by the default. Size is the number of characters in the seed. (Where different grammars yield the same .GIF, minimum-median-maximum values are given.) **v** is the angle through which the turtle is turned (left or right, - or +). **sc** is the number of 0.2 pixels to move forward (on F). Steps is the number of turtle moves to interpret the grammar (at depth **it**).

Used	Image	size	bytes	Sep	Nov	inc	Size	v	str	it	sc	Steps
38		28×32	140	1	2	1	58	60		3	5	192
110		28×42	140	2	5	3	66-119-119	60	1.†	2	10	64
877		49×1	47	25	29	4	56-68-69	0	†	2	5	48
249		10×3	49	2	2	0	56	5-6		2	4	48
24		82×94	491	1	1	0	55	60		4	5	768
3279		10×12	64	59	91	32	0-64-69	60	†	2	5	48
170		15×14	73	6	7	1	57	60		2	5	48
31		14×14	76	2	3	1	67	-72	2.	2	5	80
11		45×16	90	1	1	0	93	9		2	5	48
21		24×17	98	0	1	1	56	60	3.	2	5	96

Default start string **str** is F++F++F.
1. F+F+F+F
2. +F+F+F+F+F
3. F++F++F3t5F+rc34+c++'l44FrF'15

†A few start symbols differ, sometimes radically, yet yeild the same image.

During the trial evolution was allowed to exploit a hole where by it generated 997 (2%) invisible agents. Crossover created these by ensuring **v**=0. The hole was fixed after the trial.

The evolution of large and complex fractal patterns suggest that Pfeiffer is already pressing up against the 2000 steps limit. After the trial, this limit was relaxed significantly without undue hardship.

We must admit to having been caught out by the significant start up delay. This was not a feature of the original Netscape 4 implementation but arose as a "finishing touch" during porting to other browsers. One of the original motivations for using Javascript as opposed to using Java was that Java applets had come with a painful start up overhead. This delay was removed after the trial.

6.1   Real Time Performance

On average each .GIF takes 300mS to generate and occupies 66 bytes. On average each seed takes 60 bytes. On a fast link (2Mb/S) the time to process each each new seed should be dominated by drawing the .GIF. Even on a 9k6 baud line, the average data transfer time should be only 140mS. Thus, ignoring processing time in the user's web browser and network latency, Pfeiffer should be able to process between 2 and 3 fractal images per second. In contrast typical maximum rates are 0.5-1.0 per second (mean 0.73). This suggests performance is dominated by network (including server) latency and browser overhead. To some extent these are outside our control. Together these suggest there is little performance gain to be had within the existing system design.

Pfeiffer gathers a lot of data but some additional data might be helpful. For example the type of computer/browser being used. Also mostly the data gathered is about successful operation, little is said about things that failed. On a less technical front, there is no attempt to gather user feed back. E.g. what did they think about it? Was it difficult to use? Why did they stop? Did they find it boring?

Surprisingly the computational power of a standard (350MHz) PC is only just sufficient. Smoothly animating the movement of a population of 25 .GIF images across a browsers screen can fully load it. One reason for moving to a Java implementation would be to display the L-system directly thus removing the network delays associated with crossover. However one could expect similar CPU loading issues with Java animations as with Javascript animations. This would need careful investigation.

6.2   Non-portability

It was somewhat disappointing to discover that so recent a language as Javascript is seriously non-portable. Not between different computers. (Almost all development was on computers of the same type, running the same or similar operating systems) but between different browsers. So code running in one browser would behave radically differently when run on the same machine in a different browser.

Portability was less of an issue on the server. Debugging and development tools are problematic in both server and browser. Development of Javascript was much the more painful.

7 Future: Breeding "Intelligent" Agents

Our agents are very limited. We feel they need to be able to evolve to react to their environment. They need to be able to evolve to predict their environment. Of course this makes requirements of both the agent and the environment. Also, perhaps crucially, it needs to be able to effect the environment, and predict what those effects will do for it (and for others). While L-systems have been mainly used (as we have done here) to create static structures, they can describe networks. Those networks could contain sensory and active elements, they could contain processing elements (as in artificial neural networks [Gruau, 1994; Hornby and Pollack, 2002], or even GP like communicating computational processes).

There is a strand of thought in which intelligence came from a co-evolutionary struggle between members of the same species [Ridley, 1993]. If true, can intelligence arise in isolated agents? Or are interacting/communicating agents needed?

A problem with simulated worlds has been hosting sufficient complexity so as to be challenging but still allowing agents to be able make predictions about what will happen next and what will happen to me or to others if I do this. The Internet hosts tides of data. This data is not random. It aught to be possible to harness it to give a suitable virtual environment.

We have fallen for the usual trap of constructing a two dimensional world (on the computer screen). However is there any hope of evolving artificial life (and thereby artificial intelligence) in two dimensions? Obviously three dimensions are sufficient but computer simulations offer many dimensions ($N \gg 3$).

8 Conclusions

Lindenmayer grammars can be used as the basis for a linear genetic programming (GP) system and evolve interesting fractal like patterns. Many new patterns have been evolved, some exploiting the L-system to produce some regularities and re-use of motifs. It is feasible to represent individual agent's genetic material (seed/chromosome) with a variable length text string without defined fixed semantic fields and using crossover at the character level. The representation allows a huge degree of redundancy to evolve. The "fitness landscape" clearly contains a huge degree of "neutrality" [Smith et al., 2002] and evolution is using it. Yet, we are still only using a small part of a complete Lindenmayer grammar (e.g. the seeds do not use branching primitives, [or]). This loose representation allows the location etc. (as well as the meaning) of the L-system to evolve. Gene duplication, translocation and other genetic operations could be supported by such a general representation.

One of the original hopes was that "fitness" would arise intrinsically from the simulation. As well as user actions, one could imagine selection being based on aspects of the fractal patterns, their production or transfer across the Internet and their interaction with other agents. However, perhaps due to poor user interface exacerbated by the asynchronous nature of the image update system, evolution appears to have been undirected.

In terms of harvesting spare CPU cycles, the project confirms it can be done using Javascript and user's web browser but this experiment did not show it to be worthwhile. The project does hint at some successes. World wide distributed evolution is clearly feasible. (A single server prooved suficient but this must represent a bottleneck for much bigger experiments.) Perhaps more importantly one can recruit users (which are much more valuable than their CPUs) to assist in guided evolution. Finally animated tools are an attractive way to spread evolutionary computation.

Acknowledgements. I would like to thank Birger Nielsen for use of his perl Lindemayer interpretter http://www.246.dk/lsystems.html, Maarten Keijzer and the much put upon reviewers.

References

Chong and Langdon, 1999. Fuey Sian Chong and W. B. Langdon. Java based distributed genetic programming on the internet. In W. Banzhaf, *et al.*, editors, *GECCO*, p1229. Morgan Kaufmann. Full text in Birmingham UK technical report CSRP-99-7.

Dawkins, 1986. Richard Dawkins. *The blind Watchmaker*. Harlow : Longman Scientific and Technical, 1986.

Goldberg, 1989. David E. Goldberg. *Genetic Algorithms in Search Optimization and Machine Learning*. Addison-Wesley, 1989.

Gruau, 1994. F. Gruau. *Neural Network Synthesis using Cellular Encoding and the Genetic Algorithm*. PhD thesis, Laboratoire de l'Informatique du Parallilisme, Ecole Normale Supirieure de Lyon, France, 1994.

Hemberg et al., 2001. Martin Hemberg, Una-May O'Reilly, and Peter Nordin. GENR8 - A design tool for surface generation. In Erik D. Goodman, editor, *GECCO Late Breaking Papers*, pp160–167, San Francisco, 9-11 July 2001.

Hornby and Pollack, 2002. Gregory S. Hornby and Jordan B. Pollack. Creating high-level components with a generative representation for body-brain evolution. *Artificial Life*, 8(3):223–246, 2002.

Jacob, 2001. Christian Jacob. *Illustrating Evolutionary Computation with Mathematica*. Morgan Kaufmann, 2001.

Mock, 1998. Kenrick J. Mock. Wildwood: The evolution of L-system plants for virtual environments. In *Proceedings of the 1998 IEEE World Congress on Computational Intelligence*, pp476–480, Anchorage, Alaska, USA, 5-9 May 1998. IEEE Press.

O'Neill and Ryan, 2001. Michael O'Neill and Conor Ryan. Grammatical evolution. *IEEE Transactions on Evolutionary Computation*, 5(4):349–358, 2001.

Ortega et al., 2003. Alfonso Ortega, Abdel latif Abu Dalhoum, and Manuel Alfonseca. Grammatical evolution to design fractal curves with a given dimension. *IBM Journal Research and Development*, 47(4):483–493, July 2003.

Ridley, 1993. Matt Ridley. *The Red Queen, Sex and the Evolution of Human Nature*. Penquin, 1993.

Sims, 1994. Karl Sims. Evolving 3D morphology and behaviour by competition. In R. Brooks and P. Maes, editors, *Artificial Life IV Proceedings*, pp28–39. MIT Press.

Smith et al., 2002. Tom Smith, Phil Husbands, Paul Layzell, and Michael O'Shea. Fitness landscapes and evolvability. *Evolutionary Computation*, 10(1):1–34, 2002.

Reusing Code in Genetic Programming

Edgar Galván López[1], Riccardo Poli[1], and Carlos A. Coello Coello[2]

[1] University of Essex, Colchester, CO4 3SQ, UK
{egalva,rpoli}essex.ac.uk
[2] Depto. Ing. Eléctrica, Sección de Computación
Av. Instituto Politécnico Nacional No. 2508
Col. San Pedro Zacatenco, México, D.F. 07300, MEXICO
ccoello@cs.cinvestav.mx

Abstract. In this paper we propose an approach to Genetic Programming based on code reuse and we test it in the design of combinational logic circuits at the gate-level. The circuits evolved by our algorithm are compared with circuits produced by human designers, by Particle Swarm Optimization, by an n-cardinality GA and by Cartesian Genetic Programming.

Keywords: Genetic programming, code reuse, logic circuit design, evolvable hardware.

1   Introduction

In Genetic Programming (GP) [7,10] programs are expressed as syntax trees. This form of GP has been applied successfully to a number of difficult problems like image enhancement, magnetic resonance data classification, etc. [2]. The reuse of code is a very important characteristic in human programming. So, several attempts have been made to introduce the ability to reuse code in GP.

For example, one can reuse code using Automatically Defined Functions (ADFs) [7,8]. The problem with this approach is discovering good ADFs. ADFs behave differently in different parts of a program when they have different arguments. So, in order to discover if an ADF is good, GP has to spend additional computation to discover with which parameters the ADF can be used properly. Code reuse is also possible with Parallel Distributed Genetic Programming (PDGP) [14,15,16]. Programs are represented in PDGP as graphs with nodes representing program primitives and links representing the flow of control and results. So, PDGP can be used to either evolve parallel programs or to produce sequential programs with shared (reused) subtrees. Another technique to reuse code is the Multiple Interacting Programs (MIPs) approach proposed in [1]. A MIPs individual is equivalent to a neural network where the computation performed in each unit is not fixed but is performed by an evolved equation. Each unit's equation is represented by a GP syntax tree.

The design of combinational logic circuits is generally considered an activity that requires certain human creativity and knowledge. Traditionally this has

M. Keijzer et al. (Eds.): EuroGP 2004, LNCS 3003, pp. 359–368, 2004.
© Springer-Verlag Berlin Heidelberg 2004

been performed with techniques based on Boolean algebra, for example: Karnaugh Maps [6,18], the Quine-McCluskey Algorithm [21,17] and ESPRESSO [3].

More recently the problem of designing combinational logic circuits has been attacked with various evolutionary techniques, an area called *Evolvable Hardware* [7,19,20]. Evolvable Hardware research can be sub-divided into two main categories: intrinsic evolution, which is carried out through building and testing electronic hardware, and extrinsic evolution, carried out through simulations. Extrinsic evolution is the approach used in the work presented here.

Louis [12] was one of the first to use genetic algorithms for combinational logic design. In his thesis [11], Louis uses a genetic operator called *masked crossover* which adapts itself to the encoding and is able to exploit specific information about the problem domain.

Coello *et al.* [4] developed an approach using a two-dimensional matrix in which each matrix element is a gate (AND, OR, NOT, XOR, WIRE). The goal was to produce fully functional designs which were also minimal. They tried to achieve this by maximizing the use of WIRE gates, once feasible circuits have been found. In this work the authors reported good result for small problems. This approach, however, is highly sensitive to the values of the parameters adopted, namely the size of the matrix which, if not chosen properly, may prevent the GA from converging.

Coello *et al.* [5] used the same circuit representation as in the work mentioned above but this time used Particle Swarm Optimization (PSO) to design the circuits. Instead of using the usual PSO's real-valued representation, they used a binary encoding in order to facilitate representing circuits. The algorithm produced competitive results with respect to an n-cardinality Genetic Algorithm (NGA), but its performance seriously degraded when dealing with circuits with more than one output.

When appropriate terminals, functions and fitness functions are defined, standard GP can go beyond the production of programs and can be used to evolve circuits. The approach in [9] was, for example, to use primitives that can grow a circuit starting from an initial embryonic circuit including only a power supply, a load, and a modifiable wire. This approach has been mostly used to evolve analogue circuits and controllers.

Miller *et al.* [13] developed a technique called Cartesian Genetic Programming (CGP). In CGP a program is seen as a rectangular array of nodes. Each node may implement any convenient programming construct. In this representation, all cells are assumed to have three inputs and one output and all cell connections are feed-forward. With this technique, Miller *et al.* obtained good results for complex problems, including the three-bit multiplier and the even-*4* parity circuit. However, the approach normally requires a very high number of fitness function evaluations.

The main purpose of the present work is to explore a new GP technique, called *Encapsulated GP* (EGP), which allows the reuse of code within GP trees. In this work we will use evolvable hardware problems to test EGP. The paper is organized as follows. Section 2 contains a description of the algorithm used. We provide experimental results in Section 3. We discuss these in Section 4 and we draw some conclusions in Section 5.

2   Encapsulation Genetic Programming

2.1   Terminal and Functional Set

The representation used in our work is a tree-like one as suggested by Koza [7]. The function set for circuits with more than one output is {*AND, OR, NOT, XOR*}. For practical reasons, the functions are internally represented with numbers as indicated in Table 1. Boolean algebra notation (see third column in Table 1) is instead used to compare the results found by EGP with those produced with others techniques. In this notation the absence of a symbol between two terminals indicates the presence of an *AND*. Also, we use the relations A *NOR* B = *NOT*(A *OR* B) and A *NAND* B = *NOT*(A *AND* B) to represent NOR and NAND, respectively.

The terminal set consists of the inputs of the circuit. These are defined with the letters {*a,b,c,...*}. The terminal set includes also a special *encapsulation terminal, p*, which will be explained later. We use the *"Grow"* initialisation method, which allows the selection of nodes from the whole primitive set until the depth limit is reached.

Once we have defined the terminal and functional sets, we proceed to generate the individuals in the population. For this we have used the *postfix* representation. We chose this representation because it is easy for the computer to execute, using a stack-based interpreter (see Section 2.2).

2.2   Interpreter of Genomes

To evaluate each individual, it is necessary to use an expressions' evaluator (interpreter of genomes). Ours is based on a stack, and works in the following way. It reads characters from left to right. If the character read is a terminal, then its corresponding value is stored in a stack. If the character read is a function (see Table 1), then the values for its arguments will be taken from the stack for evaluation and the result of this evaluation will be stored on the top of the stack (see Figure 1). This procedure is repeated until the end of the expression is reached.

Table 1. Function set (first column). The second column reports the character used in our implementation, while the third shows the corresponding Boolean algebra notation.

Boolean Operators	Representation	Symbol
NOT	1	'
OR	2	+
NOR	3	(see text)
AND	4	(see text)
NAND	5	(see text)
XOR	6	⊕

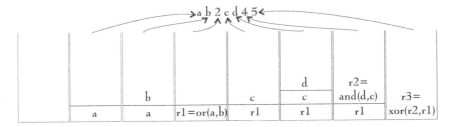

Fig. 1. Contents of the stack at different stages of the interpretation of the program ab2cd45.

2.3   Encapsulation Terminal

The method proposed in this paper does not only allow reusing code but it also allows evolving graph-like structures, which could encode, for example, combinational logic circuits. This is the result of using the p terminal symbol, which works as follows:

- Once the individuals in the population have been generated, every individual is checked to see if it contains p's at the genotype level. If an individual contains this symbol, we assign one point within the individual to which this p refers.
- If the p symbol points to a function symbol, the p symbol effectively represents the sub-tree rooted at that function.
- If the p symbol points to a terminal symbol, the p symbol simply represents that node.

2.4   Genetic Operators

The genetic operators used in EGP are: tournament selection, crossover, mutation and elitism.

The crossover operator works as usual: 1) two individuals are selected from the population; 2) we randomly select a crossover point in each parent; 3) we swap the sub-trees rooted at the crossover points. An important difference is that, if the sub-tree swapped contained a p symbol, the p symbol's pointer is *not* changed (Figure 2 illustrates this behaviour).[1] This means that, as a result of crossing over, the code represented by p's *may* be in individuals different from the one containing the p symbols. Figure 3 shows the typical pattern of reuse resulting from repeated applications of crossover.

The mutation operator works as follows: 1) an individual is selected in the population; 2) a random node is selected; 3) the node is replaced with a different random primitive, taken from the primitive set. In our algorithm, if the node

---

[1] There is an exception to this rule: we prevent a p symbol from referring to a sub-tree that contains the same p since this would lead to an infinite loop. We do this by reassigning the positions to which the p in question is pointing to.

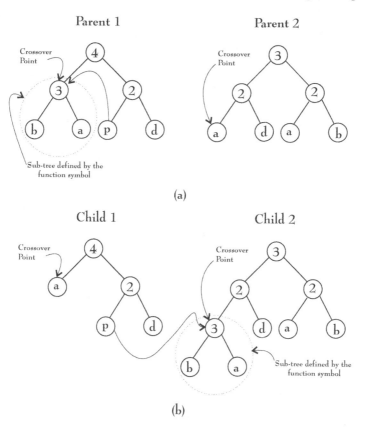

(a)

(b)

Fig. 2. Two parent trees *before* applying the crossover operator (a) and the children obtained *after* applying the crossover operator (b).

selected contains a reference point from a p symbol, then we replace first this p with the sub-tree it points to and then, we apply the mutation operator.

Elitism is in charge of guaranteeing that the best individual in the current generation passes intact to the following generation.

2.5   Fitness Function

The fitness function that we used for circuit design works in two stages: at the beginning of the search, the fitness of a genotype is the number of correct output bits (raw fitness). Once the fitness has reached the maximum number of correct outputs bits, we try to optimize the circuits by giving a higher fitness to individuals with shorter encodings.

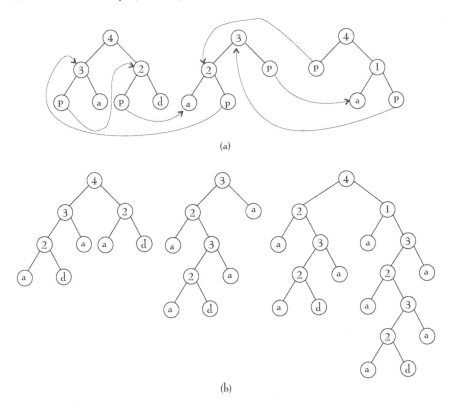

Fig. 3. Example of typical pattern of code reuse in EGP. After a few generations individuals contain numerous p symbols pointing at each other's code (a). The corresponding, logically-equivalent population shows a high degree of similarity between individuals (b).

3   Experimental Results

We used several evolvable hardware problems of different complexity taken from the literature to test EGP. Our results were compared with those obtained by human designers, by NGA [4], by PSO [5] and by CGP [13].

After a series of preliminary experiments we decided to use a crossover rate of 70% and a mutation rate of 30%. In all runs we kept the best individual of each generation (elitism). For all the examples, the we performed 20 independent runs.

3.1   Two-Bit Adder

Our first example is a two-bit adder with 4 inputs and 3 outputs.

The parameters used in this example are the following: population size = 560, maximum number of generations = 700.

Table 2. Comparison of results between an NGA, Karnaugh Maps plus Boolean algebra, the PSO algorithm and EGP on the two-bit adder problem.

NGA	PSO
$F_1 = B \oplus D$	$F_1 = B \oplus D$
$F_2 = (A \oplus C) \oplus BD$	$F_2 = (BD) \oplus (A \oplus C)$
$F_3 = AC + BD(A \oplus C)$	$F_3 = (AC) + ((BD)(A \oplus C))$
7 gates	7 gates
2 ANDs, 1 OR, 4 XORs	3 XORs, 3 ANDs, 1 OR
Karnaugh Maps plus Boolean algebra	**EGP**
$F_1 = A \oplus D$	$F_1 = AC + ((BC)(A \oplus C))$
$F_2 = (A \oplus C)D' + ((A \oplus C) \oplus B)D$	$F_2 = (BC) \oplus (A \oplus C)$
$F_3 = AC + BD(A + C)$	$F_3 = B \oplus D$
12 gates	7 gates
5 ANDs, 3 ORs, 3 XORs, 1 NOT	3 ANDs, 3 XORs, 1 OR

All the runs found the feasible region[2]. That is in all runs the program could solve the problem. The best result found in this example contained 7 gates (3 ANDs, 3 XORs, 1 OR), and 10% of the runs found circuits with this number of gates.

The results produced by EGP in this example were competitive w.r.t. those produced using Karnaugh Maps, *NGA* and PSO (see Table 2).

3.2 Two-Bit Multiplier

Our second example is a two-bit multiplier with 4 inputs and 4 outputs.

The parameters used in this example are the following: population size = 450, maximum number of generations = 500.

Again, we obtained interesting results. All the runs performed were able to reach the feasible region. The best result found in this example contained 7 gates (5 ANDs, 2 XORs) and 15% of the runs found circuits with this number of gates.

The results produced by EGP in this example were compared against those produced using Karnaugh Maps plus Boolean algebra, the NGA and CGP (see Table 3).

3.3 Katz

Our third example is the Katz circuit with 4 inputs and 3 outputs.

The parameters used in this example are the following: population size = 880, maximum number of generations = 4,000.

In 30% of the runs EGP found the feasible zone. The best result found in this example contained 19 gates (4 AND, 7 XORs, 4 ORs, 4 NOTs) and 5% of the runs found circuits with this number of gates.

---

[2] The feasible region is the area of the search space containing circuits that match all the outputs of the problem's truth table.

Table 3. Comparison of results between the NGA, Karnaugh Maps plus Boolean algebra, CGP and EGP on the two-bit multiplier problem.

NGA	CGP
$F_1 = (BD)(AC)$	$F_1 = (AD)(BC)$
$F_2 = AC \oplus ((BD)(AC))$	$F_2 = ((AD)(BC)) \oplus AB$
$F_3 = BC \oplus AD$	$F_3 = AD \oplus BC$
$F_4 = BD$	$F_4 = CD$
7 gates	7 gates
5 ANDs, 2 XORs	5 ANDs , 2 XORs
Karnaugh Maps plus Boolean algebra	**EGP**
$F_1 = (AB)(CD)$	$F_1 = (AD)(BC)$
$F_2 = AC(BD)'$	$F_2 = ((AD)(BC) \oplus A)C$
$F_3 = BC \oplus AD$	$F_3 = AD \oplus BC$
$F_4 = BD$	$F_4 = BD$
8 gates	7 gates
6 ANDs, 1 XOR, 1 NOT	5 ANDs, 2 XORs

Table 4. Comparison of results between Karnaugh Maps plus Boolean algebra, Quine-McCluskey Procedure and EGP on the Katz problem.

Karnaugh Maps plus Boolean algebra
$F_1 = (A\oplus)'(B \oplus D)'$
$F_2 = B'D(A' + C) + A'C$
$F_3 = BD'(A + C') + AC'$
19 gates
2 XORs, 4 ORs, 7 ANDs, 6 NOTs
Quine-McCluskey Procedure
$F_1 = (A \oplus C)'(B \oplus D)'$
$F_2 = A'C + (A \oplus C)'(B'D)$
$F_3 = (F_1 + F_2)'$
13 gates
2 XORs, 2 ORs, 4 ANDs, 5 NOTs
EGP
$F_1 = (A \oplus C')(B \oplus D')$
$F_2 = (C + (D' + D)')(((C \oplus D) + B)A)'$
$F_3 = (((DB \oplus A) \oplus B) + (C \oplus A)) \oplus C$
19 gates
4 ANDs, 7 XORs, 4 ORs, 4 NOTs

The results produced by our system in this example were compared against those produced using Karnaugh Maps plus Boolean algebra and Quine-McCluskey Procedure (see Table 4).

4   Discussion

On the test problems reported above, our algorithm has shown very competitive results with respect to other approaches that employ other types of evolutionary algorithms. Although results are not improved with respect to those previously reported, our approach consistently reaches the feasible region (which does not always happens with other methods). We believe the good performance of EGP is largely due to its ability to reuse code (as indicated by the large number of p's used in all the solutions found). In tests with larger (and more difficult) circuits, the algorithm has shown promise, but more tests are needed in order to allow a fair assessment of its performance.

5   Conclusions and Future Work

We have presented EGP, a new genetic programming approach to evolve programs with a high degree of code reuse. The approach has been validated using test functions taken from the evolvable hardware literature. Comparison between EGP and other heuristics has shown that our approach can consistently reach the feasible region of the three test problems used while converging to the best-known solutions for two of them.

In our future work we plan to extend our algorithm in several ways. The ideas behind our algorithm are general and, thus, EGP can be adopted in other application domains in which code reuse (and/or graph-like representations) may be beneficial. Also, we are interested in extending EGP by adding self-adaptation mechanisms that would make preliminary runs and parameter tuning unnecessary. We would also like to in incorporate multi-objective optimization concepts to improve the search capabilities of EGP.

Acknowledgements. The first author thanks the Mexican Consejo Nacional de Ciencia y Tecnología (CONACyT) for support to pursue graduate studies at University of Essex. The third author also acknowledges support from CONA-CyT (project No. 34201-A). Finally, the Essex authors would like to thank the members of the NEC (Natural and Evolutionary Computation) group for helpful comments and discussion.

References

1. P. J. Angeline. Multiple Interacting Programs: A Representation for Evolving Complex Behaviors. *Cybernetics and Systems*, 29(8):779–806, November. 1998.
2. W. Banzhaf, P. Nordin, R. E. Keller, and F. D. Francone. *Genetic Programming An Introduction*. Morgan Kaufmann Publishiers, Inc, San Francisco, CA, 1998.
3. R. K. Brayton, G. D. Hachtel, C. T. McMullen, and A. L. Sangiovanni-Vincentelli. *Logic Minimization Algorithms for VLSI Synthesis*. Kluwer Academic Publishers, 1984.

4. C. A. C. Coello, A. D. Christiansen, and A. H. Aguirre. Use of Evolutionary Techniques to Automate the Design of Combinational Circuits. *International Journal of Smart Engineering System Design*, 2(4):229–314, June. 2000.

5. C. A. C. Coello, E. H. Luna, and A. H. Aguirre. Use of particle swarm optimization to design combinational logic circuits. In *Evolvable Systems: From Biology to Hardware. 5th International Conference, ICES 2003*, volume 2606, pages 398–409, Trondheim, Norway, March. 2003. Springer, Lecture Notes in Computer Science.

6. M. Karnaugh. A map method for synthesis of combinational logic circuits. *Transactions of the AIEE, Communications and Electronics*, 72(I):593–599, November. 1953.

7. J. R. Koza. *Genetic Programming: On the Programming of Computers by Means of Natural Selection*. The MIT Press, Cambridge, Massachusetts, 1992.

8. J. R. Koza. *Genetic Programming II: Automatic Discovery of Reusable Programs*. The MIT Press, Cambridge, Massachusetts, 1994.

9. J. R. Koza, F. H. Bennet, D. Andre, and M. A. Keane. *Genetic Programming III: Darwinian Invention and Problem Solving*. Morgan Kauffman Publishiers, Inc, 1999.

10. W. B. Langdon and R. Poli. *Foundations of Genetic Programming*. Springer, 2002.

11. S. J. Louis. *Genetic Algorithms as a Computational Tool for Design*. PhD thesis, Department of Computer Science, Indiana University, 1993.

12. S. J. Louis and G. J. Rawlins. Designer Genetic Algorithms: Genetic Algorithms in Structure Design. In *Proceedings of the 4th International Conference on Genetic Algorithms*, pages 53–60, San Diego California, . 1991. Morgan Kaufmann Publishiers, Inc.

13. J. F. Miller, D. Job, and V. K. Vassilev. Principles in the Evolutionary Design of Digital Circuits - Part I. *Journal of Genetic Programming and Evolvable Machines*, 1(1):8–35, . 2000.

14. R. Poli. Some Steps Towards a Form of Parallel Distributed Genetic Programming. In *Proceedings of the 1st Online Workshop on Soft Computing*, pages 290–295, Nagoya, August. 1996.

15. R. Poli. Discovery of Symbolic, Neuro-Symbolic and Neural Networks with Parallel Distributed Genetic Programming. In *Procedures of 3rd. International Conference on Artificial Neural Networks and Genetic Algorithms, ICANNGA 1997*, pages 419–423, Norwich, April. 1997. Springer.

16. R. Poli. Parallel Distributed Genetic Programming. In D. Corne, M. Dorigo, and F. Glover, editors, *New Ideas in Optimization*, pages 403–431, London, 1999. McGraw-Hill.

17. W. V. Quine. A way to simplify truth functions. *American Mathematical Monthly*, 62(9):627–631, November. 1955.

18. C. E. Shannon. Minimization of boolean functions. *Bell Systems Technical Journal*, 35(5):1417–1444., 1956.

19. J. Torresen. A Divide-and-Conquer Approach to Evolvable Hardware. In *2nd International Conference, ICES 1998*, volume 1478, pages 57–65, Lausanne, Switzerland, September. 1998. Springer, Lecture Notes in Computer Science.

20. J. Torresen. Evolvable Hardware - The Coming Hardware Design Method? In *Neuro-fuzzy techniques for Intelligent Information Systems*, pages 435–449. N. Kazabov and R. Kozma (editors), Physica-Verlag (Springer-Verlag), . 1999.

21. E. W. Veitch. A Chart Method for Simplifying Boolean Functions. *Proceedings of the ACM*, pages 127–133, May. 1952.

Exploiting Reflection in Object Oriented Genetic Programming

Simon M. Lucas

Dept. of Computer Science
University of Essex, Colchester CO4 3SQ, UK
sml@essex.ac.uk

Abstract. Most programs currently written by humans are object-oriented ones. Two of the greatest benefits of object oriented programming are the separation of interface from implementation, and the notion that an object may have state. This paper describes a simple system that enables object-oriented programs to be evolved. The system exploits reflection to automatically discover features about the environment (the existing classes and objects) in which it is to operate. This enables us to evolve object-oriented programs for the given problem domain with the minimum of effort. Currently, we are only evolving method implementations. Future work will explore how we can also evolve interfaces and classes, which should be beneficial to the automatic generation of structured solutions to complex problems. We demonstrate the system with the aid of an evolutionary art example.

1 Introduction

The majority of programs currently being developed by programmers are written in object-oriented languages such as Java, C++, C# and Smalltalk. In contrast, the vast majority of evolved programs use an expression tree representation. Evolving program trees was first done by Cramer [1], and later re-discovered and popularised by Koza [2]. Koza went on to introduce automatically defined functions (ADFs) [3], which provide a degree of program modularity, and can significantly improve the performance of the evolutionary algorithm. Teller [4] introduced indexed memory to allow functions to have state (making them, mathematically speaking, not functions any more, unless we consider the memory as an additional argument to the function).

Some applications can get by with functions that operate only on primitive data types, such as general classes of number. Many types of program, however, can be much more elegantly and compactly expressed by using additional data structures, such as arrays, vectors, matrices and various collections (e.g. lists, sets and maps for example). Strongly Typed GP (Montana, [5]) was developed to support this, and restricts the evolved program tree to call functions with arguments of the correct type. This can drastically reduce the size of the search space, while still allowing all sensible solutions to be reachable. Other alternatives to standard tree-based GP include Linear GP [1,6,7], where a program

M. Keijzer et al. (Eds.): EuroGP 2004, LNCS 3003, pp. 369–378, 2004.

is specified as a sequence of instructions, and Cartesian GP [8], where nodes are positioned and connected with some spatial constraints. Also of interest are GraphGP [9], Linear Graph GP [10], and Grammatical Evolution [11], in which trees are generated by a context-free grammar.

Of more direct relevance this paper is the work of Bruce[12,13] on object oriented genetic programming (OOGP), and of Langdon[14] on evolving abstract data types. Langdon and Bruce independently evolved data types such as stacks and queues. Bruce investigated the difficulty of evolving methods that needed to cooperate such that some shared memory would be used in a compatible way. For example, when implementing a stack it is vital that the push and pop methods cooperate properly. Both Bruce and Langdon, however, focused mostly on evolving tree-type expressions to implement particular methods.

The most similar prior work to this paper is Abbott's initial exploration of OOGP [15]. Abbott also uses reflection to make method invocations, and mentions the ability to exploit existing class libraries as an advantage of the approach, though the the parity problem he uses as an example does not demonstrate this, and instead uses specially defined classes and methods to help solve the problem.

Abbott raises doubts regarding whether the evolution of new classes is really feasible. This is clearly a fundamental point, since without the definition of new classes and interfaces, we are only doing a very limited form of object oriented programming. Indeed, much of the difficulty of software design lies in the identification of useful abstractions. The high level design involves identifying appropriate classes and interfaces. When we make a good job of this, implementing the methods is usually relatively straightforward. On the other hand, if we make no attempt at the higher level design, then the method implementations tend to be complex, poorly structured, hard to maintain and offer very little re-use.

While there are many impressive achievements reported in the recent book of Koza et al [16], most of the evolved programs and circuits are relatively small, typically having tens of nodes rather than hundreds or thousands. Making GP scale up to larger systems is still a challenge, and the space in which we search is of fundamental importance.

To quote Koza [2]:

> "if we are interested in getting computers to solve problems without being explicitly programmed, the structures that we really need are COMPUTER PROGRAMS"

Whether we use standard GP or OOGP, we can still theoretically search some space containing all possible computer programs. However, different representations (and their associated operators) structure the space in different ways, and this can have important implications for how evolvable the structures are in that space.

There is also an important practical point. When we evolve a program in standard GP we begin by specifying the set of functions and terminals. How we choose these can be critical to the success of the evolutionary process. It is also a criticism levelled at GP as a general machine learning method: that the choice of function set strongly biases the search. Hence, the user in making this choice has already partially solving the problem, or in the worst case, prevented a good solution from being found.

In practice, when a programmer writes OO software, they typically make extensive use of existing class libraries. This paper investigates a simple but powerful idea: the use of reflection to enable evolutionary algorithms to directly exploit such class libraries.

2   Evolving Object-Oriented Programs

Currently, there seems to be very little work being done on OOGP. At the time of writing, a *Google* search for the phrase "Object Oriented Genetic Programming" returned only 32 pages, compared with 75,900 pages for "Genetic Programming". Of these 32 hits, the majority referred to object oriented implementations of standard tree-based GP.

There are many reasons why we should explore the idea of evolving object-oriented programs:

- To directly exploit the power of existing OO class libraries.
- To better model real-world problems where objects have state.
- To better integrate evolved object classes with an existing project.
- For a certain class of problem, OO programs might be more *evolvable* than expression trees. Object classes (with fields and methods) may provide a more appropriate unit of evolution than function-trees.
- The OO paradigm seems to promote better software re-use than the functional paradigm that standard GP is based on. Evolved OO programs might include classes that can be re-used in other applications.
- The OO paradigm suggests additional genetic operators based on sub-classing existing classes, defining new interfaces.
- Evolution is also possible at the object level, where the state of the objects evolve rather than the program code.

These points surely warrant further study. Well written OO programs can be a joy to read, understand and modify. One interesting aspect of OOGP is whether we can evolve OO software that is similarly well designed. Also of interest here are Object Oriented Software Metrics [17], both in aiding the objective analysis of evolved programs, and perhaps building these metrics into the fitness function used during evolution.

We wish to stimulate interest in this under-explored area. We will show how easy it is to evolve object oriented programs with the aid of the Java Reflection API. Reflection allows a program to discover at run time the class (type) of an object, the methods that can be invoked on objects of a class, whether the methods are class or instance methods, and the fields of an object. For each method we can look up its return type and the types of its parameters.

Using this information it is straightforward to randomly generate a program as a sequence of method invocations on a set of objects. This means that we can write an entirely generic OOGP system that will evolve method implementations to match a specified interface. If this approach fails to converge in practice, owing to the size of the search space, we are still free to then restrict the space by applying prior knowledge of the problem domain by restricting the set of existing methods to be used.

3   Our Reflection-Based OOGP Implementation

Suppose we have written an object-oriented program, but wish to evolve some parts of it. The standard way to approach this using toolkits such as ECJ [18] is to define a set of functions that are appropriate to the problem at hand, and then evolve an expression-tree that uses those functions. For each function it is necessary to write a new Java Class definition that sub-classes GPNode. This involves some straightforward but slightly tedious manual effort for each new class of problem to be addressed.

3.1   The Java Reflection API

An interesting alternative is to use reflection to determine directly the set of possible methods and variables to be used. Manual intervention is still possible, in that we can specify the set of object classes and/or methods to be considered, but it is no longer necessary to write wrapper classes or methods to invoke these.

Reflection in an OO language is where a program is able to discover things about itself at run time, such as the class of an object, the fields associated with it, its superclass, the set of interfaces it implements, its set of constructors, and the set of methods that can be invoked on it. Java has classes called Method for each method defined for a class. By getting a reference to the Method object, we can then invoke the corresponding method. Using reflection we can generate and evolve the objects constructed by a program, and the methods invoked on those objects. In languages such as Smalltalk or certain OO variants of LISP, it is even possible to generate new classes at run-time. In Java, this is not easy to do directly - it involves auto-generating Java source files, compiling them, and then loading the compiled classes. However, we can even define As a minimum, all the user of the system need do is specify which method implementations should be evolved, the set of objects to invoke methods on, and the set of objects to use as arguments. Then, to evolve each method implementation, the user also specifies which objects should be used to select the possible

3.2   Evolving Method Implementations

Given a method signature (i.e. its return type and list of parameter types), we wish evolve the code that implements the method.

We consider a method implementation to be a sequence of *Instructions*. Each Instruction consists of a Method reference (the Method to be invoked), an Object reference (the Object to invoke it on), and an array of Objects - which are the arguments to the method. The Object reference is ignored if the method is static (i.e. a class method and not an instance method). The array of arguments may be either null or zero length if the method to be invoked takes no parameters.

To avoid confusion with existing Java Reflection classes, such as `Method` we call our implementation of a method a `Program`. Our implementation of `Program` allows the random generation of programs if a specified size n, simply by making n calls top the Instruction Generator. The use of a sequence is reminiscent of Linear GP. We allow programs to be mutated by adding a new randomly generated instruction or deleting an existing one - in the prototype, these events are equally likely.

3.3   Random Instruction Generation

To assist in generating programs we implemented a class called `Instruction Generator`. This takes two arguments: a set of active objects that we wish to allow methods to be invoked on, and a set of argument objects: objects that we wish to select the set of arguments from.

We use reflection to get the set of methods callable on each object. In Java there are two alternative ways of doing this, with the reflection methods called `getDeclaredMethods()` and `getMethods()`. The former gets all the methods declared in this class i.e. public, protected and private ones, but not any inherited methods. The latter gets all the inherited public methods. Actually, in Java Reflection, the private and protected modifiers only express preferences, and can be overridden. Hence, it is possible to discover the set of all methods that can be called on an object by calling `getDeclaredMethods()` first on the class of that object, then the superclass of the object and so on until we reach Object, the root of Java's Object hierarchy.

Using this we build up two look-up tables called methodLut and typedArgs, both of type HashMap from Java's Collections API. The purpose of methodLut is to provide direct access to the set of callable methods for each active Object - hence methodLut is keyed on the active object, and each entry in methodLut is a collection of methods. To be considered callable, each of the method's parameters must have an object of an appropriate type in the argument set. In order to aid this check, we organise the set of argument objects into the typedArgs HashMap. The key for typedArgs is the type of parameter (i.e. an instance of Class), while each entry in the map is a set of objects of that type. Each object may have many entries in the type map, one for each parameter type that it can be passed as. In other words, an Object is entered in the map for its own Class and for all its super-classes, and for all the interfaces implemented by all those classes.

There is a slight problem with the above description: we use the set of active objects and the set of argument objects to construct the set of instructions, where each instruction is a method to be invoked on a particular object using a particular set of objects as arguments. What we also need is to be able to run the same program (sequence of instructions), but using different objects as arguments, and different objects to invoke them on. For example, if we are evolving a program to draw a picture, then each new version of the program may need to draw the picture on a different Graphics Object. There are several possible solutions that allow this, such as storing the actors and arguments sets in an array, and then having the instruction storing the index of the actor or argument. Then, by changing the object stored at that index, we can achieve the desired effect.

The solution we preferred, however, is to define an `ObjectHolder` class, which has two fields: `Class objectClass`, and `Object objectValue`. This structure provides local fine-grain control of the object classes and values.

3.4   Primitive Arguments

Methods that take primitive arguments (such as `int` or `double` have to be handled specially, since Java draws a distinction between Objects and Primitives. This distinction is made for the sake of efficiency, but means that we have to write extra code to deal with this. When invoking a Method using reflection, the set of arguments to the method is passed to an array of Object (i.e. of type `Object[]`). However, it is not possible to place primitives in such an array - instead we must fill the array with Object-based wrappers (such as Integer and Double). The reflection API will then automatically extract the underlying primitive values from these Objects, which in Java are immutable. Worse still, for our purposes here, the Integer class is declared final from our point of view, which precludes the possibility of defining our own sub-class of the wrapper class i.e. the Java language does not permit a class definition of the form `MyInteger extends Integer`.

3.5   Timing Results

In order to judge the overheads involved in running this form of GP, we studied the cost of computing the sum of squares of the set of integers from zero to $n-1$. Each integer in the range is first cast to a double before being being multiplied by itself. This showed that using reflection for a method invocation can be over 100 times slower than making a direct method call. Whether this is an issue depends on the complexity of the method being called, but it is a potential problem with our approach.

4   Example Application: Evolutionary Art

Here we choose an application where we already have a number of useful classes defined for the problem domain. The objective is to provide an implementation of an evolvable picture, for use in an evolutionary art application. We've decoupled the picture evolution and drawing from the rest of the program (that deals with the GUI, for example) by defining an interface for an Evolvable Picture. This is shown in Figure 1. This takes just two method - one for producing a mutated child, and the other for drawing itself on a Java Graphics Object.

```
public interface EvolvablePicture {
    // gets a randomly varied child
    public EvolvablePicture getChild();

    // draw on the graphics object
    public void draw(Graphics g, Dimension d);
}
```

Fig. 1. The interface for an Evolvable Picture

```
public class EvolvableObjectPainter implements EvolvablePicture {
    Program p;
    ObjectHolder graphics;
    static int len = 20; // the starting length for progs

    public EvolvableObjectPainter() {
        ArrayList active = new ArrayList();
        graphics = new ObjectHolder( Graphics2D.class );
        active.add( graphics );
        ArrayList args = new ArrayList();
        // ... add some numbers to args...
        args.add( new Integer(1) );
        // .. lines omitted

        InstructionGenerator gen =
            new InstructionGenerator(active, args);
        p = new Program( gen, len, null );
    }
        // ... two-arg constructor used below omitted
    public EvolvablePicture getChild() {
        System.out.println("Chose: " + p);
        return new EvolvableObjectPainter(p.mutatedCopy(), graphics);
    }

    public void draw(Graphics g, Dimension d) {
        graphics.setObject( g );
        p.execute();
    }
}
```

Fig. 2. OOGP Implementation of the Evolvable Picture interface

Figure 2 shows most of our implementation of the Evolvable Picture interface that exploits our OOGP system. There are a few points to note. We use an ObjectHolder to hold a reference to the current graphics object, and also to specify the type (class) of object that it will hold. Then, each call to draw updates the object to be the current Graphics object.

The implementation of the getChild method is very simple - and mainly involves calling the two-argument constructor with a mutated version of the

```
java.awt.Graphics.fillArc(int,int,int,int,int,int) :
  : 100 : 10 : 100 : 1 : 100 : 100
java.awt.Graphics.fillArc(int,int,int,int,int,int) :
  : 100 : 100 : 100 : 10 : 10 : 100
java.awt.Graphics.drawRect(int,int,int,int) :
  : 100 : 100 : 100 : 25
java.awt.Graphics.setColor(java.awt.Color) :
  : java.awt.Color[r=64,g=93,b=251]
java.awt.Graphics.drawOval(int,int,int,int) :
  : 100 : 25 : 1 : 25
java.awt.Graphics2D.translate(double,double) :
  : -0.2617993877991494 : 0.5235987755982988
  ...
```

Fig. 3. Sample evolved picture program

program. The other main part of our `EvolvableObjectPainter` is the default
constructor. Here we simply set up the `ArrayLists` of active objects and of
argument objects. For the argument objects, we put a handful of Double and
Integer numbers in there - we've omitted these for space reasons.

Our evolvable art GUI allows picture evolution by having the user click his
preferred image to breed from by mutation at each generation. Using this with
the `EvolvableObjectPainter` implementation described above successfully exploited the Java Graphics API, and Figure 4 shows the twelve pictures displayed
on generation 30 of one of the runs.

Note that the type-safe Instruction Generation described above is very important in cutting the size of the search space. For example, given a Graphics2D
object, there are 92 public methods that can be called, many of which take
several arguments. Given our set of constants (about 10) that we set up in the
constructor, this would lead to a huge set of possible `Instructions`, many of
which would lead to invocation exceptions without proper type checking in advance. A fragment of an evolved program is shown in Figure 3. Note that all the
method calls shown were generated automatically using reflection.

5   Conclusions

The set of class libraries or APIs that are associated with a language such as Java,
both those supplied as part of the language platform, and additions provided by
third parties, are the end result of a long software design process. Together, they
are based on hundreds of expert man years of effort, and provide a vast source of
knowledge useful in the construction of real-world problems. They distill much of
what the computer science community knows about writing software for practical
applications.

The main contribution of this paper has been to demonstrate how it is possible to tap into this knowledge source, and evolve interesting programs that are
able to exploit these class libraries given only the smallest and most easily pro-

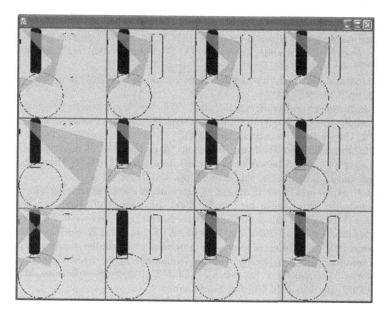

Fig. 4. Running the Evolvable Picture application. All the drawing methods used were picked out by the evolutionary algorithm with the aid of reflection on a Java Graphics2D object.

vided of clues, such as a method signature and a set of objects to use as actors and parameters. There is a huge potential for future exploitation.

An important challenge is to evolve programs that are not only simple and efficient, but perhaps well designed in terms of developing and deploying re-usable class libraries. What sort of environment do we need in order for something like the Java *Collections* API to evolve?

Acknowledgements. The author(s) would like to thank the members of the X group at the University of Y for useful discussions of this work.

References

1. Nichael Lynn , "A representation for the adaptive generation of simple sequential programs", in *Proceedings of an International Conference on Genetic Algorithms and the Applications*, John J. Grefenstette, Ed., Carnegie-Mellon University, Pittsburgh, PA, USA, 24-26 July 1985, pp. 183–187.
2. J.R. Koza, *Genetic Programming: on the programming of computers by means of natural selection*, MIT Press, Cambridge, MA, (1992).
3. J.R. Koza, *Genetic ProgrammingII: automatic discovery of reusable programs*, MIT Press, Cambridge, MA, (1994).

4. Astro Teller, "Turing completeness in the language of genetic programming with indexed memory", in *Proceedings of the 1994 IEEE World Congress on Computational Intelligence*, Orlando, Florida, USA, 27-29 June 1994, vol. 1, pp. 136–141, IEEE Press.

5. D.J. Montana, "Strongly typed genetic programming", *Evolutionary Computation*, vol. 3, pp. 199–230, (1995).

6. Markus Brameier and Wolfgang Banzhaf, "Effective linear genetic programming", Interner Bericht des Sonderforschungsbereichs 531 *Computational Intelligence* CI–108/01, Universität Dortmund, April 2001.

7. Markus Brameier and Wolfgang Banzhaf, "A comparison of linear genetic programming and neural networks in medical data mining", *IEEE Transactions on Evolutionary Computation*, vol. 5, no. 1, pp. 17–26, 2001.

8. Julian F. Miller and Peter Thomson, "Cartesian genetic programming", in *Genetic Programming, Proceedings of EuroGP'2000*, Riccardo Poli, Wolfgang Banzhaf, William B. Langdon, Julian F. Miller, Peter Nordin, and Terence C. Fogarty, Eds., Edinburgh, 15-16 April 2000, vol. 1802 of *LNCS*, pp. 121–132, Springer-Verlag.

9. Riccardo Poli, "Evolution of graph-like programs with parallel distributed genetic programming", in *Genetic Algorithms: Proceedings of the Seventh International Conference*, Thomas Back, Ed., Michigan State University, East Lansing, MI, USA, 19-23 1997, pp. 346–353, Morgan Kaufmann.

10. Wolfgang Kantschik and Wolfgang Banzhaf, "Linear-graph GP – A new GP structure", in *Proceedings of the 4th European Conference on Genetic Programming, EuroGP 2002*, Evelyne Lutton, James A. Foster, Julian Miller, Conor Ryan, and Andrea G. B. Tettamanzi, Eds., Kinsale, Ireland, 3-5 2002, vol. 2278, pp. 83–92, Springer-Verlag.

11. M O'Neill and C Ryan, "Grammatical evolution", *IEEE Transactions on Evolutionary Computation*, vol. 5, pp. 349–358, (2001).

12. Wilker Shane Bruce, *The Application of Genetic Programming to the Automatic Generation of Object-Oriented Programs*, PhD thesis, School of Computer and Information Sciences, Nova Southeastern University, 3100 SW 9th Avenue, Fort Lauderdale, Florida 33315, USA, December 1995.

13. Wilker Shane Bruce, "Automatic generation of object-oriented programs using genetic programming", in *Genetic Programming 1996: Proceedings of the First Annual Conference*, John R. Koza, David E. Goldberg, David B. Fogel, and Rick L. Riolo, Eds., Stanford University, CA, USA, 1996, pp. 267–272, MIT Press.

14. William B. Langdon, "Evolving data structures with genetic programming", in *Proc. of the Sixth Int. Conf. on Genetic Algorithms*, Larry J. Eshelman, Ed., San Francisco, CA, 1995, pp. 295–302, Morgan Kaufmann.

15. Russ Abbott, "Object-oriented genetic programming: An initial implementation", in *International Conference on Machine Learning: Models, Technologies and Applications*, 2003, pp. 24–27.

16. John R. Koza, *Genetic Programming IV: Routine Human-Competitive Machine Intelligence*, Kluwer Academic Publishers, 2003.

17. M. Lorenz and J. Kidd, *Object-Oriented Software Metrics*, Prentice Hall, 1994.

18. Sean Luke, "A Java-based Evolutionary Computation and Genetic Programming Research System", http://www.cs.umd.edu/projects/plus/ec/ecj/.

Evolutionary Feature Construction Using Information Gain and Gini Index

Mohammed A. Muharram and George D. Smith

School of Computing Sciences
UEA Norwich, Norwich, England
m.muharram@uea.ac.uk, gds@cmp.uea.ac.uk

Abstract. Feature construction using genetic programming is carried out to study the effect on the performance of a range of classification algorithms with the inclusion of the evolved attributes. Two different fitness functions are used in the genetic program, one based on information gain and the other based on the gini index. The classification algorithms used are three classification tree algorithms, namely C5, CART, CHAID and an MLP neural network. The intention of the research is to ascertain if the decision tree classification algorithms benefit more using features constructed using a genetic programme whose fitness function incorporates the same fundamental learning mechanism as the splitting criteria of the associated decision tree.

1 Introduction

The research presented in this paper addresses the question of whether or not a decision tree algorithm benefits more than another classifier, with the inclusion of an attribute evolved using a genetic program (GP) whose fitness function is based on the splitting criterion of the decision tree. Previously, [9] evolved attributes using a GP and compared the classification performance of C4.5 using the original attributes with that of C4.5 using the augmented attribute set which included a new evolved attribute. Their results were mixed, with some data sets showing an improvement in classification accuracy using the augmented attribute set, whilst others showed no significant difference. It is notable that the fitness function used by the GP in [9] was based on *Information Gain Ratio*, the splitting criterion used in C4.5.

This work was further explored by [7] who argued that using a GP whose fitness function is the same as the decision tree splitting criterion might introduce some bias in the results. They also used a GP with fitness function based on *Information Gain*, but, in addition to using C5 to perform the classification, they used two other decision tree algorithms, namely CHAID/XAID [2] and CART [3], as well as a multi-layer perceptron neural net (MLP). Their results show that, in general, all classification algorithms can benefit from the inclusion of an evolved attribute but it is by no means guaranteed. The performance of C5 was certainly improved more than the other classifiers on 2 of the 5 data sets used, in one case attaining 100% accuracy on both training and test sets

M. Keijzer et al. (Eds.): EuroGP 2004, LNCS 3003, pp. 379–388, 2004.

for all 10 fold samples, but this gain was not consistent over all the data sets considered.

The research presented in this paper extends this work by using a GP whose fitness function is based on either *Information Gain* (IG), as before, or the *Gini Index* (GI), the splitting criterion used in CART [3]. This allows us to test the dependence of the potential improvement of the classifier on the actual fitness function used.

The remainder of the paper is structured as follows: Section 2 presents a brief review of attribute construction and the use of GP to evolve features, or attributes. Section 3 describes the experimental methodology, the details of the data sets used and the parameters and settings used in the GP. The results are presented in Section 4 and a summary in Section 5.

2   Attribute Construction

When constructing classification models from data sets, the data is normally presented as a fixed number of features, or *attributes*, one of which is the discrete valued, dependent variable, or *class*. The purpose of classification is to find a description of the class variable based on some or all of the other predicting variables. The representation of this description varies depending on the particular induction technique used, and includes decision trees, rules, artificial neural networks, Bayesian classifiers, and many others, see [12].

The success of any classification algorithm depends on its ability to represent any inherent pattern in the data set, and hence depends on the set of predictive attributes available, or its attribute vector. If the set of available attributes does not include one or more powerfully predictive attributes, this will limit the performance of classification algorithms that are unable to "combine" these attributes in any way. Techniques such as tree induction typically assess the predictive ability of attributes on a one-by-one basis. At each internal node of the tree, each attribute is analysed in turn to measure its predictive power in terms of the class output. Any *combination* of predicting attributes which presents a much stronger prediction may therefore be missed, if the operators available to the induction process are insufficient to identify that combination.

One approach to overcome this problem is to allow the induction process the flexibility to identify and 'construct' these powerfully predictive combinations. For instance, in [11],where the authors use a feed forward neural network to extract knowledge from corporate accounting reports, the first hidden layer of nodes were inclined to construct ratios of the raw data. It is widely recognised that accounting ratios, rather than the basic accounting data, are more useful in terms of what can be deduced about a company's financial status. Turning to decision trees, OC1 is an oblique tree induction technique designed for use with continuous real-valued attributes. During the induction stage, OC1 considers linear combinations of attributes, and partitions the data set into both oblique and axis-parallel hyperplanes, [8].

Another approach is to construct new attributes which are combinations of the original attributes, the objective of the construction technique being to identify highly predictive combinations of the original attribute set and hence, by including such combinations as new features (attributes), to improve the predictive power of the attribute vector, see [6]. In this paper, we restrict our attention to the use of *genetic programming* [5] to evolve new attributes.

There are essentially two approaches to constructing attributes in relation to data mining; one method is as a separate, independent pre-processing stage, in which the new attributes are constructed before the classification algorithm is applied to build the model [6,1]. The second approach is an integration of construction and induction, in which new attributes are constructed within the induction process. The latter is therefore a hybrid induction algorithm, often referred to as *interleaving* [13].

In a recent study [9], Otero et al. use genetic programming as a pre-processing, attribute construction technique. For each data set used, and for each trial in a 10xCV (cross validation) test, a single new attribute was evolved using a GP with *Information Gain Ratio* as the fitness function of the GP. Classification using C4.5 was applied to the data set, both with and without the new attribute and the results showed a significant improvement in the performance of C4.5 with the use of the newly evolved attribute in 2 of the 4 data sets used. However, in this study, it is notable that the objective function of the feature construction GP and the subsequent classification algorithm, C4.5, both use *Information Gain Ratio*. Would a different classification algorithm benefit as much?

Muharram and Smith [7] address this question by using a GP, with *Information Gain* as the fitness, to construct a new attribute, and by analysing the improvement in performance of four different classifiers, including C5, when this new attribute was included in the attribute vector. In one of the five data sets (Abalone), they found no significant difference in classification accuracy with the inclusion of the newly evolved attribute for any of the classification techniques. In 3 data sets used, the performance of all algorithms improved and only for one data set (Wine) was C5 the only algorithm to improve on the accuracy whilst all others suffered a deterioration in performance.

The research presented in this paper follows on from the work of [9] and [7] by adopting two different fitness functions in the attribute construction GP, one based on *Information Gain*, as before, the other based on the *Gini Index*, the splitting criterion used in CART, see [3].

3   Experimental Details

3.1   Data Sets

In this paper, we are primarily addressing the performance of a decision tree classifier when a new, potentially more powerfully predictive attribute is introduced. A decision tree is typically constructed using a greedy, iterative process, wherein, during the induction stage, each internal decision node is associated with a test on one of the predicting attributes, the particular test being chosen to optimise a measure relating to the splitting criterion. Successors of the internal nodes are formed and the process is repeated at each successor node. In C4.5, for instance, the splitting criterion is the *Information Gain Ratio*, see [10], whilst in CART (Classification and Regression Trees), the splitting criterion is the Gini index [3].

The experiments are performed on 5 data sets, all from the UCI data repository[1]. Table 1 shows the number of cases, classes and attributes for each data set. Note that our GP considers all attributes to be real-valued variables. Thus the single Boolean attribute in the Abalone data set is considered as real-valued for the purposes of this study.

Table 1. Data Sets used in experimental work.

Data Set	Cases	Classes	Attributes
Abalone	4177	28	8
Balance-scale	625	3	4
BUPA Liver Disorder	345	2	6
Waveform	300	3	21
Wine	178	3	13

3.2   Methodology

The main aim of this work is to ascertain if classification using a decision tree is biased in any way by the inclusion of a constructed attribute which has been evolved by a GP whose fitness function is based on the splitting criteria of the decision tree. For the fitness function of the GP therefore, we use one of two measures, namely *Information Gain* (GI) (the basis of the splitting criterion used in C5) and the *Gini Index* (GI).

The attribute construction stage is a pre-processing stage prior to the classification stage. For the classification, we use four algorithms as in [7]:

1. C5, a descendant of C4.5, a decision tree algorithm whose splitting criterion is based on *Information Gain Ratio*, see [10];
2. CART, a decision tree algorithm whose splitting criterion is based on the *Gini Index*, see [3];
3. CHAID, a decision tree algorithm whose splitting criterion is based on achieving a threshold level of significance in a chi-squared test, see [4].
4. MLP ANN.

For each data set we use 10-fold cross validation (CV) to compute the error rate. Thus the data set is firstly partitioned into 10 subsets. For each trial, 9 of the 10 subsets are used as the training set whilst the remaining set is used as the test set.

---

[1] www.ics.uci.edu/~mlearn/MLRepository.html

The methodology is as follows: For each data set and for each 10-fold trial:

Original. Apply each classification algorithm to the training set (original attributes only) and evaluate resulting models on test set.

Augmented-IG. Evolve a single, new attribute from the training set using GP with IG as the fitness function; apply each classification algorithm on augmented training set (original attribute set plus IG-evolved attribute). Evaluate resulting model on the test set.

Augmented-GI. Evolve a single, new attribute from the training set using GP with GI as the fitness function; apply each classification algorithm on augmented training set (original attribute set plus GI-evolved attribute). Evaluate resulting model on the test set.

For both the classification using original attributes and those using the augmented sets, we then determine the average error rate over the 10 trials for each algorithm and for each data set. These are referred to respectively as *Original*, *Augmented-IG* and *Augmented-GI* in the results tables in the following section.

Note that, like [9] and [7], the attribute construction is a pre-processing technique. Thus, in this current work, for each data set and for each classification technique, the GP was run 20 times and the classification technique 30 times. Note also that, for each trial, a different attribute may be evolved by the GP, even when the same fitness function is used.

3.3   The GP

The GP is designed to construct real-valued attributes from the original (assumed) real-valued attributes of the data set. Thus the terminal set consists of all the original attributes plus the constant "1", whilst the function set consists of the arithmetic operators +,-,*,/.

The initial population is created using a ramped half-and-half method, and the size is fixed at 600. The GP was run for 100 iterations.

The selection method used is tournament, with a tournament size of 7. Mutation and crossover are fairly standard, with mutation replacing nodes with like nodes, and crossover swapping subtrees. Mutation rate is 50%, whilst crossover rate is 70%. The fitness of an evolved attribute is measured as it would be at a branch node of the decision tree, whether IG or the GI is used.

Finally, Otero et al. [9] showed that limiting the size of the tree, and hence the complexity of the constructed attribute, made little difference to the results. Muharram and Smith [7] also limit the size of the constructed trees, choosing an upper limit of 40 nodes. For the experiments reported in the following section, no such upper limit was adopted.

4   Results

4.1   Error Rates

In Tables 2 to 5, we present the error rates (for the test sets) averaged over the 10xCV trials. In each table, the second column shows the error rate achieved by the induction technique using the original attribute set. The figure after the ± is the standard deviation of the accuracies over the 10 trials. In the third column, we show the error rates achieved by the induction technique on the augmented attribute set, i.e. the original attributes plus the single evolved attribute using IG as the fitness. In the final column, we show the error rates achieved when the GI is used as the fitness. [Note that, in each of the 10 runs necessary for 10xCV, a new attribute is evolved from scratch.]

Table 2. Error rates for the Abalone data set.

Abalone	Original	Augmented-IG	Augmented-GI
C5	79.26 ± 1.21	79.09 ± 2.06	80.07 ± 2.40
CHAID	76.45 ± 1.61	74.77 ± 2.62	75.40 ± 2.34
CART	74.69 ± 1.76	73.02 ± 2.55	73.86 ± 2.43
ANN	72.45 ± 1.93	72.49 ± 2.74	73.14 ± 2.79

It is clear from Table 2 that the Abalone data set continues to prove difficult. For all classification algorithms, the error rates in the test sets are significant, even with the evolved attribute. Arguably, the Augmented-IG errors are marginally better than the Augmented-GI, but the standard deviations make this inconclusive. In this respect, these results are in keeping with those of [9] and [7].

Table 3. Error rates for the Balance-scale data set.

Balance-scale	Original	Augmented-IG	Augmented-GI
C5	22.42 ± 6.20	0.00 ± 0.00	0.00 ± 0.00
CHAID	28.39 ± 5.17	5.65 ± 2.55	5.49 ± 2.30
CART	22.74 ± 5.01	0.00 ± 0.00	0.00 ± 0.00
ANN	10.00 ± 3.79	9.36 ± 4.01	9.19 ± 3.65

On the other hand, when we look at the results for the Balance data set, in Table 3, we see a number of interesting features. Firstly, restricting attention to the *Original* column, we note that the ANN is performing significantly better than the decision tree algorithms. This suggests that, for this data set, it is possible to construct some powerfully predictive attributes from the original attribute set. Sure enough, we observe, from the *Augmented-IG* and *Augmented-GI* columns in Table 3, significant improvement in performance for all decision tree classifiers; indeed, the accuracies of all the decision tree techniques are improved by around 23%. Furthermore, and more interestingly, we note that both C5 and CART achieve 0% error (on all training and test sets) with the inclusion of the evolved attribute, irrespective of which fitness function is used.

The ANN, although having a better performance than the other classifiers with the original attributes, also improves performance with the augmented attribute set, but not so dramatically, and indeed less significantly if we take the standard deviations into account.

Table 4. Error rates for the BUPA data set.

BUPA	Original	Augmented-IG	Augmented-GI
C5	36.47 ± 7.99	32.35 ± 6.50	32.94 ± 8.75
CHAID	40.00 ± 9.73	30.00 ± 6.17	32.06 ± 8.14
CART	32.35 ± 7.21	30.29 ± 8.77	31.18 ± 7.87
ANN	37.65 ± 7.18	35.29 ± 10.47	31.47 ± 8.66

Table 4 shows the average error rates for the BUPA data set. Once again, all classifiers have improved their performance with the addition of the evolved attributes. However, it is notable that neither C5 nor CART appear to be benefiting more from the addition of the attributes evolved using IG and GI respectively. The story is much the same with the Waveform data set, see Table 5, with all classifiers showing an improvement with the inclusion of an evolved attribute, but with neither C5 nor CART achieving any additional enhancement.

Table 5. Error rates for the Waveform data set.

Waveform	Original	Augmented-IG	Augmented-GI
C5	22.94 ± 2.23	19.54 ± 1.64	19.64 ± 2.37
CHAID	28.36 ± 1.81	24.92 ± 2.30	24.64 ± 2.12
CART	24.58 ± 2.61	20.02 ± 1.71	19.54 ± 1.76
ANN	17.15 ± 7.41	15.20 ± 2.29	15.77 ± 2.28

Finally, turning attention to the Wine data set, the results in Table 6 once again indicate the potential for any classification algorithm to benefit from the inclusion of evolved, highly predictive variables. The ANN, despite achieving around 96.5% accuracy with the original attribute vector, still manages to improve its performance with both augmented sets, attaining 100% accuracy over a number of the 10-fold test sets. Here the *Augmented-GI* set appears to giving marginally better results than the *Augmented-IG* set, but the standard deviations are too large to make this significant.

Table 6. Error rates for the Wine data set.

Wine	Original	Augmented-IG	Augmented-GI
C5	6.47 ± 7.04	5.29 ± 7.04	4.12 ± 4.84
CHAID	17.06 ± 8.06	17.65 ± 8.77	15.29 ± 7.94
CART	10.59 ± 9.92	5.88 ± 8.32	3.53 ± 3.04
ANN	3.53 ± 7.44	2.94 ± 5.72	1.76 ± 2.84

The results shown in Tables 2 to 6 generally support those of [9] and [7], in that attribute construction using genetic programming can generate improvements in the performance of a classifier, sometimes significantly so, as in the case of the Balance-scale data set.

However, we can claim here that the improvement in performance, if any, of the classifiers is not significantly dependent on which measure is used in the GP to evolve the attributes. If we measure the absolute improvement in performance for each classifier, averaged out over all the data sets, then, using the attributes evolved using IG, C5 manages an overall 6.26% improvement in accuracy, CHAID achieves a 7.45% improvement, CART 7.15% and ANN 1.10%. With the attribute evolved using the GI, C5 achieves a 6.16% improvement, CHAID achieves a 7.48% improvement, CART 7.37% and ANN 1.89%. It cannot be concluded from these results, therefore, that C5 (resp. CART) has an advantage over the other classifiers with the inclusion of a feature evolved using a GP with IG (resp. GI) as a fitness measure.

4.2   Tree Size

We turn our attention now to the issue of the size of the resultant decision tree when the evolved attributes are included in the attribute set.

In Table 7, for each data set and for each tree induction algorithm, there are three entries, one for each of the three techniques (Original, Augmented-IG, Augmented-GI). The numbers represent the average number of nodes in the tree over the 10 fold trials. The number in brackets is the average depth of the tree.

For the Abalone data, it is interesting to note the wide variation in the sizes of the tree, despite there being no corresponding wide variation in the accuracies achieved (see Table 2). Significantly, there appears to be no great reduction in the size of the tree with the introduction of evolved attributes. The Balance data set, however, presents a significant reduction in tree size, with both IG and GI- augmented attribute vectors. Indeed, the GP consistently evolves the key relationship between the four original attributes $((f_1 * f_2)/(f_3 * f_4))$ and the resulting trees (in C5 and CART) split twice on this evolved variable, giving 4 nodes in all, not including root. Even taking the complexity of the evolved attribute into consideration, therefore, there is still a large reduction in complexity. Interestingly here, CHAID trees, although equally small, do not attain the 100% accuracy of either C5 or CART.

Table 7. Average tree size for classification by C5, CART and CHAID. Each entry represents the number of nodes in the tree averaged over the 10 fold trials. The number in brackets is the average depth of the tree. Both measures do not include the root.

Data set	C5			CART			CHAID		
	Orig.	Aug-IG	Aug-GI	Orig.	Aug-IG	Aug-GI	Orig.	Aug-IG	Aug-GI
Abalone	2120	2038	2038	59.8	54.2	54.6	101.1	101.7	100.2
	(22.6)	(22)	(22)	(8.1)	(7.4)	(8.0)	(5.9)	(6.1)	(5.9)
Balance	79.8	4	4	81.2	4	4	42.7	3.8	4.5
	(8.7)	(2)	(2)	(7.2)	(2)	(2)	(4.4)	(1.4)	(1.6)
BUPA	60.9	27	25.4	44.2	32	28.6	12.4	9.5	8.8
	(9.1)	(7.5)	(7.2)	(6.7)	(7.5)	6.5)	(3.8)	(2.8)	(2.8)
Wave	352.4	274.6	258.2	52.4	47.2	43.8	376.8	335.8	337.9
	(15.2)	(14.5)	(14.9)	(7.5)	(6.3)	(6.5)	(7.2)	(6.2)	(7.5)
Wine	8.8	4.6	6.2	13	5.2	5.4	10.6	9.1	10.9
	(3.2)	(2.3)	(2.8)	(4)	(2.3)	(2.5)	(2.1)	(1.8)	(2.2)

CHAID trees for the BUPA data set are much smaller in comparison to the others, especially with the augmented attribute vectors, and yet Table 4 shows there is very little to choose between the performance of these algorithms. For the Waveform data set, there is a less significant reduction in the size/depth of the tree, consistent with the less significant reduction in error rate. In the case of CHAID, in fact, the Augmented-GI technique produces thinner, deeper trees than the Original set. A similar result is seen for the Wine data set.

As one would expect, the most significant improvements in classification correspond to the largest reductions in tree size, namely for the Balance data set. However, the peculiarities of the different algorithms outweigh any trend that might be present in Table 7.

5 Conclusions

In this paper, we have used a GP to evolve a new attribute which is a non-linear function of the original, real-valued attributes. This was done as a pre-processing stage in a data mining exercise to build classification models for a number of public domain data sets. The GP used information gain or the gini index as a fitness function.

We compared the performance of 4 classifiers (C5, CHAID, CART and ANN) with and without the new attribute, to ascertain if C5 or CART was in any way benefiting from the inclusion of an attribute evolved using information gain or gini index respectively. We have found no evidence that any algorithm has an advantage over the other classifiers, and that, in general, all classifiers benefit from the inclusion of an evolved attribute. Only in one data set did we notice a dramatic improvement for C5 and CART (100% accuracy on all 10 fold test trials) whilst the performance of the other classifiers improved less dramatically.

Whilst this study was primarily aimed at decision tree algorithms, and their potential to benefit from the inclusion of an attribute evolved using a GP with information gain/gini index as a fitness function, a fuller study is underway to investigate the effect on classifier performance when attributes are evolved using a more generic fitness function.

Acknowledgments. The first author would like to acknowledge financial support from his parents and from the Yemen Education Ministry.

References

1. H. Bensusan and I. Kuscu. Constructive induction using genetic programming. In T. Fogarty and G. Venturini, editors, *Proceedings of Int. Conf. Machine Learning, Evolutionary Computing and Machine Learning Workshop*, 1996.
2. D. Biggs, B. de Ville, and E. Suen. A method of choosing multiway partitions for classification and decision trees. *J. of Applied Statistics*, 18:49–62, 1991.
3. L. Breiman, J. H. Friedman, R. A. Olshen, and C. J. Stone. *Classification and Regression Trees*. Wadsworth, Inc. Belmont, California, 1984.
4. G. V. Kass. An exploratory technique for investigating large quantities of categorical data. *Applied Statistics*, 29:119–127, 1980.
5. J. Koza. *Genetic Programming: On the Programming of Computers by Means of Natural Selection*. MIT Press, 1992.
6. I. Kuscu. A genetic constructive induction model. In P. J. Angeline, Z. Michalewicz, M. Schoenauer, X. Yao, and A. Zalzala, editors, *Proc of Congress on Evolutionary Computation*, volume 1, pages 212–217. IEEE Press, 1999.
7. M. A. Muharram and G. D. Smith. The effect of evolved attributes on classification algorithms. In *Proceedings of 16th Australian Joint Conference on Artificial Intelligence*, 2003.
8. S.K. Murthy and S. Salzberg. A system for induction of oblique decision trees. *Journal of Artificial Intelligence Research*, 2:1–32, 1994.
9. F. E. B. Otero, M. M. S. Silva, A. A. Freitas, and J. C. Nievola. Genetic programming for attribute construction in data mining. In *Genetic Programming: Proc. 6th European Conf. (EuroGP-2003), LNCS*, volume 2610, pages 384–393. Springer, 2003.
10. J. R. Quinlan. *C4.5: Programs for Machine Learning*. Morgan Kaufmann, San Mateo, 1993.
11. D. Treigueiros and R. H. Berry. The application of neural network based methods to the extraction of knowledge from accounting reports. In *Proceedings of 24th Annual Hawaii Int. Conf. on System Sciences IV*, pages 137–146, 1991.
12. I. H. Witten and E. Frank. *Data Mining: Practical machine learning tools and techniques with Java*. Morgan Kaufmann, CA, 1999.
13. Zijian Zheng. Effects of different types of new attribute on constructive induction. In *Proc of 8th Int. Conf. on Tools with Artifical Intelligence (ICTAI'96)*, pages 254–257. IEEE, 1996.

On the Evolution of Evolutionary Algorithms

Jorge Tavares[1], Penousal Machado[1,2], Amílcar Cardoso[1],
Francisco B. Pereira[1,2], and Ernesto Costa[1]

[1] Centre for Informatics and Systems of the University of Coimbra,
Pólo II - Pinhal de Marrocos, 3030 Coimbra, Portugal
[2] Instituto Superior de Engenharia de Coimbra,
Quinta da Nora, 3030 Coimbra, Portugal
{jast,machado,amilcar,xico,ernesto}@dei.uc.pt

Abstract. In this paper we discuss the evolution of several components of a traditional Evolutionary Algorithm, such as genotype to phenotype mappings and genetic operators, presenting a formalized description of how this can be attained. We then focus on the evolution of mapping functions, for which we present experimental results achieved with a meta-evolutionary scheme.

1 Introduction

In order to achieve competitive results with an Evolutionary Computation (EC) approach, it is often required the development of problem specific operators, representations, and fine tuning of parameters. As a result, much of the EC research practice focuses on these aspects. To avoid these difficulties, researchers have proposed the evolution of these EC components. We believe that the evolution of parameters, operators and representations may contribute to performance improvements, give insight to the idiosyncrasies of particular problems, and alleviate the burden of EC researchers.

We propose the evolution of several components of an EC algorithm, and present the results attained in the evolution of the genotype-phenotype mapping procedure [1]. In section 2 we make a brief perusal of related research. Next, in section 3, we study different ways of evolving EC components, presenting a formalization. The experimental results are presented in section 4, which also comprises their analysis. Finally, we draw some overall conclusions and give pointers for future research.

2 Related Work

The area of Adaptive Evolutionary Computation (AEC) focuses on the evolution of specific parameters of EC algorithms. Angeline [2] makes a formal definition and classification of AEC, proposing three levels of adaptation: population-level, individual-level and component-level.

There are several AEC approaches that allow the dynamic resizing of the genotype, allowing its expansion and contraction according to environmental

M. Keijzer et al. (Eds.): EuroGP 2004, LNCS 3003, pp. 389–398, 2004.

requirements. Angeline and Pollack [3] propose the co-evolution of: a high-level representational language suited to the environment; and of a dynamic GA where the genotype size varies. Also related to genotype-phenotype mapping, is the work of Altenberg [4] about the notion of "evolvability" - the ability of a population to produce variants fitter than previous existing one's. In [5,6] Altenberg explores the concept of Genome Growth, a constructional selection method in which the degree of freedom of the representation is increased incrementally. This work is directly connected to the concepts presented by Dawkins in [7], where he clearly differentiates genetics, the study of the relationships between genotypes in successive generations, from embryology, the study of the relationships between genotype and phenotype in any one generation. This leads us to the concept of embryogeny, the process of growth that defines how a genotype is mapped onto a phenotype, and to the work of Bentley. In [8], the use of such growth processes within evolutionary systems is studied. Three main types of EC embryogenies are identified and explained: external, explicit and implicit. A comparative study between these different types, using an evolutionary design problem, is also presented.

Another aspect that can be subject of self adaptation is the set of genetic operators. The most straightforward approach is to try to select, from a pre-defined set, the most useful operator according to the environment. A paradigmatic example of this type of approach can be found in [9], which describes an AEC algorithm that dynamically chooses the crossover operator to apply, and adjusts the crossover probability. The self adaptation of crossover parameters is also described in [10], where the adaptation of parameters governing the selection of a crossover point, and amount of crossover operations is described.

The evolution of the genetic operators is the obvious next step. In [11], Teller describes how genetic operators can be evolved using PADO, a graph based GP system. In [12] GP is extended to a co-evolutionary model, allowing the co-evolution of candidate solutions and genetic operators. The evolving genetic operators are applied to the population of candidate solutions, and also to themselves. Another approach to the evolution of genetic operators is described in [13]. In this study, an additional level of recombination operators is introduced, which performs the recombination of a pool of operators. In [14] Spector and Robinson discuss how an autoconstructive evolutionary system can be attained using a language called Push. In the proposed system the individuals are responsible for the production of their own children.

3   Evolving EC Components

Historically EC is divided into four families namely: Evolution Strategies (ES); Evolutionary Programming (EP); Genetic Algorithms (GA); and Genetic Programming (GP). In spite of their differences they can all be seen as particular instances of the Generic Evolutionary Algorithm (GEA) presented in figure 1.

The first step is the creation of a random set of genotypes, $G(0)$. These genotypes are converted to phenotypes through the application of a mapping

```
t ← 0
G(0)   ← generate_random(t)
P(0)   ← map(G(0))
F(0)   ← eval(P(0))
while  stop criterion not met  do
        G'(t)        ← sel(G(t), P(t), F(t))
        G''(t)       ← op(G'(t))
        G(t + 1)     ← gen(G(t), G''(t))
        P(t + 1)     ← map(G(t + 1))
        F(t + 1)     ← eval(P(t + 1))
        t ← t + 1
end while
return result
```

Fig. 1. Generic Evolutionary Algorithm.

function (*map*). In most cases there isn't a clear distinction between genotype and phenotype, so this step is typically omitted. The next step consists on the evaluation of the individuals. This is performed at the phenotype level using a fitness function, *eval*.

The main evolutionary cycle follows. A set of parents is selected, using *sel*, followed by the application of genetic operators, *op*, which yields a new set of genotypes, $G''(t)$. The next steps consist in the generation of the phenotypes and their evaluation. The evolutionary cycle continues until some termination criterion is met.

3.1   Meta-evolution

The most obvious approach to the evolution of EC components is the use of meta-evolution.

Let's assume that we are interested in evolving one of the components of EC, for instance the mapping function, and that we resort to GP to evolve populations of these functions. Each genotype, G_i^{map}, will be an encoding of a candidate mapping function; once expressed, via map^{map}, it will result in a phenotype, P_i^{map}. We need to define: sel^{map}, op^{map} and gen^{map}. Like map^{map} and $eval^{map}$ these functions will be static. Therefore, we can use standard GP selection, operators and replacement strategy.

We also need to evaluate the mapping functions, which implies developing a fitness function, $eval^{map}$. One possibility is to use a set of rules that specify the characteristics that are considered desirable in a mapping function, and assign fitness based on the accordance with those rules. We propose an alternative approach.

Since we are mainly interested in mapping functions that promote the discovery of good solutions for an original problem, we run, for each mapping function being evaluated, P_i^{map}, a lower level EC algorithm in which P_i^{map} is used as mapping function. Fitness is assigned using a function similar to the one presented in figure 2. Thus, the fitness of each phenotype is the result of a lower level EC. This result can indicate: the fitness of the best individual (at the lower level); the time necessary to reach the optimum; the average fitness of the last population; etc.

$$
\begin{aligned}
&eval^{map}(P^{map}) \\
&\quad \textbf{for } i = 1 \textbf{ to } \#(P^{map}) \textbf{ do} \\
&\qquad F_i^{map} \leftarrow GEA(P_i^{map}) \\
&\quad \textbf{endfor} \\
&\quad \textbf{return } average(F^{map})
\end{aligned}
$$

Fig. 2. Meta-level fitness function.

It should be more or less obvious that we can employ the exact same strategy to evolve: *sel*, *op*, *gen* or *eval*. If we are evolving evaluation functions, the lower level EC is guided by P_i^{eval}. However, we are interested in a P_i^{eval} which allows the discovery of individuals which are fit accordingly to some original fitness function. As such, the return value of GEA should reflect its performance according to this original function.

The main problem of the architecture presented in this section is its high computational cost. In the next section we make a brief description of alternative approaches, which are, potentially, less time consuming.

3.2   Other Approaches

One of the alternatives is to use a standard EC approach in which each genotype, G_i is composed by:

– G_i^{sol} – the encoding of a candidate solution to some original problem, and
– G_i^{Δ} – where Δ is a tuple; each of its elements being an encoding of one of the following functions $\{map, sel, op, gen, eval\}$. Different elements correspond to different functions.

Likewise, the phenotype of an individual, P_i, is composed by a candidate solution, P_i^{sol}, and by a set of functions P_i^{Δ}. We name this approach *dual-evolution*.

Assuming that *map* is part of Δ, the phenotype is calculated in two steps. First, a static mapping function is applied to G_i^{Δ} yielding P_i^{Δ}. Then, the mapping function associated with the individual, P_i^{map}, is applied to G_i^{sol}, resulting in P_i^{sol}. Needless to say, if *map* is not a part of Δ, a static mapping function is used. If *op* is part of Δ, the generation of descendants must be changed. This can be done pretty much in the same way: apply conventional EC operators to G_i^{Δ}, and apply P_i^{op} to G_i^{sol}.

This approach is appropriate for operators that take as input a single geno-type. Evolving operators for sexual reproduction is slightly more complicated. Let's assume that individuals i and j where selected for sexual reproduction, and, without loss of generality, that this operation yields two descendants i' and j'. $G_{i'}^{\Delta}$ and $G_{j'}^{\Delta}$ are created by applying standard operators. $G_{i'}^{sol}$ and $G_{j'}^{sol}$ are created through the calculation of $P_i^{op}(G_i^{sol}, G_j^{sol})$, and $P_j^{op}(G_j^{sol}, G_i^{sol})$, respectively.

The integration of other elements can pose some problems. Since both com-ponents, (Δ, sol), of the individual share a single fitness value, the evolution of $eval$, sel or gen, can easily lead to stagnation. For example, if an individual is responsible for its own evaluation, then all it must do to dominate the population is assign himself a extremely high value.

One option is to consider the original fitness function as a survival fitness, which determines the chances of reaching adult age, and thus of being a possible candidate for reproduction (sel) or part of the next generation (gen). When an individual i is selected for mating it uses its own fitness function, P_i^{eval}, to evaluate a set of mating candidates.

This approach can also be used for sel: if i is selected for mating, it uses P_i^{sel} to select its matting partners. In this case the input to P_i^{sel} could be the static fitness values of the other individuals; the fitness values i assigns to the other individuals (using P_i^{eval}); or both. We were unable to find an elegant way of integrating gen that doesn't lead to stagnation.

An alternative to dual-evolution is using a co-evolutionary approach, which can be considered as an intermediate level between dual and meta-evolution. In a co-evolutionary approach we would have one population composed by candi-date solutions to a given problem. Each of the remaining populations would be composed by a specific EC component that we wish to evolve. This approach will be analyzed in a future paper.

4   Experimental Results

To test our ideas we decided to apply meta-evolution to evolve mapping func-tions. We use a two level meta-evolution scheme composed by a GP algorithm and a GA. At the higher level we have the GP algorithm, which is used to evolve the mapping functions. At the lower level we have the GA, whose task is finding the maximum value of a mathematical function. The goal is to evolve mappings that help the GA to accomplish its task.

The function being optimized by the GA, $f(x)$, is defined over the interval $[0, 1]$, and is the sum of $f_{peak}(x)$ and $f_{wave}(x)$, which are specified as follows:

$$f_{peak}(x) = max(0, |1 - 2|x - peak| - (1 - \frac{1}{r})| \times 0.1 \times r) \qquad (1)$$

$$f_{wave}(x) = cos(2\pi \times r \times (x - peak)) \qquad (2)$$

f_{wave} creates a sine wave with r repetitions in the $[0, 1]$ interval, returning values between -1 and 1. By adding f_{peak} we change the values of one of the repetitions, making it reach a maximum value of 1.1. In figure 3 we present a graph of $f(x)$. To increase the complexity of the problem, variable r is set to 100, which means that the wave function repeats itself 100 times in the $[0, 1]$ interval.

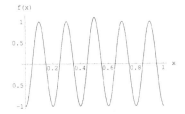

Fig. 3. Test function, $r = 5$, $peak = 0.5$

By changing the value of the variable $peak$ we can change the coordinate of the maximum of $f(x)$. This ability to change the maximum is fundamental. If this value doesn't change the GP algorithm could find programs that output a constant x value corresponding to the maximum of $f(x)$. This isn't, obviously, the desired behavior. What we aim to achieve is a GP program that transforms the search space in a way that helps the GA to find the maximum value. Thus, for each value of x the GP programs should compute a new value, x'. The reorganization of the search space induced by the x to x' transformation should make the task of finding the optimum easier.

To ensure that it is possible to find a good mapping function we decided to design one by hand. We were able to develop the following function:

$$g_{optimal}(x) = \frac{x + floor(frac(x \times 10000) \times r)}{r} \qquad (3)$$

Where $frac$ returns the fractional part. This function has the effect of folding the space r times, and then expanding it back to $[0, 1]$. By using this mapping function the topology of the search space is changed, resulting in a less convoluted fitness landscape. In figure 4 we present a chart of this mapping function, $g_{optimal}(x)$, and of the search space resulting from its application, $f(g_{optimal}(x))$.

To assign fitness, we run, for each GP individual, $mapping_j$ a GA. Each GA genotype, G_i^{sol}, is a binary string of size 50, encoding a value, G_i^{sol}, in the $[0, 1]$ interval. The GP individual is used as mapping function for the GA. The value $G_i'^{sol}$ will be mapped to x_i' (thus, $x_i' = mapping_j(G_i'^{sol})$). x_i' is then used as the x coordinate for the function being optimized by the GA, f.

In order to get a good estimate of the quality of the mapping $functions$ we perform 30 runs of the GA for each GP individual. To prevent the specialization of the GP individuals, the value of $peak$ is randomly chosen at the beginning of each GA run. The fitness the GP individual is equal to the average fitness of the best individual of the last population of the lower level GA.

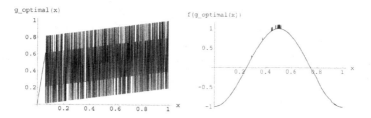

Fig. 4. On the left $g_{optimal}(x)$; on the right $f(g_{optimal}(x))$, $r = 5$.

We use the following function and terminal sets:

- $f\text{-}set = \{+, -, \%, \times, floor, frac\}$, where $\%$ is the protected division.
- $t\text{-}set = \{G_i'^{sol}, 1, 10, 100\}$, where $G_i'^{sol}$ is a variable holding the value of the GA genotype that is currently being mapped.

The settings for the GP algorithm were the following: Population size = 100; Number of generations 500; Swap-Tree crossover; Generate Random Tree mutation; Crossover probability = 70%; Mutation probability=20%; Maximum tree depth = 10.

The settings for the GA where the following: Population size = 100; Number of generations = 50; Two point crossover; Swap Mutation; Crossover probability = 70%; Mutation probability=$\{1\%, 2.5\%, 5\%\}$.

4.1   Analysis of the Results

The chart on figure 5 shows the evolution of the fitness of the best individual during the evolutionary process. An overview of the results shows that the GP algorithm is able to improve the fitness of the mapping functions. This indicates that the GP is able to find useful mappings for $f(x)$.

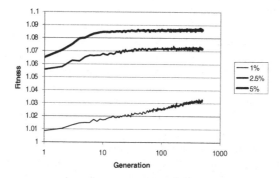

Fig. 5. Evolution of the fitness of the best individual. Averages of 30 independent runs

The main objective of our approach is to find a mapping function that consistently improves the performance of the GA algorithm. To evaluate the experimental results we need some reference points. Therefore, we conducted a series of experiments in which the mapping function was not subjected to evolution. In these tests we used the following static mapping functions: $g_{optimal}$, already described; and $g_{identity}$ with $g_{identity}(x) = G'^{sol}$. These results will be compared with the ones obtained using as mapping functions the best individuals of each GP run, $g_{evolved}$.

Table 1 shows the average fitness of the best individual of the last population of a traditional GA (Number of generations $= 100$) using as mapping functions $g_{identity}$, $g_{optimal}$ and $g_{evolved}$. The results are averages of 100 runs for the static mappings and of 3000 runs for the evolved mappings (100 runs per each evolved mapping).

Table 1. Average fitness of the best individual of the last population. The entries in bold indicate a statistically significant difference between these values and the corresponding $g_{identity}$ values ($\alpha = 0.01$).

Mutation	$g_{identity}$	$g_{optimal}$	$g_{evolved}$
1%	1.02713	**1.08763**	**1.04738**
2.5%	1.03442	**1.09731**	**1.07736**
5%	1.03995	**1.09964**	**1.09020**

As expected using $g_{optimal}$ considerably improves the performance of the algorithm, yielding averages close to the maximum attainable value, 1.1. Table 1 shows that the use of the evolved mapping functions significantly improves the performance of the GA. However, the results attained are inferior to the ones achieved using $g_{optimal}$. This difference diminishes as the mutation rate increases.

To get a better grasp of how the use of the evolved mapping functions alter the GA, we present, in figure 6, the evolution of the fitness of the best individual during the GA run.

For static mappings the fitness increases abruptly in the first generations, stagnating for the remainder of the run; with the evolved mappings the fitness increases steadily during the entire run. An analysis of the evolution of the average fitness of the GA populations gives insight to how the evolved mappings are improving the GA performance. As figure 7 shows, the use of evolved mappings decreases significantly the average fitness of the populations. These results, in combination with the ones presented in figure 6, indicate that the evolved mappings improve the performance of the GA by promoting phenotypic diversity, preventing the early stagnation of the GA runs.

The evolved mappings aren't similar to $g_{optimal}$, which can't be considered surprising. As is often the case when analyzing the results of a GP program, it isn't clear how the evolved mappings solve the problem of improving the GA

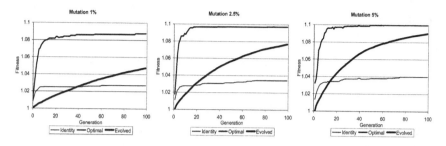

Fig. 6. Evolution of the fitness of the best individual.

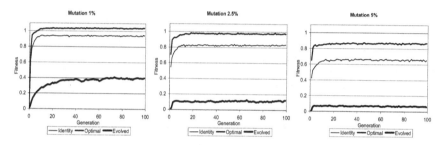

Fig. 7. Evolution of the average fitness of the GA populations.

performance. The charts suggest that reducing the number of GA generations used in the GP fitness assignment procedure, thus increasing the difficulty of the evolved mappings task, may lead to mappings closer to $g_{optimal}$. Additionally, taking into account the average of the GA populations when assigning a fitness value for the GP individuals, may also prove useful to achieve mappings closer to $g_{optimal}$.

5   Conclusions and Further Work

In this paper we discussed the extension of the canonical EC algorithm, presenting a formalization. The proposed changes involve the evolution of several components of EC which are typically static. The evolution of these components may prove useful in improving the EC performance, lessen the burden of researchers, and provide indications about the characteristics of the problems being solve.

The attained results are promising, and provide pointers for the improvement of the approach. Future research will include: making a wider set of experiments; applying the proposed approach to a different set of domains; and using dual-evolution and co-evolution to evolve EC components.

References

1. Banzhaf, W.: Genotype-phenotype-mapping and neutral variation – A case study in genetic programming. In Davidor, Y., Schwefel, H.P., Männer, R., eds.: Parallel Problem Solving from Nature III. Volume 866., Jerusalem, Springer-Verlag (1994) 322–332
2. Angeline, P.J.: Adaptive and self-adaptive evolutionary computations. In: Computational Intelligence: A Dynamic Systems Perspective. IEEE Press (1995)
3. Angeline, P.J., Pollack, J.B.: Coevolving high-level representations. In: Artificial Life III. Volume XVII of SFI Studies in the Sciences of Complexity. (1994) 55–71
4. Altenberg, L.: The evolution of evolvability in genetic programming. In Kinnear, K.E., ed.: Advances in Genetic Programming. MIT Press, Cambridge, MA (1994) 47–74
5. Altenberg, L.: Evolving better representations through selective genome growth. In: Proceedings of the 1st IEEE Conference on Evolutionary Computation. Part 1 (of 2), Piscataway N.J., IEEE (1994) 182–187
6. Altenberg, L.: Genome growth and the evolution of the genotype-phenotype map. In Banzhaf, W., Eeckman, F.H., eds.: Evolution as a Computational Process. Springer-Verlag, Berlin (1995) 205–259
7. Dawkins, R.: The evolution of evolvability. In Langton, C.G., ed.: Artificial Life, SFI Studies in the Sciences of Complexity. Volume VI., Addison-Wesley (1989) 201–220
8. Bentley, P., Kumar, S.: Three ways to grow designs: A comparison of embryogenies for an evolutionary design problem. In Banzhaf, W., Daida, J., Eiben, A.E., Garzon, M.H., Honavar, V., Jakiela, M., Smith, R.E., eds.: Proceedings of the Genetic and Evolutionary Computation Conference. Volume 1., Orlando, Florida, USA, Morgan Kaufmann (1999) 35–43
9. Spears, W.M.: Adapting crossover in evolutionary algorithms. In: Proc. of the Fourth Annual Conference on Evolutionary Programming, Cambridge, MA, MIT Press (1995) 367–384
10. Angeline, P.J.: Two self-adaptive crossover operators for genetic programming. In: Advances in Genetic Programming 2. MIT Press, Cambridge, MA, USA (1996) 89–110
11. Teller, A.: Evolving programmers: The co-evolution of intelligent recombination operators. In Angeline, P.J., Kinnear, Jr., K.E., eds.: Advances in Genetic Programming 2. MIT Press, Cambridge, MA, USA (1996) 45–68
12. Edmonds, B.: Meta-genetic programming: Co-evolving the operators of variation. CPM Report 98-32, Centre for Policy Modelling, Manchester Metropolitan University, UK, Aytoun St., Manchester, M1 3GH. UK (1998)
13. Kantschik, W., Dittrich, P., Brameier, M., Banzhaf, W.: Meta-evolution in graph GP. In: Genetic Programming: Second European Workshop EuroGP'99, Springer (1999) 15–28
14. Spector, L., Robinson, A.: Genetic programming and autoconstructive evolution with the push programming language. Genetic Programming and Evolvable Machines 3 (2002) 7–40

Genetic Programming with Gradient Descent Search for Multiclass Object Classification

Mengjie Zhang and Will Smart

School of Mathematical and Computer Science
Victoria University of Wellington,
P. O. Box 600, Wellington, New Zealand
{mengjie,smartwill}@mcs.vuw.ac.nz

Abstract. This paper describes an approach to the use of gradient descent search in genetic programming (GP) for object classification problems. Gradient descent search is introduced to the GP mechanism and is embedded into the genetic beam search, which allows the evolutionary learning process to globally follow the beam search and locally follow the gradient descent search. Two different methods, an online gradient descent scheme and an offline gradient descent scheme, are developed and compared with the basic GP method on three image data sets with object classification problems of increasing difficulty. The results suggest that both the online and the offline gradient descent GP methods outperform the basic GP method in terms of both classification accuracy and training efficiency and that the online scheme achieved better performance than the offline scheme.

1 Introduction

Since the early 1990s, there has been a number of reports on applying genetic programming techniques to object recognition problems [1,2,3,4,5,6,7]. Typically, these GP systems used image features as the terminal set, arithmetic and conditional operators as the function set, and classification accuracy, error rate or similar measures as the fitness function. During the evolutionary process, selection, crossover and mutation operators were applied to the genetic beam search to find good solutions. While most of these GP systems achieved reasonably good results, they usually spent a long time on training. Accordingly, the evolutionary process was often stopped when a maximum number of generations was reached, rather than an ideal solution was found.

Gradient descent is a long term established search technique. This technique can guarantee to find a local minima for a particular task. While the local minima might not be the best solution, it often meets the request of that task.

The goal of this paper is to apply the gradient descent search to genetic programming for multiclass object classification problems, and to investigate whether this approach can perform better than the basic GP approach in terms of training efficiency and classification performance. While the meta-search [8] and diversity of constants [9] in GP have been investigated, we will describe a different approach.

M. Keijzer et al. (Eds.): EuroGP 2004, LNCS 3003, pp. 399–408, 2004.
© Springer-Verlag Berlin Heidelberg 2004

2   GP Applied to Object Classification

In the basic GP approach, we used the tree-structure to represent genetic programs [10]. The ramped half-and-half method was used for generating programs in the initial population and for the mutation operator [11]. The proportional selection mechanism and the reproduction [12], crossover and mutation operators [13] were used in the learning and evolutionary process.

2.1   Terminals and Functions

Terminals. In this approach, we used two kinds of terminals: *feature terminals* and *numeric parameter terminals*.

Feature terminals form the inputs from the environment. The feature terminals considered in this approach are the means and variances of certain regions in object cutout images. Two such regions were used, the entire object cutout image and the central square region. This makes four feature terminals. The values of the feature terminals would remain unchanged in the evolutionary process, although different objects usually have different feature values.

Numeric parameter terminals are floating point numbers randomly generated using a uniform distribution at the beginning of evolution. Unlike feature terminals, the values of this kind of terminals are the same for all object images. In the basic GP approach, they would remain unchanged during the evolutionary recombination. In our gradient descent algorithm, they will be changed and updated (see section 3).

Functions. In the function set, the four standard arithmetic and a conditional operation were used to form the function set:

$$FuncSet = \{+, -, *, /, if\} \tag{1}$$

The $+$, $-$, $/$ and $*$ operators are addition, subtraction, multiplication and "protected" division with two arguments. The *if* function takes three arguments. If the first argument is negative, the *if* function returns its second argument; otherwise, it returns its third argument.

2.2   Fitness Function

We used classification accuracy on the training set as the fitness function. The classification accuracy of a genetic program classifier refers to the number of object images that are correctly classified by the genetic program classifier as a proportion of the total number of object images in the training set.

In this approach, we used a variant version of the *program classification map* [12] to perform object classification. This variation situates class regions sequentially on the floating point number line. The object image will be classified to the class of the region that the program output with the object image input falls into. Class region boundaries start at some negative number, and end at the same positive number. Boundaries between the starting point and the end point are allocated with an identical interval of 1.0. For example, a five class problem would have the following classification map.

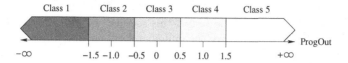

2.3   Parameters and Termination Criteria

The parameter values used in this approach are shown in table 1. The learning process is terminated when one of the following conditions is met:

– The classification problem has been solved on the training set, that is, all objects of interest in the training set have been correctly classified without any missing objects or false alarms for any class.
– The accuracy on the validation set starts falling down.
– The number of generations reaches the pre-defined number, *max-generations*.

Table 1. Parameters used for GP training for the three datasets.

Parameter Names	Shape	coin1	coin2	Parameter Names	Shape	coin1	coin2
population-size	300	300	500	reproduction-rate	20%	20%	20%
initial-max-depth	3	3	3	cross-rate	50%	50%	50%
max-depth	5	6	8	mutation-rate	30%	30%	30%
max-generations	51	51	51	cross-term	15%	15%	15%
object-size	16×16	70×70	70×70	cross-func	85%	85%	85%

3   Gradient Descent Applied to Genetic Programming

This section describes how to apply the gradient descent search to genetic programming. Both the online scheme and the offline scheme were considered.

In our GP system, the parameters to be applied to the gradient descent algorithm are the numeric parameter terminals in each individual program. We assume that a continuous cost surface/function C can be formed from a genetic program P for a given classification task based on a set of numeric parameter terminals. To improve the system performance, the gradient descent search is applied to take steps "downhill" on the C from the current numeric parameter terminal T.

The gradient of C is found as the vector of partial derivatives with respect to the parameter values. This gradient vector points along the surface, in the direction of maximum-slope at the point used in the derivation. Changing the parameters proportionally to this vector (negatively, as it points to "uphill") will move the system down the surface C. If we use O_i to represent the value of the ith (numeric parameter) terminal T and y to represent the output of the genetic program P, then the distance moved (the change of O_i) should therefore be:

$$\Delta O_i = -\alpha \cdot \frac{\partial C}{\partial O_i} = -\alpha \cdot \frac{\partial C}{\partial y} \cdot \frac{\partial y}{\partial O_i} \tag{2}$$

where α is a search factor. In the rest of this section, we will address the three parts — $\frac{\partial C}{\partial y}$, $\frac{\partial y}{\partial O_i}$ and α, then give the online and offline algorithms.

3.1   Cost Function and Partial Derivative $\frac{\partial C}{\partial y}$

We used half of the squared difference between the program actual output (y) and the desired output (Y) as the cost function:

$$C = \frac{(y - Y)^2}{2} \tag{3}$$

Accordingly, the partial derivative of the cost function with respect to the genetic program would be:

$$\frac{\partial C}{\partial y} = \frac{\partial(\frac{(y-Y)^2}{2})}{\partial y} = y - Y \tag{4}$$

The corresponding desired output Y is calculated as follows.

$$Y = \mathbf{class} - \frac{\mathbf{numclass} + 1}{2} \tag{5}$$

where **class** is the class label of the object and **numclass** is the total number of classes. For example, for a five class problem as described in section 2.2, the desired outputs are $-2, -1, 0, 1$ and 2 for object classes 1, 2, 3, 4 and 5, respectively.

3.2   Partial Derivative $\frac{\partial y}{\partial O_i}$

We use the program shown in figure 1 as an example to describe the chain rule for the calculation of $\frac{\partial y}{\partial O_i}$.

In this program, nodes 1 and 3 are functions, node 4 is a feature terminal and nodes 2 and 5 are numeric terminals. Accordingly, the gradient vector should contain values from the partial derivatives from nodes 2 and 5. The partial derivatives of the genetic program with respect to node 2 and node 5 are:

$$\frac{\partial y}{\partial O_2} = \frac{\partial(O_2 O_3)}{\partial O_2} = O_3$$

$$\frac{\partial y}{\partial O_5} = \frac{\partial(O_2 O_3)}{\partial O_5} = \frac{\partial(O_2 O_3)}{\partial O_3} \cdot \frac{\partial O_3}{\partial O_5} = \frac{\partial(O_2 O_3)}{\partial O_3} \cdot \frac{\partial(O_4 + O_5)}{\partial O_5} = O_2 \cdot 1 = O_2$$

As O_2 and O_3 can be obtained from evaluation of the program, these gradients can be calculated accordingly. In other words, using the chain rule the gradients can be broken down to evaluated values and derived operators.

The partial derivatives of the various functions/operators used in this approach are listed in table 2.

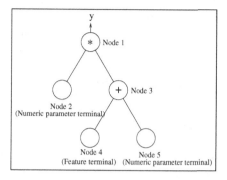

Fig. 1. Sample partial derivatives of numeric terminals in a genetic program.

Table 2. Partial derivatives of operators in the function set.

Function f	meanings	$\frac{\partial f}{\partial a_1}$	$\frac{\partial f}{\partial a_2}$	$\frac{\partial f}{\partial a_3}$
$(+\ a_1\ a_2)$	$a_1 + a_2$	1	1	$-$
$(-\ a_1\ a_2)$	$a_1 - a_2$	1	-1	$-$
$(*\ a_1\ a_2)$	$a_1 \times a_2$	a_2	a_1	$-$
$(/\ a_1\ a_2)$	$a_1 \div a_2$	a_2^{-1}	$-a_1 \times a_2^{-2}$	$-$
$(\text{if } a_1\ a_2\ a_3)$	if $a_1 < 0$ then a_2 else a_3	0 0	1 if $a_1 < 0$ 0 if $a_1 \geq 0$	0 if $a_1 < 0$ 1 if $a_1 \geq 0$

3.3   Search Factor α

In the online scheme, the search factor α in equation 3 was defined to be proportional to the inversed sum of the square gradients on all numeric parameter terminals along the cost surface, as shown in equation 6.

$$\alpha = \eta \cdot \frac{1}{\sum_i^N \left(\frac{\partial y}{\partial O_i}\right)^2} \tag{6}$$

where N is the number of numeric parameter terminals in the program and η is a learning rate defined by the user. In the offline scheme, we directly used the user defined learning rate η as the search factor.

3.4   Online Gradient Descent Algorithm

The online gradient descent algorithm in GP is summarised as follows. For each program on each object, do the following:

– Evaluate the program, save the outputs of all nodes in the program.
– Calculate the partial derivative of the cost function on the program $\frac{\partial C}{\partial y}$ using equations 4 and 5.
– Calculate the partial derivatives of the program on numeric parameter terminals $\frac{\partial y}{\partial O_i}$ using the chain rule and table 2.

- Calculate the search factor α using equation 6.
- Calculate the change of each numeric parameter terminal using equation 2.
- Update the numeric parameter terminals using $(O_i)_{new} = O_i + \Delta O_i$.

3.5   Offline Gradient Descent Algorithm

The offline learning algorithm is similar to the online learning algorithm except that the search factor α simply takes the value of the learning rate η rather than using equation 6 and that the change of each numeric terminal in a program is based on the sum of all object examples in the training set rather than on each single object. Accordingly, the numeric parameter terminals will be only updated after a whole cycle of all examples in the training set.

It is important to note that the gradient descent algorithms do not replace *any* of the normal genetic operators that produce populations from generation to generation. Instead, the gradient descent algorithms augment the existing GP system by locally applying gradient descent search to each program in the current population in a particular generation.

4   Image Data Sets

We used three image data sets in the experiments. Example images are shown in figure 2.

The first set of images (figure 2 (a)) was generated to give well defined objects against a noisy background. The pixels of the objects were produced using a Gaussian generator with different means and variances for each class. Four classes of 713 small objects were cut out from these images to form the classification data set *shape*. The four classes are: black circles, light grey squares, white circles, and grey noisy background. This set was considered to include an easy object classification problem.

The second data set (*coin1*, figure 2 (b)) was intended to be harder than data set 1 and consisted of scanned 5 cent and 10 cent New Zealand coins. There are five classes of 480 object cutouts: 5 cent heads, 5 cent tails, 10 cent heads

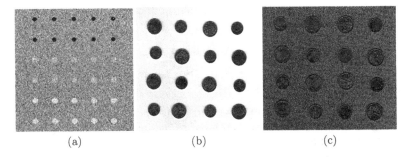

(a)   (b)   (c)

Fig. 2. Example images from Shape (a), Coin1 (b) and Coin2 (c)

and 10 cent tails, and a relatively uniform background. The coins were located in different locations with arbitrary orientations. These images were scanned with a resolution of 75pt and some of them were not clear to human eyes. The classification problem here is fairly hard.

The third data set (*coin2*, figure 2 (c)) also consisted of five classes of object cutouts, but the background was highly clustered, which makes the classification problems much harder. Human eyes also have difficulty to distinguish heads from tails for either 5 cent or 10 cent coins. Thus, the three data sets provide object classification problems of increasing difficulty.

The object cutout images in each of the these data sets were equally split into three separate data sets: one third for the training set used directly for learning the genetic program classifiers, one third for the validation set for controlling overfitting, and one third for the test set for measuring the performance of the learned program classifiers.

5   Results and Discussion

This section presents the results of our GP approach with both the online and the offline gradient descent algorithms on the three data sets and compare them with the results of the basic GP approach without the gradient descent search. For all cases, 10 runs were carried out and the mean results on the test set are presented.

5.1   Shape Data Set

Table 3 shows the results on the Shape data set using different learning rates. The first line shows that the basic GP approach without using the gradient descent algorithm (η is 0.0) achieved an average accuracy of 99.48% over 10 runs on the test set and the average number of generations of the 10 runs spent on the training process was 9.56.

For data set *shape*, the online gradient descent algorithm achieved the best performance of all the three methods in terms of both classification accuracy and training generations. In particular, using the online gradient descent algorithm at learning rates of 0.2, 0.4, 0.7 and 1.0, ideal performances were achieved and only one generation[1] was required for the evolutionary learning process. This was considerably faster than the basic GP approach. While the offline algorithm also achieved better accuracy and a faster training than the basic GP approach for these learning rates, it was not as good as the online algorithm for this data set.

---

[1] One generation in GP with the two gradient descent algorithms usually requires a slightly longer time than that in the basic GP approach. However, this could be considerably improved by only applying the gradient descent algorithm to the top 5% of the programs in the population. In this case, the actual times for a single generation in the three methods would be still very similar.

Table 3. Results of the shape data set.

Dataset	η	Generations			Accuracy (%)		
		Basic	Online	Offline	Basic	Online	Offline
	0.0	9.56	–	–	99.48	–	–
	0.2	–	1.00	3.20	–	100.00	99.77
Shape	0.4	–	1.00	2.20	–	100.00	99.86
	0.7	–	1.00	2.80	–	100.00	99.81
	1.0	–	1.00	3.30	–	100.00	99.63
	1.4	–	1.00	5.50	–	99.95	99.77

Table 4. Results of the two *coin* data sets.

Dataset	η	Generations			Accuracy (%)		
		Basic	Online	Offline	Basic	Online	Offline
	0.0	51.00	–	–	82.12	–	–
	0.2	–	20.40	35.70	–	98.94	94.19
Coin1	0.4	–	25.40	43.40	–	98.94	93.06
	0.7	–	23.30	46.60	–	98.81	91.81
	1.0	–	36.70	47.30	–	97.69	92.44
	1.4	–	34.00	37.50	–	97.94	94.38
	0.0	51.00	–	–	73.83	–	–
	0.2	–	51.00	51.00	–	83.50	72.17
Coin2	0.4	–	51.00	51.00	–	82.83	77.67
	0.7	–	50.20	51.00	–	85.17	78.83
	1.0	–	51.00	51.00	–	86.50	84.17
	1.4	–	51.00	51.00	–	80.83	79.00

5.2   Coin Data Sets

As shown in table 4, the results for the two coin data sets show a similar pattern
to the *shape* dataset. In both data sets, for all the learning rates investigated here,
the accuracy performances of the GP approach with the two gradient descent
algorithms were almost always superior to those without the gradient descent
search. Again, the online algorithm was better than the offline algorithm on
these data sets. These results suggests that a combination of the basic genetic
beam search with the gradient descent search could find better genetic program
classifiers than the genetic beam search only for these object classification tasks.

   In terms of the number of generations used in the training process, the GP
approach with the two gradient descent algorithms required fewer generations
to achieve good results for dataset *coin1*. For example, the approach with
the online algorithm at a learning rate of 0.2 only used 20.4 generations and
achieved 98.94% accuracy, while the basic GP approach used 51 generations
but only obtained 82.12%. For dataset *coin2*, all the GP approaches used
almost all the 51 generations (one of the stopping criteria). However, after
examining the internal behaviour of the evolutionary process, we found that
the method with the online gradient descent algorithm could found the best
solution at generations 10-20 in all the cases while the basic method found the

best program at generations 45-51 in almost all the cases. The offline algorithm was a bit slower than the online algorithm, but still much faster than the basic GP method. These results suggest that the GP approach with the gradient descent search is faster to find the best solution than without.

For dataset *coin2*, the accuracy performance could not be improved with even more generations. This is probably because only four simple features were used in the terminal set, which were not sufficient for this difficult task.

The results also show that different performances were obtained if different learning rates were used. It did not appear to have a reliable way to determine a good learning rate. As in neural networks, this learning parameter needs an empirical search through tuning certain experiments. However, if this can lead to considerably better results, this price is worth to pay. Our experiments suggest that a learning rate between 0.2 to 1.0 is a good starting point for object classification problems.

6   Conclusions

The goal of this paper is to develop an approach to integrating gradient descent search to genetic programming (GP) and to investigate whether the hybrid approach is better than the basic GP approach for object classification problems. This goal was achieved by introducing and embedding the gradient descent search into the genetic beam search to form the online and offline gradient descent algorithms, allowing the evolutionary process to globally follow the beam search and locally follow the gradient descent search to find good solutions.

On all the data sets investigated here, the two GP methods with the gradient descent search achieved better results than the method without in both classification accuracy and training generations. In particular, the online gradient descent algorithm suited the best to these classification problems. As expected, the performances on the three image data sets deteriorated as the degree of difficulty of the object classification problem was increased.

Although developed for object classification problems, this method is expected to be applied to general classification and prediction tasks.

For future work, we will investigate whether the performance on the difficult coin data sets can be improved if more features are added to the terminal set. We will also investigate the power and reliability of the gradient descent GP methods on even more difficult image classification problems such as face recognition problems and satellite image detection problems, and compare the performance with other long-term established methods such as decision trees, neural networks, and support vector machines.

References

1. David Andre. Automatically defined features: The simultaneous evolution of 2-dimensional feature detectors and an algorithm for using them. In Kenneth E. Kinnear, editor, *Advances in Genetic Programming*, pages 477–494. MIT Press, 1994.

2. Daniel Howard, Simon C. Roberts, and Richard Brankin. Target detection in SAR imagery by genetic programming. *Advances in Engineering Software*, 30:303–311, 1999.

3. Thomas Loveard and Victor Ciesielski. Representing classification problems in genetic programming. In *Proceedings of the Congress on Evolutionary Computation*, volume 2, pages 1070–1077, COEX, World Trade Center, 159 Samseong-dong, Gangnam-gu, Seoul, Korea, 27-30 May 2001. IEEE Press.

4. Andy Song, Vic Ciesielski, and Hugh Williams. Texture classifiers generated by genetic programming. In David B. Fogel, Mohamed A. El-Sharkawi, Xin Yao, Garry Greenwood, Hitoshi Iba, Paul Marrow, and Mark Shackleton, editors, *Proceedings of the 2002 Congress on Evolutionary Computation CEC2002*, pages 243–248. IEEE Press, 2002.

5. Walter Alden Tackett. Genetic programming for feature discovery and image discrimination. In Stephanie Forrest, editor, *Proceedings of the 5th International Conference on Genetic Algorithms, ICGA-93*, pages 303–309, University of Illinois at Urbana-Champaign, 17-21 July 1993. Morgan Kaufmann.

6. Jay F. Winkeler and B. S. Manjunath. Genetic programming for object detection. In John R. Koza, Kalyanmoy Deb, Marco Dorigo, David B. Fogel, Max Garzon, Hitoshi Iba, and Rick L. Riolo, editors, *Genetic Programming 1997: Proceedings of the Second Annual Conference*, pages 330–335, Stanford University, CA, USA, 13-16 July 1997. Morgan Kaufmann.

7. Mengjie Zhang and Victor Ciesielski. Genetic programming for multiple class object detection. In Norman Foo, editor, *Proceedings of the 12th Australian Joint Conference on Artificial Intelligence (AI'99)*, pages 180–192, Sydney, Australia, December 1999. Springer-Verlag Berlin Heidelberg. Lecture Notes in Artificial Intelligence (LNAI Volume 1747).

8. Thomas Loveard. Genetic programming with meta-search: Searching for a successful population within the classification domain. In E. Costa C. Ryan, T. Soule, M. Keijzer, E. Tsang, R. Poli, editor, *Proceedings of the Sixth European Conference on Genetic Programming (EuroGP-2003)*, volume 2610 of *LNCS*, pages 119–129, Essex, UK, 2003. Springer Verlag.

9. Conor Ryan and Maarten Keijzer. An analysis of diversity of constants of genetic programming. In E. Costa C. Ryan, T. Soule, M. Keijzer, E. Tsang, R. Poli, editor, *Proceedings of the Sixth European Conference on Genetic Programming (EuroGP-2003)*, volume 2610 of *LNCS*, pages 404–413, Essex, UK, 2003. Springer Verlag.

10. John R. Koza. *Genetic programming : on the programming of computers by means of natural selection*. Cambridge, Mass. : MIT Press, London, England, 1992.

11. Wolfgang Banzhaf, Peter Nordin, Robert E. Keller, and Frank D. Francone. *Genetic Programming: An Introduction on the Automatic Evolution of computer programs and its Applications*. San Francisco, Calif. : Morgan Kaufmann Publishers; Heidelburg : Dpunkt-verlag, 1998. Subject: Genetic programming (Computer science); ISBN: 1-55860-510-X.

12. Mengjie Zhang, Victor Ciesielski, and Peter Andreae. A domain independent window-approach to multiclass object detection using genetic programming. *EURASIP Journal on Signal Processing, Special Issue on Genetic and Evolutionary Computation for Signal Processing and Image Analysis*, 2003(8):841–859, 2003.

13. John R. Koza. *Genetic Programming II: Automatic Discovery of Reusable Programs*. Cambridge, Mass. : MIT Press, London, England, 1994.

Author Index

Lecture Notes in Computer Science

For information about Vols. 1–2881

please contact your bookseller or Springer-Verlag